Islam and
Liberal Citizenship

Islam and Liberal Citizenship

The Search for an Overlapping Consensus

ANDREW F. MARCH

OXFORD
UNIVERSITY PRESS

OXFORD
UNIVERSITY PRESS

Oxford University Press, Inc., publishes works that further
Oxford University's objective of excellence
in research, scholarship, and education.

Oxford New York
Auckland Cape Town Dar es Salaam Hong Kong Karachi
Kuala Lumpur Madrid Melbourne Mexico City Nairobi
New Delhi Shanghai Taipei Toronto

With offices in
Argentina Austria Brazil Chile Czech Republic France Greece
Guatemala Hungary Italy Japan Poland Portugal Singapore
South Korea Switzerland Thailand Turkey Ukraine Vietnam

Published by Oxford University Press, Inc.
198 Madison Avenue, New York, New York 10016
www.oup.com

First issued as an Oxford University Press paperback, 2011

Library of Congress Cataloging-in-Publication Data
March, Andrew F., 1976-
Islam and liberal citizenship : the search for an overlapping consensus /
Andrew F. March.
p. cm.
Includes bibliographical references and index.
ISBN 978-0-19-533096-0 (hardcover); 978-0-19-983858-5 (paperback)
1. Citizenship (Islamic law). 2. Muslims—Non-Muslim countries.
3. Pluralism—Religious aspects—Islam. 4. Liberalism—Religious
aspects—Islam. 5. Citizenship—Europe. 6. Liberalism—Europe.
7. Islam and secularism—Europe. I. Title.
KBP2430.M37 2009
340.5'9—dc22 2008026903

9 8 7 6 5 4 3 2 1

Printed in the United States of America

To my parents

Acknowledgments

My DPhil dissertation advisors, Michael Freeden and Sohail Hashmi, were as supportive and encouraging of the earliest form of this somewhat experimental project as could possibly be hoped.

Christopher Melchert was exceedingly generous with his time, answering many a banal question, reading overlong chapters, and providing crucial support in my initial efforts to navigate Islamic sources—all beyond the call of duty for an informal, unofficial mentor. Akram Nadvi and Yahya Michot of the Oxford Centre for Islamic Studies (OXCIS) were generous and patient with my many questions and impromptu office visits. Mark Muehlhaeuser of the OXCIS library provided not only much valuable assistance but also enjoyable company on an almost daily basis for nearly two years. David Miller, Elizabeth Frazer, and Tariq Ramadan provided valuable and much needed critical feedback during the various examinations of the thesis on which this book is based. Guy Kahane and Edward Kanterian provided valuable philosophical perspective and much valued friendship during these years. In addition to the Oxford Centre for Islamic Studies, the staffs of the Bodleian Library (particularly the Radcliffe Camera), the Oxford Oriental Institute Library, and the Institut Français du Proche-Orient (IFPO) Library (Damascus) were supportive and friendly.

While writing this book, I was supported generously by the Marshall Aid Commemoration Commission, the Beeston Scholarship of St. John's College (Oxford), and the Becket Institute at Oxford University. Michigan State University's James Madison College and Yale University's Political Science Department have provided excellent support and working conditions for me since 2005.

Between this book's earliest manifestation as a doctoral dissertation and now, I have benefited from discussions with, among numerous others, Mohammad Fadel, Sherman Jackson, Steven Kautz, Naz Modirzadeh, Micah Schwartzman, Yasir Qadhi, Jonathan Quong, and the editors and anonymous reviewers of *American Political Science Review* and *Philosophy & Public Affairs*. I have also benefited from the response and discussion at seminars, conference panels, and invited talks at, in roughly chronological order, the Becket Institute (St. Hugh's College, Oxford), the Oxford Centre for Islamic Studies, the Second World Congress for Middle Eastern Studies (Amman, Jordan), the Middle East Studies Association (MESA), Michigan State University's Muslim Studies Program, George Washington University's Political Science Department, Middlebury College's Clifford Symposium, and Harvard University's Kennedy School of Government. My thanks are also due to the students of both iterations of "Comparative Political Theory: Islam and Liberalism" at Michigan State's James Madison College (spring 2007) and Yale (fall 2007), respectively. Matthew Ingalls read almost the entire manuscript (chapters 3 and 5 through 8) and improved it immensely in the areas of Arabic translation and transliteration, English style and clarity, and factual and interpretive accuracy. I am in his debt. Finally, I would like to thank Theo Calderara of Oxford University Press for his support and patience, as well as the editorial and production staff both known to me (Meechal Hoffman and Linda Donnelly) and unknown, and the copyeditor, Joy Matkowski.

This volume was published with the assistance of the Frederick W. Hilles Publication Fund of Yale University.

A version of chapter 4 was published previously as "Liberal Citizenship and the Search for an Overlapping Consensus: The Case of Muslim Minorities," *Philosophy & Public Affairs*, vol. 34, no. 4 (Fall 2006), 373–421.

Parts of chapters 1, 5, and 6 were included in "Islamic Foundations for a Social Contract in Non-Muslim Liberal Democracies," *American Political Science Review*, Vol. 101, No. 2, May 2007, pp. 235–252.

I discuss some of the themes of chapter 7 in "Sources of Moral Obligation to Non-Muslims in the 'Jurisprudence of Muslim Minorities' (Fiqh al-aqalliyyāt) Discourse," *Islamic Law and Society*, 16:1 (2009).

My constant companion, joy, and reason for being for the last decade has been my son, Tamir, who has had a vague awareness of this book's preparation. That his awareness has been so vague, and the impact of the work involved for this book on him so slight, is due in great measure to his grandparents, to whom goes my immense, but insufficient, gratitude. That this book is not better is due to many factors, but the most tangible of them is the fact that it was produced in its substance prior to the advent of my wife, Naz. In the subsequent two years, I have been blessed with a glimpse of the conditions of joy, inspiration and intellectual partnership in which all my future endeavors will unfold. It is already difficult to recognize what came before.

Contents

Introduction: Moral Conflict, Political Liberalism, and Islamic Ethics, 3

Part I: Justificatory Comparative Political Theory: The Search for Overlapping Consensus through "Conjecture," 17

1. Purposes: The Place of Justificatory Comparative Political Theory, 23
2. Methods: The Ethics of Comparative Ethics, 65

Part II: Islam and Liberal Citizenship: Patterns of Moral Disagreement and Principled Reconciliation, 97

3. Islamic Objections to Citizenship in Non-Muslim Liberal Democracies, 103
4. Identifying Equilibrium: An Ideal-Typical Islamic Doctrine of Citizenship, 135

Part III: Islamic Affirmations of Liberal Citizenship, 163

5. Residence in a Non-Muslim State, 165
6. Loyalty to a Non-Muslim State, 181
7. Recognition of Non-Muslims and Moral Pluralism, 207
8. Solidarity with Non-Muslims, 237

Islam and Liberal Citizenship

Introduction

Moral Conflict, Political Liberalism, and Islamic Ethics

This book examines whether Muslims, *qua* Muslims, can regard as religiously and morally legitimate the terms of citizenship in a non-Muslim liberal democracy. This involves asking what is involved doctrinally in constructing as religiously legitimate practices such requirements as living in and being loyal to a non-Muslim state, regarding non-Muslims as political equals with whom one might cooperate socially and politically, contributing to non-Muslim welfare, and participating in non-Muslim political systems.

Although I am focusing in this book specifically on the relationship between Islamic doctrine and liberal citizenship, the inquiry itself is a generic one. All religious and philosophical doctrines or, indeed, noncomprehensive collections of beliefs and preferences can be presumed to provide their bearers with a wide set of motivations for action, some of which may conflict with liberal terms of social cooperation. These questions would be of interest even without the recent public examples of value conflict in Western societies, simply because Islam is an important comprehensive doctrine that has achieved a critical presence in existing liberal democracies recently enough for there not to exist a significant philosophical literature on its relationship to liberalism and citizenship. Lest it be thought that asking these questions suggests a *particular* background suspicion or mistrust of Islamic political ethics, it should be borne in mind not only that these questions can be and are posed to all non-Islamic doctrines flourishing in liberal societies but also that these very questions are the subject of earnest, and constant, internal debate among Muslim religious scholars and intellectuals. That internal debate provides the material for this book.

An immediate caveat is in order here. This book does not aim to provide any of the following: a full account of the historical evolution of Islamic doctrine in context or a "genealogy" of Islamic approaches to secularism, an anthropological or sociological study of the practices or views of actual Muslim citizens or communities in Western democracies, a political-psychological study of the creation of motivations on the part of individuals or communities and the status of religious doctrine as an independent variable in those motivations, a political analysis of the long-term motivations or trustworthiness of various political groups or actors within Western Muslim communities, or a historical or genealogical criticism of how contemporary Western, liberal societies "construct the Muslim (as) Other." I believe this book is fully compatible with and complementary to the many excellent such studies in print;[1] however, the present study is, rather, a work of political theory that seeks to analyze Islamic (as opposed to Muslim) attitudes toward shared citizenship through a methodology of comparative political ethics. It is a study of Muslim citizenship in non-Muslim liberal democracies *as a religious problem for believing Muslims.*

The questions raised in this book are familiar ones, as is their framing. They are echoed in the popular and academic discussions of whether "Islam" might be "compatible" with some core liberal value or institution—democracy, human rights, gender equality, just war theory, or even "modernity" at large. There are many good reasons to be skeptical of or dissatisfied with such questions and approaches. They may encourage either a stereotypical negative treatment of Islamic ethics or, alternatively, a superficial and unserious dismissal of the reality of genuine (and perhaps reasonable) moral disagreement.[2] They may gravely overstate the extent to which political conflict can be explained through the consciously affirmed moral and religious beliefs of participants in such conflicts and may thus exaggerate the benefits to be gained by establishing the compatibility of Islam with this or that moral principle. They may suggest that all of the accommodation, reform, or growth in terms of deep moral commitments has to take place on the side of Muslims.[3] They may provide an apologetic ideological cover for the injustices committed by actors who claim to endorse liberalism, human rights, and modernity.[4] They may confuse the explanatory order of things by thinking that political goals are determined by ideological, moral, or religious beliefs.

These objections are appropriate, and their force raises a series of problems that I seek to address in the first two chapters of this book. In those chapters, I seek to make the case that a comparative ethics that does in the end aim at some form of consensus, convergence, or moral agreement is worth pursuing and can be done in a serious way that gives these reasonable reservations their due. In this book, I aim to take the fact of moral disagreement seriously in its own terms while remaining cognizant of the complexities of lived human experience and the limits of formal ethical theorizing. It is driven by a first-order value commitment to a particular conception of justice and citizenship but is not unreflective or uncritical about that conception, and still less of any given political context in which that conception is publicly appropriated. It is motivated by the aim of principled moral reconciliation, but it also seeks to do justice to the richness, subtlety, and complexity of Islamic political ethics.

The methodology that I believe allows this balance to be struck is presented in Part I, but I would like to draw attention here to one argument in favor of this approach. Consider the following hypothetical, idealized reservation about a study that aims at demonstrating the compatibility between Islam and liberal citizenship:

> The search for "compatibility" obscures many other fascinating stories to be told about our present historical moment. It is insensitive to the myriad ways in which problems and conflicts are ideologically constructed on all sides. It does not do justice to the way in which identities and moral commitments are the historical products of many things in addition to formal religious doctrine or rational inquiry, namely the pervasive effects of power imbalances. Islam is many things in addition to a collection of doctrines and rules—it is a cultural and civilizational identity which is available for mobilization and appropriation out of all sorts of political, social, cultural and psychological needs. It is also an identity which is a source of anxiety for a very powerful political-economic-cultural apparatus—again, out of all sorts of political, social, cultural and psychological needs. We should not assume that all episodes of conflict or disagreement between "Muslims" and non-Muslims point to a straightforward case of moral disagreement without regard for the historico-political context in which those disagreements become salient. Besides, it is much more likely that the background fact of moral disagreement is something which is mobilized by people in power to place the debate (whether they know it or not) on grounds which are convenient for them.[5]

I view this book not only as perfectly compatible with the above statements but also, in a curious way, affirmative of some of their underlying suspicions and commitments.[6] There is no doubt that complex and confusing historical moments are often presented by persons with first-order normative value commitments (and, of course, with vested interests) as instances of a *certain kind* of moral conflict. Invariably, this presentation frames the debate in ways that vindicate our own normative commitments and the methodologies from which they are derived.

Take the recurring disputes over the boundary between freedom of expression and religious sensitivity in Europe and North America (from the Rushdie affair to the Danish cartoons). For certain liberals, these disputes are a matter of convincing a group of citizens why freedom of expression cannot normally be curtailed to accommodate religious conceptions of dignity and the sacred.[7] For Muslims (and, indeed, others), they may be a case of secularism's inability to take faith seriously[8] or perhaps the West's need to provoke and degrade Muslims and Islam.[9] For critical social theorists, they may be a case of Europeans' historically unaware and un-self-critical preoccupation with Muslims as an internal Other[10] and of Muslims' un-self-confident fixation on Islam as an identity held together by a series of symbols, signs, and disembodied rules, which is itself a product of their historical subjugation by Western colonialism.

Awareness of this tendency should lead anyone to a certain self-restraint. Perhaps what we choose to emphasize as the core issue in a given moral conflict is not the whole story. How do we know whether we are dealing with a conflict between two incompatible but similarly elaborate and autonomous moral *doctrines* or a conflict between groups of *people* situated in a pathological power relationship? Inevitably, both are the case, so how do we begin to untangle the web of complacent self-descriptions, historical shadows, and power interests? How can we be sure of the motivations and anxieties of parties in a conflict? How can we be sure that we are evaluating a certain tendency, ideology, or trend in terms of its most sophisticated manifestation, rather than its crudest and least self-aware?

One way is by evaluating the moral conflict in question in terms of the difference between what the various parties value and what they wish to see prevail. Conflict over whether to permit cartoons of the Prophet Muhammad may be many things—evidence of Europe's historically situated anxiety about Islam and its own Muslim population,[11] Muslims' postcolonial lack of self-confidence, secularism's inability to take religious belief seriously, Muslims' admirable resistance to Western arrogance—but it is for that no less about whether to permit offensive cartoons of the Prophet Muhammad in an existing, multicultural, secular democracy. Conflict over whether to permit girls to wear the headscarf in French schools may be many things—evidence of the West's obsession with "saving brown women from brown men,"[12] the desire of Muslim men to reassert patriarchal authority over Muslim women, an instance of France's misguided approach to religion and republican desire to create certain kinds of subjects—but it is for that no less about whether to permit girls to wear a headscarf in school. Conflict over whether Canada should allow Muslim arbitration courts may be many things—a manifestation of Canadians' fear of Muslim "barbarians at the gates,"[13] a sign of Westerners' hypocrisy and double standards when it comes to Islam, evidence that Muslim communities are determined to avoid assimilation into Canadian society—but it is for that no less about whether a country committed to both civic equality and religious freedom should allow Muslim arbitration courts. Thus, a first step is to isolate what precisely is immediately at stake in terms of competing claims about what is just, good, or permissible. Of course, this is not a call to treat instances of moral disagreement outside their broader historical and power context; context is an important factor in assessing the morality of a given course of action. But while that context *may* show that a given instance of moral disagreement is "actually about" something else (power, racism, Islamophobia, integration, class), it may not do that. We certainly cannot assume from the outset that that is the case. Hence, all the more reason to attempt to isolate the moral-doctrinal elements from the context-power elements for the purposes of clarity and rigor. Differently put, we cannot assume (from the outset of an inquiry) that there is one *single* power context that is determinant of an event's morality *tout court*.

A second step is to isolate what *precisely* about these competing claims is *Islamic* or *liberal*. Is there a *tradition* to thinking in these terms?[14] Are the claims or demands being advanced the *only ones* that can be advanced in the name of Islam or liberalism? How *central* to those moral traditions are the claims or demands? Do these demands or claims tend to emerge in *other social or power contexts*? Are they claims that *inherently* or only *contingently* reinforce certain power dynamics?

Thus, this approach to moral conflict and consensus discards the description of conflict in broad civilizational terms, as if Islam were some grand metaphysical reality and liberalism nothing more than the ideology of late modern capitalism. Although deep causality or grand narrative may be illuminating, it is not always clear that it prescribes a better mode of engaging contemporaries publicly across moral divides. In place of an integrated understanding of civilizational commitments according to which Western liberalism and Islamic ethics meet one another wholesale, this study thus proposes approaching moral conflict in terms of the *specific* points of contact between political liberalism as an ideal theory of social cooperation and Islamic doctrine as a tradition of systematic thought about what Muslims may legitimately regard as permissible. In place of a time-slice view of contemporary Islamic sensibilities, this study seeks to place contemporary Islamic positions in the context of a *juridical and ethical tradition*.[15] In place of an emphasis on the tangled interests and motivations of particular actors, this study abstracts from the details and complexities of particular political contexts in order to theorize an *ideal moral encounter*. The aim is to clarify our understanding of the sources of moral disagreement and what is required for principled moral reconciliation.

The hope is not just moral consensus but also to deflate and to demystify some of the rhetoric surrounding moral disagreement. A typical antagonistic approach to Islamic political ethics is to assert that all undemocratic, antiliberal, or violent Islamic practices are inevitable by-products of an essential Islamic code or ethos. A typical apologetic response to such statements is to place the criticized practices in the context of colonialism or contemporary political antagonism, or to make a distinction between the Islam of medieval legal scholars and the more complex cultural or political practices of particular communities. This book can contribute to that debate. By studying the patterns of moral disagreement in their *specific points of contact*, by studying Islamic moral commitments in terms of a *juridical and ethical tradition*, and by abstracting ourselves from a political analysis of current events to something like an *ideal moral encounter*, it is possible to better understand whether a given political conflict actually has at its root a principled moral disagreement between competing ethical systems. Sometimes there will be evidence of a longer standing conflict of ideals or values. Sometimes liberal terms of citizenship will be shown to be compatible with even very conservative Islamic conceptions of moral obligation. At other times, liberal terms of citizenship will be shown to require substantial revision of long-standing Islamic commitments. *At no point do we assume that actual political conflict and the consciousness of real persons can be reduced to formal religious or philosophical commitments*,[16] but by taking those commitments seriously enough to study them in their own terms, we avoid both the simplistic judgment that all political conflict between Muslims and non-Muslims is reducible to essential cultural, moral, or religious features and the slightly less simplistic judgment that all such political conflict is a proxy for some kind of anticolonial or counterhegemonic resistance.

A further way of avoiding confusion about the purposes of this study is to make explicit the radically different interest various types of scholarship have in the terms *Muslim* and *Islamic.* To fix ideas, let us simplify the distinction as one between an interest in Muslim/Islamic as an *identity* and Muslim/Islamic as a *set of beliefs.* When I pose the question "Can Muslims regard as legitimate the terms of citizenship in a non-Muslim liberal democracy?" a host of perfectly reasonable objections immediately present themselves. These objections are related to the views previously presented in objection to the interest in the "compatibility" between Islam and this or that belief, system, or practice: Why should we assume Muslims are any more hostile to liberal citizenship than any other citizens? Doesn't this recall the degrading, and often racist, suspicions about whether Catholics and Jews could be good American citizens? Why should we assume that Islamic religious texts explain the motivations and interests of actual Muslim citizens rather than focus on their lived practices? Doesn't the discourse on whether Muslims can be good liberal citizens contribute to a dominant understanding of Muslims as illiberal and dangerous, and isn't there something of a double standard in how this discourse is mobilized in Western societies?

All of these objections to the organizing question of this book raise crucial and valid moral concerns. They presume, however, an *identity-based* approach to the study of religious or cultural political encounters, in the sense that "Muslim" and "Islamic" are presumed to function as ascriptive cultural markers of persons and the communities they comprise. There are good reasons, of course, to focus on Muslim and Islamic "identity," as opposed to formal religious doctrine, not the least of which is the fact that many persons themselves are as deeply committed to their public cultural identities as they are to their considered beliefs. Of course, the more compelling reasons are the ways in which nominal identities serve to shape political loyalties, personal consciousness, and social esteem. It is impossible to live socially outside of the range of ascriptive identities by which others recognize us, and it is to a large extent impossible to achieve the social respect necessary for stable individual self-esteem without our ascriptive identities themselves in some way being respected and recognized. That is true for all of us in all times and places, but it is hard to think of a social identity at the present time in the West that is as mobilized, as vilified, as glorified, as scrutinized, and as reified as are "Muslim" and "Islamic." It is thus natural to assume that raising questions about moral disagreement in a diverse society must address the experiences of all persons who might be identified according to the same ascriptive monikers of the groups at the core of a given moral disagreement, in this case "Muslim" and "Islamic."

By contrast, I wish to state as clearly as possible that for me the terms "Muslim" and "Islamic" serve to identify a *set of beliefs* or rather, more accurately, a *tradition of argumentation about the formulation of religious doctrine.* It is, of course, not easy in the case of actual individuals or communities to cleanly separate commitment to an identity from commitment to beliefs. In the case of Islam, the claim is often that the "identity" is derived precisely from a commitment to certain beliefs. Furthermore, the commitment to a certain social identity can be an important factor in the selection of beliefs. Where what we can call identity commitments and belief commitments overlap, it might be impossible to identify primary motivations. For example, the popularity of certain radical Islamic *beliefs* (both in the West and in Muslim-majority countries) often coincides with a very public affirmation of an Islamic *identity.* What is the order of causality here? Does a higher-order desire to be as Islamic (in the identity sense) as possible lead to an elective affinity for certain beliefs? Or, rather, does the conviction that certain beliefs are true result in a natural adoption of the public markings of an Islamic identity and a political commitment to a certain imagined community? Do political events affecting a certain cultural community (in the identity sense) create the conditions for certain beliefs to be adopted as true? Or, rather, is the background fact of certain beliefs being held what creates the terms by which that cultural community was constructed in the first place? Take the case of Islamic *jihād* doctrines. Can we know whether a given Muslim who supports or approves of the activities of so-called jihadi groups does so because of a prior moral belief derived from Islamic doctrine or because of psychological factors related to the dynamics of conflict and "the love of one's own"?

For all of these reasons, it is often extremely difficult to even identify the "moral disagreement" in question, especially when such disagreements take place in a larger context of political antagonism. Traditions of religious doctrine and belief are often (if not always) entangled with the political and social needs of particular communities. It is, for that reason, all the more important to be cautious, precise, and rigorous in speaking about the nature of moral disagreement. My own way of attempting to be more cautious and precise and to avoid making unsubstantiated claims is to limit my focus to the study of traditions of Islamic *internal doctrinal arguments* on the problem of liberal citizenship without expecting that such a study will explain the totality of moral relationships between Muslim *communities* and Western societies.

This distinction I make between identities and beliefs, and my preference for focusing on the latter, is not derived from a methodological or political agenda exogenous to Islam. *All of the substantive questions, problems, and debates I focus on in this book are derived entirely from internal Islamic sources.* Consider the following passage by European Muslim intellectual Tariq Ramadan:

> There are a number of issues which should be tackled and discussed in the debate about the Muslim presence in Europe. To give a clear answer about the Islamic legality and conditions for staying in a non-Muslim society is, of course, of great importance but it is still not sufficient: it is also necessary to determine what Muslims' responsibilities and rights towards their new societies are. For, as soon as

> their Religion is respected and their freedom assured, they become part of the host countries' constitution and law. This has to be clarified for Muslims living in the West: i.e., what does it mean to be part of a Western society? Is there a limit or an exception to respect for the law and the constitution? Is there any discrepancy between respecting Western laws and being faithful to the teachings of the Qur'ān and the *Sunna*? Can a Muslim be a true and trustworthy citizen of a European country or has he or she simply the right to apply for Western nationality?[17]

It is clear that the concern with the deep, principled congruence between liberal and Islamic conceptions of justice, the good, and social solidarity is in absolutely equal measure an endogenous Islamic and liberal concern.

Philosophical Motivations

There is another way in which this book contributes to a common debate (both academic and popular) about the conflict between liberalism, secularism, and religion. Of course, political liberalism is committed to a certain form of secularism. This form holds that in modern conditions it is not reasonable to expect that all persons in a given society will be united around a religious foundation for public deliberation, never mind a single religious doctrine; because legitimate political power ought to justify itself to all persons subject to it, public deliberation ought to be conducted in terms of a "public reason" that is accessible to all persons regardless of their religious beliefs. This is the dominant contemporary philosophical understanding of the separation of church and state. Although this understanding also seeks to limit "secular" public reason by not allowing it to proceed on grounds that explicitly deny the truth or value of religious beliefs, it nonetheless does not allow religious doctrine or law to triumph in coercive state institutions. When the two conflict, public reason trumps religious reason. Even if it tries to do so without negating religion, it does not allow that religious truth be brought to bear on society at large.

For many believers, that alone is tantamount to denying religion. For them, there is no neutral space where religion is neither affirmed nor denied. By not affirming it, it is denied. And yet, we are asking for a religious justification of this state of affairs. How could this possibly be? How could there be religious reasons for religion being superseded by secular authority, even secular authority that does not seek to transform all believers into unbelievers? Thus, it is often claimed, there is a necessary and inevitable existential conflict between religion and liberalism.[18] There are, therefore, only two ways for religious citizens to be liberal citizens: One, their religious beliefs may be *replaced* by new ones, at least those beliefs that conflict with liberal justice; two, their religious beliefs may be *augmented* by new ones. A believer may come to accept liberal freedoms—including the freedoms to blaspheme, to apostatize, and to sin—but only by *replacing* her former belief that religion prohibited these freedoms with views from outside religion or by *acquiring* a new belief from outside religion while not thinking about (or while forgetting) what God might have said on the matter.

Is there a third option? Might it be the case, despite what seem to be irreconcilable conflicts of authority, that religious doctrine can provide believers with some account of why and when secular authority is legitimate, why and when unbelievers can be embraced in at least civic friendship, why and when it is permissible to allow sin to go unvanquished? Is it possible that affirmations of liberal citizenship might emerge from *within* religion, or at least receive doctrinal justification on grounds entirely *internal* to religion? This knot has often been thought irresolvable even in the case of Christianity; could it possibly be the case that a religion like Islam, with an utterly unambiguous claim to worldly authority, could provide *principled* reasons for this self-restraint?

This is the main question this book addresses. My main starting premise is that this question need not be treated in grand terms, as if the politico-theological question needed to be treated as a *proof* in need of *axiomatic* demonstration in one way or another. What if the question were an open one, subject to historical or "empirical" treatment? By the latter, I mean that whether a believer regards a social or political context as fundamentally incompatible with religious commitment is a question that demands study into *particular* political demands and theological beliefs. Does *this* religious ethical tradition have the resources to endorse *this* context of social cooperation? Is it reasonable to hope that political institutions we are committed to for our own moral reasons can be the object of commitment for different reasons that our fellow citizens find authoritative? Given the broader state of religious and philosophical disagreement on how to live, may we at least hope for compatibility between most religious and philosophical views on how to live *together*?

The idea of "compatibility" or agreement is something that comes easily to the moral imagination. We encounter conflict in the world, and one intuitive response is to seek out commonality with our moral contemporaries. Often, we are magnanimous enough to imagine that what we believe to be a fair resolution of a conflict must have some echo in the other's moral perspective. The idea of grounding cooperation on what is worthy of being agreed to by all parties or of searching for moral foundations for cooperation from a variety of disparate sources is also an approach to moral conflict with strong appeal within political philosophy.

In *Political Liberalism*, John Rawls writes: "There are many reasonable comprehensive doctrines that understand the wider realm of values to be congruent with, or supportive of, or else not in conflict with, political values as these are specified by a political conception of justice for a democratic regime."[19] When it is, in fact, the case that comprehensive religious and philosophical "doctrines endorse the political conception [of justice], *each from its own point of view*,"[20] society enjoys what Rawls refers to as an "overlapping consensus." Because a liberal society ought not to impose on its citizens a single religion or philosophical doctrine, the dilemma of instability arising from deep moral disagreement (which a liberal society creates and tolerates) is resolved or moderated not when we all come to share a moral doctrine but "when the doctrines making up the [overlapping] consensus are affirmed by society's politically active citizens and the requirements of justice are not too much in conflict with citizens' essential interests."[21] The claim is that metaphysical disagreement that results in different conceptions of value and how to live need not preclude principled agreement on the terms of political cooperation. Even religious doctrines are presumed to have the resources to provide an internal account of the legitimacy of a liberal political order: "Here I shall suppose—perhaps too optimistically—that, except for certain kinds of fundamentalism, all the main historical religions admit of such an account and thus may be seen as reasonable comprehensive doctrines."[22]

How optimistic indeed is Rawls being here? Can a political conception of justice based on the values of individual freedom and civic equality be affirmed by those believing in revealed conceptions of truth and justice that allow—indeed, require—that the community uphold extensive, paternalist forms of authority? Can individuals who believe in the truth of their ethical doctrines recognize the authority of governments not founded with the express purpose of advancing those doctrines? Does recognition of a purely political conception of justice require that believers bracket their religious beliefs or that they find within their religious beliefs affirmation of values that can underpin the political conception?

These questions have, at times, been answered in the affirmative in relation to the ethical pluralism to be found in Western constitutional democracies. Many Christians of various sects and denominations, for example, have found ways of both upholding the truth claims of their religion and adopting the political values required to recognize the legitimacy of constitutional democracy. A yet stronger claim is that the liberal political values that support constitutional democracy, particularly individual autonomy and civic equality, are generally embedded in Western political culture and found even in those "comprehensive ethical doctrines" that are not otherwise forms of liberalism. That is, not only do many Christians, for example, as heirs to a broader Western political tradition, believe in civic equality *in addition to and apart from* their religious beliefs but also they draw precisely on those religious beliefs in order to affirm the distinctively political values necessary for democratic legitimacy.

Increasingly, however, Western political communities are composed of citizens endorsing doctrines and beliefs other than those drawn from, sustained by, or shown to be compatible with secular political traditions, including ones based on Islam and other non-Western traditions. Does this fact add a new dimension to our attempts to deal with ethical pluralism in Western societies? Any arguments for the legitimacy of political liberalism based on the existence of a common post-Reformation or post-Enlightenment shared tradition of secularism and political liberties (separate from attempts to show a theological basis for these values) would, for one, seem to be inapplicable. Beyond this, however, in the face of an increasingly complex cultural and ethical pluralism, are we at all compelled to ask how the specific doctrines held by citizens of a liberal state might overlap with our conceptions of justice? In this book, this question takes the following form: Is there an interpretation of Islamic moral commitments, one not in great conflict with orthodox, Sunni[23] Islam, by which Islam may be considered among the doctrines that understand the wider realm of values to be congruent with, or supportive of, or else not in conflict with, political values as these are specified by a political conception of justice for a democratic regime? Can there be an Islamic doctrine of citizenship in liberal democracies?

Comparative Ethics

This book is not simply a work of scholarship, in the sense of studying Islamic thought in its historical context. It is, rather, in some ways an exercise in what Rawls referred to as "conjecture," or the attempt to argue for the existence of an "overlapping consensus" between a liberal political conception of justice or citizenship and a particular comprehensive ethical doctrine *that is not one's own*. Such a project must be understood partly as a *civic exercise*, in the way that an inquiry into normative public principles would be. The objective is not to provide the most convincing account of why certain claims are advanced as "Islamic" in a given context, what the necessary (historical, political, psychological) conditions are for such a claim being so advanced, or what the implications are of such claims being advanced. Rather, the aim is to investigate what is involved Islamically in arguing for the religious legitimacy of liberal citizenship in such a way that believers (particularly those open to arguments *against* liberal citizenship) might be convinced. Thus, this project is best understood as an exercise in comparative ethics because it treats both liberalism and Islam as first-order moral traditions that provide justificatory reasons for their adherents and that are presumed to have the capacity to both conflict and overlap.

It is not the place of a non-Muslim political theorist to determine how the Islamic revelatory sources are best converted into truth claims or normative judgments. In addition to the complexity of moral consciousness experienced by actual persons acknowledged previously, a multiplicity of intellectual and spiritual traditions exist that give shape to the idea of "Islamic ethics." However, the aim of this book is neither simply to pay homage to the bare fact that Islam is a complex and polyvalent living tradition nor to add to the apologetic literature in opposition to the crude and uninformed claims about Islam's essential dangerousness ("What about Rumi?"). I take those points for granted but do not see them as adequate accounts of internal Islamic understandings of the margin and the periphery in formal moral justification. Rather, I conceive of comparative ethics as the effort to structure a rigorous encounter between two serious and widely endorsed systems of thought. It is my claim that the corpus that best suits this purpose from within Islam is the tradition of Islamic law, broadly within which I include Qur'anic exegesis (*tafsīr*), *ḥadīth* commentary, jurisprudence (*uṣūl al-fiqh*), and substantive legal-ethical rulings (*furūʿ al-fiqh*, or *aḥkām*). This book thus analyzes Islamic sources, mostly juridical, and aims at a relatively comprehensive survey of existing views and arguments on the problem of liberal citizenship with some claim to stem from orthodox Islamic methods and commitments, putting what I will call "compatible views" into a context of relative orthodoxy or centrality. Further, it involves analyzing the underlying moral reasoning of views that ostensibly endorse the terms of liberal citizenship, recognizing the complexity and ambiguity found within religious polemics.

Outline of Chapters

This book is divided into three parts with a total of eight chapters. Part I, "Justificatory Comparative Political Theory: The Search for Overlapping Consensus through 'Conjecture,'" outlines the methodological and analytic framework that I adopt and develop to defend a conception of liberal citizenship and structure an investigation in Islamic discourses. Chapter 1, "Purposes: The Place of Justificatory Comparative Political Theory," argues why political theorists interested in liberal citizenship (but not necessarily interested in Islam) might be interested in an inquiry of this nature and defends it against a number of anticipated criticisms. Chapter 2, "Methods: The Ethics of Comparative Ethics," develops a method for engaging in this form of comparative political theory, with special reference to religion, again anticipating a series of important objections and reservations, some of them discussed above.

Part II, "Islam and Liberal Citizenship: Patterns of Moral Disagreement and Principled Reconciliation," is divided into two chapters. Chapter 3, "Islamic Objections to Citizenship in non-Muslim Liberal Democracies," presents the range of Islamic arguments found in both classical and contemporary sources that problematize liberal citizenship. The aim in this chapter is merely to provide evidence that liberal citizenship *can be* contested within formal Islamic religious doctrine. These internal Islamic discourses show that before we can discuss the central liberal concerns of justifying state neutrality and individual freedoms to revise one's conception of the good, it is necessary to look at a series of questions related to Muslim belonging, loyalty, and solidarity in a non-Muslim state. *There is, however, no case made or suggested that, because of these Islamic juridical-doctrinal debates, actual Muslim citizens (in the cultural, identity sense) must experience liberal citizenship as problematic.*

Based on this background ideal-typical case against liberal citizenship, I argue in chapter 4, "Identifying Equilibrium: An Ideal-Typical Islamic Doctrine of Citizenship," what views emerging from within Islamic doctrine on the questions discussed in chapter 3 would be regarded as reasonable from the perspective of political liberalism while requiring the least revision of traditional Islamic commitments. I refer to this as the search for a certain kind of equilibrium. I argue that political liberalism has a preference for an Islamic doctrine of citizenship that would be the *least demanding possible* for committed Muslims in the sense of requiring minimal departure from traditional or widely held beliefs (thus including in an overlapping consensus the widest possible spectrum of Islamic commitments) while remaining fully compatible with justice and a well-ordered society (thus not making the overlapping consensus "political in the wrong way"). I argue in this chapter for a certain set of ideal-typical Islamic statements that would be representative of a reasonable affirmation of liberal citizenship; I then use these statements as the benchmark for my analysis of Islamic polemics in the final part.

Part III, "Islamic Affirmations of Liberal Citizenship," has four chapters that all respond to the main doctrines presented in chapter 3 contra liberal citizenship. All four chapters demonstrate that very strong and authentically Islamic arguments exist for accepting all of the core demands of citizenship, many being found even in medieval works of Islamic jurisprudence. Crucially, Islamic arguments shown to support the idea of an overlapping consensus also vindicate many of the claims of Rawlsian political liberalism to be a more appealing form of liberalism to nonliberals precisely because of its abstention from claims to metaphysical truth.

Chapter 5, "Residence in a Non-Muslim State," examines the classical and contemporary arguments for permitting legal residence within a non-Muslim state. The emphasis in this chapter is not only on the technical Islamic arguments against the prohibition of such residence (encountered in chapter 3) but also on the treatments of the underlying reasons for discouraging residence and of the conditions under which residence is regarded as legitimate. Chapter 6, "Loyalty to a Non-Muslim State," examines Islamic discussions on when Muslims can exhibit loyalty to non-Muslim states, particularly through contributing to their self-defense. This chapter focuses heavily on the Islamic legal discourse on contract, particularly the notion of the *amān* contract of mutual security, which Islamic jurists from the earliest times to the present have used to justify what I argue amounts to a social contract of (at the least) loyal residence and political obligation. Chapter 7, "Recognition of Non-Muslims and Moral Pluralism," builds on the doctrines discussed in the preceding chapters by examining Islamic affirmations of the potential permanence of moral disagreement (which in a liberal society cannot be confined to recognition of "Abrahamic fraternity" with Jews and Christians) and the idea that "justice" (as opposed to contingent accommodation) is the standard by which political relations with non-Muslims are regulated. These discourses centralize the Islamic commitment to proselytizing (*da'wa*), which remains essentially ambiguous from a liberal perspective. This chapter thus considers whether and in what circumstances a privileging of the possibilities for proselytizing can be regarded as compatible with a moral commitment to liberal citizenship. Chapter 8, "Solidarity with Non-Muslims," treats the liberal conceptions of civic friendship and social cooperation in terms of two tangible requirements, a willingness to contribute to the political and social welfare of those who do not share one's conception of truth and a willingness to participate in a non-Islamic political system. This chapter emphasizes long-standing Islamic distinctions between cooperation for this-worldly ("political" in the Rawlsian sense) goods and for spiritual or metaphysical aims. These final two chapters also reveal some creative and possibly inspiring attempts by contemporary Islamic scholars (not otherwise “reformist” or “modernist” thinkers) to theorize and theologize the moral character of relationships with non-Muslims in the context of shared social cooperation beyond the (already significant) resources provided by the legal tradition.

PART I

Justificatory Comparative Political Theory

The Search for Overlapping Consensus through "Conjecture"

Contemporary political philosophy is rich in treatments of ethical and cultural diversity. Critics of liberalism claim that it fails to take seriously the claims of culture in general and minority cultures in particular. Liberals claim that multiculturalism and group rights fit comfortably within a liberal framework, while differing on just how accommodating liberal political systems should be of nonliberal minorities, as well as on what features of liberalism make it fair to cultural minorities. The substantive values of nonliberal perspectives, for their part, are usually assumed to be either excluded or outweighed by "universal" liberal claims. But treatments of their specific claims and their own attempts to relate to liberal norms and expectations tend not to be the fare of political theory.

The emphasis on "comprehensive doctrines" to be found in Rawls's later work does not characterize much of the literature on multiculturalism and minority rights. In addition to the conflict emerging from the type of pluralism envisaged by Rawls—that of groups seeking to use the state to impose or advantage a vision of the good life derived from a relatively elaborate philosophical or religious doctrine—contemporary political philosophy has also grappled with the demands of less philosophically grounded pluralism. While Rawls seems to imagine a more or less symmetrical conflict between worldviews,[1] the broader literature on multiculturalism and group rights is concerned with various asymmetrical power relationships and the ways in which the interests of women, racial minorities, subnational ethnic and linguistic groups, native populations, and religious minorities may not be fully protected by traditional liberal conceptions of equal citizenship on an individual basis. The themes of asymmetry and power permeate the multiculturalism debate: Critics of universal citizenship seek to point out the asymmetries in power held by various groups; many liberals concede this while refusing to neglect the concurrent asymmetry between those minority groups and their individual members.

Theories of liberal neutrality and multiculturalism have thus developed as a way of preserving universal, equal citizenship in the conditions of both religious and/or ethical pluralism and the group demands of minority or marginal cultural groups. The fact of "reasonable moral pluralism" leads to a liberalism that seeks to justify basic political institutions without reference to any single controversial doctrine. The fact of cultural pluralism leads to calls for policies to assist the survival of minority groups, to offer group-based representation, to provide exemptions from public duties, to alter traditional conceptions of the cultural basis of political communities, to establish forms of differential treatment, or simply to "recognize" the particularity of various group experiences.

The presence of Islam within liberal democracies intersects all of these philosophical, ethical, and social debates insofar as *Islam* is a (Rawlsian) comprehensive ethical doctrine and *Muslim communities* constitute cultural, and often racial and linguistic, minority groups. Moreover, the practice of Islam represents a textbook illustration of both the appeals and the challenges of liberal neutrality. On the one hand, liberals would claim that Muslim minorities benefit from the religious neutrality of secular, liberal democracies. Muslims in the West do not face the stark choice between political rights and the practice of their religion. As a minority community, Muslims enjoy protections against certain majority impositions. On the other hand, the practice of Islam free from the state imposition of Christianity, atheism, or another doctrine directly incompatible with Islamic truth claims is balanced by the protection of individual Muslims from communal authority. Muslims in liberal democracies enjoy rights deriving from the value of individual autonomy that do not figure in traditional elaborations of Islamic law, particularly the right to freedom of conscience (including apostasy), the right to free speech (including blasphemy), and the right of free marriage (including for women). Similarly, liberal neutrality may not provide Muslim communities with all the rights and protections they may find desirable, such as protection from offensive speech. Furthermore, there are questions related to Muslim citizenship in liberal democracies that are particular to Islamic legal and ethical discourses and rarely considered by liberal political philosophers. The very questions of living in a non-Muslim country, cooperating with non-Muslims, and exhibiting loyalty to non-Muslim authorities are all very much contested within Islamic legal-political thought. It is clear that Islamic citizenship in liberal democracies faces not only all of the cultural, social, and political problems faced by all cultural and racial minorities in the West but also, on top of these, problems of a distinctly ethical, conscientious, and doctrinal nature.

The aim of this book is thus to examine whether Muslims *qua* Muslims can regard as religiously legitimate the demands of citizenship in liberal democracy. This involves asking whether requirements such as living in and being loyal to a non-Muslim state, regarding non-Muslims as political equals with whom one might cooperate socially and politically, and allowing fellow Muslims to practice or not practice their religion as they see fit can be regarded as legitimate practices. At worst, one would look for attitudes, values, and proclamations that regard such concessions as necessary evils given the minority status of Muslims in liberal democracies, but one day perhaps to be overcome in the conditions of a pious majority. At best, one would look for statements that portray cooperation with non-Muslims and freedom of conscience for Muslims as values sanctioned or even encouraged by Islamic texts, that is, as *Islamic* values. Thus, this is primarily a search for a religiously based ethical *doctrine*. By contrast, the liberalization of individual Muslims or of whole societies, whether that means abandoning religious belief or enriching one's repertoire of beliefs with liberal values expressly regarded as new or exogenous to religion, is properly regarded as a sociological phenomenon. That process may be more historically important, sociologically interesting, or politically reliable as a path to the stability of liberal institutions, but it is not the object of this inquiry.

This type of inquiry is a form of *comparative political theory*. What is comparative about it is the attempt to pose similar questions across philosophical and ethical traditions with the aim of identifying the possible grounds for consensus. It differs from the traditional concerns of hermeneutics, discourse analysis, genealogy, or intellectual history to the extent that it is concerned with a particular form of normative argumentation, or justification. Comparative political theory (what I will also refer to as "conjecture," following Rawls, or simply as comparative ethics) on my understanding does not pretend to be disinterested or value-neutral. It is openly concerned with justifying certain normative principles from different philosophical, ethical, or religious foundations.

The need for this type of comparative political theory is not necessarily assumed by Western political theorists. A philosopher might ask the following questions: Given that the liberal political conception of justice is derived and justified independently of those doctrines, what need does it have to be justifiable within them? Why should we care whether Muslims (or the Amish, or Southern Baptists, or Mormons, or hedonists) have the resources *within* their religious doctrines to become the kinds of citizens that political liberalism requires them to be? Shouldn't nonliberals simply be asked to accept the principles of justice (if they are to be reasonable, that is)? What if we discover that there is no foundation for an overlapping consensus between political liberalism and a given comprehensive doctrine? Would that detract at all from our liberal commitment to equal rights and individual liberties? Would it lead to any meaningful conclusions about the status of the holders of that doctrine as citizens? Furthermore, isn't the whole inquiry a bit contradictory? Isn't it the very point that these are *nonliberal* doctrines that by definition prioritize the good and the true over the right? Aren't theories of justice supposed to be independent of the accommodation of power or considerations of popularity? Isn't that what makes them theories of justice rather than theories of prudence, social stability, or political decision making?[2]

Other theorists (perhaps various communitarians, multiculturalists, or critical theorists) might object to the liberal bias in the methodology. After all, isn't it assumed here that it is liberal values that we are trying to find the foundation or justification for in nonliberal doctrines and not the other way around? Isn't there an assumption operating that for various doctrines and traditions to be treated with respect (as "reasonable" in Rawls's terms) that they must be able to find the resources to become certain types of liberals? Isn't this approach just another form of intellectual hegemony designed to undercut minority traditions by more subtle means? Rephrasing, there might be at least three important reservations about this form of comparative political theory.

First, theorizing across existing doctrines is based on nothing more than historical contingency and thus has *no justificatory force*. The moral force of intersubjective agreements is that they are not based merely on self-interest or strategy but that they can be justified from the standpoint of all human beings. Merely pointing out that a value or a norm can also be found in another ethical tradition does not advance this constructivist moral claim. The approach is either anthropological or sociological (in that it may be of empirical or historical interest) or else political (in that it may represent a path to social stability or accommodation), but it is of no inherent philosophical or ethical interest. *We have nothing to learn, as it were, about how we should organize our societies from studying, for example, Islamic texts, insofar as we cannot take their claims literally or seriously consider adopting them as our own.*

In addition to these concerns, it is not clear that, where one might aspire to a normative consensus or a deliberative outcome between citizens, one is looking for a consensus between *doctrines*. Part of the aspiration of political constructivism, discourse ethics, deliberative democracy, and public reason is that citizens will be able to appeal to each other *qua* citizens and not merely *qua* rationalists, Christians, Muslims, and so on. We aspire toward agreement precisely based on arguments that citizens can endorse regardless of whether these arguments are grounded in their more controversial beliefs. Thus, when we do engage intellectually with nonliberal cultural or religious groups over a particular policy dispute (such as the Danish cartoon affair, abortion, or school prayer) and are willing to examine our received beliefs in light of the views they advance, what is important to us are not the arguments put forward from within their ethical traditions (i.e., arguments that presume the veracity of those traditions in order to be accessible) but only arguments that can be "translated" into a form of public reason. For example, we are willing to consider how far our defense of freedom of speech can be carried in the Danish cartoons affair but only in relation to other publicly accessible political values, like protection against offense or respect for beliefs, and not, for example, Qur'anic or doctrinal injunctions against insulting the Prophet. We are willing to debate Christians on the morality of abortion but only in terms of whether it is *reasonable* for us to consider a first-trimester fetus as a human and not whether it is *divinely ordained* for us to do so.

Thus, seeking to ground the ethical values that support a commitment to public reason, discourse ethics, or deliberative democracy in comprehensive doctrines, as opposed to public reason, may be something that we actually want to avoid. There might be a special force to this concern for those invested in political liberalism's commitment to a free-standing public justification. Because a political conception of justice is not justified by a public appeal to its truth and instead relies on its relation to truth or rationality remaining ambiguous, "trying to pry open the specific affirmations that relate the political conception to moral truth [might] compromise the purity of a merely political conception of justice."[3]

Second, to the extent that one of the purposes of comparative political theory is to find consensus, the project is *implausible.* It is chimerical to assume that one will always be able to arrive at similar enough conclusions (even about how to disagree) from different first principles. Furthermore, such intersubjective agreement between parties based on different comprehensive values or principles will be inherently unstable and unreliable, if not purely tactical on the part of actors. This objection is put most forcefully from within a liberal perspective by Brian Barry. For Barry, the liberal requirement that nonliberals tolerate behavior they regard as wrong cannot be sweetened by public self-restraint in the way that tolerance is justified (say, through arguments based on "neutrality" or "reasonableness"). "We have to abandon as illusory the hope that people might be left undisturbed in the dogmatic slumbers while somehow being cajoled into accepting liberal policy prescriptions. Dogmatism must give way to scepticism before the appropriately attenuated concept of wrongness can become attractive. . . . There is no way that non-liberals can be sold the principle of neutrality without first injecting a large dose of liberalism into their outlook."[4] Because persons who not only hold comprehensive doctrines but also hold them dogmatically will have little interest in looking outside those doctrines for moral arguments or motivations, they will not regard themselves as morally bound to a liberal political conception of justice should they acquire political power. Thus, even if an overlapping consensus can be shown between *some* doctrines, short of all non-(politically)liberal doctrines disappearing, we are no closer to understanding what to do about such "unreasonable" pluralism. In fact, the commitment to a public language of neutrality and reasonableness may deprive liberals of crucial resources for combating intolerant, illiberal doctrines operating in society.

Third, "justificatory" comparative political theory is really a form of *cultural hegemony* with a human face. The assertion is that minority cultures are obliged to become liberal to a certain extent in order to enjoy equal citizenship or recognition as valuable expressions of human experience. This reveals the inherent paradox in liberal claims to neutrality or universality: On the one hand, political liberalism claims to be a doctrine that tolerates nonliberal forms of life and conceptions of the good, yet on the other, it requires that doctrines, associations, or communities eligible for this toleration already exhibit enough liberalism to be able to share in this project of mutual toleration. This objection is put forcefully by Bhikhu Parekh:

> A widespread consensus among comprehensive doctrines then
> might not be available and yet it is badly needed to make political

> liberalism viable. Rawls's society has no choice but to *create* one. Since liberal values are embodied in the basic structure of society and enjoy enormous power and prestige, Rawls hopes that all, or at least most, comprehensive doctrines would over time adjust to and be informed by political liberalism. Since the latter is grounded in comprehensive liberalism, this would mean the dominance of the latter over other comprehensive doctrines. Rawls's political liberalism is, or could be seen by some as, not a principled and self-limiting moral position but a political device with a large hidden agenda.[5]

It is clear from these criticisms that this type of inquiry is open to criticism from both flanks: that, in carefully testing liberalism's appeal to nonliberals, it is too agnostic about liberal foundations and that, in searching for resources to "liberalize" nonliberal doctrines, it is too uncritical of them. There may not be a fully satisfactory response to much of this. Nonetheless, even if direct and final refutations of these concerns may be lacking, one can still call into question the extent to which they are important and argue for other values and purposes of theorizing that are neglected by these objections. In the following two chapters, I first examine the purposes of theorizing across ethical doctrines in various meta-ethical approaches and then summarize why, and to what extent, liberal political theorists should be interested in the comprehensive views of nonliberal fellow citizens. I then examine some moral and methodological problems in comparing ethical traditions with the aim of justifying common principles, refute some common objections or reservations, and propose a set of principles for guiding this form of inquiry.

I

Purposes: The Place of Justificatory Comparative Political Theory

So why do we need an Islamic doctrine of citizenship in liberal democracies, any more than we need a Catholic, Mormon, Amish, or hedonist doctrine of citizenship? Why is it not enough to determine through public reasoning what is reasonable for the state or political community to demand of its citizens and leave it at that? If citizens comply with just laws and act in a way that allows a well-ordered democratic society to enjoy stability, is it even proper for political theorists to be inquiring into what comprehensive beliefs citizens should hold?

The concern with the possibility of an overlapping consensus or support for liberal institutions from comprehensive doctrines is part of a long tradition in political theory of addressing moral psychology, human motivations, and the conditions for stability. Political philosophers have often concerned themselves not only with justifying their normative theories but also with addressing how those theories can overcome the many barriers standing in the way of a just society: ignorance, greed, envy, superstition, amour propre, ideology, and so on. Some philosophers have imagined that the inherent intellectual and moral limitations of the masses of ordinary people create a need for additional institutional or policy mechanisms to increase the likelihood that they will support just and good regimes. Plato thus anticipated that the ordinary citizens of his *kallipolis* would need to be taught a number of "noble lies" for them to assent voluntarily to the rule of the highest class. Others, including utilitarians such as John Stuart Mill, have traditionally put great emphasis on the ability of education to narrow the gap between the beliefs of ordinary citizens and the true, good, or rational guiding philosophy of the society.[1] Yet in these theories, these subsequent mechanisms are remedies for dilemmas that, however anticipated, arise from outside the theory itself. Others have imagined that the very implementationof the proposed ideal society would inherently bring about a resolution of the problem of stability. Theorists such as Rousseau and Marx, who imagined that greed, selfishness, and egotism are not innate human features but rather the products of socialization in existing institutions, thus asserted that the implementation of an ideal order (the true republic or communism, respectively) would itself by necessity remove the root causes of the opposition to justice or freedom.

The later work of John Rawls contains a unique contribution to this tradition. For Rawls, in addition to all of the familiar obstacles placed by human nature, a well-ordered society is also threatened by the efforts of persons to advance, through the state, aims derived from their conceptions of the good (or "comprehensive doctrines"). Such persons are not necessarily ignorant or selfish in the ways imagined by Plato, Hobbes, or Marx. They do not use the values and symbols of a conception of the good simply as a mask or legitimation for material self-interest. Nor does Rawls declare that certain conceptions of the good are false, and that *these doctrines* must be overcome or transcended. Rather, Rawls argues that intrasocietal disagreement about truth, the good, the valuable, and the rational is an inevitable feature of human life in the conditions of freedom. A public language of justification based on the truth of any single doctrine will either face perennial opposition from some segment of the population or rely on state coercion (including indoctrination) to secure assent. Thus, however sincere or well motivated they are in their adherence to their deepest philosophical beliefs, persons who seek to impose those beliefs through the state are fundamentally *unreasonable* in the sense of being unwilling to "propose and abide by fair terms of cooperation" or by failing to recognize fellow citizens as free and equal. Citizens so motivated will thus have little to no loyalty to a liberal political regime.

The problem of stability in political liberalism is thus twofold: First, many citizens will be motivated to oppose a liberal political order in the name of what they believe to be true, rational, or good. Second, the liberal political order itself does not publicly claim to be true or rational and thus does not provide its citizens with a complete philosophical account of how liberal principles fit into a larger conception of a well-lived life, an account that could be used to answer the claims of those who believe that their true beliefs ought to inform the basic structure of society.

The idea of an overlapping consensus thus largely functions as a way of showing how a just and well-ordered society is *possible*: If one of the main threats to the stability of a just society is the impact of undemocratic and unreasonable comprehensive doctrines (in addition to selfishness, envy, irrationality, class conflict, and the like), then at least *that* threat can be removed or mitigated when "there are many reasonable comprehensive doctrines that understand the wider realm of values to be congruent with, or supportive of, or else not in conflict with, political values as these are specified by a political conception of justice for a democratic regime."[2] If one of the requirements of political liberalism is that it not take sides in deep philosophical questions about truth, then at least that vulnerability can be overcome when citizens are able to relate a liberal conception of justice in some way to their own conception of truth.

A fuller account of these ideas is elaborated later. However, it is important to stress that the interest in political and social stability need not derive from a commitment to any *particular* normative or justificatory project, such as (Rawlsian) political liberalism. Whatever the strength of rational arguments for liberal principles, we can easily recognize that actual agents often require additional motivations for action, without thinking that those motivations provide independent philosophical justification.[3] On an aggregate level, we can acknowledge that liberal institutions are more stable when a persistent majority of citizens do not hold comprehensive views that declare those institutions to be illegitimate, thus contributing to a range of social goods about which liberals care, such as stability, social order, trust, harmony, efficient decision making, solidarity, social integration, political legitimacy, and respect for rights.[4] Perhaps, following Tocqueville, we feel that the stability of a democratic society relies at some level on "the different concepts men adopt, the various opinions which prevail among them and to the whole collection of ideas which shape mental habits."[5] One may feel that the appeal to religious beliefs for such support is an unfortunate, perhaps even cynical, tactic for achieving social stability,[6] or one may argue in principle that all beliefs are ultimately derived from controversial metaphysical commitments and that the appeal to another's value commitments in moral argumentation is all we have.[7] However, unless one believes that religious or philosophical doctrines never provide their adherents with motivations for action, or that they ought not to be indulged by appealing to them to endorse the reasonableness of liberal terms of social cooperation, one has no reason to be indifferent to an investigation of their capacity to support or oppose liberal conceptions of justice or citizenship.

Although to be interested in whether the comprehensive doctrines in a society are part of an overlapping consensus does not require taking sides in the debate on the philosophical or justificatory role of an overlapping consensus, it is true that political liberals—those who believe that political justification in public should not refer to any single controversial comprehensive metaphysical doctrine or conception of the good—have special reasons for being interested in the prospects for an overlapping consensus in any given political society. In what follows I outline the place of the idea of an overlapping consensus in political liberalism and show that the liberal interest in the existence of such a consensus in the case of any *particular* comprehensive doctrine is primarily political rather than justificatory. However, while this book presumes a commitment to a liberal conception of citizenship as a framework for morally evaluating Islamic views on membership in non-Muslim liberal democracies, and draws on Rawls's idea of an overlapping consensus as a way of structuring our interest in Islamic ethics, I believe this inquiry is robust vis-à-vis many ongoing debates about the desirability, success, or possibility of the specific justificatory scheme laid out in Rawls's later work. For this reason, after my survey of Rawls's concept of an overlapping consensus, I examine two popular alternatives to political liberalism (Habermas's and Benhabib's views on discourse ethics and deliberative democracy, and two forms of historical relativism). My conclusion is that the understanding of the precise value of actual consensus or agreement about the terms of social cooperation, and thus of the purpose of exploring Islamic doctrines at this book's level of detail, is actually quite comparable across these three perspectives. Thus, I believe there need arise no significant concern among political theorists broadly sympathetic to liberalism about my preferring the language of political liberalism throughout this book ("overlapping consensus," "reasonableness," "fair social cooperation," and so on).

Stability and the Overlapping Consensus in Rawlsian Political Liberalism

Much of recent philosophical liberalism is defined by a concern to defend a liberal conception of justice that is neutral not only between (reasonable) conceptions of the good in the political sphere but also in its very justification of such neutrality.[8] Rawls's earliest formulation of his theory of justice had been subjected to the criticism that not only were the principles of justice arrived at it in his original position not neutral in their effect on various conceptions of the good life but also his account of stability (how the principles of justice would come to enjoy the support of citizens subject to them) presumed that citizens would come to adopt the moral principles underlying the conception of justice as a true comprehensive doctrine. Rawls became convinced that enduring disagreement about moral, philosophical, and theological questions is the result, not of the failure of human reason, but of the so-called burdens of judgment. Those burdens include inconclusive evidence, the differential assignations of weight to facts, the indeterminacy of concepts, the influence of personal experience on judgment, and the incommensurability of values.[9] Because of the way these burdens bear on human reason, reasonable persons will—in the conditions of freedom from oppressive state power—arrive at different judgments on questions of morality and the good. This is Rawls's "fact of reasonable pluralism."[10] Disagreement that is attributable to the burdens of judgment, unlike disagreement caused by bias and self-interest, is therefore reasonable and ought to be tolerated. It is not to be regarded as a misfortune but rather as the inevitable result of life in the conditions of freedom. Because, in Rawls's own view, his account of stability in *A Theory of Justice* (that reasonable citizens will all converge on a broad moral reflective equilibrium) was fundamentally inconsistent with its own political institutions (freedom of thought and association), it was defective and needed to be revised.

Rawls's revision asserted that his principles of justice were meant to apply only to a specific object, namely, political cooperation, and not as general moral principles. This involved a revision of some of the more controversial concepts of justice as fairness—namely, the conceptions of the person, rationality, and autonomy required for the theory to be coherent—so that they did not imply a commitment to comprehensive truth-claims that might alienate citizens who (reasonably) do not endorse them. This revision allowed Rawls to advance a new account of stability that did not assume that all citizens will ultimately converge on common moral judgments in a well-ordered society. Rather, Rawls now argued that a purely political, or "freestanding," conception of justice is available for endorsement by a variety of comprehensive doctrines. While political liberalism merely proposes its principles of justice as the most reasonable or appropriate such principles for a democratic society and abstains from public philosophizing on their ultimate foundations, in civil society many citizens will find that their own religious and secular doctrines give them principled reasons for supporting the liberal terms of social cooperation.[11] The assumption here is that comprehensive doctrines play a role in providing their adherents with their conception of rationality, that is, which goals they are motivated to pursue. If a doctrine endorses a political conception of justice for reasons a person finds compelling or authoritative, we imagine that person is thus motivated to support the conception of justice. When many such doctrines provide their adherents with such reasons and motivations, we speak of an "overlapping consensus" obtaining in civil society (or the background culture of a democratic society) on the reasonableness of the terms of social cooperation.

In Rawls's words: While "it is left to citizens individually to settle how they think the values of the political domain are related to other values in their comprehensive doctrine," "the history of religion and philosophy shows that there are many reasonable ways in which the wider realm of values can be understood so as to be either congruent with, or supportive of, or else not in conflict with, the values appropriate to the special domain of the political. This makes an overlapping consensus possible, thus reducing the conflict between political and other values."[12] The long-term demonstration of stability is:

> that those who affirm the various views supporting the political conception will not withdraw their support of it should the relative strength of their view in society increase and eventually become dominant. The political conception will still be supported regardless of shifts in the distribution of political power. Each view supports the political conception for its own sake, or on its own merits. The test for this is whether the consensus is stable with respect to changes in the distribution of power among views.[13]

This indicates that the overlapping consensus is not merely a Hobbesian modus vivendi but a moral consensus between citizens.

Another way of understanding the relationship of stability to justice is via Rawls's conception of justification. Political liberalism aims at offering all citizens a *pro tanto* justification for a political conception of justice. By "*pro tanto* justification" is meant the idea that a conception of justice (or a policy within a liberal state) can be shown to be reasonable in that it requires no comprehensive or metaphysical beliefs to support it. It can be justified by using purely political values appropriate to a democratic political community with a diversity of comprehensive doctrines.[14] In political liberalism, political justification is thus *reasonable justification,* rather than justification based on an appeal to truth, the good, or the authority of a comprehensive moral or epistemological doctrine.

As such, political liberalism is limited in the scope of its claims and hence its resources to motivate individual citizens. An important feature of political liberalism's self-restraint is that public institutions do not give a philosophical or religious account of how liberal tolerance and neutrality fit into a grand theory of truth or the good. This strategy is, of course, designed to increase social unity. Religious and cultural conflicts can be avoided or mitigated by limiting governmental power to what can be justified to all reasonable citizens. However, precisely because political liberalism is a thin public philosophy and does not help citizens order their own souls so that their private purposes and public institutions are aligned, social unity might be fragile. Because some citizens might have no deep, compelling reasons to regard thin, freestanding political principles as outweighing the political principles derived from their deep and purposeful religious and philosophical beliefs, there might exist what we could call a "justificatory gap." Such citizens will thus be only contingently committed to liberal institutions as long as their relative social and demographic power requires tactical moderation and self-restraint.

Political liberalism gives the following answer to this central problem: Because liberal principles are freestanding rather than derived from a controversial doctrine of truth or the good, they are *eligible for* endorsement by a variety of such controversial doctrines. Thus, the conjecture goes, individual citizens may have their own deep and compelling philosophical and religious reasons for endorsing liberal principles. When the "citizen accepts a political conception and fills out its justification by embedding it in some way into the citizen's comprehensive doctrine as either true or reasonable,"[15] she has a "full justification" for that conception, which the conception itself studiously avoids providing. Crucially, unlike with public justification, we are not concerned about the views of other citizens who do not share our comprehensive doctrine. The search for a full justification is nonpublic, occurring privately or in communities of shared moral purposes (what is commonly called "civil society"). We may continue to regard a full justification of liberal institutions to obtain or not obtain even when fellow citizens disagree about any aspect of our reasoning. However, no citizen's (or group's) full justification is regarded as proving a *public* justification binding on any other citizen.[16] The idea of full justification is simply the claim that a purely political, freestanding public conception can receive deep philosophical or theological endorsement despite not providing one itself, which helps account for how citizens of a liberal state will be motivated to support it.

The purpose of this book is to examine the possibilities for an Islamic *full justification* of liberal citizenship, and thus I characterize this project as a work of "justificatory comparative political theory." Such a purpose distinguishes this inquiry from other projects with historiographical, anthropological, sociological, or genealogical aims.

Empirical Overlapping Consensus: Political Not Justificatory

It is important at this point to avoid confusion about the idea of "overlap" between doctrines and the philosophical interest in the *empirical* existence of a full justification of a liberal conception of justice from within any particular comprehensive doctrine. The first point that bears stressing is that the public conception of justice is not to be regarded as the product of an overlap of existing doctrines, such as might be visualized by a Venn diagram.[17] The problem of social unity in political liberalism is not resolved through a process of bargaining or negotiation between existing social groups so that the final terms of social cooperation are more or less acceptable to citizens based on their values, principles, and goals derived from their comprehensive doctrines. "The content [of the principles of justice] is not affected in any way by the particular comprehensive doctrines that may exist in a society."[18] Such a process would make political liberalism "political in the wrong way," in the sense of being a political compromise or modus vivendi designed with a particular society in a particular time period in mind.[19] Political liberalism's claim to fairness is grounded, rather, in its claim to be reasonable to all *citizens*, regardless of their comprehensive doctrines.

Second, the reasonableness of the conception of justice does not depend on the endorsement of any particular doctrine; rather, the public conception of justice must be *available* for endorsement by a variety of doctrines. A brisk or superficial reading of *Political Liberalism* might result in some confusion on this point, with some statements asserting that the empirical existence of an overlapping consensus between actual doctrines is required for the reasonableness of a conception of justice. This might in turn suggest the *need* for an inquiry into the content of those doctrines.

The ambiguity in the relationship between justice and stability is best exemplified in this passage: "Unless [justice as fairness is sufficiently stable], it is not a satisfactory political conception of justice and it must be in some way revised."[20] The clear implication here is that stability is *not* merely a political or historical concern, but a normative one:

> The problem of stability is not that of bringing others who reject a conception to share it, or to act in accordance with it, by workable sanctions, if necessary, as if the task were to find ways to impose that conception once we are convinced it is sound. Rather, *justice as fairness is not reasonable in the first place* unless in a suitable way it can win its support by addressing each citizen's reason, as explained within its own framework.[21]

But it is important to keep in mind here that at this stage of justification a citizen's moral doctrine *is part of* his reason. How else could he have good reason to reject an otherwise reasonable conception of justice? If it is purely out of obtuseness or self-interest, then we don't care about his rejection. Only if he has good reason (of which adherence to a moral doctrine is one) to reject a conception of justice do we bother to concern ourselves with the fact of disagreement.

The concern might be this: The principles of justice are supposed to be reasonable ("correct") for reasons *independent* of moral doctrines. Their reasonableness, however, does rely also on their *stability*. If they are unstable, then they are unreasonable. Their stability, in turn, relies both on their ability to inculcate a particular moral psychology among citizens and on their capacity to be endorsed by multiple comprehensive doctrines. If reasonableness relies on stability, and stability relies partly on compatibility with moral doctrines, then doesn't it follow that reasonableness relies partially on compatibility, which seems to be excluded by the first premise?

Of course, neither is the political conception of justice derived from existing comprehensive doctrines, nor is the justification of that conception contingent upon its support from within any given doctrine.[22] It is clear that an *empirically existing* overlapping consensus—understood as the endorsement of the principles of justice by the major religious and ethical doctrines in a given society—is merely a desideratum for a liberal conception seeking to enjoy popular support. The confusion arises because Rawls asserts that a political conception must, indeed, be the object of an overlapping consensus and thus enjoy stability—but only between *reasonable* comprehensive doctrines.

Opening his discussion on the idea of an overlapping consensus, Rawls writes that:

> in such a consensus, the *reasonable doctrines* endorse the political conception, each from its own point of view. Social unity is based on a consensus on the political conception; and stability is possible when the doctrines making up the consensus are affirmed by society's politically active citizens and the requirements of justice are not too much in conflict with citizens' essential interests as formed and encouraged by their social arrangements.[23]

Also: "To serve as a public basis of justification for a constitutional regime a political conception of justice must be one that can be endorsed by widely different and opposing though reasonable comprehensive doctrines."[24] In this preceding sentence, note both that the requirement is that the conception "can be endorsed" (not that it *is* endorsed) and that even that is only by "*reasonable* comprehensive doctrines."

So the question now becomes: What makes a doctrine reasonable? Remember that the reason for Rawls's revision of his theory into a freestanding, political conception of liberalism is the burdens of judgment and hence the fact of reasonable pluralism. Here, reasonableness is an epistemological quality: Views are reasonable because they are compatible with the free use of human reason under the burdens of judgment.

Consistent with this, Rawls's definition of a "reasonable comprehensive doctrine" refers to three intellectual features. A comprehensive doctrine is reasonable if it is (1) an exercise in theoretical reason,[25] (2) an exercise in practical reason,[26] and (3) based on a tradition of thought.[27] Presumably these are the features that a doctrine would acquire from the free use of human reason over a long period of time. However, precisely because these are intellectual (epistemic) features, rather than moral ones, such a definition of a reasonable comprehensive doctrine would not exclude doctrines that are clearly opposed to a liberal conception of justice, such as any theocratic or secular perfectionist doctrine. Clearly, a conception of overlapping consensus that required the endorsement of all such doctrines in a given society would be either impossible to establish or an accidental overlap of the interests and values of those doctrines and thus "political in the wrong way."

Thus, Rawls immediately reverts in the section on "Reasonable Comprehensive Doctrines" (II §3, pp. 58–66) to a discussion of "reasonable *persons*" and the views they hold. The two relevant features of a reasonable person are that reasonable persons are willing "to propose principles and standards as fair terms of cooperation and to abide by them willingly, given the assurance that others will likewise do so"[28] and that they recognize the burdens of judgment. Both of these features define reasonableness in moral terms, particularly in reference to attitudes displayed toward fellow citizens. True, recognition of the burdens of judgment refers to an attitude toward knowledge, but is also primarily of a moral nature. For the interest is not in the quality of the reasoning of the citizen about philosophical or metaphysical matters. Rather, the concern is whether the citizen recognizes the reasonableness and equal moral worth of other citizens who do not endorse her doctrine.[29]

An enormous amount of weight is placed on the burdens of judgment. Rawls believes that anyone who recognizes the burdens of judgment and hence the reasonableness of pluralism will "think it unreasonable to use political power, should [one] possess it, to repress comprehensive views that are not unreasonable, though different from [one's] own. This is because, given the fact of reasonable pluralism, a public and shared basis of justification that applies to comprehensive doctrines is lacking in the public culture of a democratic society."[30] Because the only moral reason to use state power in this way is the claim to truth, but all holders of reasonable doctrines can make this claim, "when we make such claims others, who are themselves reasonable, must count us as unreasonable . . . and so [we] endorse some form of liberty of conscience and freedom of thought."[31] Note that reasonableness excludes as unreasonable *from the outset* all forms of religious fundamentalism that would use state or, indeed, any coercive power to impose beliefs about morality or virtue.

Thus, the existence or not of an empirical overlapping consensus between doctrines flourishing in a society does no justificatory work at all. What real normative work is being done by demonstrating the possibility of an overlapping consensus on a conception of justice when that consensus needs to be demonstrated only between doctrines that are reasonable, namely, that are already compatible with the main part of that conception? To the extent that the "pluralistic consensus test"[32] seems to require only that a conception of justice emerging be the subject of agreement by those doctrines that *can* agree to it, it seems entirely superfluous philosophically. The passing of this test is already guaranteed by the definition of *reasonableness*, which also carries the justificatory burden for the conception of justice.

Instead, the overlapping consensus seems in the end to be a sociological concept and a device for normatively evaluating moral doctrines that might be held in a society. To be quite clear then: The interest on the part of liberal political philosophers in the endorsement of a liberal conception of justice by any particular doctrine (such as Islam)—that is, in the possibility for a "full justification" from within a particular doctrine—is of political, not philosophical, interest. The mere fact of Islamic rejection of this or that liberal principle is not alone evidence that we might have gotten that principle wrong. Of course, the fact that there may be a more reasonable, an equally reasonable, or another sufficiently reasonable political principle or institution may be brought to our attention by the challenge from within a comprehensive doctrine such as Islam, but this is quite different from any such doctrine having a veto over the reasonable.

Whether we are bothered by the idea that Rawls's theory overdetermines the range of moral pluralism acceptable in a society by his relatively thick conception of the reasonable or by the possibility that recognizing the burdens of judgment as a fact may be as demanding philosophically and epistemologically as skepticism or other positions from which Rawls abstains[33] need not be addressed here.[34] It suffices to deny that these facts alone constitute grounds to disregard a liberal conception of justice in its substantive aspects or that any appropriation of the idea of an overlapping consensus is incoherent. We may continue to speak of a search for an overlapping consensus in a political society as long as we do not advance confusing and self-contradictory claims about the independent normative force of such a consensus. For those who are not uncomfortable about defending the liberal terms of social cooperation as reasonable, the value of honesty ought to compel us to concede at least that we see the search for an overlapping consensus as a political project. Liberalism surely has the resources to defend itself against any charges of unfair exclusion arising from this acknowledgment.[35]

Seeing the overlapping consensus as a political or sociological concept does not deprive it of moral significance. What we are, in effect, asking is: Does our conception of justice (which we hold to be at least reasonable, if not true) have the *capacity* to be the object of moral consensus for a wide range of citizens? Consider Joshua Cohen's explanation of the value of such a moral consensus (he calls it no less than a "fundamental good"):

> First, the likelihood that social order will stably conform to the conception is increased by the existence of a moral consensus on it. Second, the existence of a moral consensus supports a variety of specific values of considerable importance. It increases social trust and harmony, supports social peace, reduces the complexity of decision making, encourages a willingness to cooperate and so reduces the costs of monitoring and enforcement, and—assuming the consensus

> is reflected in public debate and decisions—reduces alienation from public choices because citizens embrace the norms and ideals that guide those choices. Third, a consensus on norms of justice provides a way to reconcile the ideal of an association whose members are self-governing with an acknowledgement of the central role of social and political arrangements in shaping the self-conception of citizens, constraining their actions, channeling their choices, and determining the outcomes of those choices. For when a consensus on norms and values underlies and explains collective decisions, citizens whose lives are governed by those decisions might nonetheless be said to be self-governing because each endorses the considerations that produce the decisions as genuinely moral reasons and affirms their implementation.[36]

We are now in a position to answer the question posed at the beginning of this part: Of what interest is it to political liberals the way existing doctrines in a society relate to our conception of justice—whether different groups of citizens can endorse the same values for different reasons? It is of interest to the extent that three conditions obtain: (1) that it matters to holders of comprehensive doctrines how their doctrine relates to the public conception of justice; (2) that citizens' judgments on (1) have an effect on the goods named previously, namely, social order, trust, harmony, efficient decision making, social integration, political legitimacy, and autonomy; and (3) that liberals care about the goods listed in (2). The results of an inquiry into the possibility of an overlapping consensus between our conception of justice and comprehensive doctrine *D* might serve in two ways: (1) as part of our evaluation of the likelihood of realizing these fundamental social goods in a given society[37] and (2) as part of our marshaling of resources for their realization.

Discourse Ethics and Deliberative Democracy

We find a rival to Rawls's constructivism in the "discourse ethics" developed by Jürgen Habermas and his colleagues. Although sharing the commitment to both Kantian universalism and formalism, discourse ethics breaks with Rawls's neo-Kantian appeal to ideal reason developed monologically (i.e., from the standpoint of a single unencumbered subject or many such subjects in a fictitious setting) to ideal speech and argumentation between multiple situated (i.e., real) subjects. While for Rawls, moral philosophy depends on abstracting from the particular circumstances of real subjects, for Habermas, "as long as moral philosophy concerns itself with clarifying the everyday intuitions into which we are socialized, it must be able to adopt, at least virtually, the attitude of someone who participates in the communicative practice of everyday life."[38] Discourse ethics thus calls for the transformation of Kant's categorical imperative from a consistency test applied within the reasoning subject's own mind (*in foro interno*) to a test of a given maxim's capacity to be approved of by all persons to whom it might apply through a procedure of open argumentation. Morality can thus be known not through the procedure of autonomous will formation or rational agreement behind a veil of ignorance, but through actual dialogue between persons eminently aware of their interests and cultural heritage: "Only those norms can claim to be valid that meet (or could meet) with the approval of all affected in their capacity *as participants in a practical discourse*."[39]

The normative force of discourse is twofold. First, by eschewing the abstract model of social contract theories for a model of real communication in the lifeworld, discourse ethics seeks to meet the Hegelian claim that morality can never be conceived of outside particular historical horizons and is intelligible only in the context of lived ethical practices expressed through social bonds and shared forms of life (*Sittlichkeit*). Practical discourse presumes these bonds of social integration not simply as a pragmatic concession but because that is precisely the context in which moral dilemmas and claims to normativity emerge:

> Discourse ethics gives up Kant's dichotomy between an *intelligible* realm comprising duty and free will and a *phenomenal* realm comprising inclinations, subjective motives, political and social institutions, etc. The unbridgeable gap Kant saw between the intelligible and the empirical becomes, in discourse ethics, a mere tension manifesting itself in *everyday communication* as the factual force of counterfactual presuppositions.[40]

However, this nod to Hegelianism does not result in a form of moral relativism or particularism, according to which historically current norms are themselves authoritative. Just as Rawls's later concern for a socially existing overlapping consensus must not be confused with a program to derive principles of justice from existing doctrines or political culture, Habermas's program of grounding moral knowledge in practical discourses must not be confused with the crude reification of existing norms or prejudices:

> While there is an unequivocal relation between existing states of affairs and true propositions about them, the "existence" or social currency of norms says nothing about whether the norms are valid. We must distinguish between the social fact that a norm is intersubjectively recognized and its worthiness to be recognized. . . . [O]ur motives for recognizing normative claims to validity are rooted both in convictions and in sanctions, that is, they derive from a complex mixture of rational insight and force.[41]

The point of ideal argumentation for Habermas is that it allows participants, while being the sole arbiters of their own interests, to apprehend some kind of general interest. By removing threats, force, sanctions, bribes, and other inducements from the domain of persuasion, we are able to endow actual discourses with a moral quality. Just like Rawls's original position, the function of ideal discourse is essentially diagnostic; it is the formal procedure by which we know whether a norm or maxim is just: "What is expressed in normative validity is the authority of a *general will* shared by all concerned, a will that has been divested of its imperative quality and has taken on a moral quality. This will invokes a universal interest, which we can ascertain through *discourse*, that is, grasp *cognitively* from our perspective as participants."[42] The original position cannot do this because it ignores the lifeworld, the realm in which morality manifests itself. But anthropological attention to the lifeworld alone is not sufficient because it is replete with power relations and exploitation that preclude tests of universalizability and impartiality that define morality. It is not without reason then that Habermas describes "the ethics of discourse [as] pick[ing] up the basic Hegelian aspiration to redeem it with Kantian means."[43]

Why Habermas thinks discourse can do this is the second aspect of its normative force. All foundationalist moralities are troubled by the skeptic's charge that the grounding values of the theory are expressions of a particular culture's conception of the good and cannot be justified in an objective, noncircular way. The skeptic's charge is that attempts to justify values as "universal" result in three equally bad alternatives: putting up with an infinite regress, arbitrarily breaking off the chain of deduction, or making a circular argument. What posing this "trilemma" presumes, however, is a purely semantic, or logical, conception of deduction. Argumentation involves, on the other hand, *pragmatic* rules that allow bridging the logical gap left in relations that are not best characterized as "deductive." Drawing on the work of Karl-Otto Apel, Habermas then argues that merely in posing this (Münchhausen) trilemma, the skeptic:

> will have involved himself in a performative contradiction if the proponent [of the universal validity of the principle of universalization] can show that in making his argument, he has to make assumptions that are inevitable in *any* argumentation game aiming at critical examination and the propositional content of those assumptions contradicts the principle of fallibilism. This is in fact the case, since in putting forward his objection, the opponent necessarily assumes the validity of at least those logical rules that are irreplaceable if we are to understand his argument as a refutation. In taking part in the process of reasoning, even the consistent fallibilist has already accepted as valid a minimum number of unavoidable rules of criticism. Yet this state of affairs is incompatible with the principle of fallibilism.[44]

Habermas thus believes that the actual pragmatics of communication and argumentation commit the participant to certain substantive normative presuppositions, namely, equal respect, the rejection of coercion, the freedom to form opinions, the intersubjective validity of reasons, trust, and honesty. Simply by engaging in discourses based on argumentation, the skeptic acknowledges the incoherence of claims to normative validity achieved through coercion, lies, or exclusion and thus implicitly recognizes the principle of universalization that he is in the process of denying. Expounding the transcendental-pragmatic (i.e., unavoidable) rules of argumentation (which I will not reproduce here) shows, according to Apel and Habermas, that "the idea of impartiality is rooted *in* the structures of argumentation *themselves* and does not need to be *brought in* from the outside as a supplementary normative content."[45] By showing this to be true, Habermas believes that "discourse ethics improves upon Kant's unsatisfactory handling of a specific problem of justification when he evasively points to the alleged 'fact of pure reason' and argues that the effectiveness of the 'ought' is simply a matter of experience. Discourse ethics solves this problem by deriving (U) [the principle of universalization] from the universal presuppositions of argumentation."[46] In other words, while all Kantian theories (including those of John Rawls and G. H. Mead) are based on some form of ideal role taking as a guarantee of impartial judgment, Habermas believes that discourse is a superior path to this impartiality because it publicly binds all participants to the abstract, counterfactual presuppositions involved in the cooperative search for truth. All Habermas believes he has done here is justify a rule of argumentation (a formal procedure) for moral dialogue. As seen previously, any substantive norms or maxims must emerge from real discourses and not from any single theorist's armchair reasoning: "Moral justifications are dependent on argumentation actually being carried out, not for pragmatic reasons of an equalization of power, but for internal reasons, namely that real argument makes moral insight possible."[47]

These meta-ethical controversies are of interest to us here only insofar as they have some bearing on the justification of liberal principles and the place of comparative theorizing in that justification. For this, we are better off engaging with theories of deliberative democracy elaborated in large part by Habermas's associates. The first tendency we observe is that of emphasizing the greater discursive inclusiveness of discourse ethics and deliberative democracy over Rawlsian theories of public reason:

> Discourse ethics has one distinctive virtue when compared with other variants of contractarian and universalist models of normative validity: its participants feel free to introduce into the dialogue their life-world moral dilemmas and conflicts without any constraints imposed by counter-factual experiments and idealizations. Discourses do not prescribe the content of moral argument through thought experiments or definitional boundary drawings between the public and the private. Furthermore, individuals' needs as well as principles, life stories as well as moral judgments, can be freely shared with others, but discourse participants may also keep "private" aspects of their personal narratives they prefer not to share. There is no obligation of self-disclosure in the public space.[48]

For proponents of discourse ethics, contractarian or constructivist theories purchase their "more *determinate* or *concrete* content of choice and deliberation" only at the cost of "restricting the agenda of the conversation as well as abstracting away from the identity of the individuals involved."[49] Their program, by contrast, centralizes the particular perspectives of all moral beings capable of sentience, speech, and action. Our obligation of equal respect to moral or political contemporaries is the obligation to allow them to represent themselves in their own languages and narratives (or to decline to do so, a point that has deep significance for this project). There is no requirement to adopt an irreligious or acultural "public reason" as the only appropriate language for public discourse.

From the outset, then, there is an *inherent* openness to the variety of types of claims and sources of moral authority to which citizens might appeal in the public sphere. To return to the example of free speech and offense (as in the Rushdie affair or Danish cartoon controversy), whereas the (Rawlsian) political liberal might be inclined to jump to a stage of adjudication (what is to be done?) and thereby insist that all citizens appeal to public values (free speech, respect, order, and so forth), the proponent of discourse ethics is not concerned with only legislation and collective action. For her, public dialogue is a good in itself insofar as it contributes to the recognition of the particular experiences and interests of various groups. Thus, whereas the political liberal finds the decisive value for Muslims in the Rushdie affair—the religious injunction against slandering the Prophet—irrelevant for public purposes, the proponent of discourse ethics welcomes the sharing of such moral perspectives. We need to know not only their claims but also their most authentic reasons for advancing such claims. In terms of the theme of this chapter, the proponent of discourse ethics is much less likely to question the importance of examining other ethical traditions from the inside.

Nonetheless, two families of questions arise in this context. The first is the demand for precision: Of what *specific* interest is it to us how other doctrines or traditions provide answers to shared concerns or problems? What *precisely* do we think we are learning through this about viable solutions to problems of moral disagreement and about our own views? The second is the demand for justification: Why engage in this form of discourse? To what values are we ultimately appealing when we agree to limit our own reason and search for consensus with others?

Benhabib gives two very clear contexts in which moral disagreement requires not only open dialogue but also precisely engagement with particular doctrines or traditions. The first is our attempt to identify what type of problem we are facing: "Very often, moral dialogue is necessary to identify an issue as one of legislation rather than morality, of aesthetics rather than politics. Participants must not only reach understanding of the norms in question; they must also share a *situational* understanding of these norms' intended applications. What kind of practice we think a specific cultural practice is—religious or aesthetic, moral or legal—will determine which norms we think should apply to it."[50] It is obvious that when the practices we are concerned to evaluate are those of cultural or religious groups, then the categorization of which Benhabib speaks (which is an important part of evaluation) cannot proceed without direct inquiry into the explanations and descriptions of those practices by their adherents. This aspiration to situational understanding is crucial for this book. I discuss at some length in the next chapter my understanding of a basic "diagnostic" stage for the type of comparative theorizing I am proposing.

The second context is that of according recognition:

> [We] can learn the *whoness* of the other(s) only through their narratives of self-identification. The norm of universal respect enjoins me to enter the conversation insofar as one is considered a generalized other; but I can become aware of the *otherness of others*, of those aspects of their identity that make them concrete others to me, only through their own narratives. And because cultural narratives (which comprise linguistic, ethnic, religious, as well as territorial and regional accounts) are crucial to the narrative constitution of individual self-identities, such processes of interactive universalism are crucial in multicultural societies.[51]

What both of these contexts have in common is that they only occur already within the framework of a liberal democratic system. Such a system allows for a public sphere (both state institutions and civil society) in which discourses leading to recognition and moral contestation take place, and this is primarily where deliberative democracy also is to be situated.

However, it is not clear that discourse ethics is any more capable than political liberalism of grounding a rigorous argument in defense of basic liberal rights as institutionalized in a constitutional regime that could be presented to citizens or groups that do not already endorse certain minimal principles. Habermas and Apel identify two moral principles implicit in the pragmatics of argumentation: universal respect and egalitarian reciprocity. For theorists of deliberative democracy, these principles become analogous to the requirements that power be contestable and exercised neutrally for it to be legitimate, and they provide the foundation for more robust political principles, namely (in Benhabib's case), voluntary self-ascription and freedom of exit and association. However, Benhabib concedes that:

> the relationship between the metanorm of discourse ethics, the principles of universal respect, egalitarian reciprocity, and the constitutional fundamentals of liberal democracies is not one of inference or deduction. The most general premises from which such constitutions proceed—namely, the guarantee of basic human, civil, and political rights—can be viewed as embodying and contextualizing such norms in historically varying, and sociologically as well as culturally divergent, legal contexts.[52]

What this essentially concedes is that as far as an ultimate justification of its basic principles in the sphere of action (as opposed to discourse) is concerned, discourse ethics is characterized by the same presumption of consensus as is political liberalism. When arguing, one finds oneself bound to these rules *if* one wants to avoid performative contradiction. When one has the *will* to bring the sphere of action in line with moral principles, then discourse ethics offers a procedure for doing this. The bridge from discourse to action, however, is not provided for by the theory alone. Note Benhabib's comments to this effect:

> The justification of these norms through a recourse to the internal logic of argumentation situations alone will not get us very far. Such recourse is important but is clearly insufficient. The norm of universal respect presupposes a generalized moral attitude of equality toward other human beings. The boundaries of the community of moral discourse are open-ended; "all those whose interests are affected" are part of the moral conversation. But in the case of most human communities and cultures, we can take for granted neither that this generalized moral attitude toward human equality will be shared nor that other human beings will be considered worthy conversation partners in settling social, moral, and political matters. I believe that a generalized attitude of moral equality spreads in human history through conversations as well as confrontations across cultures, and through commerce as well as wars; international agreements as well as international threats contribute to its emergence. This is a sociological and historical observation. I believe in moral learning through moral transformation, and I assume that it is not the deep structure of the mind or psyche that makes us believe in universalism, but rather such historical and moral experiences. I would defend a historically enlightened universalism.[53]

For our purposes, these comments demand clarification on two matters: First, are there good reasons to believe in universal respect and egalitarian reciprocity and good arguments to put for them in something like an ideal speech situation? Second, are we interested in normative dialogue at the level of basic constitutional design, and does it matter how arguments in favor of the most basic liberal structures are compatible with nonliberal doctrines? It appears that these values are simply posited as appropriate for our historical moment and consciousness ("modernity," broadly understood, where basic equality of persons is widely accepted) as "an idealized model with which we can measure the fairness and legitimacy of existing practices and aspire to reform them, *if and when* the democratic will of the participants to do so exists."[54]

What follows from this is that the primary interest is in what goes on *within* societies enjoying basic liberal freedoms and democratic governance in terms of public debate over the most controversial normative questions. Thus, for all of its claims to a public process of unrestricted moral dialogue, it is not clear that theories of liberal democracy grounded in discourse ethics are willing to accord the legitimation of basic liberal principles from within traditionally nonliberal traditions more than the political or sociological importance granted it by Rawls's theory of political liberalism. It is clear, at least in Benhabib's elaboration, that proponents of discourse ethics see cross-cultural dialogue as primarily a political-moral imperative within civil society, rather than a philosophical requirement of justifying liberal social cooperation. She is, for example, willing to recognize pluralism and particularity in legal or political institutions "as long as these pluralist structures do not violate [the] three normative conditions . . . of *egalitarian reciprocity, voluntary self-ascription* and *freedom of exit and association.*"[55] But these three conditions are no less robust or controversial than the principles of justice proposed by Rawls, which she thinks are guilty of being based on a "separation between the background culture and the public political culture." This separation is "institutionally unstable and analytically untenable," first because:

> there are simply too many clashes and conflicts over some of the constitutional essentials to which most liberal democracies subscribe, like gender equality, bodily integrity, freedom of the person, education of children, and the practices of certain minority subcultures and groups. Since the constitutional essentials of the liberal-democratic state, embodied in its articulation of basic human, civil, and political rights, in many cases contradict the practices of ethnic and religious minorities, clashes over the interpretation and application of these principles in the light of these practices are inevitable.[56]

These observations may be valid enough (although it is hard not to see the idea of an overlapping consensus as a recognition of the need to bridge the "separation between the background culture and the public political culture"), but discourse ethics and deliberative models of democracies are no better equipped to deal with these clashes for the simple reason that the liberal "constitutional essentials" are equally off-limits for them as they are for political liberalism. In addition to defending the inviolability of the three normative conditions, she stresses that "while the Rawlsian model focuses upon 'final and coercive political power,' the deliberative model focuses upon noncoercive and nonfinal processes of opinion formation in an unrestricted public sphere."[57] The reason that the deliberative model does not focus on state power and the rights approach to social conflict is that, for the most part, it has nothing to add or detract from it as far as it goes. Deliberation and practical discourses are very much a nonbinding supplement to the legal approach to moral conflict.

Thus, while she calls "cross-cultural dialogue and coexistence real, unavoidable and necessary," what she thinks is at stake in those dialogues is relatively minor, at least from a philosophical perspective: "debates about Koran schools in postunification Germany, struggles about the rights of young Muslim women in the Pakistani community of Bradford, England, to refuse arranged marriages, and the desire of girls of Islamic faith to wear the scarf in French public schools."[58] Take the second of these three examples: Is there any doubt that she (correctly) believes the right of these girls to refuse marriage inviolable? What if there were absolutely no moral arguments for this freedom that would be convincing to Muslim community leaders and that could be put forward in the conditions of ideal discourse? Would she be willing to then concede that such freedoms could be defended by force but would not have the status of a valid norm because they are not universalizable? Or would she argue that anyone entering into this ideal discourse would find himself recognizing the principles of equal respect and egalitarian reciprocity (even toward his daughters in this case), regardless of *whatever else he believes,* and that these values would lead to consent for such freedoms? But there is no veil of ignorance in such contexts, so how is he supposed to bracket "whatever else he believes" (i.e., his religious or cultural values that lead him to believe that arranged marriages are proper and that daughters should recognize paternal authority)?

We have three possibilities at this point: (1) We can argue that the norm in question (freedom to refuse marriage) is not a valid norm until all whom it affects (including fathers) freely endorse it; (2) we can argue that it is a valid norm but some parties refuse to relinquish the power they get from not endorsing it; or (3) we can argue that it is a valid norm because it flows from the formal moral presuppositions of discourse ethics. If (1), then we give up on our universalism in this case and concede that the freedom to refuse marriage is a local prejudice, albeit one that we have good reasons for endorsing. If (2), then we have the burden of demonstrating the bad faith of our participants and are essentially committed to suggesting the falsity of the religious beliefs with which they cloak their self-interest. If (3), then we are forced to abandon Habermas's claim that discourse ethics imposes no substantive moral principles beyond the ones implicit in the rules of argumentation and to concede that discourse ethics stacks the deck no less than Rawls's original position or later concept of "reasonableness."

Further, while she writes that "'complex cultural dialogue' is not only a sociological reality, but also an epistemological vantage point with methodological implications for moral inquiry,"[59] it is not clear what this involves. Most important, it is not clear that on basic issues of citizenship and human rights, the emphasis in discourse ethics on universal respect and egalitarian reciprocity is any less restrictive than the Rawlsian definition of what a reasonable comprehensive doctrine must be. In short, the interest in an Islamic doctrine of citizenship in liberal democracies from the standpoint of discourse ethics is, as from the standpoint of political liberalism, "political" (as opposed to justificatory or epistemic) in the following ways: (1) We believe that moral norms supported by laws are more stable when they are sincerely believed in, and showing them to be compatible with religious beliefs is one way of allowing them to be sincerely believed in; (2) we now have many Muslims as our fellow citizens and, thus, "moral partners," and one way of extending to them the respect and recognition to which they are entitled is to listen to their internal discourses and consider the way our norms are compatible with them; and (3) we believe cultural and religious traditions to be battlegrounds that change over time rather than being hermetically sealed, and we are interested in how they change in order to become compatible with new historical, political, and social moments.

Furthermore, it seems quite clear that the kind of open moral discourse within civil society (not legislatures and courts) that discourse ethics and deliberative democracy call for is equally accounted for within political liberalism. Rawls and others quite clearly restrict the duty of civility (the duty to give only "public" reasons to one another) to debates over coercive legislation, not to every matter of nonprivate concern. In the broader public sphere, there are no constraints on the types of reasons or views that can be voiced. Rawls himself discusses various nonpublic forms of public discourse, including "declaration" and "witnessing" (in addition to "conjecture," which we are concerned with in this study), not to mention his famous "proviso" that religious or other metaphysical reasons can be introduced to justify legislation, provided that public reasons are provided in due course. "Declaration" involves explaining one's religious, philosophical, or otherwise nonpublic reasons for supporting the values and principles of a reasonable policy or political conception of justice. In declaring their support, citizens describe how the content of a political conception is related to, and affirmed by, their comprehensive doctrines. By contrast, "witnessing" describes those cases in which citizens disclose their comprehensive views to protest what are, from the public perspective, reasonable and legitimate political decisions—say, if Muslims were to disclose in rich detail their objections to offensive representations of the Prophet Muhammad. For these and other reasons, it is hard to see how political liberalism is subject to the charge that it limits the depth, scope, and thickness of moral dialogue in the situations in which Habermas and Benhabib call for it, or that political liberalism does not value the pursuit of the "social bases of self-respect" that seem to be at the heart of discourse ethic's wide view of public reason.

Skeptical, Relativist, and Historicist Critiques of Liberal Justification

To this point we have examined two attempts to ground liberalism in more or less universal aspects of human reason, moral psychology and speech, and the place of comparative ethical theorizing within them. However, both of those attempts, as well as other universalist theories, are clearly aware of the historical and cultural preconditions for liberal legitimacy. Rawls's later work is interspersed with constant references to "the background political culture of democratic societies," and his concern for the existence of an overlapping consensus reveals his understanding that liberal institutions cannot flourish where they compete with widely held inegalitarian and authoritarian doctrines. Furthermore, Rawls's very conception of justification begins with a historically situated consensus of some sort. "What justifies a conception of justice is not its being true to an order antecedent and given to us, but its congruence with our deeper understanding of ourselves and our aspirations, and our realization that, given our history and the traditions embedded in our public life, it is the most reasonable doctrine for us."[60] Similarly, Benhabib distances herself from Habermas's "transcendental-pragmatism":

> As opposed to . . . Habermas's strategy of a "weak transcendental argument," based on the rational reconstruction of competencies, I would like to plead for a "historically self-conscious universalism." The principles of universal respect and egalitarian reciprocity are our philosophical clarification of the constituents of the moral point of view from within the normative hermeneutic horizon of modernity.

> These principles are neither the *only allowable* interpretation of the formal constituents of the competency of postconventional moral actors nor are they unequivocal transcendental presuppositions which every rational agent, upon deep reflection, must concede to. These principles are arrived at by a process of "reflective equilibrium" in Rawlsian terms, whereby one, as a philosopher, analyzes, refines, and judges culturally defined moral intuitions in light of articulated philosophical principles. What one arrives at [at] the end of such a process of reflective equilibrium is a "thick description" of the moral presuppositions of the cultural horizon of modernity.[61]

Liberal theorists of a more perfectionist bent—that is, those who defend liberalism not on the basis of equal respect or fairness but on the basis of its ability to promote a particularly important value or good, like autonomy—also tend to be sensitive to the fact that this good, and the conditions required for valuing it, are not themselves historically and culturally neutral. Will Kymlicka defends his grounding of liberal multiculturalism on the value of autonomy through the assertion that "the idea that we have an interest in being able to assess and revise our inherited conceptions of the good is very widely shared in Western democratic societies."[62] Similarly, in the work of the contemporary perfectionist par excellence, Joseph Raz, autonomous choice has inherent value, but only in an environment that is rich in choice-worthy options. "Personal autonomy is an ideal particularly suited to the conditions of the industrial age and its aftermath with their fast changing technologies and free movement of labour. Its suitability for our conditions and the deep roots it has by now acquired in our culture contribute to the powerful case for this ideal."[63] Our own preoccupation with autonomy is thus not written into the fabric of human nature. The conditions that make autonomy a vital condition of human well-being do not exist in all societies; autonomous choice might not be a necessary component of all human flourishing or well-being. This liberal position emphasizes the need to relate political justification to the conceptions of human value and flourishing that dominate in given social contexts. And thus, although late modern conditions of rapid social change and value pluralism make liberal schemes of rights and freedoms the most appropriate, "human beings have flourished in regimes that do not shelter a liberal civil society, and there are forms of flourishing that are driven out in liberal regimes. Liberal orders, then, have no universal or apodictic authority, contrary to liberal political philosophy."[64]

There are other approaches, however, that are *entirely* skeptical of liberalism's pretensions to justification and claim that all attempts to provide philosophical foundations for liberal intuitions are misleading. Richard Rorty "should like to replace both religious and philosophical accounts of a suprahistorical ground or an end-of-history convergence with a historical narrative about the rise of liberal institutions and customs—the institutions and customs which were designed to diminish cruelty, make possible government by the consent of the governed, and permit as much domination-free communication as possible to take place."[65] Such historicist arguments usually invoke a quasi-Hegelian assertion of the social embeddedness of moral life and consciousness, a more radical Nietzschean critique of any and all claims to objectivity and moral knowledge, or a form of the Münchhausen trilemma cited by Habermas and Apel. The last involves demonstrating that attempts to ground rights or arbitrate between groups on philosophically "neutral" grounds fail because even neutrality requires justification. How do we do this, however? On what grounds should one's meta-principles be judged? And what about *those* grounds? This exposure of the underlying assumptions operating at any level of justification threatens us with *infinite regress* (it's turtles all the way down); the only way out is either *arbitrary closure* or the invocation of certain propositions about the good that themselves are inevitably controversial and thus invite the charge of *circularity*.

Such critiques often go well beyond simple observation of the *fact* of the historical and cultural preconditions for the appropriateness of liberal institutions[66] and deny the existence of any meaningful universal human nature—whether grounded in reason, psychology, or speech—that "stands beyond history." Rorty, for example, objects to the Kantian legacy of seeking to ground moral obligation in the noncontingent, nonempirical recognition of a universal rational nature of all humans. For him, liberalism requires no such foundations, no noble myths, and can be sufficiently robust with a certain type of consciousness based on the coupling of an abhorrence of cruelty and the willingness to constantly expand the "we" toward whom one feels solidarity. Rorty mocks the neo-Kantian (both constructivist and communicative) attempts to ground rights in a universal human nature but does not think this has any serious consequences for liberal legitimacy.

These arguments are, however, often used as a way of debunking liberalism's legitimacy as such,[67] particularly its moral authority to liberalize nonliberal traditional communities. In what follows, I consider both the general argument against liberalism's claim to procedural neutrality and the specific variant of the argument directed against liberals who would impose liberal rights on nonliberal cultural groups. As with the previous discussions, my primary interest is not in assessing the overall validity of the positions considered, but what their implications would be for the possibility and desirability of the form of comparative political theory I have been discussing.

For an example of the first type of argument, I draw from Rorty and Stanley Fish. For Fish, liberalism is defined not by its commitments to certain political practices, social institutions, or structures of rights, but by its claim to be able to assess the ends, values, and beliefs of society's many "ideologies" through a reason universal and independent of any worldview, prejudice, or historical contingency. On this view, the liberal concern for procedure is not one feature among the many that define it but the very thing in which "liberalism puts its faith." For him, all of liberalism rises or falls with its ability to demonstrate the existence of a conception of reason able to function in this way that "comes from nowhere, that reflects the structure of the universe or at least of the human brain."[68] Of course, for him "reasons always come from somewhere, and the somewhere they come from is precisely the realm of particular (angled, partisan, biased) assumptions and agendas." Once we see reason as just another form of belief and not something above beliefs and able to adjudicate between them, "liberal thought loses its integrity, has nothing at its center, becomes just one more competing ideology rather than a procedure." This basic dilemma is ever-present for Fish. Literary criticism is, of course, the basic paradigm: "If I am given as a reason for preferring one interpretation of a poem to another the fact that it accords with the poet's theological views, I will only hear it as a reason if it is *already* my conviction that a poet's aesthetic performance could be influenced by his theology; if, on the other hand, I see poetry and theology as independent and even antagonistic forms of life this fact will not be a reason at all, but something obviously besides the point."[69] Free speech, like liberalism, "doesn't exist" because, *pace* Dworkin and others, it can be defended only on consequentialist grounds, rather than deontological ones, and once we are defending it on consequentialist grounds, we are opening the door to limitations on speech in cases that don't violate the ultimate ends for which we protect speech in other cases. And for him, once we are limiting speech on *any* grounds, we are open to the charge of bias, arbitrariness, sectarianism—in short, of being "political." "Merit" and "fairness," merely because there is no absolute, value-neutral, apolitical way of decontesting them, are thus simply "the ideologically charged constructions of a decidedly political agenda."[70] And so on.

Fish's basic point, which unites all of these discussions, is:

> not that reasons can never be given or that they are, when given, incapable of settling disputes, but that the force they exert and their status *as* reasons depends on the already-in-place institutions of distinctions that themselves rest on a basis no firmer (no less subject to dispute) than the particulars they presently order. In short, what is and is not a reason will always be a matter of faith, that is, of the assumptions that are bedrock within a discursive system which because it rests upon them cannot (without self-destructing) call them into question.[71]

These views are essentially those advanced by Rorty (who happens to think them of less consequence for liberalism as a political project): "For liberal ironists, there is no answer to the question 'Why not be cruel?'—no noncircular theoretical backup for the belief that cruelty is horrible."[72] What both of these theorists essentially do is walk with Rawls and Habermas up to the point where they all recognize the absence of reasons that all members of a society or discursive community can recognize as the right types of reasons for moral argument. (Rawls and Habermas do not, of course, deny the dispute described in this quote from Fish. It is the very starting point of their work.) But instead of searching for foundations (meta-reasons) buried in intuition, procedure, or speech, which they think condemned to either infinite regress or circularity, Fish and Rorty are happy to confess to arbitrary closure. They deny that any rules of argumentation or speech exist prior to socially and historically embedded ones, and they assert that the claim to have found any is nothing more than a misleading rhetorical attempt to assign to one's own partisan, secular beliefs a privileged, nonpolitical status. For them, there is no nonpolitical, philosophical way out of the impasse we face when various groups not only disagree on moral or political issues but also disagree at a prior level of abstraction as to what counts as evidence toward a given position. For Fish, the implications of this are dire: "It follows then that persons embedded within *different* discursive systems will not be able to hear the other person's reasons *as* reasons, but only as errors or even delusions."[73] We are then faced with either a perpetual political stand-off between irreconcilable ideological foes, the ascendance of one over the others through brute force, or the victory of one side over the others through its success in achieving ideological hegemony, in the case of liberalism by advancing the myth that it is not one ideological competitor among many but a neutral, apolitical adjudicative mechanism.

Whatever one thinks of the force of this argument—that there is nothing more to liberalism than its claim to neutrality and its belief that reason is the only respectable human faculty, that all subjective beliefs are on the same footing, that all instances of exclusion (intolerance) are identical, that the fact of something being controversial or contingent reduces it to bias or self-interest, that contemporary liberals do not claim to be advancing a political project or a morality—it is clear that one can be attracted to it without drawing Fish's conclusion that "liberalism doesn't exist." Rorty, for example, advances a virtually identical critique of ("un-ironic") foundationalist attempts to ground liberalism philosophically, but he thinks this critique a poor reason to abandon what are for him the two constitutive liberal commitments: the commitment to reduce instances of cruelty toward those with whom one feels solidarity and the willingness to expand the group of humans with whom one feels solidarity:

> To keep this notion [of human solidarity], while granting the point about the contingently historical character of our sense of moral obligation, we need to realize that a *focus imaginarius* is none the worse for being an invention rather than (as Kant thought it) a built-in feature of the human mind. The right way to take the slogan "We have obligations to human beings simply as such" is as a means of reminding ourselves to keep trying to expand our sense of "us" as far as we can . . . to *create* a more expansive sense of solidarity than we presently have. The wrong way is to think of it as urging us to *recognize* such a solidarity as something that exists antecedently to our recognition of it. For then we leave ourselves open to the pointlessly skeptical question "Is this solidarity *real*?"[74]

In other words, for Rorty, the fact that I have no recourse to a higher court of appeal to convince you (to my own satisfaction) that my reasons should be your reasons is no reason itself for them to no longer be *my* reasons. (For Fish, it is not clear what follows from this fact for the liberal himself except maybe a greater transparency about his political commitments.) But, of course, that is precisely the concern of this book: What is the place for entering into someone else's "discursive system" and showing them that we have *different* reasons for endorsing similar political arrangements? On one reading of these skeptical (ironic, historicist, relativist, etc.) theorists, such a project is insincere at best and impossible at worst. Both Rorty[75] and Fish[76] seem to suggest at times that there is an inherent performative contradiction in trying to argue across ethical systems or worldviews, literally, like trying to agree on the rules of grammar while speaking two mutually incomprehensible languages.

For Rorty, however, the end of philosophy (or forensics) is not the end of moral persuasion. (To believe so would be to ascribe to philosophy the very status he wants to deny it.) At this point, all we can do is *redescribe* human conditions (through literature, journalism, art, etc.) in such a way that we demonstrate to people the suffering of some and the cruelty of others, in the hope that such descriptions will have the effect of altering people's sense of their own obligations to create a more just set of relations among people they consider part of "us." Advancing arguments is not the way to convince Nazis or capitalists they are wrong; redescribing social conditions and deconstructing the (earnest) arguments advanced by those who stand in the way of justice and expanding solidarity is the way to reduce the appeal of their worldview to our moral contemporaries. For Fish, also, hope is not lost. Yet, while Rorty places faith in the model of the socially conscious muckraker and satirist (the likes of Marx, Dickens, Dewey, Sinclair, and Orwell), Fish sees moral conflict along the lines of the academic conference:

> It is true that there is nowhere to go, no locus of judgment to which disputants can appeal for an authoritative announcement. But this doesn't mean that they must throw up their hands or toss the dice; it means that they must argue, thrash it out, present bodies of evidence to one another and to relevant audiences, try to change one another's mind. To be sure, the process is not guided by any unchallengeable authority, but authority, not unchallengeable but temporarily regnant, is what is fashioned in the course of it. That is to say, authority does not *preside* over the debate from a position outside it but is the prize for which the debaters vie.[77]

For him, the fear of relativism, like for Geertz,[78] is misguided:

> The poststructuralist characterization of the normative as a local rather than a transcendental realm, far from rendering ethical judgment impossible, renders it inevitable and inescapable. Antifoundationalist thought, properly understood, is not an assault on ethics but an account of the conditions—textual and revisable, to be sure—within which moments of ethical choice are always and *genuinely* emerging; it is only if ethical norms existed *elsewhere* that there would be a chance of missing them, but if they are always and already where they are they cannot be avoided.[79]

Thus, the immediate implication of this critique of the Rawlsian attempt to escape moral conflict by the retreat to a neutral vocabulary and the Habermasian attempt to engage in moral dialogue through neutral rules of engagement is the inevitability of moral conflict and dialogue in whatever discursive form is available. We might call this position "Habermas without the rules." If my earlier argument is correct, that Habermas does away with the constraints of Rawls's "public reason" in the public sphere only after the rules of communication have structured the debate in such a way that basic moral outcomes—interpersonal equality, freedom of conscience, freedom of speech—are guaranteed, Rorty and Fish want to take Habermas's critique of Rawlsian "monological" reasoning a step further and assert that there is no morality embedded in the pragmatics of speech. Thus, if we are interested in compatibility or overlapping consensus, in the justification of the basic constraints of a liberal constitution, to citizens who are not otherwise inclined toward reason or a secular morality, we must do so directly and without recourse to any philosophical devices—such as an original position, the concept of "reasonableness," or the laws of pragmatics—that overdetermine the potential outcome of moral dialogue.

It follows from this that comparative theorizing (conjecture, comparative ethics, etc.) may be *inevitable* for justification and, indeed, *as philosophical as it gets*, depending on what type of ideological change you are trying to effect in your moral contemporary. Clearly, there may be instances when you do not want to persuade an interlocutor of the acceptability of a particular policy or principle but, rather, in the superiority of your entire moral system, authoritative tradition, Foucauldian *episteme*, or whatever. This type of persuasion, on the Rorty-Fish view, takes the form not of showing the logical necessity of holding such views but the benefits that arise from doing so. ("Try this on for size and see how you like it," or "try looking at it this way," is all Rorty thinks we can say.) But at this level, it is about wholesale conversion, not compatibility or overlapping consensus. In the context of this book, this level of persuasion corresponds to the attempt to achieve consensus not through the demonstration of fairness or compatibility between worldviews but through the comprehensive secularization of believers.

But say one subscribes to the relativist view of Rorty and Fish but is not convinced that complete secularization is either necessary or desirable. What does a Rorty or a Fish do in the case of the dilemma posed by Rawls of wanting to secure the endorsement of a political conception of justice without forcing citizens to subscribe to the ethical views of a comprehensive liberalism? It is clear that they would reject the path of "public reason" as no less controversial and inauthentic than Kantian metaphysics and that they would also reject the Habermasian approach to allow more authentic discourse in the public sphere only once it has been properly set up. They see no way out of justifying the very background structure that creates the public sphere (Rawls's constitutional essentials) on (truly) wide-open terms.[80] Although Fish at times seems to suggest that this option of wholesale conversion to religious skepticism or secularism is the only possible option, rejecting the vision of a "political liberalism" where ethical and epistemic pluralism can exist on widely acceptable terms, Rorty holds out hope for a liberal skeptic who endorses a distinctly political form of liberalism. This is Rorty's "liberal ironist" who holds that "on the *public* side of our lives, *nothing* is less dubious than the worth of those [democratic] freedoms," while conceding to the critics of modernity (Rorty mentions Nietzsche, Proust, Heidegger, Foucault, Derrida; I add religious fundamentalists) that "on the private side of our lives, there may be much which is *equally* hard to doubt, for example, our love or hatred for a particular person, the need to carry out some idiosyncratic project."[81] He is quite clear that:

> The best one can do with the sort of challenges offered by Nietzsche and Heidegger is make [a] sort of indirect reply: One can ask these men to *privatize* their projects, their attempts at sublimity—to view them as irrelevant to politics and therefore compatible with the sense of human solidarity which the development of democratic institutions has facilitated. This request for privatization amounts to the request that they resolve an impending dilemma by subordinating sublimity to the desire to avoid cruelty and pain. In my view, there is nothing to back up such a request, nor need there be. There is no *neutral*, noncircular way to defend the liberal's claim that cruelty is the worst thing we can do, any more than there is a neutral way to back up Nietzsche's assertion that this claim expresses a resentful, slavish attitude, or Heidegger's that the idea of the "greatest happiness of the greatest number" is just one more bit of "metaphysics," of the "forgetfulness of Being." We cannot look back behind the processes of socialization which convinced us twentieth-century liberals of the validity of this claim and appeal to something which is more "real" or less ephemeral than the historical contingencies which brought those processes into existence.[82]

This approach is obviously irrelevant for our purposes. Although it is the case that political liberalism must also ask the religious critic of modernity to privatize his desire for sublimity, it will simply not do to view this desire as something so easily privatized, as something clearly "irrelevant to politics" (whether this can be so easily done with Nietzsche and Heidegger is something I leave to Rorty). While we are indeed asking the religious critic of liberalism to accept that a different, limited, morality of justice may operate in the public sphere than in the private, she will certainly need good reasons for doing so and need to be assured that something essential is not lost. By definition, she is someone for whom those reasons will have to be of a certain (religious) kind and not generic, public, political, or "freestanding." In fact, this is rather what Rorty does with his group of existentialists. He argues that Nietzsche, Heidegger, Proust, Foucault, Kierkegaard, Baudelaire, and others are "historicists [antimetaphysicians] in whom the desire for self-creation, for private autonomy dominates [and] tend to see socialization as antithetical to something deep within us."[83] This has traditionally led to contempt for the leveling, homogenizing institutions of modern states, but according to Rorty, this contempt is misplaced on those theorists' *own terms* for:

> the sort of autonomy which self-creating ironists like Nietzsche, Derrida, or Foucault seek is not the sort of thing that *could* ever be embodied in social institutions. Autonomy is not something which all human beings have within them and which society can release by ceasing to repress them. It is something which certain particular human beings hope to attain by self-creation, and which a few actually do. The desire to be autonomous is not relevant to the liberal's desire to avoid cruelty and pain.[84]

It is this immanent critique—surely a form of Rawls's concept of conjecture (see chapter 2)—that allows Rorty to assert the compatibility of his vision of liberalism and a particular type of doctrine that has been thought to be opposed to it and to conclude that we should think that there was an opposition to begin with only "if we think that a more comprehensive philosophical outlook would let us hold self-creation and justice, private perfection and human solidarity, in a single vision."[85]

Of course, such a comprehensive philosophical outlook is precisely how religions like Islam see themselves. In fact, this phrase from Rorty ("self-creation and justice, private perfection and human solidarity, in a single vision") is almost to the word the language of self-description used by modern Islamist thinkers. The task of demonstrating some form of compatibility, while of necessity following along the lines of requesting the privatization of the search for sublimity, self-creation, justice, and solidarity, will surely not be as simple as pointing out a simple inconsistency, misconception, or oversight, as in the case of Rorty and his existentialists. In that case, he allows himself to advance the (very modern) dichotomy between perfection/virtue and justice/solidarity that he thinks *unites* Nietzsche, Heidegger, Proust, Foucault, Kierkegaard, and Baudelaire on the one hand and Marx, Mill, Dewey, Orwell, Habermas, and Rawls on the other. Our case involves the very rejection of such an opposition. A proper description of the ambition of this book is precisely the investigation of the internal resources accessible to Muslims that would make such a dichotomy, such an opposition, first intelligible and, perhaps, acceptable. What follows from the preceding discussion is that if one accepts the epistemological propositions of someone like Rorty, one is forced to accept that this task can be accomplished *only* by justificatory comparative political theory, or conjecture, akin to what he performs on Nietzsche, Heidegger, and the others. Unlike with Rawls or Habermas, for whom philosophy still stands apart from ideology, rhetoric, and politics, for Rorty and Fish, there is no such opposition. Rhetoric, persuasion, and ideology, including comparative theorizing, are as philosophical as it gets.

The second variant of the relativist-historicist critique allows that the "constitutive features of liberalism can be given a rational defense when they are contextualized and historicized as features of late modern (or early post-modern) societies and polities,"[86] but asks implicitly: If liberalism is just "the way we do things here," what special claim does that give us to interfere with "the way they do things there" (even when "there" might be part of "here")? Let us consider an argument that is commonly put against the right of liberal states to liberalize illiberal minorities. The argument goes that some liberal multiculturalists (particularly Joseph Raz and Will Kymlicka) defend the protection of minority cultures partially on the grounds that individual autonomy requires that the individual have a flourishing cultural setting in which to choose and revise his life path(s). However, this argument for cultural preservation from individual autonomy is undermined by the fact that not all cultures are based on, or even recognize, the value of individual choice. Many cultures value only the duty of individuals to replicate traditional patterns of behavior and social organization. It is thus paradoxical to defend the right to cultural preservation on the grounds of supporting the "thick" conditions of personal choice: If individual autonomy is the prior value, then it would certainly require *interfering* with cultures rather than preserving them. This interference will, in the long run, lead to policies of assimilation and is, in fact, unfair because it denies respect for "the way of life into which they have been inducted and which is the only life they know."[87] True respect requires not introducing the alien concept of individuals as choosers or "project pursuers."

One problem with this argument is that for the most part we are dealing not with undisturbed, virgin ways of life but with communities whose members have been exposed to modernity and do possess the knowledge of other ways of life. In fact, this is virtually an assumption of the debate. The question of whether individuals have a right to leave one cultural community for another does not arise among sixth-century nomadic Arabian tribes where there is only death (and not of the metaphorical sort) outside the embrace of the tribe. Cultural groups seek special measures to punish apostates and free thinkers only when they exist in a minimally cosmopolitan world of alternative lifestyles. If liberal theory must recognize its spatial and temporal limitations to times and places where people could *possibly* choose to adopt one lifestyle over another or where communal authorities have to take special measures to prevent exit or criticism—for example, that arguments concerning what policies to adopt toward Australian Aboriginal or Native American groups *today* might not have force in a counterfactual discussion of conditions prior to the European conquest—then so be it.[88]

What follows from this is that it is very difficult to speak of "our historical moment" that is not in any way also the historical moment of most societies on the globe today. Speaking of alternative life plans, individual choice, exit from traditional communities, or individual expression is a controversial task in many ways, but in very few circumstances could one argue that it is downright *unintelligible* or *incoherent*. If it were incoherent or unintelligible, then it wouldn't be controversial. I would make an analogy with the liberal response to the communitarian charge that liberalism trivializes the importance of religion in people's lives. The liberal response is that just the opposite is true: Precisely *because* religion is so important to people, it is vital (in the conditions of religious diversity) to enforce the separation of church and state.[89] The analogy is that it is false to say that the problem with liberalism is that it is completely inappropriate to the way most people view their cultural or religious attachments; the true problem is that liberalism is all *too* appropriate: Many individuals *are* tempted to abandon traditional lifestyles that they find limiting, insufficient, irrelevant, or oppressive. Where this temptation does not exist in practice, it is hard to see liberalism as much of a threat to traditional lifestyles. Thus, from the liberal perspective the question is not whether our own preoccupation with autonomy (in the simpler Millian sense of the ability to revise life goals) is written into the fabric of human nature or is historically contingent, or whether autonomous choice is a necessary component of all human flourishing or well-being. Rather, the liberal intuition concerns the authority of some humans over others: What do we say to individuals in traditional or non-autonomy-valuing societies who demand these freedoms? Why are their desires not self-authenticating? What ultimate authority does their surrounding culture have over women, free thinkers, and the others for *us liberals*? Why should the fact that a certain society is not traditionally one in which well-being is seen in terms of autonomous choice mean that the desire of a given member of that society for such a choice is illegitimate or incoherent? (To be clear: There is not even the beginning of an argument here for justifying intervention or violence on the part of self-authorizing outsiders.)[90]

My argument is thus that the assertion of liberalism's historically contingent application might, in fact, prove too much. It might serve as an equally strong argument for the investigation of the assimilation of liberal norms into traditionally authoritarian doctrines precisely because many of the communities in which these doctrines hold sway are, in fact, living in the same historical conditions that made liberalism coherent.[91] One of those historical conditions often advanced as crucial for liberalism, in addition to the intellectual breakdown of conventional worldviews, is the existence of an autonomous "civil society." Whether this is a prior condition for the emergence of liberalism and secularism or the consequence of them is not important for this book, as my question is not the compatibility of Islam with the secularization of Muslim-majority societies but the Islamic legitimacy of Muslims living in societies where secularism and the autonomy of society are already thought to reign.

Thus, the response to the charge that liberalism may be fine as far as it goes but is only the doctrine of a particular time and place is to challenge the assumption that those societies where basic liberal rights are contested or thought to be incoherent do not themselves exhibit any number of the features of the "time and place" that make liberalism an appropriate doctrine. This may be the case for even many parts of the non-Western world where the historicist argument is thought to be strongest but, more to the point, can be assumed uncontroversially for the case study explored in this book, that of Muslims living in already existing secular civil societies. The response to the second, implied, part of this charge—that if liberalism (as an ethos or morality, not a political entity) is limited in historical scope to those societies where autonomy is both an option and something valued, then liberal criticism of the denial of autonomy to individuals in nonliberal societies has no authority—is to place the rhetorical emphasis on the self-authenticating and legitimating desire for such autonomy when and where it emerges and to ask by what authority it should be denied. Even if we may recognize the value of nonindividualist or other nonliberal conceptions of well-being, for liberals, the burden of proof is always thought to be on those in authority who claim that an individual's desire for personal freedom is a threat to the collective well-being of the group.

This attempt at demystifying the claim that liberal rights are only applicable to societies exhibiting the features of a certain period of historical development just brings us back to our treatment of Rorty and Fish. If we do not take for granted that a certain form of political liberalism cannot be endorsed by those who are not heirs to the European Enlightenment, yet are in fact committed to the virtue of certain liberal rights for individuals in groups where they have not been traditionally practiced, we are then left with the task of arguing for secularism and autonomy against traditional conceptions of virtue and well-being or, what strikes me as more consistent with liberal pretensions, for the compatibility of liberal rights from *within* traditional doctrines. The unavoidable conclusion of relativist or historicist accounts of liberalism for those still interested in defending basic liberal institutions to nonliberals (a set that includes not only Rorty but also, I believe, Raz and Kymlicka) is that this defense must take place on the basis of *substantive* appeals to concrete values or arguments. This appeal can take place in one of two ways: either the propagation of certain values (autonomy, restraint, tolerance, equality) on their own terms or by showing them to be intelligible within the traditional moral vocabulary in question.

In Defense of Justificatory Comparative Political Theory

I believe that this brief survey of Rawls's concept of an overlapping consensus and the place it gives to the search for compatibility with nonliberal but possibly reasonable doctrines in light of both Habermasian and "relativist" critiques allows us to return now to the hypothetical objections posed to such a search in the Introduction to this part. In what follows I summarize and add to the points developed previously in defense of a comparative political theory dedicated to the search for moral consensus against the two most likely objections introduced earlier, that the search for an overlapping consensus has no justificatory force and that it may be a form of hegemonic action. (I leave the response to the other objection, that the search for an overlapping consensus is chimerical in its hope for a liberalism lying underneath illiberal doctrines, for the final four chapters.)

Comparative Political Theory Has No Justificatory Force

This view holds that, rather than having justificatory force, comparative political theory is (from the perspective of philosophers) primarily anthropological or historical, in the sense that it is a search for normative principles that are of interest only because they are held by a particular moral community: This is clearly true on certain essentials. No engagement with Islamic ethics is going to lead to a concession on the right to life for apostates. Our basic commitment to civil and human rights and democratic institutions is not deeply shaken by the revelation that some people don't share it. Nonetheless, the idea that we have nothing to learn about how to organize our societies from the study of political and ethical traditions that rely on the acceptance of the authority of a particular revelation for their normative force (rather than purely on a form of secular reason, public or other) might not be as entirely true as it is intuitive. For example, we may find arguments on the just conduct of war derived from Christian just war doctrine ultimately convincing or appealing on rational grounds, without accepting them on authority. If we had not already arrived at such arguments independently, then they clearly would have enriched our ethical perspective because of their rational or intuitive appeal.

A perhaps more relevant and more plausible area in which the substantive moral content of nonliberal doctrines matters is from within the contemporary liberal debate on which exemptions from public duties, norms, or standards citizens and groups of citizens might be entitled to.[92] Contemporary liberal thought extends across a spectrum of attitudes toward nonliberal ways of life, with doctrines of neutrality, pluralism, or multiculturalism more sympathetic to the rights of communities to maintain nonliberal ways of life, and "perfectionist" or "transformative" doctrines more insistent on the need to encourage a unitary set of civic virtues and principles. However, just as a liberal theory of multiculturalism must be critical toward the coercive power of communities over their individual members, so must a liberal theory of common values be critical of state coercion of nonliberal groups or individuals where the latter's actions do not violate clear boundaries of individual rights or public order. No liberal is for complete communal authority, and no liberal is opposed to all culturally or religiously based exemptions from common duties.[93] Thus, much of the debate over multiculturalism obscures a "multicultural plateau" arrived at not merely through accommodation of historical contingency but through a wide range of core liberal principles.

Now, what if a minority community's recognition of a political form of liberalism depended on the extent to which that liberal regime allowed for the free practice of its religion? A given community, not normally known for its respect for individual autonomy, is induced to find the resources from within its authoritative texts to see individual freedom as justifiable because of the myriad other benefits offered within a well-ordered society. But the free practice of religion requires, in the case of this community, the freedom to engage in practice *x* or refrain from action *y*, which in turn requires a certain form of exemption from public duties. Our consideration of whether the exemption is justifiable will certainly not hinge merely on the community wanting it, but in the event that we find such an exemption innocuous enough to grant, our appreciation for the importance of that exemption will undoubtedly alter our conception of the proper balance between church and state, religious liberty and civic equality, communal solidarity and individual freedom. We might, in essence, end up understanding the minimum or proper demands of citizenship in a new way because of the *specific* exemption required by a specific community.

The point here is that the process by which we decide whether to change long-standing rules or offer exemptions from them cannot be decided (whether legally or politically) merely by examining the fact of a community or individual *desiring* the change or the exemption alongside the objective *costs* to others in bringing it about. Both a deliberative ("political") approach and a legal approach (such as the principle of searching for "least restrictive alternatives" to a uniform law) might require the cultural group in question to publicly defend the authoritative or binding character of the act or omission they seek protection for, as well as to demonstrate the relative importance, or centrality, of a given practice to a religious tradition. Our sense of what limits a liberal society ought to place on communal authority is thus not entirely divorced from an inquiry into the internal discourses of cultural and religious traditions. There are good reasons to be interested in the internal discourses of nonliberal traditions, both in the case of moral conflict within civil society and at the level of the normative justification of certain laws or policies outside the basic constitutional structure that creates civil society.[94]

A further area of philosophical interest for political liberals on which a study of this nature sheds light is the question of how political liberalism ought to present the public justification of a conception of justice and how much of that public presentation citizens ought to be expected to endorse. It has been frequently argued, both by political liberals and their critics, that Rawls's conception of a "reasonable citizen," "reasonable moral psychology," or a "reasonable comprehensive doctrine" and his derivation of the "fact of reasonable pluralism" from the burdens of judgment involve many substantive philosophical claims that existing comprehensive doctrines tend to deny.[95] Furthermore, some of these claims may not be necessary for a reasonable conception of justice and are likely to present philosophical obstacles to such a reasonable conception being endorsed by citizens with fully comprehensive doctrines, particularly religious ones. The insistence on these conceptions, or on the role of the burdens of judgment in explaining the reasonableness of disagreement, is that without them any overlapping consensus is going to be too thin and not represent a stable convergence of moral views. There is thus an open philosophical debate within political liberalism on the most appropriate public presentation of a political conception of justice and on the standards by which it should be judged as to whether a given comprehensive doctrine is part of an overlapping consensus.

This is a debate to which an actual investigation into the range of views within an existing comprehensive doctrine has something to contribute. Showing that there are certain aspects of Rawls's presentation of justice as fairness or reasonable political justification that do in fact present philosophical obstacles to an otherwise successful affirmation of political liberalism from within a certain comprehensive doctrine, and that this doctrine's affirmation of political liberalism is a principled one that contributes to the stability of a well-ordered society, ought to be of independent interest to philosophers. Similarly of interest to philosophical debates would be demonstrating that without, for example, a commitment to the burdens of judgment a doctrine's endorsement of political liberalism is seriously qualified or incomplete.

This should not be controversial for political liberals or philosophers committed to some form of moral or political constructivism, for whom it is uncontroversial that political philosophy must take an interest in the political, social, and psychological conditions of its reception. The universalist claims of liberalism (given that they are in their dominant strand today based on some form of discursive intersubjectivity or constructivism) are strengthened by evidence that they can be made intelligible through other vocabularies and do not make unreasonable demands on nonliberals. The argument is put more succinctly by Habermas from within discourse ethics: "The [constitutional rights and principles] must be enduringly linked with the motivations and convictions of the citizens, for without such a motivational anchoring they could not become the driving force behind the dynamically conceived project of producing an association of individuals who are free and equal."[96]

Let us not forget also that mainstream political philosophy has reached into history and culture for its own justification. Rawls's work is the best recent example of this: He justifies the use of certain values as foundations not only because of their objective value but also because of their historical occurrence and dominance. This existing consensus functions for him as a form of justification: "One is to imagine that, for the most part, [citizens] find on examination that they hold these ideals [of the person and of social cooperation], that they have taken them in part from the culture of their society."[97] Perhaps the most famous and prestigious example of such an examination is Locke's *Letter Concerning Toleration*, which grounded the separation of church and state in scripture. From this example, Stephen Macedo has argued that "liberalism needs the support of private beliefs and practices that are at least congruent with liberal politics. Liberalism depends, after all, on a certain ordering of the soul. . . . Creating a certain religious homogeneity—at least in the sense of encouraging all religions to support shared political values and virtues—is crucial and legitimate political work that liberals must hope is performed somehow."[98] It would follow, then, that the justification of liberal conceptions of justice is at least consistent with attempts to show their compatibility with various ethical traditions, and perhaps a political necessity.

The practice of this form of comparative political theory, while not hiding its normative commitments, is also an act of respect and recognition to the extent that we have "moral contemporaries" from different ethical traditions. Arguing from multiple traditions and exhibiting openness to multiple languages in the broader public sphere is one way we extend recognition to cocitizens. Even if there are limits to toleration, we may have reasons to foster a certain attitude of respect toward the religious or philosophical traditions of fellow citizens. One of the aspects of this attitude of respect is to cultivate a preference for cultural or intellectual change from within the resources of the culture in question.[99] The neutralization of oppressive aspects of an illiberal culture through the appeal to other values held in that culture carries the possibility of being more legitimate (particularly in the short term), more politically stable, more respectful, and, therefore, of generating fewer negative side effects flowing from the resentment caused by rapid, coerced cultural, moral, or intellectual change.

So much for the skepticism on the part of those committed strongly to liberal normative positions and nonreligious modes of public justification. Objections to this kind of project are, of course, much more likely to come from a quite different perspective.

Justificatory Comparative Political Theory Is a Form of Cultural Hegemony or Domination

The charge that justificatory comparative political theory is a form of cultural hegemony could take a number of forms—that political liberalism requires nonliberal citizens to adopt an alienated or inauthentic approach to their tradition, that it involves assuming a "liberal bias" in understanding the way religious and other traditions ought to respond to contemporary social and political conditions, or even that the very act of posing liberal demands and searching for congruence in Islamic sources is a form of stigmatization and marginalization that perpetuates hegemonic discourses about Islam and Muslims.

CHARGE OF ALIENATION. The charge of *alienation* is a common criticism of liberalism, particularly political liberalism. Of course, the heart of the classical republican critique of modernity and liberal politics is that "the modern state breeds aliens, whereas older political societies could only import them."[100] A person sympathetic to this critique rejects the fact of reasonable pluralism and yearns for social unity around a common conception of the good. Persons concerned about whether political liberalism is too demanding for Muslims and other nonliberal citizens, however, will not want to adopt this critique because a politics of the collective overcoming of alienation might accord religious minorities far fewer rights than political liberalism and would certainly not aim at political liberalism's justificatory inclusiveness.

So the concern has to be that in searching for an Islamic endorsement of liberal citizenship, political liberalism makes not only demands of behavior (commission or omission) but also demands of conscience. It would have to be something like the following: "It is not enough for political liberalism that Muslims perform in a certain way and obey the laws of a liberal society; political liberalism also demands that they proclaim these laws Islamically legitimate. This can be done only by approaching their sources in an alienated way."

Here it must be emphasized (something I discuss in greater detail in chapter 4) that there is no civic duty per se to proclaim publicly the grounds of an overlapping consensus, still less under the threat of state coercion. Whether or not there is a "duty of civility" to propose public reasons and explain one's political preferences in ways others could reasonably accept, there is certainly no "duty of constructing a full justification" that citizens can demand of one another. The overlapping consensus is something we hope for, based on the long-term interest in stability and social solidarity, but it would be an intolerable violation of autonomy for the state to demand that citizens construct a full justification of liberal principles and publicly elaborate it. Citizens are free to continue to *regard* the public principles of justice as being outweighed by their nonliberal comprehensive doctrines. Of course, these views cannot be regarded as immune from scrutiny or criticism by fellow citizens, but the point of the overlapping consensus is not to legitimate the stigmatization of citizens on the grounds that they hold illiberal ideas.

Thus, the concern or criticism has to be that the very idea of full justification and the search for it by outsiders (in civil society) aims at creating an alienated citizenry or an inauthentic religious doctrine merely for the purposes of social stability, that is, reasons exogenous to the religious tradition.

The result of alienation or inauthenticity may, of course, be the case. There is no guarantee ever that citizens will order their souls in such a way that public reasonableness and nonpublic truth and rationality will be congruent or coexist harmoniously. It is, in fact, part of political liberalism's self-restraint that it does not seek to guarantee this. Nor is there a guarantee that efforts on the part of citizens to assert such congruence will be convincing or satisfying to all citizens who share the same comprehensive doctrine. (The fact that Christian doctrines of toleration exist does not mean that all Christians endorse them.) Neither political liberalism itself nor the search for an overlapping consensus through conjecture promises the overcoming of alienation. They merely posit that for many citizens it may be possible. Furthermore, they posit that given the simple fact of pluralism, a politically liberal public conception has the best chance of reducing alienation among the largest possible segment of the population.

Therefore, the charge of creating alienation is either a general one in liberal polities true about all citizens and of thus of no particular relevance for the study of Islam or the practice of conjecture, or it is an open question to be settled empirically for any individual citizen, group, or comprehensive doctrine. That is, we cannot posit as a matter of fact that Muslims will be alienated from both their religion and their public sphere in a non-Muslim liberal democracy. It might be the case for some and not for others. That is an evolving social fact rather than something inherent about liberalism and Islamic moral commitments (or at least the non-Muslim comparative political theorist must hold this view).

Finally, the charge of alienation alone cannot settle matters. That would be the case only if any instance or form of alienation was a *summum malum* and the standard by which all political and social institutions were judged. But of course, that would have to be argued for, and it would have to be shown what form of public justification and account of stability would result in less alienation for a greater number of citizens, given whether the fact of reasonable pluralism is accepted. But such an argument would probably result in a comprehensive rejection of political liberalism in toto, of which the argument against the search for an overlapping consensus per se would be but a trivial component.

In fact, justificatory comparative political theory presumes a more enlightened sociology than theories of the essential incompatibility of liberal individualism and religious (including non-Western) traditions. It resists the essentializing, or ossification, of cultural and intellectual traditions by refusing to believe, in this case study, that there is "one Islam" any more than there is one liberalism defined once and for all in the 17th century. There is a certain self-contradiction in relativist critiques of liberalism and their charge that liberal constraints on cultural systems create a form of inauthenticity: If all value systems are constructed historically, what meaningful objections on grounds of "inauthenticity" can be leveled (by relativists) against historically determined processes of reinterpretation from within ethical traditions? Here, even Bhikhu Parekh finds himself in some sympathy with Rawls: "Rawls suggests that public institutions including the state should actively encourage citizens to reinterpret their comprehensive doctrines in the light of the political conception of justice. He is right to point to the inevitable and desirable interplay between public principles and comprehensive doctrines. This is how the Koran is currently reinterpreted, as the Bible once was, in the light of the democratic principles of equality of the sexes and freedom of conscience."[101]

LIBERAL BIAS. At this point, some will insist on the criticism that this inquiry involves a *liberal bias* or presumes that it is Muslims who have the onus of demonstrating the capacity of Islam to affirm liberal principles.[102] This alone, however, cannot stand as a critique. One must show successfully what precisely is unreasonable about liberal demands of citizenship. But once one agrees to do that, then there can no longer be an objection to asking normative questions per se; at best there could be a criticism of a *particular* demand that someone could possibly show to be unfair.

Yet there is no point in denying that this is a book that seeks to defend the most reasonable *liberal* terms of social cooperation; in that sense, there is a liberal bias. But the criticism would have to be not that such a bias exists but that political liberalism itself is unreasonable or false; those skeptical of political liberalism tout court are free to articulate how it is deficient morally. But in that case, the objection is not to the liberal bias of this form of inquiry, but to liberalism per se. And, indeed, this would be appropriate because the liberal interest in an Islamic affirmation of liberal citizenship is itself a generic one, not one generated by a unique anxiety about Islam.[103]

More to the point, an important restraint on this project is the *assumption of the context of some form of social cooperation in existing non-Muslim liberal democracies*. The aim is not just to read any particular Islamic text, or the entire Islamic ethical tradition, through the lens of whether it conforms to liberal standards or expectations. Nor, for that matter, is it the assumption that present-day liberal conceptions of rights or justice need to be mobilized in an evaluation of any given social context, say the Muslim majority societies of Asia and Africa. Rather, the questions posed to Islamic thinkers in this book are carefully restricted to the most reasonable requirements of an overlapping consensus as I argue for them, given the existence of social cooperation within a pluralist liberal democracy. This rationale is much less arbitrary than simply imposing liberal concerns on any given Islamic text or on Middle Eastern societies.[104]

It is also important to stress that the defense of this project and of liberal demands of citizenship in no way implies that this is the only reason for studying Islamic political thought or the only methodology for doing so. Conjecture, or justificatory comparative political theory, is distinguished from other forms of scholarship (history, anthropology, discourse analysis, genealogy, and others), but it is not designed to replace them. It is a practice, rather, that is designed to address the consciences of believing Muslims who take their tradition seriously as a source of moral and political motivation in nonpublic discourse. The point is to identify authoritative Islamic reasons for endorsing what this author regards as the most reasonable moral principles for regulating social cooperation. There is a "bias" to the extent that this book proceeds with a certain normative conception in mind, but it is not a bias that has to exclude other purposes and methods for studying Islamic political thought at other times. Indeed, this project does not seek to defend scholarly claims by the standards of inquiry in history, social science, or cultural studies. Thus, a person seeking to invoke the "liberal bias" criticism would have to show not only that such a bias exists but also that an inquiry with such a purpose *ought never to be pursued.*

While practitioners of historiography, hermeneutics, or cultural studies might assume that their approaches are somehow more favorable or sympathetic to Islamic ethical traditions than an approach that begins with the contemporary normative standards of political liberalism, I submit that the opposite may actually be the case. An important feature of my work, which is not present in many other Western forms of scholarship, is that my use of the Islamic sources ought to be of considerable interest for believing Muslims and Islamic intellectuals, particularly those who take the problem of citizenship seriously for Islamic reasons (and there are many) and take the Islamic juridical tradition seriously in formulating their views on liberal citizenship (of which there are also many). My methodology allows for a direct discussion with such fellow citizens, and a discussion not only on liberal grounds but also on Islamic grounds. The same cannot be said to the same degree for historiographical, hermeneutical, or cultural studies approaches. That is, this method generates direct responses to those believing Muslim citizens who might regard liberal citizenship as problematic, responses that those citizens have to regard as relevant because they draw from the same sources and take the Islamic juridical tradition seriously.

The same is not always true for cultural studies. Why would a call to "situate" or "explain" Islamic discourses in their historical or psychological context be of any interest whatsoever to a Muslim citizen who believes that the Islamic juridical tradition provides relevant and salient answers to her present dilemma? The approach adopted here is actually *more agnostic* about the epistemological foundations of Western scholarship and *more sensitive* to actual Islamic traditions than are some historiographical or cultural studies approaches: I do not assume that Islamic claims to understand the world with the help of a hermeneutical-epistemological and doctrinal tradition are un-self-conscious or de novo reactions to constantly self-creating historical circumstances. I do not assume that formal doctrine is always trumped by more flexible "lived practices." They may be so, but one can hardly present this as an argument to a believing Muslim who thinks that Islam actually commands certain behavior.

Consider the following problem: A Muslim citizen of a European country regards offensive and scandalous cartoons about the Prophet Muhammad to be blasphemous and worthy of prohibition. Now, the citizen in question may adopt this view for a variety of reasons. He may be under psychological stress about modernization and his children's adoption of un-Islamic habits. He may be furious at hegemonic, neo-imperialist Western foreign policies and associate the cartoons with other political attacks on Muslims. He may be committed to an Islamist political agenda that sees the cartoon controversies as a tactical opportunity. Various methods of interpretation—historiographical, genealogical, hermeneutic, psychoanalytic—may cast light on the meaning and motivations of this political demand. All of these methods are valuable modes of Western scholarship.

However, none of these results is particularly appropriate for use in the realm of public deliberation about common social norms. None of those interpretations can serve as a *public argument* that could be presented to that citizen in favor of one policy or another, at least not without a considerable degree of presumption. According to the terms of public reason, we cannot reasonably present to this citizen for the purpose of public justification any of the following statements:

> "Your opposition to these cartoons is grounded in anxiety about your encounter with modernity and your children's exposure to Western habits. Since you are not really motivated by religious commitments (because we don't really think formal religious commitments explain all that much), we do not need to publicly address the most appropriate rules for regulating free speech and offense."
>
> "You are really just caught up in the zeitgeist of mutual distrust between the West and Islam. For the record, I share your opposition to the Global War on Terror, the U.S. occupation of Iraq, and Western support for Middle Eastern dictatorships, but because your opposition to the cartoons is really about that and not really motivated by religious commitments, we do not need to publicly address the most appropriate rules for regulating free speech and offense."
>
> "You are really part of an Islamist effort to subvert liberal democracy and are using the cartoons as a pretext for a form of antidemocratic political action.[105] Because you are really motivated by a dangerous religious doctrine, and because there is no chance that you are trustworthy, we do not need to publicly address the most appropriate rules for regulating free speech and offense."

Public reason aims at addressing this citizen in terms of the actual moral conflict in question and at resolving it in a reasonable way on the basis of a public conception of justice and appropriate political goals. Conjecture, in turn, seeks to motivate fellow citizens on the basis of their comprehensive doctrine as *they* understand it. Privately (including in academic discourse), we may in fact hold any of the above views about the political, psychological or historical causes of the citizen's political demand, but we recognize that we could hardly present them *to her* as reasons for one policy or another if we are serious about treating her comprehensive doctrine as reasonable. Rather, we aspire to reasons and arguments that we believe to be of first-order, normative interest to believing Muslims who take formal Islamic doctrine seriously enough to derive principled objections to liberal principles from it in the first place.

Another way of putting this is that the justificatory form of comparative political theory is not satisfied with asserting to fellow *non-Muslims* the vague and uncontestable claim that Islam is "a diverse, polyvalent and complicated tradition" contra the representations and misrepresentations of Western media outlets; the aim is a more ambitious one: to enter into a common practice of mutual justification with actual believing Muslims about the reasonable terms of social cooperation and what Islam might be able to endorse.

STIGMATIZATION AND MARGINALIZATION. A deeper and more potent reservation about this project, however, would be that it somehow contributes to a discourse that stigmatizes or marginalizes Muslims. I take this danger and possibility very seriously but regard it as not applicable in this case. The methodology developed in this book does not assume the presence of moral conflict on the basis of stereotypes or media images but rather addresses the precise points of contestation as presented by the most systematic articulators of liberal and Islamic doctrines. The claim that Islam might object to liberal or democratic principles (just as many other comprehensive doctrines do) and can justify illiberal political action is grounded in (fairly mainstream) Islamic texts, not in clichés or the actions of marginal groups. As one prominent American Muslim scholar, Sherman Jackson, notes in a different context:

> the views of the so-called Muslim Radicals cannot be simply ignored out of fear of bringing Islam under indictment. Nor can they be dismissed as the mindless rantings of a tiny, vociferous fringe or the politically motivated dribble of simpletons who just don't understand the grand and glorious tradition of classical Islam. For, rightly or wrongly, these views constitute the going opinion in many quarters. And, the authors of these views are often men of immense standing who wield enormous authority in the Muslim world and beyond.[106]

In the case of this study, the views canvassed that raise as problematic the idea of liberal citizenship do not even belong to the "radical" (read: jihadi) trends to which Jackson refers.

Furthermore, while there is no civic duty to refrain from challenging or criticizing fellow citizens on their comprehensive views (such a duty would be a very odd form of social solidarity, indeed, and would in fact require a very high level of mutual alienation), the interest in arguing for liberal principles from within a given comprehensive doctrine clearly involves a certain amount of respect and recognition. The search for points of congruence with a particular comprehensive doctrine (which may also have the resources to object to liberalism) requires seeing that doctrine as fundamentally (or in crucial aspects) reasonable and morally respectable. If the main tenets of a doctrine were in some crucial way incompatible with the basic idea of a fair system of social cooperation, then a liberal would regard appeals to that doctrine as an impermissibly cynical tactic.

Consider an obvious case. Say that a person is seeking to increase support for a policy of more open borders. A large segment of the population opposes this, perhaps on morally reasonable grounds. Others, however, oppose it from within an unreasonable doctrine, let's say on grounds of racial or cultural superiority. One could imagine concocting arguments for open borders that would appeal to racist sentiments. To take an extreme example:

> "It is good for the United States to permit increased immigration because that way the dirty jobs that our economy requires are not performed by white people. We need a steady stream of inferior people to perform these jobs. I do not share your doctrine of white supremacy, but don't you agree, then, that white supremacists should support immigration?"

The form of conjecture envisioned in this book *excludes* appeals to such a doctrine because the arguments invoked are radically incongruent with basic liberal principles of equality and fairness. The problem of such doctrines in a well-ordered liberal society is not to appeal to them but to contain them.

Thus, we consider conjecture to be a legitimate option for justification or persuasion only when the doctrine in question is worthy of such respect and when conjecture will involve invoking arguments that are themselves morally reasonable and compatible with basic liberal principles. In this way, far from being stigmatizing of a religious tradition like Islam by assuming its illiberal nature, conjecture (justificatory comparative political theory) in fact involves an attitude of respect and recognition vis-à-vis that tradition.

This is in some ways analogous to the argument that one treats another's beliefs with respect not by granting another person sovereignty over them but rather by soberly examining their merits.

> Arguably, it is more insulting to have one's beliefs treated as though their truth or falsity were of no consequence; for that is to have one's beliefs not taken seriously *as beliefs*. . . . But to seek to immure people's beliefs so that they will never be threatened or changed is effectively to do just that. . . . Those who seek to "protect" beliefs so that they become, in effect, exhibits frozen in a social museum runs the risk of reducing them to mere objects of curiosity which make no demands for serious consideration upon those who do not already hold them . . . their efforts may be more patronizing than the attempts of others to refute them.[107]

This book does not seek to examine the truth or falsity of Islamic beliefs, but following Peter Jones, one might say that it is more insulting to have one's moral beliefs and propositions treated as though their *reasonableness* were of no consequence, for that does not take them seriously as sincere efforts to think about the social world on the basis of a comprehensive doctrine. That form of insult is appropriate for racist beliefs, but not, in my mind, for religious beliefs, including Islamic ones.

Some may regard this as something of a backhanded compliment ("We respect Islam because we assume it has the resources to support liberal terms of social cooperation"), but this objection cannot survive scrutiny. The extension of respect always involves some form of value judgment, if respect is to be at all meaningful. Perhaps others "respect Islam" because it represents a proud civilization, because it spiritually sustains vast numbers of people, because of its intellectual and artistic heritage, because it constitutes one good life among many, because many people we respect as equals find it meaningful and valuable, or even because it is presently at the vanguard of resisting neoliberal imperialism and secular hegemony. None of those reasons is fundamentally any different from asserting that justificatory comparative political theory respects Islamic moral traditions because it conjectures that those traditions might be able to support fair terms of social cooperation as political liberalism proposes them.

Naturally, believing Muslims may not be impressed by the liberal grounds for respect, but they would be no more impressed by the other reasons listed in the last paragraph, which also all fall short of recognizing Islam as true. Thus, the liberal conception of respect for comprehensive doctrines is no more arbitrary or conditional than any other set of standards. It is, however, perhaps more precise and transparent.

What I have tried to show here is that conjecture (justificatory comparative political theory) need not be rejected on any of the canvassed grounds. However, I have not shown that every exercise in conjecture in fact *succeeds* in avoiding these (or many other) objections or criticisms. Therefore, I now turn to my proposal for a reasonable method of engaging in conjecture appropriate for the aim of identifying an Islamic full justification for liberal citizenship. Many of the arguments I gave above for conjecture in fact depend on articulating a plausible methodology that avoids certain pitfalls.

2

Methods: The Ethics of Comparative Ethics

What is the methodology by which the possibility of an overlapping consensus is tested, and who is entitled to engage in it? The process of defending a certain set of public institutions from within someone else's ethical tradition ("comprehensive doctrine"), even if adherents of that tradition have not yet done so, is referred to by Rawls, perhaps unfortunately, as "conjecture," and it is included as one of his acceptable forms of nonpublic reason. He defines *conjecture* as arguing "from what we believe, or conjecture, are other people's basic doctrines, religious or secular, and try[ing] to show them that, despite what they may think, they can still endorse a reasonable political conception that can provide a basis for public reasons." As to the guidelines for this practice, Rawls says simply that "it is important that conjecture be sincere and not manipulative. We must openly explain our intentions and state that we do not assert the premises from which we argue, but that we proceed as we do to clear up what we take to be a misunderstanding on others' part, and perhaps equally on our own."[1]

Although the idea of correcting others on the aims and requirements on their own beliefs and doctrines might seem outlandish, it is, of course, the everyday stuff of political persuasion[2] among citizens.[3] Just as the idea of reconciliation through public reason sets for philosophy the task of narrowing the gap between citizens by reasoning from basic principles that we imagine all to share, persuasion intuitively begins with the search for beliefs held by other persons from which we think we can deduce conclusions that they do not at the moment endorse.

Imagine, for example, an evangelical Christian who is opposed to legalized abortion for religious reasons (leaving aside the problem of this person's views on whether religious beliefs can serve as a public basis for justification). Perhaps this person's religious beliefs provide fully for her own motivations, but she may also sincerely believe that other persons can oppose abortion for their own reasons. We could easily imagine her seeking to persuade others of the immorality of abortion on the basis of reasons that she does not find dispositive or that she does not require, given the completeness of the religious reasons already comprising her motivational set. For example, perhaps she presents to a feminist a series of arguments (allowing for the moment that we may regard feminism as a comprehensive doctrine in something like the way we regard other religious or philosophical doctrines as such) that legal abortion has actually been bad for women in ways that a feminist is likely to regard as bad. Let us assume that the evangelical Christian is entirely forthright that her own reasons for opposing abortion are religious in nature and that these reasons constitute her primary moral and political motivation. We may also assume that she declares that she does not endorse the primary beliefs, truth-claims, commitments, and aims of the feminism espoused by her interlocutor. Nonetheless, she asserts that *given* the beliefs, commitments, and motivations of feminism, a feminist ought to oppose abortion. (Let us not consider for the moment whether she believes her assertion to actually succeed in justifying her position from a feminist perspective.)

Naturally, all sorts of political or psychological factors might contribute to those arguments being received as hostile or being less persuasive than if they had been posed by someone who publicly avowed the underlying truth-claims and moral commitments of feminism. However, this is not the same as saying that the evangelical Christian had done something problematic or manipulative merely by arguing from an alien moral perspective. That is, we do not imagine ourselves to be bound by a certain *civic* duty to regard others' political or moral worldviews as inviolable or closed off from interrogation by outsiders, especially when those persons themselves are putting forward political claims based on those worldviews. Nor do we imagine that political commitments are necessarily derived from underlying moral commitments by a process that outsiders are *cognitively* incapable of apprehending. For starters, might trying to reason from within their worldview (to give them reasons that are reasons for them), far from being morally wrong, be in some way morally *required*? Do we imagine that it is sufficient for public justification to only consider what *we* think is justified from our own internal perspective?

Nonetheless, despite our familiarity with political and moral persuasion, there remains something implausible or even unsettling in the image of outsiders entering others' ethical traditions—particularly ones as elaborate and technical as, say, the Islamic legal tradition—and blithely "try[ing] to show them that, despite what they may think, they can still endorse a reasonable political conception that can provide a basis for public reasons." Skepticism about this kind of practice would seem to apply in particular when the alien tradition is a *religious* one, for religious doctrines tend to be characterized by a number of features absent in secular ones:

- Revelatory texts are literally authoritative, whereas important statements of secular comprehensive doctrines are, at best, highly prestigious.
- Religious traditions are often decidedly authoritarian, with rigid (if not unassailable) hierarchies. (It is often difficult enough for lay or low-ranking *insiders* to argue successfully for heterodox or novel interpretations, never mind outsiders.)
- Religious believers often hold that cognitive or analytic acumen is only one condition for interpreting doctrine; noncognitive and nonrational requirements might render outsiders literally incapable of apprehending the requirements of faith.
- Religious doctrine might be rigidly conscribed by final and binding authoritative statements (as in the case of the Catholic Church) or detailed, expert arguments referring to long-standing bodies of tradition (as in the case of Islam); it may simply be a matter of *fact* (more or less) what a religious tradition holds to be the political requirements of its truth-claims, which would render very difficult Rawls's description of conjecture as correcting persons on what they can and cannot support.
- While the identity of interlocutors may always matter, given the psychological conditions of opinion-formation and change, in the case of religion, believers may be particularly resistant to arguments posed by outsiders—who are, after all, persons who publicly reject the truth-claims of the religion in question.
- Finally, both believers and nonbelievers have a tendency to regard religious belief as singularly intimate and inviolable; presenting arguments to believers about the political requirements of their faith might be seen by some as an intolerable presumption in a way that arguing about secular doctrines would not be.

Taken as a whole, these observations might constitute an objection to conjecture that we can call the "religious integrity objection."[4]

In the rest of this chapter, I set out to develop a methodology for what may be called justificatory comparative political theory, conjecture, or comparative ethics. Although this book proceeds largely on this invitation by Rawls, his brief thoughts on conjecture provide insufficient guidance for one wishing to engage in it. Furthermore, we may not be comfortable accepting all of what he does suggest, especially the notion of correcting others on the implications and requirements of their own religious doctrine.

But before that, I would like to acknowledge two further reservations about trying to show that a certain position can be justified within a given religious tradition. These two objections are quite different from the previously mentioned sensitivity to religion's inherent inclination to authority and tradition. They might be called the "banality objection" and the "polyvalent traditions objection."

The *banality objection* is essentially that we should not be surprised to find an "Islamic doctrine of citizenship in liberal democracies," but none too impressed by this fact either. Texts are subject to constant interpretation and reinterpretation; pious protests aside, religious texts are no exception to this. There is no limit to what texts can be contorted to justify, and since human beings have a wide range of motivations, we should expect fully that some people use Islamic texts to justify liberal citizenship, just as Islamic texts have been used to justify every political regime under which Muslims have found themselves living. Nothing meaningful or interesting, however, can be learned from this about "Islam" or about the special legitimacy of liberal principles.

The *polyvalent traditions objection* is essentially that all religious and cultural traditions are diverse and display multiple manifestations. Thus, looking for a single Islamic doctrine of citizenship—or, indeed, taking too seriously the abstract Islamic objections to liberal citizenship—ignores this diversity and privileges an essentialized, perhaps even stereotypical, vision of Islam. Given the wide diversity of Islamic intellectual traditions and lived experiences, not to mention their *hybridity*, privileging one tradition or discourse would be arbitrary, and trying to identify a single set of Islamic arguments recognizable to all Muslim believers would be futile. Furthermore, the conjecturer looking to present Islamic arguments endorsing the liberal terms of social cooperation might neglect incompatible positions or treat the tradition in an eclectic, à la carte, context-free way.[5]

In a way, all three of these objections have something in common. They all represent a certain skepticism about the possibility, significance, or purpose of a non-Muslim identifying Islamic arguments in favor of the liberal terms of social cooperation. They all point to the difficulty of locating "Islam" as a single comprehensive doctrine in the way Rawls treats the concept.

All of these objections have a measure of truth, and I take all of them extremely seriously, to the extent that I submit that *the first aim or principle of conjecture (justificatory comparative political theory) is not truth, or even support for liberal principles per se, but "plausibility."* We are aspiring to the most *plausible* interpretation of an ethical or cultural tradition, in the sense of preserving what are generally held to be the most constitutive elements of that tradition—what makes that tradition *that* tradition and not another one—that still allows us to arrive at some sort of consensus. If the dialectical process of comparative ethics results, particularly in the case of revealed religions, in an exegetical free-for-all with little regard for the continuity of doctrinal and methodological traditions, then we would not be engaging in a process for which we could expect a wide range of interlocutors. It is no less true, however, that if the process of comparative ethics insists on an artificially integral, fossilized or pristine conception of the other ethical tradition, then we may also run the risk of irrelevance.

Ultimately, plausibility can be measured only in terms of the reception of a given claim by the discursive community toward which it is directed. In this case, our claims are directed at multiple discursive communities, each of which will have different standards for determining plausibility and will apply those standards with different levels of rigor. The communities that might be expected to evaluate the plausibility of a claim about the possibilities for an overlapping consensus between Islamic ethics and political liberalism include liberal philosophers, Muslim religious authorities, non-Muslim experts on Islam, and conscientious lay Muslims. The plausibility of a proposal for an overlapping consensus will be the relative acceptance of such a proposal by members of each of those four main discursive communities, each of which will have not only different standards of acceptability but also, possibly, mutually conflicting standards.

Taken by itself, the plausibility standard might be said to be agent-neutral. It applies equally to whether a claim about the possibilities for an overlapping consensus between Islamic ethics and political liberalism are made by a non-Muslim or a Muslim. In reality, of course, it matters greatly who is saying what. There is a weak way and a strong way in which this is the case. In the weak way, one might say that it is not the business of outsiders to "conjecture" on possible reinterpretations of another community's ethical tradition. Particularly when dealing with the interpretation of religious texts, the charge can easily be made that nonbelievers will always lack the spiritual commitment, faith, and, most of all, good will to participate in dialogue about their ethical meaning. In the strong way, the concern is with the effects of the mere fact of an outsider endorsing a given norm on the likelihood of that norm being endorsed or regarded sympathetically.

In the first case, the concern might be that the lack of authenticity on the part of a person's engagement with an ethical traditional will result in a form of *rhetorical manipulation*, or what Robert Audi has called "leveraging by reasons," which involves "giving reasons *for the audience to hold the position* . . . [trying] to move an audience to a view by noting one or more reasons there are for it from the audience's point of view."[6] Audi has in mind a slightly different scenario—namely, when religious persons give secular reasons they do not hold to justify laws or public policies (he is concerned to show why religious citizens have a fairly robust duty to be motivated by public reasons)—but it is easy to see why his concern with a form of "secular rationalization" could apply to this project. "Does it not smack of manipulation to give reasons that do not move me, in order to get others to do what I want? I use reasons as psychological levers to produce belief on a basis that does not carry my own conviction."[7]

I do not believe that all forms of engagement with another's moral reasons are manipulative and thus do not regard Audi's charge against leveraging by reasons as applicable, at least in this case. I think there are at least four good reasons for this.

First, there are some important differences between presenting a case in a nonpublic context and doing so when what is at stake is the direct public justification of a coercive law being considered. There is nothing similar at stake in a project like this. Muslim fellow citizens are not being asked to vote on a law or constitution or consent to a political arrangement on the basis of the arguments presented in this book. Nothing is being asked of anyone except that they consider the views presented here. Furthermore, even those views are limited to topics, doctrines, and claims that themselves have been put forward from within Islamic sources as public objections to some aspect of liberal citizenship. That is, this form of justification does not aim at prying open the closed-off, inward-looking conscience of private reasoners.

Second, *pace* Audi, the fact that I cannot endorse someone else's reasons does not mean that my appeal to them is insincere or patronizing, or necessarily objectionable to the person in question. There might be a good explanation why certain reasons are reasons for one person and not for another. Take efforts at persuasion based on different material *interests*. Two persons' (or groups') interests may differ for many reasons that are perfectly transparent and acceptable to the parties themselves. The efforts of one party to show another why they may not be calculating their own interests accurately is only manipulative in a morally worrisome way if there is actual deceit involved, not merely by virtue of the fact that the persuading party does not share the interest in question (and thus the reason). In the case of *moral argumentation*, there could be equally good explanations based on something like the recognition of moral pluralism. In the conditions of moral pluralism, people understand and accept that fellow citizens do not all share one's values, perspective, or object of faith. To call patronizing the effort to present reasons based on what is consistent with *another* person's religion or moral perspective, with the understanding that these are not reasons for the person presenting them, is to misplace the potential cause for offense. In such a case, it is not the *reason* that is regarded as lacking or weak (to the person presenting it) but the *entire religion or moral perspective*. That is, reasons are not always about making accurate factual or inferential connections (in which case saying, "This might convince you even although not me" would indeed seem patronizing); they are about the coherence of facts, inferences, values, commitments, and perspectives. If a person does take umbrage at the claim "your moral commitments are consistent with x," it can only be because she thinks that *her* moral commitments should be *everyone's* moral commitments. In other words, the problem would not be a non-Muslim presenting Islamic arguments she doesn't hold but, rather, not holding Islam to be true in the first place. But this can be neither Audi's concern nor ours. As with interests, it is only if the reasons or arguments themselves itself involve parody, factual error, deceit, mockery, or the effort to harm the other's welfare that we have cause to worry about it. But to regard *reasons-for-you-but-not-for-me* as somehow inherently manipulative or uncivil strikes me as a posture that laments the very fact of moral pluralism.

Third, following on the second reason, the aim is not merely to give reasons we think *persuade* a single interlocutor at the moment of engagement. That could be achieved by giving bad reasons from the internal perspective of the doctrine in question, that is, reasons based on inaccuracies or faulty inferences, even if they are believed by the person in question. This appeal to bad reasons—where the reasons are bad for reasons internal to the doctrine (i.e., in this case, bad Islamic reasons)—would indeed be cynical and manipulative. Rather, the aspiration is to give good reasons, that is, *plausible* reasons you think can withstand open scrutiny within a discursive community. "Justifying your beliefs or principles to others does not involve simply *giving others reasons that they will accept*, but in some way advancing reasons that you think are good reasons for them to accept."[8] This principle, which is part of the principle of *sincerity* in argumentation, is thus very close to what I mean by "plausibility." The idea of plausibility suggests that arguments should be convincing to a wide range of people with similar enough beliefs and skills of reasoning. The fact that arguments are presented to a wide range of people—a discursive or argumentative community of some sort—means that we cannot rely on merely clever, sophisticated, or attractive "Islamic" arguments for some norm, even if they persuade or convince a single immediately present interlocutor.

To give an example, let's say a non-Muslim (Maarti) is discussing politics and justice with a Sunni fellow citizen (Zayd). Let us imagine that the latter is poorly informed about his religion, but holds the following principle of basing his moral judgments on the authority of scholars (AS):

> (AS): *I will base my moral and political commitments on and only on views which have been established to be authoritative by the consensus of Sunni scholars.*

He informs his non-Muslim interlocutor Maarti that he cannot regard the Finnish constitution as legitimate because he has heard that Sunni scholars have all agreed that political principles must be based on the Qur'an and Sunna. In response, Maarti tells him: "But Zayd, don't you know that the Sunni scholars all regard politics as a sphere of inactivity for Muslims until the Vanished Twelfth Imam returns from Occultation?" Of course, Maarti is invoking a Shi'ite doctrine, one that Zayd, as a nominal Sunni, has no *good religious reason* to endorse but that Maarti believes Zayd, as a poorly informed Sunni, *will endorse*. If we assume that Maarti is aware of what he is doing (and also that he is not a crypto-Shi'ite recruiter), we, of course, regard this as insincere and manipulative, whether or not the norm Maarti is trying to justify (Finland's liberal constitution) is justified from our perspective, because Maarti *knows* that as a Sunni, Zayd ought not believe in the doctrine of the Occultation of the Twelfth Imam or care about the views of Shi'ite scholars.[9] And of course, if Maarti expects a wider community of Muslims who hold AS to be present, he would probably not put forth the argument in the first place because he knows how implausible it is.

Fourth, in the case of liberal justification from multiple moral perspectives, one is not trying to justify to another person something they are not willing to have applied to themselves. We are only trying to justify norms or principles in which we believe and that we wish to see applied to ourselves. That is, we not only believe that a certain norm or principle is justified from the perspective of our interlocutor but also believe it justified from our own perspective, albeit for different reasons. This is, of course, identical to the basic notion of reasonableness in political liberalism: being willing to propose *and abide by* fair terms of social cooperation, provided that others do likewise.

So, let's say a non-Muslim (Donald) is discussing war and violence with a Sunni fellow citizen (Aymān). Donald wants Aymān to affirm the following principle of nonaggression (NA):

> (NA): *In the present global environment, no war of aggression may be waged with the purpose of advancing a certain country's imperialist aims or changing another country's government. Furthermore, because there is usually disagreement on when a country or militant group actually wages war for imperialist aims, as opposed to self-defense or humanitarianism, all wars*

> *must be approved by an uncoerced, unmanipulated supermajority vote within the full General Assembly of the United Nations.*

He presents Aymān with a long list of Islamic arguments for this principle, including Qur'anic verses, *ḥadīth* reports, and the rulings of Islamic legal scholars. Eventually, Aymān is convinced and affirms principle NA. Let us assume, contrary to the Maarti-Zayd encounter, that all of Donald's Islamic arguments are plausible—that is, *good* Islamic arguments that might withstand scrutiny if the conversation were opened up to others. (See chapter 6 for some of these arguments.) Thus, Donald fulfills the sincerity requirement as presented to this point. However, let us say that Donald himself does not affirm NA or at least not for his own country. He wants to be able to free-ride on the system of global cooperation by exempting himself from NA when he deems it necessary. Thus, his argument is insincere and manipulative (even if plausible) in a morally troubling way. But note: This has nothing to do with the fact that he is trying to move Aymān on the basis of Aymān's religious beliefs, but rather because he is trying to do so in a way that takes advantage of Aymān. It is the free-riding or unjustness of acting contrary to NA that is morally problematic, and the insincerity of the justification thus counts against it in this case.

In rejecting this form of manipulation, we posit that justificatory comparative ethics must endorse a principle of *sincerity* that has two parts: (1) We ourselves endorse what we are trying to get others to endorse (and are willing to have it applied to us), and (2) we sincerely believe that that norm can be justified from the other's moral perspective in a way that can withstand open scrutiny.[10]

However, this is not to say that the "lack of authenticity" charge is not a psychological reality or even something that is unreasonable for a moral community to assert vis-à-vis meddling outsiders.[11] Indeed, it is my view that outsiders should, to the extent possible, limit their arguments to the analysis of exegesis already produced by insiders. This view is only partially offset by the fact that one of the twentieth century's great Islamic Modernist scholars dissented from it: "Qur'anic hermeneutics . . . is concerned with an understanding of its message that will enable those who have faith in it and want to live by its guidance—in both their individual and collective lives—to do so coherently and meaningfully. In this purely cognitive effort both Muslims and, in certain areas, non-Muslims can share, provided the latter have the necessary sympathy and sincerity. Pure cognition and emotive faith can be practically separated."[12] Where persons, unlike Fazlur Rahman, are not keen on such dialogue with outsiders—and in today's political climate it is easy to see why Muslims should feel this way—one ought to be mindful of politico-psychological realities.

Yet, as reasonable as it is for adherents of a tradition to be uninterested in, or even offended by, outsiders' speculations as to what they might be induced to think, there is reason for those outsiders not to be overly daunted by this. To the extent that discourse ethics relies on having willing interlocutors, it assumes that there will be those unwilling to be interlocutors. Those dogmatically opposed to ethical dialogue with outsiders are not compelled to engage in it or to read what outsiders have to say about their ethical traditions, just as they are free to ignore various modes of Western scholarship. The worst that the conjecturer has to fear from the "lack of authenticity" charge is that a target audience will not read his work, a possibility that any prudent scholar would be well advised to come to terms with as early as possible in his career.

However, I referred above to a strong way in which it might matter who is saying something, and this depends on the target audience actually reading (or at least skimming) the text in question. When dealing with cross-cultural dialogue, particularly involving religious differences in the context of background political conflict, the fact of an *outsider* asserting something about one's tradition may be good enough reason to reject the assertion. This is really a variation on the observer's paradox, where the fact of outside observation (in this case, proposition) is itself an independent variable on the outcome. On this view, conjecture is simply a more refined form of George Bush and Tony Blair quoting from the Qur'an to assert that Islam is a "religion of peace"—or, indeed, of Pat Robertson instructing women on the true interpretation of feminism. The danger here is not merely being rejected or ignored but actually delegitimizing the proposed grounds for an overlapping consensus: "If this unbeliever says my religion allows me to believe x, and clearly wants me to do so, I better believe y, and all the more fervently at that." Tariq Ramadan accuses many contemporary European Muslims precisely of adopting an approach to Islam that "tends to define what Islam is not in light of its own principles, but in contrast with what is it not, namely Western civilisation. If the latter accepts change, evolution, freedom and progress then, *logically, reasonably* and *as opposed to it*, Islam does not. Moreover, in their minds, the more one—whether an individual, group or society—refuses change, freedom and progress, the more he or they are genuinely Islamic."[13] (This is, of course, not to belittle the task of the internal reformer, which is infinitely more dangerous. Alien conjecturers face the danger of being counterproductive; internal reformers face the danger of being shunned, ridiculed, or killed.)

What, then, is the way to minimize all of these concerns, the religious integrity, banality and polyvalent traditions objections? I propose the following methodological and ethical principles for those interested in engaging in comparative ethics. They assume a commitment to the two broader principles argued for to this point, *plausibility* and *sincerity*.

Principles of Conjecture/Comparative Ethics

"Canon First," Or: Theorize from More Orthodox Sources to Less

Religious and intellectual traditions always have a wide range of views and interpretations on record, but not all of them can equally claim to be representative of the views of the majority of adherents of a given tradition. Epistemic communities develop more and less authoritative bodies of doctrine, and outside interpreters should strive to conjecture first from within the more authoritative sources. There are moral and pragmatic reasons for this assumption. The moral reasons concern our proper attitude toward contemporaries from different traditions. This attitude should be not only one of respect and sympathy but also one of humility. We should strive to make arguments based on sources, values, and principles that our interlocutor is most likely to regard as authoritative because this takes her tradition more seriously than if we *first* referred to sources or values in which she would probably have less trust.

Moreover, one must have humility before the traditions of inquiry and standards of authority in the intellectual corpus one is studying. One must assume that few outsiders understand an ethical tradition as well as an insider, and few insiders as well as learned experts. Authoritative doctrines may indeed serve to legitimate particular interests and tend toward conservatism, but one must also assume that they represent the most concerted and sincere intellectual effort to understand, in this case, texts considered divinely revealed. Where a consensus exists that a certain corpus speaks for an ethical tradition in a particularly authoritative way, one cannot refuse to refer to it without acknowledging that one is doing so and offering some form of justification.

These moral concerns are simply the more earnest face of the pragmatic concern. One presumably has an interest in a meaningful and effective exchange with moral contemporaries, and that is best achieved by mastering their ethical language in the way they speak it, rather than referring to more eccentric dialects. The point is easily illustrated if we turn the tables. An American liberal would presumably feel more respected and be more inclined to engage with a nonliberal who was sincerely trying to make the argument that liberalism ought to respect a particular practice by referring to Warren-era Supreme Court decisions or the writings of Ronald Dworkin than by referring to pre-Reconstruction Supreme Court decisions now superseded or to the writings of Stanley Fish.

The difficulties associated with this are obvious, however, and referred to in chapter 1 as the implausibility objection to comparative political theory. After all, the point of justificatory comparative political theory is to find common ground between ethical traditions, a venture worth making only if there is the experience of significant disagreement. This might be called the *paradox of comparative ethics*: On the one hand, we begin with *different* ethical traditions that have *disagreements*, and on the other, we are trying to find ground for *agreement*. If, on the one hand, there is no disagreement worth bridging, then the venture is uninteresting and banal, yet if there is no bridging of disagreements, then the venture is futile. This implies, of course, the concurrent threat of self-contradiction: One might begin by observing the existence of deep disagreement only to finish by emphasizing the possible grounds for agreement.

The canon first principle only complicates the way out of this paradox. One feels compelled to begin with the more traditional and authoritative voices, but it is precisely these voices (particularly in the Islamic tradition, where they are likely to be medieval or earlier) that are least likely to offer anything promising in the way of an overlapping consensus with modern, liberal concerns. It is, of course, the illiberal nature of traditional doctrines in general—and their most common interpretations in particular—that creates the disagreement in the first place. Nonetheless, one must first examine and present the more "orthodox" views first, if only to better understand the contours of the ethical dispute. In the event that these sources happen to contain within them views that are conducive to an overlapping consensus, as is indeed shown to be the case for most of the questions considered in this book, then the conjecturer's project can only be regarded as that much more plausible.

However, it is expected that the more orthodox sources will often fail to provide the resources for an overlapping consensus. At this point, one ought to retreat gradually to other sources from within an ethical tradition that are arguing for positions more conducive to an overlapping consensus. By way of a metaphor, we might imagine this as peeling an onion. We thus begin with those "conservative" sources that provide the points of contact and disagreement and seek points of consensus or congruence as close to them as possible. When one discourse, genre, or tradition shows no resources for consensus, we peel back one layer of the onion (as it were) at a time in search of compatibility, rather than rushing right to the most reformist or transformative discourses, that is, those most appealing to a popular liberal conscience.

I believe this is an important principle if this form of justificatory comparative ethics is going to avoid the pitfalls into which most public and popular discussions of the "compatibility of Islam and x" fall. There is no shortage of "liberal" or "moderate" Muslim intellectuals. And as I have emphasized repeatedly, I do not assume in this study that actual lay Muslim citizens of liberal democracies experience that citizenship as problematic, religiously or otherwise. Thus, if comparative ethics is going to be doing something more interesting, revealing, and challenging than merely pointing to the fact that some persons with Muslim names are perfectly capable of presenting arguments for the compatibility of Islam and liberalism, it must take seriously the sources of moral disagreement and ask cautiously and seriously *what is involved Islamically* in such disagreement being transcended. Thus, if this study puts an inordinate emphasis on a conservative mode of Islamic belief and practice, it is not because I regard that mode as more legitimate but rather because it is that mode that both has a widespread claim to internal orthodoxy and presents the deepest moral challenge to liberalism.

Similarly, in moving from the most traditional sources to other discourses gradually and with the least doctrinal revision necessary, the point is not only to say that Islamic resources exist to justify liberalism after all. What interests us in this shift are the ways in which intellectuals use authoritative texts and traditional methodologies of interpretation and argumentation to support certain norms or principles. As outsiders, we ought not impose overly rigid preconceptions of what substantive beliefs can be derived from authoritative texts, but we are certainly obliged to read texts by Muslim authors with the objective of critically analyzing the evidence they give for their reinterpretations and how these interpretations measure up to previous ones. Thus, while the conjecturer is "engaged" or "interested" in the results of the inquiry, he should not neglect the concerns of more disinterested, value-neutral hermeneutical standards. At the bare minimum, we should be willing to speculate on where a given text or argument stands in relation to others and how plausible it is likely to be to believing Muslims.

To this point, the work of the conjecturer might be characterized as diagnostic and synthetic, which captures its position in between normative theorizing and interpretation. The conjecturer is, of course, concerned to defend a particular thesis—in this case, the proposition that certain liberal norms can be justified from the standpoint of Islamic sources—but his position as an outsider to a tradition limits the extent to which he can freely argue from original sources (engage in his own exegesis). Thus, he sees his task as critically analyzing attempts by insiders to answer the specific questions he is interested in, where such attempts exist, and, where they do not, to attempt to piece together (hence, synthesis) what such answers might be on the basis of existing scholarship.

Transparency

This sensitivity to the preponderance of intellectual resources able to be deployed *against* strategies of compatibility or consensus, as well as to the ever-present mistrust of both external and internal reformers, needs to be uppermost in the mind of the conjecturer. One response to these challenges is not to exaggerate the authority or intellectual force of evidence one finds in favor of compatibility, but just the opposite: to be rigorous in citing evidence to the contrary, or being "transparent" in one's recognition of the contingent nature of consensus and of the loss involved.[14] One must keep in mind that "many of these cultural communities are not averse to self-criticism and change, but they do so in a spirit of humility rather than self-creation, and in terms of the central values and principles of their culture rather than some allegedly transcultural norms autonomously derived by an unanchored and self-sufficient reason."[15] Recognizing this requires that one consistently identify (to the best of the outsider's knowledge and understanding) how authoritative or central one's source or interpretation is, what alternative sources and arguments exist, and what types of departures or breaks are involved in adopting a given position.

Sympathy

Clearly, the purpose of searching for an overlapping consensus is to find one. One of the dangers in assuming that one is there to be found is to treat the authoritative texts of an alien tradition in too instrumental of a manner, searching only for commonality. This endeavor may come at the expense of a loss of the spirit in which members of a tradition read those same texts. One should have, thus, "sympathy" for the community in question, not in the sense of approving of the substantive ethical directives, but in trying to "enter sympathetically into the latter's world of thought, tease out its insights and deeper concerns and anxieties."[16] This is related to the principle of transparency but goes beyond simply citing contrary evidence or acknowledging that one cites from a minority tradition. The principle of sympathy requires that, for these purposes, we assume that our interlocutors or sources (particularly the ones not conducive to our purposes) are sincere in their defense of their values and that specific positions or maxims are part of an overall conception of value. The principle of sympathy requires thus that we display an understanding of the context in which statements of value or norms are made, the relative importance of various norms, and the necessity of using language in different ways. Above all, this principle requires us to reflect critically on what will count as compatibility or overlapping consensus, what reasons or statements we will accept from contemporaries as sufficiently principled. (This theme is taken up later.)

Restraint

One runs the risk of making a great many mistakes simply by being too eager to establish the possibility of consensus. In keeping with the principles of transparency and sympathy, one of the legitimate outcomes of comparative political theory (discourse ethics, etc.) might simply be a better understanding of the unbridgeable. One should be willing to say that intersubjective consensus would come only at the cost of neglecting or sacrificing beliefs that, *at this time* at least, are constitutive of what it means to be a member of a given ethical community. One should be aware from the outset of the *professional interest* one has as a comparative political theorist (conjecturer, etc.) in arriving at a certain set of results and thus also be sensitive to how this professional interest might lead to careless methods. But if one accepts from the outset that negative results are also a form of results and that much can still be gained from the process of achieving them, then perhaps one's relative credibility can be preserved. Although we wish for positive results for any number of defensible reasons, we are also interested in analyzing the patterns of thought and the process by which traditions are negotiated and reinvented. Here the interest is not merely in advocating a particular party within a tradition but in analyzing the rhetorical techniques of the various parties and their relative overall intellectual coherence.

Operationalizing Conjecture

I propose, thus, at least as a starting point, a slightly less ambitious form of conjecture, or comparative ethics, than that suggested by Rawls. I characterize it as *diagnostic, evaluative,* and *synthetic.* It involves primarily investigating the capacity of any given comprehensive ethical doctrine to provide support for an overlapping consensus on a public conception of justice or citizenship, even if adherents of that tradition have not yet done so. Such a process, as becomes clear in the following chapters, is more complex than merely reading what others have to say in light of our own concerns.

Steps one, two, and three represent the diagnostic stage of conjecture.

1. Making transparent the range of views, and reasons for those views, from within an ethical tradition that serve to reject liberal terms of social cooperation, which we can call "incompatible positions." (I do this at length in chapter 3.)
2. Articulating from the liberal perspective what precisely is sought by way of consensus or affirmation from the nonliberal tradition in question. This step requires not only familiarity with liberal conceptions of justice and citizenship but also familiarity with the outside ethical tradition and where specifically it may conflict with liberal norms. (I do this in chapter 4.[17])
3. Searching for and presenting views from within that tradition that ostensibly approve of or accept liberal terms of social cooperation, which we can call "compatible positions." The purpose is to identify what, from the perspective of the doctrine in question, is *involved* in endorsing a particular aspect of liberal citizenship: Can it be done from within the range of diversity approved by traditional schools of thought, or does it require significant departure from orthodoxy?
4. Analyzing those views in terms of the nature of their reasoning and argumentation in an attempt to judge whether the underlying foundation for those views merits accepting them as *principled* and *stable* arguments for accepting liberal terms of social cooperation. This is the "evaluative" stage of conjecture. A primary concern of political liberalism is that it not be a mere modus vivendi between conflicting social groups but rather a potentially stable social contract. Thus, for it to be said that an overlapping consensus obtains, there would have to be good reason to believe that the comprehensive ethical doctrine in question is providing principled (rather than tactical or strategic) reasons for affirming a given liberal norm or institution, such that they would continue to be valid should the group in question improve its relative position of strength in society.

An important clarification is required on this point. Within political liberalism, comprehensive doctrines are by and large seen as autonomous. Neither do they in their specific beliefs help determine the substantive content of principles of justice, nor does political liberalism determine the precise ways in which they affirm those principles.[18] Because political liberalism leaves the determination of the rational or the true to comprehensive doctrines, it cannot say what reasons each individual comprehensive doctrine will produce for affirming the reasonable.

However, political liberalism *can say* that certain reasons or arguments for abiding by liberal principles, while rational from the perspective of the comprehensive doctrine, are not sufficiently reasonable in that they do not imply a principled, moral affirmation of liberal principles but rather a tactical or strategic one. It must reserve for itself this right on the basis of its insistence that the overlapping consensus is not a modus vivendi or "political in the wrong way" but a potentially stable moral consensus. This is another way of making the point that political liberalism does not seek to persuade or create stability through "noble lies" or manipulation. Political liberalism is not interested in having all comprehensive doctrines provide reasons to support liberal institutions; it is interested in there being a consensus of reasonable comprehensive doctrines on support for liberal institutions for morally acceptable reasons.

Thus, we expect that specific formulations of doctrinal affirmations of citizenship in liberal societies will vary from one comprehensive doctrine to another, but these formulations are of interest to political theorists because they must reflect an underlying reasonableness; otherwise, they may not in the long term be contributing to social solidarity. Liberal political theorists cannot perform exegesis of Islamic texts for Muslim citizens, but they can say that given arguments derived from such exegesis are insufficiently principled from the standpoint of political liberalism and that they do not point to an overlapping consensus. And they can suggest, which is precisely what I do in this book, what types of formulations *would* be reasonable from a liberal standpoint while preserving the language and fundamental concerns of the comprehensive doctrine.

Most of my form of conjecture consists of this type of *evaluation of reasons*, rather than direct argumentation from within an alien ethical tradition. In any event, direct argumentation from within an alien ethical tradition would necessitate extensive knowledge of the tradition in question; the methodology I adopt here presumes a preference for existing arguments already articulated by persons who claim to endorse the metaphysical underpinnings of the tradition and whose views reflect its authoritative methodologies. It seems intuitive that a person wishing to engage in the more direct form of conjecture suggested by Rawls would begin where I do, by pointing out the range of views already advanced within discourses one's interlocutor is likely to regard as significant.

5. Finally, conjecture might involve presenting as a coherent overall "doctrine of citizenship" or "overlapping consensus" a series of arguments or positions drawn from a variety of sources, scholars, and time periods. This is the "synthetic" stage of conjecture. One scholar or school may be invoked as a source of a compatible position on one question and of an incompatible position on another. What the conjecturer is trying to show is that for any given question, a principled and also authentic and plausible affirmation can be given from within the ethical doctrine. The aspiration is that an individual adherent of the doctrine who is also a citizen of a liberal democracy could in good faith articulate a general doctrine of citizenship based on the synthesis of a variety of positions. Although I do not see why it should be necessary that a single scholar or school be the source of a comprehensive overlapping consensus, it is important that the positions being brought together do not contradict one another or rely on incompatible underlying foundations or methodologies.

Locating Islam as a Comprehensive Doctrine: A Note on Orthodoxy, Moral Personality, and Hybridity

What, then, figures in Islamic ethical traditions as the primary canon, or most orthodox corpus, that allows for the most plausible treatment of the dialectic of disagreement and consensus between political liberalism and Islam?

In this study, my main focus is on the tradition of Islamic jurisprudence (*fiqh*), both classical and contemporary, and the answers that it contains to the specific questions posed by this book.[19] Islamic law, of course, should not be understood as Islamic "statute law" in the sense of that which is canonized and enforced through courts but rather as the formalized Islamic search for and elaboration of ethics and social norms.[20] In particular, I focus on the growing body of "jurisprudence of Muslim minorities" (*fiqh al-aqalliyyāt al-muslima*), which addresses directly the ethical aspects of Muslims living in non-Muslim states. The simple reason for this is that the juridical sources are still used by Muslims today to orient themselves. When doctrinally minded Muslims ask themselves, "What is Islamic?" or "What does Islam allow?" (whether it is related to worship, private behavior, or political ethics), the legal sources still remain the first point of orientation for the interpretation of revelation. While the premodern sources are not regarded as final or unambiguous, they still remain relevant for modern Muslims. According to Sherman Jackson, "While Islamic law may be irrelevant or marginal to the *applied* legal order, in the hearts and minds of ever increasing numbers of Muslims, it retains its *religious* (and even cultural) authority in terms of the definition of rights and obligations. In short, Islamic law, embattled though it may be, continues to represent for the masses of Muslims inalienable, God-given rights and obligations."[21] This may be put too strongly, but even a weaker assertion more than justifies paying attention to the practice of Islamic legal argumentation.

Thus, although the overlapping consensus must be established between present-day liberal conceptions of citizenship and present-day Islamic ethics, the presentation of modern and contemporary Islamic juridical or doctrinal positions must be done in light of classical positions. This is particularly true when contemporary Muslims are engaged in reinterpretation of doctrine. Where classical sources present no incompatibility with liberal citizenship, modern Muslims tend to *see* no incompatibility; the overlapping consensus can thus be regarded as particularly stable. Where classical sources do present incompatibilities, modern Muslims inclined toward skepticism of liberal citizenship have particularly strong grounds for declaring it unacceptable; the burden is on those (Muslims or outside conjecturers) to demonstrate compatibility. The reason for this is not so much the presumption of the continuity of classical authority. In the case of Islam, there are particular virtues in beginning with the classical tradition that are related to the experience of colonialism, the rise of Western human rights standards, and the transplant of Western legal codes into the Islamic world. In addition to the fragmentation this caused for Islamic religious traditions and the degradation of Islamic scholarly standards, there is also a question of authenticity. Islamic views emerging prior to the nineteenth century are more likely to reflect purely internal Islamic priorities, agendas, and standards.[22] One should not take this point too far and end up romanticizing premodern sources as a pure expression of Islamic commitments (for one reason, the reaction to empirical social changes in Islamic societies is, of course, a perennial feature of Islamic jurisprudence), but precolonial Islamic discourses are much less likely to represent a *conscious* effort to stress (in-)compatibility with Western, liberal standards.[23] Thus, those texts are not just presumed to enjoy greater orthodox credentials, but evidence of compatibility found within them would be very strong evidence for the authenticity and stability of an overlapping consensus.

In beginning my inquiry with the range of views expressed as elaborations of Islamic practical ethics, or the precise rulings (*aḥkām*) or *fatwās* within particular schools that compose the "branches" (*furū'*) of Islamic law, it is not my assertion that the rulings of substantive law represent the highest order ethical commitments in Islam. First, the effort to elaborate Islamic positions on the part of scholars is an inherently contingent venture. It has often been observed that the core problem in Islamic jurisprudence and ethics is that of uncertainty and contingency: God's law (*sharī'a*) is eternal and authoritative, but the texts that provide guidance are subject to fallible human interpretation. For all but the least ambiguous aspects of worship, Islamic rulings on the ethics and social relations (*mu'āmalāt*) are at best *probable* interpretations of God's command, and thus disagreement on substantive rulings within the boundaries of sincere effort based on recognized methods is legitimate.[24] Second, it has been argued that the highest order ethical commitments for Muslims actually consist not in the practice of conforming to Islamic norms but in the theological inquiry into the existence of God and the practice of *searching* for God's commands through the rigorous hermeneutical methods of Islamic jurisprudence (*uṣūl al-fiqh*).[25] This is not an argument I am endorsing in this book, but it is important to be reminded of the deep moral commitments contained in Islamic theology and implied by the rigorous methods of jurisprudence.

Thus, when I say that conjecture ought to begin with the most orthodox possible sources, the assumption is most certainly not that any given substantive Islamic position represents in itself an authoritative ruling. Rather, the claim is that positions on substantive ethical commitments relating to behavior in the world most likely to be recognized as sufficiently orthodox are to be found in the discourses of Islamic rule giving (*fiqh*, *aḥkām*, or *fatwā*-issuing (*iftā*)). But more to the point, it is primarily *here* where objections to liberal citizenship are to be found; thus, counterpositions affirming liberal citizenship ought to begin here as well. This follows from the basic Rawlsian strategy of attenuating moral conflict via the philosophically (epistemically) least-demanding route. For example, for a believing Muslim who objects to demand x of liberal citizenship because of position y found within her understanding of Islamic applied ethics, the following argument might be regarding as theologically very demanding:

> You are, in fact, mistaken that Islam prohibits x because the existence of y does not in fact represent your highest order moral commitments. In fact, "*kalām*, scholastic theology, is the discipline that identifies the highest order goods within normative Islam, as it is within that discipline that the requirements for a soul's salvation—the ultimate good from the perspective of Islam—are determined."[26] Scholastic theology (not *fiqh*, from which you cite y) is where you ought to look, and if you do, you will find values that affirm or do not object to liberal citizenship.

That argument may be very compelling, or even true. It may, in fact, serve for a wide range of Muslims as their "road map" to affirming liberal public reason. And we may, as it turns out, have to fall back to an argument like that. However, it ought to be acknowledged that invoking this argument is very demanding on the person in question in the sense that it involves her revising a wide range of very basic views. We do not reject this strategy on principle, but prefer an argument like the following:

> You claim that the existence of ruling y from within *fiqh* prohibits you from affirming x. I recognize that you are deriving your practical moral commitments from within Islamic substantive law. Are you aware of rulings y^1 and y^2 on this same question from scholars who are using the same hermeneutical methods as the scholar who asserted position y? These two rulings do not reject demand x yet take seriously the same underlying evidence and moral commitments as position y.

Thus, the primary reason for beginning with Islamic substantive law (including from the premodern period) is that it is one major source of the principled opposition to liberal citizenship. Of course, this book does not restrict itself to the classical tradition. That, in fact, would contradict my previous points about the contingent, flexible nature of *fiqh*. The classical tradition is used mostly to contextualize positions found in the contemporary period or, more important, to demonstrate the depth of points of disagreement and consensus.

Note, however, that where objections to liberal justice or citizenship are not registered as rulings of Islamic substantive law but, rather, as derived from theological commitments (say, to a particular conception of the person), then it would follow that the search for compatibility would begin within that genre. Again, this is along the Rawlsian lines of attenuating moral conflict at the level of abstraction necessary to resolve it, no more and no less. When moral conflict can be resolved by focusing on the interpretation of a shared concept, this is preferred. Only when a higher level of abstraction is necessary does one retreat to it. But this is not "abstraction for abstraction's sake. Rather, it is a way of continuing public discussion when shared understandings of lesser generality have broken down. We should be prepared to find that the deeper the conflict, the higher the level of abstraction we must ascend to get a clear and uncluttered view of its roots."[27] This insight is clearly applicable to Islamic polemics as well and is also a good defense against the misrecognition of another's moral perspective. We do not assume for another the nature and texture of their moral claim but rather respond to it, to the extent possible, in the language and tradition in which it is presented.

Readers will observe also that this book employs an eclectic approach to Islamic jurisprudence; I draw from sources across the four Sunni legal schools and across time and space. Furthermore, in the modern period Islamic jurisprudence has given way to some new genres of Islamic theorizing, and old genres (like exegesis and *fatwā*-issuing) have been appropriated by persons who would not traditionally be considered qualified. I have included some of these thinkers, such as the Muslim Brotherhood ideologue Sayyid Quṭb and Swiss Muslim reformer Tariq Ramadan, within my survey.

As to the eclectic nature of my survey, this is very much in keeping with modern Islamic practice. Both Islamic reformers and revivalists tend to downplay the significance of the boundaries between the traditional legal schools. Although various ideological trends may tend to cite one school disproportionately to others, this is due to ideological or methodological affinity, not a doctrine of absolute fidelity to a school in principle. Modern scholars refer to this practice of surveying the range of views from all schools across time and place with the aim of finding an amenable position as *takhayyur* or *talfīq*.[28] Similarly, premodern Islamic jurisprudence cultivated a genre of identifying the range of acceptable disagreement across and within schools, referred to as works of *ikhtilāf* ("difference" or "disagreement"). This is, of course, all the more in keeping with the interest in Islamic law as Islamic formal applied *ethics*—as opposed to Islamic law as something to be applied through courts, where predictability and consistency might arise as crucial values.[29] However, for believing Muslims today, fidelity to a particular school does not tend to be regarded as an obligation for lay believers or for scholars.[30]

Nor does drawing from modern works that are not, strictly speaking, works of jurisprudence contradict my general approach. Indeed, the only principle to which the outside conjecturer is absolutely committed is that of plausibility. Where it is the case that modern Muslims look to other sources or genres, such as the examples I have given of Quṭb and Ramadan, they can be invoked as examples of what a sincere, pious Muslim *might regard* as Islamic doctrine. However, it is never the case that these sources (or indeed any single nonrevelatory source) are invoked as authoritative in their own right. Rather, they are invoked as representative positions of a certain pattern or trend in Islamic discourses. Where any given source stands alone as offering a certain position, it is crucial that this fact be made transparent and that any conclusions drawn from that source take this into account.

This brief explanation should satisfy some of the criticisms introduced earlier. This form of conjecture should not taint or delegitimate any potential overlapping consensus, because the arguments are almost always drawn from mainstream, orthodox sources. The conjecturer's job is not to create Islamic arguments but to find them and analyze them in terms of their nature as reasons for action. Similarly, my eclectic approach to sources not only is in keeping with contemporary Muslim practice—that is, contemporary Muslim scholars and lay believers do not apply a rigid, historical, context-bound approach to their sources (i.e., that classical positions are *necessarily* inapplicable or that positions give guidance only for their particular context) but rather a living, appropriative one (according to which the classical sources frame the debate and allow for creative application)—but also affirms transparency as a crucial value. One is always committed to presenting the range of existing views and the relative centrality of the view one is advancing as compatible.

Three questions could reasonably be raised at this point:

One, is it possible to stably identify orthodoxy or a primary canon, in general, given the polyvalent nature of traditions and in particular in the case of modern Islam, with the absence of a "Church" and the oft-discussed "fragmentation of authority"?

Two, does treating a certain discourse (say, Islamic jurisprudence) as having a special claim to represent Islam in fact convey a certain prestige upon it and contribute to its claim to orthodoxy, perhaps at the expense of other discourses or even less systematic ways of living Islam?

Three, does treating Islam as a comprehensive ethical doctrine with canons of authoritative interpretation in fact best characterize how individual Muslims approach their tradition as well as political problems in the modern world? Are we entitled to assume that a jurisprudential argument will be persuasive to any given Muslim?

I begin by reiterating that there is no assumption anywhere in this book that any given Muslim or Muslim community can be reduced to a formal articulation of Islam. I am agnostic about the extent to which formal religious doctrine acts as an independent variable in the belief formation or political motivation of individuals and groups. That is a question for social science, or perhaps political psychology, and I acknowledge that research in those fields could affect our understanding of how important the concept of an overlapping consensus is for understanding social unity and stability.[31] Thus, to make very clear: *there is no assumption about the beliefs or motivations of any individual person with a Muslim name or adhering to a Muslim cultural tradition.*

Furthermore, it is indeed not the outsider's place to make judgments about the relative authenticity or veracity of one school of interpretation over another, and I do not wish to suggest that various internal reformers or social critics are thus insufficiently orthodox, sincere, or pious. However, this enterprise has in mind a certain ideal-typical Rawlsian Muslim citizen who takes her own tradition seriously, tends toward a formal, doctrinal understanding of religion, and self-consciously weighs the demands of citizenship against the duties of faith. It is this ideal-typical Muslim citizen, rather than one (like Rawls's "pluralist") who already sees religion as but one aspect of her identity and source of values and who already affirms an individual right to interpret her religion, who is most likely to reject on grounds of principle and conscience a non-Islamic conception of justice or citizenship regardless of more value-neutral markers of that person's well-being in a society, such as wealth, personal security, and life prospects.

Thus, we can adopt a fairly operational standard for identifying the most relevant sources: *We begin with doctrines, traditions, patterns of thought, or arguments that represent the point of conflict or moral disagreement with political liberalism.* This is all political liberalism needs to concern itself with because the point of conjecture is to attenuate moral conflict. Concerns over what constitutes the "true Islam" or where the center of gravity of Islam is located are more properly concerns for believers. They are none of the business or concern of liberal political philosophers. The rationale here for beginning with a certain set of texts is not just their conventional prestige or claim to orthodoxy; rather, the concern is a more pragmatic one grounded in the interest in full justification. Where citizens already see no tension with political liberalism, there is no need for conjecture; it is where there is a justificatory gap that we are concerned about the possibilities of congruence.

Therefore, the anxiety about identifying orthodoxy or the fear of excluding Muslims who approach Islam in a less systematic, more hybrid way need not arise. Those citizens are not excluded in any way from the normal practice of public justification, nor need they be excluded from their own search for a full justification. In fact, these citizens are much *less* likely to feel alienated from a liberal society. The (admittedly idiosyncratic) Rawlsian response to the citizen who protests that Islamic jurisprudence is not her authoritative expression of Islam is: "Fine, we may simply speak of you having a different comprehensive doctrine which has its own claim to calling itself 'Islam,' or perhaps your own personal collection of beliefs and preferences some of which are 'Islamic' in some way." There need be no single Islamic full justification of political liberalism because ultimately what we are concerned with are not doctrines per se, but citizens.

There is a further assumption that justifies the preference for conservative, orthodox sources. Because it is these sources and the believers who seek to follow them that are mostly likely to have principled objections to liberal citizenship, establishing consensus or congruence with them is thus not only a greater priority but can also be presumed to imply that liberal principles will be justified for persons with a less demanding or rigorous conception of religious obligation. In other words, evidence of congruence from within more conservative sources is very likely to suggest the *fact* of congruence from within less conservative ones (even if the "evidence," i.e., the precise arguments that happen to convince the conservative believer, cannot be presumed to sway the less conservative one). If conjecture aims at the widest possible support for a public conception of justice, then it makes sense that it would begin with the most enduring principled hindrances to that support.

Thus, for this project of conjecture to be coherent, all it needs is for Islamic beliefs to display *some* patterns of internal methodological and doctrinal consistency. If there were *no* intra-Muslim communities of shared epistemic authority, and if it were axiomatically false to say that it is possible to trace patterns of Islamic ethical justification, then the polyvalent traditions objection would succeed. However, the objection taken to that level is plainly false.

At the same time, the evolving, polyvalent, contestable nature of religious doctrine (particularly in the case of Islam with the absence of a "Church") is clearly something that conjecture relies on, even requires. Although I have stressed that it is possible to speak of Islam as having a *doctrinal* nature, that doctrine must not be understood as evolving *axiomatically* from a certain set of core and immutable defining claims or features, such that should those claims be controverted, it could be *proved* that Islam is incompatible with political liberalism.

To illustrate this, consider a debate from the Rawlsian discussion of which kinds of comprehensive doctrines in contemporary liberal democracies might be part of an overlapping consensus. Rawls's *A Theory of Justice* was originally written as a response to the utilitarian tradition that Rawls believed dominated ethics at the time. The entire purpose of his contractarian approach was to supplant utilitarianism, which he felt, among other deficiencies, did not take the difference between persons seriously enough and thus could not reliably serve as a foundation for rights. However, in *Political Liberalism*, Rawls claims that the classical utilitarianism of Bentham and Sidgwick could be part of an overlapping consensus:

> This utilitarianism supports the political conception [of justice] for such reasons as our limited knowledge of social institutions generally and of our knowledge about ongoing circumstances. It stresses further the bounds on complexity of legal and institutional rules as well as the simplicity necessary in guidelines for public reason. These and other reasons may lead the utilitarian to think a political conception of justice liberal in content a satisfactory, perhaps even the best, workable approximation to what the principle of utility, all things tallied up, would require.[32]

This optimism has been criticized by Samuel Scheffler, an otherwise sympathetic commentator on Rawls's project:

> An overlapping consensus is a consensus not just on principles of justice but also on the fundamental ideas implicit in the public political culture from which those principles are derivable. . . . Yet many of the arguments [for Rawls's principles of justice being chosen in the original position] are explicitly directed against utilitarianism. If utilitarianism is said to be included in the overlapping consensus on Rawls's two principles, then are we to imagine that utilitarians endorse Rawls's arguments for the rejection of utilitarianism even as they continue to affirm that view? This seems incoherent.
>
> Moreover, even the fundamental ideas from which the arguments for the two principles proceed [namely, the idea of society as a fair system of cooperation] . . . are ideas which, according to Rawls himself, utilitarianism does not accept. . . . If this is right, then it is

> really quite unclear how utilitarianism can be included in an overlapping consensus on Rawls's principles of justice since it rejects the fundamental ideas that serve as premises in the arguments for those principles, as well as the arguments themselves. . . .
>
> [While] a utilitarian might argue that utility will actually be maximized if Rawls's two principles are "publicly affirmed and realized as the basis of the social structure" . . . such an argument would be tantamount to conceding the inadequacy of utilitarianism.[33]

Because utilitarianism is not a cultural tradition subject to reform by its adherents but is rather defined as "the view that the principle of utility is the correct principle for society's public conception of justice,"[34] Scheffler is able to make an argument that Rawls was *plainly mistaken* to think that utilitarianism could be part of an overlapping consensus. The mere definition of utilitarianism makes the two claims incompatible. A utilitarian who endorses political liberalism or justice as fairness is, to that extent, less of a utilitarian precisely because utilitarianism is a claim about which public principles ought to guide social and political deliberation.

This is not how we understand religious doctrine. Clearly, it is possible to regard Islam, or rather certain claims about Islam, in this way. The belief that "there is no God but God and Muhammad is his Prophet" is such an axiomatic statement, definitive of "Muslimness." It is, of course, a trend among certain strains of Salafi or Wahhabi Muslims to increase the number of such statements that can be regarded as similarly "axiomatic" in the sense that contradiction of them renders a belief or a person un-Islamic. Such an approach to religion is clearly impermissible for outsiders. It would also render conjecture extremely difficult if the set of axiomatic beliefs included such beliefs as "Islam requires that Muslims never tolerate un-Islamic political or legal authority" and "Islam requires that Muslims only accept reasoning based on Islamic revelatory sources for the purposes of public justification." The fact that *some* Muslims regard such statements as axiomatic neither makes conjecture futile nor does it throw the door open to a use of Islamic sources with no regard for relative orthodoxy or authority. The driving question behind this inquiry is: What is *involved* in a believing Muslim endorsing the liberal terms of citizenship? Although that question presumes that *some* Islamic justification could always be provided, it is not satisfied with any such justification but the justification most likely to be compelling to the widest possible spectrum of believing Muslims.

Evaluating Comprehensive Responses to Liberal Demands: What Counts as Compatible?

Despite the anxieties revealed in the prior section about locating orthodoxy and entering into religious discourses as an unbeliever, it must be said that the main work of the conjecturer (at least for the questions addressed in this study) comes not in locating compatible arguments or assertions, but in analyzing them from a comparative ethical standpoint. Much of my analysis of Islamic sources consists in answering the question: Do the reasons being articulated by Islamic thinkers for accepting liberal constraints on the pursuit of the good indicate the existence of an overlapping consensus?

We return to the theme raised by the "paradox of comparative ethics" discussed previously, here emerging in a slightly different form. On the one hand, political liberalism, or liberal neutrality, wants to defend liberal principles without recourse to controversial metaphysical principles that various conceptions of the good might not be able to affirm. Thus, Rawls wants nonliberals to be able to endorse political liberalism without necessarily professing a belief in individual ethical autonomy as true or as a necessary component of the good. On the other hand, he wants those same citizens to accept the constraints imposed by liberalism (most important, the duty of restraint toward others) on grounds of principle and not mere political necessity. Thus, the reasons for affirming citizenship in a liberal democracy need not be the traditional metaphysical arguments for toleration (such as those derived from autonomy, skepticism, or value pluralism), but nor may they be characteristic of a modus vivendi (such as fear of punishment, a desire for social peace, or exhaustion from conflict).

That the overlapping consensus is not a mere political compromise is shown by the fact that the endorsement of the political conception of justice consists in an affirmation of its specific moral underpinnings: "How deep does the consensus go into citizens' comprehensive doctrines? And how specific is the conception agreed to? The consensus goes down to the fundamental ideas within which justice as fairness is worked out. It supposes agreement deep enough to reach such ideas as those of society as a fair system of cooperation and of citizens as reasonable and rational, free and equal."[35] Furthermore, not only are citizens affirming these moral conceptions but they are also doing so on grounds of principle. The "overlapping consensus . . . is affirmed on moral grounds, that is, it includes conceptions of society and of citizens as persons, as well as principles of justice, and an account of the political virtues through which those principles are embodied in human character and expressed in public life. All those who affirm the political conception start from within their own comprehensive view and draw on the religious, philosophical, and moral grounds it provides."[36]

Yet if the principles to be affirmed from the standpoint of a comprehensive doctrine include, for example, the protection of individual autonomy (even to some extent in the private sphere), and this affirmation must be of a moral nature, it would seem to follow that the overlapping consensus requires that each comprehensive doctrine include individual autonomy as one of its core values. Rawls's assertions that this value is limited to the political sphere are of dubious relevance, given the extent of the limitations this sphere imposes on the private. However, is it not precisely this type of demand of profession that the entire project of political liberalism is designed to avoid?

Thus, we find certain vague statements in a slightly different direction. "Justice as fairness is to be understood . . . as a free-standing view that expresses a political conception of justice. It does not provide a specific religious, metaphysical, or epistemological doctrine beyond what is implied by the political conception itself. The political conception is a module that *in different ways* fits into and can be supported by various reasonable comprehensive doctrines that endure in the society regulated by it."[37]

> Even if we do not, say, hold some form of the doctrine of free religious faith that supports equal liberty of conscience, our actions nevertheless imply that we believe the concern for salvation does not require anything incompatible with that liberty. . . . For many the true, or the religiously and metaphysically well-grounded, goes beyond the reasonable. The idea of an overlapping consensus leaves this step to be taken by citizens individually in line with their own comprehensive views.[38]

If we take these statements seriously, we are committed to considering for inclusion in the overlapping consensus comprehensive doctrines that do not preach a form of Lockean theology but manage to avoid rejecting liberal institutions. Given that it is inevitable that patterns of thought inhabiting this ambiguous terrain have some overlap with modus vivendi reasons for endorsing liberal systems, we are in need of a standard for determining when an argument from within a fully comprehensive ethical tradition is eligible for the overlapping consensus and when it is insufficiently principled for such inclusion.

A related troubling question is that discussed in the previous chapter, namely, the epistemic status of the burdens of judgment and the definition of the reasonable. As noted, Rawls not only uses the fact of reasonable pluralism to explain why political liberalism is not a concession to existing social facts but also defines his conceptions of a "reasonable citizen" and "reasonable comprehensive doctrine" partly based on whether the citizen or the doctrine recognizes the burdens of judgment. Thus, although Rawls insists that skepticism or value pluralism would be too epistemologically demanding or exclusionary for a public basis of justification, the burdens of judgment are not regarded as such. The question might arise: Ought we to include recognizing the burdens of judgment as one of the conditions for congruence, that is, as one of the demands of citizenship required for it to be said that a doctrine is part of an overlapping consensus? Ought we to include recognizing the burdens of judgment as one of the necessary *reasons* that doctrines give for tolerating fellow citizens, recognizing them, and establishing bonds of solidarity with them?

Rawls's own considerations are not likely to be sufficient for these purposes not only because of the ambiguous nature of his statements but also because he chooses not to address directly the question of the endorsement of the political conception by fully comprehensive doctrines with alternative conceptions of justice. Rather, where he does address the question of citizens who may not have previously seen themselves as holding a comprehensive doctrine that leads to the political conception of justice, he emphasizes the place of citizens with only partially, and generally unsystematic, comprehensive doctrines. In his "model case of an overlapping consensus," he thus cites three doctrines: a religious one with a (Lockean) doctrine of free faith, a comprehensive liberal doctrine, and a "pluralist" doctrine that is not "systematically unified." This latter doctrine is seen to contain a large number of nonpolitical values, as well as the capacity for various political ones. This unsystematic nature allows for the development of a freestanding adherence to the political conception of justice on its own merits, rather than as a "consequence of that doctrine's nonpolitical values." This unlinking of a doctrine's public and private values allows the former to "outweigh whatever values oppose them, at least under the reasonably favorable conditions that make a constitutional democracy possible."[39]

However, it will not do for our purposes to limit ourselves to such cases, as doing so avoids our main political interest in the prospects for engagement with fully comprehensive doctrines and our methodological interest in how the political values *themselves* need to be grounded in comprehensive doctrines. What types of theologically grounded arguments are we hoping to find, then? Rawls himself does not go further into religious doctrines than citing Locke's *Letter Concerning Toleration*.[40] Does inclusion in the overlapping consensus require a similar overt and robust endorsement of autonomy from within one's comprehensive doctrine, or is there some space for doctrines to find other ways of describing their relationship to liberalism?

There are good reasons to expand the overlapping consensus by endorsing the weaker version of the requirements for qualification. First, it is clear that the spirit of political liberalism is to avoid imposing philosophical or theological burdens on the endorsement of liberal citizenship: "The more things that people must believe in order to be included in such a consensus, the more difficult it will be for a consensus actually to be achieved."[41] The overwhelming preponderance of emphasis in *Political Liberalism* is placed on moral reasonableness. Our main concern is that we know other citizens consider themselves morally committed to the liberal terms of social cooperation, not that we know that they have certain attitudes to knowledge and reasoning about the good. We must thus be consistent in not overspecifying the reasons citizens may have for endorsing the political requirements of citizenship. Otherwise, given that Rawls does not significantly alter the substantive aspects of his theory of justice from *Theory* to *Political Liberalism* (i.e., illiberal minorities are still subject to the same legal constraints on their treatment of family and community members), what would be the point of presenting certain values as merely political rather than comprehensive?[42] It seems to me that the only possible virtues in retreating from the more comprehensive assumption in *Theory* are, one, to show that it can be done, that one does not have to be a comprehensive liberal to be in favor of liberal political freedoms (i.e., that it is not "sectarian") and, two, to avoid requiring citizens to *profess* belief in something they do not believe, that is, to avoid putting unnecessary philosophical barriers in the way of social unity. As Rawls says, "It is up to each comprehensive doctrine to say how the idea of the reasonable connects with its concept of truth."[43] It would be a bit much to read this as suggesting that all holders of religious doctrines *must* regard the political values or the burdens of judgment as somehow *true*, leaving it to them (obviously) to work out the scriptural exegesis for themselves. Rather,

I read this as suggesting a range of epistemic ways that citizens can come to accept the requirements of liberalism.

Second, in addition to the problem of making unrealistic substantive theological demands such as a profession of the value of ethical autonomy, overdetermining the ways in which citizens relate to the demands of liberalism may result in unreasonable rhetorical and discursive requirements. One of the common features of traditional moralities is that they often rest on a body of cumulative tradition that they take as authoritative, rather than a set of first principles that can either be rethought or reconfigured. Not all comprehensive doctrines present themselves as ideological clusters of concepts that can be contested, redefined, and rearranged, even if it is possible to derive such concepts and values hermeneutically. By way of asking, "Is this value an Islamic one?" Muslims might ask instead, "Am I allowed to do this?" or "What is this analogous to in Islamic law?" Thus, in addition to self-aware works addressing the practice of Islam in the West systematically, or ambitious tracts seeking to rethink Islam comprehensively for the modern era, we might find useful resources in less sophisticated tracts, pamphlets, and religio-legal responsa (*fatwās*) dealing with what Muslims ought to do in specific cases of conflict between traditional Islamic norms and liberal constraints. These texts may not self-consciously describe themselves as attempts to assert compatibility or overlapping consensus, but in piecemeal form may offer answers to specific problems that might add up to a pattern of compatible attitudes. Importantly, when doing so, these texts have the rhetorical advantage of conservative authority ("if even they say so . . . ") often lacking in more reformist discourses.

An excellent case in point is the famous debate between (now French president, then interior minister) Nicolas Sarkozy and Tariq Ramadan on French television. Sarkozy pressed Ramadan on the *ḥudūd* penalties in Muslim countries (such as stoning for adultery or amputation of a hand for theft), to which Ramadan replied that he supports a worldwide *moratorium* on but not abolition of these punishments. In his defense, he claimed that he has no authority to proclaim such an abolition and that, memorably, "there are texts involved."

This incident has been repeatedly invoked as a smoking gun revealing Ramadan's true intentions an as radical Islamist.[44] The claim is that Ramadan missed an opportunity to publicly side with a reformist vision of Islam and, in particular, to give hope to abused Muslim women. Of course, this strikes one initially as just the right response; after all, how *could* one ever be too firm on the question of stoning for adultery (or many other prescriptions from Islamic law)?

Except that we have seen that political liberalism presents itself as freestanding and proclaims the autonomy of comprehensive doctrines from the public conception of justice. Setting aside some of the more obvious pragmatic-political considerations for a public figure like Ramadan trying to maintain credibility with multiple publics (a non-Muslim European public and a fairly conservative worldwide Muslim one), as well as the consideration that, strictly speaking, Ramadan was not speaking about European and North American societies, the more interesting question relates to whether we are justified in demanding precise *forms* of legal and theological revision or merely principled affirmations of the *practice* of liberal democratic politics. We clearly have the right to insist that Islamic punishments never be carried out in Western liberal democracies; do we also have the right to insist that a faithful citizen must regard those punishments as having a *certain epistemological status* within Islam? Is it remotely proper—or wise—to meddle in another's theology at this level of magnitude, or do we have our own duty of self-restraint in this area?

For example, consider a Catholic who is a candidate for a judicial appointment in the United States. We clearly have a right to demand that the American Constitution be regarded as trumping Catholic doctrine when it comes to legal interpretation. It may even be appropriate to ask that candidate how she would balance her religious convictions with her civic ones. Surely, a Catholic who responds that she is "bound by the Constitution of the United States regardless of what my personal religious convictions may be or of the dictates of my Church" is fulfilling her obligation of civic loyalty. Do we *also* insist that she pronounce on the formulation of Catholic doctrine? Do we *also* insist that she presume to correct the Pope on what Catholic doctrine ought to be? Surely this would be regarded as an impermissible incursion into religious freedom. She has pronounced her commitment to her civic obligations, and we rightly leave her to figure out the relationship of these obligations to her theology or to her church.

Something analogous may have been going on with the Ramadan moratorium comment. Rather than an exercise in double-talk or evasion, what Ramadan might have been asserting by refusing to call for an abolition of *ḥudūd* punishments was a factual, rather than normative, claim. It is simply a *fact* that Tariq Ramadan has no authority to proclaim those punishments void, given the undisguisable fact that, yes, "there are texts involved." At stake is a very complex debate about reform and change in Islamic law: How does reform in Islamic law come about? Who is entitled to proclaim it? What we are entitled to demand is that Muslim citizens abandon the *political demand* to implement such things as Islamic moral punishments; how they *understand and describe* this in relation to their fourteen-century-long religious tradition is not so obviously a civic duty that we can articulate clearly and consistently.

Third, it must be remembered that there are a variety of paths to these values and constitutional essentials *for liberals.* Not all liberals are Kantians or Millians in their nonpolitical values. Rather, the defining feature of a liberal is a commitment to specific policies or rights, which can be arrived at from various ethical and philosophical commitments or even while denying the capacity of philosophy to provide such commitments. What all liberals (and many nonliberals) agree on are the limits of cultural authority over individual group members. It is these limits in the form of constitutions and laws that nonliberals encounter as potentially problematic, not just the metaphysics or epistemology behind them. They have no good reason to be mollified by a set of institutions that has a perfectly neutral justification, rather than the same set of institutions with a perfectionist foundation, except, to repeat, insofar as the perfectionist foundation would require nonliberals to publicly profess belief in something they cannot. Thus, we do better to restrict our emphasis to the policies that all liberals agree on and are largely in force in really existing liberalism rather than the various paths that lead to them. After all, it is precisely an *Islamic foundation* for these policies that we are looking for, and not another inquiry into liberal foundations or multiculturalism from a liberal perspective.

Fourth, it must be remembered that the search for an overlapping consensus derives from a very specific school of philosophical thought, namely, that *political* philosophy has the burden, not shared by other branches of ethics, of concerning itself with the conditions of its reception and its prospects for promoting both social stability and social unity. One consequence of this view is a certain flexibility in assessing the justice of existing conditions (remember Rawls's use of the phrase "*a more or less* just constitutional regime" as a legitimate and sufficient aim of a liberal society[45]), as well as a certain patience with nonliberal citizens who do not actively disrupt the social order. This suggests that assessments of the existence of or prospects for an overlapping consensus with any given comprehensive ethical doctrine may admit of a range of qualified responses. Kurt Baier, for example, suggests that consensus takes place on three dimensions: (1) "level," or degree of specificity, (2) the "extent" of support among the population, and (3) the "intensity" of agreement by those not opposing the regime.[46] Baier's suggestion that citizens holding various comprehensive doctrines can endorse political liberalism with various levels of intensity is consistent with my present argument that we must not, from the outset anyway, overdetermine the types of reasons citizens must invoke from their authoritative texts by way of reconciling themselves to the restraint required of them in a liberal society.

Thus, we do not want to be open to the charge of completely begging the question of compatibility by failing to regard as qualifying any doctrines but those expressly committed to a fully privatized, fully personal, quasi-Protestant theology. We are committed to considerable flexibility in considering how Muslims come to terms with the requirements of liberal citizenship in their own language. It is clear that we are entitled to press fellow citizens on what they regard as permissible or preferred *practices* or *outcomes* in a shared society, even if those preferences come from within religion. But even the interest in an overlapping consensus and a certain practice of comparative ethics does not mean insisting on the precise way in which religious citizens *articulate* the relationship between the demands of citizenship and their religious sources.

Throughout this book, I examine Islamic arguments by asking whether the reasons given for abiding by the demands of liberal citizenship are *principled*, whether they constitute an affirmation of the reasonableness of the demands themselves, and whether they suggest overall attitudes consistent with the general aims of a liberal political order. I presume that this leaves open a wide variety of strategies on the part of Muslim thinkers for approaching the fact that certain texts exist and have traditionally been interpreted in a certain way. The main questions for us are whether an Islamic argument implies some moral recognition of non-Muslim fellow citizens as free and equal persons eligible for relationships of solidarity and whether the permanence of religious and moral pluralism is an acceptable condition of life. Given the plethora of modus vivendi arguments for abiding non-Muslim rule, these standards are already plenty demanding. Should they be met through arguments other than ones emphasizing moral autonomy or the burdens of judgment, we ought to be willing to consider them indicative of an overlapping consensus. After all, if Muslims believe themselves morally committed to a fair system of social cooperation with non-Muslims on liberal terms, is that not the purpose of the ideas of full justification and overlapping consensus?

If the preceding discussion relates to the philosophical *depth* required for an overlapping consensus to obtain, the overlapping consensus can also be referred to in terms of the *level of detail or precision* on which it must be established. Rawls's view is that the overlapping consensus is on general points of principle, such as the general idea of society as a fair system of cooperation or of the person as politically free and equal. However, when seeking to apply the theory of full justification or overlapping consensus to a specific comprehensive doctrine, it quickly becomes clear that the inquiry must be conducted at a fairly precise, often technical, level. There are three main reasons for this:

1. *The problem of translation*: How would one begin to ask whether Islam can endorse "the basic idea of society as a fair system of cooperation" and the idea of public reason? Where would one find this in the Qur'an or the works of Islamic law? To begin this kind of inquiry, one has to understand how this conception intersects Islamic concerns and how these concerns are treated internally by Islamic traditions of scholarship. This can be done only by a thorough reading of Islamic sources on the problem of citizenship in a morally diverse society and by posing questions to those sources in their own terms. This is likely to require the translation of the language of political liberalism into a series of discrete or specific questions. Thus, even if one agreed with Rawls (and others) that a well-ordered society requires an overlapping consensus only on the general moral principles undergirding a liberal constitution, this general inquiry quickly becomes a precise one. Of course, this need not be a general statement about how to engage in conjecture or search for an overlapping consensus, but it certainly applies in the case of doctrines, such as Islam, that are conveyed through highly technical, expert discourses that emerged in contexts outside the background public culture of a modern liberal democracy that Rawls tends to address.
2. *The problem of conceptual red herrings*: How can one be sure that a general idea or concept means the same thing across doctrines? It should not surprise us to find notions of religious freedom, fairness, human dignity, fair social cooperation, the sanctity of life, or equality within various ethical traditions. However, we are not concerned with whether fellow citizens have their own conceptions of the same concepts about which we have conceptions, but rather whether they understand those conceptions to require (or even allow) the *specific* principles of justice and social cooperation as proposed by political

liberalism. Islam in the classical period had a doctrine of religious freedom in that non-Muslim subjects were not forced to convert, but this was not religious freedom as liberalism requires because Muslims were not allowed to convert out of Islam. Similarly, classical Islam is replete with calls to tolerate diversity, but this is diversity narrowly construed as Abrahamic fraternity with the People of the Book, a principle that does not necessarily allow for social solidarity with nonmonotheists. Thus, religious traditions are likely to have conceptual analogues to the basic moral principles underlying political liberalism, but these analogues are not equally likely to be understood as justifying precisely the same institutions and practices as political liberalism. The only way of being sure of congruence with the actual moral outcomes desired by liberalism is by investigating in the greatest possible detail.

3. *The problem of doctrinal idiosyncrasy*: While the political liberalism literature presumes that the main site of moral disagreement will be about the legitimate terms of public justification in a society that all citizens regard as their own, many doctrines have their own set of idiosyncratic concerns or objections to liberal citizenship. Or as in the case of Islam, perhaps they have a special set of doctrinal concerns when they find themselves in a minority condition. Thus, the search for an overlapping consensus does not involve the same sets of questions in the case of every doctrine; rather, there will be unique subjects of moral disagreement that warrant their own treatment. This point is particularly important for this book, as becomes clear in the following two chapters.

All of these concerns are driven by the basic principle of conjecture, which is that it aims at the greatest possible plausibility. Plausibility is understood in this study as the extent to which an argument for congruence or consensus represents a response to the actual moral disagreement in question and, thus, the extent to which persons who might find the objections to liberal citizenship compelling might also find compelling the efforts to mitigate those objections. As is demonstrated throughout the rest of this book, one of the consequences of a commitment to plausibility is that the demonstration of full justification for the liberal terms of social cooperation from within a given comprehensive doctrine has to take place at the level of detail required by that doctrine.

Having now made an argument for the importance of comparative political and ethical theorizing, and suggesting a number of moral and methodological guidelines for doing so, I turn now in chapter 3 to the possible Islamic objections to liberal citizenship. The purpose of this chapter is to lay out in as much detail as necessary the range and depth of existing Islamic critiques of citizenship in a non-Muslim liberal democracy, a key component of the "diagnostic" stage of justificatory comparative political theory elaborated previously. Not only is this exposition necessary for understanding what types of arguments endorsing liberal citizenship we need to look for and what those arguments need to account for vis-à-vis the Islamic tradition but also it is an important bulwark against stereotypical or impressionistic assumptions about Islamic political ethics that might arise from or result in what has come to be known as "Islamophobia." Our claim that Islamic political ethics might conflict with the liberal terms of social cooperation at very deep levels is not an assumption but rather a clear conclusion from reading a wide range of fairly mainstream texts in Islamic jurisprudence and political thought.

Thus, my inquiry into what an Islamic doctrinal affirmation of citizenship in a non-Muslim liberal democracy would consist of proceeds from the observation that grounds exist within Islamic ethics for rejecting most, if not all, aspects of such citizenship and that *some* Muslim citizens may be swayed by these views toward a principled opposition to liberal citizenship. On the basis of this elaboration of the contours of moral disagreement, we may ask what an Islamic *affirmation* of citizenship would look like. The crucial features of such an affirmation are that it be both acceptable from a liberal standpoint (i.e., that it is, in fact, an *affirmation* of the liberal terms of citizenship) and sufficiently Islamic to be plausible to believers (i.e., to help *solve* the basic problem of the rejectionist doctrine). Asking what Islamic doctrine would have to affirm for it to be said that it is providing believers with both authentic and principled reasons for endorsing liberal citizenship is best perceived as the search for a certain kind of *equilibrium*, namely, for that fully reasonable account of the minimal demands of liberal citizenship *least in conflict* with the aims and spirit of Islamic political ethics. An Islamic doctrine of citizenship in non-Muslim liberal democracies can be said to reflect equilibrium when it is as inclusive as possible of believing Muslims without violating any essential features or aims of a well-ordered liberal society. Importantly, we do not know before engaging dialectically with Islamic ethics just what the minimal demands of liberalism are and thus just how traditional or conservative a formulation of Islamic doctrine can be included in an overlapping consensus. Identifying this equilibrium is the aim of chapter 4 of this book.

PART II

Islam and Liberal Citizenship

Patterns of Moral Disagreement and Principled Reconciliation

The previous chapter raised the problem of the compatibility between liberal regimes and nonliberal conceptions of the good and discussed the circumstances in which this compatibility, or the lack thereof, might interest political theorists. The essence of the argument is that, while philosophical justification of a conception of justice does not rely on the demonstration of compatibility or consensus with other moral doctrines, the political problem of popular support for the institutions that follows from that conception does in fact largely depend on the extent to which citizens do not see an irreconcilable conflict between their conceptions of value and virtue and the extent to which they are allowed to pursue those conceptions. In addition to arguing for the fairness of liberal justice, the case for liberalism is strengthened by demonstrating that its most basic propositions—the demands of profession, commission, and omission it places on citizens—can be justified or shown to be compatible with other moral traditions.

But what is it that we are looking for support for within Islamic sources? For Rawls, the project of political liberalism expresses "the fundamental idea of a well-ordered society as a fair system of co-operation between reasonable and rational citizens regarded as free and equal"[1] and requires that agreement on the part of all citizens go at least that deep. Underpinning the conception of social cooperation is the liberal (political) conception of the individual, the view that:

> as citizens [individuals] are seen as capable of revising and changing this conception [of the good] on reasonable and rational grounds, and they may do this if they so desire. As free persons, citizens claim the right to view their persons as

> independent from and not identified with any particular such conception with its scheme of final ends. Given their moral power to form, revise, and rationally pursue a conception of the good, their public identity as free persons is not affected by changes over time in their determinate conceptions of it.[2]

Liberalism not only requires that the state not be used to impose a vision of the good life but also imposes constraints on what we can do individually or severally to coerce others privately toward acting in concert with a conception of the good. Just as one's treatment by the state—the rights and duties one derives from the relationship of citizenship—is not linked to one's membership in a particular cultural group, one's right to the protection of these freedoms in civil society by the state also cannot depend on cultural membership. There is very little disagreement among liberals (or even Western political theorists critical of liberalism) about what this entails and what types of practices nonliberals are expected to endorse through their doctrines: Substate groups cannot draw on religious or cultural authority to prevent individuals from leaving a group,[3] cannot prevent children from becoming aware of other forms of life in the society and from gaining the skills to survive in it,[4] cannot coercively impose marital decisions on family members,[5] cannot do certain things to their children that are physically harmful (like female genital mutilation or depriving children of urgent medical attention),[6] and cannot punish members in certain ways for dissenting from or criticizing communal authority.[7] Simply put, liberalism establishes a certain range of civil rights and liberties for all citizens and does not recognize the right of any cultural or religious authority to deprive its members of these rights any more than it does the state:

> The legal order must regulate men's pursuit of their religious interests so as to realize the principle of equal liberty; and it may certainly forbid religious practices such as human sacrifice, to take an extreme case. Neither religiosity nor conscientiousness suffices to protect this practice. If a religion is denied its full expression, it is presumably because it is in violation of the equal liberties of others. In general, the degree of tolerance accorded opposing moral conceptions depends upon the extent to which they can be allowed an equal place within a just system of liberty.[8]

The defining feature of liberal democracy is its protection of certain basic freedoms, particularly those of religion, conscience, speech, and association. This means that minority religious groups will not face outright threats to their religious traditions and will have their survival protected against deliberate incursions from the majority. The right of minority religious groups to survival,[9] however, cannot imply the right to impose what Will Kymlicka has termed "internal restrictions" on individual members of their groups by denying them the same rights that the majority extends to the group as a whole. Just as religious groups have rights to proselytize and to be free from forced conversion, so do individuals within those groups have the right to heresy and apostasy. The main requirement of citizenship in liberal democracies is thus that groups recognize the rights of individuals from within their own community to a form of political autonomy.

Rawls's political conception of autonomy for the individual is closely connected to his general conception of liberal society as "a fair system of cooperation between reasonable and rational citizens regarded as free and equal." Rawls's conception distinguishes society from both a community and an association, which are defined in relation to "final ends" ("religion and empire, dominion and glory; and the rights and status of individuals and classes have depended on their role in gaining those ends") or shared moral doctrines. A democratic society, rather, has certain limited, constitutionally specified ends that fall under a political conception of justice.[10] These comments essentially articulate the modern liberal notion of civil society: "that form of human association in which human beings are united not in any common purpose but instead by their subscription to an authoritative body of non-instrumental rules,"[11] that is, that the entire apparatus of the state is not used to coordinate collective action toward a single common purpose based on a sectarian conception of value and virtue. On this view, the public sphere (here limited to the institutions of the state) is the sphere of coordination of necessary collective action (areas in which society must act), the pursuit of public goods and common interests (security, general welfare, etc.), and the protection of rights. "The good"—that which gives life meaning—is something to be determined by individuals on their own or severally and pursued in society largely free from the interference of authoritative law-making bodies.

The notion that (a) there might exist a single form of well-being valid for all humans, or multiple forms all commensurable and unified within an overall morality, (b) that this conception of well-being requires communal expression and general compliance, and (c) that the state can, if necessary, be enlisted in the pursuit of this compliance is the comprehensive political worldview (or the general structure of a family of such worldviews) against which political liberalism positions itself. Liberalism abandons the search for "a more comprehensive philosophical outlook [that] would let us hold self-creation and justice, private perfection and human solidarity, in a single vision."[12] As such, liberalism does not require that citizens all subscribe to an individualist, rationalist, or skeptical conception of the meaning of life but simply that they view coercion as an inappropriate mechanism for bringing other citizens' actions into harmony with standards of virtue and personal morality derived from controversial views about human nature. In simpler terms, Rawls's terminology is a way of expressing the simple notion that laws ought not be derived from religious texts and also that laws not rely for justification on metaphysical principles that directly negate religious beliefs.

As is well known, the liberal conception of social cooperation is not the one advanced by most religious doctrines. It is, of course, *designed* to be opposed to the religious and secular doctrines that seek to base public justification on a controversial conception of truth or the good, while being at the same time fair and accessible to their adherents. As is also well known, Islam contains, among world religions, perhaps the most unequivocal claim to a political vision, the most elaborate body of legal answers to social, political, and economic questions, and the most explicit emphasis on the collective, social requirements for living a pious life.

It would be tempting to begin an inquiry into an Islamic doctrine of citizenship in liberal democracies, or Islamic support for an overlapping consensus on the terms of social cooperation, with the problems of liberal rights and freedoms and secular authority: How can believing Muslims, whose religious doctrine has, in its traditionally authoritative manifestations, called for upholding severe restrictions on social liberties as a matter of religious obligation, draw from their comprehensive beliefs to support liberal freedoms? More generally, how can believing Muslims regard as just and be loyal to any forms of governance that are not based on upholding divine law or religious aims and, what is more, ground that loyalty precisely on religious reasons? These are the deepest juridical, philosophical, and theological challenges to Islamic support for liberal institutions. What, then, could possibly be meant by the "Islamic endorsement" of the conception of society required by political liberalism?

One way of reducing the enormity of this challenge is to stage our inquiry in a special political context, that of Muslims living as minorities in existing liberal democracies. As will be seen, while one possible Muslim response to life as a minority is the demand that internal Muslim affairs (especially family law and education) be managed along *sharīʿa* lines, the assumption that Muslims are living in a society where Islamic law cannot be generally applied requires Muslim legal and political theorists to think about political life outside the normal assumptions, categories, and debates of Islamic political and legal discourses. The staging of our inquiry within this political context makes it slightly more plausible. We assume, by *positing* that we are dealing with a community that is in the minority, that using the state to impose a conception of the good is not generally part of the political imagination of the community in question. What follows is that it is precisely the aspiration to neutrality of liberal constitutions that may be appealing to Muslim minorities. They are not forced to abandon most religious practices, to convert, to culturally assimilate, or to profess something that essentially requires repudiating basic Islamic beliefs.[13] They benefit (at least from the perspective of the outside observer) from a system that does not see society primarily as uniting citizens in a single common purpose but rather as the just management of multiple private purposes, insofar as a public philosophy of shared ends and values would probably be more antagonistic to Islam than a public philosophy of neutrality.

Because we are using it to moderate the most traditional Islamic attitude (that society should be a vehicle for the general application of *sharīʿa*), this staging also means that many of Rawls's concerns need not be ours, and we must clarify what those might be instead. If the original meaning of the Rawlsian requirement to endorse a liberal conception of justice is the requirement to not see the state as a vehicle for the imposition of one's conception of the good, and I begin my inquiry by *positing* that this is not something the adherents of the comprehensive doctrine in question generally imagine as an immediate political objective, then what more do we need to find in the Islamic sources by way of compatibility with this conception?

Here it is necessary to complement our Rawlsian interest in justice with the concerns of citizenship and, more important, the idiosyncratic language of Islam. For Islamic doctrine, there are two broad problems with citizenship in non-Muslim liberal states: that those states are *non-Muslim* in character, both socially and politically, and that those states are *liberal* in character. What is important to realize is that for Islamic legal and political doctrines, a series of distinct ethical problems are raised by the former no less than by the latter. Once we recognize that for the ethical community in question, shaping general legislation in one's own image is not the only concern, we become sensitive to other political attitudes that might also fall outside an overlapping consensus. Now it is not only domination that we are concerned with from a liberal perspective but some form of internal retreat or preference for a stance of "[loyal] resident alienage" or "partial citizenship,"[14] rather than political membership and citizenship in even the moderate form proposed by political liberalism. The first requirement of citizenship in liberal democracies for minority communities is, thus, not the recognition of neutrality and secularism as a constraint upon their own use of government machinery but the recognition of the legitimacy of the political community in which they live and of their own membership in it. In the case of minority groups defined by their commitment to a particular ethical or religious doctrine, the political community must be one in which the group can feel it has an equal stake and toward which it can feel the appropriate amount of loyalty. The integration of a group of individuals freely associating in a liberal society into the general political community, and their loyalty to that political community in conflicts with other states, nations, or political communities, is primarily what I have in mind when I speak of Muslim citizens in non-Muslim states adopting a certain "doctrine of citizenship."

Similarly, while Rawls's political conception of autonomy is meant as a general attitude for citizens to adopt toward the problem of coercive authority and individual freedom, it obscures how doctrines might regard differences between fellow citizens as important in constructing various substate communities and how individuals might have different expectations from fellow citizens, depending on whether they are seen to belong to a given community of shared ends. To illustrate this: For Rawls, both the liberal requirement that religious groups not seek to use the state to force others—those not sharing their metaphysical commitments—to comply with the moral precepts flowing from those commitments and the liberal requirement that religious groups not use nonstate coercion to prevent members from leaving the group (from "revising their constitutive ends") flow from the same conception of the person as free and equal. This is consistent and coherent (in addition to elegant and parsimonious) from a liberal perspective but not necessarily so from nonliberal ones. In Islamic ethical and legal theories, it is only Muslims who are seen as objects of compulsion on moral or religious grounds; non-Muslims cannot be forced to adopt Islamic beliefs or practices, but they can be marginalized, discriminated against (in a Muslim-majority state), and generally regarded as unequal to Muslims or outside the relationship of solidarity. What this all means for our purposes is that one implication of Rawls's conception of the person—that we should not seek to force fellow citizens to adopt our conception of the good—is not intelligible to Muslims unless we specify whether those fellow citizens are Muslims or non-Muslims. Thus, we have to break down Rawls's requirement to view others as "reasonable and rational citizens regarded as free and equal" into two distinct conceptions based on the religious identity of those fellow citizens. From the Islamic perspective, the doctrinal challenge regarding non-Muslims is not their right to not be Muslim (this is widely acknowledged) but their recognition as equals and as potential objects of solidarity.

Thus, it is crucial to emphasize that this book concerns itself explicitly with Islamic thought related to Muslims living as minorities in non-Muslim states and societies—their status, their rights, their loyalties, their duties, and their well-being—and how Islamic doctrine on these questions corresponds to liberal conceptions of citizenship. It is these questions on which we first seek an overlapping consensus.

In chapter 3, I outline in greater detail precisely why Islamic thinkers have regarded the very idea of citizenship in a non-Muslim society as religiously problematic. The purpose of this chapter is not to provide a comprehensive account of Islamic positions on the questions of residence in and loyalty to a non-Muslim state and recognition of and solidarity with non-Muslims, and still less to provide a textured historical account of the positions surveyed. Rather, the point is to introduce the main classical and contemporary political, juridical, and ethical positions that could serve to ground the conscientious belief that citizenship in a non-Muslim liberal democracy is religiously impermissible. This is part of the "diagnostic stage" of conjecture. The aim is to lay out where in Islamic doctrine opposition to an overlapping consensus to the very idea of principled social cooperation with non-Muslims could be found. In light of this background, I elaborate in chapter 4 what ideal-typical Islamic positions would then be sought by a person looking to establish Islamic foundations for an overlapping consensus on the liberal terms of citizenship in a moral diverse political community.

3

Islamic Objections to Citizenship in Non-Muslim Liberal Democracies

What does a sincere, pious Muslim encounter when they ask the Rawlsian—and Islamic—question: "May I, without great contradiction, regard the terms of citizenship in a pluralist liberal democracy as acceptable from an Islamic standpoint?" From the perspective of traditional Islamic legal, political, and ethical doctrines, the idea of Muslim citizenship in non-Muslim states is deeply problematic. One can readily find within classical and modern legal discourses prohibitions on submitting to the authority of non-Muslim states, serving in their armies, contributing to their strength or welfare, participating in their political systems, and, indeed, even residing within them. These prohibitions are not mere medieval legalisms but rather reflections of a range of more general Islamic beliefs, including those that Muslims must always strive to live under Islamic law and political authority, that Muslims have obligations of loyalty (perhaps exclusively) to Muslims and Muslim polities, and that non-Muslims are not eligible for relationships of social and political solidarity.

In what follows I present in more detail the Islamic doctrinal opposition to liberal citizenship in three parts: the problem of residing in a non-Muslim state, the problem of loyalty to such a state, and the problem of solidarity with non-Muslims.[1]

Residence in a Non-Muslim State

It is significant that Year One in the Islamic tradition is not the year of Muḥammad's birth, his first revelation, his conquest of Mecca, or his death, but rather the year of his flight from persecution in his native Mecca to the city of Yāthrib (later, Medīna) twelve years into his prophecy and ten years before his death. For Muslims, this migration, known as the *hijra*, marks the point at which Muslims first constituted themselves as an autonomous political community and when Islam can be said to have emerged as a comprehensive social, economic, military, and political system. It is symbolic of something enduring in Muslim self-understanding that the Islamic era begins precisely with this political birth rather than one of the myriad other events in the Prophet's life of theological or even political significance.

In addition to symbolizing the Islamic unification of personal salvation and communal solidarity, of religious truth and political authority, the centrality of the *hijra* has posed a rather significant doctrinal problem throughout the ages. For Muḥammad's migration to Medīna was accompanied by an injunction upon his followers to do the same:

> When God had given permission to fight[2] and the clan of the Anṣār [the "helpers," those Muslims living already in Medina] had pledged their support to him in Islam and to help him and his followers, and the Muslims who had taken refuge with them, the Apostle commanded his companions, the emigrants of his people and those Muslims who were with him in Mecca, to emigrate to Medina and to link up with their brethren the Anṣār.[3]

Although it was still some time before the Muslims were joined by Muḥammad and his closest companions in Medīna, it has been often argued that this Prophetic injunction to migrate to the Islamic state inaugurated a general and permanent duty for Muslims to reside in lands ruled by Islam and to migrate from non-Islamic lands, however they may find themselves there. In the synopsis of an important contemporary scholar of Islamic law:

> It has often been argued that a just life is possible only if lived under the guidance of the Sharīʻa which, in turn, is possible only if there is an Islamic polity dedicated to the application of the Sharīʻa. That is to say, a just life is possible for a Muslim only if lived in an Islamic polity that dutifully applies the Sharīʻa. Consequently, a certain dichotomy results. On the one hand there is the abode of Islam (*dār al-Islām*) where it is possible to live an ethical life under the guidance of the Sharīʻa. On the other hand, there is the abode of unbelief (*dār al-kufr, dār al-ḥarb or dār al-shirk*) where the Sharīʻa is not applied and Islamic justice does not prevail.[4]

The affirmation of citizenship in a non-Muslim liberal democracy thus faces in Islamic doctrine a challenge at a very basic level. The size and vibrancy of Muslim communities in non-Muslim countries would seem to render this question archaic, a quintessential medieval legalism or Orientalist fixation. Indeed, as discussed at length in chapter 5, the vast majority of Muslim jurists have viewed residence in non-Muslim states as permissible in certain circumstances. Nonetheless, classically minded contemporary Muslim scholars do regard this as an active juridical question, at least in the sense of something that deserves a response.[5] More important, however, are the underlying concerns and anxieties that are often shared by scholars who permit residence in non-Muslim polities and that go to the heart of liberal citizenship.

Juridical arguments that *hijra* from *dār al-ḥarb* to *dār al-Islām* is a categorical duty for Muslims rely on a certain set of Qur'ānic verses and *ḥadīth* reports. The most oft-cited Qur'ānic verses are

> As for those whom the angels gather in death while in a state of sin against themselves the Angels will ask: "What was your plight?" They reply: "We were oppressed on earth." The [angels] will say: "Was not God's earth vast enough for you to migrate within it?" They will have their refuge in hell and how evil is such a destiny, except for those truly oppressed, those men, women and children who cannot find any means and have not been shown the way. For these there is hope that God will forgive them, for God is Forgiving and Merciful. Anyone who migrates in the path of God will find in the Earth many an abundant refuge. Whoever leaves his home in migration towards God and his Messenger, and death overtakes him, his reward with God is guaranteed, for God is Forgiving and Merciful. [Q. 4:97–100]

and

> Those who believed and migrated and struggled in the path of God with their property and their souls and those who sheltered and supported them, are friends and supporters of one another. Those who believed and did not migrate, you have no duty of protection towards them until they migrate. But if they seek your support in religion, you owe them this support, except against a people with whom you have a treaty. God sees all that you do. [Q. 8:72]

In addition, Muslim jurists point to a set of Prophetic *ḥadīth* that proclaim the permanence of the duty of *hijra*:

> The *hijra* will not come to an end until repentance comes to an end and repentance will not come to an end until the sun rises from its place of setting.[6]
>
> I am innocent of [I disown] any Muslim who lives with the polytheists, for you will not be able to tell the two apart.[7]
>
> Do not live with and associate with the polytheists. Whosoever lives with them and associates with them is like them.[8]
>
> The *hijra* will not come to an end as long as the enemy is fought.[9]

Pointing to these authoritative sources, many Muslim jurists and exegetes from the earliest stages of Islam to the present have argued that migration from non-Islamic lands to Islamic ones is, indeed, a permanent religious obligation for believers.[10] One of the most famous pronouncements on the subject (undoubtedly more for its length and rhetorical energy than for any general consensus it represents or for the authoritativeness of its author) is a *fatwā* by an Andalusian/North African Mālikī jurist, Aḥmad b. Yaḥyā al-Wansharīsī (d. 914/1508), writing at the time of the loss of Islamic lands in Spain. Before discussing at great length the moral status of Muslims who prefer to reside in non-Muslim lands, and the various operative factors (*'ilal*) that explain his position, he pronounces simply in the first line of his ruling: "*Hijra* from the land of disbelief to the land of Islam is a duty until the Day of Resurrection, as is *hijra* from lands of sin and those tainted by injustice or sedition." This matter is decisively settled for him by Q. 4:98 ("Except for those truly oppressed, those men, women and children who cannot find any means and have not been shown the way. For these there is hope that God will forgive them, for God is Forgiving and Merciful."):

> God Almighty does not accept their excuses [for not migrating], for he demonstrated that they were capable of migration in some way. Rather, the weak and oppressed who are forgiven by God for their incapacity are only those who are incapable in every way . . . and for whom there was truly no path or means open to them, such as invalids (*al-muq'ad*), prisoners (*al-ma'sūr*), the seriously ill or the very weak. Only then is forgiveness due to them, for they become like the one who is coerced into pronouncing disbelief. But even then it is necessary that they have the abiding intention to perform *hijra* if only they were able. As for him who is capable of migrating in any way or means, he is not forgiven and has wrong his soul [i.e., in a state of sin].[11]

A similar decisiveness based on a literal reading of the authoritative texts—in this case one of the previously cited *ḥadīth*—is advanced by a prominent jurist of the Ḥanafī school, who advised anyone traveling to non-Muslim lands for purposes of trade not to have intercourse with his wife or slave girl abroad "out of fear of begetting children there because it is forbidden to settle in the abode of war, [for the Prophet] said: 'I am innocent of any Muslim living with the polytheists.'"[12] This view is echoed in the interpretation of Q. 4:97–100 by twentieth-century exegete Sayyid Quṭb:

> This ruling remains valid until the end of time, transcending that particular case which the text addresses in a particular time and environment. It remains a general ruling incumbent upon all Muslims subject to pressure and persecution in any land aimed at turning them away from their faith, and yet who stay where they are in order to look after their possessions and interests or to be with their relatives and friends or because of their unwillingness to undertake the hardships of migration. Once there is a place on earth, any place, which belongs to Islam and where one can feel secure declaring one's faith and fulfilling one's religious duties, then one must migrate in

order to live under the banner of Islam and enjoy the sublime standard of life Islam affords.[13]

However categorical some jurists find these verses alone, al-Wansharīsī and others go beyond mere scriptural citation to derive from the texts the following series of arguments (*'ilal: ratio legis*, or "operative factors") that explain and substantiate the prohibition of residence (*iqāma*) in non-Muslim lands. Rather than track the historical development of juridical opinions on the duty of migration, it is more useful for our comparative purposes to account for the range of arguments that are invoked by jurists in justification of their interpretations of specific verses, or their preference for some verses or *ḥadīth* reports over others.[14]

Subjection to Non-Muslim Laws

The first explanation advanced in defense of the ban on residence in non-Muslim lands is the least flexible or subject to qualification: Muslims may not legally live in non-Muslim states because they will be subject to non-Muslim laws or authority (*tajrī 'alayhim aḥkām al-kuffār*).[15] Most of the jurists who advance this argument do not tend to consider the variety of circumstances in which Muslims may live as minorities. That is, the possibility that some non-Muslim states may grant Muslims a form of communal autonomy (including the internal application of Islamic law) does not appear to have made a difference in their reasoning. Indeed, these jurists tend to debate not whether having Muslim judges governing internal Muslim relations in a minority context mitigates the misfortune of living as a minority, but rather whether the rulings of such judges are even valid and whether those judges themselves retain their credibility.[16] Thus, for example, we find another North African Mālikī jurist, al-Māzarī (d. 536/1141), suggesting that "there is no doubt that one residing in the abode of war, if he is coerced into living there, does not lose his credibility (*lā yaqdaḥ fī 'adālatihi*), nor if his interpretation [of his religious duty] is correct, such as residing in the abode of war to plead for the rightful guidance of the people there and their deliverance from error, or for the release of prisoners. However, if their residence relies on a wrongful ruling and a deliberate forsaking of [the correct interpretation] then this does violate his credibility."[17] Despite the fact that al-Māzarī's position is clearly that only compulsion can justify residence under non-Muslim rulers, al-Wansharīsī still finds fault with it on the grounds that Muslim judges may not accept appointments from infidel rulers.[18] Thus, it is clear that for these (largely Mālikī) jurists, the status of living subordinate to and at the mercy of non-Muslim laws and political authority is a sufficient condition for prohibiting such residence, regardless of what rights and freedoms Muslims may have individually or as a community.

Similarly, jurists disposed toward this view are dismissive of the idea that Muslims may nonetheless be given the freedoms to practice their religion by non-Muslim rulers. As noted in chapter 5, those (generally non-Mālikī) jurists open to seeing migration as less than fully obligatory do so on the assumption that Muslim minorities are in a position to "manifest their religion" (*iẓhār al-dīn*) and will not be subject to oppression. Al-Wansharīsī, for example, rejects this idea not only because the full expression of Islam requires either political power or state support for Islamic law but also because even the five basic pillars of Islamic worship are such that they cannot be fully upheld in a position of subordination to unbelievers. For al-Wansharīsī, residence in non-Muslim lands causes "the loss and abandonment of prayer, fasting, paying of the *zakāh*, *jihād*, the exaltation of the word of God, bearing witness to the Truth [read: God] and protecting it [Him] from the scorn of the infidels and the derision of the immoral." For him, life outside an Islamic polity is synonymous with exposure to "impurities, filth, religious corruption and earthly scandals" that degrade the performance of even private worship.

The first duty of a Muslim is to proclaim the *shahāda* ["witness" or "attestation"; sometimes "*shahādatayn*" or the "two attestations" because of the dual content of the proclamation]—the belief that "There is no God but God and Muhammad is his Messenger." While holding this creed may seem impervious to coercion, the supreme act of private worship, for al-Wansharīsī

> one of the goals of Revelation is that the word of Islam and the declaration of its truth rest upon their open exaltation above all others, far from scorn and the symbols of disbelief. Yet cohabitation with the [infidels] in a position of shame and submission requires that this noble, exalted and lofty Word be debased and not exalted, scorned and not protected. Surely this is plenty by way of opposition to the laws of Revelation for one to refuse to bear or witness it for any period of his life except by necessity and compulsion.

Similarly, the second pillar of Islam, prayer, "which follows the bearing of witness in open and conspicuous grace, glorification and exaltation, cannot be performed or even be imagined except in total openness and grandeur, and escape from scorn and disdain. Yet in cohabitation with the unbelievers and close contact with the licentious and the debauched, prayer is exposed to neglect, scorn, ridicule and mockery." The third pillar, *zakāh*, or alms-giving, is also void for "it is well known to all men of discernment and knowledge that *zakāh* is paid to the Imam and where there is no Imam there is no payment for lack of one of the necessary conditions and thus there is no [fulfilling the requirement of the] *zakāh* [in non-Muslim lands] for the lack of a deserving beneficiary. Thus, this pillar of Islam is toppled by friendship with infidels, which involves, rather, payment to those who ask for help *against* Muslims. So it is clear what kind of direct opposition to the lawfully required practices of worship in their entirety is involved in [living in non-Muslim countries]." A pious Muslim is not even in a position to fast in non-Muslim lands for "it is conditional upon seeing the crescent moon at its first and last appearances. And in most cases the sighting is confirmed with a formal attestation, which can only be issued by the Imam or his deputies. But where there is no Imam and no deputy, there can be no attestation attesting to the month and thus doubts enter into this religious matter from its beginning to its end." With no doubt remaining that even private, voluntary acts of worship are nullified in the abode of disbelief, al-Wansharīsī concludes by wondering how "any jurist, even the most cautious and restrained, could hesitate in forbidding residence [in non-Muslim countries] with its necessary violation of the entirety of our noble Islamic principles?"[19]

Predominance of Non-Muslims over Muslims

These arguments, still grounded in the general explanation of the prohibition on Muslim residence in non-Muslim lands based on their unlawfully becoming subject to non-Muslim laws, suggest a second type of operative clause. It is clear that for some Muslim thinkers, a just political order does not only require certain collective religious practices, nor even that Muslims be governed collectively by divine law, but also that Islam and Muslims enjoy a certain predominance over non-Muslims. As cited previously, according to al-Wansharīsī, "one of the goals of the Revelation is that the word of Islam and the declaration of its truth rest upon their open exaltation *above all others*, far from scorn and the symbols of disbelief. Yet cohabitation with the [infidels] in a position of shame and submission requires that this noble, exalted and lofty Word be debased and not exalted, scorned and not protected," and that prayer, "which follows the bearing of witness in open and conspicuous grace, glorification and exaltation cannot be performed or even be imagined except in total openness and grandeur." Although Muslims of his day were subject to all manner of degradations and indignities, it appears that al-Wansharīsī is not aspiring to a status for Muslim minorities of benign neglect, where Muslims are left in relative peace and security, albeit in the shadows of church steeples, or for the status of "mutual recognition" or "parity of esteem" as found in contemporary discourses.

Consider his substantiation of his view that "as to those immigrants who curse and slander the abode of Islam and wish to return to the abode of idolatry, amongst other vile and depraved obscenities, theirs is disgrace in this world and the next. It is necessary to seize them and bring down upon them harsh punishments, to make a humiliating example of them by beatings and imprisonment, until they no longer oppose God's law." While al-Wansharīsī began his *fatwā* in a deontological vein, content to quote Q. 4:97–100 and supportive *ḥadīth*, note the litany of consequences he now associates with residence in non-Muslim lands: "For the desire for friendship with the polytheists and cohabitation with the Christians, the determination to reject *hijra*, reliance upon unbelievers and contentment to pay taxes to them, the rejection of the glory of Islam, rightful obedience to the guardians of religion, and loyalty to the rulers, their degradation and the triumph of Christian power over them, are great abominations and mortal blows, nigh akin to disbelief, may God protect us."[20] What is noteworthy in this passage is the predominance of concerns for the balance of power between Islam and Christendom. Minority status—absolutely regardless of rights or freedoms guaranteed—is an *inherent* injustice, for it embodies the inversion of the rightful relationship of glory and domination:

> God, the One and the Victorious, has created humiliation and abasement for the accursed unbelievers, and placed chains and shackles around their necks that they might travel throughout the lands and cities in them manifesting the might of Islam and the honor of its chosen Prophet. And whoever of the Muslims, whom God has preserved and made abundant, would try to shift these chains and shackles to his own neck puts himself in violation of God and His Messenger and subjects himself to the scorn and anger of the Glorious, the Almighty, and is deserving of being inverted by God with them in the fire, For God has written: "I shall certainly prevail, I and my Apostles!" Verily God is powerful, almighty! [Q. 58:21][21]

This concern cannot be dismissed as a medieval anachronism from the time when Muslim states rivaled or eclipsed non-Muslim ones in power and prestige. It is also echoed, for example, in contemporary *fatwās* issued by the Saudi Standing Committee for Scientific Research and Religious Guidance (the highest Saudi religious authority), in which they explain that their prohibition on accepting the citizenship of a non-Muslim country is partially due to "what is involved by way of submission to [unbelievers] and falling under their rule."[22] A Saudi religious scholar who fell afoul of the mainstream bureaucracy for providing a detailed juridical justification of the September 11 attacks naturally goes further in explaining that the freedom to "manifest one's religion" in a non-Muslim country "consists of anathematizing them, cursing their religion, openly criticizing them, keeping separate from them, refraining from any affection with them or reliance upon them and secluding oneself from them, and not merely praying or abstaining from their food."[23]

Strengthening Unbelievers

A third explanation of the prohibition on residence in non-Muslim lands is the possibility that it will add to the strength of unbelievers. This expression (in Arabic: *takthīr sawād al-kuffār/al-mushrikīn*, etc.) appears throughout the juridical literature across the various legal schools and is closely linked to the original context in which Muslims believe the verses 4:97–100 were revealed. Qur'anic exegetes are unanimous in holding that the verses refer to the group of Muslims who remained behind in Mecca after Muḥammad's *hijra* to Medīna.[24] Some of these Muslims were tempted to return to the pagan religion of the Arabs, and a number of them actually fought with the Meccans at the Battle of Badr (2/624), thus prompting this accusation of increasing the numerical strength of the Prophet's enemies. Many jurists have extrapolated from this original case a general concern with living where one might aid a polity that could be in conflict with a Muslim one, as was seen in al-Wansharīsī's denunciation of such things as paying taxes to non-Muslim states. This is a particular feature of jurists disposed toward seeing *hijra* as no longer an obligation (*wājib/farḍ*) but rather recommended or preferred (*mustaḥabba*; see chapter 5).

The Ḥanbalī jurist Ibn Qudāma (d. 620/1223) suggests that one of the factors for migration still being recommended even when Muslims enjoy religious freedom is the benefit of "avoiding increasing the [numbers of] the unbelievers."[25] Fellow Ḥanbalī jurist Ibn Taymiyya (d. 682/1283) does not use the expression "*takthīr al-sawād*" but advances a stronger form of the same argument. Migration is merely recommended by Ibn Taymiyya, but as to those who choose not to leave, "their helping the enemy of the Muslims by their persons or their property [*musāʿadatuhum li-ʿadūw al-muslimīn biʾl-nafs waʾl-amwāl*] is forbidden and they must avoid it by any means possible, whether through absence, intimation[26] or cajoling, and if [avoiding helping the enemy of the Muslims] is only possible through migration then it becomes a duty."[27]

We find a similar sentiment expressed in the modern period by Quṭb: "Nor does Islam tolerate that some hypocrites should be described as believers, simply because they have made the verbal declaration that there is no deity other than God and that Muhammad is His Messenger, but, at the same time, remain in the land of unfaith, *giving their support to the Muslims' enemies*. Such tolerance is, in fact, not tolerance at all but indulgence."[28] Like al-Wansharīsī (but categorically unlike the two previously cited Ḥanbalīs[29] and even other Mālikīs[30]), Quṭb's stance is that the performance of migration is something on which one's status as a Muslim may depend, placing it within the most serious category of actions. Crucially, although there is some ambiguity as to whether "increasing the numbers of the unbelievers" or the general notion of strengthening them requires direct participation in a war effort against Muslims, Quṭb makes it clear that one's very residence constitutes helping the enemies of Islam, and al-Wansharīsī helpfully includes such actions as paying general taxes among the sins one commits by residing in non-Muslim states.

Friendship with Non-Muslims

A fourth argument against residence refers not to the legal status of the land as such, but rather to the prohibition on forming bonds of friendship and solidarity with non-Muslims. This raises the implications of the broader Islamic principle of "*al-walāʾ waʾl-barāʾ*," or "loyalty and affiliation [*al-walāʾ*] (with (true) Muslims) and disassociation [*al-barāʾ*] (from infidels or sinners)." This question is treated separately later, so here I will only briefly note that certain jurists have used it to explain the impermissibility of residence in non-Muslim lands. A number of Qur'anic verses pronounce against a variety of alliances and bonds with non-Muslims, including:

> Let not the believers take the infidels for their allies in preference to the believers—for who does this has nothing to do with God—unless it be to protect yourselves from them in this way. God warns you about Himself and the final goal is to God. [Q. 3:28]

> Oh you who believe! Do not take for your intimates other than your own kind. They will continually cause you turmoil and love anything that will distress you. Loathing has already come forth from their

> mouths and what is concealed in their breasts is even greater. We have made the signs clear to you if you will use your reason. [Q. 3:118]
>
> O you who believe, do not take Jews and Christians as friends (patrons) for they are friends to each other. And who becomes friends with them becomes one of them. Verily God does not guide a wrong-doing people. [Q. 5:51]
>
> O you who believe! Do not take My enemies and your enemies as friends, offering them affection while they have denied what Truth has come unto you, driving away the Messenger of God and yourselves because you believe in God your Lord. If you have gone forth to struggle in my cause and longing for my blessing do you secretly hold affection for them? For I know all that you may conceal as well as what you do openly. And who does so has erred from the path. [Q. 60:1]

The suggested prohibition on residing in a certain territory has been linked to the suggested ban on forming friendships with non-Muslims by jurists including al-Wansharīsī[31] and modern (Saudi) Ḥanbalī jurists.[32]

Living in Sinful Environments

A closely related fifth argument is that it is sinful for Muslims to live in lands where Islam, the Prophet, and his companions are scorned and vilified and where sin and permissiveness are manifest. Saḥnūn (d. 240/854) reported that Mālik (the eponym of the Mālikī legal school) strongly disapproved of Muslims traveling to lands where the Companions of the Prophet are vilified.[33] The emphasis on the Companions suggests that Mālik was referring to Sunni-Shi'ite antagonisms, but the argument is that if even vilification of the Companions is grounds for *hijra*, then it must hold a fortiori for the vilification of the Prophet and the Qur'an, which Muslims might fear in non-Muslim lands. This duty to dissociate oneself from slander of Islam is grounded in a more general Islamic duty to dissociate oneself from any sin and evil that one is incapable of correcting. If it is presumed that an entire society is governed by un-Islamic morals, and that as a minority in such a society Muslims are not in a position to purify it, then it has often been argued that it is a duty to remove oneself from the entire sinful environment. Consider al-Wansharīsī's statement that "living amongst the unbelievers, other than *dhimmī*s or servants, is not allowed for one moment out of the day because of what will be encountered by way of impurities, filth, religious corruption and earthly scandals throughout one's life."[34] This argument is clearly applicable today, when it is common for Muslim scholars and religious authorities to associate liberal societies with social permissiveness and moral laxity (one of the terms used for liberalism is precisely "*ibāḥiyya*," or "permissiveness") and with the public disputes over the permissibility of explicit slandering of Islam and Muḥammad in novels, cartoons, and other media. Even scholars inclined toward permitting residence in non-Muslim states emphasize that it is conditional upon avoiding "the temptations that exist there [and the] permissiveness protected by their laws."[35]

Promotion of Virtue and Morality

The duty to avoid association with sin is usually linked to a concomitant duty to promote virtue and morality. The bare minimum required by this positive duty is to guarantee that one's children will be raised in an Islamic environment and that they are not in danger of straying from religion. A concern with the sustainability of Islam over generations in a non-Muslim environment is the final objection to living in such societies. It is not a purely contemporary concern; the eleventh-century Ḥanafī jurist al-Sarakhsī (quoted previously) argued that a primary reason for not settling in *dār al-ḥarb* is that one's "children might acquire the morals of non-Muslims."[36] Obviously, this is a theme that also figures frequently in contemporary discussions of the permissibility of settling in a non-Muslim state: "It is not recommended for Muslims to migrate to the lands where their next generations' religion might be at risk, unless they make every effort to safeguard [it]. Without such efforts it will be *makrūh* (reprehensible) and in some cases even *ḥarām* (forbidden) to migrate to such lands."[37]

At times, the argument is not only that social mores and cultural practices will be more permissive than in Muslim societies but also that the problem lies precisely in the liberal legal protections for those who would revise their conception of the good: "But even more dangerous than [exposure to sin] is that the children of many of these Muslims living amongst the unbelievers have deviated and the parents look at this and find that they are unable to do anything about it because the system of these unbelieving states permits sons and daughters to do as they please. Indeed it is the norm that the third generation of Muslims in these countries apostatize from Islam."[38]

This preceding survey should suffice for demonstrating that residence in non-Muslim states has itself been frequently regarded by Muslim jurists and thinkers as something impermissible or at least deeply problematic. The Qur'anic and Prophetic texts cited are often regarded as unambiguous and timeless injunctions against residing outside a Muslim polity. They are further explained by the six types of rational arguments just presented: that Muslims must not be subject to non-Muslim laws or authority, that Islam and Muslims must not be put in a position of inferiority to non-Muslims, that Muslims must avoid aiding or increasing the strength of non-Muslims, that Muslims are forbidden from forming bonds of friendship or solidarity with non-Muslims, that Muslims are required to avoid environments of sin or indecency, and that in non-Muslim environments it will be more difficult to prevent the loss of religiosity in subsequent generations.

Loyalty to a Non-Muslim State

Given that there has been a debate among jurists about whether Muslims are even permitted to reside permanently in non-Muslim states, it follows that rendering loyalty to them, including in matters of warfare, presents an even more demanding doctrinal requirement. Indeed, as shown in chapter 5, even many jurists who permit residence in non-Muslim states prefer that Muslims enjoy some form of self-seclusion (*i'tizāl*) and do not take issue with the argument that friendship with unbelievers is generally undesirable if not prohibited. This dilemma is partially symbolized by the fact that medieval Muslim scholars placed treatments of migration, residence, and behavior in non-Muslim lands as subsections of the books of law dealing with *jihād*.[39] The implications of this association are obvious. While it is indeed too simplistic to assume that all juridical discussions of non-Muslim polities and communities can be reduced to a blanket justification of aggression or antagonism, it is certainly the case that jurists view the Islamic political community both as a polity (albeit not necessarily with all of the bureaucratic features of a modern state) and as an entity toward which Muslims have ethical obligations.[40] This political community is one with universal aspirations, and it is assumed to be, at the very least, in a state of competition with other communities. A just life for a Muslim, thus, is not only performing acts of worship or avoiding sin but also serving the community of believers in any way required of him, including (perhaps especially[41]) in war for the cause of Islam (precisely which cause is the subject of later discussion).

Given this basic assumption, it is not surprising that the idea of civic loyalty to a non-Muslim state, possibly including service in a non-Muslim army, is considered aberrant.[42] The Western analogue is not Christian or humanist just war doctrines, but rather perennial state-centered expectations of civic loyalty. It is akin to asking: Are there doctrines of nationalism, patriotism, or republicanism that can themselves provide justificatory reasons for serving a foreign state? The question either meets with baffled silence or complete hostility.

That a Muslim is not allowed to kill brother Muslims in the service of a non-Muslim army is traditionally among the most uncontroversial positions in Islamic political and ethical thought. There is direct scriptural foundation for this aversion. The Qur'an proclaims:

> Never should a believer kill a believer; but (if it so happens) by mistake (compensation is due). . . . Whosoever slays a believer intentionally his reward is Hell forever, and the wrath and curse of God are upon him, and a dreadful penalty is prepared for him. [Q. 4:92–93]
>
> Do not take life which God has forbidden except for a just cause.[43] [Q. 17:33]

The definition of a just cause for taking Muslim life is provided by a well-known *ḥadīth*: "The blood of a Muslim who proclaims that there is no god but God and that I am the Messenger of God may not be legally spilt other than in one of three [instances]: a life for a life,[44] the married person who commits adultery, and one who forsakes his religion and abandons his community."[45] Other *ḥadīth* reports reinforce the general ban on killing between Muslims: "Whoever carries arms against us is not one of us."[46] "Exchanging curses with [*sibāb*] a

Muslim is sin and fighting him is unbelief."[47] "If two Muslims meet with their swords then both the killer and the killed are in the fire [for] the killed was eager to kill his opponent."[48] "None of you should point your weapon towards a brother Muslim for you do not know, perhaps Satan will tempt you to hit him and you will fall into a pit of fire."[49] "Every Muslim is inviolable to all other Muslims—his blood, his property and his honor."[50] A further *ḥadīth* seems to have implications for even noncombatant service in a non-Muslim army engaged in combat with Muslims: "Whoever assists in killing a believer even by half a word will meet God with no hope of God's mercy written on his face."[51]

Finally, among the rules established by Muḥammad for governing the various tribal and religious communities in Medina (known collectively as *al-wathīqa*, or the "Constitution of Medina") was included the following: "A believer shall not slay a believer for the sake of an unbeliever, nor shall he aid an unbeliever against a believer. Believers are friends one to the other to the exclusion of outsiders."[52]

These citations form the most explicit scriptural foundation for the prohibition against serving in a non-Muslim army engaged in hostilities with Muslims. Muslim jurists have extrapolated from these sources not only a clear prohibition against helping non-Muslims in combat against Muslims (whatever the cause) but also often the ruling that doing so constitutes apostasy. The possibility that Muslims might be in a position of serving in non-Muslim armies against Muslims seems to have occurred to most classical jurists only in the context of Muslim prisoners acting under coercion. The consensus opinion is that these prisoners must submit to torture and execution rather than raise swords against fellow Muslims on behalf of non-Muslims.[53]

With the modern period and the colonization of Muslim lands by European powers, however, the service of Muslim civilians in non-Muslim armies became a very real prospect indeed. The prominent nineteenth- and twentieth-century scholar Muḥammad Rashīd Riḍā (d. 1935) considered this situation to be the most abhorrent aspect of the offer of French citizenship to North African Muslims. He found subservience to French laws that permit acts prohibited by Islam and vice versa to be unconscionable for a Muslim, "but the gravest affliction of all is that Muslims are now compelled into military service in the enemy's army and to fight Muslims, humiliate them, force them into submission and to arrest anyone who does not respect and preserve this treaty of protection (*dhimma*)." He concluded that "if the situation is as described, then there is no disagreement amongst Muslims that the acceptance of citizenship is a clear case of apostasy and exit from the Islamic community."[54] Not surprisingly, this was also the position taken by the Ottoman government in respect to Muslim subjects of Allied states during the First World War:

> *Question*: If the states mentioned that are fighting against the Islamic government compel and force their Muslim population by threatening to kill them and even to exterminate all members of their families, is it even in this case according to the *sharīʿa* absolutely forbidden for them to fight against the troops of the Islamic countries

> and do they [by transgressing this prohibition] deserve the hell-fire, having become murderers?
>
> *Answer*: Yes.[55]

That this may indeed constitute apostasy is the position of a number of contemporary thinkers as well, including prominent cleric Yūsuf al-Qaraḍāwī.[56]

This might be considered by some sufficient to demonstrate incompatibility with a theory of civic loyalty that tolerated no exemption whatever from the duty to contribute to any of one's state's wars when called on to do so. However, the Islamic aversion to killing fellow Muslims might itself not commit a Muslim to any actual hostility toward his or her non-Muslim state. Yet positions that violate even this minimal conception of civic loyalty to a non-Muslim state can also be found in Islamic sources. I discuss three in particular here: one, the idea that Muslims might be bound to join a legitimate *jihād* against their non-Muslim state of citizenship in certain conditions; two, that supporting the self-defense efforts of a non-Muslim state of citizenship even against other non-Muslims is problematic; and, three, that the classical *jihād* doctrine that permits warfare in certain conditions against even nonaggressing infidel states is still valid, even if the conditions for its realization do not now exist and Muslim citizens of a non-Muslim state would not necessarily be required to participate.

Joining a Jihād *against One's Own Non-Muslim State*

Let us imagine a situation of hostilities between Muslim forces and a non-Muslim state. Let us further structure the assumptions of the case to make it the morally least demanding situation possible for Muslims: The conflict is assumed to take place on non-Muslim soil, and Muslims are not required by their non-Muslim state to engage in actual combat against coreligionists, either in cases of clear aggression (i.e., in cases when a neutral, disinterested observer could not regard Muslim hostilities as just) or in cases when Muslim forces are, or claim to be, responding to aggression by the non-Muslim state. For now, we are not concerned with any declaration on the part of a Muslim citizen of the unjustness of the Muslim cause, merely the declaration of the permissibility of his not aiding the hostile forces against his state of citizenship. This might be regarded as the least demanding possible declaration of civic loyalty involving combat between Muslim and non-Muslim forces.

What rejecting this demand requires from the Muslim perspective is a very specific interpretation of the doctrine of *jihād*: It requires believing not only that in certain ideal circumstances an Islamic state led by a recognized Imam is entitled (or obligated) to engage in armed *jihād* against non-Muslim states for the purposes both of defending existing Muslim communities and of enlarging the space ruled by Islam (see point 3) but also that it is the individual obligation (*farḍ 'ayn*) of every Muslim in all places to contribute to this war effort if asked to do so. That is, he or she sins or acts unvirtuously by failing to help Muslim forces subdue or do harm to a non-Muslim state in which he or she lives.

The mainstream position is that the type of *jihād* described is at the discretion of the Imam and is a collective obligation (*farḍ kifāya*), meaning that it is an obligation upon the Muslim community as a whole and it is discharged when a sufficient number of the community engage in it.[57] Only when Muslim lands are under attack does (defensive) *jihād* become an individual obligation on all able-bodied, sound-minded Muslims. In this case, some jurists have argued explicitly that Muslims living in non-Muslim states (even under an *amān*[58]) have obligations to aid their brethren. Sarakhsī, for example, argued that if a non-Muslim state attacks a Muslim state and takes Muslim prisoners, then a Muslim legal resident (*musta'min*) of that state is required to renounce his *amān* and fight to free the prisoners.[59] Yet even in this case, some jurists give a more pragmatic interpretation of the *farḍ 'ayn* in the case of defensive *jihād*. Al-Qurṭubī, for example, writes that when a Muslim land is attacked, it is the duty of all residents of *that* land to go out and fight:

> And if the residents of that land are unable to repel their enemy, then it becomes incumbent on their immediate neighbors to go out in accordance with what was made incumbent on the residents of that land until they know that they have enough strength to repel the enemy and defend the Muslims. Similarly, it becomes a duty for anyone who is aware of the weakness of the Muslims vis-à-vis their enemy and is able to help them to go to them.[60]

A particularly apposite historical example of the invocation of the universal duty to contribute to the *jihād* is the famous Ottoman *jihād fatwā* of 1914 quoted before. In it, the conflict between the Allied and Central powers is presented as aggression directed against the Islamic caliphate and thus from the Muslim perspective a defensive *jihād* to which all Muslims have a duty to contribute:

> *Question*: When it occurs that enemies attack the Islamic world, when it has been established that they seize and pillage Islamic countries and capture Muslim persons and when His Majesty the Padishah of Islam thereupon orders the jihad in the form of a general mobilization, has jihad then, according to the illustrious Qur'anic verse: "Go forth light and heavy! Struggle in God's way with your possessions and yourselves; that is best for you did you know?" (9:41), become incumbent upon all Muslims and has it become an individual duty for all Muslims in all parts of the world, to hasten to partake in the jihad with their goods and money?
> *Answer*: Yes.
>
> *Question*: Now that it has been established that Russia, England, France and the governments that support them and are allied to them, are hostile to the Islamic Caliphate, since their warships and armies attack the Seat of the Islamic Caliphate and the Imperial Dominions and strive (God forbid) for extinguishing and annihilating the exalted light of Islam, is it, in this case, also incumbent upon

> all Muslims that are being ruled by these governments, to proclaim jihad against them and to actually attack them?
> *Answer*: Yes.
>
> *Question*: If some Muslims, now that the attainment of the aim [the protection of the Ottoman empire] depends on the fact that all Muslims hasten to partake in the jihad, refrain from doing so (which God forbid), is this then, in this case, a great sin and do they deserve Divine wrath and punishment for their horrible sin?
> *Answer*: Yes.[61]

This position that expansive *jihād* is legitimate and that it may be an individual obligation on all believing Muslims is, naturally, the view adopted by the ideologues of the contemporary radical Islamist movements. The operative source is Q. 9:38–41:

> O you who believe! What is the matter with you that, when you are asked to go forth in the cause of God you cling heavily to the Earth? Do you prefer the life of this world to the Hereafter? But little is the comfort of this life, as compared with the Hereafter. Unless you go forth, He will punish you with a grievous penalty and put others in your place, but Him you would not harm in the least. For God has power over all things. (Even) if you do not help, God has helped him. . . . Go ye forth, lightly or heavily, and strive and struggle with your goods and your persons in the cause of God. That is best for you if you but knew.

Commenting on these verses, Sayyid Abul ʻAlā Mawdūdī (sometimes: Syed Abul ʻAla Maudoodi; d. 1979) writes that:

> this verse formed the basis of a legal ruling issued by the jurists regarding *jihād*. They concluded that as long as the Muslims as a whole, or the Muslims of a particular area or a section thereof, have not been summoned to *jihād*, it would remain merely *farḍ bi-al-kifāya*. However, if the Muslims are called upon by their leader to make *jihād* [it] would become obligatory on every Muslim who has been so called upon. The matter is of such vital importance that if those who fail to perform this duty without any legitimate excuse claim to be Muslims, such a claim will not be entertained.[62]

Although not specifically mentioning Muslims living in a non-Muslim state, the argument that a legitimate Islamic ruler would have to be obeyed by any Muslim whom he calls to arms, regardless of domicile, is advanced so categorically that it is hard to imagine any space for justifying ethical obligations to non-Muslims.

However, as shown in chapter 6, most scholars view Muslim residents of non-Muslim polities as bound by a mutual contract of security. Discussion on the part of jurists of when Muslims are allowed to engage in violence against such polities tends to focus on the violation of the contract on the part of the non-Muslims. The standard (if not unanimous) view is that when a non-Muslim polity threatens the security or property of Muslim residents, then the latter are relieved of their obligations and may defend themselves in any way.[63] More interesting for our purposes (since we assume that a state that would violate the rights of its citizens in this way is not a liberal one) is whether a Muslim community enjoying rights provided by a non-Muslim polity is permitted to attack that state not as part of a "classical" *jihād* of expansion but as part of a defensive *jihād*, where the Muslims who are defending themselves are residents of a foreign country. This is clearly a more plausible scenario for obvious reasons, as the lack of a legitimate Islamic Imam makes any *jihād* of expansion a purely theoretical problem, and all contemporary "jihads" (including the September 11, 2001, attacks) are regarded as defensive in one way or another. So the argument would have to be that the contract of security is broken when the non-Muslim state attacks *any* Muslims and that Muslim citizens of that state are permitted to defend not themselves but *other* Muslims.

This is, of course, precisely the logic involved in the case of violence against a non-Muslim state of citizenship, such as the July 7, 2005, attacks in London—that it is justified on the grounds that war against any Muslims (in Iraq, Afghanistan, Palestine) warrants retaliation by all Muslims. Although contemporary jihadi movements are eager to place their views in the context of an unchanging and unambiguous Islamic ethical and legal tradition, it is difficult to find analogous sources in the classical tradition. In premodern jurisprudence, warfare was rarely conceived as a self-help affair outside the guidance of a military leader. Furthermore, most of what goes by the name of "jihad" for these groups are attacks on civilians with the purpose of creating a certain political outcome. The tactical use of violence against civilians in this way does not seem to be part of the classical literature because it presumes a political context of democratic accountability to a constituent population.[64]

Given the lack of a clear classical analogue in the books of law, the contemporary justification of such violence tends to center around five arguments: First, this form of violence (terrorism) is covered by the moral principle of "treatment in kind" or "reciprocity" (*al-mu'āmala bi'l-mithl*); because non-Muslims are killing Muslim civilians, it is permissible for Muslims to do the same to them. A number of Qur'anic verses can be invoked for this principle:

> And fight not against them near the Sacred Mosque unless they fight against you there first; but if they fight against you, slay them. [Q. 2:191]
>
> Fight during the sacred months if you are attacked for a violation of sanctity is [subject to the law of] just retribution. Thus, if anyone commits aggression against you, attack him just as he has attacked you—but remain conscious of God, and know that God is with those who are conscious of Him. [Q. 2:194]

The Saudi Arabian dissident Shaykh 'Abd al-'Azīz ibn Ṣāliḥ al-Jarbū' writes in his justification of the September 11 attacks that group punishment for perfidy or an attack on Muslims is permissible. He cites both the eleventh-century Andalusian scholar Ibn Ḥazm's (d. 1064)[65] commentary on the episode in Medīna when the Prophet massacred the Banī Qurayẓa tribe on grounds of perfidy and the fourteenth-century Syrian scholar Ibn Qayyim al-Jawziyya's (d. 1350) *Zād al-ma'ād*: "If a part of a people violates or reneges on a treaty or agreement and the rest of the people consents to this then the entire population becomes in violation of it, and thus subject to treatment as a warring people."[66] An unattributed text justifying the July 7, 2005, bombings in London states explicitly that "we are permitted to do to the infidels as they do to us."[67] The text cites two additional Qur'anic verses for this: 16:126 ("If you punish [*'āqabtum*] then punish in the manner in which you were punished"; the text does not quote the rest of the verse: "if you are patient then that is the best course for those who are patient") and 42:39–40 ("Those who when an injustice afflicts them help themselves. The recompense for an injury is an equal injury"). The text also quotes Ibn Taymiyya's judgment (in his *Fatāwā*) that it is permissible to cut the enemy's trees and burn their crops if they have done this to Muslims and a number of other classical scholars on the subject of reciprocity in war.

A second argument is that the basic principle or default position (*al-aṣl*) of relations with all infidel, "*jāhilī*" regimes and societies is warfare anyway. This argument tends to deny that there is a binding mutual contract of security in the first place, or that it is negated by the non-Muslim violence against Muslims.[68] Jarbū' also argues at numerous points that the "fate of unbelievers is a matter of indifference to Muslims" (8–9) and that Muslims are not permitted to mourn or regret calamities that befall unbelievers (14–15). These latter points are the first arguments invoked in favor of the July 7, 2005, attacks in the text "al-Ta'ṣīl li-mashrū'iyyat mā jarā fī Landan." The argument is that Muslims have no presumed moral obligation to non-Muslims in the first place on the principle of *al-walā wa'l-barā'*. Thus, the first positive justification of such violence is to diminish its very status as an ethical dilemma.

On the technical matter that interests us here, the "London bombing text" also makes clear that any moral obligation to non-Muslims is confined to states of peace determined by mutual contract, which British attacks on Muslims have negated: "There is no room for doubt that Britain is an infidel state at war with the entirety of Muslims (*'umūm al-muslimīn*) and there is no disputation on this except on the part of grave sinners."[69] However, the text does not address specifically the status of Muslim citizens of Britain; it treats the problem of a treaty between Muslims and Britain generally. Given how central the idea of contract is to the justification of civic loyalty (as shown in chapter 6), this omission is glaring. The closest the text comes is to invoke Muḥammad's dictum that "war is deceit" (*al-ḥarb khud'a*) to justify the failure of the British citizens to formally declare their intentions.

A third argument is that, in the special case of democratic states where non-Muslims have freely elected the governments who are attacking Muslims, those civilians are complicit in those attacks. Jarbū' writes: "Participation by voting in the decision to massacre Muslims, exporting shame and indecency to

Islam and Muslims and participating in the corruption of Muslims and diverting them from their religion" makes American civilians a legitimate target.[70] The London bombing text also states clearly that "any Briton who voted for fighting is a combatant, or at least aids and abets combat."[71]

A fourth argument is that any explicit *amān*, or contract of security, is binding only on Muslims who voluntary entered a non-Muslim country. Muslims born in a non-Muslim country did not choose to be born there and did not autonomously enter into a contract and are thus permitted to engage in hostilities.[72]

A fifth argument used to declare the lack of a binding covenant of mutual security focuses not on acts of war directed against other Muslims but on domestic security measures. The primary (if not sole) example of this is the media statement by Omar Bakri Muhammad, the supposed leader of the "al-Muhajiroun" Salafi group in the United Kingdom. He had previously declared on multiple occasions that while he supported terrorist acts against Western powers he regarded Muslims living in those countries as bound by the "covenant of security" (*'aqd al-amān*), which is discussed in chapter 6. However, on January 10, 2005, he is reported to have declared that British counterterrorism measures violated the British guarantee of security and peace to the Muslim community and thus rendered void the mutual covenant of security, making it permissible for British Muslims to attack British interests.[73] Like the previous argument on native-born versus naturalized citizens, it is not clear whether there has been any elaborate, scholarly formulation of this position. However, unlike the previous argument, it does seem to enjoy a certain theoretical plausibility (albeit not in its particular application to the British case): If it can be shown that a liberal state formally and consistently applied different sets of constitutional rights to Muslim citizens on arbitrary grounds, then the initial Islamic foundation for their obligations to that state could be said to no longer obtain.

Contributing to the Self-Defense of a Non-Muslim State

One also finds in juridical sources a frequent antipathy to Muslims helping non-Muslims when it is viewed that the cause is the advancement of a non-Islamic faith or conception of truth. The roots of this antipathy are manifold: Not only might such help be seen as directly detracting from the Islamic cause, but even if there is no direct harm to Islam or Muslims, advancing the cause, increasing the strength, or upholding the rule of unbelievers is something prohibited to Muslims. As discussed in the prior survey of the positions on migration, Muslim jurists often advance a total ethical stance according to which actions are judged partially on whether they are beneficial for Islam and Muslims. In a famous *fatwā*, the fourteenth-century jurist and theologian Ibn Taymiyya proclaimed that "helping those who depart from the Islamic *sharī'a* is forbidden."[74] This wording seems to leave him indifferent to the status of relations between such people and Muslims. Similarly, the contemporary Bosnian Salafi scholar Sulejman Topoljak writes that even if Muslims find themselves with no choice but to join non-Muslims in battle, "it is necessary that Muslims intend by engaging in such fighting only to bring about benefit to Muslims, and to elevate the word of God, without intending to bring about the strengthening of the unbelievers, befriending them or elevating the word of unbelief."[75]

In addition, there is also a clear divine command at stake in such cases. Muslims, it is often argued, have the obligation to preserve their own lives, which are made inviolable by God; to expose themselves to harm or potential death is something that is licit only in certain circumstances. Helping unbelievers is not to be found among the legitimate grounds for sacrificing one's life.[76]

Furthermore, it has been argued that if *any* interest can be discerned for the Muslim state in Muslim minorities of non-Muslim states refusing to fight, then this trumps any duties that might be thought owed to the state of citizenship. The Ottoman *jihād fatwā* previously quoted again gives an appropriate historical example:

> *Question*: Is it in this case for the Muslims that are in the present war under the rule of England, France, Russia, Serbia, Montenegro and their allies, *since it is detrimental to the Islamic Caliphate*, a great sin to fight against Germany and Austria which are the allies of the Supreme Islamic Government and do they deserve a painful punishment?
> *Answer*: Yes.

What is noteworthy from this (not forgetting, of course, that state-issued rulings are problematic as an exemplar of the Islamic juridical methodology) is that it forbids fighting against non-Muslim states allied with the Sultan, regardless of the attitude of the aggressor states toward the Muslim populations in question, with the reason being simply that it is not in Ottoman state's political interest, with no other consideration of justice.

Two quotations from prominent Ḥanafī jurists I believe encapsulate the consensus juridical opinion on this question from the classical sources:

> I asked: If some Muslims were in the *dār al-ḥarb* under an *amān* and that territory were attacked by people of *another territory of war*, do you think it would be lawful for those Muslims to fight on their side?
>
> He replied: No . . . because the jurisdiction of the unbelievers prevails there and the *Muslims cannot enforce Muslim rulings*.
>
> I asked: If the Muslims were fearful of their own persons from the enemy, should they fight in defence of themselves?
>
> He replied: If the situation were thus, there would be no harm to fight in defense of themselves.[77]

> If there is a group of Muslims under an *amān* in the abode of war and that country is attacked by another non-Muslim country, then the Muslims are not allowed to fight, for fighting involves exposing oneself to danger which is only allowed for the purpose of exaltation of the Word of God, may He be glorified, and the glorification of religion, which are not present in this case. Because the laws of idolatry are dominant over them Muslims are not able to rule by the laws of

> Islam, and thus any fighting on their part would take the form of exaltation of the word of idolatry and this is not permitted unless they fear for their lives from the invaders, in which case there is no sin incurred in fighting to defend themselves rather than fighting to exalt the word of idolatry.[78]

From the Islamic perspective, thus, even in the least demanding circumstance for the Muslim conscience—when two non-Muslim states meet in battle with no direct bearing on any Muslim community or polity—almost all classical jurists are still reluctant to permit Muslims to fight in defense of a state in which they reside under an *amān*.[79] If they are to join such efforts, it is because of the need to do so for their own sake and not because of any solidarity with the non-Muslims or even recognition of their interests. In addition to the need to protect themselves and their property, other benefits include gaining necessary military training and expertise with the purpose of putting them to use at some point in the service of Muslims or the *jihād*.[80]

Topoljak gives four specific cases in which it is permitted to fight on behalf of non-Muslims against other non-Muslims but which may not be grounded on compatible reasons: (1) If Muslims are compelled to do this on pain of death. This is from the *fiqh* principle of necessity (*ḍarūra*) and thus akin to eating carrion. This is obviously not intended to serve as a justification for doing so voluntarily or out of duty. (2) If they are defending themselves, their families, and their property from the same attacking non-Muslims. (3) "It is permitted for Muslim minorities to fight with an infidel commander if he respects the Muslims, grants them their rights and if they fear that he may be defeated by someone who will oppress them, such as when the Muslims co-operated with [Ethiopian king] al-Najāshī." The *fiqh* principles that ground this argument are the general quasi-utilitarian ones of pursuing the greatest benefit and avoiding the greatest damage or perversion. (4) If Muslims fear a greater enemy, then they can cooperate with a smaller enemy. (He gives the example of Muslim forces aiding Byzantium against Persia.) In conclusion: "Muslims living as a minority in a non-Muslim state are permitted to participate with infidels in a war against their fellow-infidel enemies if there is a benefit for them in this, such as gaining their rights or improving their situation, if doing so does not result in any harm to Muslims, or if they are coerced to do so. In all other circumstances it is not permitted for them to join them in their battle against other infidels, and God knows best."[81]

There is some question as to whether points 2 through 4 might be approaching a compatible position with liberal citizenship. The reason for thinking so is that Topoljak allows for the possibility of identifying Muslim interests with those of the non-Muslim majority, and with the consideration that a Muslim would naturally prefer the state that practices the least oppression toward them. It is, of course, central to liberal justification that the rights it gives citizens, particularly minorities, give those citizens reasons to support and be loyal toward liberal institutions. Furthermore, there are prominent liberal theories of political obligation (rational egotist theories from Hobbes to Nozick) that presume that the "citizen" (if he can be so called) will be interested in the fate of his state and fellow citizens no further than it concerns his own safety and welfare. And of course, it might be argued that political liberalism cannot require as part of a doctrine of citizenship any robust or emotional attachment to one's community of citizenship, or principled altruism, beyond what is necessary to secure the equal rights of all. Thus, there is an argument to be made that even if Muslims are fighting an invading force only to defend their *own* property, families, and persons, then such is all that some theories of citizenship assume *any* citizen is doing.

The difference between Topoljak's reasoning and that of individualist theories of political obligation, however, lies in the distinction between initial motivations for endorsing a social contract and subsequent reasoning in society. A social contract may appeal to individual (or group) self-interest (whether in the form of appeals to *reciprocity* or *mutual advantage*) as a justification for the general structure of rights and duties, but it cannot allow that every discrete demand made by the state be accepted or rejected in situ by the individual according to some self-regarding utility calculus. This latter scenario seems to be precisely what Topoljak has in mind: that Muslims residing in non-Muslim states (let us presume that they enjoy the security and freedom he refers to in point 3) can adopt a stance toward a war of aggression against their state depending on whether it *directly* threatens them and their interests or whether they have more to gain by their state preserving itself or being conquered. That is, there is no suggestion of general moral duties toward a state that has fulfilled the needs of protection, respect of rights, and welfare provision, nor of the independent rights and interests of non-Muslims except when and where they align with those of Muslims. There is no question but that this justification of serving a non-Muslim state does not indicate the existence of an overlapping consensus as it stands in Topoljak's present formulation.

Recognizing the Legitimacy and Inviolability of One's Non-Muslim State

The first part of this section dealt with Islamic views on the obligations of individual Muslims toward the Muslim community when it is engaged in a conflict that may be declared by some to be a *jihād*. The discussion was restricted to consideration of the individual Muslim citizen's *behavior* within, rather than *beliefs* about, the conflict.

There may also be a further requirement of citizenship, however, to hold certain beliefs about the rights of his community of citizenship and to be able to condemn on principled grounds certain hypothetical acts of violence on the part of Muslim forces. More broadly, there might be a requirement to share certain aspects of a doctrine of when war is justified. Even if a Muslim forswears any direct participation, he holds a doctrine incompatible with liberal citizenship if he holds that a war to facilitate the spread of Islam or to change the government of a state in which Muslims are not oppressed might in some circumstances be justifiable.

This discussion strikes at the heart of interpretations of the meaning of *jihād* in Islamic discourses. In contemporary Islamic polemics, the question of *jus ad bellum* is often posed in terms of whether *jihād* is for the purpose of spreading Islam, removing barriers to its reception, and erasing disbelief (in which case it becomes extremely difficult to see how any non-Muslim violence against Muslims, even in self-defense, or indeed any claim by a non-Muslim polity to noninterference on a permanent basis can be accepted as legitimate by a Muslim), or merely for the purpose of self-defense against oppression and tyranny directed against Muslims (in which case a Muslim argument for self-restraint toward non-Muslims, and the existence of absolute rights to noninterference for them, can begin to be made). Alternatively, it is sometimes asked whether the "basis" or "basic principle" (*al-aṣl*) of relations with non-Muslims is war or peace.

The classical sources give support almost exclusively for the former, incompatible, position. ʿAbd al-Qādir notes that "our jurists have diverged on the transmission of [Islam] to the unbelievers into two camps. The first camp is the majority of the classical jurists who . . . held that the basic status of relations between Islam and unbelief is war, that peace is the exceptional condition under emergency conditions and that the source of this state of war is unbelief."[82] As was mentioned earlier in this chapter, one of the primary constructs of Muslim political geography was that of the non-Muslim world as *dār al-ḥarb*, "the abode of war." Consequently, non-Muslim residents of such countries are usually referred to as "*ḥarbīs*," the ascriptive adjective of the noun *war*. The theological-juridical basis for this ascription is clearly the view that, even if a constant state of actual warfare is not assumed, the basic status of relations between the abodes is one of war and permanent nonrecognition.[83] In the classical period, all Sunni schools "thought of the *jihad* as a war for the expansion of Islamic territory—i.e., the sphere where the norms prescribed by the Shariʿa would be paramount."[84] The application of this doctrine at the theoretical level varied, depending on the non-Muslim community. For polytheists, the legitimate Imam was to give the choice between conversion to Islam and war.[85] For People of the Book (Christians, Jews, and Zoroastrians), the choice was conversion to Islam, submission to Muslim authority through paying the poll tax (*jizya*), or war.

Classical jurists also imposed strict limits on the legitimate duration of a peace treaty, refusing to justify permanent guarantees of security to non-Muslim states regardless of the balance of power between them and Muslim forces. Underpinning these specific positions was the general point of doctrine that the object of human history is for the entire world to eventually become *dār al-Islām*, either through voluntary conversion or, if necessary, war led by a legitimate Imam. Thus, "from the jurists' perspective, non-Muslims had no right to resist Islamic military expansion, and the rules for treating the conquered peoples reflect the jurists' premise that in refusing to submit to Islam, they were doing a wrong that justified harsh treatment."[86] It is clear that articulating a compatible doctrine of just war will require for Muslim citizens of liberal democracies a more radical departure from the range of opinions articulated in the classical tradition than have the questions presented to this point.

Although Islamic Modernists of varying stripes have articulated a new doctrine of *jihād* as "defensive" war (which is discussed in chapter 6), it is, of course, a reaffirmation of the letter of the classical doctrine that characterizes the more radical contemporary Islamist movements. These groups see *jihād* as war to eradicate man-made barriers to the implementation of Islamic law. Their doctrine receives its most famous articulation, of course, in the writings of Sayyid Quṭb. In the following passage, Quṭb argues that verses in the Qur'ān that speak of peace or coexistence with unbelievers [e.g., Q. 8:61, 60:8, 2:190, 3:64] were temporary, provisional rulings abrogated by the final ruling revealed in *sūra* 9[87]:

> If Muslims today, in their present situation, cannot implement these final rulings, then they are not, now and for the time being, required to do so. For God does not charge anyone with more than he or she can do. They may resort to the provisional rulings, approaching them gradually, until such a time when they are able to implement these final rulings. But they may not twist the final texts in order to show them as consistent with the provisional ones. They may not impose their own weakness on the divine faith, which remains firm and strong. Let them fear God and not attempt to weaken God's faith under the pretext of showing it to be a religion of peace. It is certainly the religion of peace, but this must be based on saving all mankind from submission to anyone other than God. [Islam's] advocates must not be ashamed of declaring that their ultimate goal is to destroy all forces that stand in its way of liberating mankind from any shackle which prevents the free choice of adopting Islam.
>
> When people follow human codes and apply man-made laws to regulate their lives, every doctrine and code has the right to live in peace within its own area, as long as it does not entail aggression against others. In this case, coexistence of difference creeds, regimes and social orders should be the norm. But when there is a divine code requiring complete submission to God alone, and there are alongside it human systems and conditions that are man-made, advocating submission to human beings, the matter is fundamentally different. In this case, it is right that the divine system should move across barriers to liberate people from enslavement by others. They will then be free to choose their faith in a situation where people surrender themselves to God alone.[88]

Elsewhere, Quṭb makes clear that the classical doctrine of nonrecognition of non-Muslim polities ought to be revived by Muslims as part of the renewal of their religion: "No peace agreement may be made [with Christians and Jews] except on the basis of submission evident by the payment of a special tax which gives them the right to live in peace with the Muslims. . . . Never will they be forced to accept the Islamic faith. But they are not given a peaceful status unless they are bound by covenant with the Muslim community on the basis of paying the submission tax."[89] Other scholars, such as 'Abd al-Qādir, directly address the clear conflict between the affirmation of the classical doctrine and recognition of the United Nations and the present state system, arguing that Islam cannot recognize the United Nations charter as permanently binding, that it can only be honored conditionally and because of necessity, that the exchange of ambassadors does not imply any guarantee of peaceful relations between countries, and that the enduring conflict between faith and unbelief results necessarily in an Abode of Islam and an Abode of War.[90]

Thus, insofar as citizenship might require permanent recognition of the status and rights of non-Muslim political communities, there are both classical and contemporary doctrines that reject such a possibility theoretically on the basis of a reading of what the authoritative texts require by way of advancing the spread of Islam and obedience to Islamic law in this world. There are ample reasons for a Muslim to say that he or she cannot affirm on a potentially permanent basis the right of non-Muslim communities to resist military actions by a legitimate Islamic state led by a legitimate ruler undertaken with the purpose of introducing Islamic rule.

To conclude this section, the following five specific claims that can be found within Islamic doctrine might be regarded as covering the range of potentially incompatible positions on the question of civic loyalty to a non-Muslim state.

1. A Muslim may never combat another Muslim in the service of unbelievers, regardless of the cause.
2. A war for the sole purpose of expanding the space ruled by Islam and Islamic law is a just war, a legitimate form of *jihād*.
3. It may be the duty of every individual Muslim, even those residing outside the Islamic polity to contribute to a legitimate *jihād*, if so called by a legitimate Imam.
4. A Muslim may not advance the cause of unbelievers or uphold non-Islamic rulings and truth-claims.
5. A Muslim may not sacrifice his life for other than certain causes, of which defending a non-Muslim society is not one.

Solidarity with Non-Muslims

We have encountered in the previous two sections the view that Muslims should not contribute to the strength, wealth, or well-being of non-Muslim societies and polities, nor should they make alliances or friendships with them. This principle of *al-walā' wa'l-barā'*, often thought to be an injunction based on a number of Qur'anic verses and *ḥadīth* reports, has been used to ground the position that Muslims should not reside in non-Muslim countries or, if they must, that they should not contribute to such countries' self-defense, even against other non-Muslims. Such a view is the precise antithesis of a doctrine of recognition and civic solidarity that might be said to be implied by a commitment to liberal citizenship.

'Abd al-Qādir, for example, points to verse 5:51 ("O you who have believed, do not take Jews and Christians as friends [*awliyā'*: friends, allies, patrons] for they are friends to each other. And who becomes friends with them becomes one of them. Verily God does not guide a wrong-doing people.") and objects to professional and specialist employment in the West for "work amongst the transgressors[91] constitutes strengthening them, supporting them, preserving and upholding what they believe in, which is truly the very meaning of loyalty,[92] which God forbade [in 5:51]."[93]

Other Qur'anic verses are often used to the same effect. *Sūra* 60 (*al-Mumtaḥana*) deals entirely with relations with non-Muslims, and the first verse has been used in tandem with 5:51:

> O you who have believed! Do not take My enemies and your enemies as friends, offering them affection while they have denied what Truth has come unto you, driving away the Messenger of God and yourselves because you believe in God your Lord. If you have gone forth to struggle in my cause and long for my blessing do you secretly hold affection for them? For I know all that you may conceal as well as what you do openly. And who does so has erred from the path. [60:1]

Other similar verses can be found in *sūras* 3, 4, and 5, the last of which is held by Islamic scholars to be among the final revelations, which gives it greater legal authority for Islamic scholars.

> Let not the believers take the infidels for their allies in preference to [or: in exclusion of] the believers—for who does this has nothing to do with God—unless it be to protect yourselves from them in this way. God warns you about Himself and the final goal is to God. [3:28]

> Oh you who believe! Do not take for your intimates other than your own kind. They will continually cause you turmoil and love anything that will distress you. Loathing has already come forth from their mouths and what is concealed in their breasts is even greater. We have made the signs clear to you if you will use your reason. [3:118]

> Those who take unbelievers as friends rather than believers: Are they looking for honor amongst them? All honor is with God. [4:139]

> O you who believe! Do not take as friends unbelievers rather than believers. Do you want to give God a clear proof against you? [4:144]

> Can you see many of them allying with those who disbelieve? So vile indeed is what their passions make them do that God has condemned them and in suffering shall they remain. For if they truly believed in God and the Prophet and all that was bestowed on them from on high they would not take unbelievers for their allies, but many of them are iniquitous. [5:80–81]

The precise scope of the concept of *walā'* or *muwālāh* (friendship, patronage, alliance, loyalty) used in most of these verses is inherently vague. Does it cover all aspects of amicable relations between Muslims and non-Muslims, or is it limited to very specific legal or political arrangements that might come at the expense of the Muslim community?[94] Are these general injunctions (*aḥkām ʿāmma*) for all times and places, or to be read in their revelatory context (*asbāb al-nuzūl*) of Muḥammad's struggles with non-Muslim communities and polities in the seventh century? These are subtle scholarly questions, but what is clear is that Muslim writers in various times and places have seen these verses as ruling generally on the question of forming bonds of solidarity with Muslims in a non-Muslim state. Exegetes such as al-Qurṭubī and Ibn Kathīr spend very little time in specifying the range of relationships covered by the verses prohibiting *muwālāh* with non-Muslims. If they do, it is usually by way of enumerating synonyms or other general concepts like "keeping company" (*muṣāḥaba*), "befriending" (*muṣādaqa*), "mutual consultation" (*munāṣaḥa*), or "revealing the intimate concerns of believers to them" (*ifshā' aḥwāl al-mu'minīn al-bāṭina ilayhim*).[95] Modern commentators (as well as Muslim Qur'an translators) also treat the term generally and as a synonym for loyalty and friendship. ʿAbd al-Qādir, who attempts to approximate the classical jurists, defines the concept in terms of "affection," "help," "alliance," "friendship," "following," "being neighbors," and "proximity."[96]

Treating these verses and this concept as bearing on the question of citizenship would thus indeed appear to have clear justification from our standpoint because citizenship and solidarity cover the range of meanings of *muwālāh*: We are concerned with both the legal and political agreement to accept a non-Muslim state's protection and patronage and the bond of mutual concern between fellow citizens, which we might indeed consider to be a form of alliance or civic friendship. Ibn Bayya offers succinctly that "*walā'* is a certain commitment to and a relationship with people, ideas and values and must be dealt with [from a religious standpoint]."[97]

For those who read the *muwālāh* verses as having both a literal and a general application, and thus discouraging all forms of solidarity with non-Muslims, these verses are underpinned, clarified, or explained primarily by three ethico-political principles. The first is that putting one's trust in unbelievers is a form of rejection of God and His promises. This is one of the interpretations of 3:28 given by Sayyid Quṭb:

> In these verses we have a statement confirming the denunciation of those who have been given a share of God's revelations, but who have nevertheless turned their backs and refused to submit their disputes for arbitration according to God's book which lays down God's code for human life. They have rejected the Divine code which regulates the life of the universe as well as human life. [There is] a stern warning in the current passage against the believers forging an alliance with the unbelievers. Since the unbelievers have no power to control the universe, and since all power belongs to God, He alone is the guardian of the believers and their allies. How, then, can a believer be justified in forming an alliance with the enemies of God? True

> faith in God cannot be combined with an alliance with, or patronage of, the enemies of God. Hence, we have this very stern warning in verse 28, making it absolutely clear that a Muslim disowns Islam if he forgoes a relationship of alliance or patronage with someone who refuses to acknowledge God's revelation as the arbiter in life. He has cut himself off from God.[98]

In effect, Quṭb thus views this question as covered by the general injunction to "rule by what God has sent down" (5:45), which includes for him and his Islamist disciples the duty of Islamizing all political institutions through the implementation of Islamic law. Living willingly in a state dominated by non-Muslim laws and seeking protection and welfare from it is a rejection of God's sovereignty and power, whether that state has a Muslim or non-Muslim majority. For a ruler or ruling class to implement laws other than what God has revealed can only be a rejection of those laws and the God who revealed them; similarly, for individual Muslims to intentionally seek out the protection and friendship of those who so reject God, particularly when an Islamic alternative exists, can only be such a rejection. Remember from earlier in this chapter that these very verses (3:28, 3:118, 5:51, 60:1) have been viewed by classical Mālikī and modern Wahhabi jurists as ruling also on the question of residence for the very reasons given here: Living in a state implies accepting its protection and thereby committing oneself to certain duties of restraint toward it, as well as the inevitable contribution to its welfare. If one views these as an impermissible form of *muwālāh* with unbelievers, then all three aspects of citizenship addressed in this book (residence, loyalty, and solidarity) are struck down by a single principle and set of verses.

The second principle derived from these verses is that alliance and friendship with unbelievers is a betrayal of Muslims and the Islamic community on earth. This theme is particularly salient, given the generally accepted context for the revelation of the verses in question, which is the betrayal of the Islamic community by the "hypocrites" (*al-munāfiqūn*), those who pretended to be Muslim before the fall of Mecca but in fact maintained loyalties and allegiances with their Christian, Jewish, and erstwhile pagan brethren.[99] Given our discussions in the previous two sections of doctrinal opposition to Muslims aiding or strengthening non-Muslim polities, particularly at the expense of a Muslim one, this theme does not need to be dwelled on here.

The third principle is that unbelievers are inherently untrustworthy and will ultimately seek to subvert Muslim faith. This explanation for the prohibition on friendship and solidarity with non-Muslims is advanced on the basis of verses 3:118[100] and 5:51 in particular. Ibn Kathīr says simply, commenting on 5:51, that Jews and Christians are the enemies of Islam and its adherents, and allies of one another in this. Ultimately, their promises and treaties are untrustworthy.[101]

Naturally, the liberal rejoinder is that the neutral, liberal state that does not seek to use state power to advance a conception of truth will pose less of a threat to Muslim aims than states committed to a doctrine of truth in direct opposition to Islamic claims. This argument is convincing to many Muslims,[102] but certainly not to all. Some contemporary scholars do not regard the modern freedoms guaranteed by liberal regimes, and especially the aspiration to neutrality of some liberal states, as a mitigating factor on non-Muslim hostility to Islam. In fact, it is coherently argued that liberal states may in fact be worse for Muslims than avowedly Christian or Jewish states because they relegate religion to the private sphere, banish God from public morality, and give protection to immoral acts, or because of the special regard for the People of the Book accorded Christians and Jews in the Qur'an.[103] These discourses point toward an interest in an overlapping consensus with other conservative, religious doctrines in modern secular societies on either general inclinations (more religion in public) or specific points of doctrine and policy (resistance to legal protection for homosexuality, opposition to abortion, securing funding for religious schools, etc.), given the belief that secularism poses a greater threat to Islam than other faiths.[104] The latter is in fact a midway position between the various liberal ones and that of Quṭb, who naturally rejects the entire idea of shared interests with non-Muslim believers:

> A Muslim is required to show tolerance in dealing with the people of earlier revelations, but he is forbidden to have a relationship of alliance or patronage with them. His path to establish his religion and implement his unique system cannot join with theirs. No matter how kind he is to them, they will never be happy to implement his faith and establish his system. Nor will it stop them from entering other alliances to scheme against and fight the Muslims. It is too naïve to think that we and they can ever join forces to support religion in general against unbelievers and atheists. For whenever the fight is against Muslims, they join forces with the unbelievers and atheists.[105]

What both positions share, however, is a view that both the general society and the state are the locus for the implementation of the Islamic good life in a way that requires a particular form of cooperation and trust with others. The trust sought is not a form of mere promise keeping, but a shared commitment to upholding substantive moral values and combating behaviors that contradict them. The radicals and the conservatives differ primarily in terms of the comprehensiveness of consensus they demand. For Quṭb, such a level of consensus on the meaning and requirements of the Qur'an is required that very few actual Muslims, and almost no Muslim states, are worthy of solidarity. For the traditionalist conservatives, their Islamic project overlaps sufficiently with the aims of many non-Muslim conservatives to see them as trustworthy allies, at least against some forms of secularism. Thus, we have a family of positions that caution against solidarity with non-Muslims on the basis of a liberal social contract: (a) Non-Muslims will ultimately always seek to oppress and undermine Muslims when they have the chance and are thus untrustworthy; (b) true solidarity requires a shared commitment to eradicating unbelief and un-Islamic forms of power, and thus only true Muslims are trustworthy; and (c) a Muslim must live in a social environment where immorality is actively discouraged and divine authority can be acknowledged, and thus only non-Muslims who share these beliefs can be trusted.

The preceding makes a case that Islam, as a comprehensive ethical doctrine, has the resources to provide believing Muslims with reasons for rejecting some of the most basic terms of citizenship within a non-Muslim liberal democracy. As this book is not a work of historiography, it was not my aim to put all of these sources in their historical context or to speculate on the conditions in which these doctrines rather than others become mobilized. This should be a problem only if it were the case that the arguments surveyed here were articulated as applying to only a particular context, are views that are widely held to be defunct for believing Muslims, or are views that rest on methodologies, concerns, or texts no longer regarded as central to Islamic political thought, that is, if they are views that are not and could not be authoritative or compelling to present-day believing Muslims. However, as evidenced by the reference to contemporary Islamic juridical and political texts that endorse and advance these views as central to the Islamic political vision, this is clearly not the case. The general views that only Islamic political authority is just, that Muslims ought to aspire to live under such authority, that loyalty in political and martial matters is restricted to Muslim polities, and that solidarity is reserved for the community of shared moral understanding have their origins in the revelatory texts and have been reasserted frequently by a variety of religious authorities (particularly the orthodox religious scholars) across time and place.

For Islam as a comprehensive ethical doctrine to give support to an overlapping consensus on the terms of citizenship, it would thus have to provide reasons for endorsing on principled grounds positions somehow contradicting those encountered in this chapter. However, it is not enough to immediately return to the Islamic sources on the previous questions. The preceding discussion referred to, but deliberately avoiding resolving, a series of *ambiguities* related to what liberalism properly requires by way of a "doctrine of citizenship" from all (not just Muslim) citizens. Just what measure of loyalty in wartime does liberalism require of citizens? Just what ought to be the balance between the desire to bring people to one's conception of truth and the recognition of moral pluralism? Just what is a reasonable balance between the special sense of solidarity and devotion to a community of fellow believers and the feelings owed to the civic community?

Thus, it is not precisely evident what the reasonable liberal responses would be to the Islamic emphasis on *da'wa* (proselytization) in the justification of membership in a non-Muslim society, the refusal to participate in war, and the preference for solidarity with coreligionists over unbelievers. While there are often very explicit denunciations of the specific idea of citizenship in a non-Muslim society on the basis of these views, from a liberal perspective it is not immediately clear how much of the Islamic perspective has to be revised and whether any variations on these basic inclinations might be reasonable. Given that my claim is that the specific positions or legal judgments presented here are significant because they are indicative of general inclinations and attitudes within Islamic politico-legal thought, and given my avowed aim of an "equilibrium" overlapping consensus (that fully reasonable account of the minimal demands of liberal citizenship *least in conflict* with the aims and spirit of Islamic political ethics), some subtlety (and precision) appears in order for our understanding of what a reasonable Islamic response to liberal citizenship would look like. I thus turn in chapter 4 to a more abstract inquiry into the demands of liberal citizenship based on the background of opposition encountered here.

4

Identifying Equilibrium: An Ideal-Typical Islamic Doctrine of Citizenship

What is it reasonable for citizens in a liberal society to demand of Muslim fellow citizens by way of an "Islamic doctrine of citizenship" *if it is to be said that there is an overlapping consensus on the terms of social cooperation*? Given the views encountered in the previous chapter, what Islamic theological, ethical, or jurisprudential statements would be regarded as morally reasonable responses to the liberal conception of citizenship? This is an inquiry of a special nature. My interests are not directly what *policies* a liberal state should have or what *practices* on the part of citizens are compatible with justice and equality, but rather in what *views* emerging from a comprehensive doctrine are reasonable responses to the liberal terms of social cooperation. My aim is to establish, with as much precision as possible, what political liberalism demands of Muslim citizens living as minorities in liberal states by way of an ideal-typical *doctrinal affirmation of citizenship* if it is to be said that there is a consensus on the terms of social cooperation in a liberal society and thus that the comprehensive doctrine in question is providing its adherents with moral reasons for endorsing those terms. In other words, what precisely are we looking to find within Islamic sources? This is primarily an inquiry into liberal political theory, but one inspired by the special concerns, misgivings, and anxieties of a particular comprehensive doctrine.

I begin by emphasizing two distinctions. The first is between the requirements of justice and the requirements of citizenship. There are many ways in which an individual or a community can adhere to requirements of justice without actually fulfilling any duties of citizenship. This point is particularly salient for the present investigation into doctrines and the possibility of an overlapping consensus, where we are not only concerned with behavior but also with beliefs and reasons. One meets requirements of justice merely by not breaking just laws; one affirms a doctrine of citizenship only by giving certain types of reasons for not breaking them, as well as by affirming one's commitment to a particular society and political system.

The second distinction that is crucial for this study is that between a citizen and a resident alien. The notion of a resident alien, or an "alienated citizen," does not refer to legal status, but rather to someone who lives within a state, accepts some benefits of social cooperation, and renders the legal duties required of him, but does not seek to share political sovereignty with his compatriots, does not identify with the political system, and resents or is indifferent to the contribution he makes to society's welfare and security.[1] As Michael Walzer notes, some critics of liberalism argue that this is all that any member of a liberal society is or, rather, that "the modern state breeds aliens, whereas older political societies could only import them."[2] Such a critique is based on a comparison with classical republicanism and reflects a yearning for a very thick conception of citizenship.

Obviously, political liberalism is going to call for a comparatively thin conception of citizenship, but even within liberalism, there is a distinction between not breaking just laws and affirming one's citizenship. The attributes of citizenship include affirmation of the legitimacy of the political community as it is constituted, of one's contribution to its welfare and that of fellow citizens as a result of social cooperation, and of one's willingness to participate politically. This is an understanding of citizenship, whatever disagreements persist about its precise minimum requirements, as a moral choice rather than legal status. The goals and values of political liberalism—a well-ordered society, fairness, shared political sovereignty, democracy, distributive justice, stability arising from an overlapping consensus—point beyond citizenship as law-abidingness to a morally motivated commitment to a political community, the rights of fellow citizens, and a political system. Unlike matters of justice, it is not necessarily the case that the desire to avoid civic integration into a particular society, or even a desire to withdraw from it in some way, is necessarily unjust, unreasonable, or morally reprehensible. However, a doctrine of resident alienage—political quietism mixed with alienation from the community and its political system—is precisely what political liberalism seeks to avoid through its philosophy of public justification.

Based on the views encountered in the previous chapter, here I examine the contours of a reasonable Islamic affirmation of citizenship—a doctrine that is as loyal as possible to traditional Islamic aims while avoiding a stance of resident alienage or partial citizenship—in three parts: residence, loyalty, and recognition/solidarity. In all of what follows, the question is to identify only what would be indicative of an affirmation of citizenship, not what is independently morally justifiable.

Residence in a Non-Muslim State

As seen in the previous chapter, the affirmation of citizenship in a non-Muslim liberal democracy faces in classical Islamic doctrine a challenge at a very basic level. Classical Islamic law has dealt at length with the problem of Muslims residing in non-Muslim states, both in the sense of states with non-Muslim majority populations and in the sense of states run by non-Muslim law. The question in the Islamic sources takes the form of whether it is lawful for a Muslim to reside in the non-Muslim world (what is often referred to as *dār al-ḥarb* (the "abode of war") or *dār al-kufr* (the "abode of unbelief")) or whether a Muslim is obligated to migrate (perform *hijra*) to the "Abode of Islam" (*dār al-Islām*). Thus, when speaking of Muslim citizens of liberal democracies, the debate over citizenship begins with whether a Muslim may even regard a non-Muslim majority society run by non-Islamic law as a place where she may reside.

There is a tradition in Islamic law of regarding such residence as impermissible. In classical jurisprudence, this position was advanced mostly by the Mālikī school of law (predominant in North Africa), but in the modern period it has been advanced by Saudi adherents of the Wahhabi doctrine, as well as some revivalist thinkers not adhering to any single school, such as the Egyptian Sayyid Qutb. Although these authorities often claim that there is a categorical divine command to migrate from spheres of non-Muslim rule based on two Qur'anic verses and a number of reports of Prophetic speech (*ḥadīth*), more interesting for comparative political theory are the substantive arguments in favor of, or explanations of, this divine command. Muslim thinkers who regard residence in a non-Muslim polity as unlawful generally advance six types of rational arguments: (1) that Muslims must not be subject to non-Muslim laws or authority, (2) that Islam and Muslims must not be put in a position of inferiority to non-Muslims, (3) that Muslims must avoid aiding or increasing the strength of non-Muslims, (4) that Muslims are forbidden from forming bonds of friendship or solidarity with non-Muslims, (5) that Muslims are required to avoid environments of sin or indecency, and (6) that in non-Muslim environments, it will be more difficult to prevent the loss of religiosity in subsequent generations.

What is important for our purposes is that the reasons given for prohibiting residence are precisely objections to relationships with non-Muslims characteristic of bonds of citizenship. Thus, there is something crucial to emphasize for anyone wishing to explore the possibility of an overlapping consensus: that not only is it necessary to find Muslim scholars disagreeing with the idea of a prohibition on residence in a non-Muslim state but also the justifications and conditions for such residence must address these underlying objections in a way consistent with liberal terms of social cooperation; we are interested in residence in a society to which one can *belong*. To be sure, liberalism clearly does not preclude the forming of subnational communities (based on religion, culture, national origins, class, occupation, ideology, region, lifestyle, etc.). However, while these substate communities may claim a more profound or sublime sense of loyalty than the state or wider society, they should not claim predominance in the political sphere to the extent of denying the legitimacy of political arrangements that seek to protect the rights of all individuals constituting the political community, and by asserting a parallel political authority. The response of "internal retreat" violates liberal requirements of citizenship once it includes the claim to communal political-legal authority over members at the expense of the generally binding legal system. Although liberal pluralism is committed to providing certain conditions for the survival of minority groups and to protecting the right to association, these conditions cannot include general exemptions from all basic duties that apply to all citizens equally, including duties to pay taxes and obey the same laws.

A natural demand for the Islamic political imagination is for some such form of Muslim communal autonomy within individual non-Muslim states, characterized, in the first order, by the application of Islamic family law for Muslims and perhaps any other areas of the Islamic social code[3] that concern purely internal Muslim relations. For example, as discussed at length in chapter 5, classical Muslim jurists who permitted Muslim residence in non-Muslim states were adamant that it was only under the condition that Muslims were secure in their persons, faith, and property and that they had the freedom to "manifest their religion." However, there is an inherent ambiguity here as to whether "manifesting one's religion" refers to something like the religious liberties protected by a liberal state or to communal autonomy. Some jurists argue for the more demanding condition of communal autonomy; some are clearly content with private religious liberties. The role of the conjecturer in this case is to rigorously examine the arguments advanced (usually advanced in a very different context than that of a modern liberal state) and test whether the nature of the conditions for accepting a certain demand are compatible with political liberalism.

A further question relates to the realm of the ends communities seek to advance within liberal democracies. The crucial example here is the emphasis placed by Muslim thinkers on the duty of proselytizing (*da'wa*, or "calling," in Arabic). As also shown in chapter 5, Muslim jurists from the Middle Ages to the present have seen residence in non-Muslim lands as a desideratum precisely because of the opportunities it gives for spreading the Islamic message. Clearly, liberalism cannot object to a group's wish to win adherents through peaceful missionary activities. There is no question of a violation of justice here. In fact, there is an element to this justification that is *deeply affirmative* of a liberal social order, insofar as it refers to a benefit accruing to Muslims that is a core value in liberal societies, namely, religious freedom (both to proselytize and to convert). However, the conjecturer may see in this a motivation that in fact violates the spirit of citizenship if a doctrine justifies residence and belonging in a society *merely* to advance the group's communal aims. The concerns liberals have about such a justification are that (1) it risks seeing non-Muslims only as potential converts and not as free and equal citizens, (2) it does not preclude the Islamization of the state if the group someday finds itself a majority, and thus (3) it may reveal a shallow commitment to the society and state as (potentially permanently) pluralistic and secular. The general concern is that any acceptance of liberal institutions or constraints is purely tactical, rather than grounded in a principled acknowledgment of the fact of reasonable pluralism. Contrast the justification of residence from *da'wa* with a justification that points to a benefit accruing to Muslims from core liberal policies that is not merely a potential *consequence* of those policies but *intrinsic* to them, say, the inherent goodness of living in a society where one is unafraid of the arbitrary exercise of power.

Thus, there is another way in addition to seeking to assert parallel or contradictory political authority in which a minority community could fail to affirm its citizenship within a political community, and that is by passively accepting a state's political authority but seeking to avoid any meaningful contribution to it. Loyal resident alienage is a very plausible Islamic response to living in a non-Muslim society. The response would justify residence and basic political obligation but call for no meaningful engagement with the society, contribution to its self-defense or welfare, or participation in its political system. It would also place great emphasis on the conversion of non-Muslims and eventual transformation of the society and political system. There would be no call for breaking existing laws, but certainly for their ultimate Islamization. The inevitable insistence that such doctrines would result in law-abiding citizens is irrelevant; the underlying reasons and comprehensive beliefs are not contributing to support for social cooperation on liberal terms, that is, to the overlapping consensus.

To be clear: Groups that choose not to integrate themselves culturally, economically, socially, or politically into the wider society in order to pursue a collective vision of the good (such as the Amish, Dukhobors, or Haredim ubiquitous in the multicultural liberalism literature) are not, by virtue of their rejection of the wider society and its public sphere, violating any particular requirement of justice. While I am required as a citizen to regard my share of collective sovereignty as *no more* than equal to everyone else's, I am not required (by justice) to regard my own share with any great sentimentality. I am not, in most liberal democracies, required to vote. I am not required to regard my political community (nation) as my most *precious* loyalty or even one that trumps others in all contexts.[4] I am not required to cultivate a range of specific and demanding civic virtues. This is not to suggest that ghettoization might not be a political problem or something to be addressed by liberal governments. It is also not to suggest that the desire to enhance social solidarity, integration, or a civic ethos is an inappropriate object of political action or education, merely that it is difficult to assert that a group consciously turning its back on modern society and choosing to live solely in pursuit of the good is, *in this alone*, violating a requirement of justice.[5] However, this book argues that an overlapping consensus can be sought not only on requirements of justice but also on conceptions of citizenship. There is clearly an overlap to the extent that one is a citizen of a political system, and each political system is founded on a conception of justice, but as I have shown, a wide range of questions that relate to membership and belonging are not covered by justice. The need to examine these questions is particularly strong in the case of communities that—unlike the Amish, Dukhobors, or Haredim—see themselves as adhering to a universal, proselytizing faith.

Thus, the conjecturer would first seek consensus in the terms for legitimating residence in a non-Muslim state. She is not looking merely for Muslim scholars who permit such residence but for those who do so for reasons compatible with the aims of a liberal political order, reasons that would give the Muslim citizen authentic and principled reasons for regarding his state of residence as a place he can live along the terms liberalism prescribes. Based on my reading of the treatment of this question in Islamic sources, I submit that a stable and compatible doctrine of residence in a non-Muslim state would require affirmation of the following positions:

R1: The authoritative texts cited in favor of the prohibition on residence do not necessarily dictate the conclusions advanced by those jurists; there are other authoritative texts that lead to contradictory rulings, and there are reasons to regard these as more authoritative than the texts cited by pro-hijra jurists.

R2: It may be possible to fulfill the basic duty to "manifest one's religion" even in the absence of sovereign Muslim political authority and under non-Muslim political and legal authority.

R3: While great benefits to Islam, including its possible spread and the strengthening of Muslim communities, can be gained by living in non-Muslim lands, this is not the only way in which Muslims are permitted to regard their life in those societies.

Chapter 5 begins this inquiry by examining arguments for residence in a non-Muslim state from the perspective of political liberalism and the interest in an overlapping consensus on the terms of social cooperation.

Loyalty to a Non-Muslim State

Residing in a non-Muslim state, even on the "right" terms and for the "right" reasons, does not alone establish a doctrine of citizenship. A second aspect of the affirmation of belonging required of minority ethical or religious communities is the question of competing loyalties between the state of citizenship and other states or communities. The questions that we are interested in here are what it means to be loyal to one's state, what other loyalties may be consistent with that loyalty, and for what reasons it is legitimate to refuse to fight. This also requires some elaboration with special reference to Islamic concerns. These questions have traditionally been addressed in response to the pacifism of certain Christian sects, to refusal in the vein of Hobbesian individualism, and to liberal humanist or cosmopolitan objections to injustice against other humans. The Islamic case is special, however, because objections to fighting come not from pacifism, individual self-preservation, or cosmopolitanism but rather from a doctrine of loyalty to the global political community of fellow Muslims (the *umma*). The concern arises that refusal may point to nothing more than a rejection of civic commitment to a non-Muslim society.

As demonstrated in the previous chapter, Muslim citizens have traditional doctrines prohibiting service in a non-Muslim army and discouraging identification with the interests of a non-Muslim state. In the interests of being systematic, I present the following five specific points of Islamic doctrine as covering the range of potentially incompatible positions on the question of civic loyalty to a non-Muslim state (see the previous chapter for the sources underpinning these positions).

1. A Muslim may never combat another Muslim in the service of unbelievers, regardless of the cause.
2. A war for the sole purpose of expanding the space ruled by Islam and Islamic law is a just war, a legitimate form of *jihād*.
3. It may be the duty of every individual Muslim, even those residing outside the Islamic polity, to contribute to a legitimate *jihād*, if so called by a legitimate Imam.
4. A Muslim may not advance the cause of unbelievers or uphold non-Islamic rulings and truth-claims.
5. A Muslim may not sacrifice his life for other than certain causes, of which defending a non-Muslim society is not one.

Without making any assumptions about the popularity of these positions among any present-day Muslim community, it is plain that there is a very explicit doctrinal background that could cause a Muslim to doubt the legitimacy of her loyalty to a non-Muslim state. From the perspective of political liberalism, the most problematic views are the following: that a Muslim may not recognize his non-Muslim state's unqualified right to existence, that he may not regard himself as under any personal duty of restraint toward his state of citizenship, and that he may not feel he can defend his state of residence, even against a non-Muslim aggressor, solely because of the non-Islamic character of that society's political system. What then would a Muslim citizen have to proclaim for it to be said that he is balancing his loyalties to his community of fellow believers and his duty to his state of citizenship?

Two obvious, or near-obvious, positions can be immediately established:

L1: Hostilities on the part of Muslim forces against a non-Muslim state are justified only in self-defense or to counter aggression and not to facilitate the spread of Islam or to change the government of a state in which Muslims are not oppressed.

I argue later that there is considerable scope for reasonable disagreement on just war theory; however, a citizen who holds that it may be just for another state to invade his state for the sole purpose of changing its political system, when that political system does not oppress him, is not being reasonable, in the most basic sense of proposing and being willing to abide by fair terms of social cooperation. Of course, the fundamentalist may feel that merely by being forced to live under non-Islamic law she is being oppressed. But this is not inconsistent with her acknowledging that she enjoys equal civil rights and liberties to those of all other citizens. She may feel that her non-Muslim fellow citizens are oppressed as well by being "forced to live under man-made law." It is also not inconsistent with her recognizing that being denied equal liberal rights (to property, fair trial, freedom of religion, freedom of expression, etc.)

would be an additional and different form of oppression. Thus, L1 refers to a situation in which Muslims are treated as free and equal citizens within a secular political regime. Controlling for what the Muslim and the liberal would both regard as "oppression" (unequal civil rights), the reasonable Muslim citizen regards the mere fact of secular legislation as insufficient grounds for forcible regime change.

Note that L1 excludes from an overlapping consensus the following variation on position (2):

> (2a) A war for the sole purpose of expanding the space ruled by Islam and Islamic law is a just war, a legitimate form of *jihād*. However, not every single Muslim is required to join in such efforts or regard his participation as an individual duty. Muslims residing in non-Muslim states are required to uphold their tacit or express promise to those states not to harm them.[6]

Although asserting (2) or (2a) need not qualify as a crime,[7] the views in those statements characterize doctrines well outside the most flexible and inclusive possible overlapping consensus. In terms of a doctrine of citizenship, our understanding of the requirement that religious or cultural minorities see their membership in a liberal society as legitimate would obviously imply the principled condemnation of violence used against it, not just personal abstention from such violence.

A second principle of loyalty thus follows:

> L2: In conflicts between a non-Muslim state in which Muslims live and a Muslim force, a Muslim may forswear on grounds of principle any active aid to the Muslim force and promise to engage in no violent activities against their non-Muslim state.

My phrasing of this principle is neutral as to the cause and moral status of the war. That is, should the Muslim or non-Muslim state be regarded as the aggressor, a Muslim citizen should regard a liberal state of citizenship as inviolable in this way. From the Islamic perspective, this in fact involves two separate positions: that a Muslim need not contribute to the fulfillment of the collective duty to expand the realm of Islam and that a Muslim need not discharge his individual duty to contribute to the self-defense of Muslim lands by attacking his state of residence or citizenship. It is clearly the latter that is more problematic from an Islamic standpoint (although, as cited previously, even many of the more radical Islamist groups operating in Western countries affirm it). However, even from a liberal perspective, it requires justification and clarification.

Consider a citizen who feels that his state is waging an unjust war or maintaining an unjust law. Liberalism holds that political obligation does not always require obedience in these cases.[8] Refusal to fight in an unjust war or to obey an unjust law is thus not generally considered a rejection of one's citizenship in what is otherwise a liberal democracy. Two questions then confront us: On what grounds may a citizen regard a war (or law) as unjust? What forms of opposition to these injustices, in addition to refusal, are consistent with affirmation of one's citizenship in such a state?

On the first question, the first observation from the liberal perspective is that while the burdens of judgment will result in reasonable pluralism about the moral status of certain wars, some objections to war will be clearly unreasonable, or incompatible with the basic moral reasoning of other citizens. For example, a common Islamic response to the wars in Afghanistan and Iraq is that they are unjust simply because of the religious identities of the parties—a Muslim must oppose these wars simply because non-Muslims are attacking Muslims. This view makes no distinctions based on cause, war aims, or conduct within war. The view is that a Muslim may not regard his non-Muslim state's use of force against any Muslim as legitimate for any reason, even self-defense. This form of reasoning is thus outright unreasonable in failing to recognize fellow citizens as enjoying a basic moral status. Any further reasoning about the permissibility of various forms of resistance to unjust wars already rests on premises that reveal a basic unreasonableness and, thus, a lack of affirmation of liberal citizenship.

However, this form of unreasonableness need not be the case. First, it may be the case that there is reasonable disagreement on the actual motives and necessity of a given war.[9] Thus, an unreasonable citizen says the United States acted unjustly in responding to the September 11 attacks by invading Afghanistan because a non-Muslim state may never attack Muslims. There is no disputation here that the September 11 attacks were the work of an entity in Afghanistan, that military response would be an effective prevention of future attacks, or even that a military response would involve unjust collateral damage. A reasonable citizen, on the other hand, might say that the United States acted wrongly in invading because it was not necessary or effective for preventing future attacks or that it could not be done without intolerable collateral damage. We may regard this citizen as wrong or as not demonstrating to a sufficient degree that his position proves the invasion unjust but concede that he advances reasons that are consistent with recognizing his fellow citizens' legitimate rights.[10]

Also, it may perfectly well be the case that a domestically liberal state acts illiberally, even unjustly, abroad. There might be a consensus between various just war doctrines that *in this case* the war was unprovoked, disproportionate, or motivated by some other purpose, such as power, glory, domination, economic gain, or territorial expansion. Even if a Muslim citizen who advances this objection is largely motivated by the fact of Muslim suffering (she does not raise similar objections or skepticisms about her state's wars against non-Muslim states, or does not raise them so vociferously), she may still be supported by a range of comprehensive doctrines in her view that the war is unjust, just as some Black Nationalists in the 1960s may have been largely motivated by particularist sentiments but still correct in their condemnation of racist policies.

So let us grant that a Muslim citizen may regard one of her state's wars as unjust and that she may be strongly supported in this view by other just war doctrines. The question then arises as to what forms of disobedience or opposition are compatible with support for liberal citizenship. (Again, the question is not simply what ought to be *permitted* in a liberal society but whether we think a citizen who *believes* that x is justified is capable of giving support to liberal terms of social cooperation.) The most plausible argument that one could take up violent action against their liberal state of citizenship yet still not be advancing a general doctrine incompatible with citizenship in that state would be something like the following:

1. To view something as unjust may be reasonably interpreted as to will it to cease. To will something to cease must also imply that some actions taken toward that end are willed. Unjust actions may thus be countered with actions designed to stop them.
2. Such actions, to be morally permissible, must be necessary, proportionate, and directed at the morally responsible agents.
3. Many unjust actions involve violence. Peaceful acts of resistance may be either ineffectual or impose further unbearable costs on those already transgressed against. Violent acts may thus be more effective than nonviolent ones and, if proportionate to the original injustice and directed only at morally responsible agents, not instances of a further injustice.

Let us pause here. What I think is fairly uncontroversial is that a loyal citizen may wish for his state's unjust actions to cease and recognize that certain countervailing actions may be necessary. In the case of an unjust war of aggression, he may also recognize the right of other peoples to resist, just as he claims this right for himself. Thus, I see no incoherence or disloyalty in his recognizing that the violence directed against his state's military forces by other forces legitimately resisting is legitimate. In this recognition, he is merely expressing his wish for his liberal state to act more justly.

However, our question deals with such a citizen taking a further step and actively helping the resistance to injustice, specifically through direct violent action. The argument would thus have to involve something like:

4. All moral agents have a duty to advance justice. If violent action in resistance to initial aggression is deemed to be justified in principle, no autonomous moral agent's action in support of this justified resistance can be deemed unjustified, as long as it remains within the bounds of proportionality and is directed at morally responsible agents.

The argument here is essentially that if the liberal state of citizenship acts so unjustly in the first place, it surrenders any legitimate expectation of loyalty. An apposite example is that of John Brown (or, rather, "John Brown," since I do not wish to be responsible for accuracy or nuance in historical interpretation). Can it be said that "John Brown," in violently attacking agents of slavery when the responsible political authorities had failed to do so, is thereby demonstrating adherence to a comprehensive doctrine incompatible with liberal citizenship? That is, why is the ideal-typical position "I pledge loyalty to my political community and promise to defend it against aggressors but make no commitment to supporting or even tolerating in its own injustices" so different from the position "I consent to obey the laws of my society legitimately enacted so long as they do not violate fundamental principles of justice"? And if the former is not obviously of a different nature morally from the latter, could we not imagine that similar standards of reasonableness would be met by an ideal-typical Islamic position something like "I pledge loyalty to my non-Muslim state of residence so long as it respects my rights, provides me with security, and does not transgress egregiously against my brother Muslims"?

To understand why something like L2 is still required, we must accept certain beliefs about the relationship that is formed by citizenship and the nature of democratic commitment. To be committed to citizenship in a liberal democracy is, perhaps, to be committed primarily to realizing certain values and principles. That is why loyalty to a state or nation can never be absolute, because such a state or nation is only worthy of loyalty as much as it is itself loyal to those principles over a long period of time. However, an affirmation of citizenship, rather than a commitment to justice, is not just an affirmation of those principles in the abstract but an affirmation of a particular long-term project of realizing those principles. Moreover, political community, however intimately defined in terms of principles of justice, is also an exercise and a practice of pursuing many other things besides justice, such as welfare, solidarity, and prosperity, and all of this in the real cauldron of history and through the actions of real people with the normal range of human motivations.

Thus, the traditional liberal justification of civil disobedience and the refusal to fight presumes a certain stance of "loyal opposition" where the citizen disobeys or refuses, not out of either selfishness or rejection of her membership in the political community, but precisely in affirmation of that membership. The citizen who disobeys out of principle does not do so lightly or in response to every policy with which she disagrees. Furthermore, she often expects and accepts punishment for this disobedience, not just resignedly or even for propagandistic effect, but to express her overall commitment to the rule of law and the democratic community that sustains it. This stance also draws on (but, in turn, is limited by) the belief in the capacity of democratic institutions to (eventually) rectify injustices and on the citizen's long-term commitment to the community's development in the direction of justice.

By contrast, violence represents an exit from the community and a disavowal of the democratic process that disobedience and refusal (including, say, a refusal to pay the proportion of one's taxes that support an unjust war) do not. This is not to say that such an exit may never be a morally reasonable response. It may. But it is not "citizenship." It is not a commitment to sustaining, supporting, and reforming the institutions of a political system one endorses. It is not a commitment to a long-term relationship that may at times disappoint but, in balance, satisfies more than any other. Of course, a political system may prove itself over a sufficiently long period to be too corrupt or too indifferent to its historical ideals. But with an exit via the resort to violence in such a case, it is no longer clear that we are dealing with our central concern: endorsement of reasonable terms of social cooperation in a liberal democracy. This may be the case with my reference to "John Brown," insofar as the United States prior to the Civil War was not a just society.

To return to our specific inquiry, here is a current example. A Muslim citizen who regards the present U.S. occupation of Iraq as unjust would not be advancing an unreasonable view. Furthermore, Islamic doctrine gives this citizen far more resources for defending this view than the simplistic "non-Muslims may never attack Muslims" attitude I presented earlier. She may give reasons similar enough to those non-Muslim citizens may offer: The war was unprovoked, it has resulted in intolerable civilian casualties, and the United States is not obviously materially disinterested. These views could result in the reasonable position that violent resistance against this occupation is morally justified (which is not to say that it is the only or the most reasonable position). As I argued before, this conclusion is susceptible to the further argument that therefore any moral agent is justified in aiding this just resistance, even violently. On this view, it is the unjust war, not the citizen's unreasonable comprehensive doctrine, that has produced this situation.

According to the reasoning I presented, the response of the political liberal can only be that this person has given up on the capacity of democratic communities to correct their mistakes and has demonstrated a certain disinterest in her own long-term investment in the community's moral progress. And this, to be clear, all presumes the *charitable* interpretation of the citizen's reasoning: that it is based on considerations of justice that are potentially part of an overlapping consensus, and not a cruder form of Muslim communalism or in-group solidarity. We thus defend L2 on these grounds: If a Muslim citizen regards a war waged by his state of citizenship as unjust for reasons that are potentially reasonable or principled, then his decision to oppose this war through violent action reflects, if not itself injustice, then a repudiation of the long-term relationship that characterizes citizenship; if this citizen regards a war waged by his state of citizenship as unjust for reasons that reflect rather a basic lack of recognition of that state's legitimate rights, then his comprehensive doctrine is not reasonable to begin with in the way required by political liberalism.

We come now to a much more complicated set of questions about when it becomes unreasonable for Muslim citizens to fight in or otherwise support the self-defense efforts of the society that has guaranteed them security and equal rights and liberties and, in general, provided the conditions of their daily life. Let us begin by assuming that affirming the right of one's political community to defend itself against aggression (L1) is both a necessary and *sufficient* just war doctrine for a citizen to hold. That it is sufficient suggests that this is all a citizen must proclaim; a citizen who refuses to fight in an unjust war abroad cannot be accused of holding a doctrine incompatible with liberal citizenship. I accept as established the traditional liberal right to conscientious refusal to fight in wars that can be regarded as unjust from a moral perspective.[11] Even a citizen who refuses to fight in a war that may be just but not one of self-defense—think of humanitarian invasions or preventive wars—can hardly be accused of denying that his society enjoys the basic right to self-defense.

Thus, whether requests for conscientious objection may be part of a comprehensive moral doctrine compatible with liberal citizenship can be problematic only if the war is one of self-defense and if the reasons that motivate certain citizens to so refuse reflect an underlying unwillingness to propose and abide by fair terms of cooperation and a lack of recognition of their political community's basic legitimate rights.[12] The concern in the case of Islam as a comprehensive doctrine is that because it commands believers to defend their Muslim-majority political community, their unwillingness to fight for their non-Muslim political community may reflect indifference, lack of commitment, or, in the worst case, contempt for that community's legitimate interests.

Let us begin with the most difficult situation from an Islamic perspective, when a Muslim may be required to defend a state of citizenship against a Muslim force. Based on the original Islamic positions (1) and (2) we might encounter the following position:

> (1') No Muslim is permitted to fight in a non-Muslim army, even to defend a territory in which he lives and is not oppressed, when the opposing force is a Muslim one.

Here we pick up where our discussion in defense of L2 left off. This position seems to strain the boundaries of tolerance and appear analogous to an ethnic or national minority during a war between his state of citizenship and the country of his coethnics. What distinguishes the two cases, however, is that in the national minority case we have a *simple* clash of loyalties between national communities: The minority would prefer to live with its coethnics and makes no pretense of membership in another *nation*. In the Muslim case, however, we might be dealing with a religious obligation to never kill another Muslim. He might not reject the host community as such, and might be willing to defend it against non-Muslim aggressors, but faces a conflict of obligations and prefers not to shed certain kinds of blood. He seems not to have clearly chosen his fellow citizens over his fellow Muslims, but it is also not yet clear that he has done the reverse.

If he proclaims himself unwilling to kill fellow Muslims but also unwilling to aid them or damage his fellow citizens by any acts of commission (i.e., he affirms L2), we may just be willing to recognize this neutrality as a sufficient declaration of civic loyalty. To even consider a position like (1') for inclusion in an overlapping consensus, we would first require that it be combined with L2 in something like the following way:

> (1a) No Muslim is permitted to fight in a non-Muslim army, even to defend a territory in which he lives and is not oppressed, when the opposing force is a Muslim one. However, if the Muslim has been given security, treated fairly, and allowed to manifest his religion in that territory, he may not join the forces of the invading Muslim army and may not engage in any acts of sabotage or obstruction of the non-Muslim state's efforts to defend itself.

What we are specifically looking to establish is that the citizen does no harm to the society's vital interests by any of his actions or refusals to act, and that he is committed to no declaration of the illegitimacy of the acts performed by his fellow citizens (i.e., he also affirms L1). The latter requirement refers again to the *reasons* used by a citizen to justify positions such as (1') or (1a). We want to know both that the citizen seeks exemption because of a specific divine imperative not to kill fellow Muslims (rather than out of a desire to see his state of citizenship conquered) and that his promise to engage in no acts of sabotage or betrayal are advanced for *principled* reasons (rather than a desire to avoid punishment).

Thus, the following statements might support the claim that a citizen can assert (1') and (1a) and still be holding a doctrine eligible for the overlapping consensus:

> (1b) No Muslim is permitted to fight in a non-Muslim army, even to defend a territory in which he lives and is not oppressed, when the opposing force is a Muslim one because the Qur'an and *ḥadīth* have proclaimed it a sin for a Muslim to kill a fellow Muslim.

This position makes it clear that he fears angering God by doing something rather than supports the efforts of an invading Muslim force to conquer a non-Muslim state. Similarly, we prefer an elaboration of (1a) along the following grounds:

> (1c) If the Muslim has been given security, treated fairly, and allowed to manifest his religion in that territory, he may not join the forces of the invading Muslim army and may not engage in any acts of sabotage or obstruction of the non-Muslim state's efforts to defend itself because he has to that point accepted the protection and benefits of living in that state and thus contracted himself not to harm it.

This addendum to (1a) makes it clear that the Muslim citizen feels a certain moral obligation to the non-Muslim society and his non-Muslim fellow citizens, insofar as he considers the duty not to violate contracts or promises a moral obligation derived from religion. He not only fears worldly punishment for acting against the interests of his state, but divine punishment for committing a sin. For our purposes, this demonstrates that he is capable of proposing and abiding by fair terms of social cooperation.

However, let us consider that the liberal state has enacted a policy of *conscription* for the war of self-defense. The argument might be made then that what the dissenting citizen is requesting is an unfair exemption from the duty to perform an act that all citizens have the obligation to perform, like paying taxes. Why should a citizen's personal conscience not be grounds for an exemption from all demands of commission? What is additionally problematic is that the citizen has not declared certain acts as unjust per se but only when done to certain people. It might thus be claimed that the individual does not in fact have a conscientious objection at all because he does not assert universal principles applying to the conduct of war but rather arbitrary principles, depending on the identity of the agent and the object. Our question is, thus, whether this privileging of a claim of another community over the claim of one's fellow citizens is a violation of the duties of citizenship.

I want to consider the idea that it depends on the precise weight of each claim. If one's moral claim to an individual whom he regards as a fellow member of a special community of humans is to not kill him or do him grave damage, and the claim to another political community (in which he enjoys protection and freedom) is that of discharging his individual share of a collective duty that does not rely for success on his individual performance, then our specifically *liberal* conception of citizenship ought to tolerate exemption on these grounds. By contrast, declaring that one's lack of recognition of the political community (even one in which one is not oppressed) forbids one from contributing to its welfare through paying fair taxes demonstrates an indifference to the community and its legitimate interests in a way that refusing to kill for it does not. The point here is that the (Islamic) duty not to kill fellow Muslims is not symmetrical to the (civic) duty to discharge one's share of a collective obligation. The former is far weightier than the latter.

What I believe this suggests is that holding specifically position (1b) does not commit the Muslim in question to the position that he has no obligations to his state of citizenship or that *any* duty to fellow Muslims (no matter how trivial) outweighs *any* duty to fellow citizens (no matter how weighty). Thus, what is determinant in this case are three factors: (a) that the duty to fellow Muslims is particularly weighty in a moral sense (the duty not to kill), (b) that his exemption from a collective duty will itself not result in the society's inability to achieve a legitimate and necessary goal, and (c) that he has not proclaimed the *illegitimacy* of a non-Muslim society's efforts to defend itself, even against Muslim forces. Thus, we may say that a Muslim citizen who affirms L1 and L2, who explains his support for L2 though a statement like (1c) (i.e., that his promise not to harm his political community is *principled*), and who explains his request for exemption through a statement like (1b) (i.e., that it is based on a desire to avoid sin and next-worldly punishment, not a desire for the defeat of his political community) is affirming reasonable views about the rights of his political community and his duties toward it.

This discussion has, however, revealed the precise limits of the balancing act between the two competing loyalties. The preceding discussion assumes that the reasonable Muslim citizen is making an earnest effort to discharge both his civic and his religious obligations and that there may be an equilibrium where he does no vital harm to either community. This equilibrium is disturbed, however, when it is imagined that the self-defense efforts of a society require for success the contribution of all adult citizens. Let us also suppose that he regards noncombatant service as impermissible, say, according to the *ḥadīth*: "He who kills a believer by even half a word will meet God with no hope of His mercy written on his face." However improbable this may be, given modern warfare, let us suppose that a Muslim community does vital damage to its political society even by remaining passive, and does so for no other reason than the narrow one of wishing not to kill fellow Muslims. Only here does it become clear that the failure to choose between communities becomes, in fact, a choice. The Muslim may assert no wish for his society to be conquered (L1) but is in fact wishing for this *less* than he wishes to obey God, as he imagines God requires. Here he joins the class of partial citizens or semialiens, along with all committed pacifists.

From the perspective of political liberalism, the most blatantly problematic request for exemption is when a non-Muslim state is seeking to defend itself against the aggression of another *non-Muslim* force. We can synthesize the sentiments expressed in the Islamic positions (4) and (5) into the following plausible statement:

> (4') No Muslim is permitted to fight in any non-Muslim army, even to defend a territory in which he lives and is not oppressed, and even when the aggressing force is not a Muslim one.

This case appears to represent repudiation of citizenship in this state, and perhaps even the form of loyal resident alienage that Walzer discusses. It is enough to say that a doctrine that declares it impermissible for Muslims to help defend a society in which they live, are not oppressed, and are not facing a conflict of loyalties fails to recognize the legitimacy of the political community and its reasonable interests. What is decisive in this case is that the Muslim citizen seems to have no absolute doctrine of pacifism and no conflicting moral or religious obligation to another community or agent that is being violated in the act of aiding the legitimate self-defense of the community. The weakness of the reasons for refusal seems to suggest a simple failure to regard the community in which he lives as one in which he has a stake and the welfare and security of which are of crucial importance to him, attitudes that are both foundational to the spirit of citizenship.

However, even this case may be more complicated than it appears. The crucial factor in determining whether a Muslim can assert (4') and still be said to hold a doctrine of citizenship compatible with that of political liberalism are the types of reasons cited in defense of it. Consider the following synthesis of the views supporting position (4):

> (4a) No Muslim is permitted to fight in any non-Muslim army, even to defend a territory in which he lives and is not oppressed, and even when the aggressing force is not a Muslim one, because it is impermissible for him to advance the cause of unbelievers or to uphold the laws of unbelief.

In this case, the reasons advanced in support of a refusal to contribute do, in fact, reveal an utter lack of solidarity with fellow citizens—something approaching an attitude of contempt. Non-Muslims cannot be supported no matter what their treatment of Muslims has been, simply because of their comprehensive doctrine. However, consider:

(4b) No Muslim is permitted to fight in any non-Muslim army, even to defend a territory in which he lives and is not oppressed, and even when the aggressing force is not a Muslim one, because his life has been made sacred and it is impermissible to expose oneself to danger except for the purpose of exaltation of the Word of God, and the glorification of religion, which are not present in this case.

This justification seems at first glance similar if one understands "the exaltation of religion" as a euphemism for fighting for Muslim communal interests. However, what if one understands it to be a divine imperative to not expose something sacred and inviolable (a Muslim's own life) to mortal danger, except in a few expressly delineated cases? We might interpret the Muslim invoking (4b) as saying: "Strictly speaking, we can't die for this cause because God has not permitted it, and it would thus be a sin to do so; however, under the terms of citizenship, we are not allowed to violate your legitimate interests through any form of betrayal, and we are allowed to contribute in noncombatant capacities." Here it becomes clear that the reasons invoked for exemption are (a) sincerely held and of a principled nature, (b) not grounded in indifference or contempt for one's non-Muslim fellow citizens, and (c) not incompatible with contributing to the state of citizenship in nonviolent ways that are also on principled grounds. In fact, like the case of refusing to fight against an aggressing Muslim force when the survival of the society depends on such contribution, the Muslim citizen whose *only reason* for refusing to fight is his belief that God has not allowed him to die for this reason is approaching the traditional grounds for refusal advanced by Quakers or other Christian pacifists. In such a case, we might judge that (4b) represents a doctrine compatible with political liberalism but creating a hybrid citizen-alien doctrine, whereas (4') alone and (4a) are blatantly incompatible.

If this is correct, and if it is also correct that a Muslim's abstention from a war of self-defense against an aggressing Muslim force is reasonable when he has affirmed L1 and L2, and explained his abstention according to (1b) and (1c), then the only additional principle of civic loyalty required from Islamic sources would be the following:

L3: In conflicts when the non-Muslim state in which Muslims live is under attack by another non-Muslim force, and thus no conflict of loyalty or theological imperative is at stake, it is permissible to contribute in some substantive way to the self-defense efforts of the non-Muslim state.

Leaving the meaning of "substantive contribution" vague enough to include both combatant and noncombatant service, I submit that this position represents an equilibrium between the concerns of political liberalism and those of Islamic doctrine. Note that it is always possible that a Muslim could affirm on principled, Islamic grounds such noncombatant service even against an aggressing Muslim force (especially if he asserts L1), which would represent a more robust version of this position.

Chapter 6 is devoted to Islamic affirmations of these three broad positions.

Recognition of and Solidarity with Non-Muslims

Implicit in the preceding discussions of residence and loyalty was an attitude not only toward a particular space or government but also toward the other citizens living in that society. Much of what was discussed in the previous two sections points to an attitude of recognition on the part of Muslims toward non-Muslims, insofar as we require Muslims to view non-Muslims not *merely* as potential converts and non-Muslim societies as potential objects of loyalty. Affirmation of the inviolability of non-Muslim life and property as a basic religious duty arising from a contract between two parties would go a long way toward grounding the recognition of equality in the public sphere, which is a basic requirement of citizenship in a pluralist society. The topics covered in the previous section do not, however, necessarily lead to a doctrine of recognition or civic solidarity, understood as a willingness to contribute to common social and political goals in a condition of equality. Such willingness, I submit, would suggest a more robust recognition of the other as a civic equal than does the mere recognition of the state as having valid claims on subjects enjoying its protection. The latter could conceivably be achieved under a rubric of relations between distinct communities or units, as it has indeed traditionally been conceived in Islamic juridical and political theories.

Recall from the section on residence in a non-Muslim state that there is a tradition in Islamic jurisprudence that prohibits living in a non-Muslim state because Muslims are forbidden from forming bonds of friendship or solidarity with non-Muslims. This view is often thought to be an injunction based on a number of Qur'anic verses, including:

> Let not the believers take the infidels for their allies in preference to the believers—for who does this has nothing to do with God—unless it be to protect yourselves from them in this way. God warns you about Himself and the final goal is to God. [3:28]
>
> Oh you who believe! Do not take for your intimates other than your own kind. They will continually cause you turmoil and love anything that will distress you. Loathing has already come forth from their mouths and what is concealed in their breasts is even greater. We have made the signs clear to you if you will use your reason. [3:118]

As discussed in the previous chapter, for those who read the "*muwālāh* verses" as having both a literal and a general application, and thus as discouraging all forms of solidarity with non-Muslims, these verses are underpinned, clarified, or explained primarily by three ethico-political principles: that putting one's trust in unbelievers is a form of rejection of God and His promises, that alliance and friendship with unbelievers is a betrayal of Muslims and the Islamic community on earth, and that unbelievers are inherently untrustworthy and will ultimately seek to subvert Muslim faith. For many Muslim scholars, from conservative-traditionalists to more radical revivalists, secular self-restraint on the part of non-Muslim states does not mitigate the basic mistrust, given the view that both the general society and the state ought to be the locus for the implementation of the Islamic good life in a way that requires a particular form of cooperation and trust with others. The trust sought is not a form of mere promise keeping, but a shared commitment to uphold substantive moral values and combat behaviors that contradict them. Thus, we have a family of positions that caution against solidarity with non-Muslims on the basis of a liberal social contract. Scholars inclined toward this position who still see residence in non-Muslim lands as permissible tend to recommend some form of self-segregation for Muslim communities or endorse political obligation on the grounds that these lands will someday have Muslim majorities. A very small number take the medieval designation of non-Muslim lands as the "abode of war" literally and claim that the ethics of war permit Muslims to regard non-Muslim life, property, and honor as licit.[13]

This is the Islamic background to our emphasis on the need to ground Islamically a doctrine of recognition and social solidarity. The very idea of forming meaningful bonds of affection and cooperation with non-Muslims is rejected by some classical and contemporary fundamentalist thinkers. Bearing this in mind, what would political liberalism require by way of an alternative Islamic doctrine of recognition and solidarity with fellow citizens regarded as "moral others"?

This question of the moral other (or the differentiation between out-group and in-group moral others) is more of a concern of Continental political thought, where it is often treated in terms of the concept of "recognition." It is an important theme, for example, in Habermas's discourse ethics and Charles Taylor's neo-Hegelian communitarianism, both of which consider that the rights-based approach of Rawls, Dworkin, Ackerman, and others is necessary but not sufficient for grounding the totality of our moral obligations to fellow citizens, many of which are present more in informal relations than in formal ones. These theorists are sensitive to the ways in which institutions in both the public sphere and civil society are paramount in the creation of socialized human "selves." Taylor writes:

> Our identity is partly shaped by recognition or its absence, often by the *mis*recognition of others, and so a person or group of people can suffer real damage, real distortion, if the people or society around them mirror back to them a confining or demeaning or contemptible picture of themselves. Nonrecognition or misrecognition can inflict harm, can be a form of oppression, imprisoning someone in a false, distorted, and reduced mode of being. . . . Misrecognition shows not just a lack of due respect. It can inflict a grievous wound, saddling its victims with a crippling self-hatred. Due recognition is not just a courtesy we owe people. It is a vital human need.[14]

Seyla Benhabib:

> We should view human cultures as constant creations, recreations, and negotiations of imaginary boundaries between "we" and the "other(s)." The "other" is always also within us and is one of us.

> A self is a self only because it distinguishes itself from a real, or more often than not imagined, "other." Struggles for recognition among individuals and groups are really efforts to negate the status of "otherness," insofar as otherness is taken to entail disrespect, domination, and inequality. Individuals struggle to attain respect, self-worth, freedom and equality while also retaining some sense of selfhood. I argue that the task of *democratic equality* is to create the impartial institutions in the public sphere and civil society where this struggle for the recognition of cultural differences and the contestation for cultural narratives can take place without domination.[15]

When dealing with the context of multiculturalism, the obligation to extend recognition to the other is primarily the obligation of the social majority or dominant group. To the extent that "American nationhood" has been constructed as "white" or, at least, "not-black," the duty of recognition consists in negating this construction. To the extent that French selfhood is defined as "not-Muslim" or "not-Arab," theorists of recognition will see a duty to redefine such selfhood in terms that do not result in the inherent marginalization of the original imaginary. These concerns lead to a constant sensitivity to the informal, subtle, and often disguised attempts to assert a "universal selfhood" around particular and local characteristics.

It is these insights that in cultural and social movements lead to the frequent emphasis not merely on rectifying legal injustices but on altering social attitudes toward marginalized and overburdened groups. It is crucial to this thinking that altering such attitudes or images is not instrumental, or functional, in securing more "fundamental" political and economic rights. Thinking on recognition, "voice," "presence," and such matters has emphasized how domination can persist even after the equalization of formal political rights, as well as the *inherent* harm in failing to recognize the experiences and perspectives of certain groups.

It would be wrong to say that these are themes ignored or belittled by Rawlsian or other liberal theories of justice. Rawls, for example, includes "the social bases of self-respect" among his primary goods, which might be an analogue to the concept of recognition. Raz writes that since, "for most people, membership in their cultural group is a major determinant of their sense of who they are . . . slighting one's culture, persecuting it, holding it up for ridicule, slighting its value, etc., affect members of that group. Such conduct hurts them and offends their dignity."[16] Furthermore, the rigorous emphasis on equality and the exclusion of morally arbitrary characteristics from among the legitimate reasons for distributing social goods unequally give rights liberals a certain language for talking about recognition and informal oppression. It is perhaps best to see the two traditions as complementary, with different priorities and emphases. Rights go only so far, but it is important to remember that it is precisely our *liberal value commitments* that make us concerned not only about formal freedoms but also the value of those freedoms, not only about formal equality but also substantive equality of opportunity.

There is, thus, a wide range of moral obligations *toward* Muslim minorities grounded in the duty of recognition, in addition to the legally protected freedoms of speech, religion, and association, that liberals are willing to acknowledge. For example, to the extent that public space is used at the moment for cultural and religious expression by the majority (nativity scenes, etc.), it should also be open to minorities for this use.[17] Media outlets, as well as political institutions, should not only take into account the interests and perspectives of cultural minorities (or oppressed groups as such, which do not have to be a minority) but also should be open to those groups to speak publicly for themselves in the most authentic way possible. Steps should be taken to counter aggressive and unfair portrayals of groups in the media. The heritage and practice of Islam should be publicly affirmed as valuable, rather than merely tolerated in private. And so on.

To which points, the liberal makes two qualifications. The first is that there are clear limits to recognition. The obvious limits on our tolerance of *practices* ("No free exercise for Aztecs," as William Galston likes to say[18]) implies a similar limit on our duty to refrain from public criticism. Our duty not to stigmatize, perpetuate harmful stereotypes, or treat an entire civilizational tradition as worthless cannot constitute a taboo on intercultural comparisons or criticism. As mentioned in my introduction to Part I, a multicultural liberal is someone sensitive not only to the asymmetries in power between dominant groups and subaltern groups but also to those between individuals within groups and is unimpressed by arguments that members of socially privileged groups are doing wrong by criticizing internal practices of minority groups that may involve the oppression of vulnerable members within those groups. Liberal value commitments to equality of opportunity, neutrality, freedom of association, and toleration help ground a liberal multiculturalism, but liberals will hold "that appeals to 'cultural diversity' and pluralism under no circumstances trump the value of basic liberal rights."[19] The requirement to recognize the value of cultures and other experiences is not an obligation to abstain from intercultural comparisons of value,[20] or an obligation to the cultural products of a given tradition, but primarily an obligation to *persons*. One of the ways in which we treat them equally and with respect is to try to enter into their system of cultural production with sympathy and not assume that their equality is contingent upon their conversion to our cultural system, but given that this is a commitment to *persons* (and not cultures as such), we may have other commitments to those same persons that trump that of cultural recognition.

The second is that the requirement of recognition goes both ways. Although it is usually the majority or the dominant group that has failed to recognize the groups it has oppressed (and thus rather absurd to talk about an obligation on the part of African Americans or women to "recognize" the white, male experience), in certain cases, the demand of mutual recognition between weaker and stronger parties might not be absurd. A group might be weak and oppressed in a certain context but powerful in another, or the powerful, dominating group might be in some way threatened by the other. To take three examples, Protestants in Northern Ireland, Jews in Israel, and whites in

South Africa all constitute dominant groups who have been the subject of resistance to their superior position by their respective "others." But in each case, the stronger group's position of dominance and policy of oppression conceals (or is the open response to) an inherent insecurity, usually caused by their own nonnative status and "the other's" demographic superiority and national aspirations. A group may be wealthy, politically hegemonic, and militarily unassailable but still lack something it needs for a secure, confident existence that only the other can give. A group may be poor, politically dispossessed, and left with limited means of resistance, but possessed of a certain cultural authenticity or demographic confidence. It is thus not absurd or unreasonable in these cases for the three groups in question, while conceding rights or rectifying past injustices, to demand from their respective weaker "other" some form of recognition not only of *their* right to live where they do securely but of the authenticity of their legitimate experiences and desires.

The second context in which mutual recognition might not be an absurd demand is when the community is defined not in historically contingent or cultural terms but in religious, doctrinal terms. There are groups that see their continuity (their definition of what makes them *that* community rather than another) precisely in terms of commonly held, authoritatively articulated beliefs about value, truth, and the good.[21] One such belief on which a religious community might have the resources to issue guidance is what attitude a believer should adopt toward unbelievers: whether a believer can legitimately reside in the same community with them and regard them as having independent moral value.[22] Islam is such a religion, and, I have tried to show here, liberalism is such a doctrine of social cooperation that requires particular answers to these questions. Thus, it is not absurd or unfair in a liberal society, while extending recognition to Muslim communities (and Islam as such), to require a form of mutual recognition from those communities in the form of authoritative or intellectually formalized statements in favor of joint citizenship with non-Muslims.

While liberalism is characterized by its protection of a more or less autonomous civil society in which individuals are free to form a variety of allegiances and bonds of solidarity along any lines they choose (race, class, religion, culture, hobbies, etc.), it envisions a public sphere in which citizens act as equals. This translates into a requirement that, whatever bonds of solidarity and association an individual may hold, she must regard all fellow citizens, even those we do not regard as sharing in our most cherished and important final goals and ends, as particular kinds of equals. Although I may regard myself as a Catholic first, second, and third in terms of what I consider to be my most constitutive identity, may limit virtually all of my social and personal contacts to fellow Catholics, and may regard non-Catholics as moral aliens in a profound sense, at the political level, I must recognize non-Catholics as persons entitled to the same rights as myself and persons with whom I might cooperate and feel solidarity. This is not a requirement to consider their final ends and values as equally worthwhile to mine, as equally correct in an absolute sense, but simply to regard others as having an equal share in the exercise of collective political authority.

Note that this does not require *excessive* solidarity. I am not required to put this political conception of equality in a position of absolute priority over my other conceptions of solidarity. The moral other can be one whom—in our own minds—we simply suffer ungladly. I am not required to want him as my neighbor, my business partner, or my son-in-law. I am not required to regard his metaphysical beliefs as equally true as mine or his values as equally worthy. I am not required even to take his errant ways as a given and forgo the hopes of persuading him of the error of his ways, as long as I don't regard him as a potential object for coercion in matters that do not harm me in certain ways and do not regard him socially as *merely* a potential object of conversion. In the Islamic context, this involves examining the treatment of non-Muslims as groups with whom one might make contracts, cooperate, and form common goals.

Note also that this does not require liberals to be indifferent to or uninterested in more sociological concerns about the prospects for democracy and solidarity in a society in which such attitudes of disdain, avoidance, or mistrust are widely and intensely held and cohere around a limited number of cleavages. Just as we might be concerned about the effects of cultural pluralism on solidarity—that is, when many citizens hold the just-described attitudes of mistrust and alienation toward fellow citizens who differ racially, ethnically, or linguistically—we might observe neutrally that a society in which most citizens are divided into groups based on conceptions of the good that merely *tolerate* each other publicly but do not generally interact privately is a society that will lack the levels of interpersonal trust and deep commitment to the public conception of justice necessary for surviving political conflict. For our purposes, however, we are forced to say that such private attitudes are not in themselves a violation of any doctrinal requirements of citizenship in liberal democracies. Here I have in mind a certain conceivable Islamic attitude of avoidance toward non-Muslim fellow citizens. A Muslim might not want to convert non-Muslims or transform the state, but limit all potentially corrupting contact with them for himself and his family. He might see non-Muslims as moral inferiors, perhaps even hell-bound, and ritually unclean. How far can such attitudes of avoidance go before departing from the overlapping consensus, which must be divorced from sociological concerns about the possible consequences of the generalization of such attitudes?

I believe the proper liberal position to be that a liberal society can tolerate such private attitudes so long as there is no articulation of a doctrine of the absolute religious *impermissibility* of sharing in a certain limited number of public ends, including the common defense, social order, and public welfare. A formal doctrine of the permissibility of shared civic friendship with non-Muslims would involve doctrinal affirmations of both *recognition* and *solidarity*.

A general doctrine of recognition, I submit, would have two main pillars: first, recognition of a right not to be Muslim and some acceptance of pluralism and difference as a potentially permanent feature of social life and, second, an affirmation of relationships based on justice between communities. Together, these two pillars would contribute toward a positive conception of recognition and respect for non-Muslims, beyond mere tolerance in the "negative" sense of mutual forbearance.

I have discussed briefly the problems liberalism has with Islamic justifications of sharing political space with non-Muslims solely on the grounds that they may someday become Muslims. On the one hand, the fact of reasonable pluralism is a central organizing principle for liberal justification. Political liberalism goes to great lengths to convince nonliberals, particularly religious believers, that it advances no truth claims contrary to their metaphysical beliefs and, thus, that believers need not repudiate their own claims to truth. However, a core feature of reasonableness is being able to see fellow citizens as free and equal self-authenticating sources of valid claims and interests. One of the implications of this view is that, given the burdens of judgment, diversity in beliefs and life choices is an inevitable feature of free and open societies. Thus, although liberalism upholds the freedom to proselytize on the basis of the right to revise one's conception of the good, it is doubtful that a citizen can support liberal citizenship to even a minimal degree without *accepting* that many of his fellow citizens may never convert to Islam. Mutual recognition between citizens thus requires that this diversity be accepted, even as we try to win adherents to our way of life. I thus submit that the first pillar of a doctrine of recognition would include as an extension of the earlier principle R3 an acceptance of religious pluralism something like the following:

> RP: Religious disagreement is an inevitable feature of human life, perhaps divinely ordained. Although a Muslim has a duty to make the Islamic message known and to call to it, it is understood that not all unbelievers will hear or heed this call. It is permissible to live in societies even where there is little or no prospect of Islam becoming a majority religion, and it is permissible to maintain civic relationships with unbelievers even after they have heard and failed to accept the invitation to Islam.

I have phrased this rather deliberately to express the idea of diversity and minority status as a potentially permanent condition. Although this principle could have many varieties, the idea is to exclude from an overlapping consensus those (rather common) justifications of political obligation that rest on the premise that some day (even centuries hence) present-day non-Muslim societies will have Muslim majorities that can thus create Islamic states. A further important note is that Abrahamic fraternity or shared monotheism is not a sufficient ground for civic solidarity in a politically liberal society that does not distinguish between citizens on the basis of metaphysical beliefs. Recognition must also be extended to atheists, agnostics, and non-Abrahamic believers.

That Muslims have reason to believe that sharing social space with non-Muslims is a permanent condition to be tolerated, or a necessity out of which virtue can be made, implies very little about the nature of relations between communities in that social space. It certainly does not imply that members of different communities have the same moral standing or that they are entitled to the same standards of treatment. Medieval Islamic public law granted non-Muslims in Muslim states significant rights to noninterference but nothing approaching equality of rights or status. Thus, as a second building block of our doctrine of recognition of the other, we require Islamic reasons for regarding relations with non-Muslims in a single society as relations of *justice between equals*. This requirement opens up extremely complex questions of the substantive content of justice (see my discussion later on this in relation to political participation), but a doctrine of mutual recognition would not be complete with something like the following:

> J: Relations between Muslims and non-Muslims are governed by standards of justice, rather than the ethics of war or contingent accommodation. Minimal standards of justice require civic equality and procedural impartiality toward all persons, regardless of their religious identity.

Building on this, these more passive aspects of recognition must also be supplemented with a more positive doctrine of solidarity. Rawls has referred to liberal society as a "fair system of cooperation," that is, as one based on *reciprocity* as opposed to mutual advantage, impartiality, mere socially coordinated activity, a fixed natural order, or a system of traditional hierarchy justified by religious authority or aristocratic values. For Rawls, *reciprocity* is the idea that "all who are engaged in cooperation and who do their part as the rules and procedure require, are to benefit in an appropriate way as assessed by a suitable benchmark of comparison,"[23] a conception that lies between impartiality (being moved by the general good) and mutual advantage (everyone benefiting with respect to their present or expected future situation). I am not concerned here to vindicate a particular conception of distributive justice but merely the basic idea of citizenship as social cooperation: of contributing to the welfare (directly and indirectly) of fellow citizens (including those who do not share your conception of the good) and of sharing political sovereignty. One cannot speak of a comprehensive doctrine as affirming citizenship in a society when at the same time it seeks to avoid contributing to the welfare of fellow citizens merely because they do not share a conception of truth or of the good. This willingness to so contribute is what I have in mind by "solidarity."

We have seen throughout the two chapters in this part that contributing to the welfare and strength of non-Muslims is something to which some Muslim jurists and exegetes have objected. They have objected to contributing to the material well-being of non-Muslims both because this increases the relative strength of non-Muslim states and societies over Muslim ones and because they see such mutual aid as belonging to a relationship of love, fraternity, and solidarity that can be established only with fellow Muslims. A Muslim has no libertarian objection to the redistribution of his wealth in principle but may have such an objection when it occurs across confessional boundaries and through the coercive powers of a non-Muslim state. However, it is unavoidable even in a Nozickian minimal state that sharing political space involves, in countless ways, sharing the burdens of social life. We contribute to one another's welfare not only through forced redistribution but also even as a double effect of pursuing our own goals. Given the sources we have encountered that discourage contributing to the welfare of non-Muslims, an overlapping consensus would require some contrary declaration in favor of *solidarity* such as:

> S: It is permissible for a Muslim to form common social, economic, and civic goals with non-Muslims. It is understood that in sharing social and political space Muslims benefit from this and in turn contribute to the material welfare of non-Muslims, to which there is no Islamic objection.

In addition to the willingness to contribute to the material welfare of non-Muslims, a crucial aspect of solidarity relates to sharing political sovereignty. With this question of political participation, we reach a hinge between the two broad problems with citizenship in non-Muslim liberal states that I identified earlier: one, in those states being *non-Muslim* in character, both socially and politically, and, two, in those states being *liberal* in character. It is readily conceivable that a Muslim could affirm residence on liberal terms, forswear any assistance to aggressive foreign powers (including Muslim ones), recognize the acceptability of religious pluralism, and even gladly contribute to the secular welfare of non-Muslims, yet find it impermissible to contribute to the formulation of non-Islamic legislation. Even if this person disavowed any interest in using political institutions to impose an Islamic conception of government, one would still have to say that his comprehensive doctrine is not fully supportive of an overlapping consensus because of the failure to recognize the legitimacy of political institutions, for "to be a citizen is to be committed to a political system, not merely to the survival of the society that system organizes, but to the survival of the particular organization and also to all those purposes beyond survival that the organization sets for itself. Residence alone cannot and does not generate such a commitment."[24]

Yet, when speaking of the legitimacy of political institutions, we immediately enter into very deep and complex questions of justice. The question from the Islamic perspective immediately becomes whether any non-Islamic forms of legislation can be just. That none can is not an obvious or universally accepted Islamic position. To be sure, any reconstruction of a comprehensive Islamic doctrine of citizenship in a liberal democracy (Muslim-minority or not) would require addressing this; however, doing so satisfactorily would require exceeding the constraints of the present inquiry. Nonetheless, we can address this question here in the context of solidarity with non-Muslims. (Thus, my reference to political participation was as a "hinge" issue.)

Although to be regarded as holding a doctrine of citizenship, a citizen need not consider political participation as part of his conception of the good, he should at least regard it as *permissible* in relation to his conception of the good, and if he in fact does not participate, then his reasons should be such that they do not constitute rejection of or ingratitude toward what other citizens do when they perform the necessary task of political participation. Furthermore, his reasons for participating must be such that they do not undermine or reject the liberal terms of social cooperation.[25] Clearly, examples of the latter would be various long-term strategies to "Islamize" political institutions, including political participation in the present institutions as an acceptable tactic. More ambiguous attitudes would be those that reveal unease with liberal institutions but justify political participation exclusively as a means of securing certain benefits *for Muslims*. Let us suppose that the benefits in question are themselves compatible with liberal conceptions of justice and a well-ordered society; might such a justification be compatible with liberal citizenship?

Consider the following three positions:

1. My conception of the good is based on the pursuit of purely private happiness. I have no objection to the political order around me—it provides me with all the security and freedom I need to be happy—but nor do I feel the need to be a part of it. Should this political order be threatened by forces that would replace it with one more hostile to my interest in security and freedom, I would have no objection to defending it, but otherwise I am happy to let others handle the administration of things.
2. My conception of the good is based on the pursuit of happiness. I have certain interests that I share with some citizens but not with all. Influencing politicians through various forms of political participation is an important way in which I advance those interests. Otherwise, where our group interest is not affected, I have very little interest in political participation.
3. My conception of the good is based on the pursuit of salvation, which I think can be best achieved through government on the basis of a divine law. I understand that in this society the majority of the population does not share my understanding of what divine law requires. This society gives me the security, freedom, and dignity to follow my most important religious practices and, thus, I would defend it against harm and destruction. I do not begrudge my unbelieving fellow citizens their worldly happiness, and I do not resent my contribution to their welfare. However, while I will obey all laws of this society that do not oppress me, I do not feel any need to contribute to the making of those laws. For me, political participation is only justified to pursue social benefits for coreligionists, which may or may not overlap with the interests of others.

The first and third statements are expressions of nonparticipation based on one's conception of the good that, I believe, are nonetheless affirmations of citizenship (as opposed to mere resident alienage) because of the way they affirm the legitimacy of what other citizens do when they participate in political life (and even a certain gratitude for it). If we can assume that many non-Muslim citizens of contemporary liberal democracies hold conceptions of the good conforming to the first or second template, then an Islamic argument that views nonparticipation as the norm and participation justified only to pursue Muslim self-interest is equally compatible with liberal citizenship *if it presumes an argument something like the third template as the underlying Islamic position*, rather than a position of gradual Islamization or an even more indifferent attitude to non-Muslims. (This argument presumes that the individual in question is also affirming all the previously mentioned beliefs about the permissibility of loyalty, recognition, tolerance, and contributing to non-Muslim welfare.) What is decisive is that although the motivation is largely to advance Muslim communal interests, this citizen does not view benefits that accrue to non-Muslims as a double effect as something otherwise impermissible or unfortunate. Thus, the final aspect of a doctrine of recognition and solidarity would be an affirmation of the permissibility of participating in a non-Muslim political system along the following lines:

> PP: It is permissible for a Muslim to participate in a political system that is not based on Islamic justice or public justification. Such participation is an appropriate way to advance certain interests of Muslim communities, particularly in worldly matters, interests that may overlap with those of non-Muslim fellow citizens.

Chapters 7 and 8 of this book, "Recognition of Non-Muslims and Moral Pluralism" and "Solidarity with Non-Muslims," respectively, address these questions of whether Islamic doctrine can give Muslims moral reasons for regarding non-Muslims as political equals, contributing to their welfare, and joining them in common civic purposes, including through political participation.

Although this book does not satisfactorily address the central liberal questions of whether Muslims can regard any non-Islamic forms of governance as substantively just, whether liberal regimes can be so regarded, and how Muslims can justify the liberal requirement of self-restraint toward fellow Muslims while encouraging Islamic conceptions of virtue and morality, the concerns of political liberalism are omnipresent throughout the following four chapters. This is the case primarily in three ways: First, in addressing the non-Muslim nature of societies in which Muslims live as minorities, the emphasis is always on *the terms of association* required by political liberalism; second, in addressing the reasons that Muslim scholars give for accepting those terms of association, the emphasis is always on the *nature of those reasons* and their compatibility with my understanding of the overlapping consensus; third, the question is paramount throughout *whether political liberalism fulfills its ambition* to earn the loyalty of nonliberal groups over other forms of liberalism or other forms of non-Islamic governance. These discussions will go a long way toward suggesting how Muslims may indeed regard liberal principles of justice as overlapping with the most important concerns of Islamic conceptions of justice—the successful demonstration of which would point to a more comprehensive overlapping consensus—but they will not establish the case entirely.

PART III

Islamic Affirmations of Liberal Citizenship

5

Residence in a Non-Muslim State

Those whom the angels gather in death while in a state of sin against themselves they will ask: "What was your plight?" They reply: "We were oppressed on earth." The [angels] will say: "Was not God's earth vast enough for you to migrate within it?" They will have their refuge in hell and how evil is such a destiny, except for those truly oppressed, those men, women and children who cannot find any means and have not been shown the way. For these there is hope that God will forgive them, for God is Forgiving and Merciful. Anyone who migrates in the path of God will find in the Earth many an abundant refuge. Whoever leaves his home in migration towards God and his Messenger, and death overtakes him, his reward with God is guaranteed, for God is Forgiving and Merciful.

—Qur'an, *Sūrat al-Nisā'* (4): 4:97–100

In chapter 3, I outlined the tradition of juridical doctrines that hold that residence in a non-Muslim polity is either impermissible or deeply problematic. One finds both the argument that the issue is settled by divine text (Q. 4:97–100 and 8:72) and six main explanatory arguments: that Muslims must not be subject to non-Muslim laws or authority, that Islam and Muslims must not be put in a position of inferiority to non-Muslims, that Muslims must avoid aiding or increasing the strength of non-Muslims, that Muslims are forbidden from forming bonds of friendship or solidarity with non-Muslims, that Muslims are required to avoid environments of sin or indecency, and that in non-Muslim environments, it will be more difficult to prevent the loss of religiosity in subsequent generations. The six explanatory arguments are more widely held than the narrow juridical ruling that residence is prohibited by God. They also clearly display moral objections to the relationships with non-Muslims that are characteristic of citizenship and civic friendship.

In chapter 4, I thus argued that an Islamic doctrine of citizenship in non-Muslim liberal democracies would include something like the following positions:

R1: The authoritative texts cited in favor of the prohibition on residence do not necessarily dictate the conclusions advanced by those jurists; there are other authoritative texts that lead to contradictory rulings, and there are reasons to regard these as more authoritative than the texts cited by pro-hijra jurists.

R2: It may be possible to fulfill the basic duty to "manifest one's religion" even in the absence of sovereign Muslim political authority and under non-Muslim political and legal authority.

R3: Although great benefits to Islam, including its possible spread and the strengthening of Muslim communities, can be gained by living in non-Muslim lands, this is not the only way in which Muslims are permitted to regard their life in those societies.

I now turn in this chapter to an exploration of Islamic foundations for these views.

The first argument of those jurists who do not believe that migrating from a non-Muslim polity is a categorical and permanent duty for all Muslims rests on a contextualization of verses 4:97–100. The basic juridical position is best summed up by canonical *ḥadīth* collector Abū Dāwūd:

> *Hijra* was at the beginning of Islam recommended but not obligatory, and this is based on Q. 4:100: "And whoever migrates in the cause of God will find in the earth many an abundant refuge." This verse came down when the oppression of the polytheists against the Muslims was intensifying and thus the Prophet migrated to Medina and the Muslims were commanded to migrate as well to be in his presence that they might be with him and help one another should something befall them, and that they might learn their religion and come to understand it from him. There was great fear at that time of the Quraysh, but when Mecca was conquered and submitted, this same meaning [of *hijra*] was retained and the obligation of migrating was lifted and it returned to being recommended and preferred. There are thus two *hijras*: the one that has ended is the obligation and the one that remains is the recommendation.[1]

It is this position that one finds consistently endorsed by most non-Mālikī jurists and exegetes,[2] as well as some modern-day Mālikīs.[3] To the point that the duty to migrate was abrogated after the conquest of Mecca, jurists cite a number of *ḥadīth* that contradict or dilute the implications of the ones cited by the pro-*hijra* jurists:[4]

> There is no migration after the conquest [of Mecca] but rather *jihād* and intent. And if you are called out to fight, then do so.[5]

> 'Ā'isha is reported to have said: "There is no *hijra* today. Before, a believer had to flee with his religion to the Messenger of God, fearing seduction and persecution away from his religion. But from today God has made Islam manifest and a believer can worship his Lord wherever he may be."[6]

> 'Umar [the third Caliph] is reported to have said: "There is no migration after the death of the Prophet."[7]

> A man came to the Prophet and said: "I want to give my allegiance to you by performing *hijra*." The Prophet responded: "The *hijra* has ended with those who performed it [before the conquest] but you can give allegiance through submitting to God, *jihād* and good deeds."[8]

Furthermore, in adjudicating between the implications of the two sets of *ḥadīth*, some scholars have cast doubts on the authenticity of some of the pro-*hijra ḥadīth*. Abū Dāwūd, for example, argues that "the *isnād* of the *ḥadīth* of Ibn 'Abbās ["there is no *hijra* after the conquest"] is uninterrupted (*mutaṣṣil*), whereas the *isnād* of the *ḥadīth* of Mu'āwiya is interrupted (*mursal*)."[9] As part of the contextualization and historicization of the sources used by the pro-*hijra* jurists, it is also often argued that the verses and *ḥadīth* reports both refer to a situation in which Muslims were at war with the *specific* non-Muslims in question,[10] and in a context in which an Islamic state existed that claimed the right to protect all Muslims. On a purely technical-pragmatic note, then, it is not rare to find jurists and other thinkers arguing that in a period of history where no caliphate or obvious successor Islamic state exists, nor one that could possibly accommodate all Muslims actually living as minorities or in non-Islamic states (including those with majority Muslim populations), the duty of migration cannot possibly be regarded as practicable. This view is pronounced parsimoniously by one of the preeminent Saudi jurists of recent years, Ibn 'Uthaymīn (whose colleagues were quoted in chapter 3 as pronouncing the duty to migrate as absolute): "If we say it is *ḥarām* [forbidden] for them to settle amongst non-Muslims, then where is the Islamic state that will accept them and allow them to settle there? Indeed there is none."[11]

The first position (R1) seems to be widely affirmed. However, it should be noted that both the technical argument (there is no divine prohibition on residence) and the pragmatic argument (to where would Muslims migrate?) are consistent with a variety of positions incompatible with the liberal conception of citizenship, mainly that an obligation to migrate could obtain should a successor to the caliphate come into existence, that Muslims may have an obligation to bring some form of Islamic legal order into existence even in Muslim-minority lands, and that Muslims are always required to support other Muslims during hostilities, no matter what the cause of war. What else, then, have Muslim jurists had to say about the terms and conditions under which Muslims may reside in non-Muslim polities?

The crucial conditions underlying the technical arguments for the permissibility of residing in a non-Muslim land are, of course, the Muslims' security, their lack of fear of seduction away from Islam (*al-fitna fī'l-dīn*), and their freedom to "manifest [their] religion" (*iẓhār al-dīn*). In fact, many jurists and exegetes do not see the freedom to practice religion as a mitigating factor on a general ban supposedly implied by Q. 4:97–100, but rather read these verses themselves as requiring migration only because of the oppression experienced in Mecca. The argument is that those verses refer to Muslims who were oppressed (*kunnā mustaḍ'afīn fī'l-arḍ*), harried, and constantly being induced to abandon Islam.[12] Thus, the obligation to migrate is only for those who find themselves in this condition. For all others, jurists arrive at a variety of recommendations. Some argue that residence in non-Muslim lands where one is safe and can "manifest one's religion" (*iẓhār al-dīn*; *iqāmat al-dīn*, etc.) is permitted, but that migration is still preferred (recommended, meritorious: *mustaḥabb*) to avoid the negative consequences of such residence discussed in chapter 3, such as increasing the strength of non-Muslims.[13] Other jurists, however, go so far as to argue that residence in non-Muslim lands, given the conditions of security and freedom, is even *recommended* (*mustaḥabb*),[14] in rare cases *required*,[15] or that "if a Muslim is able to manifest his religion (*iẓhār dīnihi*) in one of the unbeliever's countries, this country becomes a part of *dār al-Islām*."[16] The argument in these cases is invariably that Muslims residing in non-Muslim lands may be the cause of the eventual return of Islam (in the cases of conquered lands) or of its spread, grounded in the belief that Islam is a universal religion, that the entire earth belongs to God, and that Muslims have the duty of "calling" (*al-da'wa*) to Islam. Given this paramount duty, how is it possible that residence in non-Muslim lands could be forbidden? ask contemporary Muslim jurists.[17]

These texts leave two important questions for our comparative purposes and methodology. The first concerns what Muslim jurists mean when they refer to freedom from seduction from religion (*al-fitna fī'l-dīn*) and the freedom to manifest (*iẓhār*) or practice/uphold (*iqāma*) one's religion. Do these discourses include a conception of practicing one's religion that is consistent with liberal restraints on communal and paternal authority over group and family members (R2), or do they presume some form of communal autonomy within non-Muslim states where certain areas of Islamic law will be applied? Second, what type of argument is the argument from *da'wa*? Is the justification of residence in non-Muslim lands based primarily on the duty to call to Islam a justification compatible with the liberal conception of citizenship (R3)?

Iẓhār al-dīn

Muslim jurists have expressed the condition of enjoying religious freedom in a non-Muslim polity in a number of ways, including *iẓhār al-dīn* (manifesting religion), *iqāmat al-dīn* (practicing/upholding religion), *iẓhār sharā'i' al-Islām* (manifesting the prescriptions of religious law), *iẓhār sha'ā'ir al-Islām* (manifesting the rituals of Islam), and *al-qiyām bi-wājibāt al-Islām* (performing the duties of Islam), with the first two being the most common. The majority of these jurists do not specify what these terms require. Indeed, Abou El Fadl remarks that "there is no consensus among jurists with regard to the level of freedom necessary for Muslims in a non-Muslim territory. Perhaps the vagueness of their expressions on this point indicates that the jurists did not wish to articulate a fixed, non-negotiable rule that might be difficult to apply to specific situations, especially situations in which Muslim territory is occupied by non-Muslims."[18] Even scholars who refer in some way to a duty to "live according to the *Sharī'a*" in non-Muslim lands do not always discuss whether this requires coercive political authority or, indeed, whether present freedoms guaranteed by liberal states permit such a life. For example, one finds a certain Shaykh Muhammad al-Hanooti, a member of the North American Fiqh Council, responding to the question of migration in the following way:

> The goal [of a Muslim] to take this worldly life as a place for arrangements to enter paradise. If one can accomplish this goal wherever in the world, it is legitimate for him/her to be there. If not, then one should move to another territory where he/she can have a better investment to go to Paradise. Therefore, immigration to a non-Muslim country is allowed on the contingency that the Muslim should be able to maintain his way of life and practice Islam within the Shariah laws and rules.[19]

He declines to specify whether "practicing Islam within the Shariah laws and rules" is a matter of personal ethics and worship or upholding rules related to family and punitive law. This failure to specify any obvious clashes with the liberal system, and the implication that the final judgment is to be made by the individual believer, might be read optimistically as a compatible position. Thus, the essential question in Islamic juridical terms is whether the duty to manifest or practice religion is satisfied by the rituals of worship (*'ibādāt*) or only by some quasi-political authority applying the laws of social relations (*mu'āmalāt*).

The concern, within our inquiry into an Islamic doctrine of citizenship in a non-Muslim state compatible with the liberal conception, is that Muslim jurists will insist that religious freedom for Muslim communities entail some form of communal autonomy, with substate institutions of authority competent to enforce Islamic family, commercial, and certain criminal codes. Indeed, a number of jurists have suggested this more or less explicitly. A later Mālikī jurist qualified the standard position of his school by arguing that migration is not necessary if the laws of Islam are applied to Muslims.[20] Similarly, a number of Ḥanafīs are on record advancing a similar condition, stricter than their school is known for.[21] Helpfully, the prominent Shāfi'ī al-Nawawī distinguishes between levels of religious freedom by contrasting the conditions of *self-protection* (*al-imtinā'*: related to refusal, abstention, forbearance, etc.) and *segregation* (*al-i'tizāl*: related to self-seclusion, withdrawal, disassociation, etc.). For al-Nawawī, the second more demanding condition is clearly analogous to some form of parallel political authority, as demonstrated by his expectation that such a community will be in a position to challenge the wider non-Muslim polity. He writes that if:

> they are capable of self-protection and segregation, then it is obligatory that they reside in *dār al-ḥarb* because its [legal] status is actually *dār al-Islām*, and if they were to migrate then it would then become *dār al-ḥarb* which is forbidden. And while living there it is necessary for them to call the polytheists to Islam by argumentation or by fighting.[22]

It is al-Nawawī's position on a condition *without* this form of communal autonomy that was quoted previously:

> And if they are capable of self-protection but not [complete] segregation or calling for fighting, then *hijra* is not obligatory. In fact, if one hopes that by remaining Islam might spread in his place of residence, then it is obligatory that he reside there and not migrate, as well as if it is hoped that Islam might prevail there in the future. Yet, if one is weak in *dār al-kufr* and is not able to manifest one's religion then one's residence there is forbidden.

It is clear that for al-Nawawī, at least, the preferred position is the former, one clearly incompatible with liberal norms, while the second, one potentially compatible, is still permitted. Such a preference can be expected to also be present in contemporary Muslim discourses. Indeed, certain semiliberal states with Muslim minorities, such as India and Israel, have systems whereby at the very least family law is administered on a communal-sectarian basis rather than one of universal civic equality. It is thus not surprising that such preferences should also be present among the largely immigrant Muslim populations of the West. Most often, this is expressed as an anxiety about the religion of future generations:

> If you do not take full care to safeguard your religious life and arrange for the religious education and upbringing of your children and make sure that your future generations remain true to Islam, then your living in this country is a sin and you are in grave danger. For us Muslims it is permitted to live only in a country where we can live with our distinctive qualities and observe our duties. If it is not possible in this environment or you feel you cannot carry out your religious obligations, it is not permissible for you to stay. It is your duty to see that you live here distinctly as Muslims. You should build your own society and ensure that your children will remain Muslims after you.[23]

This quotation does not mention political authority or Islamic law specifically, but political liberalism is hostile to the idea that communities have a right to *ensure* that subsequent generations will adhere to the same conception of the good as any present generation, because such guarantees can come only at the expense of the equal rights and freedoms of those subsequent generations.

It may be argued in defense that Nadwi does not necessarily have in mind anything in the way of coercive authority; however, it suffices to respond that where liberal institutions are committed to protecting any individuals seeking to revise their conception of the good, it is to be expected that a certain number of any generation will, in fact, be "seduced" away from the Islam of their parents or other figures of authority, just as a certain number will convert to Islam as a result of Muslims' legitimate proselytization. To be fair, Nadwi's statement is laden with ambiguities; however, it is clear that at the very least there is a deep ambivalence, if not hostility, to the fact that Muslims are required to yield a certain measure of paternal and communal authority over family and group members in liberal states.

However, in addition to those thinkers who see the practice of Islam complete *only* when it comprises an entire way of life, including some manifestation of communal power, there is a parallel tradition of speaking specifically about "duties of religion" (*wājibāt al-dīn*), "to fulfill the obligations of religion" (*iqāmat al-dīn*), or even simply worship (*'ibāda*) in the minority context.[24] For example, analyzing Ibn Taymiyya's usage of "*iqāmat al-dīn*" as the condition for not migrating, Yahya Michot acknowledges the ambiguity in the phrase but argues that the jurist is operating with an individual rather than collective understanding of its requirements: "Certes, le concepte n'est pas très précis et pourrait impliquer beaucoup plus qu-une simple practique de l'Islam—on aimerait dire: 'en bon père de famille.' Ce qui par contre est indubitable, c'est que, dans le fetwa de Mardin, Ibn Taymiyya parle de la chose au singulier, pas au pluriel. De cette mise en œuvre de la religion, il fait donc d'abord une affaire individuelle, personnelle, non pas collective ou communautaire."[25]

Particularly helpful here is the previously cited *fatwā* of twentieth-century Syrian jurist and exegete Muḥammad Rashīd Riḍā, which was his response to a questioner (*mustaftī*) from Bosnia inquiring into whether *hijra* was required from the Muslims of Bosnia after that territory's incorporation into Hapsburg Austria. This *fatwā* is important because Riḍā actually specifies what constitutes seduction away from religion ("*al-fitna min al-dīn*"), the condition that virtually all jurists agree mandates emigration, unlike most of the classical jurists. Riḍā writes:

> *Hijra* is not required for those who are able to practice their religion [*iqāmat dīnihi*] free from seduction away from it, *that is, coerced abandonment of religion or the prohibition on performing religious duties.* And this is akin to what 'Ā'isha is reported to have said in [the *ḥadīth* collection of] al-Bukhārī when she was asked about *hijra*: "There is no *hijra* today. Before a believer fled with his religion to God and His Messenger out of fear of temptation away from it, but today God has made Islam manifest and a believer may worship his Lord wherever he may be."[26]

Further on, he denies arguments that worship and marriage are invalid under non-Muslim rule: "There is no difference between the worship and marriage of a Muslim in *dār al-kufr* and a Muslim in *dār al-Islām* but only in the ordinances of political, civil and military relations."[27] The implication of Riḍā's justification of life lived in these conditions is that the latter ordinances are not prerequisites for living a just life or securing salvation.

A more satisfactory treatment of this problem would involve a much deeper investigation of plausible Islamic arguments for strictly noncoercive maintenance of Islamic ideals of virtue and the good. Because such an investigation goes beyond the narrower task set for this study, I will limit this present discussion of what jurists mean when they speak of freedom from "seduction away from religion" and freedom to manifest one's religion to the previous demonstration that most jurists prefer vagueness to precise descriptions of conditions, and that within those texts that are less vague the range of positions includes both calls for communal authority and calls for satisfaction with freedom of worship and practice. I believe this is sufficient at this point for demonstrating that we are not proceeding based on a radical misunderstanding of some obvious and universally held conception of manifesting, practicing, or upholding religion.[28] Naturally, Islamic jurists regard some implementation of divine law as a religious duty; however, the preponderance of scholars who regard "manifesting religion" as a crucial condition for legitimate residence in a non-Muslim polity do not clearly insist on the most robust understanding of that requirement (namely, *sharīʿa* courts). We may thus note that widespread affirmations of R2 exist without thereby deducing that this constitutes a more positive affirmation of liberal justice.

Daʿwa

The invariably concomitant justification of life lived in a non-Muslim society is that Muslims will be in a position to help the spread of Islam through their numbers and their proselytizing: "Residing in [one of the unbeliever's countries] is better than migrating because it is hoped that others will convert to Islam through him."[29] The desire to proselytize and win adherents to one's way of life is clearly itself not something to which a liberal can object. In fact, one might argue that the very purpose of liberal institutions is to protect action on this desire. Furthermore, I believe that the Muslim literature on *daʿwa* is a potential source for the implicit acceptance of liberal constraints because of its emphasis on private, noncoercive means for converting both non-Muslims and wayward Muslims to an Islamic conception of virtue and the good. This theme is pursued throughout the course of this book, particularly in chapters 7 and 8.

Nonetheless, a justification of residence in non-Muslim states based on the duty to proselytize could be seen to conflict with the liberal conception of citizenship in a number of potential ways. As argued in chapter 4, the concerns liberals have about such a justification are that, first, it risks seeing non-Muslims only as potential converts and not as free and equal citizens; second, it does not preclude the Islamization of the state if the group someday finds itself a majority;[30] and thus, third, it may reveal a shallow commitment to the society and state as (potentially permanently) pluralistic and secular. The general concern is that any acceptance of liberal institutions or constraints will be purely tactical, rather than grounded in a principled acknowledgment of the fact of reasonable pluralism.

For example, consider the position of Syed Abul Hasan Ali Nadwi (quoted previously): "Your stay here is correct; not only justified but an act of worship if it is a source of preaching and propagation of faith. But if not, then I have great misgivings."[31] Like the previous statement of his, this one is deeply ambiguous. Optimistically, one could read it as merely reminding Muslims that they have a duty to call to Islam no matter where they find themselves. However, it could easily be read also as a warning against accepting liberal systems for what they are, against accepting pluralism as a permanent fact of social life, and especially against developing moral commitments to these societies. The notion of parallel commitments as a citizen and as a propagator of one's conception of the good does not seem to figure. In (slight) contrast, note the wording of Canadian-Muslim scholar Shaykh Ahmad Kutty, who also describes residence in non-Muslim countries as something that can be transformed into "worship": "The economic migrants living in the West can transform their *hijrah* into an act of *'ibadah* (worship) if they change their intention and dedicate themselves to be ambassadors of Islam in their new home."[32] Here Kutty first argues that the duty to migrate ended with the conquest of Mecca, and residence in non-Muslim lands is permitted as long as Muslims enjoy security and the freedom to practice religion. The function of *da'wa* for him is not the primary (or sole) justification of residence, but an act that transforms residence from something merely permitted to something sacred. There would appear to be space in such a construction for disentangling one's commitments to a country of citizenship and the duty to promote one's conception of the good by making the second—the act of "worship"—into a more sublime, but not exclusionary, reason.

Another ambiguous position is that of Yūsuf al-Qaraḍāwī:

> There can be no questioning of the permissibility of residing in a non-Muslim country, or in "*dār al-kufr*," as it is referred to by the jurists, for if we were to forbid it, as some scholars imagine, we would close the door to the call to Islam and its spread throughout the world. [Had this been done] then the Islam of old would have been restricted to the Arabian peninsula and not left it. For if we read history and reflect upon it properly we find that the spread of Islam into the lands that we today refer to as the Arabic and Islamic worlds occurred through the influence of individual Muslims, merchants, Sufis and others like them, who migrated from their countries to those lands in Asia and Africa and mixed with the local people, worked together with them and in turn were liked by them for their good morals and sincerity, as was their religion which had implanted these virtues in them. Thus people entered our religion en masse and individually.[33]

As with Nadwi's statement, nothing in this explicitly rejects pluralism and liberal constitutions, but Qaraḍāwī's analogy between Muslim emigration to

Europe and early migration to "lands we today refer to as the Islamic world" raises questions about the level of principled and authentic commitment to non-Muslim-majority societies that Qaraḍāwī (and others who speak of the Islamization of Western societies) is willing to recognize. What if there were no serious prospect of mass conversion or of the eventual predominance of Islam in these lands? Would Qaraḍāwī still be content with the vision of Muslims living indefinitely in a pluralist society and a neutral state? What if Muslims were to eventually achieve a social majority in one of these states, in no small measure thanks to present liberal freedoms? Would Qaraḍāwī argue that Muslims have an obligation to preserve a liberal, neutral state that guaranteed to other citizens the freedoms from which Muslims benefited? The least that can be said is that the juridical framework in which Qaraḍāwī operates does not tend to pose these sorts of questions to the Islamic sources (ignoring any other political and ideological commitments that may also explain the silence). His jurisprudential (*fiqhī*) discourse is committed to the slightest possible departure from traditional rulings and beliefs compatible with the "pragmatism" and innovative reasoning (*ijtihād*) that he claims are the centerpieces of his "minority *fiqh*."

By contrast, consider the vision of *da'wa* presented by Swiss-Muslim philosopher Tariq Ramadan. For Ramadan, *da'wa* is the duty to "present Islam, explain the content of this Faith and the Islamic teaching as a whole,"[34] and

> must not be confused with either proselytism or efforts to convert: the duty of the Muslim is to spread the Message and to make it known, no more no less. Whether someone accepts Islam or not is not the Muslim's concern for the inclination of every individual heart depends on God's Will. The notion of *da'wa* is based on one principle which is the right of every human being to make *a choice based on knowledge* and this is why Muslims are asked to spread the knowledge of Islam among Muslims as well as non-Muslims.[35]

This articulation is clearly grounded in the public values of political liberalism: mutual recognition, restraint, and individual freedom. In fact, these values are partially derived from his comprehensive commitments: *da'wa* is actually a moral responsibility to increase knowledge and the range of choice in society for the good of others and of truth; the Sunni doctrine of predestination is turned into an argument for restraint.[36]

Similar to Nadwi's, Kutty's, and Qaraḍāwī's argument that fulfilling the obligation of *da'wa* transforms residence in non-Muslim lands into a form of worship and those lands themselves into a *particularly* virtuous place to be, Ramadan offers a vision of how living in the West is not a compromise or something to be compensated for, but a *particularly* Islamic form of living. This he does through his linking of the concept of *da'wa* with that of *shahāda*, bearing witness. In the narrow sense, *shahāda* refers to the first pillar of Islam, bearing witness that "There is no God but God, and Muḥammad is His Messenger." For Ramadan, however, it signifies a Muslim's full and comprehensive expression of himself as a moral being. It is the duty to publicly bear witness that transforms life in the West into an act of worship: "Wherever a Muslim, saying the *shahāda*, is in security and is able to perform his/her fundamental religious duties, he/she is *at home*, for the Prophet taught us that the whole world is a mosque. This means that Muslims living in Europe, individuals as well as communities, can not only live in Europe, but that they uphold a great responsibility for they provide their societies with a testimony based on Faith, spirituality, values, a sense of limits and a permanent human and social commitment."[37] This differs from the narrow, proselytizing arguments of Nadwi and Qaraḍāwī in its insistence on mutual responsibility and the emphasis on the expression of one's values universally in the public sphere in the conditions of pluralism.

But in addition to this general injunction to bear witness, both Qaraḍāwī and Ramadan see the West as a particularly crucial arena for this mission. Again, however, there is a marked difference in emphasis and justification. For Qaraḍāwī, the West is too powerful to forgo attempts to influence it: "It is necessary for Muslims—with their distinguishing virtue of possessing a universal message—to have a presence in the West, considering that it is the West that has come to lead the world and direct it politically, economically and culturally." The implications of this for Qaraḍāwī are twofold: that Muslims need to be in the West to help other Muslims already living there (and to call to Islam) and also to influence it to the benefit of Muslims, rather than "leaving the powerful and influential West to the penetration of the Jews."[38] Ramadan also begins by emphasizing the centrality of the West in the world and the urgency of Muslim influence there:

> Muslims settled in the West are at the *centre*, at the *heart*, at the *head* of the system which produces the symbolic apparatus of Westernization. In this very specific space, at the *centre*, and far more exactingly still than at the *periphery*, Muslims must *bear witness*, they must be *witnesses* to what they are and to their own values. Indeed, the whole world is a *land of testimony* [*dār al-shahāda*] but there is a specific space, bearing an incomparable symbolic charge, which is the heart of the whole system and in which millions of Muslims now live. At the centre, more than anywhere else, the axial principle of *shahāda* takes on its full meaning.[39]

By contrast, however, Ramadan emphasizes not merely the need to maximize Muslim interests in the West but rather the Muslim duty to participate in it dialectically out of a sense of belonging and responsibility:

> the European environment is a *space of responsibility* for Muslims. This is exactly the meaning of the notion of "*space of testimony*" [*dār al-shahāda*] that we propose here, a notion that totally reverses perspectives: whereas Muslims have, for years, been wondering whether and how they would be accepted, the in-depth study and evaluation of the Western environment entrusts them, in light of their Islamic frame of reference, with a most important mission. . . . Muslims now attain, in the *space of testimony*, the meaning of an essential duty and of an exacting responsibility: to contribute, wherever they are, to

> promoting good and equity within and through *human brotherhood*. Muslim's outlook must now change from the reality of "protection" alone to that of an authentic "contribution."[40]

Furthermore, when he expounds on the content of the Islamic duty to "enjoin justice" or "promote good and equity," this takes on a particularly political (in the Rawlsian sense) cast: He understands the Muslim's duty to bear witness to Islamic values as a duty to be involved in society in the areas of "unemployment, marginalisation, delinquency, reform of legal, economic, social and political systems," and so forth, that is, precisely the sort of civic goals appropriate in a politically liberal regime.

Unlike the more traditionally minded Islamic scholars, Ramadan is self-consciously engaged in a search for overlapping consensus. If anything, Ramadan's position might be more liberal than is required by political liberalism, for I submit that that there is nothing incompatible in wanting to convert others as such to one's conception of the good and of truth, merely that one's attachment to one's political community, and one's recognition of fellow citizens, should not be *limited* to one's desire to convert them. Also, although I have been critical here of some of the aspects of the more traditional, juridical approach represented by Qaraḍāwī and others, I do not mean to rule out these sources as potentially giving support to an overlapping consensus. This question will be fully answered only through the discussions in chapter 6 on Islamic arguments for being loyal to non-Muslim states in the way that is required by political liberalism, and in chapter 7 on recognition of non-Muslims. Here I merely wish to elaborate on the tensions inherent in *da'wa*-based justifications for residence in non-Muslim lands and to show that they can be expressed in forms that are both compatible and incompatible with the demands of citizenship and that it is not always apparent from the *da'wa*-based arguments alone whether a given thinker is articulating a compatible doctrine. I return to the question of *da'wa* a number of times in the forthcoming chapters, at greatest length in chapter 7.

I must also mention here a final approach to the question of *hijra* in which Muslims may find a justification for living in non-Muslim lands. This position differs radically from the other approaches in that it does not limit the discussion of the duty to migrate to a purely geographic or political context but rather sees *hijra* as a spiritual concept, grounded in the individual duty to avoid sin. A number of Prophetic Traditions are used to justify this identification, including the following:

> A bedouin came to the Messenger of God and asked him: "O Messenger of God, inform us about the *hijra*. Is it to you wherever you might be or to a specific land? And when you die does it lapse?" The [Prophet] said: "*Hijra* is migration from all abominations whether manifest or hidden and that you maintain the prayer and render the *zakāh*, and then you are an emigrant."[41]
>
> The Messenger of God was asked: "Which *hijra* is superior?" He said: "That you migrate from [avoid] that which your Lord has abominated."[42]

> The emigrant is one who flees from [shuns, avoids; *hajara*] that which God has prohibited.[43]
>
> Be devoted to God wherever you are.[44]

For the richest and most elaborate exemplar of this argument, we turn to a remarkable series of *fatāwā* by the fourteenth-century Ḥanbalī jurist Ibn Taymiyya, in which he consistently and exclusively addresses the question of migration from the abode of war in terms of the Islamic duty to avoid sin and sinners wherever they may be. In these texts, Ibn Taymiyya relies on the shared etymological derivation of *hijra* (migration) and *hajara* (avoidance, abandonment, ignoring, ostracizing) from the root h-j-r[45] to suggest in general that the concepts are linked spiritually and even juridically, and specifically to advance the argument that the former is in fact a derivative duty of the latter. Thus, when asked about the duty of migration, Ibn Taymiyya responds: "And on the question of migration (*hijra*) from the abode of war and perversion to the abode of Islam and faith, this is avoidance (*hajr*) on the part of one living amongst unbelievers and hypocrites who do not allow him to do what God commanded him to do."[46] Elsewhere: "As to the question of the migration of a Muslim from the abode of war, what is meant by this is that a Muslim must avoid evil things and those who engage in them, whose company harms him, except in the case of an overriding need or interest [for remaining with them]."[47] Rather than elaborate on the specific social or political conditions that might actually require a physical migration, he instead develops his views on the forms and functions of avoidance, which include educating and rebuking sinning or lax Muslims. In a subsequent *fatwā*, he elaborates on the connection between migration and the repudiation of sin:

> *Hijra* is a form of rebuke, and punishment is a form of *hijra*, which is in fact the renouncing and repudiation of evil. For the Prophet said: "The emigrant (*al-muhājir*) is one who avoids (*hajara*) evil" and [elsewhere] ". . . one who avoids what God has forbidden him." This is the migration/repudiation as piety (*hijrat al-taqwā*). And there is also migration/repudiation as rebuke (*hijrat al-ta'zīr*) and migration/repudiation as *jihād*, as in the migration/repudiation of the three who hung back from the *jihād* where [the Prophet] commanded the Muslims to avoid them (*amara bi-hajrihim*) until repentance was granted to them. Thus, migration is at times a form of devotion and piety, if it consists in avoiding sin. To this we have the words of the Almighty: "When you meet those who indulge in [idle] talk about Our verses, turn away from them until they begin to talk of something else. And if Satan should make you forget this, then once you remember again remain no longer in the company of the unjust. For those who are devoted to God are in no way accountable for them except to remind them [of God, and] perhaps they will turn again to Him." [Q. 6:68–69] And at other times it is a form of *jihād*, commanding the right and forbidding the wrong and the imposing of sanctions, and consists in punishing those who transgress and are unjust.[48]

The unavoidable conclusion of his linking the question of migration from a non-Muslim society to that of dealing with sin in any society is that the objective political, institutional, or even demographic facts cannot be regarded as absolutely determinant. The objective situation that matters for Ibn Taymiyya is the presence of sin or corruption, whether in a Muslim or non-Muslim society.[49] The Muslim's duty is to avoid, repudiate, rebuke, or overturn this state of affairs, depending on his relative strength[50] and the chances that his actions will result in a worse state of affairs.[51] Furthermore, the subjective factor that ultimately determines the Muslim's justness is the intention behind his deeds.[52] Therefore, if a Muslim is in a position in which the most he can achieve is to personally avoid the company of sinners, rather than publicly rebuke them or otherwise forbid their actions, then he is clearly preserving his moral status in the way possible, given his circumstances and the concern for his general interests. Given that Ibn Taymiyya explicitly permits residence in non-Muslim lands where Muslims have the freedom to practice their religion, it is a plausible reading of the present texts that they are less concerned with a Muslim always residing in Muslim-majority lands than with his consistency in personally disassociating himself from sin. A contemporary Muslim might regard this as a relatively apolitical requirement that can be fulfilled or neglected in both Muslim and non-Muslim societies.[53]

Conclusion

Muslim jurists and exegetes have thus advanced roughly six arguments for the legitimacy of living permanently in a non-Muslim state: First, that the authoritative texts cited in favor of a ban do not necessarily dictate the conclusions advanced by those jurists; second, that there are other authoritative texts (namely, other *ḥadīth* reports) that directly lead to contradictory rulings and that there are reasons to regard these as more authoritative than the texts cited by pro-*hijra* jurists; third, that it may be possible to fulfill the basic Islamic duty to "manifest one's religion" even in the absence of sovereign Muslim political authority; fourth, that even if there were reasons to believe that *hijra* is a religious duty, it is practically infeasible for masses of Muslim communities to migrate from one country to another and, moreover, it is not obvious to which country they would migrate today in the absence of an Islamic caliphate or imamate; fifth, that great benefits to Islam, including its possible spread and the strengthening of Muslim communities, can be gained by living in non-Muslim lands; and, sixth, that the duty to migrate can be understand as a spiritual duty to avoid sin and sinners in one's own life rather than merely as a duty to live in a certain state.

Arguments one, two, four, and six amount to a technical Islamic affirmation of principle R1, which I argued in the previous chapter was necessary for a doctrine of citizenship. Argument three is that, although Islamic jurists would certainly prefer some form of Islamic legal authority for Muslim communities, this is not an absolute requirement of residence, and thus R2 is affirmed. Argument five raises the concern about whether Islamic goals related to residing in non-Muslim polities, namely, the interest in spreading Islam, might reveal an underlying rejection of liberal pluralism. There are clearly scholars who are explicit in their hope that Islam will someday be a majority religion in Western (particularly European) countries and thus in a position to alter their political and legal systems. However, this aim is not, strictly speaking, required or necessarily implied by the interest in *da'wa*. It is possible to conceive of life in a non-Muslim society as producing such benefits to Islam and Muslims without those benefits inherently contradicting a liberal order, thus affirming R3.

Establishing the permissibility of residing in a non-Muslim state, however, does not exhaust the demands of the conception of society as introduced in the previous chapter. In addition to the reservations discussed about some of the arguments for residence in non-Muslim lands, it was argued that the conception of society required by liberalism, particularly of minority communities, involves not only the toleration of the political community but also affirmation of one's membership in it. Affirming the legitimacy of one's (potentially permanent) physical presence in such a space—the problem addressed by the juridical discourse on *hijra* and *iqāma*—is only a prerequisite to endorsing such a conception.[54] As we will see, some thinkers that were used here to demonstrate favorable attitudes toward residence are explicitly opposed to Muslims fulfilling duties of citizenship such as military service, or even adopting the citizenship of these countries in the first place.[55] Like the question of *hijra*, the question of contributing to the self-defense of a non-Muslim state relates to the problem of balancing loyalties between a state of residence and the global community of believers, and this question thus serves as the complement to this chapter's discussion of residence in a non-Muslim state. It is to that question that we now turn.

6

Loyalty to a Non-Muslim State

Fulfill the Covenant of God when you have entered into it and do not break your oaths after you have affirmed them for you have made God your guarantor and God knows all that you do.

—Qur'an, *Sūrat al-Naḥl* (16):91

It is not righteousness to turn your faces towards East or West, but rather righteousness is . . . to fulfill the contracts which you make.

—Qur'an, *Sūrat al-Baqara* (2):177

In chapter 3, we came across a tradition of Islamic doctrines that constitute the Islamic foundation for rejecting civic loyalty to a non-Muslim state. Views akin to the following five positions are ubiquitous in Islamic juridical discourses:

1. A Muslim may never combat another Muslim in the service of unbelievers regardless of the cause.
2. A war for the sole purpose of expanding the space ruled by Islam and Islamic law is a just war, a legitimate form of *jihād*.
3. It may be the duty of every individual Muslim, even those residing outside the Islamic polity to contribute to a legitimate *jihād*, if so called by a legitimate Imam.
4. A Muslim may not advance the cause of unbelievers or uphold non-Islamic rulings and truth-claims.
5. A Muslim may not sacrifice his life for other than certain causes, of which defending a non-Muslim society is not one.

Given that, taken individually or together, these principles deny that a Muslim resident of a non-Muslim state may develop even minimal bonds of loyalty to it, especially when that might detract from loyalty to the Muslim community, I have argued that an Islamic doctrine of citizenship would require some formulation of contrary principles.

It is appropriate here to summarize my discussion from chapter 4 of what political liberalism might regard as the proper demands on citizens in terms of patriotism and contributing to a state's self-defense. Traditional liberal justifications of conscientious objection to unjust wars, or general exemption from fighting in the case of committed pacifists, do not apply in the case of believing Muslim citizens. In their case, a reluctance to fight may be the consequence of the principle of *al-walā' wa'l-barā'*: their solidarity with a community of fellow believers across citizenship boundaries or, inversely, even when hostilities do not concern Muslims on either side, their unwillingness to form deep bonds of solidarity with non-Muslims at all. The basic idea of greater solidarity with Muslims does not *necessarily* result in a doctrine contrary to the demands of citizenship from the perspective of political liberalism because communal solidarity is one of those components of a conception of the good that might be reasonable. Political liberalism does not demand that a deep, robust, emotional commitment to one's political community and its system of governance be part of one's comprehensive conception of the good. If a conception of the good involves a special concern for a certain community of fellow believers, then political liberalism objects only insofar as this special concern prescribes attitudes or actions that violate the legitimate *political* rights and needs of the community of citizenship. I thus argued that Muslim citizens of liberal democracies can avoid this violation by endorsing on principled grounds the following positions:

> L1. Hostilities on the part of Muslim forces against a non-Muslim state are justified only in self-defense or to counter aggression and not to facilitate the spread of Islam or to change the government of a state in which Muslims are not oppressed.

Our concept of a doctrine of citizenship does not overlap with our conception of what is legitimately punishable in society. There may be acts that are legitimately punishable in a liberal democracy that at the same time do not constitute a *doctrinal* rejection of citizenship in a liberal democracy. It will be obvious, for example, that my position reserves for the citizen the space to exempt himself from a draft or conscription during virtually any war conducted outside the homeland not directly required for self-defense without being accused of general civic disloyalty. However, a state may be justified in punishing citizens for disobeying generally binding legislation enacted through democratic procedures. Yet from the standpoint of political liberalism, it cannot be said that a citizen who prefers not to kill or be killed except when the survival or safety of his state are at stake and when his personal contribution through violent action is required is the bearer of a *doctrine* that violates the overlapping consensus sought by liberalism. Similarly, there may be acts that are not legitimately punishable in a liberal democracy that at the same time do constitute such a rejection. It might be unjust to punish a citizen who simply *proclaims* a doctrine of *jihād* that holds that war undertaken by Muslim forces against a non-Muslim state for the purposes of advancing Islam or Muslim interests is legitimate, or that commands absolute solidarity with any Muslim in all cases of conflict between Muslims and non-Muslims, yet does not directly incite violence against his state of citizenship. Nonetheless, such a doctrine would clearly indicate that this citizen does not affirm a comprehensive ethical doctrine that gives support to a liberal conception of justice or citizenship.

> L2. In conflicts between a non-Muslim state in which Muslims live and a Muslim force, a Muslim may forswear on grounds of principle any active aid to the Muslim force and promise to engage in no violent activities against her non-Muslim state.

I argued that so long as her contribution to the war efforts in the form of participation in combat is not indispensable to the success of those efforts, such a position constitutes part of a doctrine of loyalty compatible with liberalism.

> L3. In conflicts when the state in which Muslims live is under attack by a non-Muslim force, and thus no conflict of loyalty or theological imperative is at stake, it is permissible to contribute directly to the self-defense efforts of the non-Muslim state.

If, however, a Muslim considers it a sin to sacrifice his life for a cause other than one specified in holy texts, then political liberalism would at least require him to regard it as permissible to contribute to the self-defense efforts in other ways. The concern from the standpoint of liberalism in the event that a Muslim citizen prefers not to engage in combat is that the reasons for this be grounded in some theological imperative to not commit an act that may be a double effect of serving the non-Muslim state, and not an indifference or contempt for the legitimate interests of that state.

In what follows, I explore Islamic resources for these three positions characteristic of a minimal doctrine of civic loyalty. I argue that one finds even in classical Islamic jurisprudence an important resource for grounding the level of loyalty to a non-Muslim state required of Muslims in the strict emphasis on the obligation to uphold oaths, promises, and contracts, including with non-Muslims. This commitment to contract allows even very "orthodox" Islamic scholars to affirm L2. By contrast, L3 seems to require supplementing classical views with new ones or creatively interpreting the legal reasoning of classical scholars. However, L1 is a clear case where Muslims will have to depart from classical jurisprudence and endorse the efforts of Modernists to revise the classical *jihād* doctrine.

The *amān*: Foundation for a Contract of Civic Loyalty

The most prominent contemporary advocate of the notion that Muslims can fully and without contradiction embrace their citizenship in European countries has written: "Contracts determine our status, fix our duties and rights and direct the nature and scope of our actions. Once agreed, the terms of a covenant should be respected and if there is a point which seems to work against Muslim rights—or even their conscience as Believers—this has to be discussed and negotiated since Muslims are, unilaterally, not allowed to breach a treaty."[1] Ramadan argues further that "millions of Muslims have tacitly or explicitly recognized the binding character of the constitution or the laws of the country they enter into and then live in. By signing a work contract or asking for a visa, they acknowledge the validity and authority of the constitution, the laws and the state all at once."[2] He concludes from this a robust and principled position of political obligation to non-Muslim states of citizenship:

> One can then see that it is clearly in the name of faithfulness to the Islamic teachings of *Sharīʿa* and *fiqh* that Muslims can live in the West, and that it is their duty to respect the law of the country. In other words, Islamic law and jurisprudence *order* a Muslim individual to submit to the framework of positive law in force in his country of residence in the name of the tacit moral covenant which already underlies his very presence. To put it differently again, *implementing the Sharīʿa,* for a Muslim citizen or resident in Europe, is explicitly to respect the constitutional and legal framework of the country in which he is a citizen. Whereas one might have feared a *conflict of loyalties,* one cannot but note that it is in fact the reverse, since faithfulness to Islamic teachings results in an even more exacting legal *implementation* in the new environment. *Loyalty to one's faith and conscience requires firm and honest loyalty to one's country*: the *Sharīʿa* requires honest citizenship within the frame of reference constituted by the positive law of the European country concerned.[3]

In what follows, I examine further this idea of contract in classical and contemporary juridical works. The question to be addressed here is to what extent the duty to uphold contracts can ground compatible responses to the specific demands of civic loyalty as I characterize them.

A series of Qur'anic verses exhort Muslims to honor any contract (usually *ʿahd* or *ʿaqd,* sometimes *mīthāq*) into which they enter:

> It is not righteousness to turn your faces towards East or West, but rather righteousness is . . . to fulfill the contracts which you make. [2:177]

> O you who believe! Fulfill all contracts. [5:1]

> Fulfill God's covenant when you have entered into it and break not your oaths after asserting them, for you thereby make God your guarantor. [Q. 16:91]

> Fulfill every contract for contracts will be answered for [on the Day of Reckoning]. [Q. 17:34]

> It is those who are endued with understanding that receive admonition, those who fulfill the covenant of God and do not violate their agreements. [13:19]

There is also a famous *ḥadīth* reported through multiple chains (*ḥadīth muta wātir*) and in multiple forms about the sinfulness of breaching contracts:

> When God gathers all earlier and later generations of mankind on the Day of Judgment he will raise a flag for every person who betrays a trust (*ghādir*) so it might be said that this is the perfidy of so-and-so, son of so-and-so.[4]

In addition to these texts that deal generally with the status of promises and contracts, a number of revelatory texts apply this duty to the context of military conflict with non-Muslims. Verse 8:72 (discussed also in the previous chapter on migration) speaks of those who failed to join the Islamic community through migration: "If they [Muslims living amongst non-Muslims] seek your aid in religion, it is your duty to help them, except against a people with whom you have a treaty."

A *ḥadīth* reported in Muslim's *Ṣaḥīḥ* applies at a personal level the principle of upholding promises not to fight them provided to non-Muslims. It is reported that a Companion of the Prophet, Ḥudhayfa ibn al-Yamān, said:

> Nothing prevented me from being present at the Battle of Badr except this incident: I came out with my father Ḥusayl to participate in the Battle but we were caught by some Qurayshi unbelievers. They said: "Do you intend to go to Muḥammad?" We said: "We do not intend to go to him but we wish to go back to Medina." So they took from us a covenant in the name of God that we would turn back to Medina and would not fight on the side of Muḥammad. So when we came to the Messenger of God and related the incident to him he said: "Both of you proceed to Medina. We will fulfill the covenant made with them but seek God's help against them."[5]

Although the episode does not deal with a contract with non-Muslims arising as a consequence of legal residence, it seems to be a perfect example of the justification of some Muslims refraining from fighting nonbelievers because of a promise made to them. The fact that the *ḥadīth* is situated during the lifetime of Muḥammad (when there can be no question about a Muslim's fealty to the leader of the community and his obligation to participate in *jihād*) can only add to its potency as a guide for Muslim behavior in nonapostolic times.[6]

Jurists from across the Sunni schools are quite clear that contracts made with non-Muslims are as morally binding as those made with Muslims. Muslim behavior in a non-Muslim state is generally treated in relation to the legal concept of *amān*, the formal guarantee of security from a potentially hostile entity that is a form of contract imposing obligations on both sides. Jurists are unanimous in holding that the enjoyment of *amān* imposes on the Muslim certain moral and sometimes legal obligations to the non-Muslim entity in question.[7] Sarakhsī declared that "it is abhorred for a Muslim who requests an *amān* from them [by swearing] on his religion to deceive or betray them, for treachery [*ghadr*] is forbidden in Islam. The Prophet said: 'He who betrays a trust will have a flag stuck in his anus on the Day of Judgment so that his betrayal may be known.'"[8] The Ḥanbalī Ibn Qudāma agrees with, and in fact goes beyond, the Ḥanafī position:

> Whoever enters the land of the enemy under an *amān* shall not cheat them in transactions. [This] is forbidden, because they only gave the *amān* under the condition of refraining from deceit or betrayal, and of his [guarantee of] security to them from himself. Even if this [contract] is not explicitly pronounced it is still binding because it is presumed. For this same reason, whoever comes to one of our lands from one of theirs under an *amān* and betrays us thereby violates his contract. So if this is established then it is not permitted [for a Muslim] to betray them, because this is deceit [*ghadr*], which is not permitted in our religion. The Prophet said: "Muslims are bound by their terms." [*al-muslimūn 'inda shurūṭihim*] If a Muslim under an *amān* steals, cheats or borrows something from a non-Muslim and then flees to *dār al-Islām* then if the non-Muslim goes there under an *amān* Muslim authorities are obligated to provide for the return of his property as if he had taken it from a Muslim.[9]

Note a number of additional elements to this basic position, most important: (like many Western doctrines of political obligation) a recognition of tacit agreements, the usage of parity and reciprocity as operative ethical values, and the legal point that Muslim authorities may in fact enforce the rights of non-Muslims.[10]

For most contemporary Islamic scholars, the question of general political obligation to a non-Muslim state falls under the rubric of the duty to uphold contracts, including the duty to obey laws relating to war. Once a Muslim has accepted the security of a non-Muslim state, he is bound to follow all of its laws, including paying taxes that contribute to general social welfare.[11] In one *fatwā*, a scholar responds that Muslims should continue to obey the law and pay taxes to the American government even during a war against a Muslim country because there is a general obligation to abide by the laws of one's country and because "falling in trouble with the law is worse than the fact that part of your taxes is used by the government to display some sort of anti-Islam campaigns, such as giving full and blind support to the Israeli atrocities in Palestine."[12]

There are at least two interpretations of such a position: On one reading, it could be seen as part of the Sunni tradition of quietism developed as a doctrine of political obligation to tyrannical regimes during centuries of unjust rule in Muslim countries. This tradition is summed up by the popular proverb: "Better one hundred years of tyranny than one day of civil unrest [*fitna*]." This first interpretation gives a Muslim reasons to act in accordance with his civic duties, but not reasons to *choose* or *endorse* such duties as a liberal regime would impose. Furthermore, it is not clear that the reason for obeying laws stems from a recognition of the moral status of other citizens, of the rights of the wider society, or of the legitimacy of the regime. It is consistent with a purely instrumental, self-regarding attitude of judging what is in the best interests of the Muslim community.

On a different reading, it could be seen as an attempt to balance ethical obligations, concluding in this case that the duty to uphold a contract is greater than the duty not to contribute proportionally to an unjust policy. This is akin to another traditional Sunni position, a rival to the above one: "There can be no obedience to man [*makhlūq*; lit: a created being] in disobedience to God [*khāliq*; lit: the Creator]." This second interpretation invites a certain interrogation of one's political regime in light of one's metaphysically derived, ethical commitments, not dissimilar from the form of comparative political theory developed in this study. Thus, in another *fatwā*, Qaṭari scholar 'Alī Muḥyī al-Dīn al-Qara Dāghī argues that the duty not to lie obligates a Muslim to pay taxes to a non-Muslim state, but that the duty "to abide by the laws of the country [only holds] so long as they do not contradict the Laws of God. If there is such a contradiction, no one should be obeyed at the expense of disobeying God."[13] This approach, when resulting in the endorsement of performing civic duties, is obviously more indicative of a genuine overlapping consensus than the quietist approach because it involves a judgment that those duties are either reasonable or at least not objectionable from an Islamic standpoint. Of course, this position results in problems of its own, namely, that Muslims will not endorse liberal citizenship as such but rather assume a line-item approach of picking and choosing which laws do not involve "disobedience to the Creator."[14]

This is not a problem that can be resolved definitively. Although liberal doctrines of civil disobedience might support Muslim refusal in some cases—say, refusing to comply with the French or Turkish headscarf bans—such doctrines do not constitute a general acquiescence to a private veto over every law. But we should not be distracted at the moment by this wider question of political obligation. Part of what we are seeking to establish by addressing liberal citizenship question by question in this study is whether any individual basic obligation of citizenship involves such "disobedience to the Creator." What I believe the Islamic insistence on adherence to contracts shows, however, is precisely that justice, generally speaking, applies across religious differences: In principle, Muslims are required to regard duties arising out of contracts with non-Muslims as binding unless the duties involve performing a prohibited act; paying taxes[15] and in general following the laws of a non-Muslim state that protect the rights of non-Muslims are not presumed *in themselves* to involve disobedience to the Creator.

On this chapter's narrower question of loyalty in wartime, however, Muslim jurists are able to speak more precisely. It is quite clear for the majority that this duty to honor contracts (*al-wafā' bi'l-'aqd*) and to abide by conditions freely endorsed (*al-muslimūn 'inda shurūṭihim*) overrides for many jurists any general duty to contribute to an Islamic polity's military efforts against a state of residence. Indicative here are the juridical treatments on the behavior of Muslim prisoners. Note how seriously the canonical thirteenth-century Shāfi'ī jurist al-Nawawī takes the act of agreeing to conditions:

> If they capture [a Muslim soldier] then he is obligated to flee as soon as he can. If they free him without condition then he is obligated to

> try and fights them because they are unbelievers with no guarantee of security. But if they free him on the condition that he is under a guarantee of security [*amān*] from them, then they are also under a guarantee of security from him. If they guarantee his security and ask for a guarantee from him then it is forbidden for him to fight them or steal their property on the basis of what the Almighty has said: "O you who have believed! Fulfill all contracts." [5:1] But if they violate their guarantee to him then he may do so as well to them. If they free him under a guarantee of safety but without asking for one themselves, then even in this case the majority say that they are still under such a guarantee on his part because of their placing him under a guarantee.[16]

Ibn Qudāma advances a similar position with the addendum that even the condition to remain in the country rather than return to the Islamic polity must be honored, again "for the Prophet said: 'Muslims are bound by their conditions.'"[17] Although the jurists in question do not seem to directly address the obligations of Muslims residing in or visiting non-Muslim countries for nonmartial purposes toward the war effort of a Muslim polity, the only reasonable interpretation is that if this applies to prisoners during wartime, then it does a fortiori to nonprisoners and noncombatants who reside or enter there willingly under an *amān*. The duty to honor contracts, even tacit ones, is binding on all Muslims, and entering a non-Muslim land is only done under an *amān*, which is regarded as a contract that includes among its conditions the obligation to do no harm to non-Muslim interests. If a Muslim decides that it is his duty to serve in a *jihād* or otherwise advance Muslim interests over non-Muslim ones, then jurists (as we saw with the Sarakhsī quote in the previous section) require that he first renounce his *amān* as a way of honorably advising non-Muslims of his intentions.

This value, articulated deeply and widely in the classical legal tradition, is the most common Islamic justification for honoring non-Muslim interests while residing in non-Muslim lands. The European Council for *Fatwa* and Research:

> prescribes adherence to what has been demonstrated in the texts of the Book and the Sunna and has been agreed upon by the jurists by way of loyalty to the terms of the contract of *amān* and the conditions of residence and citizenship in the countries of Europe in which they live. Amongst the most important things which are required of them are: 1. That they consider the lives, property and honor of non-Muslims to be inviolable according to the requirements of the contract under which they entered these countries and remained residing in them, for God has said: "Fulfill every contract for contracts will be answered for [on the Day of Reckoning]." [17:34] [and] 2. That they respect the laws of these countries which have sheltered them, and protected them and have made it possible for them to enjoy all the guarantees of a dignified life, for God has said: "Is there any reward for good but good?" [55:60][18]

The vice chairman of this council, Fayṣāl Mawlawī, in another text refers to the contemporary system of visas and naturalization as the legal and moral equivalent of the former *amān* and exhorts fidelity to their terms.[19]

In fact, Mawlawī and Qaraḍāwī extract from the duty to honor contracts an even more robust position than my original wording, which refers only to a Muslim's behavior when his state of citizenship itself is under attack. Qaraḍāwī argues that even when the duty of *jihād* does obtain, it can be discharged in a variety of ways: "As for Muslims living beyond the territories, they are required to back the wronged with all means possible. Thus, *jihād* is not confined to fighting in the battlefield. There are many forms of support. A Muslim can give out charity, boycott the products of the enemy, etc."[20] Referring to the 2003 invasion of Iraq, a war that Mawlawī refers to as "aggression" and thus potentially a situation of defensive *jihād*, contribution to which would then be an individual obligation on all Muslims (*farḍ 'ayn*), he writes that "Muslims are bound by conventions they concluded with these [non-Muslim invading] countries, such as nationality or residence. Therefore, they are exempted from fighting along with the Iraqi people, for Allah says '. . . if they seek help from you in the matter of religion then it is your duty to help them except against a folk between whom and you there is a treaty' [Q. 8.72]." Furthermore, although Muslims may in no circumstances participate in that war on the non-Muslim side, "they are not [even] allowed to evade taxes [in their host countries] because of the conventions they concluded with these countries. Also, they are not allowed to attack the military institutions."[21] Thus, according to Mawlawī, not only do Muslim citizens of non-Muslim states have no right to sabotage their states' efforts of self-defense but also they are not even allowed to damage the interests of their state of citizenship when it is engaged in what is regarded as a war of aggression against a Muslim country.[22] It is also argued occasionally that the principle of reciprocity (*al-mu'āmala bi'l-mithl*), which some use to justify violence against civilians or one's state of citizenship (see chapter 3), "is limited to that which is considered virtuous in Islam. For example, if the enemy violates the honor of Muslim women, Muslims do not violate the honor of their women. If they kill women, children and the weak, Muslims do not respond by doing the same. If they starve prisoners of war to death, Muslims do not reciprocate."[23]

Mawlawī, Qaraḍawī, and the European Council for *Fatwa* and Research represent what we might refer to as the neo-classical strand of contemporary Islamic ethical thought, insofar as they seek to articulate their positions as much as possible within the framework of the classical juridical tradition and thus claim a certain conservative authority and authenticity. As I have previously argued, the articulation of compatible positions from within such conservative or canonical discourses represents particularly strong evidence of a plausible overlapping consensus. In this case, it seems quite clear that there are very stable Islamic foundations for a principled, religiously grounded affirmation of our first statement of loyalty, the abstention from and repudiation of any acts damaging to one's state of citizenship when it is engaged in conflict even with a Muslim force or entity.

Defending a Non-Muslim State

Because Muslims do not proclaim a general doctrine of pacifism, and because national defense is a legitimate state activity to which all citizens must in general be willing to contribute, I argued earlier that an Islamic doctrine of loyalty to a non-Muslim state would include the justification of direct contribution to self-defense efforts when the aggressing force is a non-Muslim one. Such a position was not generally advocated by the classical jurists, who held that it is generally impermissible to contribute to the military strength of non-Muslims, and is on that basis often rejected by contemporary Muslim scholars. A rare exception was the early (eighth-century) scholar Sufyān al-Thawrī, who argued that it was permissible for Muslim prisoners of non-Muslims to fight the non-Muslim enemies of their captors, because all non-Muslims were enemies anyway.[24]

It is not rare, however, for contemporary neo-classical scholars—some of whom hold that fighting fellow Muslims on behalf of non-Muslims constitutes apostasy—to assert that there is no moral dilemma in serving in non-Muslim armies against other non-Muslim armies. The closest that the authoritative texts come to addressing such a situation are the reports on the experiences of the Muslim community living in exile in Abyssinia before Muḥammad's migration to Yāthrib (Medīna). This precedent we have seen introduced earlier in relation to the permissibility of residing in and submitting to the authority of non-Muslim states. The Christian king of Abyssinia, al-Najāshī (the Negus), is often used as the paradigmatic non-Muslim but just ruler whom Muslims are commanded to honor with their loyalty. The canonical account of the Prophetic biography (the *sīra* of Ibn Isḥāq) reports that during the Muslim stay in Abyssinia, "a rebel rose to snatch his kingdom from him, and I never knew us to be so sad as we were at that, in our anxiety lest this fellow would get the better of the Negus, and that a man would arise who did not know our case as well as he did. We prayed to God to give the Negus victory over his enemy and to establish him in his own country. [When he was victorious] we lived in the happiest conditions until we came to the apostle of God in Mecca."[25] Although the Muslims in Abyssinia did not join the Abyssinian army and contribute directly to defense efforts, the implication is clearly that Muslims may form deep sympathies (expressed here through active prayer) with just non-Muslim states and rulers (the latter of which we may be tempted to compare to political systems), particularly in their conflicts with aggressors.[26]

Yet, the contemporary statements permitting actual military service are not generally based on *positive* textual evidence of the permissibility of this and are usually satisfied with noting the various restrictions on such service. In his book devoted entirely to Muslim minority issues, Qaraḍāwī simply remarks: "Muslims are confronted with the question of mandatory military service in these countries, and there is no objection to this unless such a country declares war against a Muslim country."[27] In an Internet *fatwā* (in response to a question posed by this author), he elaborates on this, naming three conditions on joining a non-Muslim army: "1. One should not take part in a war that goes against his belief and religion. 2. One should adopt Islamic morals of justice and equity and not to transgress against others. 3. One should practice *da'wa* (preaching Islam) whether among his colleagues or among the soldiers of the enemy."[28] In the same response was included the view of another scholar, the Canadian Muslim Shaykh Ahmad Kutty, who likewise emphasized not the Muslim or non-Muslim character of the state but the ethical status of the war:

> Muslims who are citizens are definitely allowed to serve in the armies of their own country, regardless of whether it is a Muslim country or predominately non-Muslim country. They are also allowed to fight wars that are legitimate and ethical. But they are not allowed to fight in a war of aggression; for all wars of aggression are unlawful in Islam. War in Islam is sanctioned only either in self-defense or to remove oppression and tyranny. So Muslim soldiers cannot fight in wars which are considered unjust and unethical. They can excuse themselves on grounds of moral conscience.

These positions represent a significant break with the juridical tradition they are supposed to represent in both content and methodology. Classical jurists were anything but indifferent to the identities of the various parties in a conflict or political situation; it was in fact largely this that determined the ethical status of wars and governments. Further, the classical doctrine of *jihād* allowed, even required, wars that would by today's standards of international law be regarded as wars of aggression. The position that one's willingness to participate in a war depends on the ethical status of that war, while tacitly suggesting that non-Muslim countries may be sometimes justified in engaging in war, seems to be approaching a suggestion that the Islamic doctrine of just war should not be expected to conflict greatly with non-Islamic ones. These views are discussed in more detail in the following section.

The methodology developed in this study largely involves analysis of the types of reasons advanced for a position. In the case of the positions here, the primary reason for holding that it is permissible to serve in a non-Muslim army is merely that this is not one of the things *specifically* forbidden by the revelatory texts. Thus, one can do whatever is not specifically forbidden, which in this case includes fighting brother Muslims, contributing to a war of aggression (i.e., violating a principle of *jus ad bellum*), or aggressing within war (i.e., violating a principle of *jus in bello*). The response to the variety of arguments against serving in a non-Muslim army—that it is wrong to add to the strength of unbelievers, that one is not allowed to befriend or associate with them at all, that one cannot uphold the law of unbelief, that war is only just when it is to advance the cause of Islam—is one of silence rather than direct engagement or refutation. An explanation might lie in the fact that the scholars seem to see this question resolved by their broader understandings of just war and *jihād*. For scholars who genuinely assert an Islamic just war doctrine that is more reflective of contemporary international law than the classical Islamic doctrine, the question of serving in a non-Muslim army is obviously not as thorny as it is for those seeking to rehabilitate the classical doctrine. The specific arguments against serving in a non-Muslim army in any context are all preempted by the modernist rethinking of the *jihād* doctrine. In any event, regardless of the connection to wider beliefs on war, legitimating service in a non-Muslim army simply on the grounds that nothing in Islam forbids it is an acceptable form of the type of argument we are looking for: It is an Islamic argument (rather than an argument grounded in public reason), and it is principled. The only potential question relates to its strength or plausibility: If we are aware of Islamic arguments against such service that rely on authoritative texts, then the Muslim believer looking for guidance may not be satisfied with anything less than direct refutation of the incompatible positions or at least similar citation of evidence.

There have been other attempts to deal with this question. In a 1907 *fatwā* on Russian Muslims participating in the Russo-Japanese War that is invoked by a number of contemporary scholars, Rashīd Riḍā did "not consider that fighting on behalf of the Muslims of Russia against Japan is disobedience to God nor forbidden by *sharī'a*, and in fact may be one of the things rewarded by God if engaged in with the correct intention."[29] He proceeds to outline two rationales for fighting in the Russian army that would qualify as correct intention. These qualify as Islamic arguments that we can analyze in terms of compatibility.

The first is most likely constitutive of a compatible position: "His obedience to the state protects his brothers from amongst the state's subjects from any oppression or evil that may befall them if the state is an oppressive, autocratic one; it makes them equal to any other citizen in rights and privileges if it is a representative, just state; and it benefits them in other ways if the state is in between." The concerns in this statement all relate to benefits that accrue to the Muslim community from participating in the war and have nothing to do with either obligations to the state of citizenship or the justness of the war in question. A concern with advancing the interests of Muslim communities is also central in the justifications of many contemporary scholars of Muslims serving in non-Muslim armies. The argument is that there may be a certain general communal interest (*maṣlaḥa*) in the performance of otherwise forbidden acts. Both the structure and the substance of this form of argument raise some important concerns about compatibility. For example, in the *fatwā* cited earlier in which Qaraḍāwī declares fighting fellow Muslims on behalf of non-Muslims "unbelief," he goes on to say that Muslims should be willing to accept noncombatant positions to avoid *accusations* of "high treason" that would "pose a threat to the Muslim community and also disrupt the course of *da'wa*" and that "individuals should not set their conscience at ease and refuse to participate in the war, if this will endanger the whole Muslim community. This is based on the juristic rule, which states that the lesser harm may be borne to prevent a greater harm, the private harm may be borne to prevent a general one and the right of the group takes precedence over that of the individual."[30] This *fatwā* is not directly relevant to our present discussion (since it deals with fighting Muslims, which is uniformly held to be impermissible), but it serves as a cruder and more obvious example of justifications for performing certain acts that are not actually arguments for an overlapping consensus because they still hold the acts to be wrong and unjust.

Thus, the concern is that Riḍā's rationale might be read as implying more problematic positions, including (1) that if none of the benefits here described will in fact accrue to Muslims, then there is no justification for aiding non-Muslims; (2) that if the benefits accrue, then Muslims are permitted to engage in whatever acts secure them, including unjust wars; and (3) that even if Muslims are permitted to join non-Muslim armies to secure benefits for themselves, there is no suggestion that the cause of the non-Muslim state is in itself just or reasonable. Thus, there might be a reading of Riḍā's first rationale that sees it as either insufficiently principled or principled in the wrong way (i.e., only concerned with the interests of Muslims).

The case for the compatibility of Riḍā's rationale with a liberal conception of citizenship rests in his recognition of some states as "representative and just." This statement alone constitutes a major step toward an overlapping consensus in its suggestion that states might be at the same time non-Muslim and just, quite a break indeed from the implications of some jurists and thinkers we have encountered that equated non-Muslim states' unjustness precisely with their non-Muslimness. More specifically, however, he seems to be accepting the desirability of a social contract in which Muslims enjoy equality with non-Muslims in exchange for sharing the same duties. Even if his comprehensive motivations are the welfare of a given substate community, his longer term means for increasing that welfare is precisely the greater integration of the Muslim population as citizens in a non-Muslim state. In terms of our interest in the specifically Islamic grounding of the desirability or acceptability of this type of social contract, we can infer a similar type of "negative" or "no prohibition [*'adam al-taḥrīm*]" justification that we found with Kutty and Qaraḍāwī: if there is nothing specifically contrary to Islamic requirements in a given act, then it is in that way the object of an overlapping consensus.

Note that this argument would also resolve the dilemma of dealing with the *fatwā* on its consequentialist interpretation from the previous paragraph: It doesn't matter if the jurist is advancing consequentialist or unprincipled reasons for doing something if he does not think that these are reasons for doing something that would otherwise be impermissible or sinful, as is the case with Qaraḍāwī's justification for taking noncombatant positions in wars against Muslim forces. The consequentialist justification can simply be an added benefit to one's conception of the good, but the legitimation of the act is the statement that nothing in the conception of the good contradicts it.

Riḍā also offers a second rationale for serving in a non-Muslim army, which requires separate analysis:

> The knowledge and practice of war remain amongst the most important facets of social life for human beings. Thus, if they are forbidden for a certain people then that people is weakened, and the weak are never but humiliated and degraded. It is thus better for Muslims who are subjects of those states that they participate like the ordinary people of those nations in the basic elements of social life, strengthened by their strength and made proud by their pride, rather than

> being weak and degraded by their religion, for Islam does not permit that its adherents chose weakness and subjugation over strength and pride. Thus, if they choose the latter [by not serving in the Russian army] they are incapable of preserving their religion. . . . [We] advise Muslims to choose pride over humiliation whatever the source of pride and strength may be over weakness and consider that preserving Islam outside of its abode requires this.

The question to be addressed here is whether Riḍā's emphasis on strength and pride for Muslims, as well as military knowledge, is a questionable justification for discharging a civic duty. Consider the response of Topoljak (cited briefly in chapter 3) that "participation in the army of a non-Muslim country with the intention of training and gaining fighting skills is permitted, even required."[31] He gives the examples of those Muslims who had been trained in non-Muslim armies but later used those skills in the wars in Bosnia and the Caucasus, and in fact he cites this *fatwā* by Riḍā. What is problematic about Topoljak's argument are the auxiliary beliefs by which they are legitimated: namely, that Muslims ought not be citizens of a non-Muslim country if the Islamic state exists, that there is a duty to prepare for *jihād* in the classical sense, and that Muslims are not supposed to strengthen non-Muslims if they can help it. For Topoljak, serving in a non-Muslim army is justified by the principle of necessity (*ḍarūra*) as the only way of acquiring the skills to discharge a duty that is directly hostile to the interests and rights of a non-Muslim state, a further step away from compatibility with liberal citizenship than Qaraḍāwī's principle of utility/interest (*maṣlaḥa*).

For Riḍā, despite some similar use of language, it appears that the benefit in question is quite different. He speaks generally in terms of "strength" (*quwwa*) and "pride" (*'izza*) without referring, as does Topoljak, to *jihād* or to the acquisition of these qualities at the expense of non-Muslims or in order to use military skills against them. Thus, his understanding of these qualities does not seem to be incompatible with the aims of a liberal democratic society, if enjoying a status of equality in relation to non-Muslims constitutes "strength" and "pride." Given his historical context, the alternative for him was probably a situation of hostility, marginalization, and suspicion. Countering this potentially destructive majority-minority dynamic through insisting on full inclusion and full participation is precisely the response that liberalism prefers for minority communities to articulate.

There is thus another way in which comprehensive doctrines can articulate compatible responses, and that is by pointing out the benefits that accrue to a conception of the good as a double effect. Like the "utilitarian" interpretation of Riḍā's first acceptable intention behind joining a non-Muslim army, this justification depends on the "no prohibition" or "no contradiction" justification. A holder of a comprehensive doctrine can first assert that there is no contradiction between a given demand and the comprehensive doctrine, or even articulate a compatible affirmation of the reasonableness of the demand, and then show how other benefits also accrue to the holder's pursuit of his private conception of the good as a double effect of the given civic duty in question. Even though the citizen is affirming a civic duty for a different set of reasons than the ones for which it is required by the state, as long as these private motivations are not contradictory to, or undermining of, the legitimate rights and interests of the state (as is the Topoljak *jihād*-preparation motivation), there is no reason not to regard them as legitimate nonpublic supplementary justifications for a citizen.

For example, there may be certain motivations for joining an army derived from individualist conceptions of the good, including the desire to achieve high physical fitness, the desire to develop or operate cutting-edge technology, the desire to enjoy the solidarity of a cohesive organization, the desire to achieve a certain self-image or self-esteem, the desire to acquire martial skills, the desire to exercise authority over other people, the desire to acquire for free skills for later application in the labor market, or the desire for a challenging and gratifying career. One can also see how the activities of a military may advance the values of a range of comprehensive ethical doctrines. A rather bizarre but apropos case recently occurred within the Royal Navy, which in October 2004 allowed one of its technicians to be officially registered as a Satanist and enjoy the right to engage in certain religious rituals while onboard ship. According to the individual in question, his decision to enter the armed forces was a direct consequence of his comprehensive beliefs: He found that service in the military was one way of acting on his comprehensive belief in vengeance.[32] Communitarian conceptions of the good may also provide citizens who belong to minority groups with motivations for joining their state's military forces. Minority communities in the United States and Israel, for example, have found military service as a path to acceptance by the wider national community and a means of communal advancement. Although the goods aspired to should be the unconditional right of citizens rather than conditional upon (especially voluntary) military service, this is another example of a nonpublic reason that is clearly compatible with the demands of citizenship.

The motivation of serving one's country may coexist with all of these nonpublic motivations in a variety of ways—from benign indifference through unquestioned affirmation to equal fervor—but the liberal state can hardly insist that it is itself a basic civic duty to perform other basic civic duties for the sole reason that they *are* duties or for the *same reasons* that make them duties. In all of these cases, citizens find that the activities they engage in as citizens are activities they want to engage in *anyway* and thus can affirm the demands of a liberal state as acceptable from within their comprehensive doctrines. Given that they find the general aims of the military, and the internal rules and practices, not in contradiction with any of their comprehensive beliefs, and that their aims do not contradict those of a well-ordered society, one might say that this is a possible path to an overlapping consensus. I wish here to suggest a clear analogy between these motivations and Riḍā's three justifications of service in a non-Muslim army: as something that might earn Muslims equal treatment in a non-Muslim democracy, as a way of acquiring the military knowledge that Islam prescribes, and as a path to communal strength and pride. They are compatible motivations because, even though there is no direct consideration of the interests of the non-Muslim community, all of these goals are themselves consistent with the aims of a liberal society (i.e., a Muslim can both pursue these aims without violating any of the legitimate interests of a non-Muslim society, and he can hold these motivations *alongside* a recognition of non-Muslim rights without incoherence or self-contradiction), and because they presume the desirability of integration into that community.

Perhaps the objection can still be made that a true overlapping doctrine on the question of contributing to the self-defense of one's state must include (whatever else it includes by way of supplementary beliefs) the belief that one's fellow citizens' interests are legitimate and important to the person in question, and that this is, at least partially, *why* he serves in a military. This belief was accounted for to a certain extent in the discussion on contracts. A fuller account requires entering into the more complex area of Islamic doctrines of just war. This is, as noted previously, precisely where many contemporary Muslim jurists place the present question—in the context of their general views on just war. For many of them, serving a non-Muslim army is not a discrete technical question, as it may have been for the classical jurists, but related to their modernist doctrine of *jihād* as a purely defensive war. This shift to a more universal just war doctrine, based on conditions that apply to both Muslims and non-Muslims, is a far more stable and substantive foundation for an overlapping consensus than a technicality.

Permanent Recognition of Non-Muslim States

Verse 8:61 of the Qur'an reads: "If they incline towards peace, then incline to it as well and place your trust in God." The precise character of the moral-doctrinal demand made by liberalism on Muslim citizens is summarized in a virtuoso way in Sayyid Quṭb's commentary on this verse:

> I have dwelt rather extensively on the provisional nature of the rule outlined in this verse, which requires the Prophet and the Muslims to reciprocate any inclination to peace by the unbelievers. My aim is to clarify a certain aspect of confusion that arises from the spiritual and intellectual defeatism reflected in the work of many of those who write about Islamic *jihād*. Such people feel the pressure of modern values that prevail in international relations. Lacking a clear understanding of Islam as they are, they find it too much for the divine faith to adopt a single and permanent approach towards all humanity, giving all people a choice between three alternatives: acceptance of Islam, payment of *jizya* or being at war with Islam. . . . Such writers try to impose a different interpretation on Qur'ānic statements and *aḥādīth* so that they can be seen to be in line with the situation in our present world with all its pressures on contemporary Muslims. They find the single approach of Islam and the three choices it offers too hard to swallow. Such writers often interpret statements that have a

> provisional nature or qualified application as final, permanent and having general and universal application. When they tackle the final statements they interpret these in the light of those provisional ones to which they have applied a final import. Thus, they come up with the idea that Islamic *jihād* is merely a defensive operation to protect Muslim people and their land when they are attacked, and that Islam will always accept any offer of peace. To them, peace is merely a state of non-belligerence which, in practical terms, means that the other camp will not attack the land of Islam. According to their understanding, Islam should shrink inside its borders at all times. It has no right to call on others to accept its message or to submit to God's law, unless such a call takes the form of a speech, statement or bulletin. When it comes to material forces, Islam has no right to attack the ruling forces in *jāhiliyyah* societies unless it first comes under attack, in which case Islam is right to defend itself.[33]

Affirming the "defeatist," "defensive" interpretation of the Islamic doctrine of *jihād*, according to which non-Muslim states have the right to equal recognition with Muslim states, is precisely what is required for a Muslim citizen of a liberal democracy for it be to be claimed that her conception of the good provides her with reasons to endorse the liberal conception of citizenship in a pluralist society. This topic of Islamic theories of international relations requires separate monographic treatment on its own,[34] but in what follows, I attempt to discuss briefly the grounds on which a Muslim citizen might affirm the legitimate rights of self-defense of her non-Muslim state of citizenship.

There is no lack of verses in the Qur'an that exhort believers to adopt an attitude of mutual tolerance and nonaggression with unbelievers. In addition to the verse quoted before, one finds:

> Fight in the cause of God those who fight you, but do not transgress limits, for God does not love transgressors. [2:190]
>
> And fight them until there is no more tumult or oppression and there prevail justice and faith in God, but if they cease let there be no hostility except to those who practice oppression. [2:193]
>
> If they withdraw from you but fight you not and (instead) send you (guarantees of) peace, then God opens no way for you (to war against them). [4:90]
>
> Do not say to him who offers you a greeting of peace, "You are not a believer," seeking the chance goods of the present life. [4:94]
>
> God does not forbid you, with regard to those who do not fight you for your faith nor drive you from your homes, from dealing kindly and justly with them. For God loves the just. [60:8]

Whereas the classical doctrine articulates no absolute right to recognition for non-Muslim polities, "modernist authors underline the defensive aspect of *jihād*, and hold that *jihād* outside Islamic territory is only permitted when the peaceful propagation of Islam is being hindered or when Muslims living amongst unbelievers are oppressed."[35] The main questions for our purposes relate to the types of arguments advanced by these "Modernist" Muslim jurists and scholars in favor of a doctrine of *jihād* as defensive war: Do any of the doctrines articulated by these thinkers in fact overlap with modern standards of permanent recognition, and do the reasons given for restraint and tolerance meet the ethical standards that I have been developing in this study?

The most frequent argument for a "defensive" conception of *jihād* is in two parts. First, it is argued that the vast majority of Qur'anic verses on fighting and warfare prescribe a doctrine of defensive war. This argument holds that the more "aggressive" verses are best understood in the context of the hostility faced by the first generation of Muslims from the pagan Arabs rather than as a general attitude toward non-Muslims or as the higher stage of God's revelation on the ethics of war, abrogating the chronologically previous "peaceful verses." Second, it is argued that the basic "positive" duty underpinning *jihād* is not the duty to eradicate unbelief or remove non-Islamic forms of rule, but rather the duty of *da'wa*, that is, to call non-Muslims to the universal message of Islam. Thus, should the right to proselytize be unmolested in non-Muslim lands and should there be an accord of mutual nonaggression, then there are no grounds for aggression against such non-Muslim states.

The modern Islamist (revivalist) argument for a Qur'anic foundation to "offensive" *jihād*, as expounded by Quṭb, Mawdudi, and others, rests on the theory of successive stages to God's injunctions on war, with later verses establishing the final guidelines on war and relations with unbelievers and in the process abrogating (*naskh*) the previous, temporary verses. In contrast, Modernist scholars tend to examine all of the verses on a particular subject matter coequally and attempt to arrive at an interpretation based on consideration of all of them together in their textual as well as historico-revelatory context.[36] Following this methodology, a wide range of Islamic scholars in the modern period have been swayed by the large number of verses, such as those cited here, that enjoin restraint, reciprocity, and faithfulness to contracts and declare that the basic principle (*al-aṣl*) of relations between Muslims and non-Muslims is peace and invitation to Islam.[37] The argument is usually advanced not that there is a conflict between the verses that needs to be explained or mitigated, but rather that they (and the historical behavior of the Prophet and his successors[38]) all affirm the same essential message, especially when the more "aggressive" verses are read not in isolation but as part of longer passages: that violence is justified only in response to aggression, oppression, or treachery, such as that faced by Muḥammad and his followers from the pagan Arabs and the Byzantine and Persian empires.

In relation to the verses from *Sūra* 9 that are central to justifications of "expansive *jihād*," modernist authors are quick to point out that the entire chapter clearly deals with the specific antagonism between the early Muslim community and the pagan Arabs, as the classical exegetical tradition unambiguously asserted, and in particular, the pagans' violation of existing treaties with the Muslim polity.[39] Even within this context, Muslims are still exhorted to observe the standards of restraint and reciprocity called for in chronologically previous chapters. Verse 9:4 declares that "[The treaties are not dissolved] with those pagans with whom you have entered into an alliance and who have not subsequently betrayed you, nor aided anyone against you. So fulfill your obligations with them until the end, for God loves the righteous." The surrounding verses are replete with descriptions of the pagans' perfidy (9:8: "If they get the better of you, they will not observe towards you any bond or treaty") and excesses (9:13: "Will you not fight a people who violated their oaths, plotted to expel the Messenger, and were the first to attack you?") in such a way that both treats this as the ultimate *casus belli* and not the pagans' mere paganism (9:12: "*If* they break their oaths after their covenant and revile your religion, *then* fight the leaders of unbelief so they may desist." Emphasis added), and clearly gives the passages a contextual and contingent character. Arguing, as the revivalists do, that this *Sūra* establishes a *basic* principle of antagonism between believers and unbelievers requires not only extracting verses from their unambiguous context but also, in certain cases, citing only half or partial verses. The general principle of mutual restraint and recognition between Muslims and others is thus, according to the modernists, the manifest implications of the entirety of revelation on the subject of fighting, including verses from *Sūra* 9 and other chapters.

What the Modernist scholars do not address, however, is why the medieval religious scholars who constructed the classical *jihād* doctrine were also confused about the lessons to be drawn from the Qur'an and the Prophet's *sunna*. This is a general dilemma in Islamic Modernist thought and an important reason for this book's adoption of the principles of comparative ethics defended in chapter 2. This lacuna is addressed directly by Sherman Jackson (an American convert to Islam who is trained in both Western and Islamic modes of scholarship) in an effort to theorize a modern Islamic just war doctrine while openly acknowledging that such efforts involve significant departures from classical doctrine and the practice of the Prophet and his followers.

Like the Modernist scholars cited here, Jackson treats the revelatory sources in their context, but he expands that context to include not just the immediate conflict with the Meccan polytheists, but the general state of affairs in late antiquity. For Jackson (following Fred Donner[40]), the Qur'an observes and takes for granted (rather than prescribes as an innovation) the world as existing in a "state of war." The idea of permanent recognition of other entities (tribes, cities, empires) simply did not exist at the time of revelation and the early growth of the Muslim community. Thus the Qur'anic treatment of war first of all simply "reflected the social, historical and political realities of 7th century Arabia."[41] Qur'anic exhortations to fight and its emphasis on the absolute loyalty due the Islamic community reflect the need to "break the early Muslims' emotional, psychological and even material dependency on the 'old order' by forcing them to affirm their commitment to Islam by way of a willingness to fight—in accordance with the existing norm—for the life and integrity of the new religion."[42] Thus, like the Modernists, Jackson sees the Qur'anic exhortations in the context of the war for survival with the Meccan enemies.

However, Jackson also sees a clear application of these lessons to the later juridical tradition, which is where one finds the concepts of *dār al-ḥarb* and *jihād al-ṭalab* (expansive, missionary *jihād*), because the "state of war" characteristic of pre-modern Arabia "characterized the pre-modern world in general. . . . Muslim juristic writings continued to reflect the logic of the 'state of war' and the assumption that only Muslims would permit Muslims to remain Muslims. They continued to see jihad not only as *a* means of guaranteeing the security and freedom of the Muslims but as virtually the *only* means of doing so."[43] In other words, the failure of the premodern juridical tradition to assert a doctrine of mutual recognition with non-Muslim polities need not imply that what is central to the Islamic political imagination is the utopian commitment to a world governed by Islam but rather that doctrines of mutual recognition were simply not part of the medieval "imaginary" at all. Where were the corresponding *doctrines* of recognition from non-Muslim quarters? Given that the underlying circumstances that gave rise to the classical doctrine have changed, that is, that doctrines of mutual recognition are now available, there is every reason for the Islamic doctrines to change.

Jackson invokes classical methods of jurisprudence (*uṣūl al-fiqh*) to buttress this latter claim. Against the misconceptions of both some Muslims and non-Muslims, Jackson shows that legal dynamism (within the confines of the texts) is the normal assumption of Islamic law. He quotes thirteenth-century Mālikī jurist Shihāb al-Dīn al-Qarāfī's view that "Holding to rulings that have been deduced on the basis of custom even after this custom has changed is a violation of Unanimous Consensus [*ijmā'*, the fourth source of Islamic law] and an open display of ignorance of religion."[44] If it is true, then, that the Qur'anic prescriptions and juristic interpretations on war were both based on an interaction with temporally determined circumstances ("custom"), then with the change of those customs, it is in fact a *requirement* of the rules of classical jurisprudence that Islamic rules be revised.

Crucially, Jackson sees this kind of reasoning as potentially compelling even to Revivalist thinkers like Sayyid Quṭb, who also endorse a "dynamic" reading of the Qur'an that requires an engagement with changing circumstances. He focuses in particular on Quṭb's interpretation of Q. 9:29 ("Fight those who do not believe in God and the Last Day and do not forbid that which God and His Messenger have forbidden and do not practice proper religion, among those who were given the Book until they pay the poll-tax and they are subdued"), which relies not on an immutable Divine command but rather on the observation of Jewish and Christian hostility as "*an historical fact.*" Because it is "clear that it is Qutb's belief that Jews and Christians (which one senses he uses as a catch-all for the West) are inherently hostile towards Muslims that informs his reading of 9:29" to the exclusion of other possible interpretations:

> Qutb's understanding of the Qur'anic doctrine on Muslim–non-Muslim relations is as informed by his own reading *into* the text as it is by his attempt to extract meaning *from* the text. For the Qur'an clearly establishes a range of possible attitudes and behaviors on the part of Jews and Christians towards Muslims. Moreover, at least as many if not more exegetes, classical and modern, hold chapter five

> (which speaks of Christian love for Muslims) to be the last-revealed chapter as hold chapter nine to be so. As such, on purely formal grounds, one could just as rightly argue that chapter five reflects the final teaching on Muslim–non-Muslim relations. What brings Qutb to privilege 9:29 and to construe it in the manner he does seems to be his *historical assessment*, based in part on his own experience, of the attitude of Jews and Christians towards Muslims. On this assessment, one would have to admit that whether we employ his "dynamic" method or the classical jurisprudence exemplified by al-Qarafi, Qutb is certainly correct in the conclusion he draws. But, it is equally true, on both approaches, that this conclusion could be overturned, assuming a different *historical assessment*. In other words, assuming that Jews and Christians are no longer active enemies of Muslims, or that there are political mechanisms in place that prevent them from acting on this hostility, even Qutb (or his followers), *on his own methodology*, could be convinced to modify his interpretation of 9:29. In sum, assuming an overall "state of peace," even Qutb might be forced to concede that there is no obligation to wage jihad against Jews and Christians.[45]

Jackson is doubtlessly being optimistic when he reduces the classical and Revivalist commitment to expansive *jihād* as based ultimately on an empirical assessment that non-Muslims will always be dangerous to Muslims. As we saw in the extended quotation that opened this section (extracted from Quṭb's commentary on Q. 8:61), the threat posed by non-Muslims is just *one* rationale for expansive *jihād*. Equally important seems to be the belief that in Islam there is a *categorical* Divine command to not passively tolerate systems of unbelief when capacities permit. Nonetheless, there is thus some reason to believe that even though doctrines of mutual recognition (as required by L1) are a substantive revision of a broad premodern juridical consensus, they may have the capacity to persuade Muslims committed to the idea of an orthodox interpretation of Islam, which itself, as Jackson shows, need not involve a commitment to the letter of existing juridical positions.

The Modernist doctrine of just war, however, is not quite as simple as a bare doctrine of mutual nonaggression. The Qur'an-based arguments for restraint are often embedded within a broader argument about the universal nature of the Islamic mission and the duty of Muslims to proselytize. For these theorists, their emphasis on the importance of *da'wa* exempts them from any charge of passivity, defeatism, or insularity. Not only do they match the "Revivalists" in their insistence on bringing the message of Islam to unbelievers in all places and at all times but also "protecting the right to call to Islam" figures as a legitimate *casus belli* for some of these writers.[46] There is enough ambiguity in the formulation and use of this expression to call for its examination in terms of the aims and methodology of this study, which I do later. First, however, it is important to show how relating the ethics of war to the duty to proselytize enables Modernist theorists to argue for a defensive conception of *jihād*.

The argument advanced is that *da'wa*, rather than some categorical duty to overturn man-made laws or systems of rule, is the value ultimately behind the offensive *jihād* doctrine from which Modernist theorists are eager to distance themselves. Once this is asserted, then it is further argued that the crucial variable in determining the stance toward a non-Muslim polity is its policy toward Islamic missionaries. Protection of the freedom to preach the Islamic message guarantees it absolute immunity from hostility:

> Islam, after the spread of its call around the world and the reaching of its message to all mankind, does not forbid in reality the establishment of nations and states with a variety of legal systems, *if they preserve a posture of neutrality towards the Islamic call*, or make treaties of friendship and peace with Muslims, and of non-aggression with Muslim states. These states enjoy *absolute* freedom and the right to exist with whichever legal systems they want: because the Qur'ān recognizes the existence of multiple communities [" *'ālamīn'* "] ("Blessed is he who revealed the Proof/Discernment [*al-furqān*: the Qur'ān] to his servant that he may be a Warner for all people." [25: 1]) and forbids Muslims to take oaths through deception in order to violate contracts, and to fall into injustice, indecency, wickedness and sin through fearing the proliferation of nations or forbidding that one nation should become more numerous than another.[47]

More important, it is an article of faith for Modernist theorists that *da'wa* is a strictly noncoercive enterprise by its very nature and essence.[48] These theorists further argue, therefore, that if the ultimate value and goal is spreading the Islamic message, then all political acts and state policies must be judged in terms of their impact on this project. It is thus frequently pointed out not only that coercion is strictly antithetical to the nature of religious conversion but also that proselytizing flourishes best in an atmosphere of peace and charity and that a posture of hostility toward non-Muslim communities can only harm the long-term interests of *da'wa* if it serves to alienate non-Muslims from the essentially just and peaceful Islamic message.[49] Reciprocating recognition is thus both a categorical duty based on divine command and in the enlightened self-interest of Islamic communal aims.

There is no question about the general ethical nature or "sincerity" of argumentation on the basis of Qur'anic exegesis and a central religious value and objective (in this case, *da'wa*). Rather, what is left to be examined is whether what is understood by "self-defense" is more or less that which is understood in international law or whether the Islamic modernist notion of "defending the Islamic mission" opens the way for justifying wars that are not, strictly speaking, defensive. The question is essentially whether there is a genuine distinction between the notion of *da'wa* as noncoercive employed by the Modernists and that employed by Revivalists such as Sayyid Quṭb, for whom "defending the Islamic mission" and "protecting freedom of religion" serve as euphemisms for overturning secular political systems.[50]

Most of these authors clearly are not, in fact, developing a "crypto-Revivalism" that uses "defending the Islamic mission" as a euphemism for establishing an Islamic social order. Most of them are, in fact, eager to compare the "true" *jihād* doctrine to international law.[51] Zuḥaylī in particular seems anxious to avoid any ambiguity in his just war doctrine and how it differs from classical ones:

> As for a non-Muslim nation which did not initiate hostilities, did not obstruct Islamic missionaries, and left them free to present their religion to whomever wishes: it is not permissible to fight it nor to sever peaceful relations with it. The guarantee of security [*amān*] between it and Muslims is firm [*thābit*], not based on a payment of money or a specific treaty, but because the basic principle [of relations with non-Muslims; *al-aṣl*] is peace. The basic principles of international relations in Islam do not allow for war to be considered as a foundation of these relations, for this is not consistent with the sublimity of the Islamic mission and its universal inclination which is not realized except through peace.[52]

Whether individual thinkers see defensive *jihād* as analogous to modern international standards, however, is not really the point. Let us assume that the thinkers in question are advancing a doctrine whereby a liberal state that protects the freedom of Muslims to call non-Muslims to Islam is immune from hostility. Thus, Muslim citizens of such states can refer to these doctrines and the Qur'anic verses on which they are based to justify their recognition of the right to exist of their specific states of citizenship. The problem to be discussed is that these doctrines would seem to justify, in theory, wars that respond to a non-Muslim state's actions against the Islamic mission that fall short of both aggression against another state and serious oppression against a domestic population. Such wars would thus not be wars of self-defense, wars of humanitarian intervention, or even wars of Islamic revolution, but some underdetermined fourth kind that seeks to create a space for the freedom to practice and proselytize Islam.[53] 'Abd al-Qādir, for example, uses a variety of expressions to describe actions or policies that nullify the state of mutual nonaggression, some of which are vague: "seduction away from religion" (*al-fitna 'an al-dīn*[54]), "barring missionary activities" (*al-ṣadd 'an al-da'wa*), "hostility towards religion or the Islamic state" (*al-i'tidā' 'alā'l-dīn aw 'alā'l-dawla al-islāmiyya*), or "violating treaties" (*al-naqḍ li'l-'uhūd*). War can legitimately be waged for the purposes of "aiding the oppressed" (*nuṣrat al-mustaḍ'afīn*) or "removing those who do evil" (*izālat al-ṭawāghīt*[55]). Thus, for 'Abd al-Qādir, although "it is the duty of the state to provide [missionaries] with everything which work in the field of proselytizing demands, including the preservation of peaceful relations between Muslims and others," he declares that if "the country in question calls for war either by attempting to tempt these missionaries away from their religion or to block their missionary activities, then it is necessary to fight them for temptation away from religion is an assault on the holiest thing in human life."[56] A literal reading of this passage would seem to render a wide range of societies, such as the former Communist countries, vulnerable to hostility for reasons that liberalism would not regard as sufficient for hostile action. Thus, in this sense there is no shared conception of *jus ad bellum* with liberalism, but a shared notion that liberal democracies should be inviolable. Does this count for an overlapping consensus?

One might find troublesome two possible implications of this position: first, that it might seem to imply certain fundamental attitudes toward non-Muslim societies that are in the long run incompatible with other professed attitudes of tolerance and recognition; second, that it might result in principled support for the policies of other (Muslim) states that contradict the aims of one's (liberal) state of citizenship. The first concern is, more specifically, that this doctrine enshrines an inequality between Muslim and non-Muslim societies. Nowhere (in my reading) is there the suggestion that the right to proselytize is a universal right that would be guaranteed to non-Muslim missionaries in Muslim-majority societies. Similarly, while liberalism would certainly be committed to the freedom to proselytize as a general principle, no liberal would consider military action a proportionate response to the failure to guarantee such a freedom. Thus, the second concern: that a Muslim citizen of a liberal democracy adhering strictly to the letter of the Modernist *jihād* doctrine would find herself bound to support a *jihād* for the purpose of "opening" a nonliberal, non-Muslim state to Islamic missionary activity, regardless of how this might affect the particular interests of her state of citizenship or the general interests of preserving international law.

Ultimately, however, I think these concerns, however reasonable it may be to press them vis-à-vis these doctrines qua doctrines of international relations (rather than doctrines of citizenship), go beyond what can be legitimately built into the relationship between a citizen and his state. For one, the concerns all relate to a Muslim citizen's attitude toward *other* political communities, yet the wider principles of international relations are themselves controversial, vague, and underdetermined. It is not obvious either what general principles of international relations a liberal state should be committed to or what specific policies are justifiable. A liberal state might choose to advance international principles of justice that diminish its own sovereignty, it might choose ad hoc alliances with other states for its own welfare, or it might prefer a policy of strict neutrality and isolation. Reasonable disagreement about these policies is the norm; there is no shared principle of international relations intrinsic to the terms of (domestic) citizenship. Beyond a concern with protecting its own vital interests, it is not clear why a state should concern itself with its citizens' attitudes toward other states' security as a necessary element of the basic social contract.

This discussion is separate from such problems as enforcing laws related to funding militant groups or international extradition agreements. First, we are only dealing at the moment with *beliefs* related to just war, not specific actions in an armed conflict. Second, let us assume that laws that allow a state to punish a citizen for aiding a foreign terrorist group are legitimate; it is not obvious that what a person guilty of such a crime (for example, an Irish American who contributed funds to the Provisional IRA) has done is to violate his social contract with his specific state of citizenship. Third, in the case of Muslims following the Modernist *jihād* doctrine, it is not clear that it is the liberal (or non-Muslim) character of their own state that generates the conflict of loyalties. In fact, the character of the state of citizenship seems to be quite irrelevant. Fourth, many Muslim theorists derive from the duty to abide by contracts with non-Muslim states a general duty to obey all the laws of that state and argue for a general exemption from the duty to join a *jihād*. Fifth, and finally, the general obligation to aid beleaguered Muslims is often argued to be limited by verse 8:72: "If believers seek your aid in religion it is your duty to help them except against a people with whom you have a treaty of mutual alliance."

Pressing the objection to a citizen supporting a war to open a foreign, nonliberal state to Islamic missionary activity would require doing so consistently. As I discussed earlier, the special identification of Muslim citizens with the global Islamic community can be treated as analogous (not identical) to both the special bond ethnic or cultural minorities may feel with their comembers in other states and the solidarity felt by communities joined together by shared ideological or moral commitments. Deeming an Islamic belief in the legitimacy of this type of *jihād* as something that negates an (otherwise) overlapping consensus might require a similar judgment on American citizens who support national, ethnic, or religious movements for altering governments or borders in such places as Ireland, Israel, and the Balkans, or who have held sympathy for the replacement of oppressive foreign regimes with new ones (whether Marxist, democratic, or other) through force. It is thus quite clear that Modernist doctrines of *jihād* that argue for the absolute recognition of states that allow for unrestricted missionary activities and do not aggress against Muslim communities provide sturdy and principled foundations for loyalty to a non-Muslim state of citizenship. Concomitant arguments for the lack of similar inviolability for states without the freedom to proselytize do not render this loyalty void or insufficient.

Conclusion

In this chapter we have built on the discussions of permanent residence begun in the previous one. Whereas the discussion of residence established the permissibility of living under the authority of a regime that guaranteed Muslims religious freedom, the discussions of contract and just war in this chapter have sought to add a further dimension of moral obligation toward a state of citizenship. Alone, neither of the discussions is sufficient for an Islamic affirmation of the conception of society proposed by political liberalism. The first discussion on *hijra* and residence leaves the possibility of Muslims residing in non-Muslim states as (in spirit) permanent resident aliens. This discussion on contract, loyalty, and recognition leaves the possibility of justifying only temporary, ad hoc contracts with non-Muslim states. However, articulating all of the individual positions examined in the past two chapters in tandem, as part of a single, coherent doctrine, brings us a considerable distance toward a *general* social contract with a non-Muslim state. What we have shown to this point is that there are firm, religiously grounded values and principles, some with deep roots in the classical juridical tradition, for affirming residence in a liberal democracy and recognizing the legitimate rights to existence and security of such a state that meet the requirements of an overlapping consensus.

Much of what we have already encountered in Islamic discourses seems richer and more comprehensive than the conclusions I have allowed myself to draw from them. The treatment of contract on the part of some Islamic theorists seems to allow for much more than pacts of mutual nonaggression, and our brief look at the Modernist discourse on *jihād* seems to go much deeper than principles of international relations, since Modernist theorists treat *jihād* as a problem of how to fulfill Islam's inherent universalism and how to deal with error and falsehood in the world. Yet it would also be consistent with all that I have demonstrated in the previous two chapters to argue against the political integration of Muslims into a non-Muslim state and the formation of meaningful bonds of civic solidarity with non-Muslim fellow citizens. The relationship established by the Islamic sources to this point, while contributing to a thicker doctrine of citizenship, is best described as one (from the Islamic perspective) of clientage between a non-Muslim state and its Muslim residents. Such a relationship is not without its moral duties and bonds, but it lacks any commitment to positive common civic purposes with non-Muslim fellow citizens separate from attempts to convert them. In chapter 4, I referred to a certain "conception of the other" based on the recognition of fellow citizens who do not necessarily share one's comprehensive metaphysical beliefs as requisite for a robust affirmation of citizenship in a liberal democracy. I now turn to address what an Islamic affirmation of such a conception might require.

7

Recognition of Non-Muslims and Moral Pluralism

Let not the believers take the infidels for their allies in preference to the believers—for who does this has nothing to do with God—unless it be to protect yourselves from them in this way. God warns you about Himself and the final goal is to God.

—Qur'an, *Sūrat Āl 'Imrān* (3):28

Had your Lord willed all those who live on the Earth would surely have attained to faith, so could you then compel the people to believe, despite the fact that no one can attain to faith except by God's leave and that He leaves this evil upon those who do not use their reason.

—Qur'an, *Sūrat Yūnus* (10):99–100

Much of what was argued in the previous chapter implied an attitude of recognition on the part of Muslims towards non-Muslims, insofar as we found Muslim jurists arguing that contractual bonds between Muslims and non-Muslims bestow upon the latter strict claims against the former. Affirmation of the inviolability of non-Muslim property, honor, and life as a basic religious duty arising from contract between two parties goes a long way toward grounding the recognition of equality in the public sphere, which is a basic requirement of citizenship in a pluralist society. The topics covered in the previous chapter do not, however, necessarily lead to a doctrine of civic solidarity, understood as a willingness to contribute to common social and political goals in a condition of equality. Such willingness, I argue, would suggest a more robust recognition of the other as a civic equal than does the mere recognition of the society or state as having valid claims on subjects enjoying its protection. The latter could conceivably be achieved under a rubric of relations between distinct communities or polities, as it has indeed traditionally been conceived in Islamic juridical and political theories. Most of what I argued in the previous chapter could be coherently advanced alongside a view that Muslims in non-Muslim liberal democracies are something akin to resident aliens (in spirit) rather than citizens. This would certainly be the best characterization of the assumptions of the classical jurists we surveyed in that chapter. It is thus clear that a satisfactory affirmation of duty of recognition, for which I argued in chapter 4, must include recognition of the validity of justice across groups in a diverse society and the acceptability of contributing to the general welfare of such a society through such acts as paying taxes and participating in non-Islamic governments. It is important to note here, however, that while I am attempting to collapse the problem of recognition into concrete, almost technical questions, my belief is that these questions are the best way of revealing which concrete political practices are consistent with more abstract ethical, even metaphysical, beliefs about the other.

My discussion of recognition and solidarity is broken down in the following way: I first examine in this chapter the recognition of difference as such in Islamic discourses. A general doctrine of recognition, I argue, would consist of two main pillars. One is the recognition of a right not to be Muslim and some acceptance of pluralism and difference as a potentially permanent feature of social life, which I characterized in chapter 4 in the following way:

> RP: Religious disagreement is an inevitable feature of human life, perhaps divinely ordained. Although a Muslim has a duty to make the Islamic message known and to call to it, it is understood that not all unbelievers will hear or heed this call. It is permissible to live in societies even where there is little or no prospect of Islam becoming a majority religion, and it is permissible to maintain civic relationships with unbelievers even after they have heard and failed to accept the invitation to Islam.

Second, recognition involves an affirmation of "justice" as the regulatory principle of relations between communities divided by metaphysical beliefs:

> J: Relations between Muslims and non-Muslims are governed by standards of justice, rather than the ethics of war or contingent accommodation. Minimal standards of justice require civic equality and procedural impartiality toward all persons regardless of their religious identity.

Together, these two pillars would contribute toward a positive conception of recognition and respect for non-Muslims, beyond mere tolerance in the "negative" sense. To give greater depth to the affirmation of these two principles, I round out this chapter with a further discussion of the Islamic discourse on *da'wa*, in which I argue that for all of its ambiguities it reveals in some of its articulations a deep and principled intersubjective recognition of non-Muslims, and also with some exegetical treatments of the verses in the Qur'an that seem to prohibit friendship with non-Muslims (what I call the "*muwālāh* verses"), introducing the ways in which some Islamic religious scholars do not regard these verses as prohibiting civic relationships.

There is an inherent tension, even in the most orthodox sources, between the refusal to form close bonds and relationships with non-Muslims (based on the principle of *al-walā wa'l-barā'*) and the Islamic inclination to universalism, which involves seeing all non-Muslims as potential Muslims. Indeed, this tension between antipathy and openness is generated by a single belief, that of the superiority of Islam. Thus, even apart from specific doctrinal and legal elaborations on the duty of "tolerance" or on the precise political guarantees to non-Muslims within a single state, it is obvious that because of the centrality of *da'wa* to Islamic discourses an attitude of mere mistrust, antipathy, or indifference toward non-Muslims will never be a fully Islamic position. Or as Fayṣal Mawlawī demands: "Can you call someone [to Islam] while harboring feelings of hatred towards him?! Or making plans to fight him?"[1]

As alluded to earlier, I construct an Islamic doctrine of recognition in two parts. A doctrine of recognition, I submit, would consist of at least two beliefs: (a) that religious difference is a normal, tolerable social condition and thus that there is a right to not be Muslim and (b) that there are obligations of justice that apply across this difference. This chapter concludes with a discussion of the role of *da'wa* in legitimating an attitude of recognition toward non-Muslims, as well as alternative interpretations of the Qur'anic verses (3:28, 3:118, 5:51, 60:1, the "*muwālāh* verses") encountered in chapter 3.

The Inevitability of Religious Disagreement

Three points of Islamic doctrine are frequently invoked to imply a general Islamic doctrine of recognition of the other or of pluralism but are, in fact, insufficient for the requirements of citizenship in a liberal democracy. The first theme that proves to be a red herring for us is the Islamic doctrine of ethnic, racial, tribal, national, and linguistic equality. It is a mainstay of Islamic doctrine that no such differences of origin between believers are to be recognized. Verse 49:13, for example, proclaims "O mankind! We created you from a single pair of male and female and made you into nations and tribes that you may know each other. The most honored amongst you in the eyes of God is the most righteous and pious. Verily God is all-knowing and informed of all things." The problem, of course, is that this position does not preclude a strict doctrine of inequality for non-Muslims.[2] The duty to "know one another" does not extend necessarily to other religions or ethical doctrines, which would indeed provide a very powerful—almost Millian—argument for liberal institutions. In fact, it is clear how the verse might be enlisted for the justification of radical *inequality* between believers and unbelievers, albeit across ethnic divisions: "The most honored amongst you in the eyes of God is the *most righteous and pious*." To be sure, liberal citizenship does indeed require the racial, ethnic, and linguistic blindness that Islam exhorts, and thus we might expect believing Muslims to be particularly faithful adherents to liberal principles of racial and ethnic equality, but it requires more.

A second theme frequently surfacing in Muslim apologetic literature is Islam's recognition of prior revelations and prophets in the Abrahamic tradition and its tolerance for the "People of the Book" (*ahl al-kitāb*). A significant number of Qur'anic verses speak of the duty to recognize the practices of Scripturary (*kitābī*) communities, and such verses are frequently used to point to an Islamic tradition of religious pluralism and tolerance.[3] A frequent citation is verse 5:48:

> And unto you we have revealed this Scripture in truth, confirming the scripture that came before it and guarding it in safety. So judge between them according to what God has revealed and do not follow their errors about what has come to you by way of truth. To each among you have We prescribed a law and a way. And if God had so willed he would have made you a single people, but (His Plan is) to test you in what He has given you; so strive to outdo one another in all virtues. The goal of you all is to God; it is He that will show you the truth of the matters in which you dispute.

The context for this verse, and numerous others that speak of the inevitability of diversity within the Abrahamic family (2:62, 2:213, 4:163, 5:43, 5:47), is the Muslim response to the competing truth claims of the three monotheistic religions toward the end of Muḥammad's prophecy. Islamic law later extended privileges of limited self-government to Jewish and Christian communities, deemed Jewish and Christian women permissible in marriage to Muslim men, and allowed Scripturaries to avoid war or conversion through paying tribute or the *jizya* poll tax.[4] By medieval standards, such policies constitute a tradition of relative intercommunal tolerance.

Our problem, of course, is that it is not enough to establish a doctrine of merely *religious* pluralism that would ground recognition and tolerance on a common belief in God or, more narrowly, seek a coalition with "the People of the Book" referred to in Islamic scripture.[5] Such arguments are clearly insufficient within a liberal context that seeks to establish solidarity on the basis of shared citizenship independent of controversial metaphysical beliefs. Solidarity with non-Muslim but believing fellow citizens in a liberal democracy not only says nothing about nonbelieving citizens but also may, in fact, contribute to a coalition within a liberal democracy opposed to liberal institutions. What is required is some reason to affirm tolerance toward non-Muslims entirely regardless of their religious beliefs, whether by identifying separate verses or by arguing that the verses that enjoin tolerance to fellow Scripturaries or "getting to know one another" across ethnic difference somehow imply the same for all humans, including unbelievers.[6]

In fact, it is not rare for scholars to take Qur'anic verses that discuss how the primordial religious unity of mankind was disrupted for good as a matter of divine will and wisdom and conclude that the lesson for Muslims is not merely intramonotheist mutual toleration but the general doctrine that "the divine wisdom behind difference is to set a task for mankind to compete amongst one another in good deeds, for God has created them to differ; difference is thus a divine practice."[7] Thus, where the copious verses dealing with *religious* disagreement are interpreted to apply for modern Muslims to moral disagreement in general, this tradition of thought might not be a red herring at all. However, to the extent that political liberalism would insist not merely on acceptance or tolerance of disagreement but on the recognition of its reasonableness, it is hard to escape the conclusion that moral views departing from revealed monotheism will lack the substantive recognition that Islamic sources have been able to accord Judaism and Christianity.

A third red herring is the tradition of recognizing uncertainty in religious judgment and hence "legitimate religious difference," or *ikhtilāf.* As is well known, Islamic law is the province of jurists, not the state. As such, what traditionally defined a ruling (*ḥukm*) as Islamic was the methodology by which it was derived.[8] Disagreement about methods (*uṣūl al-fiqh*) such as defined the co-orthodox legal schools (*madhāhib*), about the application of those methods to concrete problems, or about the interpretation of vague or ambiguous texts (both Qur'anic verses and *ḥadīth* reports) are all regarded as legitimate reasons for doctrinal diversity.[9] This tradition of recognizing an intra-Islamic "fact of reasonable pluralism" is undoubtedly an important factor in allowing for the creation of an Islamic doctrine of citizenship in non-Muslim liberal democracies. It is this pluralism that allows even classical jurisprudence to produce concrete positions or rulings which I have argued constitute Islamic reasons for endorsing certain aspects of liberal citizenship. It is also what allows new rulings and doctrines to address new situations in the modern period without requiring a manifest repudiation of the *idea* of Islamic law. However, the fact that there is an Islamic tradition of dealing with moral pluralism (*ikhtilāf*) must not be interpreted as itself providing evidence for the Islamic acceptability of moral pluralism *as political liberalism understands it.* The Islamic conception of *ikhtilāf,* indispensable as it is, is not an endorsement of *all* reasonable disagreement; it is by definition bounded by a commitment to the truth of Islam and to the methods of *uṣūl al-fiqh.* It is precisely the rejection of those metaphysical and epistemological commitments (definitive of political liberalism) that mark the fact of *unreasonable* pluralism from the Islamic perspective. Thus, like the obligations to "know one another" and to recognize the special status of Jews and Christians, the concept of *ikhtilāf* as traditionally understood might in fact be an Islamic reason to *reject* political liberalism. Clearly, we need something else.

For textually inclined believing Muslims, the most likely path to an affirmation of the acceptability of social cooperation with persons with no religious or metaphysical affinity is an appropriation of the verses revealed to Muslims during the pre-*hijra*, Meccan period. A number of these verses speak of religious diversity in a way that does not presume religious belief or a monotheistic revelation in the Abrahamic tradition as a condition for recognition:

> If it distresses you that those who deny the truth turn their back on you, why then if you can go down deep into the Earth or ascend a ladder to heaven and bring them a [more convincing] message [then do so, but remember] if God had so willed then he surely would have gathered them all under His guidance. So do not be one of the ignorant. [6:35]

> The final evidence of all truth lies with God alone and had He so willed, He would have guided you all to truth. [6:149]
>
> Had your Lord willed all those who live on the Earth would surely have attained to faith, so could you then compel the people to believe, despite the fact that no one can attain to faith except by God's leave and that He leaves this evil upon those who do not use their reason. [10:99–100]
>
> If your Lord had willed he could have made mankind a single people, but they do not cease to disagree, except for those whom God has bestowed his mercy. And for this He has created them. [11:118–119]
>
> Say: "O unbelievers! I do not worship what you worship and you do not worship what I worship. And never will I worship what you have worshipped, and never will you worship what I worship. You have your religion and I have mine!" [109:1–6]

Other verses, often but not exclusively Meccan, refer again to differences between Muslims, Jews, and Christians but speak of judgment belonging only to God in a way that could possibly apply to religious disagreement in general:

> Because of this [the doubts amongst holders of prior revelations], call [to God] and stay on the straight path as you have been commanded and do not follow their whims, but say: "I believe in whatever revelation God has bestowed from on high and I have been ordered to bring about equity between you. God is our Lord as well as yours. We shall account for our deeds and you for yours. Let there be no contention between us. God will bring us together and to him is our final goal." [42:15]
>
> Unto every community We have appointed ways of worship, which they ought to observe. Thus do not let them draw you into disputes but summon them all to your Lord. And if they try to argue with you say: "God knows best of what you do and God will judge between you on the Day of Resurrection with regard to that on which you were wont to differ." [22:68–69]

The Qur'an, in particular the chapters revealed before the *hijra* to Medina, during the first Meccan period, is indeed filled with verses describing Muḥammad as "not a warden" or "only a warner" to mankind (e.g., 4:80, 6:66–67, 6:106–7, 34:28, 42:48, 88:21–24), proclaiming that no one shall bear another's burden in the afterlife (6:164, 17:15, 34:25, 35:18, 39:7, 53:38), and that God will be the judge of matters on which mankind disagrees (2:113, 3:55, 5:48, 6:164, 7:87, 10:93, 16:92, 16:124, 22:69, 32:25, 39:3, 39:46, 45:17).

The relationship of the Meccan verses to the entirety of the Islamic message is the subject of particular ideological controversy in Islamic polemics. On one extreme, at least one modern school of thought has based a theory of Islamic reformation for the modern era on the more spiritual and metaphysical, as well as socially accommodating, nature of the earlier Meccan verses.[10]

However, this school has been deemed heretical by some Sunni scholars (its founder, Maḥmūd Muḥammad Ṭāhā, was hanged by the Islamist government in Sudan on grounds of apostasy), and it would be troubling if believing Muslims had to commit themselves to these metaphysical and hermeneutical views for these Meccan verses to be thought instructive on the question of moral pluralism. The more orthodox view, of course, is that God revealed the Islamic message to Muslims progressively, and thus in the event of contradiction between Qur'anic verses, later revelations are presumed to have greater authority than, and will often be said to abrogate, earlier ones. Thus, the Medinan revelations, which give guidance to Muḥammad as a judge and political authority, represent God's true intentions for Muslims as a political community, with all that that entails.

What makes the Meccan verses of particular interest for this study is not only that they are *generally* held to be more supportive of "reformist" doctrines[11] but also that they address life lived by Muslims in a minority context, where access to state-coercive power is not expected. Furthermore, whereas the later Medinan verses address intercommunal relations in a context where the dominant non-Muslim communities are Christian or Jewish, the Meccan verses address a situation where Muslims are dealing with polytheists, with whom no religious affinity whatsoever is to be had. Thus, one need not adopt the controversial "second message" doctrine of Ṭāhā (which posits that the Meccan verses reveal the true nature of Islam as such) to entertain the idea that the Meccan revelations show a path to an authentic Islamic life *in certain circumstances.*

This seems to be the position of Yūsuf al-Qaraḍāwī, for example, who sees the "Meccan Qur'an" as containing the purest statement of Islam's universal aspirations and thus openness to unbelievers.[12] In addressing the question of Muslim residence in the West, he cites 11:118 and comments that "whoever would wish to group all mankind into one religion or one sect it is as though he opposes divine will." He further cites 42:15 and 22:68–69 to justify his claim that "Islam takes an interest in all people without regard for their religion, whatever it may be."[13] Importantly, this concern is not grounded in a presumption of the *other's* monotheism but exclusively in the *Muslim's* monotheism: All souls belong to God and are thus subject to a certain regard and respect; the pious Muslim wants these souls to be saved but knows that their infidelity or belief, and ultimate judgment, is God's will.

In another *fatwā* on the subject of whether Jews and Christians are regarded as "infidels" (*kuffār*) in Islam, Qaraḍāwī comes very close to addressing the dilemma discussed in political liberalism under the rubric of the burdens of judgment when he asks: "How do we reconcile our belief in the infidelity of the People of the Book and our call to tolerate them?"[14] He first seeks to diffuse the question by asserting the fact that to hold a belief is to hold it to be true and thus to hold that others who deny it are "unbelievers" in the truth of that belief. He points out that this is the case for any doctrine, religious or secular, and not unique to Islam. We can regard this as analogous to the basic "fact of pluralism" in the Rawlsian sense of multiple incompatible doctrines coexisting in society. The Rawlsian question is then, "What do we regard as the cause of this basic fact of pluralism, and thus how ought that pluralism to be regarded morally and politically? Why should we restrain ourselves in the realm of public justification to include people whom we may think are wrong?" Qaraḍāwī similarly proceeds, upon demystifying the question of "infidelity," by noting that this general fact of incompatibility between doctrines "suggests an important question which demands an answer: How did Islam solve this puzzle? I mean, how does a Muslim tolerate one whom he regards as an unbeliever in his religion?"[15]

Qaraḍāwī gives a number of intriguing answers to this problem beyond platitudes about "respecting the dignity of others." Importantly, while the question asks about tolerance toward Jews and Christians (thus raising the problem I discussed previously about Abrahamic or monotheistic fraternity as a template for recognition), Qaraḍāwī's answers do not refer to any basic religious commonality. The first is that "the Muslim regards differences between people in religion to be a fact according to the will of God Almighty, Who bestowed on his creation this form of freedom and choice in action and omission,"[16] quoting Q. 18:29: "Let he who wishes believe and he who wishes disbelieve." And 11:118–119: "If your Lord had willed he could have made mankind a single people, but they do not cease to disagree, except for those whom God has bestowed his mercy. And for this He has created them."[17] Again, these are Meccan verses that do not assume that those refusing to adopt Islam are already Abrahamic monotheists. Because of the trust they have in the goodness and wisdom of God's will, "Muslims do not think for a single day that they might compel people to all become Muslims just as God (May He Be Exalted) said to His Messenger 'If it had been your Lord's will then all on earth would have believed. Will you then compel them until they believe?' [10:99]."

A second argument is the theological point that "Muslims are not charged with holding unbelievers accountable for their unbelief, or for punishing the errant for their error, for the time for that is not this world but rather the Day of Reckoning." This is on the basis of the previously cited verses 22: 68–69, 42:15, and 5:118 ("If You cause them to suffer—verily, they are Your servants; and if You forgive them—verily, You alone art almighty, truly wise!"). Qaraḍāwī's conclusion from this is to distinguish one's judgment of the other's infidelity from one's social and political commitments to him: "For this reason, the Muslim's conscience is at ease and he finds no conflict between his conviction in the unbeliever's unbelief and the demand to be just and equitable towards him."[18]

Certain Meccan verses thus give a believing Muslim potentially authentic and powerful reasons for regarding religious disagreement as a natural, divinely ordained state of affairs, and for regarding pluralistic societies as the field of some of his most important religious activities, namely, bearing witness to the Islamic message, summoning unbelievers to Islam, defending Islam's virtues through reason and in goodwill, and standing for justice. Clearly, such beliefs have been held to be compatible with a variety of political arrangements. Acknowledging that God may have ordained that some people will not believe and that there will always be communities of unbelievers in any society is not inconsistent with preferring a political system based on religious doctrines and giving social advantages to believers. The "pluralism as divine injunction" alone is not a strong enough belief to result in a doctrine of liberal equality, particularly in a Muslim-majority society. However, in a Muslim-minority society, where liberal freedoms already exist and provide advantages to Muslim communities, the belief that living with nonbelievers is both God's will and a prerequisite for performing certain acts vital to a virtuous life (calling to Islam, defending it in a rational manner, advocating justice) is an important pillar of a doctrine of citizenship in such a society.

Recall from chapter 1 that one of the central critical questions for political liberals is whether something like the recognition of the burdens of judgment is necessary for a principled affirmation of the fact of reasonable pluralism and, thus, for a doctrine to be reasonable. I believe that the "pluralism as divine injunction" doctrine is ambiguous on this question. The idea of a "fact of reasonable pluralism" is intended to do two main things. First, it is intended to explain why moral disagreement is likely to be an enduring feature of free societies rather than something that could plausibly disappear under ideal circumstances. Second, it is supposed to give a strong normative reason for why political justification must be "public" in a particular way, namely, in that it restricts itself to beliefs and values that can be presumed to be held in common.

The "pluralism as divine injunction" doctrine clearly serves for Muslim scholars to explain why moral disagreement is likely to be an enduring feature of human societies, and it clearly gives very strong reasons for accepting this feature as something other than a failure of Muslims to create certain sociopolitical conditions. However, it is not clear that this basic attitude of tolerance implies that Muslims not ought to expect that the conditions and circumstances for as many persons as possible to accept the truth of Islam could not be created by humans. Furthermore, it by no means follows that the public language of justification ought to be limited to accommodate those who hold errant views—albeit understandably and tolerably. Axiomatic or inferential reasoning in religious traditions functions in a different way than it does in philosophical doctrines. The fact of "pluralism as divine injunction" does not *necessarily* result in a doctrine of justificatory neutrality, as it might in a secular, philosophical system, if the same texts that declare pluralism to be a divine injunction *also* command that morality be promoted, that moral judgment be referred to God, and that his revelation be spread.

Thus, although it is often argued that contemporary liberalism derives its commitment to public justification from its foundational value of respect for persons and recognition of their moral personality, we cannot be so hasty to assume that all statements of recognition, respect, or toleration in other traditions will equally result in a commitment to neutrality of justification. To be sure, those values of recognition, respect, or toleration themselves are crucial components of a doctrine of citizenship, but to fill them out in a satisfactory way from an Islamic perspective I believe will require more than the basic idea that moral pluralism is a divine injunction. We need other values and moral commitments.

Justice across Communities

That Muslims have reason to believe that sharing social space with non-Muslims is a permanent condition to be tolerated, or a necessity out of which virtue can be made, implies very little about the nature of relations between communities in that social space. It certainly does not imply that members of different communities have the same moral standing or that they are entitled to the same standards of treatment. Thus, as a second building block of our doctrine of recognition, we are interested in exploring Islamic reasons for regarding relations with non-Muslims in a single society as relations of justice between equals.

The notion inherent in the last chapter's semitechnical discussion of contract is often addressed in Islamic discourses in a much more explicit, general, and theoretical way. Numerous Qur'anic verses exhort believers to uphold justice (*'adl*) and equity (*qisṭ*) in all cases, including in their interactions with unbelievers:

> Believers, be steadfast in upholding equity, bearing witness to the truth of God, even if it be against yourselves, or your parents and kin. Whether the person be rich or poor, God's claim takes precedence over the claims of either of them. Do not then follow your own whims lest you swerve from justice. If you distort the truth or decline to do justice, God is aware of all that you do. [4:135]

> Believers, be steadfast in your devotion to God, bearing witness to the truth in all equity. Never allow your hatred of a people to lead you astray from justice. Be just, this is closer to righteousness and be God-fearing for surely God is aware of all you do. [5:8]

> It may be that God will grant love and friendship between you and those whom you now hold as enemies for God is All-Powerful, and God is Oft-Forgiving, Most-Merciful. God does not forbid you from dealing justly and equitably with those who do not fight you for your religion nor expel you from your homes, for God loves the equitable. [60:7–8]

Indeed, the *fatwā* by Qaraḍāwī cited previously on the question of religious pluralism concludes the discussion of how to make sense of tolerance toward infidels by invoking Q. 60:8 to argue that "the Muslim has faith that God commands justice and loves equity and calls to noble characteristics even with idolaters, and that He hates injustice and punishes the transgressors, even if the injustice was on the part of a Muslims towards an unbeliever."[19] Similarly, Rāshid al-Ghannūshī writes that "Islam did not command justice only for Muslims but for mankind generally, and this is perfectly clear in the Qur'ān, where justice is an obligation that must be observed even when one is dealing with one's enemy."[20] This is a general position that is universally affirmed, even by theorists we have used as exemplars of incompatible doctrines on other questions. Quṭb, quoting 4:135, remarks that "the trust [Muslims] have been assigned is to maintain justice, in its absolute sense, in every situation. It guarantees justice between people, giving everyone, Muslim or non-Muslim, their rights. In their entitlement to justice, all people, believers and unbelievers, are equal in God's sight, as we have seen in the incident involving the Jewish man in Madina."[21] This view (or at the very least, rhetoric) is consistent with classical exegesis. The ninth- and tenth-century historian and exegete al-Ṭabarī writes on verse 60:8 that "it is correctly stated that towards all peoples and religions you must treat them justly and equitably. God has made this a general ruling in this verse and He did not later make it merely applicable in specific cases and did not abrogate it. God loves the just and those who give people their rights."[22] Similarly categorical is Ibn Taymiyya's commentary on the same verse: "No one is permitted to treat anyone else unjustly, even if he is an unbeliever."[23]

Obviously, authors such as al-Ṭabarī, Ibn Taymiyya, Quṭb, and Qaraḍāwī are operating with a different substantive conception of justice than will be enforced in a liberal regime. An additional problem with the orthodox claim that Islam "guarantees justice between people, giving everyone, Muslim or non-Muslim, their rights" is that according to classical Islamic civil law, these are not *equal* rights.[24] "In their entitlement to justice, all people, believers and unbelievers, are equal in God's sight" in the same way that all citizens of Plato's republic are equal with their radically unequal rights and duties.

Once again, in the Muslim-minority context, there is reason to believe that this question about the type of justice Muslim jurists or ideologues would extend to all subjects of the state is less of a concern. Clearly, as discussed before, the potential exists for severe dispute over what justice requires even where Muslims are a minority,[25] but what these texts show is that what is *not* likely to be a matter of dispute among serious Islamic thinkers is that basic idea that the demands of justice apply equally to non-Muslims, that "justice" is the proper standard for dealing with all fellow citizens. The common Islamic and liberal commitment to procedural justice reveals a shared powerful resource for grounding a doctrine of *moral recognition*, despite obvious differences on what sorts of actions should be liable for punishment. A famous story, for example, has Ibn Taymiyya defending the right of a Christian accused of insulting the Prophet on the grounds of insufficient evidence, without, of course, questioning the rule that insulting the Prophet merits punishment.[26] Thus, for the moment we are concerned not to make the point that Islamic conceptions of justness overlap with liberal ones but, rather, that the moral obligation to uphold "justice" even toward infidels (those likely to be damned) constitutes a form of recognition of the moral worth of the other in a sociopolitical context. It is merely one piece of a larger doctrinal attitude toward life in non-Muslim societies.

In a contemporary context, consider the views of Lebanese Ayatollah Muḥammad Faḍl Allāh on the situation that "some [Muslim thinkers] look at Western institutions as a form of prey or booty which one ought to gain as much from as possible even through dishonorable means such as fraud, forgery and deceit, and some consider that stealing from unbelievers is permissible based on certain *fatāwā*."[27] Faḍl Allāh's response articulates precisely the attitude of recognition that we are seeking to establish in this section:

> Through our studies of Islamic ethics we find that they are not divided into various parts, for example, one way of dealing with Muslims and another with non-Muslims such that it is permissible to lie to a non-Muslim and mandatory to tell the truth to a Muslim. For the question does not relate to the identity of the other but to the integrity of the person himself. There is a *ḥadīth* that says: "He who is not trustworthy has no religion, even if he fasts and prays." Thus, Islamic ethics represent the values which emanate through the Muslim person, whether the morality which relates to his personal state or to his relations with the other, because Islam wants the Muslim person to respect the other (except in the case of war, which has its own ethical rules). For the person remains a person in your treatment of him and your respect for him. Thus, we reject any unethical behavior towards non-Muslims in a state of peace with you, based on the words of the Almighty [quoting 60:8]. Equity is giving each his right and on this basis you are not allowed to violate his right, or to treat him in such a way as you have no right to do, such as stealing his money, violating a contract you have with him, or harming him in any circumstance.[28]

What is crucial about this passage is that the recognition of the rights of non-Muslims in a given society is not based merely on a specific promise or contract but rather on a general, divinely ordained attitude of recognition and respect for the dignity of the other. While Faḍl Allāh is a Shi'ite scholar, his argument is not phrased in Shi'ite sectarian metaphysics or hermeneutics, and similar statements can be found in Sunni texts.[29]

This position, of course, must be considered in light of classical Islamic theories of moral obligation. Islamic moral theology according to the ("orthodox") doctrine of Ash'arism does not proceed in general on the basis of natural rights but rather on the basis of theistic subjectivism or voluntarism, that is, the doctrine that *all* moral rights and obligations obtain because God has chosen them and informed us of them. He could have done otherwise (that is, given us different rights and duties or none at all), and our nature or reason is only an accidental (rather than necessary) guide to them. That is, all rights and claims are "statutory" in the sense of being created by God in the act of revelation.[30]

The situation becomes rather more complicated in the case of non-Muslims, as has been discussed at length in earlier chapters. Although it is true that in a theological sense, *all* "God's slaves have no original rights whatsoever, no rights apart from those granted by God,"[31] the act of revealing the Qur'an and Islam to Muslims created an absolute relationship of moral obligation *between Muslims* as a matter of *fact* (that is, by an act of God's grace and mercy, not necessity on His part). Muslims' lives, property, and honor are inviolable by virtue of being Muslim; Muslims require no special contract or political relationship for these rights to take effect. Strictly speaking, the same cannot be said of the comprehensive relationship with non-Muslims. According to classical doctrine, an adult, non-Muslim male living outside an Islamic polity in a state with no legal treaty with an Islamic polity (in the "Abode of War") is licit—he has no immunity from violence. Muslims, we might say, are in a state of basic moral nonobligation (*barāʾa*) to him. It is only through *specific contractual relationships* that moral obligations arise. (This is the meaning of the classical ethico-legal category of such persons as "*ḥarbīs*": they were residents of the Abode of War (*dār al-ḥarb*) and as such had no legal or moral rights until they became *mustaʾmīns* or *dhimmīs*.) As was discussed in previous chapters, these contractual relationships can occur from actions on the part of Islamic authorities or individual Muslims, as in the case of the *amān*.

Thus, how are we to understand such statements as "Islam wants the Muslim person to respect the other (except in the case of war, which has its own ethical rules)"? I would like to suggest three possibilities.

The first is that language about absolute obligations of justice to non-Muslims because of their basic humanity and the Muslim's own sense of dignity is primarily rhetorical. This is not to say that such passages are insincere or a form of legitimate dissimulation (*taqiyya*). Rather, it is merely to say that all of the actual moral work is being done by the concept of contract. Note that Faḍl Allāh acknowledges the distinct ethics of war (which, itself, is far from unique to Islam) and "reject[s] any unethical behavior towards non-Muslims *in a state of peace with you*." As noted, many contemporary Islamic scholars regard the basic state of relations between Muslims and non-Muslims as one of peace, and this does indeed raise foundational questions about moral obligation in Islam. However, the scholars we are discussing here (Ṭabarī, Ibn Taymiyya, Quṭb, just as representative figures) do not subscribe to this doctrine; they regard the basic status of relations as one of nonrecognition. Thus, to find them speaking about obligations of justice and equity to non-Muslims presumes that there is a background authorizing contractual relationship. In the cases cited here of the exegesis of Ṭabarī, Ibn Taymiyya, and Quṭb, that relationship is the *dhimmī* status of protection that the Islamic state extends as a contract. In the case of Faḍl Allāh, Qaraḍāwī, and Ghannūshī, that relationship is the *amān* contract of mutual obligation for Muslims living in a non-Muslim state. Thus, we are simply back to our discussion from chapter 6 on the inviolability of contracts. The language encountered here of a relationship of justice is powerful and sincere but theologically redundant, since it assumes that the relationship of justice is contracted into.

The second interpretation is a variation on the first, and one to which I alluded in the previous chapter. It is that we may interpret the idea of contract as endowing non-Muslims with a general moral status. They are worthy of entering into contracts with; they are *eligible* for relationships of justice and moral obligation. I see no reason to be particularly troubled by two possible objections: (1) that the moral obligation in the cases of contract is to God or one's own soul and (2) that particular contracts are weak ground for a commitment to justice.

First, the concern about the weakness of a contractualist approach is mitigated by the important fact that while specific obligations emerge from contracts, there is a general, "statutory" injunction to enter into them. Muslims have no choice, theologically and morally speaking, but to enter into contractual relationships with non-Muslims when the conditions demand it, which they do in the case of legal residence in a non-Muslim state. In this sense, we might say that the obligation of justice toward non-Muslims *is* a "statutory" one. Furthermore, the first objection is likely to be an inescapable feature of theological ethics and is also a problem not limited to the relationship with unbelievers. Why could we not say that a Muslim's motivation to refrain from harming fellow Muslims or his own soul is equally grounded in an obligation to God or even in a fear of punishment? In fact, that the moral force of any contract is based on these deeper values of *respect for self* (for lying and deceit is a negation of one's own moral nature) counts strongly in its favor; respect for one's own moral personality must be distinguished sharply from the rational pursuit of self-interest.

As to the second objection, it is true that the belief in natural rights or one's own natural duty to advance justice would provide deeper foundations. However, the same problem arises with all contractualist or constructivist approaches to ethics and justice, including Rawls's. If one conceives of moral obligations not in realist terms but as arising out of actual relationships of social cooperation, where the duty to justify (the duty of civility) emerges, it is not always easy to understand one's moral obligations outside that relationship. Thus, for example, whereas the famous "hard cases" such as abortion, animal rights, the rights of the disabled, the rights of noncitizens or even slavery are frequently raised as cases where political liberalism fails to provide sufficient moral resources for public deliberation,[32] the argument might be made that it is not that liberalism as a comprehensive doctrine lacks the moral resources for thinking about these questions but rather that the general constructivist approach to *political morality* brackets questions about persons or other entities outside the relationship of cooperation.[33] But what is crucial in both Islamic and constructivist approaches is that the willingness to create moral obligations through ideal or actual contracts presumes a certain moral equality of the other.

There is, however, a third possibility. I believe it is possible to discern a certain desire on the part of Islamic scholars to theorize a more comprehensive moral relationship with non-Muslims and non-Islamic societies than is permitted by classical constructs. To this point, I believe we have encountered three main discourses for thinking about moral obligation in Islamic traditions: the "statutory," the contractualist, and the consequentialist-utilitarian. The first draws on divine commands and thus might be referred to as "deontological." The second points to the permissibility of entering into contracts with non-Muslims of variable content and thus might be referred to as "constructivist." The third considers the overall benefits to Muslim communities and ultimate Islamic aims in accepting less than ideal political arrangements, including those that require upholding obligations to non-Muslims or advancing their interests. What, then, would a more "comprehensive" or "qualitative" understanding of the relationship of recognition and moral obligation consist in? I believe that some such attitude is actually behind statements like Faḍl Allāh's (and those of others such as Mawlawī and Ghannūshī, not to mention more self-conscious Modernists such as Mohammad Hashim Kamali[34] and perhaps Tariq Ramadan). In the rest of this chapter, I try to show this by examining Islamic treatments of the obligation to engage in *da'wa* and of the meaning of the classical prohibition on relationships of *muwālāh*—loyalty and affection—with non-Muslims.

Da'wa

It is impossible to discuss the Islamic ethics of recognition and coexistence without discussing the question of proselytizing (*da'wa*). Some contemporary scholars—using the linguistic template of the classical debate on whether the "basic principle" (*al-aṣl*) of relations with non-Muslims is peace or war—hold that the obligation of *da'wa* today characterizes the very essence of relations with non-Muslims, that is, that the "basic principle" of relations with non-Muslims is *da'wa*.[35] We discussed in chapters 3 and 5 some of the basic problems with reducing the legitimization of peaceful coexistence in non-Muslim states to the possibility for winning new adherents to Islam, namely, that (1) it risks seeing non-Muslims only as potential converts and not as free and equal citizens, (2) it does not preclude the Islamization of the state if the group someday finds itself a majority, and thus, (3) it may reveal a shallow commitment to the society and state as (permanently) pluralistic and secular. The general concern is that any acceptance of liberal institutions or constraints will be purely tactical, rather than grounded on a principled acknowledgment of the fact of reasonable pluralism.

The converse of this is that *da'wa* implies a noncoercive approach to the inculcation of belief and virtue, that it involves recognizing the common humanity and potential for salvation of all humans, and that it requires a certain integration into and concern for the wider non-Muslim society. Here I focus on the way the ethics of *da'wa* reveal certain values of recognition of the other that are crucial to citizenship in a pluralist democracy.

Three Qur'anic verses in particular are used by scholars in discussing how *da'wa* should be carried out:

> Call to your Lord's path with wisdom and kindly exhortation, and argue with them in the most kindly manner, for, behold, your Lord knows best who strays from His path, and best knows who are the rightly-guided. [16:125]
>
> Say [O Prophet]: "This is my way. I am calling you all to God with perception [*baṣīra*] I and all who follow me." [12:108]
>
> There is no coercion in religion. Truth stands out clearly from falsehood. [2:256]

In discussing these verses and the methodology of *da'wa* in non-Muslim lands, Muslim thinkers frequently emphasize a number of themes and values that are ripe for appropriation into a doctrine of recognition. Four in particular stand out, which I organize here around phrases and terms found in the preceding verses: (1) Good-willed exhortation [*al-maw'iẓa al-ḥasana*], (2) argumentation [*jadal*], (3) noncoercion [*Lā ikrāh*], and (4) wisdom [*ḥikma*].

The phrase *al-maw'iẓa al-ḥasana*, found in Q. 16:125, translatable as "kindly exhortation" or "good-willed warning," has been used by exegetes and scholars as calling for a posture of goodwill, friendship, patience, and sincerity toward nonbelievers, as well as engagement with and commitment to one's wider society. Faḍl Allāh describes such a form of exhortation, warning, and preaching as a mode of inviting to Islam that allows the addressed to feel as though "your role is one of friend and giver of good advice, who seeks that which will benefit him [the other] and make him happy."[36] He points to a number of other Qur'anic verses that corroborate this view that disagreement and opposition that fall short of aggression can be met with patience and restraint: "Repel evil with that which is kindlier. Then there will be friendship and affection between you and him in place of enmity" [41:34]. "Tell my servants that they should only say those things which are best, for Satan sows dissent amongst them and is a clear enemy to man" [17:53]. "And if they [non-Muslims] greet you, you should respond with an even kinder greeting or one just as kind" [4:85].

Similar views on the part of prominent contemporary scholar Fayṣal Mawlawī have already been encountered in our discussion of war and loyalty. Recall that Mawlawī summarized the modernist position on whether the basic principle of relations between Muslims and non-Muslims ought to be a state of peace or aggression by challenging: "Can you call someone [to Islam] while harboring feelings of hatred towards him?! Or making plans to fight him? Under such conditions can you call him with wisdom and good-willed warning [*al-maw'iẓa al-ḥasana*]?" However, he derives from the duty to invite to Islam in a spirit of "good-willed warning" much more than a position of mutual non-aggression. He speaks, importantly, of *'āṭifa* for non-Muslims, which has a literal meaning of attachment, sympathy, affection, liking, but when transferred to a social, intercommunal context, can be understand as analogous to a conception of civic solidarity, or at least as providing a foundation for accepting it. He asks, "How can a Muslim be a caller of humanity to Islam when he is reluctant even to initiate a greeting, or speak to him a kind word, to the point that non-Muslims suspect that in the Muslim's heart there is no affection [*'āṭifa*] for them. . . . If there does not exist a form of affection or respect or good will between you and non-Muslims, then you will never succeed in calling to Islam."[37] This concern of his with whether a Muslim may feel "love" or "affection" for non-Muslims merits some dwelling on.

The need for justifying such sentiments was shown in chapter 3, where verses 3:28,[38] 3:118,[39] and 4:144[40] and their interpretations were introduced. Mawlawī's response to this dilemma is to argue that what is forbidden are two specific states: having affection for those who fight Muslims because of their faith and, concerning peaceful non-Muslims, loving them *on account of* their unbelief. "But if there is an unbeliever who does not fight God and His Apostle and displays certain positive characteristics and esteemed values then there is no harm in appreciating these characteristics or values in him because they are drawn from the store of his God-given nature, and thus they are acceptable from a religious standpoint."[41] There are two distinct ideas in operation here that are powerful, religiously grounded reasons for recognizing and forming bonds of solidarity with non-Muslims.

The first is that there is a sphere of social interaction where humans form bonds of trust and affection separate from religion. Such bonds and feelings are clearly inferior to the bonds formed by religion or shared moral purposes but are legitimate within their own sphere, and a Muslim can be sincere in valuing them. These bonds may be based on common interests, shared experiences, or secular virtues. "There cannot be love in your heart for a non-Muslim because of his unbelief, but there may be for other considerations. He may be honest, and you can love him for his honesty. He may be faithful to contracts and you love him for this . . . or for his morals, wisdom, reason, or your closeness and shared interests. It is only blameworthy if it involves something explicitly forbidden."[42] He refers to this as *ḥubb fiṭrī*, or "innate love" (from the Islamic idea that all humans share a common innate nature, *fiṭra*), to be distinguished from *ḥubb 'aqā'idī*, "creedal love," the affection between persons who share religious beliefs. All humans are endowed with a common instinctive nature and thus share certain basic needs, passions, and inclinations. The common pursuit of these can result in love, affection, and solidarity across creedal lines.[43] Mawlawī is even willing to refer to these bonds as a form of brotherhood. Contrary to the belief that brotherhood is only religious,[44] Mawlawī argues that there are various forms of brotherhood, including "human brotherhood, national brotherhood, familial brotherhood and Islamic brotherhood, which exceeds all others in strength if it is present. And if Islamic brotherhood is absent, then there remain all these other forms."[45] As to verse 49:10 ("Only believers are brothers"), "it means that believers can be but brothers to one another, but it does not restrict brotherhood to believers. For brotherhood between believers and unbelievers has other reasons, such as shared nationality, humanity or interests. The strongest bond of religious brotherhood is not the only kind nor does it forbid one of these other kinds developing between me and a non-Muslim."[46] These ideas are quite widespread among scholars of the pragmatic, Muslim Brotherhood school of thought. Qaraḍāwī similarly distinguishes between human brotherhood and religious brotherhood by noting that while the latter is the more sublime, it does not exclude either more general or more particular forms of brotherhood with non-Muslims.[47]

There is clearly a close parallel between these ideas and the liberal conception of solidarity between citizens. His bifurcation of solidarity based on shared interests, secular values, and proximity and that based on shared metaphysical beliefs closely mirrors the understanding of solidarity according to the Rawlsian form of political liberalism. Political liberalism conceives of political community as organized precisely around common principles of justice and such common goals as can be justified by purely political, worldly, and social needs. This seems to be the exact understanding of the type of community and solidarity that can develop between Muslims and non-Muslims, according to Mawlawī. A further commonality between the liberal and Islamic conceptions is their shared universality: The bonds of shared interest or *ḥubb fiṭrī* ("innate love") can develop among humans anywhere and without regard to cultural, racial, or ethnic differences. Some of the claims of political liberalism appear to be vindicated here, particularly its main aspiration that, in excluding metaphysical claims and goals from the language of political justification, more citizens with a wider range of comprehensive ethical doctrines can affirm its claims to political validity. Here, Mawlawī seems to be saying something similar: Islam would prefer to be expressed through a community where politics and metaphysics are fused. But given the reality of sharing political space with non-Muslims, it is preferable to limit solidarity and political power to that which all humans have in common. Were non-Muslim states to make wider claims to metaphysical truth, then it might be more difficult for Muslims to affirm citizenship within them.

This solidarity based on shared needs is complemented by a second idea implicit in Mawlawī's understanding of *da'wa* through "good-willed warning." Consider the following statements: "We conclude that there can and must be affection and love towards a person whom you wish to call to God and that this affection is a small piece of the affection that God wills be directed towards him. This is the foundation which is considered to be stronger and weightier than all that which opposes it." Although it is natural for bonds of love and affection to arise among neighbors and cocitizens, "this affection has nothing to do with [shared] faith, but rather is connected exclusively to religious considerations as far as we Muslims are concerned. For God has commanded us to bestow mercy on all mankind as a part of faith."[48] This statement helps alleviate some of our general concerns about the compatibility of the aims of *da'wa* with citizenship in a pluralist society. On this view, *da'wa* is not merely motivated by the aim of winning adherents to one's way of life but rather by a desire to extend to the other a good (perhaps the greatest good) unconditionally. This motivation reflects a very authentic and deeply sincere form of recognition of the moral status and importance of the other.

The second important theme in the *da'wa* literature is that of argumentation [*jadal*]. In Q. 16:125, Muslims are instructed to "argue with them in the most kindly manner" [*jādilhum bi'latī hiya aḥsan*]. The second part of this injunction we have dealt with; here we are concerned with how the very command to argue can imply an attitude of recognition. A central feature of the Muslim understanding of *da'wa*, and of Islam itself, is the belief that faith need not conflict with reason. Faḍl Allāh, in discussing the methodology of *da'wa*, goes so far as to compare *da'wa* with the scientific method: He emphasizes the need to erase all preconceptions and prejudices, to present evidence and proofs, and to follow the rules of deduction and logical inference.[49]

For our purposes, we are not so much concerned with Islamic beliefs about the precise relationship between faith and reason, or doctrines of the rational proof of Qur'anic inimitability, as with the ethical implications of the commitment to rational debate. Not unlike some of the principles of discourse ethics and deliberative democracy (a comparison to which I return later), the Islamic commitment to invite to Islam through reason and proof is a commitment to transparency, honesty, respect, and a position of discursive equality between inviter and invitee. Faḍl Allāh writes that "this is the call which lays out its message clearly and openly without confusion, obscurity or distortion."[50] Also not unlike theorists of discourse and deliberation, many Islamic thinkers reject an antagonistic, conflictual, zero-sum form of *da'wa* and debate in favor of something more collaborative and open-ended.[51] This commitment to transparency, simplicity, and honesty reflects a belief in the manifest truth and superiority of the Islamic message but, applied to the methodology of *da'wa*, reflects also a commitment to an attitude of intersubjective respect and recognition toward non-Muslims.

The attitude suggested by the requirement of open, rational argumentation is enhanced by the rejection of coercion in proselytizing. In addition to Q. 2:256 cited previously, Q. 10.99 reads: "If it had been your Lord's will then all on earth would have believed. Will you then compel them until they believe?" It is a staple of Islamic discourses that *da'wa* must be undertaken free from any spirit of aggression or coercion, that the only faith that counts with God is that which is sincere and freely adopted, and that the moral value of acts or beliefs is derived only from their intent.

The subject of coercion clearly demands a more technical philosophical discussion about what precisely constitutes coercion and free will. What is clear is that a theological belief in the existence of free will, or a belief in morality requiring right intentions or motivations, does not necessarily result in the endorsement of any particular kind of political institutions. There is no necessary intellectual contradiction in believing that faith must be voluntary and sincere while also believing that the state is called on to advantage a particular doctrine or way of life. There is also no necessary intellectual contradiction in believing that faith must be voluntary and sincere for it to count with God, while believing that society is justified in punishing behavior or thought that violates divine command. Islamic thinkers are usually quite clear on this. Faḍl Allāh, for example, in discussing the implications of Q. 2:256, writes that, *da'wa* "leaves others to take responsibility for themselves. For mankind is in the first and last reckoning responsible for its faith or unbelief." But he quickly adds:

> All of this is within the bounds of *da'wa* in its specific purview when the conflict is between ideas or doctrines as such. However, when *da'wa* shifts to the realm of the state, which organizes the affairs and lives of people according to a particular doctrine, and the conflict shifts to a war between the Islamic entity and the entity of unbelief or a conflict between two states, the position of *da'wa* then also shifts. The method changes and the matter takes on a new direction, focusing now on protecting the Islamic entity and the state of truth.[52]

For classical and classically minded Islamic thinkers, the question of religious tolerance and freedom of choice is never merely about individuals' right to believe what they wish and seek out information about various ways of life; the discussion almost always assumes such concepts as an Islamic "public order" or an Islamic "entity" that there is an obligation to preserve and defend. This results in such positions as a ban on non-Islamic propagation within Islamic polities, punishment for any heresy or "slander" of Islamic beliefs, punishment for "sins against oneself" or against God,[53] or Quṭb's position, introduced in the previous chapter, that true religious liberty is removing all barriers to obeying God's law (namely, any non-Islamic legal and political systems) so humankind can be "free" to choose Islam. The implication is often that the Qur'anic phrase "*lā ikrāha fī'l-dīn*" is almost a descriptive statement: It is simply a matter of fact that faith cannot arise out of coercion; coercion cannot *cause* faith and save the unbeliever. But acts that in the liberal tradition might be referred to as coercion may have other justifications, like upholding Islamic honor or public order or, more precisely, fulfilling the Islamic obligation to "command the right and forbid the wrong."

Once again, we must emphasize our focus on the minority political context, where the standard rejection of coercing faith based on Q. 2:256 and 10:99 may yet result in certain values or orientations supportive of liberal institutions. What is clear is that the recognition that coercion cannot cause belief, and the concomitant belief that one then ought not try to cause belief through coercion, is not sufficient to necessarily result in the endorsement of liberal institutions. However, what we are considering at the moment are precisely Islamic beliefs about *how to cause faith*, how to bring about faith in others. This is what *da'wa* involves, rather than (at least directly) defending an Islamic public order or an Islamic polity. Thus, insofar as Muslim thinkers regard residence in non-Muslim liberal democracies largely as a space for *da'wa*, for inviting to Islam, it is deeply significant for our interest in recognition that these efforts are universally regarded by Muslim thinkers to proceed entirely free from any inclination towards force, deception, or coercion. Although such an understanding may be insufficient to ground support for liberal neutrality in Muslim-majority societies, it contributes toward a respect for the autonomy, equality, and intellect of the non-Muslim other in a society already governed by liberal institutions.

A fourth concept, wisdom [*ḥikma*], also comes from Q. 16:125. According to most commentators, the injunction to "call to your Lord's path with wisdom" essentially involves adapting one's methods and approaches according to time and place. Faḍl Allāh refers mostly to the need to understand one's circumstances and realities, to be more flexible in addressing non-Muslims in order to be more relevant and effective.[54] This notion raises clear questions about the motivations implied by this interest in appropriateness, flexibility, and efficacy: Is this simply a tactical imperative, grounded not in any concern about the genuine needs or interests of the other but merely in a desire to win as many adherents to Islam as possible? Note that the same concern applies to the duties to preach and argue in a kindly manner. Is the injunction to approach non-Muslims with kindness, openness, and respect valid or compelling simply because alienating non-Muslims is counterproductive to the aims of *da'wa*? At one point, Faḍl Allāh suggests that one must make the addressed "*feel as though* you are a fellow-traveler on a journey towards truth, and that you respect him and his ideas," not that one must indeed be so, and describes arguing in the best manner as "the best practical method to arrive at that goal" [of winning adherents to Islam].[55]

Without denying the possibility that some may approach *da'wa* without a genuine respect for or recognition of the other, there are a number of possible responses to this challenge. The first is one we have suggested before in other contexts: that what is crucial here is not the explanation or justification given by certain exegetes of a divine injunction, but the mere fact that the action or attitude in question *is a command*. The attempt to explain why the command might be there may reveal tactical considerations, preferences, or inclinations, but the justification and reason for acting in such a way lies in the command itself, not in the explanation. If the result is to produce an attitude of recognition and tolerance in the political sphere, then the religiously authoritative nature of the command can be deemed sufficiently ethical for the demands of Rawlsian political liberalism.

There is a further, more interesting, reason for thinking that the command to call to Islam with wisdom might be constitutive of a genuine attitude of recognition, even on its more pragmatic, tactical interpretation. To the extent that "wisdom" is understood as inviting to Islam in a way appropriate for one's social surroundings, it is a call for *knowing the other* and *integrating with the wider society*, which are inclinations to both recognition and solidarity. It is largely in the name of *da'wa* that Muslim thinkers call for this. Mawlawī, for example, writes that the preliminary forms of relations between Muslims and non-Muslims crucial for *da'wa* (before attaining the stage of *ḥubb fiṭrī* discussed earlier) are mutual knowledge (*al-ta'āruf*), coexistence, and cooperation, adding that "we are a part of the society in which we live: Although a Muslim feels a part of the Islamic community . . . when he chooses to live in the West and chooses to be a part of this society in which he lives, then he must also think about this society—its issues, worries and problems—from his Islamic perspective. This is what requires him to look into the matters of the Islamic call in the West."[56] This is a common sentiment in Islamic writings on *da'wa* and living in non-Muslim countries.[57] I have argued that a minimal conception of citizenship, as opposed to what I have been referring to as "resident alienage," requires some affirmation of positive relationships to fellow citizens and a willingness to contribute to common welfare; it is clear that the Muslim understanding of the means and aims of *da'wa* contains powerful motivations for such integration and involvement.

As alluded to earlier, some comparison with Habermasian discourse ethics and theories of deliberative democracy might be in order here. Briefly, Habermas believes that the actual pragmatics of communication and argumentation commit participants to certain substantive normative presuppositions, namely, equal respect, the rejection of coercion, the freedom to form opinions, the intersubjective validity of reasons, trust, and honesty. Simply by engaging in discourses based on argumentation, participants acknowledge the incoherence of claims to normative validity achieved through coercion, lies, or exclusion and thus implicitly endorse various principles of recognition.[58]

To be sure, there are important differences between discourse and *da'wa* in their assumptions and motivations. First and chief among them is that discourse ethics is presented by its advocates as the *search* for truth; ethical knowledge is not posited beforehand. Islamic *da'wa* obviously presumes the result and the norm sought before contact with the other. Second, unlike discourse or deliberation, *da'wa* is not necessarily reciprocal. Habermas discusses empathy and putting oneself in the other's position, but this is not something called for in *da'wa* except in the most limited way. Although *da'wa* theorists do speak of listening to and getting to know the other, this is either purely instrumental to the aim of conversion or sincere but unrelated to the search for truth. The idea cannot be seriously entertained by Muslims that the actual process of debate and dialogue might result in greater ethical knowledge or a change of heart by Muslim "callers." Quite the opposite: The *da'wa* literature is replete with admonitions about who is allowed to engage in *da'wa*, on the moral and intellectual preparations they must make in advance to be immune to the inevitable opposition they will face, and even against engaging in too much arguing with nonbelievers, lest they get bogged down in obscurantist debates.[59]

Yet, while *da'wa* is strategic in a certain sense, or at least there is certainly the possibility for strategic thinking or motivations, the ethics of *da'wa* do in some sense incline toward the values of discourse ethics and deliberative democracy. Although *da'wa* may call for a certain cultivation of the other to create a positive identification with Islam and Muslims, this cannot be compared with strategic action proper, which uses the promise of threats and rewards to motivate action by the other. Just as in communicative action, where "one seeks *rationally* to *motivate* another by relying on the illocutionary binding/bonding effect of the offer contained in his speech act,"[60] the aim of *da'wa* is to genuinely motivate the other towards accepting Islam for the right reasons. Just as the "structure of communication rules out all external or internal coercion other than the force of the better argument and thereby also neutralizes all motives other than the cooperative search for truth,"[61] *da'wa* forbids coercion or threats as a motivating tactic and nullifies any motive for either spreading or accepting Islam other than the search for truth and salvation. Conversion must be voluntary, sincere, and for the right reasons. One cannot lie or deceive to bring about conversion. Just as in discourse and deliberation, everyone is allowed to question all assertions, introduce any assertions, and express attitudes, desires, and needs; *da'wa* does not presume that the non-Muslim must be silent and passive. It is true that the Muslim is not looking to the non-Muslim for truth, but his confidence in Islam's perfection allows him to welcome any concerns, objections, or (mis-)perceptions of the other. Finally, as in both discourse and deliberation, the *process* of *da'wa* itself has a certain value. *Da'wa* proponents do not expect everyone to convert, but there is a value placed on merely engaging with the other and presenting Islam to him. A Muslim "caller" (*dā'ī*) can discharge his obligation merely by engaging with non-Muslims, which he cannot do through a conversion brought about by ignoble means. The attention that Muslim theorists devote to the methodology and procedure of *da'wa* reveals the value placed on merely exposing others to Islam in a way that preserves the dignity of both parties.

In short, *da'wa* does not share the epistemic ambitions of discourse ethics or the community-building ambitions of deliberative democracy, but in the social context, there is a shared result of recognizing the other. Goodwill, transparency, honesty, sincerity, reason, freedom of choice, noncoercion, patience, openness to getting to know the other, and respect are all *da'wa* values that might be interpreted as comparable to Habermas's, thereby revealing certain implicit attitudes of recognition.

The "*Muwālāh* Verses"

Chapter 3 introduced a series of verses seeming to forbid friendship or alliance (*muwālāh/walā'*) with unbelievers, which was regarded as a doctrine potentially obstructive of bonds of recognition and solidarity between Muslims and nonbelievers. Here, before turning to the next chapter on solidarity, I examine interpretations of the *muwālāh* verses that do not forbid the types of relationships required between citizens in a liberal democracy.

In his exegesis of the Q. 3:28, Rashīd Riḍā says that only "those who are without knowledge and interpret the Qur'ān whimsically claim that the verse does not permit Muslims to ally themselves or come to agreement with others, even if this is in their interest and despite the fact that the Prophet himself made alliances with certain polytheists. In fact, some religious zealots claim ignorantly that this verse forbids any cooperation or association with them, or trusting them in any matter at all."[62] In opposition to this view Riḍā argues that there are three elements to a proper interpretation of the ban on *muwālāh*. The first is that, as with the verses on war and fighting, they refer strictly to those non-Muslims who aggress against and fight Muslims and emphasize that the circumstances of revelation (*asbāb al-nuzūl*) of this and the other *muwālāh* verses are the betrayal of the Muslim community by Muslims to Meccan pagans who were engaged in active combat with Muslims.[63] Decisive for him in this judgment are verses 60:7–8 (". . . God does not forbid you from dealing justly and equitably with those who do not fight you for your religion nor expel you from your homes, for God loves the equitable") and the fact that the Prophet himself established bonds of friendship, trust, and alliance with various non-Muslim individuals and states both before and after his migration from Mecca.[64] The second, related, point that Riḍā emphasizes is that Q. 3:28, 4:139, and 4:144 all refer to taking non-Muslim allies *rather than* or *in preference to* believers: *min dūn al-mu'minīn*. Thus, what becomes forbidden is allying with them at the expense of Muslims and Muslim interests.[65]

Third and finally, Riḍā understands the reference to *muwālāh* as approving of non-Muslims' unbelief and allying with them in pursuit of these aims.[66] Encapsulating these latter two points, he quotes his mentor Muḥammad 'Abduh, who argued that what is forbidden is anything that results in abandonment (*khidhlān*) of religion, harm (*īdhā'*) to its people, or damage (*iḍā'a*) to their interests. "But what opposes this, such as trade or *other social interactions of a secular nature*, is not included amongst that which is forbidden because it does not involve any opposition to God and His Apostle or any opposition or resistance to their religion."[67]

Contemporary Mauritanian scholar (and, along with Qaraḍāwī and Mawlawī, a leading scholar of the European Council for *Fatwa* and Research) 'Abd Allāh Ibn Bayya approaches the question along terms similar to Mawlawī's handling of the question of "love and brotherhood." He notes that "*walā'* is any firm bond which ties people together in a special, close and intimate relationship which give rise to obligations, rights and duties." Note first that there is a certain reversal of the traditional order of causality. Whereas the traditional question is whether certain relationships are eligible for *walā'* (and the obligations it implies) in the first place, Ibn Bayya's point of departure is that certain such relationships of *walā'* already exist and that certain moral obligations are thus unavoidable. He then makes the distinction between various types of such relationships, the first being based on shared creed, the second on familial ties, and the third on contract. "The highest and most exalted of these loyalties is that based on creed which includes faith in basic pillars of religion, the shared practice of rituals and adherence to moral virtue. This relationship of loyalty is not incompatible with loyalty to a homeland which binds people together into a contract of citizenship and defends its territory against aggression."[68] Further on, he suggests that loyalties can be seen as concentric circles or as steps in a pyramid, with religious loyalty at the summit, "but this does not exclude loyalty to a nation or homeland."[69]

As with Mawlawī's discussion, Ibn Bayya seems to find modern, liberal conceptions of citizenship and political community conducive to Islamic modes of justification of the minority condition. If anything, Ibn Bayya is more explicit in his endorsement of contemporary European norms for European Muslims. He begins a lengthy discussion titled "On Citizenship" by describing the various components of the modern understanding of national citizenship and how it differs from premodern ones: It expresses a reciprocal, mutual (*mutabādil*) relationship between individuals living on a territory not necessarily bound by descent, religion, or common memory; its framework is a constitution and system of laws; it is similar to a voluntary association of cooperation based on contractual belonging; and those belonging to it as of today have the same rights as the longest standing members.[70] His interpretive understanding of liberal conceptions of citizenship is thus nearly identical to the liberal self-description. Ibn Bayya even cites Habermas's conception of constitutional patriotism, or "the feelings of an individual towards his own membership in a civil society established on the basis of participation in certain basic values," as the ideal expression of the modern conception of "citizenship as a voluntary bond joined within national horizons and ruled by a constitution" and suggests that this conception "is the most important bridge to the respect and acceptance of religious values in all human societies which is compatible with Islam's conception of human coexistence. A Muslim doesn't find an objection to it but rather cooperates with it."[71]

Thus, Ibn Bayya's point about the compatibility of multiple loyalties is quite specific and interesting for this study, for his statement (quoted previously) that religious loyalty does not exclude national loyalty continues by adding the qualification "*according to the conception of citizenship to which we have pointed*"—that is, the modern liberal conception—"for it is not incompatible with religious loyalty insofar as the contract of citizenship does not imply leaving one's religion, abandoning rituals or limitations on the freedom for a Muslim to live his faith." Ibn Bayya's endorsement of this conception of citizenship is not only negative, however. He argues that the "circle" that makes up the compact of citizenship provides much good that is "demanded by religion and desired by nature," including:

> The right to life, justice, equality, freedoms, protection of property, protection against arbitrary imprisonment and torture, the right to social security for the poor, elderly and ill, cooperation between individuals in society for the general welfare, as well as all of the duties and obligations which follow, such as paying taxes, defending the homeland against aggression, obeying the law and upholding the contract of citizenship all of which falls under the religious obligation to be loyal to contracts and their requirements which itself falls under loyalty to religion: "O you who believe! Fulfill all contracts."[72]

Of course, these goods that are "demanded by religion" and are thus encompassed by (the broader circle of) Islamic religious commitments are clearly not only secular ("political" in the Rawlsian sense) but also meant to evoke liberal self-descriptions. He is even more explicit than this, though. He takes pains to enumerate the:

> great values of secularism [*'almāniyya*] and neutrality [*al-muḥāyida*] which are regarded positively, including: (1) respect for convictions; (2) neutrality between religions; (3) the recognition of both individual and collective human rights and the state's protection of them; (4) the right of disagreement, diversity and transformation of the characteristics of individuals and groups; (5) and the right of access to courts to realize and enforce one's rights, the setting of obligations on individuals with respect for law, paying taxes by way of participation in national efforts to construct institutions, and defense against aggression.[73]

Finally, he defends secularism against some of its Muslim critics, who put forward an interpretation of secularism as a system that "departs from neutrality and interferes in the particular characteristics of peoples and nations, and functions as a tool of control over convictions." This, he submits, is a "distortion of the basic meaning of secularism which [does not require] submission to a single comprehensive ideological trend which might wish to impose its particular concepts constructed on its own prejudices."[74]

So here we have a quite unmistakable endorsement of secularism and citizenship on liberal terms as a system that is beneficial for Muslim minorities and that is asserted to be compatible with Islamic commitments. It is also noteworthy that this endorsement comes not from a savvy media figure living in a Western country, like Tariq Ramadan, but a senior, traditionalist Mālikī religious scholar from Mauritania writing in Arabic; these passages cannot be dismissed as rhetoric for consumption within some cross-cultural or ecumenical dialogue. However, it is appropriate to ask just what is Islamic about these arguments. As I argued at some length in chapter 2, an "Islamic argument" is not just the judgment or opinion of someone with a Muslim name or writing about Islamic themes. Of course, in the banal sense, "Islam" is just what its adherents believe it to be; however, a study like this involves a search for more concrete Islamic doctrinal demonstrations or efforts to fit these kinds of statements of judgment into broader theories of Islamic moral commitment. This search does not imply the assumption that the only authentic Islamic beliefs or values are those that can be shown to have direct textual derivation but rather the assumption that Islamic law and ethics (like Western ethical discourses) are not just assertions of opinion or authority but involve standards of argumentation and demonstration that establish how a moral claim can be evaluated and can be carried from one discursive situation to another.

Ibn Bayya does not fail to draw on Qur'anic verses, although it is not obvious that they are causing the full extent of the beliefs presented here. The first verse used to ground his robust affirmation of the virtues of secularism is, as quoted previously, Q. 5:1: "O you who believe! Fulfill all contracts." As seen in the last chapter, the obligation to uphold contracts can give strong reasons for *honoring* secular systems, although it is not clear where it gives any particular reasons to *value* all of the goods provided by secular systems or, more precisely, to *choose* a system that limits coercive social action to these goods. A second verse introduced seems more apropos: "And never let your hatred of people who would bar you from the Inviolable House of Worship lead you into the sin of aggression: but rather help one another in furthering kindness [*al-birr*, which can imply religious devoutness as well as charity] and God-consciousness, and do not help one another in furthering evil and enmity" [Q. 5:2]. As Ibn Bayya notes, this verse clearly refers to the relationship with the Meccan polytheists with whom the Muslims were at war, "so how could it not permit [cooperation] with peaceful citizens?"[75] It is clear how such verses could give warrant to the civic principle of cooperation in worldly matters, possibly on grounds of solidarity (this verses resurfaces in the next chapter on political participation), but this still seems quite remote from the enthusiasm displayed by Ibn Bayya for secularism, neutrality, and modern citizenship. Why, for example, would this verse not also ground cooperation with Jewish and Christian fellow monotheists *against* strict secularism and all of the equal liberties it has been shown to protect ("... help one another in furthering kindness [*al-birr*] and *God-consciousness...*")?

Thus, another approach for Ibn Bayya is to step back from the texts and simply note the substantive overlap in broader values and aims. After enumerating the "great values of secularism and neutrality" (the five points quoted previously), he observes that "all of this does not contradict the great values to which the revealed religions called, especially Islam, which calls to kindness, affection and human brotherhood [*al-birr wa'l-maḥabba wa'l-ukhūwa al-insāniyya*]" and that devotion to one's homeland and fellow citizens is validation by both reason and revelation.[76] Here it is hard not to recall Rawls's claim that, even without explicit metaphysical grounding, the values of fair social cooperation are simply "very great values" that have intuitive appeal for persons who enjoy them. Although it does not resolve the concern expressed here about the concrete Islamic metaphysical grounding for such principles, it is noteworthy to hear an echo of these claims in an otherwise fairly technical work of modern Islamic jurisprudence. Although Ibn Bayya does not elaborate on this here, in the next chapter we encounter efforts to fit the pursuit of purely secular, worldly goods into a larger and longer standing Islamic conception of the good and the legitimate purposes of law and social cooperation (to wit, the tradition of speculating on the "purposes of *sharīʿa*" (*maqāṣid al-sharīʿa*).

The final perspective on the question of loyalty and belonging within a secular context that Ibn Bayya introduces by way of response to (unnamed) Islamic skeptics is what I have been calling the "no prohibition" (*ʿadam al-taḥrīm*) argument, although he chooses to frame it in terms of the obligation on Muslims to avoid evil. He begins by noting that evil has its degrees and ranks, with the evil of losing religion entirely at the top, closely followed by the evil of participating in sins and prohibited acts. The acts of forming bonds of loyalty and affection with non-Muslims only rise to the rank of an evil to be avoided when they come at the expense of such bonds with Muslims—*min dūn al-muʾminīn*.[77] Once again, he repeats his basic point that the very extensive and incontrovertible obligations that Muslims have to one another are not "a suspended wall keeping out all secular [*dunyawī*; lit.: this-worldly, mundane] relationships with other people which do not impinge upon or attack the foundations of belief; nay, cooperation with people to advance common interests [*maṣāliḥ*] and repel harm, the mutual exchange with them of affection and cooperation with them in accordance with the law of morality is all in keeping with the words of the Exalted 'speak goodness unto people.'"[78]

This debate finds a slightly more precise and doctrinally systematic elaboration in ʿAbd al-Qādir's treatise on Muslim minorities. He concurs with Riḍā that the *muwālāh* verses are not absolute in the sense of applying to both peaceful and warring unbelievers, but that "God has prescribed hostility and antagonism only to those who fight God, His Apostle and the believers. There is no prohibition on friendship with unbelievers who do not harm believers."[79] He arrives at this position for reasons identical to Riḍā's (and Ibn Bayya's[80]): The verses all emphasize non-Muslim aggression and the idea of befriending them "in exclusion of the believers" (*min dūn al-muʾminīn*), the Prophet himself turned to non-Muslims for help, and other generally held rulings, such as the permissibility of marrying Christian and Jewish women, show that the ban on befriending non-Muslims cannot be general in application.

ʿAbd al-Qādir's efforts are interesting, however, because he makes more of an effort to consider what forms of alliance are permitted and to apply these views to a contemporary political context. Therein, we encounter what are by now rather familiar views. In terms of alliance between political entities, he writes that there must be an overwhelming need for this and the "word of unbelief" may not be dominant, but that alliance is "not *muwālāh* unless it is to the benefit of the unbelievers and their word is ascendant. Such a situation is humiliation for religion and its adherents." Non-Muslim lands are permissible as refuges if Muslims are in danger and no other Muslims are in a position to help, as with the case of those whom Muḥammad sent to Abyssinia during the first Meccan period. Within this context, it is permissible to cooperate with them in the spheres of economics, science/knowledge, and even military "coordination" (*tansīq*) under the supervision of Muslim authorities. This also covers treating unbelievers with kindness (*al-iḥsān, bi'l-luṭf*); tolerating them; being charitable, hospitable, and equitable toward them; exchanging gifts; lending and borrowing; and visiting them, among other interactions.[81]

Possibly drawing from 'Abduh's and Riḍā's treatment, he reserves the term *muwālāh* for situations in which there is a form of setback, subjugation, or disappointment (*khidhlān*) for religion, harm to its people, and a neglect of their interests, as well as an aggrandizement of unbelievers and a strengthening of them over Muslims, without regard to whether the unbelievers in question are peaceful or warring. This can happen in two ways: (a) being pleased with their unbelief or having affection for them because of it, or (b) "relying" on them.

The first way (a) involves associating too intimately with them on a *religious* basis, ascribing truth to their doctrine, or seeing no difference between it and Islam in regard to their respective truth-claims. "This includes approving of their doctrines or religious rituals, or ascribing truth to them, as well as aiding them in ways which strengthen and affirm them in their unbelief. This results in a defeat for religion and belief." He refers to this, quoting Ibn Taymiyya, as "*muwālāh bi'l-qalb*"—"allying one's heart [to them]"—and emphasizes that the only hatred a Muslim feels is toward what the unbeliever holds by way of error and idolatry, not toward him personally.[82] However, various forms of special consideration, approval and recognition of unbelievers with good characters/morals, or personal relations with unbelieving children, wives, or other relatives do not constitute *muwālāh*.

The second way (b) involves not merely forming bonds of trust with unbelievers but being pliable or submissive to them, flattering them, being obsequious, and the like, as well as asking them for help or allying with them against Muslims, imitating them, or aggrandizing them and spreading their doctrines and ideas.[83] The crucial element for him and others is clearly how intimately linked the political and the religious are in a given alliance or friendship. For 'Abd al-Qādir, "tolerance consists in inter-personal treatment, not in the doctrinal concept or in the social system. Good treatment does not mean loyalty or assistance in religion, or recognition that the religions revealed before Muḥammad's prophecy are accepted by God and that Islam can stand with them in a single front against atheism."[84] Others have also recently interpreted the ban to refer to adopting unbelievers' characteristics related to their religion, doctrines, beliefs, or rituals, not as neighbors or citizens.[85]

Is this understanding of the permissible forms of friendship with unbelievers compatible with bonds of citizenship in general and with the conception advanced by political liberalism in particular? The area of ambiguity that remains is whether living under a political order that advances values other than Islamic ones constitutes a form of subordination, subservience, or "defeat" for religion forbidden by even the Modernist theorists. Among the conditions under which Muslims may forge alliances with non-Muslims, 'Abd al-Qādir lists that the "word of Islam" must be ascendant over (*ẓāhira 'alā*) that of unbelievers. Such a term suggests that he has in mind alliances between states (for how could even Muslim jurists expect that the word of Islam will be ascendant in a non-Muslim state?), but to the extent that citizenship is a form of formal alliance or contract, it is reasonable to ask whether the ascendance of non-Islamic aims or doctrines might render bonds of citizenship similarly unacceptable.

Does the liberal nature, specifically the *politically* liberal nature, of a non-Muslim state have any bearing on this discussion? On one reading, if living as a minority under a non-Islamic government is *in itself* the form of subordination or subservience deemed to be forbidden, then it doesn't particularly matter what form of government exists in such a country.[86] Yet, we already have Riḍā, 'Abd al-Qādir, Qaraḍāwī, Ibn Bayya, and others on record permitting residence in such states. So either they are only justifying a form of resident alienage according to which Muslims would reside in such states but seek to avoid any form of political integration, or they are open to the possibility that the terms of citizenship in certain states may not result in a form of *muwālāh* that they reject. There are at least two very strong reasons for arguing that a politically liberal regime comes as close as possible to avoiding the conditions that Islamic theorists find unacceptable.

The first main condition that was seen to constitute the unacceptable form of *muwālāh* was forming political alliances to the exclusion of (*min dūn*) and in opposition to fellow Muslims. Muṣṭafā al-Ṭaḥḥān, for example, was cited previously as having no objection to living with non-Muslims as neighbors and citizens, but (citing Qaraḍāwī's authority) "it is necessary that a Muslim's loyalty not be to another community at the expense of his own." The second condition was if Muslims were required to ally with non-Muslims in expressly religious or doctrinal matters, advancing the aims or prominence of another creed.

Political liberalism can advance a case that it requires neither of these from Muslim citizens. The last chapter explored in some detail the requirements of loyalty to a non-Muslim liberal democracy. We took seriously a Muslim's concern not to find himself betraying the welfare or interests of fellow Muslims simply because it is in the interest of his non-Muslim state or political community. In cases where a Muslim entity or force was clearly the aggressor against a Muslim's state of citizenship, we showed that the Muslim citizen has very strong religious reasons for opposing such actions and contributing to the non-Muslim state's efforts of self-defense in a civilian capacity. In turn, I argued that the liberal state can in good conscience accommodate the Muslim citizen's desire not to kill fellow Muslims.

As to the second condition, we again have reason to point to the advantage of political liberalism's commitment to neutrality and "epistemic abstinence." In disavowing any claim to metaphysical truth as the basis for justice, in requiring of citizens no such affirmations in order to participate politically, and in establishing no collective goals that require adherence to a controversial metaphysical doctrine, political liberalism can retort that it requires of Muslim citizens no statement whatsoever about the truth or superiority of any one religion, doctrine, or way of life. Given that Muslim jurists are prepared to allow residence even in states that exhibit no such restraint, their very discourse on *muwālāh* reveals Islam-specific reasons why Muslims should be more willing to take a step beyond resident alienage toward citizenship in a politically liberal state than in any other non-Muslim regime.[87]

The discussion of which forms of "loyalty" or "civic friendship" with non-Muslims are Islamically permissible moves the discussion of recognition away from the more passive acceptance of the other's unbelief to more positive forms of active cooperation for mutual benefit. What I am suggesting is that there is a concern on the part of Islamic scholars to think about the moral relationship with non-Muslims, non-Muslim societies, and non-Islamic states in ways that exceed the confines of the classical constructs. This alone should not be surprising, except that the classical constructs get us quite far already. As demonstrated in the preceding three chapters, the three main Islamic approaches to moral obligation (the "statutory-deontological," the "constructivist-contractualist" and the "consequentialist-utilitarian") are quite robust. Islamic scholars discern a divine command to treat non-Muslims with justice and equity and to enter into certain kinds of contractual relationships with them. They allow for the construction of more specific moral obligations arising out of contracts (as long as they do not require explicit disobedience to God, although what would entail this is not usually spelled out once and for all). And they imagine a wide variety of ways in which abiding by the terms of social cooperation as presented by non-Muslim states might be good for Muslims. Those approaches alone would probably suffice for theorizing liberal citizenship, and were it the case that contemporary Islamic scholars as conservative as Qaraḍāwī and Mawlawī (both of whom are active in the Muslim Brotherhood) were concerned to articulate a "public" doctrine of something like loyal resident alienage (while in more "private," Islamic circles downplaying obligations to non-Muslims), they would almost certainly restrict themselves to them. However, they do not. Even their Arabic-language texts written for internal Islamic consumption display a concern to more comprehensively theorize and theologize the relationship with non-Muslims. This approach to moral obligation I refer to as "comprehensive-qualitative," as it goes beyond the demands of justice and equitable treatment to imagine a relationship of concern and overlapping interests. This approach is not without its problems; I have repeatedly emphasized the ambiguous nature of relying on *da'wa* and would not suggest that the scholars encountered here are themselves committed to liberal conceptions of justice based on principled self-restraint. Nonetheless, I do maintain that these trends are significant for an understanding of evolving Islamic ethical and political discourses and that they are authentic grounds for an Islamic approach to moral obligation *qua* recognition of the other. I continue this discussion in the next chapter, where I treat the idea of solidarity arising from social cooperation.

8

Solidarity with Non-Muslims

It may be that God will grant love and friendship between you and those whom you now hold as enemies for God is All-Powerful, and God is Oft-Forgiving, Most-Merciful. God does not forbid you from dealing justly and equitably with those who do not fight you for your religion nor expel you from your homes, for God loves the equitable.
—Qur'an, *Sūrat al-Mumtaḥana* (60): 7–8

To this point, most of our questions have been negative in character: whether Muslims can *refrain* from migrating or betraying a state of residence, for example. Even our discussion of recognition to this point has focused largely on passive acceptance of non-Muslims' unbelief. To speak of a doctrine of citizenship, however, rather than a state of resident alienage, suggests certain basic positive duties as well toward fellow citizens. What these are is obviously fiercely contested in liberal political theory; here I do not seek to vindicate a particular conception of social justice or civic duty, but rather the mere idea that Muslims may find themselves contributing to the welfare of non-Muslims, even indirectly and involuntary through taxation or as a double effect of pursuing one's own interests. In this chapter, I examine Islamic arguments for the permissibility of such contributions.

To avoid confusion, my argument is not that the belief must be held that such contribution and participation are part and parcel of an Islamic conception of the good life or that they are aspects of virtue. Such assertions would be a very thick instance of an overlapping consensus, but what the comparative theorist in this case is interested in establishing is merely an Islamic foundation for the belief that contributing to the welfare of non-Muslim societies and participating in their political life are permissible and not in conflict with any core Islamic conception of the good or of justice. I articulated in chapter 4 what I regard as the "equilibrium" statement of a commitment to solidarity with non-Muslims in the following two principles:

S: It is permissible for a Muslim to form common social, economic, and civic goals with non-Muslims. It is understood that in sharing social and political space Muslims benefit from this and in turn contribute to the material welfare of non-Muslims, to which there is no Islamic objection.

PP: It is permissible for a Muslim to participate in a political system not based on Islamic justice or Islamic public justification. Such participation is an appropriate way to advance certain interests of Muslim communities, particularly in worldly matters, interests that may overlap with those of non-Muslim fellow citizens.

Together with the views introduced in the previous chapter, I submit that these principles of solidarity and political participation are sufficient to demonstrate a "conception of the other" compatible with liberal conceptions of citizenship.

Contribution to Non-Muslim Welfare

The first thing to be reemphasized is that the general notions of charity, contributing to the welfare of others, and sacrificing for the sake of one's political community are central to Islamic religious ethics. This is best exemplified by the obligation, one of the five basic pillars of religious practice, to render *zakāh*, often translated as "alms tax." This does not establish our case, however, as the *zakāh* has very specific religious understandings and implications, and it cannot be argued that the forms of contribution a Muslim makes to the welfare of a non-Muslim society are equivalent to the *zakāh*.[1] In addition to this specific obligation, however, numerous Qur'anic verses urge believers toward charity and responsibility for the welfare of others, including:

> It is not righteousness that ye turn your faces towards East or West; but it is righteousness to believe in God, the Last Day, the Angels, the Book, and the Messengers; to spend of your substance out of love for Him, for your kin, for orphans, for the needy, for the wayfarer, for those who ask, and for the ransom of slaves; to be steadfast in prayer, and practice regular charity, to fulfill the contracts which you have made; and to be firm and patient, in pain (or suffering) and adversity, and throughout all periods of panic. Such are the people of truth, the God-fearing. [2:177]
>
> Serve God, and make not any partners with Him in His divinity. Do good to parents, kinsfolk, orphans, those in need, neighbors who are near, neighbors who are strangers, the companion by your side, the wayfarer and those whom your right hands possess: for God loves

> not the arrogant, the vainglorious. Nor join those who are miserly or enjoin others to miserliness, or hide the bounties which God has bestowed on them. [4:36–37]
>
> Truly man was created very impatient. . . . Not so those devoted to prayer . . . and those in whose wealth there is a share for the needy and the indigent. [70:19–25]

In considering the Islamic value of charity in the context of citizenship, what is relevant is that in a non-Muslim liberal democracy contribution to the welfare of others may be enforced by state structures and that it cannot be limited to members of one's substate moral community.

The idea of such contributions being enforced by state structures as an obligation of political justice is itself not objectionable from a Muslim standpoint. As discussed in the chapter 3, the collection of the *zakāh* has traditionally been regarded as one of the duties of a legitimate ruler.[2] In a more modern framework, speaking about the general duty to be charitable, Sayyid Quṭb, for example, notes that that the "Islamic view of social organization" entrusts social security to "government machinery when the smaller, more directly involved machinery of the family becomes incapable of meeting the challenge."[3] This is, of course, in relation to a Muslim-majority society, but it serves to demonstrate that the idea of the state intervening to secure a certain pattern of wealth distribution should itself not pose a doctrinal challenge for Muslim citizens of non-Muslim states.

Bearing in mind some of the statements we encountered in chapter 3 on avoiding contributing to the strength of unbelievers, what requires more explicit justification is the idea of making such contributions to a non-Muslim society or political community. Thus, here the focus is on the cross-communal nature of social obligations in a liberal democracy. Furthermore, as argued in chapter 6, we do not regard general endorsements of political obligation (calls to obey the law of any state in which one lives in relative security and freedom) as endorsements of active citizenship or participation in any such society. We are thus interested in positive reasons for regarding the substantive requirements of life in a liberal democracy as reasonable or acceptable.

Nothing in the verses quoted previously limits the obligation of charity to fellow believers, and exegetes have not tended to read in such a restriction. Even Quṭb, in commenting on 4:36–37, interprets the verses as "an order to extend charity to certain groups of one's immediate family and of the human family at large."[4] Some classical exegetes, in fact, interpreted the phrase "neighbors who are near, neighbors who are strangers" from 4:36 as referring to Muslims and non-Muslims, respectively, a reading that expressly includes non-Muslims within the sphere of social obligation.[5] There is even a tradition holding that the Caliph 'Umar, in assigning an allowance from the public treasury for poor non-Muslims, interpreted the two expressions from Q. 9:60 (cited previously as the authoritative verse on the allocation of the *zakāh*) for "poor" and "needy" (*al-fuqarā'* and *al-masākīn*) as referring in turn to Muslims and non-Muslims.[6]

A particularly categorical and unambiguous treatment is that of the thirteenth-century Mālikī jurist and exegete al-Qurṭubī, who writes (on Q. 4:36): "The instruction of good treatment of neighbors is recommended whether they be Muslims or unbelievers. This is the correct reading. 'Good treatment' (*al-iḥsān*) has the meaning of charity (*al-muwāsāh*), good relations, refraining from harming them, and protecting them from harm."[7] He notes further that all scholars are of the consensus that no part of this verse is abrogated by subsequently revealed verses. Thus, in this vein, in addition to the "political obligation" justification for paying taxes to a non-Muslim state, some contemporary scholars refer directly to the goodness of the purposes to which they are put.[8] Qaṭari scholar 'Alī Muḥyī al-Dīn al-Qara Dāghī, for example, responds to a question about the permissibility of paying taxes to a non-Muslim state that may adopt some anti-Muslim policies that "we should bear in mind that income taxes bring about benefit to society, as they may be spent in different legitimate ways such as on refugees, the needy, infrastructure, etc."[9] He further cites Q. 5:48, which concludes by exhorting Jews, Christians, and Muslims to all "compete with each other in good works."[10]

A number of other values and orientations serve to give this exhortation to charity a more comprehensive philosophical foundation for affirming solidarity and mutual concern with non-Muslims. We have already encountered in the discussions on *da'wa* and *muwālāh* certain views on contributing to non-Muslim welfare. The *da'wa* discourse revealed both a weak and a strong form of solidarity with non-Muslims. The weak form held that *da'wa* requires a certain integration into and concern for the wider non-Muslim society. On this view, *da'wa* is the higher value and objective, but a certain concern for non-Muslims and their societies—which we are assuming here to validate nonvoluntary contributions to such societies—may be not only compatible with but also even supportive of or necessary for the aims of *da'wa*. This sentiment is comparable to what we are regarding as the mainstream understanding of permissible and impermissible forms of *muwālāh*: The verses in question are held to permit co-operation and friendship with non-Muslims in civil and secular matters. When one adds to this the general Islamic call for charity and generosity, without any strong reason for thinking it is restricted to Muslims, one has a strong reason for expressing the form of solidarity required with non-Muslims in a liberal state. Mawlawī describes "cooperation" (*al-ta'āmul*) as one of the basic stages of relations with non-Muslims (resulting in the stage of "affection" (*'āṭifa*) or "innate love" (*ḥubb fiṭrī*)), pointing out the numerous occasions when the Prophet joined with non-Muslims to advance just secular causes. He marvels that "one may find it difficult to bear after these juridical questions that you can advance your own interests and at the same time the interests of non-Muslims," even giving a remarkably Rawlsian argument: "If there are certain matters which we consider religiously ordained or legitimate [*shar'ī*], and non-Muslims adopt them *for different reasons* then we can co-operate with them towards the realization of them as long as they are considered legal for us."[11]

It is also common for Muslim scholars to situate the question of contributing to non-Muslim societies as an aspect of the Islamic duty to "command the right and forbid the wrong." The logic here is very similar to that of *da'wa* and the arguments for cooperating in secular matters with non-Muslims, to the extent that the basic question is how Muslims can bring about Islamically desirable ends in non-Muslim lands.[12] For example, when Tariq Ramadan expounds on the content of the Islamic duty to "enjoin justice" or "promote good and equity," this takes on a particularly political (in the Rawlsian sense) cast: He understands the Muslim's duty to bear witness to Islamic values as a duty to be involved in society in the areas of "unemployment, marginalisation, delinquency, reform of legal, economic, social and political systems,"[13] that is, precisely the sort of civic goals appropriate in a politically liberal regime. By contrast, for a genuinely strict Salafī scholar, "enjoining justice" would point toward the direct confrontation of sin or scandalous behavior, such as in the infamous Danish cartoon incident. Similarly, an unattributed article on the *IslamOnline* Web site justifies contribution to non-Muslim societies and active social engagement within the context of this duty: "We Muslims are commanded to improve the societies we live in, to enjoin the good and forbid the wrong. It's not enough to do that just among ourselves. We have to be an active part of our societies, not only to gain our own rights, but to see that right and justice prevail. The important thing is to work with the non-Muslims around us to improve society (and to try to gradually shape it to our standards)."[14]

Of course, as the final parenthetical statement suggests, these are all the same arguments given for cooperating with non-Muslims in the pursuit of illiberal aims.[15] For the purposes of our wider inquiry into support for liberal institutions, this point needs to be borne in mind. At the moment, this need not concern us, however, for the understanding here is that the sorts of goods Rawls has in mind as "political" are what Mawlawī and others refer to as "social" or "worldly," and that they can be legitimately pursued with non-Muslims. The point is that the goods Muslims are commanded to pursue *include* a wide range of secular goods, including education, economic prosperity, public health, and public order, as part of the general Islamic conception of welfare. Although the aims of *da'wa* and "commanding right and forbidding wrong" can justify the pursuit of illiberal aims in a non-Muslim society, this does not detract from the strength of their support for the pursuit of *other* aims compatible with political liberalism.

There was also a stronger view, likewise attributable to Fayṣal Mawlawī, which held *da'wa* itself to be one way of discharging a yet higher duty. In Mawlawī's words, "God has commanded us to bestow mercy on all mankind as a part of faith." Here the focus is not only on the non-Muslim's ultimate duty to save himself, and on all humankind's duty to God, but also on what is due him in this world: "We conclude that there can and must be affection and love towards a person whom you wish to call to God and that this affection is a small piece of the affection that God wills be directed towards him. This is the foundation which is considered to be stronger and weightier than all that which opposes it."[16] The foundational belief for *da'wa* is, of course, Islamic universalism, which itself presumes certain commonalities among all humans, including a common origin, nature, and purpose. This is a common theme in contemporary Islamic treatments of living in a shared political space with non-Muslims. Scholars often point to the numerous Qur'anic verses that are addressed to humankind in general (including 2:21, 4:1, 4:174, 10:57, 34:28), as well as those that speak of God's beneficent intentions for humankind, among the most popular being Q. 17:70: "We have honored the sons of Adam, provided them with transport on land and sea, given them for sustenance things good and pure, and conferred on them special favors, above a great part of Our creation."[17] The beliefs that the message of Islam is directed toward all humanity; that all humankind shares a common origin, nature, and purpose; and that God's creation was an act of love for humankind are often reduced by contemporary scholars to the simple formula that "Islam seeks to bring benefit and improvement to all people and all races."[18] Although the "benefit to humanity" implied is, of course, comprehensive in nature[19] and "controversial" in the Rawlsian sense, the argument of contemporary scholars is that it is un-Islamic to regret one's own proportional contribution to the welfare (material, inter alia) of people whom God wishes to bless.

Participating in Non-Islamic Governments

Our earlier discussion of the permissibility of residence in non-Muslim states (chapter 5) touched on the problem of submitting to non-Muslim rule or legislation. For those who were seen to view residence as impermissible, it was this condition that was held to explain the ban most convincingly. Conversely, it was shown that a large number of jurists have held that residence is permissible even without Muslim self-rule on Islamic lines. Our subsequent discussion of loyalty to a non-Muslim polity focused on the Islamic duty to adhere to contracts, including the tacit conditions implied by accepting a state's protection. Some Muslim scholars extract widely from this duty, arguing not only that one may not betray one's state in wartime but also that one must obey all the laws of a land in which one accepts security. The argument from contract is thus the most frequently invoked justification (along with, of course, the juridical principle of "necessity making the forbidden permissible") for obeying non-Muslim, and un-Islamic, political and legal authority.[20]

This is obviously not the same thing as arguing that such authority may be just or may act justly or, differently put, that a Muslim would have reasons to choose or voluntarily endorse such authority. Living in a non-Muslim land, recognizing its right to security, and accepting the unbelief of fellow citizens are all crucial components of a doctrine of citizenship in a non-Muslim state. None of them suggests, however, any belief in the justness or acceptability of the political institutions of such a state, which is required if Muslims are to affirm their own citizenship within such states (as opposed to mere contribution to a society). It is obvious that the more orthodox juridical sources we are privileging in this work are not likely to ground a Muslim's fealty to such political systems on the general acceptability or justness of their being un-Islamic. It would, in fact, be folly to ignore the reserve with which contemporary Muslim neo-classical thinkers treat secular, liberal politico-legal systems, even outside the Muslim world. Is a doctrine of loyal resident alienage thus as far as these sources can be pushed?

Here I think much depends on the questions one poses to the sources. Although I believe that there is important work to be done on how Muslim jurists understand the general purposes of the *sharī'a* (*maqāṣid al-sharī'a*), in particular, the five essential interests it serves to protect (*al-ḍarūriyyāt al-khamsa*),[21] and whether these purposes can be shown to be fulfilled by non-Islamic legal systems, thus rendering them in some way "just," demonstrating this with sufficient rigor would exceed the bounds of the present discussion. However, a frequent question in Islamic treatments of the minority condition is whether it is permissible to participate in non-Islamic governments, either through voting or through accepting appointments.[22] This topic bears directly on the question of solidarity and recognition. Although it may allow us a brief glimpse at how Muslim theorists might regard the actions of a non-Muslim liberal regime as substantively just, the question of immediate interest concerns political participation as a indication of Muslim willingness to share political sovereignty with non-Muslims. Thus, we are operating with a fine distinction between the political system of a non-Muslim liberal democracy qua liberal democratic political system and qua non-Muslim political system. Yet, while we are for the moment focusing primarily on the latter dimension, the former nonetheless remains our standard for evaluating the compatibility of arguments for participation. The question of political participation is thus a *hinge issue* between the aspects of citizenship relating to living in a non-Muslim political space and those relating to political justice.

The ultimate inseparability of addressing political participation as an issue of solidarity and as an issue of justice is obvious once we begin to examine Islamic arguments for participation. The main arguments *against* participation are the following: (1) It involves taking non-Muslims as patrons in the way proscribed by the Qur'an, (2) it involves "inclining toward" those who do wrong ("And incline not to those who do wrong, or the fire will seize you; and you have no protectors other than God, nor shall you be helped" (11:113)), (3) it involves accepting and legitimating the status quo of non-Islamic rule and man-made legislation, and (4) it will result in assimilation to non-Muslim society.[23]

Not surprisingly, many contemporary Muslim scholars respond to fundamentalist arguments that participation in a non-Islamic system is a sin by pointing out the need to advance the Islamic conception of good by all legitimate means. Just as *da'wa* requires a certain integration into a non-Muslim society, so can political participation, including coalitions with non-Muslim religious groups, be a legitimate means for advancing illiberal aims. One scholar, echoing American right-wing Christian claims, even mentions the rulings of the U.S. Supreme Court under Chief Justice Earl Warren as something Muslim political participation might eventually undo:

> The Warren Court in the 1950s began to turn the constitution into anti-religion until it became what it is today, supportive of all kind of

> evils. If Muslim justices sit in that position, the same constitution has the potential (theoretically speaking) of being supportive of Islamic rules and values. Non-participation of Muslims in the political process is saying that "I do not care and I will let the opportunity of Islamization pass by." How would you answer Allah? Actually, the alternative is even worse, that is, indifference and complacency to the evils.[24]

This quotation exemplifies a species of arguments that justify political participation as part of a long-term strategy of general Islamization or as the best available means of "commanding right and forbidding wrong," where the wrongs intended to be confronted largely include acts protected as matters of personal liberty by liberal regimes.[25] Thus, although in one sense certain arguments for participation in a (heretofore) non-Muslim political system can be construed as a position of solidarity qua concern for non-Muslim souls, such arguments do not affirm civic solidarity within liberal constraints. These are not justifications of sharing political sovereignty and collective responsibility but rather a weighing of relative evils;[26] they are invariably presented as consistent with the complete rejection of democracy as a system that Muslims might *choose* for themselves.[27]

Even without exploring the possibility of a more comprehensive overlap between liberal and Islamic conceptions of political justice alluded to earlier, there are currents of Islamic thought that focus on the permissible forms of political cooperation between Muslims and non-Muslims within liberal constraints. The dominant strategy of justification hovers between two arguments: that there is no prohibition (*'adam al-taḥrīm*) on collaborating with unbelievers in secular matters and that pursuing secular forms of welfare and justice is itself a religious injunction. Although these arguments are advanced by scholars who may be highly conservative, even "Revivalist" on some readings,[28] they differ from their intellectual brethren who call for using political freedoms to advance Islamic conceptions of morality in focusing primarily on using non-Islamic institutions toward secular aims, although there is often a creative ambiguity in the identification of the aims and values to be pursued.

I begin, then, with an example of how both the problem of political participation is treated as less controversial than it in reality is and how there is vagueness in the description of the purposes of and the constraints on political participation. Ibn Bayya notes simply (claiming to express the considered conclusions of the European Council for *Fatwa* and Research) that "the basic principle is the legitimacy of political participation by Muslims in Europe, and the specific evaluation of it varies from permissibility, to recommendation to necessity based on what the Exalted One said: 'help one another in furthering kindness [*al-birr*] and God-consciousness, and do not help one another in furthering evil and enmity' [5:2] as well as on the fact that it is considered amongst the requirements of citizenship."[29] He includes within political participation joining civic associations and political parties, voting, and running for office and then specifies two sets of "general rules and precepts" (*ḍawābiṭ*):

> upholding Islamic morals such as truthfulness, justice, loyalty and trustworthiness (*al-ṣidq wa'l-'adl wa'l-wafā' wa'l-amāna*), respect for the plurality of differing opinion, fair competition with opponents and the avoidance of violence. [Further rules include] voting in elections on the condition of upholding [religiously] legitimate, moral and legal principles, which include the clarity of purpose in serving society, avoiding deception and defamation, and impartiality from personal whims and interests.[30]

Without a more detailed specification of the terms and their Islamic derivation, these rules seem to largely reinforce the basic idea of fidelity to contracts and the impermissibility of perfidy. This is not to say they are insincere, but it is hard to discern the extent of his theorization of such commitments as "respect for the plurality of differing opinion" and "fair electoral competition." Similar vagueness in definition and derivation is to be found in his listing of the legitimate goals and purposes of political participation in Europe: "the protection of rights and freedoms, and the defense of moral and spiritual values and of the Muslim presence in those countries and their legitimate interests."[31] It is not clear how much we learn about the precise, principled negotiation of the Islamic and the liberal taking place in the thought of scholars like Ibn Bayya in these statements. They are clearly designed to legitimate the *idea* of legal participation in non-Muslim political systems against its opponents and to leave open the possibility that present liberal terms of such participation are not invalid. However, without more precise internal Islamic reasoning and the consideration of alternatives, not much more can be deduced from these statements.

I think, rather, that more is to be learned from looking at the ways in which scholars have justified political participation and its limits with the presumption that it is, at the very least, Islamically problematic and questionable.

A particularly popular Qur'anic story for scholars seeking to justify participation in a non-Muslim political system has always been that of Joseph (Yūsuf) in Pharaonic Egypt, who, according to verse 12:55 ("Appoint me over the storehouses of the land. I am a capable guardian and know things well."), accepted appointment as a minister of the pagan pharaoh of Egypt. Muhammad Al-Mukhtar al-Shanqiti, an American Muslim scholar, cites the example of Joseph to argue that "cooperating with non-Muslims in worldly affairs is permissible as long as that will bring benefits to Muslims and will help establish justice or ward off injustice. Hence, there is nothing prohibited in Muslims' participating in elections run in non-Muslim countries, especially when such participation accrues benefits to Muslims or wards off harm."[32] Two features of this position are particularly noteworthy. The first is that scholars citing the story of Joseph do not limit their conception of welfare and of the good to the spiritual and the moral but focus more intensely on secular and political aspects of welfare. The second is that, bearing in mind the interest in benefiting Muslim communities, the notion of benefiting or cooperating with non-Muslims is affirmed. Shanqiti thus writes that "Muslims who participate in the US elections should not have selfish objectives in doing so; that is, they should not aim at achieving the welfare of the Muslim minority only. Rather, they should aim at rescuing the whole American nation . . . in the same way that Prophet Yusuf saved a pagan people from famine."

This reading of the story of Joseph is supported by traditional exegesis. Some exegetes merely note in relation to the verse that it provides "evidence of the permissibility of accepting appointments from an unbeliever if one knows that this is the only means of establishing justice and moral policies."[33] The question of accepting appointment from an unjust or unbelieving ruler receives more detailed treatment in the exegesis of Shāfiʿī scholar al-Māwardī:

> If the authority in question is unjust then scholars are divided as to the permissibility of taking appointments from him into two positions: the first is that it is still permitted if one acts justly in what he has been assigned, because Joseph was appointed by Pharaoh[34] and because the consideration is of the justness and validity in his deeds and not in the deeds of others. The second position is that this is not permitted because of what it entails by way of loyalty to the unjust and support for them, and absolving them by executing their plans. This camp gives two explanations for Joseph's appointment by Pharaoh: first, that this Pharaoh was upright [*ṣāliḥ*] whereas the Pharaoh of Moses was tyrannical. Second, that the consideration for him was over [the king's] dominions and not his actions, and he [Joseph] was thus free from subservience to him. The more correct application of these two positions is to separate and classify what he is being assigned from the unjust into three categories: first, what one is allowed to do because it does not involve independent authoritative judgment in its execution (*min ghayr ijtihād fī tanfīdhihi*), such as the collection and distribution of charity. Second, what one is not allowed to perform alone because it requires authoritative judgment, such as the distribution of war booty; thus one may not accept such appointments from the unjust ruler because he will administer [such goods] unlawfully and will apply his discretionary judgment over that which he has no right. Third, what one may accept appointment over if it involves some independent authority, such as judging cases and making rulings, and the duty to obey [the unjust ruler] is removed. Thus, if it is a matter of carrying out a ruling between two conflicting parties or mediating between two subjects, then it is permitted; however, if is a matter of [merely administering] an imposed decision then it is not permitted.[35]

There are three main themes and points that stand out from Māwardī's synopsis of the range of legal disputation (*ikhtilāf*).[36] The first is that non-Muslim rulers, and by extension non-Muslim political systems, can be "just" or "upright" or can act justly even while being non-Muslim. The confusion here arises because of the frequent overlap in the conceptions of "justice" and "belief." Believing, submitting to God, and performing one's religious obligations are crucial aspects of justice. Contemporary Lebanese Shi'ite Ayatollah Muḥammad Faḍl Allāh addresses this problem directly by suggesting that there are (applicable here) two kinds of injustice: first, direct infringement on people's rights in society and, second, the very act of opposing or neglecting God's law, or being an unbeliever. Non-Muslims can be just in this sense of not oppressing people or depriving them of their social rights while still being unjust toward themselves and God.[37] Crucially, even the party referred to by Māwardī as not permitting loyalty to or support for unjust rulers allows that the pagan pharaoh of Joseph may have been "upright" or "virtuous" (*ṣāliḥ*), and we have seen that the Christian king of Abyssinia (al-Najāshī/the Negus) is often referred to as "just" (*'ādil*), even before his conversion to Islam.

Along this line, Rāshid al-Ghannūshī, while not addressing in detail which substantive aspects of justice non-Muslims may exemplify, advances a particularly explicit nonutopian vision of how Muslims may pursue the Islamic conception of justice in a non-Muslim state:

> An Islamic government is based on a number of values which if accomplished in their totality would result in a perfect or near-perfect system. But it may not be possible for all such values to be implemented, and therefore some must suffice in certain circumstances in order for a just government to exist. A just government, even if not Islamic, is considered very close to the Islamic one, because justice is the most important feature of an Islamic government, and it has been said that justice is the law of God.[38]

Ghannūshī's views are largely based on the jurisprudential doctrine of the fourteenth-century Andalusian scholar al-Shāṭibī, in particular the view—introduced previously—that divine law has been revealed to protect the five basic human interests of faith, life, property, intellect, and lineage. Although beginning from these precepts does not preclude substantive disagreement about even the basic demands of justice (for example, does the basic human interest in having faith protected result in liberal freedoms of conscience or in curtailments on the right to blasphemy and scandalous speech?), in this case, it is clearly a strategy designed to encourage Muslims to focus on the broadest conception of human needs and welfare rather than the desire to rule by everything "which God has revealed" (or which Islamic legal scholars have derived). For his part, Ghannūshī refers to "preventing the evils of dictatorship, foreign domination, or local anarchy" as "aims of the *sharī'a*," which can be attained in non-Muslim states and which are clearly congruent with liberal justice.

The second suggestion in these treatments is that one can pursue just actions within a non-Muslim regime. The ambiguity here is whether justice is defined in exclusively Islamic terms and whether a requirement for acting justly is having complete autonomy to implement Islamic rulings. Al-Ālūsī, for example, writes that one may request appointment[39] from an unjust ruler if "the supplicant is one who is able to uphold justice and implement the rulings of the *sharī'a*."[40] The conditions of the Joseph example, however, and the prior point about how non-Muslims may act justly make it obvious that the jurists are not restricting participation to such ideal conditions as complete control over the legal system. Sunni scholar 'Abd al-Qādir, like his Shi'ite counterpart Faḍl Allāh, seeks to directly confront the disjunction between the vagueness of the classical sources and the clarity of contemporary realities. He notes that most classical scholars regard serving under a non-Muslim "sultan" as permissible if the person is able to uphold justice and "implement the rulings of the *sharī'a*, if that is the only way to bring about rights, and if this enables him to benefit the worthy and protect them from harm."[41] He does not answer whether "implementing the rulings of the *sharī'a*" means acting in the broad outline or intent of Islamic law, merely acting justly, not violating any express religious injunctions or prohibitions, or implementing Islamic law in its specificity (*furū'*). He, quite accurately, acknowledges that today, however, all states have their own legal systems and do not allow people to apply whatever legal codes or conception of justice they please. He notes that some hold that it is thus not permissible for a Muslim to accept the appointment of an unbeliever in order to uphold and apply non-Islamic laws and judgments but that acting in civil or secular matters where one is in the position to bring about justice and welfare (particularly to Muslims) is permissible. What is important for such scholars is that one is able to separate the fact of being a *mutawālī* (appointee, client, etc., with its implications and intonations of subservience) from the actual actions performed; one does certain things within a non-Muslim state to advance the cause of justice or bring about benefits to Muslims, not to advance unbelief or injustice.[42]

Perhaps the most direct and remarkable statement approaching what liberal jurisprudence refers to as "self-restraint" on the part of legislators or state officials comes not from a contemporary thinker like Tariq Ramadan or Khaled Abou El Fadel but from Ibn Taymiyya in his discussion of the Abyssinian king al-Najāshi (the Negus). As mentioned briefly in chapter 6, Muḥammad sent a group of followers to Abyssinia to escape persecution in Mecca "for the king there will not tolerate injustice and it is a friendly country."[43] We have seen this example used already as justifying residence in non-Muslim lands, loyalty to a non-Muslim state, support for a non-Muslim state's self-defense efforts, and regarding it as "just." Islamic tradition holds that this king later converted to Islam on the invitation of the Prophet[44] but was unable to rule "according to the Qur'ān" because of the majority sentiments of his Christian population. Ibn Taymiyya comments on this in the following way: "We know definitely that he could not implement the law of the Qur'ān in his community because his people would not have permitted him to. Despite that, the Negus and all those who are similar to him found their way to the pleasure of God in eternity although they could not abide by the laws of Islam, and could only rule using that which could be implemented in the given circumstances."[45]

Obviously, one wants to be cautious in deriving too much from a statement such as this. Clearly, any Islamic legal scholar would see the Negus's restraint as an unfortunate necessity rather than a position of principle, and something to gradually disappear. However, the notions that one can personally live a just life and attain salvation, can act justly in a political context, and can be sensitive to the sensibilities of a majority non-Muslim population, all while ruling and acting by other than "the law of the Qur'ān," are powerfully and unambiguously expressed here by a scholar often appropriated by the most utopian and uncompromising Revivalist thinkers.

The third implication of the Joseph story is that acting justly can consist in service to a non-Muslim[46] people, such as acting to save the pagan Egyptians from famine. This is emphasized much more strongly in the contemporary sources. Tariq Ramadan, for example, writes that "to defend justice cannot be to defend Muslims only: the best witness of the excellence (*iḥsān*) of the Islamic way of life lies in respecting the ideal of justice over and above the failings of Muslim believers."[47] Qaraḍāwī justifies political participation on grounds of pursuing welfare for both Muslims and others: "What urges a Muslim to engage in politics is the fact that he is required to show care for others and concern himself with the problems of his Muslim brothers."[48] Shanqiti emphasizes in the previously cited *fatwā* "issues related to public welfare, which a Muslim is enjoined to participate in achieving, whether for the favor of Muslims inside or outside America, or even in relation to non-Muslims." These comments complement our previous discussions on justice across communities and on contributing to non-Muslim welfare by showing that such a contribution is not only permitted but also is itself an independent argument in favor of political participation.

Scholars drawing from the example of Joseph to justify political participation also cite examples from the life of the Prophet Muḥammad that support the practice of cooperation in secular matters. ʿAbd al-Qādir raises another dilemma of political participation, that of voting for non-Muslims who otherwise hold non-Islamic aims or beliefs. He writes that this is permissible to gain rights or other benefits for Muslims on the basis of a number of examples of the Prophet accepting the support, intervention, and protection of non-Muslims.[49] These examples include treaties with pagan Arabs as well as with Jews and Christians both before and after his migration to Medina. Another popular example is that of the "*ḥilf al-fuḍūl*," a pact among pre-Islamic Arabian tribes in Mecca to "support the wronged, maintain close relations with relatives and take good care of them. The Prophet did witness the signing of the alliance prior to his prophethood and said afterwards that if he were to be invited to a similar alliance in Islam he would have accepted without reservation. He further stressed that any good and noble contract made in the pre-Islamic era is automatically endorsed by Islam."[50] Ghannūshī not only extracts from this that the "community of believers may participate in an alliance aimed at preventing injustice and oppression" but also goes on to speak of "serving the interests of mankind, protecting human rights, recognizing the authority of the people and rotating power-holding through a system of elections. The faithful can pursue all these noble objectives even with those who do not share the same faith or ideology." One does not need to see the surplus of meaning in this comment of the Prophet that Ghannūshī does in order to observe its affirmation of recognizing and participating in non-Muslim authority in the service of overlapping conceptions of public good.

For contemporary scholars, two considerations in particular are thus central in discussing the permissibility of political participation in a non-Muslim state (whether through voting or accepting political appointments): the range of acts one may engage in or support and the types of benefits for Muslims that one is in a position to pursue. The discussions surrounding the former question are particularly supportive of the view that a politically liberal regime is best placed to gain the support of nonliberal communities. Although we have encountered the view that the secularism of liberal states poses a challenge for Muslim loyalty to those states, a more frequent view—introduced in the previous chapter in the discussion of the "*muwālāh* verses"—is that the religious neutrality of liberal political institutions alleviates Muslim concerns about offering loyalty to non-Islamic comprehensive, metaphysical doctrines.

In the *fatwā* by American Muslim scholar Shanqiti that we have been discussing, he writes that:

> taking part in the US elections is not a sign of affiliation to the polytheists, nor is it a kind of support for the oppressors. Judging parliaments to be gatherings of disbelief and polytheism is inappropriate, as this does not take into account the complicated nature of such parliaments. The US Congress, for instance, is not a religious organization, as the American constitution neither supports a certain religion nor restricts another. The US Congress is not, thus, a gathering of disbelief, even though its members are disbelievers. Also, it is not a gathering of belief, even if there are Muslim members in it. It is a neutral political body in relation to matters of religion, according to the American constitution. The US Congress can only tackle issues related to public welfare, which a Muslim is enjoined to participate in achieving, whether for the favor of Muslims inside or outside America, or even in relation to non-Muslims.

Sheikh Muhammad Al-Hanooti, a member of the North American Fiqh Council, echoes these views: "In the US, religion is not a priority in politics. On the contrary, politicians are secular in demonstrating what they are targeting. Of that secularism, we have perhaps more than 60% of our welfare and interests to be run through a polling system. Schooling, sanitation, zoning, social services, police, court, medication, finance, business, sports, recreation, etc. are run by people that are elected to office. Are you going to tell me that I am loyal or giving allegiance to the *kuffar* (non-Muslims) because I want to lead myself in the way that can get a school for my children, good sanitation for my neighborhood or good cooperation with the police to protect me?"[51] This is also the official position of the European Council for *Fatwa* and Research, which uses the previously cited examples of the Prophet's behavior to argue that:

> it is permissible for Muslims to engage with non-Muslims in commercial transactions, peace treaties and covenants according to the rules and conditions prevalent in those countries. Mutual cooperation in worldly affairs goes far to encompass all citizens who share a

> common destiny, neighborhood and sometimes kinship. This may be extended to include economic and commercial fields. . . . Elections in the modern world systems have become a means through which people choose candidates and judge the programmes they adopt. Muslims living in such societies enjoy rights and are bound to uphold certain duties. If they fail to uphold those duties they are no more entitled to receive the rights, for the rights meet the duties. Thus, Muslims' participation in elections is a national duty; in addition it falls under cooperation on that which is good and righteous for society and warding off harms from it.[52]

This awkwardly articulated position in fact probably goes well beyond the most common liberal conceptions of civic duty in the direction of positive participation.

Although this form of argument is designed to show merely that there is no prohibition on participating in non-Muslim political systems, scholars attempt to place it within broader Islamic juridical and ethical theory. In this case, it is a matter of arguing that the pragmatic pursuit of *part* of the Islamic conception of the good or of secular welfare and the balancing of costs and benefits are *general* principles of Islamic jurisprudence. We opened this discussion with a quote that rejected democracy as a principle but allowed that certain Islamic objectives might be advanced through democratic means. Such justifications of political participation in a non-Muslim society are obviously not supportive of liberal institutions when the idea of shared ends with non-Muslims is tolerated merely as a necessarily evil, when the objectives to be pursued are illiberal ones, and when the idea of ultimately introducing Islamic forms of rule is advanced. However, liberal theory obviously cannot exclude all reasons for fulfilling civic duties that are based on benefits to a given substate community or to a given conception of the good. Thus, in addition to the forms of rhetoric we encountered earlier, there are a number of related arguments for political participation that emphasize the possible benefits for Muslims in such participation but may be regarded as supportive of the liberal political order.

The first such argument is the one we have seen articulated by Rāshid al-Ghannūshī based on his reading of Shāṭibī's jurisprudence. This argument basically holds that the Muslim's duty is "to work towards preserving whatever can be preserved of the aims of *sharī'a*," understood broadly as the five basic human interests of life, faith, property, intellect, and lineage. This emphasis on the ultimate purposes of Divine law serves to deflect attention from both particular, technical rulings of Islamic law and the un-Islamic forms of behavior permitted in non-Muslim states. Instead, non-Islamic governments can been seen as *sufficiently* just because of the general human interests they protect (such interests include for Ghannūshī, both in Muslim-majority and -minority political contexts, "independence, development, social solidarity, civil liberties, human rights, political pluralism, independence of the judiciary, freedom of the press, or liberty for mosques and Islamic activities"), possibly resulting in a legitimate form of governance that he calls "the government of rationale" as opposed to "the government of *sharī'a*." The crucial measure of Ghannūshī's doctrine of how to share political space with non-Muslims is how he addresses the question of social coalitions with non-Muslims. Here, he sides firmly with liberal secular groups over other nonliberal religious ones: "Can any Muslim community afford to hesitate in participating in the establishment of a secular democratic system if it is unable to establish an Islamic democratic one? The answer is no. It is the religious duty of Muslims, as individuals and as communities, to contribute to the efforts to establish such a system."[53] This goes for Muslim minorities in particular, who have no hope of establishing Islamic rule. "The best option for such minorities is to enter into alliances with secular democratic groups. They can then work towards the establishment of a secular democratic government which will respect human rights, ensuring security and freedom of expression and belief—essential requirements of mankind that Islam has come to fulfill."[54]

Like Tariq Ramadan, Ghannūshī is articulating a self-consciously liberal doctrine of citizenship, and it is not clear what in his views here represent attempts to formulate Islamic doctrine on the basis of a methodology and what are his judgments about what is prudent. The more conservative juridical tradition, however, also contains certain resources of its own for similar forms of pragmatism. Speaking about Muslim-majority societies, Yūsuf al-Qaraḍāwī argues that the basic principle (*al-aṣl*) is that it is forbidden to participate in a non-Islamic government but that there are certain grounds for exception: (a) reducing evil and injustice to the extent that one can, (b) committing the lesser of two evils (*akhaff al-ḍararayn*), and (c) descending from the higher example to the lower reality.[55] These three grounds for participating are linked to certain general principles of Islamic jurisprudence (*qawā'id fiqhiyya*: maxims or rules that jurists refer to when arriving at a ruling that is not resolved by the authoritative sources[56]), including "necessity makes the forbidden permissible" (*al-ḍarūra tubīḥ al-maḥẓūrāt*), "hardship brings about relief" (*al-mashaqqa tajlib al-taysīr*), "do no injury nor reciprocate an injury" (*lā ḍarar wa lā ḍirār*), and "relieve hardship" (*raf' al-ḥaraj*). The conditions that Qaraḍāwī imposes on such participation are illuminating. They include (a) that there be some responsibility, independence, and authority, rather than merely being the executor of another's will, and (b) that the regime not be characterized by injustice and tyranny and known for its antagonism to human rights. This means that a Muslim may not participate in dictatorial regimes that tyrannize their populations but "only in a regime based on democracy which respects human faculties." And another condition is (c), that there be the right to oppose everything that contradicts Islam in a clear way, or at least to refrain from it.[57]

The first condition we encountered in Māwardī's discussion of the Joseph example. It is not entirely clear what is meant by "responsibility, independence and authority," but if the form of political participation in question is voting or even serving in legislatures, then one enjoys autonomy equal to that of any similarly placed citizen. As for administration or bureaucratic positions, one could easily imagine this condition being invoked in favor both of a Muslim citizen applying her specialist or technical talents to social or civic purposes and of her resigning a position where she feels compelled toward acting contrary to personal conscience. Combined with the third condition, one sees emerging an Islamic doctrine of how to deal with un-Islamic aspects of a political system to which one is otherwise loyal and committed. Although this is not exactly a strict doctrine of liberal self-restraint (Qaraḍāwī does not oppose certain illiberal laws supportive of Islamic values or interests), it points toward how a Muslim may remain loyal to a system that is "sufficiently just" in terms of the rights and freedoms it protects but also tolerates behavior forbidden by Islam. Qaraḍāwī's second condition on political participation also offers another strong indication that liberal regimes may be regarded as more just than other non-Islamic regimes.[58]

This pragmatic position has deep roots in Islamic legal thinking. While those (such as Ghannūshī or Ramadan) seeking to argue for the justness of non-Islamic regimes generally quote Shāṭibī, those (such as Qaraḍāwī or 'Abd al-Qādir) arguing for a more modest pragmatism refer to the authority of Ibn Taymiyya, namely, his view that "the *sharī'a* came to bring about and perfect welfare, and to reduce and negate corruption."[59] Qaraḍāwī refers to this basic consequentialist form of thinking as *"fiqh al-muwāzanāt,"* or "the jurisprudence of balancing [costs and benefits]."[60] The application of this methodology to our present question results in the fairly anodyne recommendation to Muslim minorities to develop a "disciplined openness and flexibility so that they do not become cramped, isolated and withdrawn from their societies, but rather contribute to them positively, give them the best they have to offer and take from them the best they have to offer. Thus the Islamic community achieves that most difficult balance: preservation without obscurity and participation without assimilation."[61]

This form of justifying political participation in non-Muslim states emphasizes two main themes: the duty to command and forbid, suppress evil, combat injustice, and the like, and the possibility of securing benefits (*maṣāliḥ*, sing.: *maṣlaḥa*[62]) for Muslims. As for the first, there is little more to add to our previous treatment. Although there are secular evils to be stamped out, and some scholars are apt to emphasize them over morality questions, there is no avoiding the fact that most conservative or traditionalist Muslim scholars (and many pious lay believers) would regard as a clear-cut political victory illiberal legislation passed by a non-Muslim parliament that bans certain behavior noxious to a Muslim sensibility. 'Abd al-Qādir writes that a Muslim can be elected to a non-Islamic legislature but may not agree to anything that contradicts the law of his Lord and must demand that which that law requires.[63] Yet within this broad consensus, there are important differences of priority and emphasis; that one can justify participating for *other* reasons and that one can justify participating even when a regime fails to suppress certain "evils" are the reasons for not regarding a scholar's interest in "forbidding wrong" as definitively incompatible with liberal citizenship.[64]

'Abd al-Qādir also gives a particularly succinct summary of the second theme, the argument from *maṣlaḥa*: "working within the institutions of unbelief is permissible if it is in defense of basic needs and necessities, or if it is to advance the interests of Islam and Muslims, for example, to combat injustice or to bring about some advantage to the Muslim community within a given country. But if it is to advance a private interest or individual ambitions then it is impermissible."[65] He invokes another principle of jurisprudence, citing Ibn Taymiyya: "That without which something required (or recommended) cannot be realized, is itself required (or recommended)." (*Mā lā yatimm al-wājib (al-mustaḥabb) ilā bihi huwa wājib (mustaḥabb).*) The obvious question raised by this statement relates to what sorts of interests or benefits these scholars imagine being advanced by political participation. There is strong reason to believe that the reference to *maṣlaḥa* generally signifies an interest in secular, public goods. It was al-Ghazālī who introduced the concept in its mature form, defining its substance as everything that helps humankind preserve the five necessary interests of life, religion, intellect, property, and lineage.[66] Shāṭibī in turn writes: "I mean by *maṣlaḥa* that which concerns the subsistence of human life, the completion of man's livelihood, and the acquisition of what his emotional and intellectual qualities require of him."[67] The use of *maṣlaḥa* as an ethico-legal concept obviously requires much more rigorous and technical treatment than there is space for here.[68] However, what is important to establish at this point is that the largely secular implications of the concept of *maṣlaḥa*[69] help answer one of our two main concerns about its use as a justification for political participation. That concern is that the conception of welfare advanced by Muslim scholars might involve aims that are themselves incompatible with a liberal political order. As opposed to the use of concepts such as "commanding right and forbidding wrong" or "reducing evil in society," the reliance on *maṣlaḥa* generally signifies a pragmatic approach to the public sphere and an emphasis on goods compatible with a liberal political order.

American Muslim scholar Muzammil Siddiqi claims, for example, that "it is in the best *maslahah* (welfare) of Muslims to participate in the system" because as minorities "they must protect their lives, their properties and their rights to live in peace. In order to protect their own rights and to promote the good things in the society, if it is necessary for them to participate in the political system of non-Islamic states, then it is their duty to do so."[70] It is also common for scholars to speak about the possibility of using political participation to change specific policies of non-Muslim states. The foreign policy of Western states toward the Islamic world is obviously a common theme.[71] True, it cannot be said (at this point) that most of the scholars we are quoting would in any way object to some political outcomes that are incompatible with a liberal political order, such as the forms of "internal restrictions" discussed by Kymlicka that set limitations on exit from or criticism of one's community. Getting non-Muslim states to recognize Muslim personal law or ban offensive, scandalous, or blasphemous speech would, without a doubt, be regarded as enormous victories by the likes of 'Abd al-Qādir or Qaraḍāwī. However, there are two countervailing considerations: that these scholars do not limit the benefits they seek to secure through participation to such incompatible aims and that they do not speak of these incompatible aims as conditions on residence or political participation. For the most part, they have in mind either general conceptions of human welfare (as evidenced previously by the emphasis on the secular as the appropriate domain for cooperation with non-Muslims) or Muslim-specific aims that are nonetheless compatible with competitive democracy. For example, there is nothing about using democratic means to direct social spending toward eligible Muslim communities, to secure recognition for religious schools, or even to support foreign policies beneficial to the welfare of Muslims in Muslim-majority countries, which suggests an illegitimately tactical attitude to democracy. Furthermore, in addition to specific policies or outcomes, there is a more interesting tendency to speak of the *inherent* benefit of being a community that participates politically. 'Abd al-Qādir endorses Qaraḍāwī's sentiments quoted previously ("that Muslims do not become cramped, isolated and withdrawn from their societies") and argues that not participating leads to "marginalization and remaining in darkness."[72] Thus, the focus on Muslim welfare goes beyond mere checklists of desired policies or reforms.

The other possible theoretical concern with justifying political participation on the basis of the pursuit of Muslim welfare is that it might suggest a certain sectarianism or group egotism, that is, an exclusive concern with Muslim welfare and seeking to limit (or even merely regretting) the corollary benefits that accrue for those outside one's particular community. As seen previously, 'Abd al-Qādir justifies political participation "if the goal is to advance the interests of Islam and Muslims" but claims that if there are no such benefits, then he has not encountered a jurist who has permitted it.

The argument that participation is permitted only if it produces some benefit for Muslims is certainly problematic for our interest in participation as a feature of recognition and solidarity, but I submit that it is not an obviously incompatible reason for civic engagement. Political participation is not required in a liberal democracy. Although a thicker conception of citizenship might assert that one must take up one's share of collective sovereignty and responsibility in order to be a true citizen, other conceptions may be more appropriate for a complex, large, and impersonal political community. Consider the three following positions, introduced at the end of chapter 4:

1. My conception of the good is based on the pursuit of purely private happiness. I have no objection to the political order around me—it provides me with all the security and freedom I need to be happy—but nor do I feel the need to be a part of it. Should this political order be threatened by forces which would replace it with one more hostile to my interest in security and freedom, I would have no objection to defending it through voting or speaking out, but otherwise I am happy to let others handle the administration of things.
2. My conception of the good is based on the pursuit of happiness. I have certain interests that I share with some citizens but not with all. Influencing politicians through various forms of political participation is an important way in which I advance those interests. Otherwise, where our group interest is not affected, I have very little interest in political participation.

3. My conception of the good is based on the pursuit of salvation, which I think can be best achieved through government on the basis of a divine law. I understand that in this society the majority of the population does not share my understanding of what divine law requires. This society gives me the security, freedom, and dignity to follow my most important religious practices and thus I would defend it against harm and destruction. I do not begrudge my unbelieving fellow citizens their worldly happiness, and I do not resent my contribution to their welfare. However, while I will obey all laws of this society which do not oppress me, I do not feel any need to contribute to the making of those laws.

My suggestion here is that the Islamic justification of political participation to advance Muslim communal aims is something like an amalgam of the second and third positions. As I argued in chapter 4, if we can assume that many citizens of contemporary liberal democracies hold conceptions of the good conforming to the first and second templates, then an Islamic argument for participation based solely on Muslim self-interest is equally compatible with liberal citizenship *if it presumes an attitude something like the third template as the underlying Islamic position,* rather than a position of gradual Islamization (as seen in the M. Amir Ali piece) or an even more indifferent attitude toward non-Muslims. What is decisive is that although the motivation to participate is largely to advance Muslim communal interests, this citizen does not view benefits that accrue to non-Muslims as a double effect as something otherwise impermissible or unfortunate.

Some normative theories of democracy presume that all any individuals or groups seek when they participate in politics is to benefit themselves. That is, many citizens hold a conception of the good something along the lines of the first and second templates and enter political life only to secure goods and benefits for themselves and others like them. Egotistical motives are presumed on the part of all sorts of social actors; those motives themselves are not indicative of an uncivic attitude unless they involve the two features discussed before: the pursuit of goods incompatible with a liberal political order or hostility to the welfare of other citizens "on principle." We have shown that Islamic justifications for political participation *can but do not need* to display these two features; the understanding of "Islamic interests or welfare" does not necessarily involve results contradictory to the wider aims of the liberal society and does not necessarily resent or regret any benefits also accruing to non-Muslims.

This is an important difference between arguments for participation based on the methodology of *fiqh al-muwāzanāt* or the pursuit of *maṣlaḥa* and the arguments we encountered at the beginning of this section based on the duty to forbid the wrong. In addition to the wider and more flexible nature of the concept of "welfare," the crucial feature about the argument from *maṣlaḥa* or "balancing" (*al-muwāzanāt*) is that one is responding to existing conditions. One is finding benefits within certain known parameters. Thus, although one may not necessarily hold a comprehensive belief in liberal democracy as the most just form of government, one's arguments for participating within it are not necessarily part of a strategy for undermining it, as with the M. Amir Ali text. We thus make a distinction between (1) a person's wider beliefs about long-term political objectives or justifiable policies and (2) his arguments for voting here and now: (1) can be incompatible with political liberalism while (2) might not be, and (1) does not necessarily imply (2). A person can hope for an Islamic political system in general (or even someday in the West) but at the same time give reasons for voting that are not dependent on that wish and are not in themselves incompatible with liberal citizenship. We have seen a range of motivations for political participation that are compatible with liberal democracy, either permissible egotistical aims or collective ones that overlap with secular conceptions of justice or the good.[73] The assumption of the comparative political theorist is that the sincere lay Muslim may in good faith take compatible arguments for political participation (or any of the other questions we have examined in this study) without necessarily subscribing to the wider, possibly incompatible views.

In this chapter, we have built on the discussions of permanent residency, civic loyalty, and recognition begun in the previous three. I argued at the end of chapter 6 that affirmations of residence and civic loyalty could be consistent with arguing against the political integration of Muslims into a non-Muslim state and the formation of meaningful bonds of civic solidarity with non-Muslim fellow citizens. In the preceding two chapters, I have shown that powerful, authentically Islamic arguments exist for a thicker doctrine of citizenship. These include arguments for accepting ethical pluralism in society, insisting on standards of justice across religious and moral communities, forming bonds of friendship and commitment with non-Muslims, contributing to non-Muslim welfare, and, finally, participating in non-Muslim political systems. Crucially, not only have the terms of friendship, cooperation, and political participation with non-Muslims been shown to overlap with political liberalism's conception of public and social (i.e., secular) goods but also some Islamic scholars have been seen to view liberalism's restriction of the political sphere to such secular goods as the main legitimating factor in permitting civic bonds with non-Muslims and integration into non-Muslim social and political life. This chapter has thus demonstrated both an Islamic foundation for solidarity with non-Muslims and evidence of political liberalism's claim that it can be supported more easily by nonliberal doctrines than other forms of liberalism.

At this point, I believe that it is difficult to maintain the distinction between citizenship and justice on which this book has been based. I have characterized that distinction as one between the problems of moral obligation to a non-Muslim political community and of substantive theological affirmation of distinctly liberal political institutions. While I have presumed liberal terms of social cooperation and a liberal conception of an overlapping consensus as the criteria for a comparative evaluation of Islamic doctrinal debates on life in a non-Muslim society, and I believe that I have demonstrated that liberal freedoms and nonmetaphysical terms of public justification appear to be attractive to Islamic scholars as a way of distinguishing between various non-Islamic regimes, this book has not sought to examine what would be involved in a more comprehensive Islamic affirmation of liberal justice per se. With the question of political participation, though, I believe that the questions pertaining to "citizenship" rather than "justice"—broadly: loyalty, belonging, and membership in a particular kind of society, as opposed to concrete questions of which kinds of acts are eligible for promotion or prohibition by coercive authority—reach their end. Our examination of the debates on residence, loyalty, recognition, and solidarity have covered significant ground and, I believe, reveal powerful and internally plausible Islamic resources for thinking about a comprehensive relationship of moral obligation with non-Muslims. Building on this would require opening up an inquiry into very sophisticated debates on moral psychology, the evaluation and classification of types of moral acts, commanding right and forbidding wrong, and the applicability of traditional Islamic justifications of moral coercion in non-Islamic polities, to name just a few. Such an inquiry, complementary with this one as it may be, demands to be treated separately, as I indeed hope to be able to do in future studies.

Conclusion

Tradition and Creativity in Grounding Moral Obligation to Non-Muslims

This book began by noting Rawls's assumption in *Political Liberalism* that "there are many reasonable comprehensive doctrines that understand the wider realm of values to be congruent with, or supportive of, or else not in conflict with, political values as these are specified by a political conception of justice for a democratic regime" and that "except for certain kinds of fundamentalism, all the main historical religions . . . may be seen as reasonable comprehensive doctrines." The preceding chapters can be understood as an attempt to take up the invitation implicit in this statement and in Rawls's belief that liberal democratic regimes partially rely for their stability on the existence of an "overlapping consensus" of such reasonable doctrines on certain basic questions of justice and social cooperation.

Yet, the first consequence of opening an inquiry into the compatibility of a given comprehensive doctrine with a liberal political order is an exposure to the unique concerns, aims, and demands of that doctrine. This is likely to result in an additional set of questions, above and beyond the central question of how adherents of a comprehensive doctrine can find reasons from within it for supporting a political regime that does not privilege that, or any other, doctrine. In the case of formal Islamic doctrine, a wide range of questions exists about the permissibility of residing in non-Muslim states, being subject to their laws, being loyal to them, and forming bonds of solidarity with their other residents. These questions, taken together, bring us into a domain of political thought with perhaps as long a tradition as thought on the problem of justice, namely, the problem of citizenship.

The question of citizenship is, above all, a question of belonging, loyalty, solidarity, and participation. There is, I have repeatedly emphasized, an overlap with questions of justice. There is no obligation grounded in justice *to desire to belong* to this or that political community, but if you do wish to belong, then liberal justice prescribes belonging on certain terms. There is no obligation grounded in justice to be loyal to this or that political community, but liberalism holds that it is unjust to deny to others the same rights to security that they have provided for you. Yet, despite this overlap—which we might say is a necessary consequence of the fact that all citizenship is loyalty to a political system, and all political systems proclaim a conception of justice—there is a difference of emphasis between the two clauses of each of the two previous sentences. The first clauses relate to the identity of the community in question; the second to its terms of cooperation. Most of this book has focused on questions related to the first clauses: Are there plausible Islamic reasons for justifying belonging, loyalty, solidarity to *non-Muslim societies* in the first place? Time and again, this inquiry into the possibilities of citizenship has brought us up against the deeper questions of liberal justice, but for various reasons, that conception of justice (on my understanding of it) has figured as a constraint on Islamic reasons for belonging, rather than as a direct object of Islamic justification itself. The feasibility of such deferral reached its limits in our final discussion on Islamic arguments for participation in non-Muslim governments. I referred to that question as a "hinge issue" because it is the final question to be discussed as a problem of citizenship, yet can be fully treated only as a problem of justice because the question of political participation is infused with the question of the legitimacy of non-Islamic rule as such.

This wider justification of accepting a non-Islamic form of rule as *legitimate* or *just* is something I hope to study in a future work. I have thus been very clear from the beginning that a comprehensive doctrine of citizenship in liberal democracies would require a few pieces missing from this study, chiefly an argument for the *substantive justness* of liberal orders despite their being un-Islamic and a justification of the liberal duty of *self-restraint* toward errant, sinning Muslims. In addition, some more detailed treatment of the range of Islamic conceptions of the good life and how it can be lived outside Islamic political authority would thicken such a doctrine of citizenship.

The results of this investigation into Islamic foundations for citizenship in non-Muslim states give us surprisingly strong reasons to be optimistic about the prospects for such a doctrine. Here I wish to summarize the arguments surveyed in the previous four chapters and then comment briefly on some of the general aims and questions of this study, including our hermeneutic and historical interest in how Islamic scholars present their arguments as relating to Islamic tradition, and finally our interest in the basic claim of political liberalism to appeal more to nonliberal citizens than other forms of liberal justification and, thus, to be more appropriate for a diverse society.

Chapter 5 examined debates over residence in non-Muslim states. It was shown (in chapter 3) that a certain tradition in Islamic law declared such residence to be impermissible, both on the claim that there is a divine prohibition to this effect and also, more interesting for our purposes, because residence involves other prohibited conditions, including subordination to non-Muslim law and contribution to the strength of non-Muslim polities or the welfare of non-Muslim communities. This tradition denies that basic religious freedoms can be enjoyed in such states and that a pious Muslim can live a good or just life while under non-Muslim political authority and surrounded by moral laxity.

Contrary to this position, a more dominant tradition within Islamic jurisprudence rejects the claim that a clear divine prohibition on residence in non-Muslim lands exists. This tradition asserts that if certain conditions are met, residence is permissible. The central condition is that the freedom to "manifest one's religion" (*iẓhār al-dīn*) must exist. I noted that there are good reasons to suspect that Islamic conceptions of what constitutes religious practice differ from liberal notions of religious freedom. Indeed, numerous Muslim jurists were cited as calling for forms of political autonomy that would not normally be acceptable from a liberal standpoint. However, although the demand for the application of some areas of Islamic law within Muslim minority communities is frequently invoked, both classical and modern scholars have argued that such communal autonomy is not a necessary condition for residence. That is, while the expression "to manifest one's religion" remains (perhaps deliberately) vague, I cited evidence that it is not unambiguously a reference to substate political authority over Muslim communities. Scholars arguing along these lines also frequently invoke the possible benefits to Muslims of living in non-Muslim states. The benefit we primarily concerned ourselves with was the freedom to proselytize, or to engage in *da'wa*. The concern—omnipresent in this study—is that while peaceful proselytizing surely violates no requirements of justice, a justification of residence and obedience simply on the grounds that it will facilitate the spread of Islam may reveal a purely tactical affirmation of the demands of citizenship, including support for democratic institutions and recognition of non-Muslim fellow citizens. I concluded by noting that certain conceptions of *da'wa* (most notably that of Tariq Ramadan) put less emphasis on conversion than on bearing witness to one's moral standards and that even the emphasis on conversion need not contradict the aims of a liberal political order.

Chapter 6 dealt with the problem of loyalty toward a non-Muslim state of citizenship, both in terms of obeying its laws and in terms of contributing to its self-defense. Again, I began by introducing doctrines in chapter 3 that deny that such a duty could ever be acceptable from an Islamic standpoint. The essence of such incompatible doctrines is to be found in the Islamic conception of community. Islam, for all Muslim legal scholars, is more than a theology or even a moral code; it must be embodied in certain communal relationships, ideally culminating in authority over the social order (which must not be confused with the demand for a "state" in the modern Weberian sense of the term). This view entails a very strict code of loyalty to all fellow Muslims and legitimate Muslim polities, and it rejects certain forms of loyalty or subordination to non-Muslims. This general view attains its purest form in the classical doctrine of the *jihād*, which legitimated war for the purpose of bringing new territories into the orbit of Islamic authority.

Yet, equally entrenched in Islamic jurisprudence is the duty to uphold contracts, even with non-Muslims. Medieval scholars assumed that Muslims visiting or residing in non-Muslim states would be doing so under a mutual guarantee of security, or an *amān*. Both medieval and modern Muslim scholars have argued that a Muslim who accepts the security of a non-Muslim state finds himself with a very strict set of duties toward that state, duties that can be argued to fulfill liberal demands of civic loyalty, including a duty to avoid harming or betraying it (even during a legitimate war against that state) and to obey laws that do not require manifest rebellion against God. Like many liberal contract theorists, Muslim jurists have argued that such duties can arise from even tacit consent, demonstrated by one's willingness to benefit from a state's security, public order, and welfare. Crucial to a genuine doctrine of loyalty, modern Islamic reformists have also revised the doctrine of *jihād*, arguing now that war is only justified in self-defense or to defend oppressed Muslim communities, a view that allows Muslim citizens to regard their non-Muslim state of citizenship as immune to aggression and entitled to defend itself, even against Muslim forces. Once again, central to this reformulation is the emphasis on *da'wa*. Numerous contemporary scholars insist that a general attitude of hostility or aggression toward non-Muslims is entirely inconsistent with and subversive of the Islamic interest in conveying the Islamic message (*bulūgh al-da'wa*), which, they argue, is the actual value underpinning the classical *jihād* doctrine.

Chapters 7 and 8 dealt more explicitly with relationships between citizens, namely, the duty to recognize the equality of citizens who do not share one's own conception of the good and to accept the bonds of solidarity arising from social cooperation, which may include participating in political processes. Again, these chapters respond to the doctrines presented in chapter 3 that reject the equality of non-Muslims and the very idea of demonstrating "loyalty" (*walā'*, or *muwālāh*) toward them, contributing to their welfare, or participating in their political system.

The reconstruction of a contrary doctrine consisted of two parts: recognition (chapter 7) and solidarity (chapter 8). Recognition was held to consist in turn of two views: (a) that moral disagreement is a normal, tolerable social condition and thus that there is a right not to be Muslim and (b) that there are obligations of justice that apply across this difference. Both views were shown to have deep support from the most traditional and conservative Islamic sources. Here, the inevitable emphasis on the role of *da'wa* was found to be unambiguously constructive. *Da'wa*, on its modern understanding, invokes a number of values and insists on certain practices—goodwill, transparency, honesty, sincerity, reason, freedom of choice, noncoercion, patience, openness to getting to know the other, and respect—that reveal certain implicit attitudes of recognition. A refutation of the view that "loyalty" (*muwālāh*) toward non-Muslims is prohibited was found in the views of a wide range of Muslim scholars that the operative Qur'anic verses that seem to prohibit such loyalty all refer strictly to those non-Muslims who aggress against and fight Muslims, emphasizing that the circumstances of revelation (*asbāb al-nuzūl*) of this and the other *muwālāh* verses are the betrayal of the Muslim community by members to Meccan pagans in active combat with Muslims.

The conception of solidarity in chapter 8 focused on the general idea of contributing to the welfare of non-Muslims and the more specific idea that this might take the form of sharing political sovereignty. Both were shown to have support in Islamic juridical discourses. Crucial to the acceptance of such solidarity, for Muslim scholars, was the restriction of the scope of solidarity and political activity to strictly secular areas. Although it is not rare for Muslim scholars and intellectuals to speak of the possibility of a coalition with Christian religious groups in the pursuit of illiberal aims, far more predominant was the insistence that Muslims not be drawn into contributing to religious or doctrinal aims directly contrary to Islamic ones. The (Rawlsian) ideal of restricting political action to the procurement of common, "political" goods is frequently echoed in Islamic discourses.

Thus, in all the areas in which this book set out to investigate the possibility of an overlapping consensus, Islamic views compatible with liberal conceptions of the demands of citizenship can be found. Furthermore, there was surprisingly strong support from classical, conservative jurisprudence, particularly on questions relating to the terms of residence, loyalty to a state of residence, recognition of religious difference, and contribution to non-Muslim welfare. Remember that I argued that political liberalism has a preference for demonstrating compatibility with the most orthodox possible views. Despite the existence of incompatible views and doctrines on all the questions surveyed, it is highly significant that the core demands of a social contract in non-Muslim states are capable of receiving support from the most orthodox of Islamic jurisprudential sources.

This is, of course, not to deny that some areas required departure from the classical sources. Serving in a non-Muslim army, integration into a non-Muslim polity, and sharing aims with non-Muslims were all practices either ignored by classical jurists or rejected by them. And of course, the classical *jihād* doctrine, which maintains that non-Muslim spaces have no unconditional right to exist (even if their Muslim residents have duties toward them), is something that would have to be superseded by a Modernist doctrine for it to be said that a doctrine of citizenship obtains. Yet, not only self-conscious "reformers" but also what I have termed "neo-classical" jurists found grounds for legitimating these positions. The particular grounds or arguments have been surveyed at length; here I wish merely to note three general ways in which contemporary scholars dealt with either contradiction with or the silence of the classical sources.

The first pattern is that of broad, general, conservative statements followed by clarification or qualification. The works of Khālid 'Abd al-Qādir and Sulejman Topoljak (Tūbūlyāk) on the "jurisprudence of Muslim minorities" (*fiqh al-aqalliyyāt*) are good examples. Both scholars were quoted at some points as broadly rejecting the very idea of citizenship in or loyalty to a non-Muslim polity. However, these statements were often followed by more detailed treatments of specific practices or situations that strongly diluted the initial rejection. Often, the subsequent, more detailed discussion involved not merely legitimizing compromise with or accommodation of reality but an argument that specific demands or practices do not actually equate to the practices covered by the general ban. Khaled Abou El Fadl suggests that this is very much in keeping with the traditional practice of Islamic law, which "creatively responds to the socio-political dynamics of society placed within a specific historical context. . . . This creative process is expressed primarily through the subtleties of language, and hence, unless one focuses on the details of the juridical linguistic practice, one would not be able to notice, much less appraise, the dynamics of the legal discourse."[1] That is, the pattern of bold, ostentatious proclamations of fealty to tradition, followed by quieter, subtler attention to detail, is very much in keeping with Islamic juridical tradition.

The second pattern is a general claim about the inherent flexibility, pragmatism, and eudaemonism of *sharīʿa*, without necessarily invoking the general doctrine of the "purposes of *sharīʿa*." Here, the emphasis is on cost-benefit analysis (or *fiqh al-muwāzanāt* ("the jurisprudence of balancing")) for each individual practice, where the potential "benefits" (*maṣlaḥa*; pl. *maṣāliḥ*) can be either the material welfare of Muslims or advancing an Islamic conception of the good. Yūsuf al-Qaraḍāwī, ʿAbd Allāh Ibn Bayya, and other popular jurists are the prime examples. They exhort a pragmatism and flexibility that is sensitive to the dangers of conflict, without developing a doctrine of the good life independent from the classical rulings. Ibn Taymiyya is the classical jurist often invoked to justify this pragmatic approach, which is probably the predominant one in contemporary Islamic discourses.

The third pattern is a slightly more self-conscious, bolder version of the second. It emphasizes the general substantive aims (*maqāṣid al-sharīʿa*) of Islamic law and ethics (such as the "necessary goods" or *ḍarūriyyāt*), without necessarily claiming that this constitutes or necessitates a general rethinking or reworking of *sharīʿa* (à la Abdullahi an-Na'im). Rāshid al-Ghannūshī and Tariq Ramadan are the main exemplars of this practice surveyed in this book, although it can also be seen in the thought of scholars such as Rashīd Riḍā, ʿAbd Allāh Ibn Bayya, and Yūsuf al-Qaraḍāwī. Both Ghannūshī and Ramadan present their arguments as flowing from the corpus of classical Islamic doctrine, but this they do not define merely in terms of the specific rulings (*aḥkām*) reached by the legal schools but also in terms of the "purposes [*maqāṣid*] of *sharīʿa*," which are what ground (and thus trump) specific rulings. This methodology allows them to be practical in relation to the concrete circumstances in which Muslims live, yet claim for this practicality a traditional foundation. The legal theories of the fourteenth-century Andalusian scholar al-Shāṭibī are the point of reference for these scholars.

What is clear for all of these (often overlapping) approaches is that their task of making the lives of Muslims in non-Muslim states palatable and legitimate is made significantly easier when one assumes that the non-Muslim state in question proclaims a public philosophy similar to Rawls's political liberalism. Although some critics of the later Rawls have claimed that his retreat in the area of liberalism's epistemic claims is superficial and unlikely to appease groups who are bothered by actual policies rather than metaphysical foundations, Islamic law constitutes an ethical doctrine that appears to be able to compromise much less on areas of public profession than on areas of actual policy.

Very often, it is precisely what states ask Muslims to *proclaim* that scholars are concerned about. Political liberalism's "epistemic abstinence" allows Muslim scholars to redescribe situations in a way that makes them permissible from an Islamic perspective, bearing in mind Abou El Fadl's point about Islamic law's capacity for creativity being "expressed primarily through the subtleties of language." Here, we have a concrete instantiation of how the aims of political liberalism intersect the concerns of one particular comprehensive ethical doctrine.[2]

Thus, when Muslim scholars can say that serving in a non-Muslim army, cooperating with non-Muslims, paying taxes to a non-Muslim state, or participating in a non-Muslim political situation do not require "exalting the word of unbelief" or rejecting Islamic truth claims, those practices take on an entirely different ethical significance than if they took place in a state that proclaimed a perfectionist doctrine. Muslim jurists are able to describe these practices in exactly the way a Rawlsian liberal would: as necessary or reasonable demands of social cooperation, rather than duties arising from a shared conception of truth or virtue. Although some Muslim scholars object to the liberal state's nonreligious foundation and claim to prefer to live as a minority in a Christian state, far more prefer—if the state is not going to be founded on Islam—that it be active only in "political" matters, rather than spiritual ones. These jurists seem to be making the precise calculation that Rawls supposes either parties in the original position or citizens living under a "constitutional consensus" will: that the most reasonable and rational response to ethical pluralism is to limit the range of political cooperation to secular, civil areas and to prefer state neutrality on questions of truth.

Yet, it would be a mistake to assume that, therefore, all of these Islamic scholars are approaching citizenship in non-Muslim liberal democracies from a purely defensive posture—while holding their noses, as it were. Surely, this is the case for the premodern jurists, as well as the likes of contemporary scholars ʿAbd al-Qādir, Topoljak, and perhaps in some cases even Qaraḍāwī. However, the responses of other scholars seemed to suggest an intellectual accommodation of the spiritual purposes of life and political reality in a way perfectly compatible with Rawlsian political liberalism. Tariq Ramadan's concept of Western states as an "abode of witness" (*dār al-shahāda*) and a place where life can be *particularly* virtuous is one such view.[3] Similar is Fayṣal Mawlawī's insistence on the necessity for "innate love" (*ḥubb fiṭrī*) towards non-Muslims and his conclusion that "there can and must be affection and love towards a person whom you wish to call to God and that this affection is a small piece of the affection that God wills be directed towards him. This is the foundation which is considered to be stronger and weightier than all that which opposes it."[4] Ibn Bayya's enthusiastic description of the "great values" of secularism and neutrality is another example. Such views lead us away from the fear that political liberalism may be "political in the wrong way" by suggesting that a pious Muslim may see a non-Muslim political community as a place where his deepest and most important aims may be fulfilled and as a "community with whose moral unity or participatory politics he can beguile himself."[5]

This move beyond a minimalist Islamic accommodation of liberal citizenship is exemplified in the way in which the moral relationship with non-Muslims and a non-Muslim political community is theorized and theologized. Recalling the problematic status of this relationship in some Islamic discourses,[6] one can observe four main ways of thinking about moral obligation to non-Muslims and non-Islamic polities, which map on generally to how moral obligations are constructed in Islamic ethics. For the purposes of drawing comparisons with Western ethical theory, I would like to suggest that we can refer to these four approaches to moral obligation as "statutory-deontological," "constructivist-contractualist," "consequentialist-utilitarian," and (idiosyncratically) "comprehensive-qualitative."

The statutory-deontological approach to moral obligation to non-Muslims refers to the appeal to those divine commands found in revelation that provide direct answers to moral questions. Of course, in the broad sense, all Islamic ethical theorizing will have some relationship to revelation. However, I have in mind here two specific modes of reasoning. The first is to point to specific texts that make the case that the sources are on record as demanding *these rights* (for non-Muslims). This approach is very powerful in the Muslim-majority context, where revelation speaks directly to the standards by which Jews and Christians should be accommodated within the Islamic *nomos.* (Revelation is, of course, less specific in the legislative sense for the minority condition, which may in fact be of benefit to contemporary Islamic scholars.) For the purposes of the form of (justificatory) comparative ethics adopted in this book, however, this approach is either insufficient or directly problematic for three main reasons. First, this form of the deontological approach might limit moral obligation to *those rights* enumerated in revelation. Second, an approach based solely on this might thus coexist with a broader attitude of nonobligation (*barā'*) to non-Muslims. Examples of this are the texts quoted in chapter 3 by contemporary Salafis or so-called Wahhabis, such as 'Abd al-'Azīz ibn Sāliḥ al-Jarbū', who presume that the "basic status" (*al-aṣl*) of relations with non-Muslims is war or nonobligation, which they then modify by reference to specific obligations found in scripture. Third, although specific points of revelation might contingently overlap with other ethical systems, this deontological approach might object to moral dialogue about rights, duties, and social cooperation that does not proceed on the basis of Islamic reason (such as political constructivism or public reason).

The deontological approach, however, is by no means limited to the identification of specific texts that ground specific obligations. Much more important is that the sources (particularly Qur'anic verses) enjoin a *general attitude* of treating all persons (including non-Muslims) with "justice" or "equity" (*'adāla, qisṭ*)[7] and of remaining faithful to contracts.[8] What is crucial about this form of the deontological approach to moral obligation—which I take to be characteristic of a generally held Islamic attitude—is that the recognition of the rights of non-Muslims in a given society is not based merely on a specific promise or contract but rather on a general, divinely ordained attitude of recognition and respect for the dignity of the other. In fact, the moral force of any contract is based on these deeper values of respect for self (for lying and deceit is a negation of one's own moral nature) and recognition of the other. Thus, in addition to any substantive legal or moral duties that might be enumerated, this implies a general attitude of *moral recognition*; non-Muslims cannot be treated instrumentally, and their rights and claims (whatever they are) cannot easily be dismissed, even if Muslim interests could be shown to benefit from this.

However, even this source of moral obligation, as important and powerful as it is, has its limitations for our purposes of theorizing a doctrine of citizenship compatible with political liberalism. The main problem, of course, is that there could be serious substantive disagreements about what violates justice. To give an extreme example only to make the point (and not to suggest that this is something alive in the Islamic moral-political imagination), premodern Islamic law allowed slavery and enumerated the conditions under which it could be practiced "justly." More to the point, there is no obvious contradiction between the basic concept of "justice" and defending general social rules against blasphemy or offensive speech or in calling for some form of nonterritorial autonomy for Muslim communities (particularly in the areas of family law), both demands that (perhaps unlike slavery) are clearly plausible in the modern context.

A second broad approach to grounding moral obligation is derived from the general Islamic permissibility of entering into contracts and the general Islamic requirement of honoring them, which I am thus referring to as the "contractualist" or "constructivist" approach. As discussed at length in chapter 6, the relevant discourse here is on the contract of *amān* with a non-Muslim society and state, which is how Muslim jurists have traditionally discussed life in a non-Muslim society, including the basic terms of social cooperation. Jurists from across the Sunni schools are quite clear that contracts made with non-Muslims, including the *amān*, are as morally binding as those made with Muslims. They are unanimous in holding that the enjoyment of *amān* imposes on Muslims certain moral and sometimes legal obligations to the non-Muslim entity in question. As shown in that chapter, the moral obligations Muslims are permitted to consent to (thus "constructing" new moral obligations not necessarily delineated in revelation) include the basic terms of a social contract of political obligation and inviolability in wartime. An important moral feature of this approach is that its primary emphasis is on the *inherent* (Islamic) permissibility and fairness of the terms of the contract, not on the secondary benefits that might accrue by consenting.

However, as deep and powerful this source of moral obligation is (I have argued in this book and elsewhere that it is probably sufficient for grounding the basic terms of the liberal social contract), it also suffers certain limitations in constructing a complete doctrine of citizenship or in theorizing a comprehensive moral relationship with non-Muslim societies. Five such limitations were observed in the preceding chapters (particularly chapter 6): (1) Obligation might be construed as to the idea of contract (i.e., to God), not necessarily to the non-Muslim agent or unit; (2) if something is not contracted to explicitly, the obligation might not be regarded as existing; (3) what Muslims are allowed to contract themselves to is always contested; (4) there is disagreement on what renders the contract void;[9] and (5) contract involves the idea of reciprocity (*al-mu'āmala bi'l-mithl*), which is inherently ambiguous from a moral perspective.[10]

A third approach to moral obligation found in Islamic discourses might be referred to as "consequentialist-utilitarian." This was referred to previously as the pragmatic approach to Islamic law and moral commitments exemplified by Ibn Taymiyya, Rashīd Riḍā, Yusūf al-Qaraḍāwī, and others. This approach presumes something like the contract scenario discussed before, at least in the sense of Muslim communities being faced with social and political circumstances not necessarily of their choosing. However, this mode of legitimizing moral obligation to non-Muslim societies differs in crucial ways. Although the discussion is usually bounded by the outer limits of what is regarded as unambiguously impermissible (thus overlapping with contractualist approaches), its substance centers on how accepting certain social and political facts may or may not benefit Muslims. Such reasoning differs according to whether the act in question is regarded as otherwise impermissible (e.g., serving in a non-Muslim army against Muslims), ambiguous in its moral status (e.g., participating in non-Muslim political systems), or presumed permissible (e.g., residing in a non-Muslim land). In turn, the types of benefit or utility tend to be of three kinds: the fulfillment of other greater Islamic religious duties (e.g., the arguments of Shaybānī and Sarakhsī that it is permissible to fight with a non-Muslim ruler to protect Muslim life and property), the advancement of certain Islamic social or political goals (e.g., the myriad arguments encountered throughout this book that appeal to the goal of advancing *da'wa*), and the secular welfare of Muslims (e.g., Riḍā's argument for military service as a way of securing political freedoms).

Some of the best examples of these types of arguments encountered in this book related to the problems of defending a non-Muslim state and participating in a non-Muslim political system. Neither is clearly prohibited by an unambiguous revelatory text (unless one holds that Q. 4:96–100 forbids such residence in the first place); arguments that they are impermissible or undesirable are derived inferentially from overall Islamic commitments. Furthermore, neither is clearly something *due* to the non-Muslim society (certainly according to Islamic reason, and possibly also according to liberal reason) as a basic matter of reciprocity, thus distinguishing these aspects of citizenship from the obligation to not violate a society's laws or security, which Islamic law treats as a clear matter of contractual obligation. These acts might be regarded in Islamic discourses as supererogatory contributions to non-Muslim welfare. It is thus not surprising that the substantive justification for performing them consists in speculating on the benefits that might accrue to Muslims in two of the senses discussed previously: Muslims can either advance "Islamic aims" through them (such as advancing the cause of *da'wa* or, in the case of political participation, influencing public policy in an "Islamic" direction) or advance the secular welfare of Muslims.

Much of the discussion in chapters 5 through 8 involved analyzing specific instances of consequentialist-utilitarian justifications for civic duties in a non-

Muslim liberal democracy in terms of their moral reasoning. I have suggested that there can be no single verdict on such forms of reasoning. At times, it is quite clear that Islamic scholars do not regard the act in question as normally impermissible in the first place (examples include voting and serving in non-Muslim armies against other non-Muslims) and that the consequentialist-utilitarian calculus does not involve any aims contrary to the interests of a well-ordered society. However, the defects and insufficiency of a consequentialist-utilitarian approach to grounding moral obligation to non-Muslim societies should be obvious. It often reflects little or no interest in the rights or interests of non-Muslims. It often implicitly or explicitly sanctions illiberal social goals if they could be achieved. And importantly, it does not involve any substantive judgment that the liberal terms of social cooperation have any independent validity or moral standing; the consequentialist-utilitarian approach is also that used to make sense of Muslim life in authoritarian and tyrannical regimes or (as in the case of Ibn Taymiyya's classical treatise on *Siyāsa shar'iyya*) to justify seemingly un-Islamic acts on the part of a Muslim ruler.

The bulk of Islamic discourses on moral obligation to non-Muslim societies take one of the three prior routes: the statutory-deontological, the contractualist-constructivist, or the consequentialist-utilitarian. However, I would like to bring attention to the tendency, particularly in recent writings, for Islamic scholars (even ones, like Fayṣal Mawlawī, who cannot be described as reformist or liberal) to go beyond these standard ways of thinking about moral obligation toward what I tentatively refer to as a "comprehensive-qualitative" approach to theorizing and theologizing the rights and welfare of others.

I refer to this mode of thinking as comprehensive-qualitative because it is grounded in an overall consideration of the quality and purpose of social relationships with non-Muslims and how they relate to the broader aim of living an Islamic life. This mode, thus, goes beyond considerations of the permissible and the forbidden into the realm of what relationships Muslims might voluntarily choose for themselves noninstrumentally. I suggest that the evidence for this mode of theorizing moral relationships with non-Muslim societies is in greatest evidence in some instances of the copious references to the centrality of the Islamic mission (*da'wa*) to life in non-Muslim societies, as well as the discussions on the goodness in contributing to non-Muslim welfare because "Islam seeks to bring benefit and improvement to all people and all races," based on the belief that "God has blessed and honored all the sons of Adam."

The idea of *da'wa* as an activity that legitimates life in non-Muslim societies was encountered in each of the four chapters dealing with Islamic responses to the minority condition. Its importance, particularly for thinkers broadly sympathetic to the ideas and methods of the Muslim Brotherhood, cannot be exaggerated. Indeed, scholars such as Qaraḍāwī and Mawlawī have written explicitly that they regard the classical debate over whether the "basic principle" (*al-aṣl*) of relations with unbelievers is war or peace to be dissolved; the basic principle of those relations is *da'wa*. In each of those chapters, I stressed the essential ambiguity of the moral nature of the *da'wa* argument for integration into non-Muslim communities. Briefly, the reservations about *da'wa* are the following: that it might reflect an instrumental attitude to non-Muslim societies and political systems, that the recognition of moral and religious pluralism in the conditions of state neutrality might be a realistic response to the minority condition and thus temporary, that with the desire to convert non-Muslims they might not be recognized as "self-authenticating sources of valid claims" but only as potential Muslims, and that the emphasis on *da'wa* might imply an ultimate objective of Islamizing the society and potentially the state. Of course, these objections take place on a special plane. They are not objections to the *practice* of *da'wa*, which, of course, is no more objectionable an act in a free society than any other use of freedom. Rather, they are reservations about whether arguments for liberal citizenship that rest largely on the possibilities for *da'wa*-as-conversion reflect a sincere moral affirmation of liberal citizenship (an overlapping consensus).

However, my argument for *da'wa* as a source of moral obligation goes beyond the fact that it is a legitimate exercise of religious freedom. Certain scholarly treatments of the practice and purpose of *da'wa* reflect an attempt to provide a comprehensive Islamic account of the moral relationship with non-Muslims based as much on theological as on juridical reasoning. The ethics of *da'wa* (based on the four themes of good-willed exhortation (*al-maw'iẓa al-ḥasana*), argumentation (*jadal*), noncoercion (*lā ikrāh*), and wisdom (*ḥikma*)), I believe, allow Islamic scholars to imagine two distinct kinds of relationship with non-Muslims: a *relationship of moral argument* and a *relationship of civic friendship*.

As I argued in chapter 7, the idea of a common relationship of argumentation is derived from the belief that the Qu'ran commands Muslims to call to Islam "with wisdom and kindly exhortation, and argue in the most kindly manner"[11] and "with the power of reason and discernment."[12] Not unlike some of the principles of discourse ethics and deliberative democracy, the Islamic commitment to invite to Islam through reason and proof is a commitment to transparency, honesty, and respect and a position of discursive equality between inviter and invitee. Also not unlike theorists of discourse and deliberation, many Islamic thinkers reject an antagonistic, zero-sum form of *da'wa* and debate in favor of something more collaborative and open-ended. By defining the long-term social relationship with non-Muslims around the Islamic moral obligation to call to Islam, Islamic scholars might be seen as theorizing, first, an intellectual and moral relationship with non-Muslims based on the practice of moral argumentation. Although the concept of *da'wa* does not align perfectly with philosophical conceptions of recognition through moral argumentation (which aspire to either truth or reasonable agreement as the outcome of discourse), it shares the idea that the pragmatics of moral argumentation require both a comprehensive recognition of the other's moral personality and an open-ended commitment to nonstrategic and noncoercive moral persuasion. In this way, using *da'wa* as a core framework for theorizing citizenship in a non-Muslim society allows scholars to theologize a comprehensive moral relationship with non-Muslims that goes beyond the juridical mode of setting boundaries (if only contingently) between the permissible and the forbidden.

Da'wa also allows scholars to theorize the relationship with non-Muslims and non-Muslim societies as one of civic friendship or mutual concern. Fayṣal Mawlawī, for example, derives from the duty to invite to Islam in a spirit of "good-willed warning" much more than a position of mutual nonaggression. He speaks of "*'āṭifa*" for non-Muslims, which has a literal meaning of attachment, sympathy, affection, or liking, but when transferred to a social, intercommunal context can be understand as analogous to our concept of civic solidarity, or at least as providing a foundation for accepting it. "We conclude that there can and must be affection and love towards a person whom you wish to call to God and that this affection is a small piece of the affection that God wills be directed towards him. This is the foundation which is considered to be stronger and weightier than all that which opposes it." Although it is natural for bonds of love and affection to arise among neighbors and cocitizens, "this affection has nothing to do with [shared] faith, but rather is connected exclusively to religious considerations as far as we Muslims are concerned. For God has commanded us to bestow mercy on all mankind as a part of faith."[13] This concern of his with whether a Muslim may feel "love" or "affection" for non-Muslims requires him to account for how a sphere of social interaction where humans form bonds of trust and affection separate from religion is to be understood. He suggests, thus, the possibility of a relationship of *ḥubb fiṭrī*, or "innate love" (from the Islamic idea that all humans share a common innate nature, *fiṭra*), to be distinguished from *ḥubb 'aqā'idī*, "creedal love," the affection between persons who share religious beliefs. All humans are endowed with a common instinctive nature and thus share certain basic needs, passions, and inclinations. The common pursuit of these can result in love, affection, and solidarity across creedal lines.

Similarly, the idea of calling to Islam with "wisdom" is explicated without reducing it to the tactical. To the extent that wisdom is understood as inviting to Islam in a way appropriate for one's social surroundings, it is a call for *knowing the other* and *integrating with the wider society*, which are inclinations to both recognition and solidarity. It is largely in the name of *da'wa* that Muslim thinkers call for this. Mawlawī, for example, writes that the preliminary forms of relations between Muslims and non-Muslims (before attaining the stage of *ḥubb fiṭrī* discussed previously) crucial for *da'wa* are mutual knowledge (*al-ta'āruf*), coexistence, and cooperation, adding that "we are a part of the society in which we live: Although a Muslim feels a part of the Islamic community . . . when he chooses to live in the West and chooses to be a part of this society in which he lives, then he must also think about this society—its issues, worries and problems—from his Islamic perspective."[14] In this way, *da'wa* also intersects the problem of political participation. Although the idea of participating in a non-Islamic political system is regarded by some as a substantive problem for Islamic jurisprudence, scholars who regard it as *permissible* (in the juridical sense) or *beneficial* (for Muslims) often go further to describe it as *virtuous*—in the way described here of seeing the welfare of non-Muslims as a religious concern for Muslims committed to *da'wa* and Islamic moral universalism.

In this way, we see not only deeper theological grounds for a comprehensive moral relationship but also the vindication of some of the claims of political liberalism. Rawls believed that political liberalism's main virtue was that, in excluding metaphysical claims and goals from the political, more citizens with a wider range of comprehensive ethical doctrines could affirm its claims to political validity. Here, certain Islamic scholars (such as Mawlawī, Ibn Bayya, Ghannūshī, Ramadan, and others) seem to be saying something similar: Islam would prefer to be expressed through a community where politics and metaphysics are fused. But given the reality of sharing political space with non-Muslims, it is preferable to limit solidarity and political power to that which all humans have in common. Were non-Muslim states to make wider claims to metaphysical truth, then it might be more difficult for Muslims to affirm citizenship within them. However, that limited political space also can be infused with deep theological meaning for Muslims, justifying the claim that a liberal polity's own self-restraint need not mean that the practice of liberal citizenship is one devoid of meaning, purpose, and inspiration.

Looking Ahead: Outlines of a Research Agenda

The questions studied in this book under the banner of "citizenship"—residence, political obligation, loyalty, recognition, solidarity, political participation—are neither sufficient for a comprehensive understanding of the relationship between Islam and political liberalism nor most reflective of the concerns (sociopolitical or religious) of practicing Muslims in existing liberal democracies. My choice of these questions should not be interpreted as suggesting that there is an actual crisis of some sort related to the debates studied in the preceding chapters.

Rather, this book is an experiment in a certain comparative way of studying Islamic legal, ethical, and political thought and, as such, preliminary to a longer term study of Islamic debates on justice, law, virtue, autonomy, and equality in non-Muslim liberal democracies. As noted at the beginning of this conclusion, a number of topics were raised in this book without being addressed remotely exhaustively. For instance, the question of moral pluralism is a puzzle for political liberalism and Islam both. Political liberalism's normativity is often held to rest on the idea that disagreement about moral truth and the good is inherently reasonable because of the burdens of judgment; political liberalism is thus normative (not a modus vivendi) but not a sectarian doctrine because the burdens of judgment do not amount to philosophical skepticism. However, there is a genuine puzzle, particularly for religious doctrines, to believe that your belief is the true one (which political liberalism must allow for, if it is not to declare in favor of skepticism or antifoundationalism) but at the same time believe that another's (false) belief is somehow reasonable so that your accommodation of him is principled. This puzzle goes well beyond the classical liberal problem of toleration; what is being asked for is not that we not persecute the wrong or the immoral but that we act reasonably toward them by not justifying political power on the basis of reasons they could not accept. The question then is whether all citizens—to be reasonable—must have this *specific* account of the fact of reasonable pluralism (based on the burdens of judgment) or whether other accounts of why humans disagree (read: why some fail to accept truth) can result in an acceptance not only of toleration but also of neutrality and public reason. This is a complex question, and there is certainly much more to be said on the Islamic side of it than my brief treatment in chapter 7. The same can certainly be said for the evolving Islamic debates on *da'wa* and political participation and how they relate to the ideas of recognition and solidarity.

In addition to my research into Islamic debates, this book may also advance research on how political theorists might fruitfully *compare* political and ethical traditions. Although I by no means believe that all comparative inquiries must have the justificatory interests of this study, I have tried to advance some arguments (in the first two chapters) for why this is one intriguing way of studying religious politico-ethical thought and for how it can be done satisfactorily. As academic interest in non-Western (particularly Islamic) traditions increases, a literature will also certainly expand on the purposes, as well as the ethical, epistemic, and methodological presuppositions, for engaging in comparative inquiry.[15]

A further agenda for future research is how the formal inquiry pursued in this book might intersect and interact with research in the empirical disciplines of anthropology, sociology, political science, and history. This book *deliberately* abstains from ambitious claims about the actual experience of Muslim communities with liberal citizenship that only those disciplines could confirm. At the same time, even a formal inquiry of this kind must have *some* correspondence to reality. (This parallels the problems faced by constructivist theories of justice and obligation that aim to be both philosophical and practical.) As I argued in the first chapter, the liberal interest in an overlapping consensus is itself of largely sociological interest (even if it remains a theoretical construct). And the use of even elite Islamic doctrinal debates would be compromised if they bore *no* similarity to the practice of arguing about Islamic beliefs in contemporary Islamic epistemic communities. A study of this kind cannot help but solicit response from empirically minded social scientists.

Caution here applies, however. There is no way a study that seeks to stage an encounter between political liberalism and Islamic doctrine can do justice to the social scientist's or historian's interest in change, context, flexibility, and the conditions within which persons act. However, the existence of such complexity in the social and cultural arena need not render trivial this book's interest in *formal Islamic reasons* for endorsing a certain ideal-typical form of social cooperation. Indeed, it cannot do so as long as there continues a lived practice of thinking and arguing about Islamic commitments on the basis of shared methodologies and of presenting those commitments publicly. Thus, the response to the anthropologist's exhortation to "look at lived practices" is to insist that debating Islamic moral commitments in the context of a rich and long-standing tradition *is* a lived practice, one of many lived practices for actual Muslims. As I insisted in the introduction and in chapter 2, there is a way in which the interest in formal doctrine is *deeply affirmative* of Muslim fellow citizens because it regards Islamic commitments not just as socially contingent responses to external circumstances but also as semiautonomous expressions of first-order moral commitments that ought to be treated in a certain way in the public context of civic discourse. Admittedly, some of the particular questions studied in this book (Can Muslims reside in non-Muslim polities? Can they serve in non-Muslim armies? Can they participate in non-Muslim political systems?) cry out for the skeptic's retort that these are *practices* to which even conservative, normatively committed Muslims have long ago reconciled themselves. This retort is well placed. I offer two responses. First, whether or not there is an actual crisis of conscience for many believing Muslims on these particular questions (it is quite clear that the most consistent and conscientious rejection of the very idea of membership and belonging in a non-Muslim society is limited to the so-called Salafī groups[16]), they are actively debated by Islamic scholars, and those arguments are of great interest to political theorists. Second, that skeptical retort is not so naturally presented to some of the more abstract, theological questions that are part of this inquiry's wider focus. For example, is it clear that an inquiry into Ghazālī's moral psychology or Shāṭibī's theory of the *maqāṣid al-sharīʿa* (the purposes of law) and how they might contribute to a theological foundation for an overlapping consensus would be negated by empirical evidence that many Muslims are unaware of those doctrines? Is it clear that an inquiry into modern debates within Catholic theological circles on liberalism, democracy, and secular authority requires for its internal coherence a study of the actual beliefs of nominal Catholics? When dealing with deeper intellectual or theological critiques, it is not clear that purchase on the ground ought to be the primary criterion of evaluation.

Thus, although an inquiry of this nature occupies a space somewhere between the study of texts and social science, it is appropriate to assert its independence from the latter. However, that is not to say that there could not be fruitful cooperation. Comparative questions could also be posed from within the empirical disciplines: Do non-Muslim legal, political, and ethical theories (including liberal ones) actually influence Islamic debates? Are there interesting sociological and demographic patterns to be discerned in when and by whom the various Islamic views surveyed here are adopted? Are Western political institutions perceived as liberal or neutral between conceptions of the good? Do normatively committed Muslims perceive secularism and neutrality as fairer and more desirable than policies that may proceed on the basis of un-Islamic metaphysical reasoning but have a substantive moral overlap with Islamic norms (such as those advanced by other conservative religious groups)? Does there seem to be an empirical overlapping consensus on basic questions of justice? If so, does something like the formal affirmation of such a consensus (as pursued in this book) seem to play a role or, rather, something like Rawls's prediction that in a well-ordered liberal society, most persons will be "pluralists" in the sense of having an unsystematic approach to political values? Do political challenges in existing liberal democracies tend to be expressed in terms of "Islamic reason" or, rather, according to concepts of values admissible under "public reason"? Does public reason seem to create alienation or insincere "translation" of nonpublic aims, or does it tend to be regarded as a sufficient and reasonable language of public political discourse? Of course, these empirical questions cannot displace philosophy (or, perhaps, for the normatively committed Muslim, Islamic doctrine), but they could be a fruitful way of bridging the study of "Islam as a belief system" and "Muslims as social communities" without collapsing either into the other.[17]

Finally, let me repeat my assertion from the introduction that a formal study of this kind can contribute to ongoing debates about how to study instances of social conflict that at least appear to involve some substantive moral disagreement. Imagine two ideal-typical options for structuring an inquiry into such instances (for example, debates over abortion, gay marriage, free speech, or religious freedom). The first option is to seek to reconstruct the best possible arguments for the various positions, including those based on religious or other nonpublic reasoning, thus identifying the contours of the moral disagreement in its most sophisticated and challenging form. We would then seek to assess the force of the various arguments or ask what would be involved in arriving at some form of principled moral reconciliation, leaving the various viewpoints with as much internal integrity as possible. The second option is to merely note that certain social phenomena are sometimes *presented* as symmetrical disagreements between autonomous moral viewpoints but in fact are best examined as instances of the exercise of some form of power by one group over another, or perhaps as the unconscious response of one group to its disadvantaged power situation. Here the questions become: How does this situation come to be described in this way? Why do certain groups prefer to frame public debates in this way? How are certain acts categorized, and what are the implications of this? Why would a group regard its interests as best advanced by this policy or discourse?

These approaches, the normative and the critical, are often viewed as incompatible, or one is viewed by its adherents as clearly superior, more relevant, or more illuminating than its rival. Perhaps one of the rival claims is valid. However, I regard it as a potentially productive avenue of research to experiment with ways in which both approaches could be enhanced by the other. Normative inquiries often take the self-conscious public demands as their object of analysis. Critical inquiry's focus on broader social or power conditions can be assimilated by normative theory either as a factor with weight in normative inquiries or as an independent object of justification. Similarly, investigations into patterns of moral argumentation experienced within various communities can be read alongside critical inquiries. In the case of Islam, critical inquiries often seek (reasonably) to compensate for unbalanced and uninformed public descriptions of Islamic beliefs and the motivations of certain actors by scrutinizing the assumptions, categories, and practices of liberal societies. However, while this form of scholarship need not be "apologetic" in any conventional sense, the price for challenging liberal assumptions in creative and powerful ways is often an incurious and superficial approach to Islamic beliefs. The desire to problematize certain liberal categories may fail to provide a more detailed understanding of nonliberal (in this case, Islamic) arguments and categories. In this way, certain critical approaches may be no less normative or alien to traditions such as Islamic ethics than liberal ones. They may thus also serve to "misrecognize" Islamic discourses no less than liberal approaches. Here, approaches to Islamic discourses such as that developed in this book might be helpful. It is *possible* that Islamic moral arguments will appear in liberal societies that spring from a tradition of thought that predates the encounter with liberalism. It is *possible* that those arguments will refer to concerns, desires, and anxieties not generated by the power apparatus of Western liberal democracies. It is thus possible that our own (liberal or critical) understandings of the sources and meaning of contemporary moral disagreement will emerge altered from the inquiry into Islamic ethical discourses as they are conducted internally.

Notes

INTRODUCTION

1. There is a vast and growing literature on Muslim minorities in Europe and North America within the disciplines of political science, anthropology, and sociology. Some of the most prominent include the numerous studies of Jocelyne Cesari (e.g., *When Islam and Democracy Meet: Muslims in Europe and in the United States* (New York: Palgrave Macmillan, 2004) and *European Muslims and the Secular State*, ed. with Seán McLoughlin (Burlington, Vt.: Ashgate, 2005)), Jørgen S. Nielsen (e.g., *Towards a European Islam* (New York: St. Martin's Press, 1999), *Muslims in Western Europe* (Edinburgh: Edinburgh University Press, 1992), and *Muslim Networks and Transnational Communities in and across Europe*, ed. with Stefano Allievi (Leiden; Boston: Brill, 2003)), and W. A. R. Shadid and P. S. van Koningsveld (editors of *Political Participation and Identities of Muslims in non-Muslim States* (Kampen, Neth.: Kok Phaos, 1996), *Religious Freedom and the Neutrality of the State: The Position of Islam in the European Union* (Leuven; Sterling, Va.: Peeters, 2002), *Intercultural Relations and Religious Authorities: Muslims in the European Union* (Leuven; Dudley, Mass.: Peeters, 2002), and *Muslims in the Margin: Political Responses to the Presence of Islam in Western Europe* (Kampen, Neth.: Kok Pharos, 1996).

2. "It is the extremist, fundamentalist Islamic groups and their ideologues who are the enemies of the West, invoking the wrath of God, and they are far removed from the great and canonical works of Arabic, Persian, Urdu, and other writing" (Akeel Bilgrami ("Occidentalism, the Very Idea: An Essay on Enlightenment and Enchantment," *Critical Inquiry*, vol. 32, no. 3 (Spring 2006), pp. 390–91)). "An image has been created not merely of the indivisibility of religion and state, but of religious doctrine determining the political trajectory of Muslim states—including their inability to accept the notion of popular sovereignty or to implement democratic reforms. Nothing could be further from the truth" (Mohammed Ayoob, "Political Islam: Image and Reality," *World Policy Journal*, vol. 21, no. 3 (Fall 2004), pp. 1–14).

3. "It is striking that the normative claims of liberal conceptions such as tolerance are taken at face value [in inquiries into the compatibility of Islam with liberalism or democracy], and no attention is paid to the contradictions, struggles, and problems that these ideals actually embody. As scholars of liberalism have shown, the historical trajectory of a concept like tolerance encompasses violent struggles that dispossessed peoples have had to wage to be considered legitimate members of liberal societies—not to mention the ongoing battles about what it means 'to tolerate' someone or something, who does the tolerating and who is tolerated, under what circumstances, and toward what end" (Saba Mahmood, "Questioning Liberalism, Too," *Boston Review: A Political and Literary Forum* (April/May 2003), p. 19.

4. Akeel Bilgrami (in "Occidentalism, the Very Idea") describes Ian Buruma and Avishai Margalit as speaking in their book, *Occidentalism: The West in the Eyes of Its Enemies*, in a "cold war voice" for describing Islamist anti-Western ideologues as

> enemies of the West [who] have confused what is the essence of the West—scientific rationality and liberal democracy— . . . and have unfairly and *illicitly extended* their perhaps justified anger against Western conquest and colonization and corporate exploitation to a generalized opposition to the West *as defined by those principles* [of scientific rationality and liberal democracy]. The West is advised not to feel so guilty by these illicit extension and derivations that it gives up on its essential commitments to its defining principles. (p. 386)

5. For the broad outlines of this perspective, see Bilgrami, "Occidentalism, the Very Idea"; Talal Asad, *Genealogies of Religion: Discipline and Reasons of Power in Christianity and Islam* (Baltimore: Johns Hopkins University Press, 1993), particularly chapter 7, "Multiculturalism and British Identity in the Wake of the Rushdie Affair"; and Asad, *Formations of the Secular: Christianity, Islam, Modernity* (Palo Alto, Calif.: Stanford University Press, 2003), particularly chapter 5, "Muslims as a 'Religious Minority' in Europe."

6. To give one example, one of the conclusions Saba Mahmood draws from her critique of investigations into the compatibility of Islam and democracy is that, "given this fraught history, [it might be] worth pausing to reflect whether other traditions, such as Islam, might have their own resources for imagining such an 'ethic that respects dissent and honors the right to adhere to different religious or non-religious convictions?'" (Mahmood, "Questioning Liberalism, Too"). My inquiry is broader than this one question of cross-confessional tolerance, but the idea of taking the resources of a nonliberal tradition seriously in its own terms is similar.

7. See, for example, Randall Hansen, "The Danish Cartoon Controversy: A Defence of Liberal Freedom," in "The Danish Cartoon Affair: Free Speech, Racism, Islamism, and Integration," *International Migration*, vol. 44, no. 5 (2006), pp. 7–16.

8. In "Reflections on Blasphemy and Social Criticism," in Hent de Vries, ed., *Religion: Beyond a Concept* (New York: Fordham University Press, 2008) Talal Asad writes:

> Philosophical criteria determining 'authentic belief' is little more than a way of devaluing moral passion, of disregarding the way passion constitutes moral actions so as to render the matter of choice irrelevant. One consequence of that devaluation is that is that it becomes difficult for the secular liberal to understand the passion that informs those for whom, rightly or wrongly, *it is impossible to remain silent when confronted with blasphemy*, for

> whom blasphemy is neither 'freedom of speech' nor the challenge of a new truth but something that seeks to disrupt a living relationship. (p. 596)

This was also presented as the Presidential and Endowed Lecture at the Humanities Institute, Stanford University, October 2006, and is available at http://townsendcenter.berkeley.edu/pubs/ASAD.pdf.

9. "If the intention of the Danish newspaper *Jyllands-Posten* was not to cause offense, there clearly was a purpose of trying to achieve some kind of victory over Muslims, to bring Muslims into line. . . . As for the republication of the cartoons across continental Europe, this was deliberately done to teach Muslims a lesson" (Tariq Modood, "The Liberal Dilemma: Integration or Vilification," in "The Danish Cartoon Affair," p. 5. Reprinted from *openDemocracy*, February 2, 2006 (http://www.opendemocracy.net/conflict-terrorism/liberal_dilemma_3249.jsp).

10. "The Rushdie affair in Britain should be seen as primarily yet another symptom of postimperial British identity in crisis, not—as most commentators have represented it—as an unhappy instance of some immigrants with difficulties adjusting to a new and more civilized world" (Asad, *Genealogies of Religion*, p. 241).

11. See Talal Asad, "Reflections on Blasphemy and Social Criticism." Asad writes: "The cartoon scandal was made to fit neatly into a wider discourse: the West's 'war on terror,' a conflict that many see as part of an intrinsic hostility between two civilizations, Islam and Europe" (p. 580).

12. Gayatri Spivak, "Can the Subaltern Speak? Speculations on Widow Sacrifice," *Wedge* 7–8 (Winter–Spring 1985), pp. 120–30.

13. Natasha Bakht, "Were Muslim Barbarians Really Knocking on the Gates of Ontario: The Religious Arbitration Controversy," *Ottawa Law Review*, Summer 2005, pp. 67–82.

14. Talal Asad's approach strikes me as congruent here: "What *are* Islamic ideas of blasphemy? Obviously not all Muslims think alike, but questions about Islamic ideas of blasphemy are aimed at a moral tradition. But even that tradition contains divergences, tensions, and instabilities that cannot be equated with an entire 'civilizational people' " ("Reflections on Blasphemy and Social Criticism," p. 589).

15. This is not the same as studying Islamic views primarily with an eye toward reconstructing their historical evolution or situating them exclusively in their historical context. That would be a very important complement to this study, which would add to our appreciation of the force and meaning of the views encountered in this book.

16. Mohammad Fadel, in addressing a similar hypothetical objection to his very similar project ("The True, the Good and the Reasonable: The Theological and Ethical Roots of Public Reason in Islamic Law," *Canadian Journal of Law and Jurisprudence*, vol. 21, no. 1 (2008), p. 12), writes that

> nothing in this Article, however, should be taken to imply that the implicit political commitments of the Islamic tradition identified in this Article can be attributed to any particular historical individual, much less a contemporary individual. Aside from the obvious fact that many Muslims have only nominal commitments to Islam, it is doubtful that even observant Muslims living in contemporary liberal societies have anything more than superficial familiarity with the doctrines discussed in this Article. Accordingly, this Article does not argue that the political commitments described below are held by any particular persons. Instead, its argument is simply that it would be reasonable to attribute this set of political commitments to persons holding the set of beliefs described in this Article.

17. Tariq Ramadan, *To Be a European Muslim* (Leicester, U.K.: Islamic Foundation, 1999), pp. 117–18.

18. Discussing the case of free speech in a liberal society, Peter Jones writes: "Muslims might come to endure attacks upon Muhammad and the Koran, not because they believe that they are obliged to by some principle that supersedes their religion (what principle could that possibly be?), but only because, in practice, that is all they can do short of leaving the society" ("Respecting Beliefs and Rebuking Rushdie," *British Journal of Political Science*, vol. 20, no. 4 (October 1990), p. 418).

19. John Rawls, *Political Liberalism* (New York: Columbia University Press, 1993), p. 169.

20. Ibid., p. 134.

21. Ibid.

22. Ibid., p. 170.

23. A major methodological cum ethical question confronting this study is the selection of sources and what this implies about my judgments about what counts as orthodox, or even Islamic. This question is addressed in the second chapter, where I discuss the general problem of locating Islam as a comprehensive doctrine and what types of texts or arguments I am interested in analyzing. My decision to draw mostly on Sunni texts does not constitute a judgment on my part that they have a more legitimate claim to orthodoxy but is rather based on more banal considerations: The vast majority of Muslims consider themselves Sunnis, and limiting my research to Sunni sources is more manageable and will preempt the problem of considering the authority of arguments from one tradition for Muslims or the other. Also, as even a prominent (and politically engaged) Shi'ite cleric concedes, "While Shi'ite jurisprudence is still crawling where the problem of Islamic minorities is concerned, we find a great Sunni historical tradition in this area" (Muḥammad ḥusayn Faḍl Allāh, *al-Hijra wa'l-ightirāb: ta'sīs fiqhī li mushkilat al-lujū' wa'l-hijra* (Beirut: Mu'assasat al-'ārif li'l-Maṭbū'āt, 1999), p. 79). This all does not mean that I am uninterested in Shi'ite sources, but when I draw from them, largely this author and Ayatollah 'Alī al-Ḥusaynī al-Sīstānī, I will restrict myself to arguments potentially accessible to non-Shi'ite Muslims or those that serve to demonstrate the depth and breadth of consensus on a certain point of doctrine. Arguments that are grounded in sectarian Shi'ite metaphysics or conceptions of politics (say, the idea that the absence of the Imam means that Shi'ites ought to be indifferent to the ordering of the secular world) would point to a separate, parallel inquiry.

PART I INTRODUCTION

1. Sometimes symmetrical in a literal sense. Rawls's understanding of the historical provenance of political liberalism, following Judith Shklar and others, is largely that it emerged from the stalemate of the post-Reformation religious wars.

2. Thomas Nagel poses similar questions rhetorically by way of entry into a consideration of the meta-ethical approach of constructivists such as Rawls: "Why should I care whether others with whom I disagree can accept or reject the grounds on which state power is exercised? Why shouldn't I discount their rejection if it is based on religious or moral or cultural values that I believe to be mistaken?" ("Moral Conflict and Political Legitimacy," *Philosophy and Public Affairs*, vol. 16, no. 3 (Summer 1987), p. 222). Joshua Cohen presents an elaboration of the objection (said to be from a conversation with G. A. Cohen) that these concerns represent a concession to de facto power arrangements and not considerations of justice ("Moral Pluralism and Politi-

cal Consensus," in David Copp, Jean Hampton, and John E Roemer, eds., *The Idea of Democracy* (Cambridge: Cambridge University Press, 1993), p. 271).

3. Larry Krasnoff, "Consensus, Stability, and Normativity in Rawls's Political Liberalism," *Journal of Philosophy*, vol. 95 (1998), p. 269.

4. See Brian Barry, "How Not to Defend Liberal Institutions," in *Liberty and Justice: Essays in Political Theory 2* (Oxford: Clarendon, 1991), pp. 34–35.

5. Bhikhu Parekh, *Rethinking Multiculturalism: Cultural Diversity and Political Theory* (Cambridge, Mass.: Harvard University Press, 2000), p. 88.

CHAPTER I

1. I am indebted to Larry Krasnoff ("Consensus, Stability, and Normativity in Rawls's Political Liberalism," pp. 269–92) for these examples and for putting Rawls's concern with stability in this context.

2. Rawls, *Political Liberalism*, p. 169. All liberal political theorists, Rawlsians or otherwise, should be able to affirm what has been suggested to this point. Whether one believes in a stronger rational foundation for liberal institutions or is skeptical of the idea of any freestanding political values, one can recognize the social and political importance of support for liberal principles from comprehensive doctrines.

3. "A philosophic justification is not to be confused with popular acceptance, rough consensus, or even probable acceptance by all reasonable parties. [But] this is not to belittle the goal of popular consensus. In the sociological sense of the word, the *legitimacy* of a liberal regime depends on widespread acceptance of its justification" (Gerald F. Gaus, *Justificatory Liberalism: An Essay on Epistemology and Political Theory* (Oxford: Oxford University Press, 1996), p. 10).

4. "Anyone attached to liberal institutions . . . is going to have to recognize that their prospects of survival depend on there being in the population a large proportion of people with a liberal outlook" (Barry, "How Not to Defend Liberal Institutions," pp. 38–39).

5. Alexis de Tocqueville, *Democracy in America* (New York: Penguin, 2003), p. 336 (from vol. I, part 2, chapter 9, "The Main Causes Which Tend to Maintain a Democratic Republic in the United States").

6. Gaus argues that this is the case only when you seek to persuade and motivate a person by appealing to values or beliefs that you not only do not hold but also consider to be irrational or unreasonable, that is, views that persist not because of the burdens of reason but in spite of them (Gerald F. Gaus, "The Rational, the Reasonable and Justification," *Journal of Political Philosophy*, vol. 3, no. 3 (1995), p. 255). Note that this is an important retort (repeated later) to the argument that seeking to justify certain liberal principles from within otherwise nonliberal traditions is somehow disrespectful or manipulative. The liberal response is that we would bother with such a project only if we have a basic respect for the tradition in the first place or if we regard the overall aims or values of the tradition as valuable and legitimate.

7. Akeel Bilgrami has argued that the liberal aspiration of justification through purely external reasons (i.e., reasons all rational subjects should endorse *in virtue of their own rationality* regardless of their substantive moral commitments) fails not only in practice but also logically and therefore that "the task of achieving secular ideals in a world in which there are strong religious and cultural identities [requires] look[ing] for reasons that will appeal even to those with these identities" "Secularism and Relativism," *boundary 2*, vol. 31, no. 2 (Summer 2004), p. 175). John Kekes: "Reasonable conflict-resolution is made possible by the traditions and conceptions of a good life to

which people who face the conflicts adhere" (*The Morality of Pluralism* (Princeton, N.J.: Princeton University Press, 1993), p. 76). And of course, Richard Rorty: "The fact that we may belong to several communities and thus have conflicting *moral* obligations, as well as conflicts between moral obligations and private commitments generates dilemmas. Such dilemmas . . . are never going to be resolved by appeal to some further, higher set of obligations which a philosophical tribunal might discover and apply. All we can do is work with the final vocabulary we have, while keeping our ears open for hints about how it might be expanded or revised" (*Contingency, Irony, and Solidarity* (Cambridge: Cambridge University Press, 1989), p. 197).

8. "I believe that liberalism depends on the acceptance of a higher-order impartiality, and that this raises serious problems about how the different orders of impartiality are to be integrated" (Nagel, "Moral Conflict and Political Legitimacy," p. 216).

9. Rawls, *Political Liberalism*, pp. 56–57.

10. The "fact of reasonable pluralism" is the central claim in *Political Liberalism*. This thesis holds that "the diversity of reasonable comprehensive religious, philosophical, and moral doctrines found in modern democratic societies is not a mere historical condition that may soon pass away; it is a permanent feature of the public culture of democracy." These reasonable doctrines "are not simply the upshot of self- and class interests, or of peoples' understandable tendency to view the political world from a limited standpoint. Instead, they are in part the work of free practical reason within the framework of free institutions" (*Political Liberalism*, pp. 36–37). And since "we are to recognize the practical impossibility of reaching reasonable and workable political agreement in judgment on the truth of comprehensive doctrines" (p. 63), we are also forced to concede that "a continuing shared understanding on one comprehensive religious, philosophical, or moral doctrine can be maintained only by the oppressive use of state power" (p. 37).

11. The idea of an overlapping consensus is not the only account of stability. Rawls also argues that the political values on which the conception of justice is based (equality, liberty, fair equality of opportunity, economic reciprocity, mutual respect) are "very great values" and hard to override. According to Rawls's moral psychology, many persons growing up in and benefiting from a liberal constitutional regime will come to internalize the moral principles that ground it, and a well-ordered liberal society will, over time, create a political culture supportive of itself. This is particularly the case for citizens who do not have fully comprehensive or elaborate comprehensive moral doctrines but rather a flexible "pluralist doctrine" that is "not systematically unified" and instead contains "a large family of nonpolitical values" (p. 155). It will be easier for such citizens to revise their nonpolitical values, ends, and beliefs to be congruent with a political conception of justice than for citizens who have a fully comprehensive doctrine, perhaps with an authoritative articulation.

12. Ibid., p. 140.

13. Ibid., p. 148.

14. Ibid.

15. Ibid., p. 386.

16. The idea of a "public justification" in Rawls's scheme is used to refer to a status when it is generally known that an overlapping consensus exists and citizens can refer to the fact that the political conception of justice is shared common ground.

17. This conception of justification as beginning with comprehensive views already existing in a society and then theorizing based on their convergence on common points of political morality is advanced by George Klosko in "Political Constructivism

in Rawls's Political Liberalism," *American Political Science Review*, vol. 91, no. 3 (September 1997), pp. 635–46.

18. Rawls, *Political Liberalism*, p. 141.

19. "We do not look to the comprehensive doctrines that in fact exist and then draw up a political conception that strikes some kind of balance of forces between them . . . [or] specify an index of [primary] goods so as to be near to those doctrines' center of gravity, so to speak. . . . [T]o do so would make it political in the wrong way" (ibid., pp. 39–40).

20. Ibid., p. 141.

21. Ibid., p. 143. Emphasis added.

22. "While we want a political conception to have a justification by reference to one or more comprehensive doctrines, it is neither presented as, nor as derived from, such a doctrine applied to the basic structure of society, as if this structure were simply another subject to which that doctrine applied" (ibid., p. 12).

23. Ibid, p. 134 (emphasis added).

24. Ibid., p. 38.

25. "It covers the major religious, philosophical, and moral aspects of human life in a more or less consistent and coherent manner. It organizes and characterizes recognized values so that they are compatible with one another and express and intelligible view of the world" (ibid., p. 59).

26. "In singling out which values to count as especially significant and how to balance them when they conflict, a reasonable comprehensive doctrine is also an exercise of practical reason" (ibid.).

27. "While a reasonable comprehensive doctrine is not necessarily fixed and unchanging, it normally belongs to, or draws upon, a tradition of thought and doctrine. Although stable over time, and not subject to sudden and unexplained changes, it tends to evolve slowly in the light of what, from its point of view, it sees as good and sufficient reasons" (ibid.).

28. Ibid., p. 49.

29. "Being reasonable is not an epistemological idea (though it has epistemological elements). Rather it is part of a political ideal of democratic citizenship that includes the idea of public reason" (ibid., p. 62).

30. Ibid., pp. 60–61.

31. Ibid., p. 61. Cf. Thomas Nagel: "The idea is that when we look at certain of our convictions from outside, however justified they may be from within, the appeal to their truth must be seen merely as an appeal to our beliefs, and should be treated as such unless those beliefs can be shown to be justifiable from a more impersonal standpoint. If not, they have to remain, for the purpose of a certain kind of moral argument, features of a personal perspective—to be respected as such but no more than that" ("Moral Conflict and Political Legitimacy," p. 230).

32. This is the phrase coined by Joshua Cohen in "Moral Pluralism and Political Consensus" to refer to the idea that a political conception of justice must be the object of an overlapping consensus if it is serve in the long term as a public basis of justification.

33. This argument is developed in Leif Wenar, "*Political Liberalism*: An Internal Critique," *Ethics*, vol. 106 (October 1995), pp. 32–63.

34. A further question would be whether the burdens of judgment alone in fact do give strong reasons for toleration of the kind envisioned by political liberalism. The argument could be made that they help explain the persistence of disagreement but

equally help those committed to the truth of their own view to explain just why it is that others fail to see the light.

35. Note Cohen's remarks: "In the case at hand, the exclusion is of a special kind. It does not amount to a deprivation of liberties or of what are conventionally understood to be the advantages of social cooperation. Instead, exclusion lies in the fact that the arguments used to justify the exercise of power depend on norms, values, and ideals that are rejected by some people whose views will as a consequence not belong to an overlapping consensus" ("Moral Pluralism," pp. 285–86). But is this exclusion arbitrary and thus unfair? One group most likely to be subject to it are "nonrationalist fundamentalists" who are not interested in defending their views on rationalist grounds but simply assert that the fact of the truth of their beliefs entitles them to enforce them:

> Faced with nonrationalist fundamentalists, it will not do to state the case for the idea of reasonable pluralism; they know that case, celebrate the limited competence of reason as a guide in human affairs, and lament the self-imposed disabilities of those who insist on proceeding within its narrow compass. Still, what they are prepared to do is to impose on those who are outside the faith in a way that—so far as others can tell—is indistinguishable from the concededly irrational practice of imposing in the name of their beliefs. To resist such imposition is not simply to affirm a disagreement with the nonrationalist fundamentalist. Instead, it is to complain about this fundamental form of unreasonableness. And finding them unreasonable in this way is sufficient to show that the exclusion is not arbitrary. (Ibid., p. 287)

36. Ibid., pp. 274–75.

37. I say "part of" our evaluation because anything more would lead to a form of intellectual, ideological, or even rhetorical determinism and exaggerate the influence that ideas as such have on individuals. This is the point of my condition (1) in this paragraph. It will not matter equally to all Muslims, Christians, Hindus, Marxists, utilitarians, and so forth what their authoritative texts or doctrines say about political values. An important theme to which Rawls often returns is that democratic legitimacy might very well depend as much on citizens *not having* overly elaborate, extensive, or specific comprehensive doctrines as on justice being compatible with particular such doctrines. That is, that while the liberal state ought to be neutral between various comprehensive conceptions of the "good life," and that it is from these quarters that the liberal state is most often attacked, it also has to justify itself and in turn can draw authority from those *citizens* subject to it, most of whom do not hold coherent, internally consistent, well-thought-out, comprehensive doctrines but rather collections of values, interests, and preferences, some of which might conflict if thought about sufficiently. (Most people do not consider it a problem that these values do not add up to a comprehensive worldview. How often is someone heard to deny that they have an "ideology"?) Rawls might be read as suggesting that in most periods of most countries' histories, the majority of citizens can be characterized in this way, or that this is a state of affairs conducive to democracy. It is only during legitimation crises or periods of serious politicization that large groups of people tend to see themselves as bearers of comprehensive doctrines, at least in the West. In fact, one might consider to what extent it is a prerequisite of a stable democracy that most people do not hold such comprehensive doctrines that, if taken seriously, would demand that the state be the vehicle for their full realization. Heavily politicized utopians are dangerous for democracy as such, and not just conflict between *various*

heavily politicized utopians. Democracy might rely rather both on some ideological consensus and lots of ideological indifference or vagueness.

38. Jürgen Habermas, "Discourse Ethics: Notes on a Program of Philosophical Justification," in *Moral Consciousness and Communicative Action* (Cambridge, Mass.: MIT Press, 2001), p. 48.

39. Ibid., p. 66.

40. Jürgen Habermas, "Morality and Ethical Life: Does Hegel's Critique of Kant Apply to Discourse Ethics?" in *Moral Consciousness and Communicative Action*, p. 203.

41. Habermas, "Discourse Ethics," p. 61.

42. Ibid., p. 74.

43. Habermas, "Morality and Ethical Life," p. 201.

44. Habermas, "Discourse Ethics," p. 81.

45. Ibid., pp. 75–76.

46. Habermas, "Morality and Ethical Life," pp. 203–4.

47. Habermas, "Discourse Ethics," p. 57.

48. Seyla Benhabib, *The Claims of Culture* (Princeton, N.J.: Princeton University Press, 2002), p. 13.

49. Ibid., p. 14.

50. Ibid., p. 12.

51. Ibid., p. 14.

52. Ibid., p. 107.

53. Ibid., pp. 38–39.

54. Ibid., p. 115.

55. Ibid., p. 19.

56. Ibid., p. 111.

57. Ibid., p. 109.

58. Ibid., p. 48.

59. Ibid.

60. Rawls, "Kantian Constructivism in Moral Theory," *Journal of Philosophy*, vol. 77 (1980), p. 519.

61. Seyla Benhabib, "Afterword: Communicative Ethics and Contemporary Controversies in Practical Philosophy," in Benhabib and Fred Dallmayr (eds.), *The Communicative Ethics Controversy* (Cambridge, Mass.: MIT Press, 1990), p. 339.

62. Will Kymlicka, *Multicultural Citizenship: A Liberal Theory of Minority Rights* (Oxford: Oxford University Press, 1995), p. 164.

63. Joseph Raz, *The Morality of Freedom* (Oxford: Clarendon, 1986), pp. 369–70.

64. John Gray, "What Is Dead and What Is Living in Liberalism?" in *Post-Liberalism: Studies in Political Thought* (London: Routledge, 1993), p. 284.

65. Richard Rorty, *Contingency, Irony, Solidarity*, p. 68.

66. Such observation is akin to Clifford Geertz's demystification of cultural relativism, which he "think[s] merely there, like Transylvania" ("Anti Anti-Relativism," *American Anthropologist*, vol. 86, no. 2 (June 1984), p. 263), or Isaiah Berlin's attempt to unlink the inquiry into what freedom is from the capacity to value or demand it.

67. See, for example, Pierre Schlag, "The Empty Circles of Liberal Justification," *Michigan Law Review*, vol. 96, no. 1 (1997), pp. 1–46.

68. Stanley Fish, *There's No Such Thing as Free Speech (. . . and It's a Good Thing Too)* (New York: Oxford University Press, 1994), p. 135.

69. Ibid., p. 135.

70. Ibid., p. 19.

71. Ibid., p. 136.

72. Rorty, *Contingency, Irony, and Solidarity*, p. xv.

73. Fish, *There's No Such Thing as Free Speech*, p. 136.

74. Rorty, *Contingency, Irony, and Solidarity*, p. 196.

75. "The existence of these two sides (like the fact that we may belong to several communities and thus have conflicting *moral* obligations, as well as conflicts between moral obligations and private commitments) generates dilemmas. Such dilemmas we shall always have with us, but they are never going to be resolved by appeal to some further, higher set of obligations which a philosophical tribunal might discover and apply. All we can do is work with the final vocabulary we have, while keeping our ears open for hints about how it might be expanded or revised" (ibid., p. 197).

76. "It follows then that persons embedded within *different* discursive systems will not be able to hear the other person's reasons *as* reasons, but only as errors or even delusions" (Fish, *There's No Such Thing as Free Speech*, p. 136).

77. Ibid., pp. 10–11.

78. "The dread of [cultural relativism] is . . . unfounded because the moral and intellectual consequences that are commonly supposed to flow from relativism—subjectivism, nihilism, incoherence, Machiavellianism, ethical idiocy, esthetic blindness, and so on—do not in fact do so and the promised rewards of escaping its clutches are illusory" (Geertz, "Anti Anti-Relativism," p. 263).

79. Ibid., p. 39.

80. "We are willing to have these discussions [about the terms of social cooperation in twenty-first-century Europe] but in DOS, not in Windows" was how this has been put to me by Yahya Michot, a Belgian-British Muslim thinker. Whereas it is widely advanced that it is the Habermasian view, rather than the Rawlsian, that allows this, my claim is that one must retreat fully to the relativist position of Rorty or Fish to fully satisfy holders of nonliberal doctrines.

81. Rorty, *Contingency, Irony, and Solidarity*, p. 197.

82. Ibid., p. 197.

83. Ibid., pp. xiii–xiv.

84. Ibid., p. 65.

85. Ibid., p. xiv.

86. Gray, "What Is Dead and What Is Living in Liberalism?" p. 284.

87. Chandran Kukathas, "Are There Any Cultural Rights?" *Political Theory*, vol. 20, no. 1 (1992), p. 125, although note that this is not Kukathas's argument.

88. One might still assert that there are *some* values that do not depend on this; there is no developmental prerequisite for condemning, say, slavery, female genital mutilation, or genocide. This may be true and may seem to point the way toward a minimal set of human rights based on human needs prior to any cultural foundation for their value. However, one might deny that these are robust enough to constitute a distinctively *liberal* ethos rather than a universal conception of *decency*.

89. It is thus not a paradox that the much more religious America defends secularism while the less religious Britain maintains the state link to the Church of England and blasphemy laws. It is only because Britain is less religious as a society (and that blasphemy laws are never enforced) that this anachronism can persist.

90. As pointed out by Will Kymlicka (*Multicultural Citizenship*, pp. 164–65), it is not incoherent to bracket such discussions of the liberal view of the desire for autonomy in nonliberal societies from discussions of what actions on the part of liberal polities toward those societies would be appropriate. Liberals are justified in thinking that the persecution of an intellectual in Egypt is wrong irrespective of the Islamic or quasi-Islamic justification of it while thinking that outside intervention to rectify

it might be wrong for other reasons. It seems that Brian Barry's attack on Kymlicka for being "soft on illiberalism" abroad (in *Culture and Equality* (Cambridge, Mass.: Harvard University Press, 2000), pp. 137–38) might be a bit excessive.

91. John Gray does, in fact, make essentially the same point when he argues that freedom is not a Western, "cultural" value as such but one appropriate to societies where no single conception of value still holds sway. Thus, while "over the long run of human history, civil societies are not the only legitimate societies, I conclude nevertheless that a liberal civil social society is the best one for cultures, such as all or virtually all contemporary cultures, which harbour a diversity of incommensurable conceptions of the good" ("What Is Dead and What Is Living in Liberalism?" p. 284).

92. For two distinct approaches to this question, see Barry, *Culture and Equality*, and Lucas Swaine, *The Liberal Conscience: Politics and Principle in a World of Religious Pluralism* (New York: Columbia University Press, 2006).

93. Even Brian Barry does not "wish to rule out the possibility that there will be cases in which both the general law and exemption are defensible. Usually, though, either the case for the law (or some version of it) is strong enough to rule out exemptions, or the case that can be made for exemptions is strong enough to suggest that there should be no law anyway" (*Culture and Equality*, p. 39).

94. Even Bhikhu Parekh, in some areas a critic of liberalism's claim to universal validity over minority subcultures, argues (*Rethinking Multiculturalism*, p. 334) for a similar form of public presentation of one's own reasons for desiring a particular law or exemption on the part of nonliberal groups:

> Adherents cannot hide behind God's authority and must accept responsibility for what they say and do in His name. It is never enough for them to say that they must do such and such things because God or the Bible or the Koran says so. The divine will is a matter of human definition and interpretation, and requires them to show why they interpret their religion in one way rather than another and why they think that their interpretation entails a particular form of behaviour. Religiously minded citizens are never excused from a rational discussion of their politically relevant beliefs and practices. Political life recognises no infallible truths, only those capable of carrying conviction with the democratic community of citizens.

95. See, in particular, Samuel Scheffler, "The Appeal of Political Liberalism," *Ethics*, vol. 105 (October 1994), pp. 4–22; and Leif Wenar, "*Political Liberalism*: An Internal Critique."

96. Jürgen Habermas, "Struggles for Recognition in the Democratic Constitutional State," in Amy Gutmann (ed.), *Multiculturalism: Examining the Politics of Recognition* (Princeton, N.J.: Princeton University Press, 1994), p. 134.

97. Rawls, "Kantian Constructivism in Moral Theory," pp. 568–69.

98. Stephen Macedo, "Transformative Constitutionalism and the Case of Religion: Defending the Moderate Hegemony of Liberalism," *Political Theory*, vol. 26, no. 1 (February 1998), pp. 64–65.

99. "Each [culture] can be improved in a way consistent with its own spirit and out of its own resources" (Joseph Raz, "Multiculturalism: A Liberal Perspective," in *Ethics in the Public Domain* (Oxford: Clarendon, 1994), p. 168).

100. Michael Walzer, "Political Alienation and Military Service," in *Obligations: Essays on Disobedience, War, and Citizenship* (Cambridge, Mass.: Harvard University Press, 1970), p. 100.

101. Parekh, *Rethinking Multiculturalism*, p. 88.

102. "What's curious to me is that in these explorations [of Islam's compatibility with democracy] Islam bears the burden of proving its compatibility with liberal ideals, and the line of question is almost never reversed. We do not ask, for example, what would it mean to take the resources of the Islamic tradition and question many of the liberal political categories and principles for the contradictions and problems they embody" (Mahmood, "Questioning Liberalism, Too").

103. A point I made in my Introduction bears repeating. Although here I am focusing specifically on the relationship between Islamic doctrine and liberal citizenship, the inquiry itself is a generic one. All comprehensive doctrines or, indeed, noncomprehensive collections of beliefs and preferences can be presumed to provide their bearers with a wide set of motivations for action, some of which may conflict with liberal terms of social cooperation. These questions would be of interest even without the more public examples of recent value conflicts in Western societies, simply because Islam is an important comprehensive doctrine that has achieved a critical presence in existing liberal democracies recently enough for there not to exist a significant philosophical literature on its relationship to liberalism and citizenship. Lest it be thought that asking these questions suggests a background suspicion or mistrust of Islamic political ethics, it should be borne in mind that these very questions are the subject of earnest, and constant, internal debate among Muslim religious scholars and intellectuals.

104. Thus, Saba Mahmood's critique (in "Questioning Liberalism, Too") of Khaled Abou El Fadl's interest in liberal democracy in the Middle East would seem to not apply to this study, or to a much lesser degree. She writes:

> I believe the reason these kinds of questions [whether the liberal meaning of tolerance is the best or the most desirable one; what does this understanding preclude, under what kinds of presuppositions, and for whom?] are seldom pursued is because of the hegemony that liberalism commands as a political ideal for many contemporary Muslim intellectuals, a hegemony that reflects the enormous disparity in power between the Anglo-European countries and what constitutes the "Muslim world" today. Indeed, the idea that the liberal political system is the best arrangement for all human societies, regardless of their diverse histories and conceptual and material resources, is rarely questioned these days. One would think that proponents of "pluralism and diversity" in the world, like Abou El Fadl, would want to explore some of the contrasting ways that questions of difference have been imagined and politically instituted within different non-liberal traditions.

105. "The prolonged and violent demonstrations against the Danish cartoons were a staged attempt by Islamists to intimidate their enemies in their own countries and in the West" (George Packer, "Fighting Faiths: Can Liberal Internationalism Be Saved?" *New Yorker*, July 10, 2006).

106. Sherman Jackson, "Jihad and the Modern World," *Journal of Islamic Law and Culture*, vol. 7, no. 1 (Spring–Summer 2002), p. 21.

107. Jones, "Respecting Beliefs and Rebuking Rushdie," p. 429.

CHAPTER 2

1. Rawls, "The Idea of Public Reason Revisited," in *The Law of Peoples* (Cambridge, Mass.: Harvard University Press, 1999), p. 156.

2. I am not identifying conjecture, or "justificatory comparative political theory," with persuasion. For a defense of persuasion against its philosophical critiques, see Bryan Garsten, *Saving Persuasion: A Defense of Rhetoric and Judgment* (Cambridge, Mass.: Harvard University Press, 2006).

3. On at least one view, all public or intersubjective justification proceeds on the basis of each person's system of beliefs. Thus, all public justification (and not mere rhetorical persuasion) involves reasoning on the basis of another's reasons, even if they are not yours. See Gaus, *Justificatory Liberalism*, particularly chapters 3, 8, and 9.

4. For an excellent analysis of the temptations, pitfalls, and costs of arguing from within an alien religious tradition in the case of international human rights activism, see Naz K. Modirzadeh, "Taking Islamic Law Seriously: INGOs and the Battle for Muslim Hearts and Minds," *Harvard Human Rights Journal*, vol. 19 (Spring 2006), pp. 191–233.

5. > Such an exercise [of reinterpreting religious texts in the light of modern values] has its dangers. It can easily violate the integrity of the texts and the tradition, charter them in the service of political and ideological fashions, encourage the government directly or indirectly to influence scholarly inquiries, and create a climate hostile to intellectual dissent. The ethos of political liberalism could easily penetrate religious and philosophical doctrines, pressure them to understand and articulate themselves in standard liberal idioms, and all but eliminate nonliberal forms of thought. Locke did this when he turned Christianity into a "reasonable" doctrine by stripping it of its theological mysteries, reducing its highly complex ethic to a simplified morality of bourgeois reciprocity, and turning churches into voluntary associations. J. S. Mill did the same with Christianity and indeed religion in general. Rawls's thought offers little protection against this persistent liberal tendency.

Parekh, *Rethinking Multiculturalism*, p. 88.

6. Robert Audi, *Religious Commitment and Secular Reason* (Cambridge: Cambridge University Press, 2000), p. 110.

7. Audi, "The Separation of Church and State and the Obligations of Citizenship," *Philosophy & Public Affairs*, vol. 18, no. 3 (Summer 1989), p. 282.

8. Gaus, *Justificatory Liberalism*, p. 139.

9. Of course, to say that such an argument is insincere and manipulative is not to say that it is morally blameworthy; it is only to say that the argument does not *justify* in the philosophical sense. Here the independent justifiability of the desired state of affairs enters and permits us to say that insincere or manipulative speech acts may be morally justified on consequentialist grounds in certain circumstances, even if they are not epistemically justified statements. In other words, it may be justified at times to lie, but we would not say that the lie creates a justified belief on the part of the manipulated person.

10. Cf. Gaus's principle of sincerity: "PS: Betty's argument justifying *N* to Alf is sincere if and only if (1) she is justified in accepting *N*; (2) she has a justified belief that *N* is justifiable in Alf's system of reasons and beliefs" (*Justificatory Liberalism*, p. 140).

11. Concerning the problem of gender equality in Islamic law, Abdullahi An-Na'im writes that "this is an internal debate for the Muslims to conduct and settle among themselves" ("The Rights of Women and International Law in the Muslim

Context," *Whittier Law Review*, vol. 9, no. 3 (1987), p. 493). Micah Schwartzman refers to this as the "cultural sovereignty objection" to conjecture ("Political Justification Beyond the Limits of Public Reason," unpublished manuscript).

12. Fazlur Rahman, *Islam and Modernity: The Transformation of an Intellectual Tradition* (Chicago: University of Chicago Press, 1982), p. 4.

13. Ramadan, *To Be a European Muslim*, p. 55.

14. This is quite different from what Rawls means by "transparency," which is merely the public assertion that one does not argue from within the tradition in question. This notion of transparency I take for granted. Micah Schwartzman refers to this as the "principle of disclosure" ("Political Justification Beyond the Limits of Public Reason").

15. Parekh, *Rethinking Multiculturalism*, p. 107.

16. Parekh, "Barry and the Dangers of Liberalism," in Paul Kelly (ed.), *Multiculturalism Reconsidered:* Culture and Equality *and Its Critics* (Oxford: Polity, 2002), p. 145.

17. A version of this chapter was previously published as Andrew F. March, "Liberal Citizenship and the Overlapping Consensus: The Case of Muslim Minorities," *Philosophy & Public Affairs*, vol. 34, no. 4 (Fall 2006), pp. 373–421.

18. "It is up to each comprehensive doctrine to say how its idea of the reasonable connects with its concept of truth" (Rawls, *Political Liberalism*, p. 94). "Citizens individually decide for themselves in what way the public political conception all affirm is related to their own more comprehensive views" (ibid., p. 38). For a helpful discussion of this question, see Krasnoff, "Consensus, Stability, and Normativity in Rawls's Political Liberalism," pp. 284–86.

19. "To speak of an 'Islamic' perspective on any particular issue, one must use sources that are transcultural and acknowledged as authoritative by Muslims of the diverse regions of Islamdom—Indonesia, India, Pakistan, Egypt, or England. The only sources that fit this description are works of *fiqh*, Islamic legal works" (A. Kevin Reinhart, "Impurity/No Danger," *History of Religions*, vol. 30, no. 1 (August 1990), p. 2). Reinhart goes perhaps too far, unless the traditions of theology (*kalām, 'aqīda, uṣūl al-dīn*) are also included. However, the basic point holds: The internal diversity of Islam, not to mention the staggering multiplicity of Muslim practices and experiences, does not mean that there are no traditions or discourses generally regarded as orthodox expressions of "normative Islam," that is, Islam as a "comprehensive ethical doctrine."

20. See A. Kevin Reinhart, "Islamic Law as Islamic Ethics," *Journal of Religious Ethics*, vol. 11, no. 2 (1993), pp. 186–203.

21. Jackson, "Jihad and the Modern World," pp. 4–5.

22. On this point, see Mohammad Fadel, "The True, the Good, and the Reasonable."

23. Which is not to say that they are not interacting with *other* alien epistemes, such as Greek philosophy, Christian theology, or Roman law.

24. Any work on Islamic jurisprudence will emphasize this basic feature of Islamic jurisprudence. See, for example, Bernard G. Weiss, *The Spirit of Islamic Law* (Athens: University of Georgia Press, 1998), chapter 5, "Probabalism and the Limits of Certainty"; Khaled Abou El Fadl, *Speaking in God's Name: Islamic Law, Authority and Women* (Oxford: Oneworld, 2001); Baber Johansen, *Contingency in a Sacred Law: Legal and Ethical Norms in the Muslim* Fiqh (Leiden: Brill, 1999); Bernard G. Weiss, *The Search for God's Law: Islamic Jurisprudence in the Writings of Sayf Al-Din Al-Amidi* (Salt Lake City: University of Utah Press, 1992); Aron Zysow, "The Economy of Cer-

tainty: An Introduction to the Typology of Islamic Legal Theory" (PhD diss., Harvard, 1984).

25. See George Hourani, "Ghāzalī on the Ethics of Action," *Journal of the American Oriental Society*, vol. 96, no. 1 (January–March 1976); and Fadel, "The True, the Good, and the Reasonable," for this argument.

26. Fadel, "The True, the Good, and the Reasonable," p. 31.

27. Rawls, *Political Liberalism*, pp. 45–46.

28. See Wael Hallaq, *A History of Islamic Legal Theories: An Introduction to Sunni* Usul al-Fiqh (Cambridge: Cambridge University Press, 1997), pp. 210, 261.

29. On this theme, see Mohammad Fadel, "The Social Logic of *Taqlīd* and the Rise of the *Mukhtaṣar*," *Islamic Law and Society*, vol. 3, no. 2 (1996), pp. 193–233.

30. "Following one of the four legal schools is not a religious obligation, for obligations are only that which God and His Apostle have made obligatory, and neither God nor His Apostle commanded Muslims to follow Abū Ḥanīfa or Mālik or any others. They commanded only obedience to the Book and the *sunna*, the only two infallible sources" ('Abd Allāh ibn al-Shaykh al-Maḥfūẓ Ibn Bayya, *Ṣinā'at al-fatwā wa-fiqh al-aqalliyāt* (Jedda/Beirut: Dār al-Minhāj, 2007), p. 408).

31. I quoted in the previous chapter Tocqueville's conception of "habits of the mind" as a possible analogue or kindred idea to Rawls's notion of a self-conscious "full justification" for liberal institutions emerging from within comprehensive doctrines. Of course, Tocqueville's broader concern with the *moeurs* that make a democratic republic stable puts equal if not greater emphasis on the less self-conscious "habits of the heart." As noted also in the previous chapter, Rawls asserts in a number of places that a full justification of a political conception of justice will be much easier to achieve for those citizens with a "pluralist" or not fully comprehensive collection of beliefs.

32. Rawls, *Political Liberalism*, p. 170.

33. Samuel Scheffler, "The Appeal of Political Liberalism," pp. 9–11.

34. Rawls, *Political Liberalism*, p. 181.

35. Ibid., p. 149.

36. Ibid., p. 147.

37. Ibid., p. 145, emphasis added.

38. Ibid., p. 153.

39. Ibid., p. 155.

40. Although, interestingly, Rawls does cite the work of Abdullahi An-Na'im in "The Idea of Public Reason Revisited" (in *The Law of Peoples*, p. 151) as evidence of the possibility of a formulation of Islam that would be part of an overlapping consensus. I do not doubt that An-Na'im's views (expressed in the text Rawls was aware of, *Towards an Islamic Reformation*) would be part of an overlapping consensus. However, for reasons I explain at more length in chapter 7, my conception of conjecture has a preference for exploring the possibilities of an overlapping consensus with views less metaphysically and hermeneutically innovative than those of An-Na'im and his mentor, Maḥmūd Muḥammad Ṭāhā. As Rawls notes, these views involve reversing the traditional understanding of the temporary and the eternal in the Qur'an and are regarded by many Sunni Muslims to be heretical (Ṭāhā was hanged for apostasy). According the principle of plausibility I adopt in this study, it would be unfortunate if a believing Muslim had to adopt the metaphysical views of Ṭāhā and An-Na'im in order to be part of an overlapping consensus. That may be the case, and of course such views can be introduced and canvassed, but the entire purpose of the methodology I develop here is to ascertain how conservative a conception of Islamic fundamental commitments can be included in an overlapping consensus, which means that it is not

enough to simply point to a text or doctrine that seems to overlap with liberal aims, no matter how sophisticated or articulate.

41. Scheffler, "The Appeal of Political Liberalism," p. 13.

42. This is not to say that there are no important policy disputes between comprehensive and political liberals. An important area is public education, where political liberals would advocate restraint in terms of the values and beliefs that can be taught to future citizens, limiting themselves to only those values crucial (not merely desirable) to producing good citizens (not persons). Some liberals, by contrast, would endorse a variation of Dewey's conception of the proper scope of public education, which extends to inculcating more robust rationalist and critical beliefs. This is a good example of how, for the political liberal, the duty of restraint in the public sphere extends to his own possible conceptions of value. (See Stephen Macedo, "Liberal Civic Education and Religious Fundamentalism: The Case of God vs. John Rawls?" *Ethics*, vol. 105, no. 3 (April 1995), pp. 468–96; and Amy Gutmann, "Civic Education and Social Diversity," *Ethics*, vol. 105, no. 3 (April 1995), pp. 557–579.)

43. Rawls, *Political Liberalism*, p. 94.

44. See Paul Berman, "Who's Afraid of Tariq Ramadan? The Islamist, the Journalist, and the Defense of Liberalism," *New Republic*, June 4, 2007.

45. Ibid., p. 15.

46. Kurt Baier, "Justice and the Aims of Political Philosophy," *Ethics*, vol. 99 (July 1989), pp. 776–77.

INTRODUCTION TO PART II

1. Rawls, *Political Liberalism*, p. 103.

2. Ibid., p. 30.

3. See Brian Barry, *Culture and Equality*, pp. 124, 128; William Galston, *Liberal Pluralism* (Cambridge: Cambridge University Press, 2002), pp. 104, 122; Joseph Raz, "Multiculturalism: A Liberal Perspective," p. 166; Chandran Kukathas, "Are There Any Cultural Rights?" pp. 117, 126–28; Parekh, *Rethinking Multiculturalism*, p. 218.

4. "Political liberalism will ask that children's education include such things as knowledge of their constitutional and civic rights so that, for example, they know that liberty of conscience exists in their society and that apostasy is not a crime, all this to ensure that their continued membership in a religious sect when they become of age is not based simply on ignorance of their basic rights or fear of punishment for offences that do not exist" (Rawls, *Political Liberalism*, p. 199). See also Ackerman, *Social Justice in the Liberal State* (New Haven: Yale University Press, 1980), pp. 153–54; Galston, *Liberal Pluralism*, pp. 93–109; Barry, *Culture and Equality*, p. 124; Raz, "Multiculturalism: A Liberal Perspective," p. 166; Parekh, *Rethinking Multiculturalism*, p. 203; Will Kymlicka, *Multicultural Citizenship*, p. 82; Amy Gutmann, "Civic Education and Social Diversity"; Macedo, "Liberal Civic Education and Religious Fundamentalism"; Richard Arneson and Ian Shapiro, "Democratic Autonomy and Religious Freedom: A Critique of *Wisconson v. Yoder*," in Ian Shapiro, ed., *Democracy's Place* (Ithaca, N.Y.: Cornell University Press, 1996).

5. See Parekh, *Rethinking Multiculturalism*, p. 275; Barry, *Culture and Equality*, p. 158; Kymlicka, *Multicultural Citizenship*, p. 41.

6. See Parekh, *Rethinking Multiculturalism*, pp. 276–77; Barry, *Culture and Equality*, p. 124; Kymlicka, *Multicultural Citizenship*, p. 41.

7. See Kymlicka, *Multicultural Citizenship*, p. 158; Parekh, *Rethinking Multiculturalism*, p. 321.

8. Rawls, *A Theory of Justice*, p. 370.

9. This is not a commitment to taking special measures to preserve any *particular* life form or culture if it is losing adherents over time because of the appeal of other life forms: "It has to be admitted that liberal multiculturalism is not opposed in principle to the assimilation of one cultural group by others. In some countries, some of the constituent cultures may lose their vitality and be gradually absorbed by others. So long as the process is not coerced, does not arise out of a lack of respect for people and their communities, and is gradual, there is nothing wrong in it. The dying of cultures is as much a part of normal life as the birth of new ones" (Raz, "Multiculturalism: A Liberal Perspective," p. 167).

10. Rawls, *Political Liberalism*, p. 41.

11. John Gray, "What Is Dead and What Is Living in Liberalism?" in *Post-Liberalism*, p. 288.

12. Rorty, *Contingency, Irony, Solidarity*, p. xiv.

13. This I take to be part of the concern (in, for example, Rawls's shifts from *A Theory of Justice* to *Political Liberalism*) to assert a freestanding public justification for liberal institutions. As has been widely noted (see Kymlicka, *Multicultural Citizenship*, p. 164), for all of Rawls's retreats, none of them comes in the area of the substantive content of justice. He keeps all the same rights, liberties, and primary goods while altering the public reasons for having them (as well as the account of stability). There is clearly a diagnostic element to this concern (we want to *know* that we are not being unfair to nonliberals, and one way to do so is to show that we could arrive at the same rights and liberties without assuming a liberal metaphysics), but I assume the concern with that, given that citizens are not treated any differently from one theory to the next, is that we think one way we might be unfair is to ask someone to affirm the truth of something (like the ultimate importance of individual autonomy) that they don't—can't—believe.

14. See Jeff Spinner-Halev, "Cultural Pluralism and Partial Citizenship," in *Multicultural Questions*, ed. Christian Joppke and Steve Lukes (Oxford: Oxford University Press, 1999), pp. 65–86.

CHAPTER 3

1. For a similar diagnosis of the main doctrinal questions and a brief overview of some of the main sources canvassed in the following chapters, see Wasif Shadid and Sjoerd van Koningsveld, "Loyalty to a Non-Muslim Government: An Analysis of Islamic Normative Discussions and of the Views of Some Contemporary Islamicists," in Shadid and van Koningsveld, eds., *Political Participation and Identities of Muslims in Non-Muslim States*, pp. 84–114.

2. Islamic tradition holds that Q. 22:39–40 ("Permission is given to those who fight because they have been wronged. God indeed has the power to help them, those who have been driven out of their houses without right only because they said 'God is our Lord.' Had God not used some men to keep back others, cloisters and churches and oratories and mosques wherein the name of God is constantly mentioned would have been destroyed. Assuredly God will help those who help Him, for verily God is the Most Powerful, Almighty.") are the first verses to address the problem of war and the first to give permission to Muslims to defend themselves. It is commonly held that these verses were revealed at the end of the first Meccan period at the time when Muhammad was preparing to depart for Medīna. See Abū Ja'far al-Ṭabarī (d. 310/923), *Jāmi' al-bayān fī ta'wīl al-Qur'ān* (Beirut: Dār al-Kutub al-'Ilmiyya, 1999), v. 9, pp. 160–166. He relates,

for example, on the authority of Ibn 'Abbās that in relation to verse Q. 22:39 ("Permission is given to those who fight because they have been wronged. God indeed has the power to help them"), "Abū Bakr said: 'It was known that there would be fighting and this was the first [such] verse to be revealed' " (p. 161).

3. Ibn Hishām, *al-Sīra al-Nabawiyya* (Cairo: Muṣṭafā al-Bābī al-Ḥalabī, 1936), v. 2, p. 111. English translation: Alfred Guillaume, *The Life of Muḥammad: A Translation of Isḥāq's* Sīrat Rasūl Allāh (London: Oxford University Press, 1955), p. 213.

4. Khaled Abou El Fadl, "Islamic Law and Muslim Minorities: The Juristic Discourse on Muslim Minorities from the Second/Eighth to the Eleventh/Seventeenth Centuries," *Islamic Law and Society*, vol 1, no. 2 (August 1994), pp. 141–42.

5. Tariq Ramadan writes that "one of the most frequent questions among Muslims living in the West is to know whether they are allowed to live in Europe or the United States or not, for these areas are part of *dār al-ḥarb* or, at least, of *dār al-kufr*. . . . The question of determining whether a Muslim was or was not permitted to live in a non-Muslim country or area appeared very early on as an issue in Islamic *fiqh*" (*To Be a European Muslim*, p. 165). See also Yūsuf al-Qaraḍāwī, *Fī fiqh al-aqalliyyāt al-muslima* (Cairo: Dār al-Shurūq, 2001), p. 25, where he lists the question of the legality of residing in a non-Muslim state as the first of the "juridical" problems facing Muslim minorities. See also Khālid 'Abd al-Qādir, *Fiqh al-aqalliyyāt al-muslima* (Tripoli: Dār al-Īmān, 1998), pp. 119–35; and Ibn Bayya, *Ṣinā'at al-fatwā wa-fiqh al-aqalliyāt*, pp. 280–85.

6. Supposedly related by the Ummayad Caliph Mu'āwiya. Recorded in Abū Dāwūd, *Sunan Abī Dāwūd, Kitāb al-Jihād* (9), *Bāb fī'l-hijra hal inqaṭa'at* (2), 2379 (Beirut: Dār Ibn Ḥazm, 1997), v. 3, p. 8; Aḥmad Ibn Ḥanbal, *al-Musnad*, 1671 (Cairo: Dār al-Ma'ārif, 1950).

7. Muḥammad is reported in the canonical collections of *ḥadīth* to have said in this in justification of his commanding that only half the blood-price be paid for Muslims killed while in prayer by a squadron of his own troops. The slaughtered Muslims were living at the time among non-Muslims. See, e.g., al-Nasā'ī, *al-Sunan al-kubrā, Kitāb al-Qasāma* (65), no. 6972 (2) (Beirut: Dār al-Kutub al-'Ilmiyya, 1991); and al-Tirmidhī, *al-Jāmi' al-ṣaḥīḥ, Kitāb al-Siyar* (22), *Bāb mā jā' fī karāhiyat al-maqām bayn aẓhur al-mushrikīn* (42), no. 1604 (Beirut: Dār al-Kutub al-'Ilmiyya, n.d.), v. 4, p. 132.

8. Abū Dāwūd, *Sunan Abī Dāwūd, Kitāb al-Jihād* (9), *Bāb al-iqāma bi-arḍ al-shirk* (182), 2787, v. 3, p. 152; al-Tirmidhī, *al-Jāmi' al-ṣaḥīḥ, Kitāb al-Siyar* (22), *Bāb mā jā' fī karāhiyat al-maqām bayn aẓhur al-mushrikīn* (42), no. 1605, v. 4, p. 133.

9. Ibn Ḥanbal, *al-Musnad*, no. 1671.

10. In chapter 5, I introduce the Islamic positions that hold that residence is permissible under certain conditions, partially on the basis of a certain set of *ḥadīth* reports that declare the *hijra* to be over with the conquest of Mecca. I note here only that there is a scholarly tradition of not regarding those *ḥadīth* reports as suspending the duty to migrate from non-Islamic lands but rather as suspending the narrow duty to migrate to where the Prophet is or to migrate away from Mecca. See Shaykh 'Abd al-'Azīz ibn Ṣāliḥ al-Jarbū', "al-I'lām bi-wujūb al-hijra min dār al-kufr ilā dār al-Islām." (This is a treatise by a contemporary Saudi scholar distributed on the Internet and is on file with the author.)

11. Ahmad b. Yahya al-Wansharīsī, *al-Mi'yār al-mu'rib wa'l-jāmi' al-mughrib 'an fatāwā ahl Ifrīqiya wa'l-Andalus wa'l-Maghrib*, ed., Muḥammad Hajjī (Rabat: Ministry of Religious Endowments and Islamic Affairs, 1981), pp. 121–22. For more on this text and its author, cf. David S. Powers, "Fatwās as Sources for Legal and Social History," *al-Qanṭara*, vol. 11 (1990), pp. 295-341. We still find an identical judgment rendered on virtually the same grounds, and in virtually the same language, by a nineteenth-century Egyptian

Mālikī. See Muḥammad b. Aḥmad 'Ulaysh (sometimes "'Illaysh," d. 1882), *Fatḥ al-'alī al-mālik fī'l-fatwā 'alā madhhab al-Imām Mālik* (Cairo: Dār al-Fikr, 1937), vol. 1, pp. 375–76.

12. Muḥammad b. Aḥmad al-Sarakhsī (d. 483/1090), *Kitāb al-Mabsūṭ* (Beirut: Dār al-Kutub al-'Ilmiyya, 2001), vol. 10, p. 84. This text remained a foundational reference for Ḥanafī law until the nineteenth century.

13. Sayyid Quṭb, *Fī Ẓilāl al-Qur'ān* (Beirut: Dār al-Shurūq, 1979), v. 2, pp. 745. English translation: *In the Shade of the Qur'ān*, Adil Salahi and Ashur Shamis, trans. and eds. (Leicester: Islamic Foundation, 2001), vol. 3, p. 286.

14. In tracking the range of positions in the classical sources, I am deeply indebted to Abou El Fadl's article, "Islamic Law and Muslim Minorities," which provides a thorough survey of the classical and medieval sources.

15. This is a view particularly popular amongst jurists of the Mālikī school of Islamic law. See 'Abd al-Salām b. Sa'īd Saḥnūn (d. 240/854), *al-Mudawwana al-kubrā* (Cairo, Dār al-Fikr, n.d.), vol. 3, p. 278; and Abū al-Walīd Muḥammad b. Aḥmad Ibn Rushd (d. 520/1126), *al-Muqaddimāt al-mumahhidāt*, ed. Sa'īd Aḥmad A'rāb (Beirut: Dār al-Gharb al-Islāmī, 1988), vol. 2, p. 151. Ibn Rushd (the grandfather of the philosopher known in the West as Averroës), citing Ibn Qāsim, a contemporary of Mālik on whose questions Saḥnūn's *Mudawwana* is based, reports that Mālik "strongly abhorred travel to the lands of war for trade by land or by sea [where] one is subject to their laws. And the grounds for his abhorrence of it is that God has made *hijra* to the lands of the Muslims obligatory for anyone who converts in the lands of disbelief so that he might be subject to the laws of Islam." He proceeds to invoke the previously cited Q. 8:72 and 4:97–98 by way of proof. This view is repeated by al-Wansharīsī (p. 124). In modern times, those who maintain the idea of a prohibition tend rather to be Saudi "Wahhabi" scholars who would otherwise incline toward the Ḥanbalī school. A prominent contemporary Mālikī, 'Abd Allāh Ibn Bayya, regards residence in non-Muslim lands as permissible for all of the same reasons traditionally held by Shāfi'ī, Ḥanafī, and Ḥanbalī scholars (*Ṣinā'at al-fatwā wa-fiqh al-aqalliyāt*, pp. 284–85).

16. Islamic law uses the term *'adāla* (lit.: "justness") to refer to a Muslim's probity, piety, and uprightness, the judgment of which determines such things as whether he can testify in court, lead prayer, or occupy public offices.

17. *Fatwā* of al-Māzarī quoted in al-Wansharīsī, *al-Mi'yār al-mu'rib*, pp. 133–34.

18. Ibid., p. 134.

19. Ibid., pp. 138–39 (all immediately preceding quotations).

20. Ibid., p. 132.

21. Ibid., pp. 137–38.

22. Ṣāliḥ ibn Muḥammad al-Shithrī, *Ḥukm al-lujū' wa'l-iqāma fī bilād al-kuffār* (Riyad: Dār al-Ḥabīb, n.d.), p. 13.

23. Shaykh 'Abd al-'Azīz ibn Ṣāliḥ al-Jarbū', "Al-ta'sīl li-mashrū'iyyat ma ḥasala li-Amrīka min tadmīr." (Like his previously cited treatise on *hijra*, this text has been available on the Internet and is on file with the author.)

24. See, for example, al-Ṭabarī, *Jāmi' al-bayān*, vol. 4, pp. 235–36; Ḥusayn Ibn Mas'ūd al-Baghawī (d. 516/1117), *Ma'ālim al-tanzīl* (Beirut: Dār al-Ma'rifa, 1987), vol. 1, p. 469; al-Zamakhsharī (d. 528/1144), *al-Kashshāf* (Beirut: Dār al-Kitāb al-'Arabī, n.d.), vol. 1, p. 555; Abū 'Abd Allāh al-Qurṭubī (d. 671/1273), *al-Jāmi' li-aḥkām al-Qur'ān*, ed. 'Abd al-Razzāq al-Mahdī (Beirut: Dār al-Kitāb al-'Arabī, 1997), vol. 5, p. 328; Ismā'īl ibn 'Umar Ibn Kathīr (774/1373), *Tafsīr al-Qur'ān al-'aẓīm* (Beirut: Dār al-Kutub al-'Ilmiyya, 1998), vol. 2, p. 343; Jalāl al-Dīn 'Abd al-Raḥmān al-Suyūṭī (d. 911/1505) *al-Durr al-manthūr fī tafsīr al-ma'thūr* (Beirut: Dār al-Kutub al-'Ilmiyya, 1990), vol. 2, p. 365. Modern exegesis: Muḥammad Rashīd Riḍā, *Tafsīr al-Qur'ān al-ḥakīm al-shahīr bi-tafsīr*

al-manār (Beirut: Dār al-Ma'rifa, 1973), vol. 5, p. 353; Sayyid Quṭb, *Fī Ẓilāl al-Qur'ān*, vol. 2, pp. 738–39, and *In the Shade of the Qur'ān*, vol. 3, p. 276. All of these exegetes use the expression "*takthīr sawād al-kuffār*" or something similar to describe the effect of the failure of certain Muslims to perform *hijra* to Medina.

25. Muwaffaq al-Dīn Ibn Qudāma (d. 620/1223), *al-Mughnī* (Cairo: Hajar, 1990), vol. 13, p. 151. This scholar was himself a migrant from Jerusalem to Damascus because of persecution at the hands of the Crusaders. This identical position is also found in the Shāfi'ī and Ḥanafī schools. See Abū Isḥāq al-Shīrāzī (d. 476/1083), *al-Muhadh-dhab fī fiqh al-Imām al-Shāfi'ī* (Beirut: Dār al-Fikr, n.d.), vol. 2, p. 227; Abū Zakariyyā' al-Nawawī (d. 676/1277), *al-Majmū' sharḥ al-Muhadhdhab* (Beirut: Dār al-Fikr, 2000), vol. 21, p. 5; and (Ḥanafī) al-Buhūtī (d. 1051/1641), *Kashshāf al-qinā'* (al-Riyāḍ: Maktabat al-Naṣr al-Ḥadītha, 1968), vol. 5, p. 44.

26. *Ta'rīḍ*, which can refer to speaking or suggesting something in an oblique, indirect, or ambiguous manner. It might include statements that are technically not lies but designed to fulfill the purpose of misleading an interrogator. Contemporary Ibn Taymiyya scholar Yahya Michot has understood this to be rather a suggestion of bribery or subornation. See Yahya Michot, *Mardin: Hégire, fuite du péché et «demeure de l'Islam»* (Beirut/Paris: al-Bouraq, 2004), p. 66.

27. Aḥmad Ibn Taymiyya (d. 682/1283), *Majmū' fatāwā Shaykh al-Islām Aḥmad Ibn Taymiyya* (Rabat: Maktabat al-Ma'ārif, 1980), vol. 28, p. 240.

28. Sayyid Quṭb, *Fī Ẓilāl al-Qur'ān*, vol. 2, pp. 732–33; *In the Shade of the Qur'ān*, vol. 3, p. 264. Emphasis added. Note that in Quṭb's text the phrase is no longer "*takthīr sawād al-kuffār*" but the less obscure "*yunāṣirūn a'dā' al-muslimīn.*"

29. However, it is noteworthy that in the modern context the most prominent Saudi Ḥanbalī jurists have advanced the more uncompromising position that *hijra* is a categorical duty and that adopting the citizenship of a non-Muslim country may constitute disbelief. The phrase "increasing the strength/numbers of the unbelievers" (*takthīr sawād al-kuffar*) figures consistently in *fatāwā* issued by the Saudi Standing Committee among their explanations for this ruling. See al-Shithrī, *Ḥukm al-lujū'*, pp. 4, 10.

30. A later Egyptian Mālikī made precisely the point that if a Muslim becomes subject to the laws of unbelievers, he should migrate. Failing to do is a sin, but not apostasy. See 'Alī al-Ṣa'īdī al-'Adawī (d. 1775), *Hāshiya 'alā kifāyat al-ṭālib al-rabbānī* (Cairo: Muṣṭafā al-Bābī al-Ḥalabī, 1952), vol. 2, p. 4.

31. Al-Wansharīsī, *al-Mi'yār al-mu'rib*, pp. 123–24.

32. Al-Shithrī, *Ḥukm al-lujū'*, pp. 3–4, 28–30.

33. Saḥnūn, *al-Mudawwana*, vol. 3, p. 278.

34. Al-Wansharīsī, *al-Mi'yār al-mu'rib*, pp. 137–38.

35. Muhammad Salih al-Munajjid, "Living in a Non-Muslim Country Seeking a Better Life," http://www.islamonline.net/fatwa/english/FatwaDisplay.asp?hFatwaID+110859. See also al-Shithrī, *Ḥukm al-lujū'*, pp. 4–5; al-Majlis al-Urubbī li'l-Iftā' wa'l-Buḥūth, *Fatāwā al-majmū'a al-ūlā* (Cairo: Maktabat al-Īmān, 1999)/European Council for *Fatwa* and Research, *First Collection of Fatwas* (Cairo: Islamic Publishing, 1999), p. 25; al-Qaraḍāwī, *Fī fiqh al-aqalliyyāt*, p. 25; Sulaymān Muḥammad Tūbūlyāk (transliteration from Bosnian of "Sulejman Topoljak"), *al-Aḥkām al-siyāsiyya li'l-aqalliyyāt al-muslima fi'l-fiqh al-Islāmī* (Beirut: Dār al-Nafā'is, 1997), p. 49.

36. Al-Sarakhsī, *al-Mabsūṭ*, vol. 10, p. 84.

37. Muzammil H. Siddiqi, "Immigration to a non-Muslim Country," http://www.islamonline.net/fatwa/english/FatwaDisplay.asp?hFatwaID+77860. See also Syed Abul Hasan Ali Nadwi, *Muslims in the West: The Message and Mission* (Leicester: Islamic

Foundation, 1983), pp. 113–14; Tūbūlyāk, *al-Aḥkām al-siyāsiyya*, p. 55; al-Majlis al-Urubbī li'l-Iftā' wa'l-Buḥūth, *Fatāwā*/European Council for *Fatwa* and Research, *First Collection of Fatwas*, p. 25; al-Qaraḍāwī, *Fī fiqh al-aqalliyyāt*, p. 25; Ibn Bayya, *Ṣinā'at al-fatwā wa-fiqh al-aqalliyāt*, p. 284.

38. Al-Shithrī, *Ḥukm al-lujū'*, p. 5.

39. Multivolume compendia of Islamic legal rulings (as opposed to books of *uṣūl* dealing with the theory of jurisprudence), as well as *ḥadīth* collections, place discussions into major sections called *kutub*, or "books". Every comprehensive collection includes as part of the treatment of the *mu'āmalāt* (interpersonal or social relations) a "Book of *Jihād*" outlining the rules of war (both *jus ad bellum* and *jus in bello*) but also, as seen here, questions related to travel to and residence in the "Abode of War."

40. Thus, even a contemporary Islamic Modernist scholar (who will surface in chapter 6 as a prominent theorist of a reformed just war doctrine for Islam) writes: "A Muslim is a firm and secular foundation for the construction of the Islamic society. He does not infringe on any of his community's rights, does not commit perfidy against it and does not betray it. He does not spy for the enemies nor does he display any kindness or inclination to them except in a small measure if it is required for the greater general interest. Nor does he help the enemies nor act in any way against the welfare of his faithful, believing community" (Wahba al-Zuḥaylī, *al-Tafsīr al-wasīṭ* (Damascus: Dār al-Fikr, 2001), vol. 1, p. 185–86.

41. Q. 4:95: "Not equal are those believers who sit [at home] and receive no hurt, and those who strive and fight in the cause of God with their goods and their persons. God has granted a grade higher to those who strive and fight with their goods and persons than to those who sit [at home]. Unto all has God promised good, but those who strive and fight has He distinguished above those who sit [at home] by a special reward."

42. I will argue for what I believe to be the reasonable demands of civic loyalty, including on the question of military service, in the next chapter.

43. The question raised by this verse is whether "life which God has forbidden" includes all innocent human life or is a specific reference to inviolable Muslim life. Either way, it covers Muslim life for sure. See note 44 for a *ḥadīth* that restricts the death penalty to those who kill fellow Muslims.

44. It should be noted that according to the law of just retaliation (*qiṣāṣ*) in most of the legal schools, a Muslim is to be killed only for killing a fellow Muslim, not an unbeliever, according to a *ḥadīth* to be found listed under the book of blood-money (*Kitāb al-Diyāt*) in Bukhārī's *Ṣaḥīḥ*. This does not preclude that a non-Muslim family may have the right to other compensation for the unlawful killing of a member. Two qualifications here apply: The Ḥanafī school applies the law of just retaliation to the homicide or manslaughter of non-Muslims as well, consistent with that school's tendency to regard territoriality more heavily than the other schools. Also, Islamic law contains the separate category of *ghīla*, or premeditated murder without anger or spite, for which some schools prescribe the death penalty regardless of the family's civil claims. (I am grateful to Mohammad Fadel for this clarification.)

45. Al-Bukhārī, *Ṣaḥīḥ*, Kitāb al-Diyāt. Also in Muslim, *Ṣaḥīḥ*, Kitāb al-Qasāma wa'l-muḥāraba, wa'l-qiṣāṣ wa'l-diyāt.

46. Al-Bukhārī, *Ṣaḥīḥ*, Kitāb al-Diyāt.

47. In al-Bukhārī, *Ṣaḥīḥ*, Kitāb al-Fitan. It is this *ḥadīth* and the next that Yūsuf al-Qaraḍāwī relies on to justify his ruling that it is not permitted to serve in a non-Muslim army against Muslims: "Islam has prohibited a Muslim to fight his fellow Muslim brother to the extent that indulging in such a fight is considered a form of

disbelief or *kufr* and a behavior pertaining to jahiliyya. The Prophet is reported to have said: 'Cursing the Muslim is lewdness and killing him is disbelief.' [And:] 'If two Muslims meet with their swords then both the killer and the killed are in the fire [for] the killed was eager to kill his opponent.'" (See http://www.islamonline.net/fatwa/english/FatwaDisplay.asp?hFatwaID=52014.)

48. Al-Bukhārī, *Ṣaḥīḥ*, Kitāb al-fitan. Also in Muslim, *Ṣaḥīḥ*, Kitāb al-fitan wa ashrāṭ al-sā'a.

49. Al-Bukhārī, *Ṣaḥīḥ*, Kitāb al-Fitan.

50. Ibn Mājah, *Sunan*, Kitāb al-Fitan.

51. Ibid.

52. Guillaume, *The Life of Muhammad*, p. 232.

53. For example, Ibn Taymiyya, *Majmū' al-fatāwā*, vol. 28, p. 539. Present-day scholars 'Abd al-Qādir and Topoljak (Tūbūlyāk) both cite this as the consensus opinion.

54. Rashīd Riḍā, *Fatāwā*, vol. 5, pp. 1749–50.

55. Ottoman Jihad Fatwa of 11 November, 1914, translated in Rudolph Peters, *Jihad in Classical and Modern Islam* (Princeton, N.J.: Markus Wiener, 1996), p. 57.

56. At http://www.islamonline.net/fatwa/english/FatwaDisplay.asp?hFatwaID==49987. See also Tūbūlyāk, *al-Aḥkām al-siyāsiyya*, p. 122, where he calls it "amongst the greatest sins and most abominable crimes."

57. See, for example, (Shāfi'ī) al-Nawawī, *al-Majmū'*, vol. 21, pp. 3–9; (Ḥanbalī) Ibn al-Qudāma, *al-Mughnī*, vol. 13, pp. 7–10; (Mālikī) Ibn Rushd (Averroës), *Bidāyat al-mujtahid wa nihāyat al-muqtaṣid* (Beirut, Dār al-Kutub al-'Ilmiyya, 1996), vol. 3, pp. 407–9.

58. An *amān* is a guarantee of safety offered to aliens visiting or residing in a territory. A person under an *amān* is a *musta'min*. The terms of Muslims living under an *amān* (*al-muslimūn al-musta'minūn*) in a non-Muslim state are explored in chapter 6 as a possible authentic Islamic resource for justifying obligations to non-Muslim states.

59. Al-Sarakhsī, *al-Mabsūṭ*, vol. 10, p. 106.

60. Al-Qurṭubī, *al-Jāmi' li-Aḥkām al-Qur'ān*, vol. 8., p. 97.

61. Ottoman Jihad Fatwa in Peters, *Jihad in Classical and Modern Islam*, pp. 56–57.

62. Sayyid Abul 'Alā Mawdūdī, *Towards Understanding the Qur'ān* (Leicester: Islamic Foundation, 1990), vol. 3, pp. 209–10.

63. See 'Abd al-Qādir, *Fiqh al-aqalliyyāt*, pp. 158–64.

64. This point is made explicitly by Shaykh 'Abd al-Mun'im Muṣṭafā Ḥalīma (Abū Baṣīr al-Ṭarṭūsī), a Syrian scholar living in London who is considered a theorist of "Salafī jihadism" but is also known for issuing a series of widely read *fatwās* forbidding suicide terrorism. He writes that "these so-called martyrdom operations are considered, as far as the method and the means used, to be a modern phenomenon, and thus it is possible that there will be room for individual religious interpretation (*ijtihād*) and legitimate difference of opinion (*ikhtilāf*) on them amongst the religious scholars" (http://www.abubaseer.bizland.com; September 23, 2005).

65. Ibn Ḥazm belonged to a now defunct legal school known as the Ẓahirī school, known for its literalism in textual interpretation. Possibly for this reason, Ibn Ḥazm's writings are popular among present-day jihadis.

66. "al-Ta'ṣīl li-mashrū'iyyat mā ḥasala li-Amrīka min tadmīr," p. 38.

67. "al-Ta'ṣīl li-mashrū'iyyat mā jarā fī Landan min tafjīrāt wa'l-radd 'alā'l-bayān al-mash'ūm li-Abī Baṣīr al-Ṭarṭūsī," p. 11. (The title "Establishing the Legitimacy of the Explosions Which Occurred in London and a Response to the Vile Declaration of Abū Baṣīr al-Ṭarṭūsī" parallels almost exactly Jarbū's text on 9/11, which it cites as its main source of authority.) This text can be found on the Internet and is on file with the author.

68. See Jarbūʿ,"al-Ta'sīl li-mashrūʿiyyat mā ḥasala li-Amrīka min tadmīr," pp. 9–10, for the argument that the basic principle (*al-aṣl*) of relations with infidels is war and p. 23 for the argument that only a caliph or "Great Imam" can make treaties with infidels binding on all Muslims.

69. "al-Ta'ṣīl li-mashrūʿiyyat mā jarā fi Landan," p. 22.

70. Jarbūʿ, "al-Ta'sīl li-mashrūʿiyyat mā ḥasala li-Amrīka min tadmīr," p. 38.

71. "al-Ta'ṣīl li-mashrūʿiyyat mā jarā fi Landan," p. 7.

72. It is not clear whether this position has been articulated formally by an Islamic legal scholar. It can be found, however, in the statements of Islamist activists in the United Kingdom. Hassan Butt, an activist who split from the U.K. Salafi groups Hizb ut-Tahrir and al-Muhajiroun over the principle that British Muslims are not permitted to engage in violence in Britain, is reported to have said:

> Now, I am not in favour of military action in Britain but if somebody did do it who was British, I would not have any trouble with that either. . . . It wouldn't necessarily be the wisest thing to do but it wouldn't be un-Islamic. . . . Most of our people, especially the youth, are British citizens. They owe nothing to the Government. They did not ask to be born here; neither did they ask to be protected by Britain. . . . They have no covenant. As far as I'm concerned, the Islamic *hukm* (order) that I follow, says that a person has no covenant whatsoever with the country in which they were born." (Aatish Taseer, "A British Jihadist," *Prospect*, issue 113, August 2005.)

Butt does not cite any Islamic text or scholar for this opinion. (The same Butt later publicly renounced jihadism and proclaimed a willingness to collaborate with British security forces (Hassan Butt, "My Plea to Fellow Muslims: You Must Renounce Terror," *Observer*, July 1, 2007).)

73. This is reported to have occurred via Webcast but then reaffirmed publicly. See *The Times*, January 17, 2005, at http://www.timesonline.co.uk/tol/news/uk/article 413387.ece.

74. Ibn Taymiyya, *Fatāwā*, vol. 28, p. 240.

75. Tūbūlyāk, *al-Aḥkām al-siyāsiyya*, p. 117.

76. See the Sarakhsī quotation given later. See also ʿAbd al-Qādir, *Fiqh al-aqalliyyāt al-muslima*, p. 170, quoting Mālik.

77. Al-Shaybānī, *The Islamic Law of Nations: Shaybānī's Siyar*, Majid Khadduri, trans. (Baltimore: Johns Hopkins University Press, 1966), p. 193. Emphasis added.

78. Al-Sarakhsī, *al-Mabsūṭ*, vol. 10, p. 106. This view is also to be found in Ibn al-Humām, vol. 6, p. 18; and Zayn ibn Ibrāhīm ibn Muḥammad Ibn Nujaym (d. 1563), *al-Baḥr al-rā'iq* (Beirut: Dār al-Maʿrifa, 1993), vol. 5, p. 107.

79. See ʿAbd al-Qādir, *Fiqh al-aqalliyyāt al-muslima*, pp. 621–22.

80. In a *fatwā* on Russian Muslims serving in the Russian army during the Russo-Japanese war, Rashīd Riḍā outlines an argument for serving in non-Muslim armies based on the Islamic obligation to acquire military knowledge and skills and to present an image of strength. (This *fatwā* is discussed at length in chapter 6 as a possible compatible doctrine. See Riḍā, *Fatāwā*, vol. 2, pp. 565–66.) Topoljak makes a similar point, with greater emphasis on the categorical duty to prepare for *jihād*, which for some Muslims may be possible only in non-Muslim armies. (See Tūbūlyāk, *al-Aḥkām al-siyāsiyya*, pp. 112–13.)

81. Tūbūlyāk, *al-Aḥkām al-siyāsiyya*, pp. 119–21.

82. ʿAbd al-Qādir, *Fiqh al-aqalliyyāt al-muslima*, p. 38.

83. Al-Nawawī: "With verses 9:5, 2:191 and 2:193 God permitted fighting [unbelievers] without qualification or condition." (al-Nawawī, *al-Majmū'*, vol. 21, p. 10.) Ibn Qudāma: "A permanent contract of protection and inviolability (*dhimma*) is only permissible on two conditions: (1) that they oblige themselves to pay the *jizya* and (2) the bindingness of Islamic rules over them." (Ibn Qudāma, *al-Mughnī*, vol. 12, pp. 763–4.) For scholarship in English: Patricia Crone, *God's Rule: Government and Islam* (New York: Columbia University Press, 2004), pp. 358–85; Majid Khadduri, *War and Peace in the Law of Islam* (Baltimore: Johns Hopkins University Press, 1955), p. 145; Bassam Tibi, "War and Peace in Islam," in Sohail Hashmi, ed., *Islamic Political Ethics* (Princeton, N.J.: Princeton University Press, 2002), p. 176.

84. Abdulaziz Sachedina, "The Development of *Jihad* in Islamic Revelation and History," in James Turner Johnson and John Kelsay, eds., *Cross, Crescent and Sword: The Justification and Limitation of War in Western and Islamic Tradition* (London: Greenwood, 1990), p. 44.

85. "All the jurists, perhaps without exception, assert that polytheism and Islam cannot exist together; the polytheists, who enjoin other gods with Allah must choose between war or Islam" (Khadduri, *War and Peace in the Law of Islam*, p. 75).

86. Ann Elizabeth Mayer, "War and Peace in the Islamic Tradition and International Law," in John Kelsay and James Turner Johnson, eds., *Just War and Jihad: Historical and Theoretical Reflections on War and Peace in Western and Islamic Traditions* (Westport, Conn.: Greenwood, 1991), p. 198.

87. 9:5: "When the forbidden months are past, then fight and slay the pagans wherever you find them. Seize them, beleaguer them, and lie in wait for them in every stratagem of war. But if they repent and establish regular prayers and practice regular charity, then open the way for them. For God is Oft-Forgiving, Most-Merciful." 9:29: "Fight those who believe not in God nor in the Last Day, nor hold forbidden that which God and His Messenger have forbidden, nor acknowledge the religion of truth, from among the People of the Book until they pay the *jizya* and feel themselves subdued."

88. Quṭb, *Fī Ẓilāl al-Qur'ān*, vol. 3, p. 1582; *In the Shade of the Qur'ān*, Salahi trans., vol. 8, p. 28.

89. Ibid., vol. 3, p. 1620 (trans., vol. 8, pp. 101–2).

90. 'Abd al-Qādir, *Fiqh al-aqalliyyāt al-muslima*, p. 185. See also the traditionalist views on war and relations between Islamic and non-Islamic lands of Moroccan-Dutch preacher 'Abd Allāh al-Ṭā'i' al-Khamlīshī, *al-Janna wa-tarīquhā al-mustaqīm wa'l-nār wa-tarīquhā al-dhamīm* (Rotterdam: Masjid al-Naṣr, 1995).

91. *Al-Mukhālifūn*, signifying those who diverge, oppose or transgress, is his standard epithet for non-Muslims, rather than *kuffār/kāfirūn* or *mushrikūn*.

92. *Muwālāh*, meaning friendship, loyalty, or patronage.

93. 'Abd al-Qādir, *Fiqh al-aqalliyyāt al-muslima*, p. 154.

94. In the earliest period of Islam, for example, the concept refers to a specific legal relationship between an Arab-Muslim patron (*mawlā*) and his non-Arab convert or freed slave client. See Ibn Bayya, *Ṣinā'at al-fatwā wa-fiqh al-aqalliyāt* (p. 299), for a reference to this in relation to the modern debate over whether Muslims may be loyal to their non-Muslim states of citizenship and non-Muslim fellow citizens.

95. See Ibn Kathīr, *Tafsīr al-Qur'ān al-'aẓīm*, vol. 2, p. 390.

96. 'Abd al-Qādir, *Fiqh al-aqalliyyāt*, p. 626.

97. Ibn Bayya, *Ṣinā'at al-fatwā wa-fiqh al-aqalliyāt*, p. 306.

98. Quṭb, *In the Shade of the Qur'ān*, Salahi and Shamis, trans., v. II, pp. 62–63.

99. See Riḍā, *Tafsīr al-manār*, v. 3, pp. 276–77, for a summary of the various theories of the context of revelation for 3:28 and 60:1.

100. See Quṭb, *In the Shade of the Qur'ān*, Salahi and Shamis, trans., vol. 2, pp. 179–81.

101. See Ibn Kathīr, *Tafsīr al-Qur'ān al-'aẓīm*, vol. 3, p. 120.

102. See Khaled Abou El Fadl, "Muslim Minorities and Self-Restraint in Liberal Democracies," *Loyola of Los Angeles Law Review*, vol. 29, no. 4 (1996), pp. 1525–42, where he argues for the superiority of liberal institutions for Muslim minorities. His argument proceeds on the basis of public reason and Muslim self-interest, so is not an example of "Islamic reason" providing grounds for an overlapping consensus. Rāshid al-Ghannūshī, a Tunisian Islamist opposition leader in exile in Britain, also frequently makes the point that it is secularism and liberalism that have made the West hospitable to Muslims and not Abrahamic fraternity. (See al-Ghannūshī, "al-Islām fī'l-gharb wa 'alāqātuhu bi'l-anẓima al-gharbiyya," in Majdī 'Aqīl Abū Shamāla, ed., *Risālat al-Muslimīn fī bilād al-gharb* (Irbid, Jordan: Dār al-Amal, 1999), pp. 90, 115.)

103. In addressing the question of whether secular, "post-Christian" societies are no longer subject to the regard doctrinally due them as "Scripturary" (*kitābī*) societies, 'Abd al-Qādir argues that the secular nature of the political system is irrelevant because Moses and Jesus were sent with only temporary and partial messages anyway, so abandoning them is not something to worry about from an Islamic perspective: "Jesus was not sent to fix relations between rulers and the ruled, or to bring a law or identify the lawful and the prohibited." Thus, present-day secularism is not a departure from Christianity but a consequence of it ('Abd al-Qādir, *Fiqh al-aqalliyyāt*, pp. 23–25.).

104. See remarks by Qaraḍāwī in http://www.islamonline.net/fatwa/english/FatwaDisplay.asp?hFatwaID=8514.

105. Quṭb, *In the Shade of the Qur'ān*, Salahi and Shamis, trans., vol. 4, p. 144. 'Abd al-Qādir also insists that the tolerance and decent treatment required toward Jews and Christians does not imply the possibility of a "single front to resist atheism" (*Fiqh al-aqalliyyāt*, p. 646).

CHAPTER 4

1. This distinction is ubiquitous in Western political theory. See, in particular, Walzer, *Obligations*, pp. 226–27: "The alienated citizen receives whatever protection the state provides and lives every day with his fellows in the shadow of that protection. But he does not participate at all in political life; he chooses not to participate. He thinks of the state as an alien though not necessarily as a hostile force, and he wants only to live in peace under its jurisdiction." Jeff Spinner-Halev prefers the term "partial citizenship" to describe the attitude (not legal status) of communities who shy away from political participation and involvement in civil society, in *The Boundaries of Citizenship: Race, Ethnicity, and Nationality in the Liberal State* (Baltimore: Johns Hopkins University Press, 1994).

2. Walzer, "Political Alienation and Military Service," in *Obligations*, p. 100.

3. Islamic law is divided between the *'ibādāt* (matters pertaining to individual worship and rituals) and *mu'āmalāt* (matters pertaining to interpersonal and social relations).

4. "The nationalist sentiment that is sometimes used to justify loyalty at the expense of justice—such as when it is said 'my country, right or wrong'—will find little support in the Qur'anic vision of justice. Loyalty to one's country and community is recommended, and so is self-exertion and sacrifice for a good cause, but not if these mean compromising on impartial justice" (Mohammad Hashim Kamali, *Freedom*,

Equality and Justice in Islam (Leicester, UK: Islamic Texts Society, 1999), p. 115). Of course, this is a sentiment clearly shared by liberals.

5. "Justice as fairness honors, as far as it can, the claims of those who wish to withdraw from the modern world in accordance with the injunctions of their religion, provided only that they acknowledge the principles of the political conception of justice and appreciate its political ideals of person and society." Rawls, *Political Liberalism*, p. 200.

6. This is the position, for example, of the British group "al-Muhajiroun" ("The Migrants"), which supports terrorist attacks against the United Kingdom and the United States but only by Muslims not legally residing in those countries. See Shaykh Muhammad Afifi al-Akiti, *Defending the Transgressed by Censuring the Reckless against the Killing of Civilians* (Birmingham, U.K.: Aqsa, 2005), p. 17.

7. Identifying unreasonable or unjust views and even being concerned with containing them is not the same task as identifying when the propagation of unjust views is grounds for coercive state action. Suppressing speech, even hate speech, is still an infringement on liberal rights, and the burden of justification rests on those who would do so to show why the stability of a liberal society requires it. See Jonathan Quong, "The Rights of Unreasonable Citizens," *Journal of Political Philosophy*, vol. 12, no. 3 (2004), pp. 328–30.

8. "A person may conscientiously refuse to comply with his duty to enter the armed forces during a particular war on the ground that the aims of the conflict are unjust. It may be that the objective sought by war is economic advantage or national power. The basic liberty of citizens cannot be interfered with to achieve these ends. And, of course, it is unjust and contrary to the law of nations to attack the liberty of other societies for these reasons. Therefore a just cause for war does not exist, and this may be sufficiently evident that a citizen is justified in refusing to discharge his legal duty." Rawls, *A Theory of Justice*, p. 381.

9. This is, of course, a nuance not raised by Rawls, who assumes that it "may be sufficiently evident" whether the war is just. But this is a genuine problem and one not caused only by the plurality of comprehensive doctrines in a society. When does a country proclaim a war to be about economic advantage or national power and fail to provide a justification that is persuasive to many of its citizens? But in present circumstances, this assumption is unwarranted. Consider the rise in wars of intervention that claim a humanitarian justification, a justification based on the need to fight nonstate terrorism, or a justification based on the need to prevent future threats from states. These wars are deeply disputed as to their nature, purpose, and necessity in ways that both wars of self-defense after a direct invasion and open military adventures are not.

10. Gaus makes the distinction between defeated, undefeated, and victorious justifications in public deliberation. My point here is that the antiwar view could fail to be victorious but also remain undefeated according to the terms of public reason. See Gaus, *Justificatory Liberalism*, pp. 144–58.

11. An individual "can maintain that, all things considered, his natural duty not to be made the agent of grave injustice and evil to another outweighs his duty to obey" (Rawls, *A Theory of Justice*, p. 380).

12. "There are likely to be moments when all residents, aliens and citizens alike, are morally obligated to defend the state that defends their everyday social life. . . . The existence of borderline cases does not call the original distinction into question" (Walzer, "Political Alienation and Military Service," in *Obligations*, pp. 105–6).

13. See Faḍl Allah, *al-Hijra wa al-ightirāb*, pp. 80–81, for a presentation and refutation of this view.

14. Charles Taylor, "The Politics of Recognition," in Amy Gutmann (ed.), *Multiculturalism: Examining the Politics of Recognition* (Princeton, N.J.: Princeton University Press, 1994), pp. 25–26.

15. Benhabib, *The Claims of Culture*, p. 8.

16. Raz, "Multiculturalism: A Liberal Perspective," p. 163.

17. Note that the principle of neutrality might also require this. However, neutrality might also require that *all* religious or sectarian expressions be excluded from public space. Theorists of recognition or discourse ethics might agree with this in some cases (say, schools or courts) but would be more sensitive to how this "neutralization" of public space might advance a false neutrality or universalism that actually serves to marginalize and stigmatize various "others" even more. This might be the critique of the French policy of *laïcité* (including the ban on head scarves in schools and other public spaces) from the difference/recognition perspective, while from the liberal perspective, such a critique is grounded in the commitment to the specific values of freedom of worship and self-expression.

18. William Galston, *Liberal Pluralism*, p. 23, and "Who's a Liberal?" *Public Interest*, Summer 2001, p. 104. The reference is to the Aztec practice of human sacrifice, which Galston takes for granted would be a practice banned in a liberal democracy.

19. Barry, *Culture and Equality*, p. 133.

20. "While [liberal multiculturalism] respects a variety of cultures, it refuses to take them at their own estimation. In particular multiculturalism urges respect for cultures which are not themselves liberal cultures—very few are. As we shall see, it does so while imposing liberal protection of individual freedom on those cultures. This in itself brings it into conflict with the cultures it urges governments to respect. The conflict is inevitable because liberal multiculturalism recognizes and respects those cultures because and to the extent that they serve true values. Since its respect of cultures is conditional and granted from a point of view outside many of them, there is little surprise that it finds itself in uneasy alliance with supporters of those cultures, sometimes joining them in a common front while at others turning against them to impose ideals of toleration and mutual respect, or to protect the members of those very cultures against oppression by their own group" (Raz, "Multiculturalism: A Liberal Perspective," p. 168).

21. Another way of putting this is that political liberals resist the collapsing of all differences of *belief*, *value*, and *practice* into differences of *identity*. See Peter Jones, "Toleration, Recognition and Identity," *Journal of Political Philosophy*, vol. 14, no. 2 (2006), pp. 123–43.)

22. As Rousseau asserted pessimistically: "Those who distinguish between civil and theological intolerance are mistaken, in my opinion. Those two types of intolerance are inseparable. It is impossible to live in peace with those one believes to be damned. To love them would be to hate God who punishes them" (Jean-Jacques Rousseau, *The Social Contract*, book 4, chapter 8, in *The Basic Political Writings* (Indianapolis: Hackett), p. 227).

23. Rawls, *Political Liberalism*, p. 16.

24. Walzer, "Political Alienation and Military Service," in *Obligations*, p. 105.

25. For example, it is possible to argue for political participation in a state that one would not wish to defend or even to see exist. (Such might be the position of some Irish Republicans in Northern Ireland or Israeli Arabs.) Similarly, it is possible to

argue that one has a duty to defend one's state and to pay taxes, but that active political participation is for whatever reason unnecessary or unvirtuous.

CHAPTER 5

1. Abū Dāwūd, *Sunan Abī Dāwūd*, v. 3, p. 8.

2. For example, al-Shaybānī, *The Islamic Law of Nations: Shaybānī's Siyar,* p. 187; al-Ṭabarī, *Jāmi' al-bayān*, v. 4, pp. 147–51; al-Khaṭṭābī and al-Baghawī in al-Nawawī, *al-Majmū'*, v. 21, p. 7; *al-Fatāwā al-Hindiyya*, (Beirut: Dār Iḥyā' al-Turāth al-'Arabī, n.d.) v. 2, pp. 232, 311–12; v. 3., p. 584 Muḥammad ibn 'Abd al-Wāḥid al-Sīwāsī Ibn al-Humām, *Sharḥ fatḥ al-qadīr* (Beirut: Dār al-Fikr, n.d.), v. 5, p. 445. Modern jurists: Muḥammad Rashīd Riḍā, *Fatāwā al-Imām Muḥammad Rashīd Riḍā* (Beirut: Dār al-Kitāb al-Jadīd, 1980), ed. Ṣalāḥ al-Dīn al-Munajjid and Yūsuf Q. Khūrī, v. 2, pp. 774–75; Jād al-Ḥaqq 'Alī Jād al-Ḥaqq, "Fatwā fī ba'ḍ aḥkām tata'allaq bi'l-aqalliyyāt al-muslima fī ghayr diyār al-muslimīn," *Majallat al-Azhar*, vol. 63, no. 6 (1991), p. 618; 'Abd al-'Azīz ibn Muḥammad Ibn al-Siddīq, *Ḥukm al-iqāma bi-bilād al-kuffār wa-bayān wujūbihā fī b'aḍ al-aḥwāl* (Tangiers: Maṭābi' al-Būghāz, 1985), p. 30; Tūbūlyāk, *al-Aḥkām al-siyāsiyya*, pp. 52–53; Qaraḍāwī, *Fī fiqh al-aqalliyyāt*, p. 38; Zuḥaylī, *al-Tafsīr al-wasīṭ*, v. 1, p. 369.

3. Ibn Bayya, *Ṣinā'at al-fatwā wa-fiqh al-aqalliyāt*, pp. 280–85, 293–94.

4. As noted in chapter 3, pro-*hijra* jurists are aware of these following *ḥadīth* reports but do not regard them as removing the general obligation to migrate from lands of unbelief. Rather, they are explained as removing the obligation to migrate from Mecca once it is no longer outside the Islamic community. (See al-Jarbū', "al-I'lām bi-wujūb al-hijra.")

5. Reported to have been the response of the Prophet to a number of companions who inquired into the status of migration after the conquest, related by the Prophet's uncle, Ibn 'Abbās. See Aḥmad Ibn Ḥanbal, *al-Musnad*, 1991, 2396, 2898, 3335, 1184; Abū Dāwūd, *Sunan Abī Dāwūd, Kitāb al-Jihād, Bāb fī'l-hijra hal inqaṭa'at*, 2380, p. 8; al-Nasā'ī, *al-Sunan al-kubrā, Kitāb al-Bay'a* (73), *Bāb dhikr al-ikhtilāf fī inqitā' al-hijra* (18), 7792 (2), v. 4, p. 426; al-Tirmidhī, *al-Jāmi' al-ṣaḥīḥ* (Beirut: Dār al-Kutub al-'Ilmiyya, n.d.), *Kitāb al-Siyar* (22), *Bāb mā jā' fī'l-hijra* (33), 1590, v. 4., p. 126; Muslim, *Ṣaḥīḥ Muslim, Kitāb al-Imāra* (33), *Bāb al-mubāya'a ba'd fatḥ Makka* (20), 85 (1353) (Beirut: Dār Iḥyā' al-Turāth al-'Arabī, n.d.), v. 3, p. 1487; al-Bukhārī, 1834, 2783, 3077, 3080 in Ibn Ḥajar al-'Asqalānī, *Fatḥ al-Bārī sharḥ Ṣaḥīḥ al-Bukhārī* (Dār al-Kutub al-'Ilmiyya, 1989), v. 4, p. 58.

6. Al-Bukhārī, 4312 in Ibn Ḥajar, v. 8, p. 32.

7. Al-Nasā'ī, *al-Sunan al-kubrā, Kitāb al-Bay'a* (73), *Bāb dhikr al-ikhtilāf fī inqitā' al-hijra* (18), 7794 (4), p. 427.

8. Muslim, *Ṣaḥīḥ Muslim, Kitāb al-Imāra* (33), *Bāb al-mubāya'a ba'd fatḥ Makka* (20), 83 (1863), v. 3, p. 1487.

9. Abū Dāwūd, *Sunan Abī Dāwūd*, v. 3, p. 8. One finds this argument repeated by other scholars, including Khaṭṭābī, Baghawī and Nawawī. It is invoked also by Qaraḍāwī and the other jurists on the European Council for Fatwa and Research.

10. Qaraḍāwī: "Also, even if the [*ḥadīth*] are authentic, it is clear that they are set in a context when the polytheists were at war with Islam. Finally, the *ḥadīth* refers to the paying of the blood price, not a general ruling on co-habitation during peacetime" (*Fī fiqh al-aqalliyyāt al-muslima*, p. 38).

11. At http://www.islamonline.net/fatwa/english/FatwaDisplay.asp?hFatwaID+110859. See also Muhammad Khalid Masud, "Being a Muslim in a Non-Muslim Polity:

Three Alternative Models," *Journal of the Institute of Muslim Minority Affairs*, vol. 10, no. 1 (January 1989); Tūbūlyāk, *al-Aḥkām al-siyāsiyya*, p. 54.

12. In fact, the argument has been made since al-Shāfi'ī that even during the Medinan period, the duty to migrate was less than absolute, as evidenced by the Prophet's permission to certain Muslims to stay in Mecca or to live in other non-Muslim lands as long as they were protected and did not fear enticement away from their religion ["*idhā lam yakhāfū al-fitna fi'l-dīn*"]. See Muḥammad ibn Idrīs al-Shāfi'ī, *al-Umm*, v. 4, p. 161 and Tūbūlyāk, *al-Aḥkām al-siyāsiyya*, pp. 50–51.

13. Abū Dāwūd, *Sunan Abī Dāwūd*, v. 3, p. 8; al-Ṭabarī, *Jāmi' al-bayān*, v. 4, pp. 147–51; al-Zamakhsharī, *al-Kashshāf*, v. 1, p. 555; Ibn Qudāma, *al-Mughnī*, vol. 13, p. 151; al-Nawawī, *al-Majmū'*, v. 21, p. 5; Ibn Taymiyya, *Majmū' al-fatāwā*, v. 28, p. 240; Ibn al-Humām, *Fatḥ al-qadīr*, v. 5, pp. 445; al-Buhūtī, *Kashshāf al-qinā'*, v. 5, p. 44;

14. Al-Māwārdī, in al-Nawawī, *al-Majmū'*, v. 21, p. 7; Abū Bakr ibn Mas'ūd al-Kāsānī in *al-Fatāwā al-Hindiyya*, v. 2, pp. 232, 311–12, v. 3, p. 584; Ibn 'Abidīn, *Radd al-muḥtār*, v. 3, 252–53.

15. Nawawī: "If one hopes that by remaining Islam might spread in his place of residence, then it is obligatory that he reside there and not migrate, as well as if it is hoped that Islam might prevail there in the future" (*al-Majmū'*, v. 21, p. 5). Also, two other Shāfi'ī scholars: Ibn Ḥajar al-Haytamī (d. 974/1566–67), *al-Fatāwā al-kubrā al-fiqhiyya*, v. 4, pp. 52–53; al-Ramlī (d. 1004/1595–96), *Nihāyat al-muḥtāj*, v. 8, p. 82.

16. Al-Māwārdī, in al-Nawawī, *al-Majmū'*, v. 21, p. 7.

17. Ibn Bayya, *Ṣinā'at al-fatwā wa-fiqh al-aqalliyāt*, p. 285; Tūbūlyāk, *al-Aḥkām al-siyāsiyya*, p. 53; Qaraḍāwī, *Fī fiqh al-aqalliyyāt al-muslima*, pp. 33–34; Ṣāliḥ ibn Fawzān ibn 'Abd Allāh al-Fawzān, *Muḥāḍarāt fi'l-'aqīda wa'l-da'wa* (Riyadh: Dār al-'Āṣima, 1992), p. 236. For these points from a Shi'ite perspective, see (Grand Ayatollah) 'Alī al-Ḥusaynī al-Sīstānī, *al-Fiqh li'l-mughtaribīn* (London/Beirut: Mu'assasat al-Imām 'Alī, 2002), pp. 63–64.

18. Abou El Fadl, "Islamic Law and Muslim Minorities," p. 159.

19. At http://www.islam-online.net/fatwa/english/FatwaDisplay.asp?hFatwaID+-77860.

20. Aḥmad al-Ṣawī (d. 1241/1825), *Bulghat al-Sālik* (Cairo: Muṣṭafā al-Bābī al-Ḥalabī, 1952), v. 1, p. 361.

21. Ibn al-Humām, *Fatḥ al-qadīr*, v. 8, p. 131; and Ibn 'Abidīn, *Radd al-muḥtār*, v. 3, pp. 252–53.

22. Al-Nawawī, *al-Majmū'*, v. 21, p. 5.

23. Nadwi, *Muslims in the West*, pp. 113–14. Nadwi was heavily involved in the Tablighi Jama'at movement, a Sunni traditionalist movement that seeks to inculcate orthodox Islamic attitudes and morals among Muslim populations through preaching, missionary, and educational activities. It tends to be quietist and focused on the religiosity of Muslim communities, rather than their governments, an attitude visible in this quotation.

24. Muḥammad ibn Aḥmad al-Shirbīnī al-Khaṭīb, *Mughnī al-muḥtāj*, v. 4, p. 239; Ibn Qudāma, *al-Mughnī*, v. 10, pp. 381, 513–15; Ibn Kathīr, *Tafsīr*, v. 1, p. 427; 'Abd Allāh ibn Aḥmad al-Nasafī (d. 710/1310), *Tafsīr al-Nasafī: Madārik al-tanzīl wa haqā'iq al-ta'wīl* (Beirut: Dār Ibn Kathīr, 1998), v. 1, p. 342.

25. Michot, *Mardin*, p. 18.

26. Riḍā, Fatwa 290, "al-Hijra wa ḥukm muslimī al-Būsna fīha," in *Fatāwā*, v. 2, pp. 773–74. Emphasis added.

27. Ibid., p. 778.

28. For example, when discussing the expressions "manifesting religion" or "manifesting the signs of Islam," Bernard Lewis writes:

> For the modern Westerner, religious freedom is defined by the phrase "freedom of worship," and means just that. But the practice of Islam means more than worship, important as that may be. It means a whole way of life, prescribed in detail by the holy texts and treatises based on them. Nor is that all. The primary duty of the Muslim as set forth not once but many times in the Qur'ān is "to command good and forbid evil." It is not enough to do good and refrain from evil as a personal choice. It is incumbent upon Muslims also to command and forbid—that is, to exercise authority. The same principle applied in general to the holy law, which must be not only obeyed but also enforced. (Bernard Lewis, "Legal and Historical Reflections on the Position of Muslim Populations under Non-Muslim Rule," *Journal of the Institute of Muslim Minority Affairs*, vol. 13, no. 1 (January 1992), p. 10)

I have shown that the sources demonstrate a much wider range of conceptions of the degrees of religious obligation and the manners in which they can be fulfilled than Lewis concedes.

29. Al-Māwardī, in al-Nawawī, *al-Majmū'*, v. 21, p. 7.

30. The notion that residence and integration in Western societies is desirable primarily as a means of influencing these societies to the political benefit of Muslims or to transform them into "Islamic societies" is not rare in Islamic discourses about the Muslim minorities in the West. See also Faḍl Allāh, *al-Hijra wa'l-ightirāb*, p. 86, where he discusses Muslim immigration to the West in terms of the "control over Western society in its entirety achieved by the Jews through their immigration and residence there."

31. Nadwi, *Muslims in the West*, pp. 113–14.

32. Shaykh Ahmad Kutty, "Is *Hijrah* (Emigration) Still Necessary?" http://www.islamonline.net/fatwa/english/FatwaDisplay.asp?hFatwaID+99040.

33. Al-Qaraḍāwī, *Fī fiqh al-aqalliyyāt al-muslima*, pp. 33–34.

34. Ramadan, *To Be a European Muslim*, p. 147.

35. Ibid., p. 134.

36. Although Ramadan is silent on whether he sees a contradiction between his statements that "the inclination of every individual heart depends on God's Will" and that it is "the right of every human being to make a choice based on knowledge."

37. Ramadan, *To Be a European Muslim*, pp. 144–45.

38. Qaraḍāwī, *Fī fiqh al-aqalliyyāt al-muslima*, p. 33.

39. Ramadan, *To Be a European Muslim*, p. 148.

40. Ibid., p. 150.

41. Ibn Ḥanbal, *al-Musnad*, 7096.

42. Ibid., 6792, 6813, 6837.

43. Ibid., 6515.

44. al-Tirmidhī, *al-Jāmi' al-ṣaḥīḥ*, 1987; Ibn Ḥanbal, *al-Musnad*, 5/153, 158, 177.

45. In English, the link might be expressed through the word *flight*: one flees a town and one flees sin or people. In the translations, however, I avoid using a single term.

46. Ibn Taymiyya, *Majmū' al-fatāwā*, v. 28, pp. 204–6.

47. Ibid., pp. 216–17.

48. Ibid., pp. 210–11.

49. He is resolute that what determines the status of a place—a building, a city, or a country—is the present and actual behavior of its inhabitants, rather than some essential, permanent or formal quality:

> That a territory might be an abode of unbelief or of faith of sinners is not a necessary attribute, but rather a contingent attribute depending on its inhabitants. Any territory in which the inhabitants are believers and pious is at that moment the abode of the Friends of God. And any territory in which the inhabitants are unbelievers is at that moment the abode of unbelief. And any territory in which the inhabitants are sinners is at that moment the abode of sin. And so it is with any others we have not mentioned that their habitation of a territory makes it their abode. (*Majmū' al-fatāwā*, v. 18, pp. 281–82)

50. "Punishing and rebuking the wrong-doer is conditional upon the capability [to do so]. Thus, the judgment of the Law has differentiated between the two kinds of *hijra* for the capable and the incapable, as well as between the paucity or abundance of the innovating wrong-doers, and their strength or weakness" (*Majmū' al-fatāwā*, v. 28, p. 211).

51. "And when [rebuking sinners] results in attainment of the good and the repulsion of evil, then it is prescribed. Yet if it results in greater corruption than that caused by the original sin, then it is not prescribed" (Ibid., p. 217).

52. Ibn Taymiyya, *Majmū' al-fatāwā*, v. 18, p. 279–80.

53. In his *fatwā* on the Muslims of Bosnia, Rashīd Riḍā makes a similar point in response to the Mālikī position that it is a duty to flee from corruption and sin. The duty, he argues, is to "uphold truth and goodness," which is possible in a wide variety of conditions. Only if one is not able to do this must one migrate, but this was not the case for early-twentieth-century Bosnians, living under Austrian rule. (See *Fatāwā*, v. 2, p. 777.)

54. Note, however, Abou El Fadl's comment on the failure of classical jurists to satisfactorily resolve the tensions and ambiguities involved in living in non-Muslim lands, including the degree to which Islam must be "manifested" and the duty to obey the laws of a host country while not violating the Sharī'a:

> Perhaps the evasiveness of Muslim jurists on the issue of a conflict between the demands of Islamic law and the demands of the *amān* [promise of security from a host state which obligates a Muslim to respect its laws and security] indicates that the only real issue to be decided is residence. Once Muslims were allowed to reside in non-Muslim territory, practical compromises were inevitable, and Muslim jurists may have realized that any attempt to control or regulate behavior was bound to be ignored by Muslim minorities living in different historical situations. (Abou El Fadl, "Islamic Law and Muslim Minorities," p. 178)

55. Tūbūlyāk: "We can say that it is not permissible for a Muslim to adopt the citizenship of a non-Muslim state, and this may be akin to apostasy in normal circumstances if there is no legitimate justification for it." (See *al-Aḥkām al-siyāsiyya*, p. 79.) Rashīd Riḍā also expressed himself vehemently against the acceptance of French citizenship on the part of North Africans under French rule; we later discuss whether his reasoning would apply as well to native-born or immigrant citizens of non-Muslim states (Riḍā, *Fatāwā*, v. 5, pp. 1748–61).

CHAPTER 6

1. Ramadan, *To be a European Muslim*, p. 162.

2. Ibid., p. 164.

3. Ibid., pp. 171–72. Emphasis in original.

4. Muslim, *Ṣaḥīḥ*, Kitāb al-Jihād wa'l-siyar.

5. Muslim, *Ṣaḥīḥ*, Kitāb al-Jihād wa'l-siyar, Bāb al-wafā' bi'l-'ahd.

6. Note however that Nawawī does not consider this *ḥadīth* to be constitutive of a general rule about keeping promises to desist from *jihād*, but rather an isolated pragmatic decision taken by the Prophet so that it wouldn't be said about his companions that they don't keep contracts (al-Nawawī, *Sharḥ Ṣaḥīḥ Muslim* (Beirut: Dār al-Qalam, 1987), v. 6, p. 386). Note also that there is extensive juridical discussion about expiating oaths and also about the invalidity of oaths or contracts to perform something forbidden or desist from something obligatory.

7. See 'Abd al-Qādir, *Fiqh al-aqalliyyāt al-muslima*, p. 160.

8. Al-Sarakhsī, *al-Mabsūṭ*, v. 10, p. 105.

9. Ibn Qudāma, *al-Mughnī*, v. 13, pp. 152–53.

10. The Ḥanafī school is known for putting a greater emphasis on territoriality than other schools. They often argue that Muslims are bound morally by the principles of Islamic law and ethics but that Islamic courts cannot claim jurisdiction over what happens in non-Muslim lands. This means that, unlike the Ḥanbalī position quoted here, most Ḥanafī jurists will not hold Muslims legally (as opposed to morally) responsible for what they do in non-Muslim countries. Thus, betrayal or fraud is a sin but not a civil crime, and Sarakhsī says it is "abhorred" for a Muslim to act in this way but refuses to prescribe an earthly punishment. Interestingly, and importantly for the question of justifying liberal freedoms for Muslims, they also apply this attitude to the enforcement of the penal code for moral crimes: "They are not bound by the laws of Islam while in the abode of war" (al-Sarakhsī, *al-Mabsūṭ*, v. 10, p. 105).

11. This principle, however, as strong a genuinely ethical motivation as it is as for acting in accordance with liberal laws, should not be mistaken for a genuine affirmation of those laws, for it is equally binding in conditions of injustice. In fact, the argument often surfaces in discussions of how Muslims should respond to injustice in their host countries, for example, American support for Israel or its own wars in Muslim countries. "Are Muslim citizens of these countries allowed to pay taxes that go toward such activities?" is a common question to muftis. That many "neo-classical" scholars (such as those cited by the popular Islam Online Web site) argue they are is no indication of an overlapping consensus on substantive questions of justice.

12. At www.islamonline.net/fatwa/english/FatwaDisplay.asp?hFatwaID=70581.

13. At www.islamonline.net/fatwa/english/FatwaDisplay.asp?hFatwaID=35886.

14. A Shi'ite voice: "If [a Muslim] agreed—even tacitly—to observe the laws of their country he is bound to honor this contract insofar as it does not involve disobedience to the holy *sharī'a*" (Sīstānī, *al-Fiqh li'-mughtaribīn*, p. 184).

15. The question of paying taxes arises here as an example of following the laws of a state and regarding the other as worthy of justice, for example, by not cheating or deceiving the state simply because the state is non-Muslim. Arguments for paying taxes because they contribute to good civic ends are discussed in chapter 8. An interesting point can be raised here. Classical jurisprudence was generally opposed to Muslim rulers imposing any taxes beyond those prescribed by *sharī'a* (such as the *jizya* on non-Muslim subjects, the *kharāj* land tax, and the *'ushr* or *ṣadaqa* tithe). One

of the most consistent areas where classical jurists are on record as condemning and chastising secular rulers is in their efforts to levy additional revenues, referred to by the jurists as *mukūs*. The argument could thus be made Islamically that Muslims ought to resist taxes levied by *any state* beyond those justified by God. Interestingly, however, this argument does not seem to figure in contemporary discourses.

16. Al-Nawawī, *al-Majmū'*, v. 21, p. 130. 'Abd al-Qādir also reports this position as an object of general consensus in Sunni *fiqh* (*Fiqh al-aqalliyyāt al-muslima*, p. 167).

17. Ibn Qudāma, *al-Mughnī*, v. 13, pp. 184–85.

18. European Council for Fatwa and Research, *Fatāwa al-majmū'a al-ūla*, pp. 19–20. Prominent Lebanese Shi'ite jurist Grand Ayatollah Muḥammad Ḥusayn Faḍl Allāh provides a similar argument in *al-Hijra wa'l-ightirāb*, pp. 80–81.

19. Fayṣal Mawlawī, "al-Mafāhīm al-asāsiyya li'l-da'wa al-islāmiyya fī bilād al-gharb," in Majdī 'Aqīl Abū Shamāla, ed., *Risālat al-Muslimīn fī bilād al-gharb* (Irbid, Jordan: Dār al-Amal, 1999), p. 222.

20. At http://www.islamonline.net/fatwa/english/FatwaDisplay.asp?hFatwaID=51564.

21. At http://www.islamonline.net/fatwa/english/FatwaDisplay.asp?hFatwaID=97351.

22. However, his use of Qur'anic evidence is rather creative. The verse in question reads in full: "As for those who have believed but have not migrated towards you, you owe no duty of protection to them until they have migrated. Yet, should they seek help from you in the matter of religion then it is your duty to help them except against a folk between whom and you there is a treaty." In other words, the verse refers to precisely the opposite circumstance from the one Mawlawī discusses: the duties of a Muslim state toward Muslims living among non-Muslims rather than Muslim minorities toward fellow Muslims in the abode of Islam. This verse has been traditionally read to impose upon the Islamic polity a duty of restraint toward non-Muslim states harboring Muslim subjects if there is a treaty between them. The verse is uniformly read as relating to the Muslims who stayed behind in Mecca or remained Bedouins rather than migrating to Medina with the Prophet. See, for example, Fakhr al-Dīn al-Rāzī (d. 606/1149), *Mafātīḥ al-ghayb* (Beirut: Dār al-Kutub al-'Ilmiyya, 1990), v. 8, pp. 165–68; al-Qurṭubī (d. 671/1273), *al-Jāmi' li-aḥkām al-Qur'ān*, v. 8, p. 37; 'Alī ibn Muḥammad Khāzin al-Baghdādī (d. 741/1341), *Lubāb al-ta'wīl fī ma'ānī al-tanzīl* (Beirut: Dār al-Kutub al-'Ilmiyya, 1995), v. 3, p. 69; Ibn Kathīr (774/1373), *Tafsīr al-Qur'ān al-'Aẓīm*, v. 4, pp. 84–86; Quṭb, *Fī Ẓilāl al-Qur'ān*, v. 3, pp. 1558–59; *In the Shade of the Qur'ān*, v. 7, pp. 212–13.

23. Jamāl al-Dīn 'Aṭiya Muḥammad, *Naḥwa fiqh jadīd li'l-aqalliyyāt* (Cairo: Dār al-Salām, 2003), p. 69.

24. 'Abd al-Qādir, *Fiqh al-aqalliyyāt al-muslima*, p. 170.

25. Guillaume, *The Life of Muhammad*, p. 153. The sources hold that the same king later converted to Islam on the invitation of the Prophet.

26. Ibn Bayya, *Ṣinā'at al-fatwā wa-fiqh al-aqalliyāt*, p. 308.

27. Qaraḍāwī, *Fī Fiqh al-aqalliyyāt*, p. 25.

28. On file with the author.

29. Riḍā, *Fatāwā*, v. 2, p. 565. This *fatwā* is used as an important point of reference by both Topoljak and 'Abd al-Qādir.

30. At http://www.islamonline.net/fatwa/english/FatwaDisplay.asp?hFatwaID=52014.

31. Tūbūlyāk, *al-Aḥkām al-siyāsiyya*, p. 113.

32. See news.bbc.co.uk/1/hi/uk/3948329.stm.

33. Quṭb, *In the Shade of the Qurʾān*, v. 7, pp. 190–91; *Fī Ẓilāl al-Qurʾān*, v. 3, p. 1546–47.

34. See Sohail Hashmi, "Interpreting the Islamic Ethics of War and Peace," in *The Ethics of War and Peace*, ed. Terry Nardin (Princeton, N.J.: Princeton University Press, 1996), 146–66; and *The Islamic Ethics of War and Peace* (Ph.D. diss., Harvard University, 1996).

35. Rudolph Peters, *Jihad in Classical and Modern Islam*, p. 122.

36. See Maḥmūd Shaltūt, *al-Qurʾān waʾl-qitāl* (Beirut: Dār al-Fatḥ, 1983), pp. 29–30, for this characterization of the preferred method of Qurʾanic exegesis, which he refers to as *"tafsīr mawḍūʿī"* (thematic exegesis).

37. Shaltūt, *al-Qurʾān waʾl-qitāl*, p. 89; Muḥammad Shadīd, *al-Jihād fīʾl-Islām* (Cairo: Muʾassasat al-Maṭbūʿāt al-Ḥadītha, n.d.), p. 119; Muḥammad Abū Zahra, *al-ʿAlāqāt al-duwaliyya fīʾl-Islām* (Cairo: al-Qawmiyya, 1964), p. 47; ʿAlī ʿAlī Manṣūr, *al-Sharīʿa al-Islāmiyya waʾl-qānūn al-duwalī al-ʿāmm* (Cairo: Lajnat al-Khubarāʾ, 1971), p. 378; ʿUthmān al-Saʿīd al-Sharqāwī, *Sharīʿat al-qitāl fīʾl-Islām* (Cairo: al-Zahrāʾ, 1972), p. 33; Wahba al-Zuḥaylī, *al-ʿAlāqāt al-duwaliyya fī al-Islām* (Beirut: Muʾassasat al-risāla, 1981), p. 93; Louay Safi, *Peace and the Limits of War* (London: International Institute of Islamic Thought, 2003), p. 27; ʿAbd al-Qādir, *Fiqh al-aqalliyyāt al-muslima*, p. 36.

38. Some theorists cite the example of Yemen, which did not oppose the Islamic call and to whom the Prophet sent missionaries rather than armies.:"The relationship of the Abode of Islam with any society which has an opposing doctrine but opens a space for invitation to Islam, and does not obstruct its missionaries or the freedom to choose Islam, is a political stance preferred over one of aggression" (ʿAbd al-Qādir, *Fiqh al-aqalliyyāt al-muslima*, p. 43).

39. Shaltūt, *al-Qurʾān waʾl-qitāl*, p. 89; Shadīd, *al-Jihād fīʾl-Islām*, p. 129; Abū Zahra, *al-ʿAlāqāt al-duwaliyya*, p. 90; al-Sharqāwī, *Sharīʿat al-qitāl*, p. 43; Muḥammad al-Būṭī, *Jihad in Islam: How to Understand and Practise It* (Damascus: Dār al-Fikr, 1995), pp. 93–97; Zuḥaylī, *al-ʿAlāqāt al-duwaliyya*, pp. 95–96; Safi, *Peace and the Limits of War*, p. 10; ʿAbd al-Qādir, *Fiqh al-aqalliyyāt al-muslima*, p. 36.

40. In Fred Donner, "The Sources of Islamic Conceptions of War," in *Just War and Jihad: Historical and Theoretical Perspectives on War and Peace in Western and Islamic Traditions*, ed. John Kelsay and James T. Johnson (New York: Greenwood, 1991), pp. 31–70.

41. Jackson, "Jihad and the Modern World," p. 11.

42. Ibid., pp. 13–14.

43. Ibid., p. 17.

44. Ibid., p. 9. He also cites a contemporary Saudi scholar and the Islamic Law Academy of the Organization of the Islamic Conference.

45. Ibid., p. 24.

46. Shaltūt, *al-Qurʾān waʾl-qitāl*, p. 89; al-Zuḥaylī, *al-ʿAlāqāt al-duwaliyya*, p. 31; ʿAbd al-Qādir, *Fiqh al-aqalliyyāt al-muslima*, p. 44.

47. Al-Zuḥaylī, *al-ʿAlāqāt al-duwaliyya*, p. 18. Emphasis added.

48. Ibid., p. 94.

49. ʿAbd al-Qādir, *Fiqh al-aqalliyyāt al-muslima*, pp. 37–44.

50. Quṭb, for example, writes that "Islam never seeks converts through compulsion or threats or pressure of any kind. It deploys facts, reasoning, explanation and persuasion." Yet he maintains this view only by not considering the imposition of an Islamic legal-political order to be a form of coercion but rather the liberation of man from the tyranny of man-made laws: "Modern man has been deprived of the right to

choose and live other than according to what is dictated by the state, using the full force of its colossal machinery, laws and powers. People are today given the choice only to adhere to the secular state system, which does not allow for a belief in God as the Creator and Master of the world, or to face annihilation." Further on:

> Islam also advocates *jihād* to guarantee the right and freedom of expression and propagation of the faith. In order for individual human beings to make the choice of whether they believe in Islam or not, nothing should stand between them and God's Message or in any way prevent them from having full and free access to it. Of the many obstacles that stand between Islam and people, foremost are the tyrannical political regimes that oppress and persecute religious believers. An objective of *jihād* is to establish the Islamic social order and defend it. It is an order that frees man from the tyranny of other men, in all its forms, by urging the submission of all to the one supreme Master." (Quṭb, *In the Shade of the Qur'ān*, v. 1, pp. 325, 329)

51. "All three of these circumstances which are demanded in order to protect the Islamic mission do not depart in practice from the rights of states recognized in modern international law, including the right to exist, the right to legitimate self-defense, the right to equality, the right to freedom, and the right to mutual respect" (al-Zuḥaylī, *al-'Alāqāt al-duwaliyya*, pp. 32–33).

52. Al-Zuḥaylī, *al-'Alāqāt al-duwaliyya*, p. 102. Further on (at p. 107) he makes explicit that this recognition is not based on the payment of some form of tribute, like the classical *kharāj* or *jizya*, which on my reading serves to ground his doctrine of recognition as a doctrine of *equal* recognition.

53. It is not clear to me, however, that an individual Muslim believer must hold this belief as a concomitant pillar of a doctrine of *jihād* as defensive war. That is, while modernist theorists advance this belief consistently enough to warrant this discussion of it as part of a general modernist just war doctrine, it seems clear that (a) their Qur'anically based justification for reciprocating nonaggression is robust and categorical enough to provide sufficient grounds for Muslims wishing to recognize the existence of their non-Muslim state of citizenship and (b) the freedoms of worship and proselytizing guaranteed by liberal democracies can figure prominently in an Islamic justification of residence and integration in a non-Muslim state without the absence of those freedoms in another society necessarily resulting in a policy of belligerence.

54. "*Fitna*" is a notoriously difficult concept to translate, as discussed in chapter 5. It can mean trial or temptation, but also tumult, turmoil, or sedition. In referring to Muslims living in non-Muslim states, it most likely invokes interference in the practice of Islam by non-Muslim authorities or majorities with the aim of seducing Muslims away from Islam or preventing them from practicing it in peace and security.

55. "*Ṭawāghīt*" is the plural form of the noun *ṭāghūt*, which can mean evil, tyranny, or even Satan.

56. 'Abd al-Qādir, *Fiqh al-aqalliyyāt al-muslima*, p. 44.

CHAPTER 7

1. Mawlawī, "al-Mafāhīm al-asāsiyya," p. 199.

2. Qaraḍāwī uses this verse to argue that Islam is open to all nations and peoples. He is silent, however, on whether this obligation extends to religious and ethical pluralism. See al-Qaraḍāwī, "al-Infitāḥ 'alā'l-gharb: muqtaḍayātuhu wa-shurūṭuhu," in Abū Shamāla, ed., *Risālat al-muslimīn fī bilād al-gharb*, p. 13.

3. See in particular Abdulaziz Sachedina, *The Islamic Roots of Democratic Pluralism* (Oxford: Oxford University Press, 2001), pp. 27–28. Compare Yūsuf al-Qaraḍāwī, *Fatāwā mu'āṣira* (Beirut: al-Maktab al-Islāmī, 2003), pp. 195–200; and Muḥammad, *Naḥwa fiqh jadīd li'l-aqalliyyāt*, pp. 80–83.

4. See, for example, Yohanan Friedmann, *Tolerance and Coercion in Islam: Interfaith Relations in the Muslim Tradition* (Cambridge: Cambridge University Press, 2003).

5. Consider 3:64: "O people of the book! Come to that belief which we have in common that we may worship none but God and not ascribe divinity to aught but him and that we shall not take human beings for our lords beside God."

6. An example of this latter possibility is 'Abd al-Qādir's argument that the secularism of Western states does not negate the regard due them as Christian (or Jewish) because those prior revelations were not intended to provide for political and legal systems in the first place. Others cite 49:13 in the context of summoning to Islam in non-Muslim societies with the implication that they are content to understand the duty to "get to know one another" as extending to religions or worldviews. For example, see Aḥmad Jā'billāh, "Qawā'id al-ta'āmul bayn al-muslimīn wa-ghayrihim fī'l-mujtama'āt al-awrubiyya"; and Mawlawī, "al-Mafāhīm al-asāsiyya," both in Abū Shamāla, ed., *Risālat al-Muslimīn fī bilād al-gharb*, pp. 41–42.

7. Muḥammad, *Naḥwa fiqh jadīd li'l-aqalliyyāt*, p. 74.

8. "As long as a jurist's view showed itself to be grounded in authentic and authoritative sources and based on recognized methods of interpretation, no one could deny him the right to express it—regardless of substance—as long as it did not violate a pre-existing Unanimous Consensus. Concomitantly, while there may be many views that could justifiably claim to represent *an* Islamic position, the only views that could claim to represent *the* Islamic position were those that were backed by unanimous consensus" (Jackson, "Jihad and the Modern World," pp. 6–7).

9. See, in particular, Khaled Abou El Fadl, *Speaking in God's Name*, pp. 9–69.

10. See Abdullahi an-Na'im, *Towards an Islamic Reformation: Civil Liberties, Human Rights, and International Law* (Syracuse, NY: Syracuse University Press, 1990); and Mohamed Khalil, *Islam and Democracy: Religion, Politics, and Power in the Middle East* (Washington, DC: USIP, 1992), both of whom adopt the theory of a "second message of Islam," developed by the late Sudanese reformer Maḥmūd Muḥammad Ṭāhā. This theory holds that the Meccan revelations, far from being superseded and abrogated by later verses, actually represent the highest and purest manifestation of Islam, to which Muslims are supposed to return after the need for the "doctrinal" phase represented by the Medinan verses has passed. On Ṭāhā's ideas, see Mohamed Mahmoud, "Mahmud Muhammad Taha's Second Message of Islam," in *Islam and Modernity: Muslim Intellectuals Respond*, ed. John Cooper, Ronald L. Nettler, and Mohamed Mahmoud (London: I. B. Tauris, 1998), pp. 105–28.

11. Wahba al-Zuḥaylī, for example, concludes at the end of his commentary on 6:35 that "this is all evidence of mankind's freedom to choose between belief and unbelief, and of the fact that all reckoning, rewarding and punishing is dependent on what persons choose for themselves by way of belief or unbelief, good or bad" (al-Zuḥaylī, *al-Tafsīr al-wasīṭ*, v. 1, p. 545).

12. Qaraḍāwī, "al-Infitāḥ 'alā'l-gharb: muqtaḍayātuhu wa shurūṭuhu," p. 8.

13. Ibid., p. 28.

14. Qaraḍāwī, *Fatāwā mu'āṣira*, p. 188. I am grateful to Mohammad Fadel for bringing this text to my attention.

15. Ibid., p. 189.

16. Ibid., p. 190.

17. Al-Zuḥaylī on 11:118: "Here is a general divine law that God Almighty is capable of making people into a single nation united in either belief or unbelief, but He left for them the choice which is the basis of all moral obligation [*al-taklīf*]. Some of them have chosen the truth and others error, and thus division and difference persevere and people continue to disagree on and to dispute matters of religion, conviction and opinion" (*al-Tafsīr al-wasīṭ*, v. 2., p. 1084).

18. Al-Qaraḍāwī, *Fatāwā mu'āṣira*, pp. 190–91.

19. Ibid., p. 191.

20. Al-Ghannūshī, *Huqūq al-muwāṭana: Huqūq ghayr al-muslim fī'l-mujtama' al-Islāmī* (Herndon, VA: International Institute of Islamic Thought, 1993), p. 48.

21. Quṭb, *In the Shade of the Qur'ān*, v. 3, p. 344. The "Jewish man" refers to an episode in Medina during which a Muslim who had stolen a shield from one of the Prophet's companions placed it in the home of a Jewish citizen of Medina and falsely accused him. When the plot was revealed, the Prophet insisted that the man be fully exonerated, at a time when the Muslim community was engaged in a wider struggle with Medinan Jews. In relation to this episode, verse 4:112 declares "He who commits a fault or a sin and then throws the blame therefore on an innocent person, burdens himself with both falsehood and a clear sin." For Quṭb, God choose to teach the nascent Muslim community the lesson that justice must be done regardless of the identity of the parties, not in spite of the enmity between Jews and Muslims at the time but precisely because of it: "The immediate objective was to purify the newly-emerging Muslim community, to treat the elements of human weakness that affected it and to eradicate narrow ties of affiliation in all their forms and guises. . . . The Muslim community needed to be seriously tested so as to purge itself of evil, weakness and ignorant practices. Its standard of justice needed to be unblemished by any worldly consideration so that it implemented justice between people regardless of any consideration of immediate interest or prejudice. God, in His wisdom, deliberately chose this particular incident at that particular time, involving as it did a Jew belonging to a community continuously scheming against the Muslims and aiming to undermine the religion of Islam" (v. 3, pp. 299–300).

22. Al-Ṭabarī, *Jāmi' al-bayān*, v. 28, p. 43. He notes that some had claimed that the verse had originally referred only to the Meccan pagans who did not take part personally in persecuting Muslims but was later abrogated by "the verse of the sword" (9:5): "Slay the pagans wherever you find them."

23. Quoted in 'Abd al-Qādir, *Fiqh al-aqalliyyāt al-muslima*, p. 647.

24. For example, the testimony of non-Muslims in court was not regarded as equal to the testimony of Muslims, three of the four Sunni legal schools held that the law of just retaliation for murder (*qiṣāṣ*; *lex talionis*) did not hold when a Muslim killed a non-Muslim and that the compensatory blood price (*diya*) was not equal, non-Muslims were not allowed to proselytize or build new houses of worship, there was often a requirement of special dress to distinguish them in public, and, of course, there was the *jizya* poll tax described by many classical jurists as serving to mark symbolically non-Muslims' subjugation. On these issues generally, see Friedmann, *Tolerance and Coercion in Islam*.

25. For example, during the Rushdie and Danish cartoon affairs, the call to limit or ban "offensive," "scandalous," or "blasphemous" speech.

26. Cited in Majid Khadduri, *The Islamic Conception of Justice* (Baltimore: Johns Hopkins University Press, 1984), pp. 180–81.

27. Ghannūshī, Mawlawī, and others also report the prevalence of the view in some Western Islamic circles that, this being the Abode of War, the relation to

non-Muslims is one of war and the situation of Muslims one of *jihād*, non-Western goods and property are licit as booty, it is permissible to file false claims for social assistance, and it is not necessary to pay taxes (al-Ghannūshī, "al-Islam fī'l-gharb wa 'alāqātuhu bi'l-anẓima al-gharbiyya," p. 112; and Mawlawī, "al-Mafāhīm al-asāsiyya," p. 220).

28. Faḍl Allāh, *al-Hijra wa'l-ightirāb*, pp. 97–99.

29. Ghannūshī mentions similar attitudes and practices of regarding non-Muslim societies as areas where the laws of war apply, referring to such practices as "criminal in the judgment of Islam."

30. See, for example, Richard M. Frank, "Moral Obligation in Classical Muslim Theology," *Journal of Religious Ethics*, vol. 11, no. 2 (Fall 1983), pp. 204–23; George Hourani, "Ethics in Classical Islam: A Conspectus," in his *Reason and Tradition in Islamic Ethics* (Cambridge: Cambridge University Press, 1985); and Bernard Weiss, chapter 2, "Divine Sovereignty and Human Subordination," in *The Spirit of Islamic Law*.

31. Weiss, *The Spirit of Islamic Law*, p. 24.

32. See, for example, Michael Sandel, "*Political Liberalism* (Review)," *Harvard Law Review*, vol. 107, no. 7 (May 1994), pp. 1765–94.

33. Martha Nussbaum gets at this problem exactly in *Frontiers of Justice: Disability, Nationality, Species Membership* (Cambridge, MA: Belknap, 2007).

34. In his numerous publications such as *Freedom, Equality and Justice in Islam* and *The Dignity of Man: An Islamic Perspective*.

35. At www.islamonline.net/fatwa/english/FatwaDisplay.asp?hFatwaID=49756.

36. Faḍl Allāh, *Uslūb al-da'wa fī'l-Qur'ān*, p. 62.

37. Mawlawī, "al-Mafāhīm al-asāsiyya," pp. 200, 211–12.

38. "Let not the believers take the infidels for their allies in preference to the believers—for who does this has nothing to do with God—unless it be to protect yourselves from them in this way. God warns you about Himself and the final goal is to God."

39. "Oh you who believe! Do not take for your intimates other than your own kind. They will continually cause you turmoil and love anything that will distress you. Loathing has already come forth from their mouths and what is concealed in their breasts is even greater. We have made the signs clear to you if you will use your reason."

40. "O you who believe! Do not take as friends unbelievers rather than believers. Do you want to give God a clear proof against you?"

41. Mawlawī, "al-Mafāhīm al-asāsiyya," pp. 212–13.

42. Ibid., pp. 210, 215–16.

43. 'Abd al-Qādir sees a similar path to recognition: "Islam recognizes [non-Muslim] societies by recognizing in a realistic [*wāqi'ī*] way their human nature" ('Abd al-Qādir, *Fiqh al-aqalliyyāt*, p. 37).

44. Based on a reading of Q. 49:10: "Only believers are brothers."

45. Mawlawī, "al-Mafāhīm al-asāsiyya," p. 218. To establish this, he first points to a series of verses (7:65, 73, 85) in which previous Abrahamic prophets were referred to as the "brothers" of their unbelieving, sinning and unjust kinsmen, and also a verse (58:22) that refers to the non-Muslim "brothers" of the first Muslims. There is a virtually identical position articulated in Qaraḍāwī, "al-Infitāḥ 'alā'l-gharb: muqtaḍayātuhu wa shurūṭuhu," pp. 8–12.

46. Mawlawī, "al-Mafāhīm al-asāsiyya," p. 219.

47. Al-Qaraḍāwī, *al-Khaṣā'is al-'āmma li'l-Islām*, p. 84.

48. Mawlawī, "al-Mafāhīm al-asāsiyya,", pp. 214–15.

49. Faḍl Allāh, *Uslūb al-da'wa*, pp. 74–75.
50. Ibid., p. 164.
51. Ibid., p. 72. See also Khurram Murad, *Da'wah among non-Muslims in the West* (Leicester, UK: Islamic Foundation, 1986), p. 21; and in the in *Risālat al-Muslimīn fī bilād al-gharb* collection of essays: Aḥmad Jā'billāh, "Qawā'id al-ta'āmul bayna al-muslimīn wa ghayrihim fī'l-mujtama'āt al-awrubiyya," pp. 45–49; 'Abdallāh al-Jadī', "Risālat al-Muslim fī bilād al-gharb," p. 130; and 'Iṣām al-Bashīr, "al-Ḥiwār sabīlunā."
52. Faḍl Allāh, *Uslūb al-da'wa*, pp. 164–65.
53. Religious obligations are often referred to as *ḥuqūq Allāh* (God's rights).
54. Faḍl Allāh, *Uslūb al-da'wa*, p. 58.
55. Ibid., p. 64.
56. Mawlawī, "al-Mafāhīm al-asāsiyya," p. 196.
57. See also, Jā'billāh, "Qawā'id al-ta'āmul," p. 53; and al-Ghannūshī, "al-Islām fī'l-gharb," p. 113, where he writes that "a foreign plant such as Islam cannot lay down its roots as long as it doesn't interact with its environment, as long as it doesn't establish cooperative relations and connections with the elements of this environment."
58. See Jürgen Habermas, "Discourse Ethics: Notes on a Program of Philosophical Justification," in his *Moral Consciousness and Communicative Action* (Cambridge, MA: MIT Press, 2001).
59. Verses 22:67–69 are often cited against entering theological disputes with non-Muslims: "To every People have We appointed rites and ceremonies which they must follow, let them not then dispute with you on the matter, but do invite (them) to your Lord: for you are assuredly on the Right Way. If they do wrangle with you, say, 'God knows best what it is you are doing.' God will judge between you on the Day of Judgment concerning the matters in which you differ."
60. Habermas, "Discourse Ethics: Notes on a Program of Philosophical Justification," p. 58.
61. Ibid., p. 89.
62. Riḍā, *Tafsīr al-Manār*, v. 3, p. 277.
63. Cf. al-Zuḥaylī, *al-Tafsīr al-wasīṭ*, v. 1, p. 186.
64. This argument is repeated almost verbatim by Qaraḍāwī (*Fatāwā mu'āṣira*, p. 193).
65. This argument is also noted in Ibn Bayya, *Ṣinā'at al-fatwā wa-fiqh al-aqalliyāt*, p. 307.
66. Again, this exact point is advanced also by Qaraḍāwī in *Fatāwā mu'āṣira*, p. 194.
67. Riḍā, *Tafsīr al-Manār*, v. 3, p. 288. Emphasis added.
68. Ibn Bayya, *Ṣinā'at al-fatwā wa-fiqh al-aqalliyāt*, pp. 292–93.
69. Ibid., p. 304.
70. Ibid., p. 302.
71. Ibid., p. 303.
72. Ibid., p. 304.
73. Ibid., p. 305.
74. Ibid., p. 306.
75. Ibid., p. 305.
76. Ibid.
77. Ibid., p. 307. He cites the exegesis of Q.3:28 of twentieth-century Tunisian scholar Muḥammad al-Ṭahir ibn 'Āshūr (d. 1973) as his authority for these views. Ibn 'Āshūr is interesting as a modern exponent and theorist of the doctrine of "the purposes of *sharī'a*" (*maqāṣid al-sharī'a*), developed in the medieval period by al-Ghazālī,

al-Shāṭibī, and others. I discuss this briefly in the next chapter because it is often used to justify political participation in non-Muslim states.

78. Ibid., p. 308.

79. ʻAbd al-Qādir, *Fiqh al-aqalliyyāt al-muslima*, p. 630.

80. "The disassociation [*barā'a*] discussed [in *sūrat al-Tawba* of the Qur'ān] is directed at the polytheists in a limited, restricted context connected to treaties, war and peace" (Ibn Bayya, *Ṣināʻat al-fatwā wa-fiqh al-aqalliyāt*, p. 301).

81. For this paragraph, see ʻAbd al-Qādir, *Fiqh al-aqalliyyāt al-muslima*, pp. 634–35.

82. Ibid., p. 637.

83. Ibid., pp. 638–39.

84. Ibid., p. 646.

85. Muṣṭafā al-Ṭaḥḥān, "al-Muslim al-dāʻiya yuḥsan al-taʻāmul maʻ al-muslim wa-ghayr al-muslim," in *Risālat al-muslimīn fī bilād al-gharb*, p. 283, citing Qaraḍāwī.

86. Indeed, it is not uncommon in certain Islamic discourses for non-Muslim liberal democracies to be compared to non-Muslim dictatorships or tyrannies, not so much in terms of the conditions Muslims face but in terms of how actively they should participate in non-Muslim political life. See M. Amir Ali, "A Case for Muslim Political Participation," *Muslim Public Affairs Committee UK*, at http://www.mpacuk.org/content/view/376/101/; and Abduljalil Sajid, "Joining Political Parties in non Muslim Countries: According to Islamic Shariah," *Muslim Public Affairs Committee UK*, at http://www.mpacuk.org/content/view/211/.

87. This interpretation of how the Islamic conception of loyalty bears on the question of citizenship is, in fact, quite commonplace among the better known neoclassical scholars active in the West.

CHAPTER 8

1. Verse 9:60 lists the proper recipients of *zakāh*: "Alms are for the poor and the needy, for those who gather them, for those whose hearts have been reconciled, for those in bondage, and in debt, for those [fighting] in the path of God, and for the wayfarer." The phrase "those whose hearts have been reconciled" is interpreted as those who have recently converted to Islam, having possibly left an existing solidarity community and in need of support. Thus, the aims of *zakāh* are exclusively religious in nature, and non-Muslims are not generally held to be appropriate recipients.

2. This was part of Wansharīsī's case that even the five pillars of Islamic worship cannot be upheld in non-Muslim societies.

3. Quṭb, *In the Shade of the Qur'ān*, v. 3, p. 146, commenting on verse 4:36.

4. Ibid., p. 145.

5. Ibn Kathīr, *Tafsīr al-Qur'ān al-ʻaẓīm*, v. 2, p. 261.

6. See Ismāʻīl al-Badawī, *Daʻā'im al-ḥukm fī'l-sharīʻa al-islāmiyya wa'l-nuẓum al-dustūriyya al-muʻāṣira* (Cairo: Dār al-Fikr, 1980), p. 525.

7. Al-Qurṭubī, *al-Jāmiʻ li-aḥkām al-Qurān*, v. 5, p. 120.

8. Much more frequently, the question is put to scholars whether the obligation to pay taxes is binding when they are put to evil purposes. The most common answer is the one we have encountered, that so long as one is party to the social contract, the duty to render loyalty (including taxes) is binding. Alternatively, a consequentialist argument is sometimes given, namely, that one risks doing more harm to oneself and the Muslim community by breaking the law than by one's proportional contribution to evil ends.

9. At www.islamonline.net/fatwa/english/FatwaDisplay.asp?hFatwaID=35886.

10. In discussing this question, many other contemporary Muslim scholars point to 5:48, which reads in full: "For every one of you We have prescribed a path and a way. If God had willed He would have made you all one community, but [He has not done so] that He may test you in what has come to you. So compete with each other in good works." However, classical exegesis seems to have read the final phrase, which some contemporary thinkers cite in the context of cross-communal solidarity, as merely exhorting each community to implement their own laws and forms of worship, not to extend charity or welfare to one another. See Ibn Kathīr, *Tafsīr al-Qur'ān al-'aẓīm*, v. 3, p. 118; al-Qurṭubī, *al-Jāmi' li-aḥkām al-Qurān*, v. 6, 137.

11. Mawlawī, "al-Mafāhīm al-asāsiyya," pp. 203–4. Emphasis added. Note also the views of British Muslim scholar Abduljalil Sajid: "Considering the issue of *walā'* [loyalty], it is evident that there's nothing wrong Islamically in having some sort of such cooperation between Muslims and non-Muslim as regards worldly affairs. According to the articles of the Madinah constitution, the residents of Madinah would cooperate in establishing justice, supporting one another in combating aggression and help one another to do righteous acts. It's clear that mutual cooperation in worldly affairs goes far to encompass all citizens who share a common destiny, neighbourhood and sometimes kinship. This may be extended to include economic and commercial fields" ("Joining Political Parties in Non Muslim Countries: According to Islamic Shariah," *Muslim Public Affairs Committee UK* (December 2004), at http://www.mpacuk.org/content/view/211/).

12. One might argue that *da'wa* is one of the acceptable means of "commanding and forbidding" (jurists speak about commanding and forbidding "by hand, by tongue, or by heart," i.e., through coercion, admonishment, or silent disapproval).

13. Ramadan, *To Be a European Muslim*, p. 147.

14. At www.islamonline.net/english/introducingislam/Tolerance/article02.shtml.

15. "Muslims should stand together along with other faith groups to rescue humanity from those who call for atheism, promiscuity, materialism, abortion, homosexuality, unisex marriages, bloodshed, misappropriation of others' property as well as those groups which enhance materialistic trends in man at the expense of his spiritual elevation" (www.islamonline.net/fatwa/english/FatwaDisplay.asp?hFatwaID=8514).

16. Note also the views of Pakistani-British Muslim scholar Khurram Murad:

> We should be kind and compassionate, just and fair, to everyone, irrespective of one's faith, race, colour, or social status, and in all situations. God has commanded us to be just and kind. Deep involvement in human welfare and service to mankind is basic to Islam and of central importance to Da'wah. The Qur'ān places these values and conduct on a par with faith in God and His worship (68:27–37; 74:42–46; 107:1–7). Why should Muslims be indifferent to the uncared for, the lonely, the old, the hungry, who live in their societies? (Khurram Murad, *Da'wah among non-Muslims in the West*, p. 23)

17. Although this verse is cited by many contemporary scholars to argue that all humankind deserves a certain quality of treatment from Muslims, most classical exegetes seemed to read it as a declaration of man's superiority over animals and his claim to the earth's natural resources. (See, for example, the commentaries of Ṭabarī and Zamakhsharī on this verse.) By the nineteenth century, however, exegete Maḥ mūd al-Ālūsi (d. 1854) read the verse as teaching that "everyone and all members of the human race, including the pious and the sinner, are endowed with dignity, nobility and honor." (See al-Ālūsī, *Rūḥ al-ma'ānī fī tafsīr al-Qur'ān al-'Aẓīm* (Cairo: Dār al-Turāth, n.d.), v. 15, p. 117.)

18. Mohammed Hashim Kamali, *The Dignity of Man: An Islamic Perspective* (Cambridge, UK: Islamic Texts Society, 1999), p. 7.

19. This attitude also has multiple possible implications, including a belief in the justness of subsuming non-Muslims into a Muslim political or social order, for the belief that "Islam seeks to bring benefit and improvement to all people and all races" is hardly a formula that obviously leads to a doctrine of political restraint or religious neutrality for the state.

20. See, for example. Faḍl Allāh, *al-Hijra wa'l-ightirāb*, pp. 88–91.

21. Faith, life, property, intellect, progeny.

22. For a similar overview of some of the main sources canvassed in this section, see also Wasif Shadid and Sjoerd van Koningsveld, "Religious Authorities of Muslims in the West: Their Views on Political Participation," in *Intercultural Relations and Religious Authorities: Muslims in the European Union*, ed. Shadid and van Koningsveld, pp. 149–68.

23. See, for example, M. Amir Ali, "A Case for Muslim Political Participation" at http://www.islamawareness.net/Politics/participate.html; and Taha Jaber al-'Alwani, "Muslims' Participation in the US Political Life," at www.islamonline.net/fatwa/en glish/FatwaDisplay.asp?hFatwaID=4743.

24. Ali, "A Case for Muslim Political Participation."

25. Michael Cook, in his magisterial study of how Muslims have understood the duty to "command the right and forbid the wrong" throughout history, argues that the dominant interpretation is that "right refers to *all* that God and His Prophet have commanded, wrong to *all* they have forbidden" (Michael Cook, *Forbidding Wrong in Islam* (Cambridge: Cambridge University Press, 2003), p. 22). To emphasize the point that this duty cannot be confused with modern, liberal notions of harm, Cook's summary of the Ḥanbalī sources (representing the most vigorous treatments of the duty) is that "the most commonly encountered forms of offence in the responsa [*fatwās*] were making music and drinking liquor—in that order. These are followed at some distance by sexual misconduct and a scatter of minor offences. On the whole, the menu is simple and repetitive" (Cook, *Commanding Right and Forbidding Wrong in Islamic Thought* (Cambridge, Cambridge University Press: 2000), p. 90). For an accessible English-language source representing an activist understanding of the individual duty to safeguard public morality, see Abū Ḥāmid al-Ghazzālī, *On Enjoining Good and Forbidding Wrong*, trans. Muhammad Nur Abdus Salam (Chicago: Kazi, 2003).

26. One of the maxims of Islamic jurisprudence is the consequentialist maxim to choose the act that will cause the least harm (*aqall al-ḍararayn*). Arguments such as the one advanced here by M. Amir Ali are essentially that participating in a non-Muslim political system is a lesser evil than failing to exert oneself toward the removal of other evils.

27. British-based cleric Haytham bin Jawwad al-Haddad explains the belief that voting in democratic elections to be unbelief (*kufr*) as arising from:

> the inability to distinguish between establishing a democratic system in which people vote for one of a number of systems, and voting to select the best individual amongst a number of candidates within an already-established system imposed upon them and which they are unable to change within the immediate future. There is no doubt that the first type is an act of Kufr, as Allah says, "Legislation is for none but Allah. He has commanded that you worship none but Him." [Qur'an, 12:41] and He says, "And whosoever does not judge by what Allah has revealed, such are the Kafirun (disbelievers)." [Qur'an, 5:44] Secondly:

> not realising that voting for a candidate or party who rules according to man-made law does not necessitate approval or acceptance for his method; this is a crucial point. (Sheikh Haytham bin Jawwad al-Haddad, "An Advice to British Muslims Regarding the Coming Elections," at http://www.as-sahwah.com/viewarticle.php?articleID=1150&%C2%A0)

28. In fact, many of these scholars echo the incompatible positions encountered previously, which call for the use of democratic institutions for nonliberal aims and even the eventual Islamization of society. My point here is that they advance other arguments as well, often prioritizing them over the "Islamization" arguments.

29. Ibn Bayya, *Ṣināʿat al-fatwā wa-fiqh al-aqalliyāt*, p. 294.

30. Ibid., p. 295.

31. Ibid., p. 294.

32. Sheikh Muhammad Al-Mukhtar al-Shanqiti, "Muslims' Participation in US Elections" (November 2003), at http://www.islam-online.net/fatwaapplication/english/display.asp?hFatwaID=106769.

33. Al-Bayḍāwī, *Tafsīr anwār al-tanzīl wa asrār al-ta'wīl*, commentary on 12:55 (extracted from digital collection at http://www.altafsir.com).

34. Presumably the point here is that Pharaoh was an otherwise unjust ruler.

35. Al-Māwardī, *Tafsīr al-nukat wa al-ʿuyūn*, commentary on 12:55 (extracted from digital collection at http://www.altafsir.com).

36. Writing roughly two centuries later, the Mālikī scholar al-Qurṭubī can still quote Māwardī word for word as having encapsulated the crucial juridical questions and range of responses. Qurṭubī's own position (recalling from chapter 3 that the Mālikīs were the most hostile to residence in non-Islamic lands) was that "this verse permits a virtuous man to work for a wicked man or an unbelieving ruler on the condition that he is given authority over his task and is not opposed or interfered with in it, and what is asked of him is useful and appropriate. However, if his work depends on the choices and whims of the wicked man then it is not permitted." He rejects the view that "this was a particular [dispensation from God] for Joseph and is not permitted today" (al-Qurṭubī, *al-Jāmiʿ li-aḥkām al-Qur'ān*, v. 9., p. 14). This latter view is not infrequent within contemporary Salafi discourses on participating in democratic elections in non-Muslim states. The argument is that Joseph was a prophet before the advent of Islam, and thus his example is not perfectly applicable to Muslim conditions. See Sajid, "Joining Political Parties in Non-Muslim Countries," for this argument.

37. Faḍl Allāh, *al-Hijra wa'l-ightirāb*, pp. 88–89.

38. Rachid Gannouchi, "Participation in Non-Islamic Government," p. 92.

39. Verse 12:55 raises two other questions for exegetes in addition to the problem of serving a non-Muslim ruler: whether one may request appointment at all, even from a Muslim ruler (there is a Prophetic *ḥadīth* against this) and whether one may praise oneself as Joseph does in the verse.

40. In al-Ālūsī, *Rūḥ al-maʿānī*, v. 13, pp. 5–6.

41. ʿAbd al-Qādir, *Fiqh al-aqalliyyāt al-Muslima*, p. 611.

42. Ibid., p. 617.

43. Guillaume, *The Life of Muhammad*, p. 146.

44. Ibid., p. 657.

45. Ibn Taymiyya, *Majmūʿ al-fatāwā*, v. 19, pp. 218–19.

46. Islamic doctrine regards all pre-Islamic prophets as "Muslim" in the general sense of worshipping God and submitting to His will. The behavior of these prophets is treated as exemplary (albeit not legally normative) for Muslims.

47. Ramadan, *To Be a European Muslim*, p. 22.

48. Qaraḍāwī, "Muslims' Participation in the US Political Life" (November 2003), at http://islamonline.net/fatwa/english/FatwaDisplay.asp?hFatwaID=4743.

49. 'Abd al-Qādir, *Fiqh al-aqalliyyāt al-Muslima*, p. 619. M. Amir Ali and others also make this point.

50. Ghannouchi, "Participation in Non-Islamic Government," p. 92.

51. Muhammad Al-Hanooti, "Voting in a Majority non-Muslim Country" (August 2003), at http://www.islamonline.net/fatwa/english/FatwaDisplay.asp?hFatwaID=14795.

52. European Council for *Fatwa* and Research, "Elections in Non-Muslim Countries: Role of Muslims" (May 2004), at http://www.islamonline.net/fatwa/english/FatwaDisplay.asp?hFatwaID==78491.

53. Ghannouchi, "Participation in Non-Islamic Government," p. 92.

54. Ibid., p. 94.

55. al-Qaraḍāwī, *Min fiqh al-dawla fī'l-Islām* (Cairo: Dār al-Shurūq, 1997), p. 180.

56. See Khaled Abou El Fadl, *Speaking in God's Name*, pp. 40–47.

57. al-Qaraḍāwī, *Min fiqh al-dawla*, pp. 184–85.

58. He is not affirming the same position as Ghannūshī, however. One can imagine him preferring a non-Muslim political system that is broadly democratic but favors religious conceptions of the good over nonreligious ones.

59. Ibn Taymiyya, *Majmū' al-fatāwā*, v. 20, p. 55.

60. See his *Priorities of the Islamic Movement in the Coming Phase* (Swansea: Awakening, 2000), pp. 47–55, 243–52.

61. al-Qaraḍāwī, *Fī Fiqh al-aqalliyyāt*, p. 35.

62. *Maṣlaḥa* in Islamic jurisprudence suggests "public interest" and gradually developed into a source for legal decisions, particularly in the works of al-Ghazālī, Ḥanbalī scholar Najm al-Dīn al-Ṭufī (d. 715/1316), and Mālikī scholar Abū Iṣḥāq al-Shāṭibī (d. 790/1388). See Bernard Weiss, *The Spirit of Islamic Law*, chapter 4, "The Venture beyond the Texts."

63. 'Abd al-Qādir, *Fiqh al-aqalliyyāt al-muslima*, p. 618.

64. Bear in mind that we are not concerned with whether any given scholar who has sought to address Muslim minority questions systematically and comprehensively, such as 'Abd al-Qādir or Qaraḍāwī, himself holds comprehensive views that would in their entirety make him a good citizen of a liberal state, unless views we are using to demonstrate compatibility are only coherent or applicable if one accepts other, incompatible, ones. It is highly unlikely that all of a scholar's views will support a liberal political order (unless they are clearly elaborated with this intent, such as the writings of Tariq Ramadan and some of Ghannūshī's texts), even on some very basic questions.

65. 'Abd al-Qādir, *Fiqh al-aqalliyyāt al-muslima*, p. 609.

66. See Felicitas Opwis, "*Maṣlaḥa* in Contemporary Islamic Legal Theory," *Islamic Law and Society*, vol. 12, no. 2 (2005), p. 188; and "*Maṣlaḥa*: An Intellectual History of a Core Concept in Islamic Legal Theory" (PhD diss., Yale University, 2001).

67. Abū Iṣḥāq al-Shāṭibī, *al-Muwāfaqāt* (al-Khubar, Saudi Arabia: Dār Ibn 'Affān, 1997), v. 2, p. 20.

68. See, in addition to Khadduri, Opwis, and Abou El Fadl, Wael Hallaq, *A History of Islamic Legal Theories*, and Muhammad Khalid Masud, *Shatibi's Philosophy of Islamic Law* (Islamabad: Islamic Research Institute, 1995).

69. Opwis argues that the post-Ghazālī legal theorists, most important, Fakhr al-Dīn al-Rāzī, Shihāb al-Dīn al-Qarāfī, Najm al-Dīn al-Ṭūfī, and, of course, al-Shāṭibī, all made important methodological and epistemological contributions to clarifying the place of *maṣlaḥa* in Islamic legal theory, but "the constituent elements of the concept

did not actually change after al-Ghazālī defined them at the end of the 5th/11th century." Similarly, modern polemics have focused on questions of epistemology and juristic methodology rather than the basic substantive meaning of *maṣlaḥa*. See Opwis, "*Maṣlaḥa* in Contemporary Islamic Legal Theory," p. 197.

70. Muzammil Siddiqi, "Muslims Participating in the US Local Councils" (October 2003), at http://www.islamonline.net/fatwa/english/FatwaDisplay.asp?hFatwaID=62236.

71. This is obviously a theme of countless texts, but Monzer Kahf's *fatwā* is interesting because it uses the question of U.S. foreign policy to emphasize civic involvement. See "Refusing to Pay Taxes to the US Due to Its Anti-Muslim Policy" (June 2002), at http://www.islamonline.net/fatwa/english/FatwaDisplay.asp?hFatwaID=70581).

72. 'Abd al-Qādir, *Fiqh al-aqalliyyāt al-Muslima*, p. 614.

73. Consider the following quotation:

> It has long been my position that any type of participation in democracy is a type of approval of that system. I have no doubt that democracy is antithetical to Islam. However, being faced with the reality of a growing Muslim population here in the UK, who for all intents and purposes consider this their home, it has become clear to me that we must participate in every aspect of society as much as possible to ensure our rights and continued existence and well being in this society. This participation most certainly includes voting for whichever party or candidate best serves the needs and interests of the UK and indeed world wide Muslim population. This does not mean approval or acceptance of the ideal of democracy, but the intention is to use the means and avenues available to benefit Muslims. The Prophet did not approve of the system of tribalism in Arabia, in fact he condemned it, but this did not stop the Prophet from accepting the protection of his uncle and the tribe of Banu Haashim. In addition to that it seems to me that the evil of participation is far less than the evil that will befall the Muslims if we do not, and the Shariah teaches us always to choose the path of lesser evil. (Shaykh Aurangzeb Khan, "Joining Political Parties in Non Muslim Countries: According to Islamic Shariah" (December 2004), at http://www.mpacuk.org/content/view/211/)

CONCLUSION

1. Khaled Abou El Fadl, *Rebellion and Violence in Islamic Law* (Cambridge: Cambridge University Press, 2001), pp. 322–23.

2. Another implication of our emphasis on the plurality of Islamic responses is the notion, often raised by Rawls, that formal doctrine alone does not explain the extent to which citizens accept a public conception of justice. People have motivations derived from a variety of sources. What can explain why a Muslim chooses the incompatible over the compatible doctrine, or one strand within the range of compatible doctrines? I have not attempted to answer this question but can say here that I find it obvious that people's reasons for finding one doctrine or another more appealing will be partly exogenous to the doctrine itself.

3. Ramadan, *To Be a European Muslim*, pp. 144–45. See chapter 5.

4. Mawlawī, "al-Mafāhīm al-asāsiyya," pp. 214–15. See chapter 7.

5. Walzer, "The Problem of Citizenship," in *Obligations*, p. 217.

6. The views presented in chapter 3 were broadly that Muslims must always strive to live under Islamic authority; non-Islamic polities may be at best adequate solutions to the secular problems of mundane life (security, trade, basic welfare) but are not legitimate in the wider senses of (a) solving these problems in the best way (that prescribed by God), (b) for the right reasons (because of the recognition of Divine guidance), and (c) allowing for the collective realization of nonsecular goals helpful to (if not crucial for) this-worldly happiness and goodness and other-worldly salvation; non-Muslim polities and societies are presumed to be in some way antagonistic to Muslim ones; and relationships of solidarity, affection, and principled moral obligation are limited to Muslims (*al-walā' wa'l-barā'*).

7. "Believers, be steadfast in upholding equity, bearing witness to the truth of God, even if it be against yourselves, or your parents and kin. Whether the person be rich or poor, God's claim takes precedence over the claims of either of them. Do not then follow your own whims lest you swerve from justice. If you distort the truth or decline to do justice, God is aware of all that you do." [4:135]

"Believers, be steadfast in your devotion to God, bearing witness to the truth in all equity. Never allow your hatred of a people to lead you astray from justice. Be just, this is closer to righteousness and be God-fearing for surely God is aware of all you do." [5:8]

"It may be that God will grant love and friendship between you and those whom you now hold as enemies for God is All-Powerful, and God is Oft-Forgiving, Most-Merciful. God does not forbid you from dealing justly and equitably with those who do not fight you for your religion nor expel you from your homes, for God loves the equitable." [60:7–8]

8. "Fulfill God's covenant when you have entered into it and break not your oaths after asserting them, for you thereby make God your guarantor." [16:91] "Fulfill every contract for contracts will be answered for [on the Day of Reckoning]." [17:34]

9. In the case of the social contract as one of mutual security guarantees, recall that some Muslim scholars regard American and British hostilities against Iraq to be a violation of the contract with *American* and *British* Muslims, or that domestic security measures constitute such a violation.

10. Insofar as it might involve a contingent commitment to moral obligations and thus implicitly contain the threat of retaliation. Also, if reciprocity is conceived of in ad hoc terms rather than as a general principle for constructing moral obligation, it might be grounded solely in tactical considerations based on self-interest. Consider Pope Benedict XVI's demand for "reciprocity" on the part of Muslim countries in the area of religious freedom. Is the suggestion that Muslims' religious freedom in Europe is contingent on the rights of Christians in the Middle East? Is the aspiration that Muslims will grant Christians similar rights to those enjoyed by European Muslims solely out of the desire to advance Muslim interests? Thus, where reciprocity operates on the ground as a tit-for-tat approach to cooperation rather than as a general feature of constructivist approaches to justice and morality, it might not be desirable in more than a very practical sense.

11. "Call to your Lord's path with wisdom and kindly exhortation, and argue with them in the most kindly manner, for, behold, your Lord knows best who strays from His path, and best knows who are the rightly-guided." [16:125]

12. "Say [O Prophet]: 'This is my way. I am calling you all to God with the power of reason and discernment, I and all who follow me.' " [12:108]

13. Mawlawī, "al-Mafāhīm al-asāsiyya," 214–15.

14. Ibid., p., 196.

15. The existing accounts of the purposes and methods of comparative political theory (chiefly Fred Dallmayr, "Beyond Monologue: For a Comparative Political Theory," *Perspectives on Politics*, vol. 2, no. 2 (June 2004), pp. 249–57; and Roxanne Euben, *Enemy in the Mirror: Islamic Fundamentalism and the Limits of Modern Rationalism* [Princeton, NJ: Princeton University Press, 1999]) strike me as unsuccessful. They lack accounts both of what makes an inquiry "comparative" (as opposed to merely broadening or illuminating) and of what particular epistemic or normative interest political theorists ought to have in any given thinker or text. The primary characteristic of this form of comparative political theory seems to be merely the study of non-Western political thought.

16. "[In Europe] there are small groups of *salafists*, doctrinaire traditionalists who seek to minimize their exchange with the surrounding non-Muslim population; they are pious exiles in a heathen land, suspicious and inward looking" (Asad, "Reflections on Blasphemy and Secular Criticism").

17. See, in particular, the work of Amaney Jamal, "The Political Participation and Engagement of Muslim Americans: Mosque Involvement and Group Consciousness," *American Politics Research*, vol. 33, no. 4 (May 2005), pp. 521–44; and Pew Research Center, *Muslim Americans: Middle Class and Mostly Mainstream*, http://pewresearch.org/assets/pdf/muslim-americans.pdf).

Bibliography

'Abd al-Qādir, Khālid. *Fiqh al-aqalliyyāt al-Muslima* (Tripoli: Dār al-Īmān, 1998).

Abou El Fadl, Khaled. "Islamic Law and Muslim Minorities: The Juristic Discourse on Muslim Minorities from the Second/Eighth to the Eleventh/Seventeenth Centuries," *Islamic Law and Society* 1:2 (August 1994), 141–187.

———. "Muslim Minorities and Self-Restraint in Liberal Democracies," *Loyola of Los Angeles Law Review* 29:4 (1996), 1525–1542.

———. *Rebellion and Violence in Islamic Law* (Cambridge: Cambridge University Press, 2001).

———. *Speaking in God's Name: Islamic Law, Authority and Women* (Oxford: Oneworld, 2001).

Abū Dāwūd, Sulaymān ibn al-Ash'ath al-Sijistānī (d. 889). *Sunan Abī Dāwūd* (Beirut: Dār Ibn Ḥazm, 1997).

Abū Shamāla, Majdī 'Aqīl, ed. *Risālat al-Muslimīn fī bilād al-gharb* (Irbid, Jordan: Dār al-Amal, 1999).

Abū Zahra, Muḥammad. *al-'Alāqāt al-duwaliyya fī al-Islām* (Cairo: al-Qawmiyya, 1964).

Ackerman, Bruce. *Social Justice in the Liberal State* (New Haven: Yale University Press, 1980).

al-'Adawī, 'Alī ibn Aḥmad al-Ṣa'īdī (d. 1775). *Ḥāshiya 'alā Kifāyat al-Ṭālib al-Rabbānī* (Cairo: Muṣṭafā al-Bābī al-Ḥalabī, 1952).

al-Akiti, Shaykh Muhammad Afifi. *Defending the Transgressed by Censuring the Reckless against the Killing of Civilians* (Birmingham, UK: Aqsa, 2005).

Ali, M. Amir. "A Case for Muslim Political Participation," *Muslim Public Affairs Committee UK* (February 2005), at http://www.islamawareness.net/Politics/participate.html.

al-Ālūsi, Maḥmūd (d. 1854). *Rūḥ al-ma'ānī fī tafsīr al-Qur'ān al-'Aẓīm* (Cairo: Dār al-Turāth, n.d.).

"al-Ta'ṣīl li-mashrū'iyyat mā jarā fī Landan min tafjīrāt wa'l-radd 'alā'l-bayān al-mash'ūm li-Abī Baṣīr al-Ṭarṭūsī" (on file with author).

al-'Alwani, Taha Jaber. "Muslims' Participation in the US Political Life" (November 2003), at http://www.islamonline.net/fatwa/english/FatwaDisplay.asp?hFatwaID=4743.

Arneson, Richard, and Ian Shapiro. "Democratic Autonomy and Religious Freedom: A Critique of *Wisconson v. Yoder*," in *Democracy's Place*, ed. Ian Shapiro (Ithaca, NY: Cornell University Press, 1996), 137–174.

Asad, Talal. *Genealogies of Religion: Discipline and Reasons of Power in Christianity and Islam* (Baltimore: Johns Hopkins University Press, 1993).

———. *Formations of the Secular: Christianity, Islam, Modernity* (Palo Alto, CA: Stanford University Press, 2003).

———. "Reflections on Blasphemy and Social Criticism," in *Religion: Beyond a Concept*, ed. Hent de Vries (New York: Fordham University Press, 2008), 580–610.

Audi, Robert. "The Separation of Church and State and the Obligations of Citizenship," *Philosophy & Public Affairs* 18.3 (Summer 1989), 259–296.

———. *Religious Commitment and Secular Reason* (Cambridge: Cambridge University Press, 2000).

Ayoob, Mohammed. "Political Islam: Image and Reality," *World Policy Journal* 21.3 (Fall 2004), 1–14.

al-Badawī, Ismā'īl. *Da'ā'im al-ḥukm fī al-sharī'a al-islāmiyya wa al-nuẓum al-dustūriyya al-mu'āṣira* (Cairo: Dār al-Fikr, 1980).

al-Baghawī, Ḥusayn Ibn Mas'ūd (d. 1117). *Ma'ālim al-Tanzīl* (Beirut: Dār al-Ma'rifa, 1987).

al-Baghdādī, 'Alī ibn Muḥammad Khāzin (d. 1341). *Lubāb al-ta'wīl ma'ānī al-tanzīl* (Beirut: Dār al-Kutub al-'Imiyya, 1995).

Baier, Kurt. "Justice and the Aims of Political Philosophy," *Ethics* 99 (July 1989), 771–790.

Bakht, Natasha. "Were Muslim Barbarians Really Knocking on the Gates of Ontario: The Religious Arbitration Controversy," *Ottawa Law Review* (Summer 2005), 67–85.

Barry, Brian. "How Not to Defend Liberal Institutions," in *Liberty and Justice: Essays in Political Theory 2* (Oxford: Clarendon, 1991).

———. *Culture and Equality* (Cambridge: Harvard University Press, 2000).

al-Bashīr, 'Iṣām. "al-Ḥiwār sabīlunā," in *Risālat al-Muslimīn fī bilād al-gharb*, ed. Majdī 'Aqīl Abū Shamāla (Irbid, Jordan: Dār al-Amal, 1999).

Benhabib, Seyla. "Afterword: Communicative Ethics and Contemporary Controversies in Practical Philosophy," in *The Communicative Ethics Controversy*, ed. Seyla Benhabib and Fred Dallmayr (Cambridge, MA: MIT Press, 1990), 330–369.

———. *The Claims of Culture* (Princeton, NJ: Princeton University Press, 2002).

Berman, Paul. "Who's Afraid of Tariq Ramadan? The Islamist, the Journalist, and the Defense of Liberalism," *New Republic*, June 4, 2007.

Bilgrami, Akeel. "Secularism and Relativism," *boundary 2*, 31:2 (Summer 2004), 173–196.

———. "Occidentalism, the Very Idea: An Essay on Enlightenment and Enchantment," *Critical Inquiry*, 32.3 (Spring 2006), 381–411.

al-Buhūtī, Manṣūr ibn Yūnus (d. 1641). *Kashshāf al-qinā'* (al-Riyāḍ: Maktabat al-Naṣr al-Ḥadītha, 1968).

al-Bukhārī, Muhammad ibn Ismā'īl (d. 870). *Jāmi' al-ṣaḥīḥ*, in Aḥmad ibn 'Alī ibn Ḥajar al-'Asqalānī (d. 1449), *Fatḥ al-bārī sharḥ Ṣaḥīḥ al-Bukhārī* (Dār al-Kutub al-'Ilmiyya, 1989).

al-Būṭī, Muḥammad Saʿīd Ramaḍān. *Jihad in Islam: How to Understand and Practise It* (Damascus: Dār al-Fikr, 1995).
Butt, Hassan. "My Plea to Fellow Muslims: You Must Renounce Terror," *The Observer*, July 1, 2007 at http://www.guardian.co.uk/commentisfree/2007/jul/01/comment.religion1.
Cesari, Jocelyne. *When Islam and Democracy Meet: Muslims in Europe and in the United States* (New York: Palgrave Macmillan, 2004).
———. *European Muslims and the Secular State*, ed. with Seán McLoughlin (Burlington, VT: Ashgate, 2005).
Cohen, Joshua. "Moral Pluralism and Political Consensus," in *The Idea of Democracy*, ed. David Copp, Jean Hampton, and John E Roemer (Cambridge: Cambridge University Press, 1993), 270–291.
Cohen, Joshua, and Deborah Chasman, eds. *Islam and the Challenge of Democracy* (Princeton, NJ: Princeton University Press, 2004).
Cook, Michael. *Commanding Right and Forbidding Wrong in Islam* (Cambridge: Cambridge University Press, 2000).
———. *Forbidding Wrong in Islam* (Cambridge: Cambridge University Press, 2003).
Crone, Patricia. *God's Rule: Government and Islam* (New York: Columbia University Press, 2004).
Dallmayr, Fred. "Beyond Monologue: For a Comparative Political Theory," *Perspectives on Politics*, vol. 2, no. 2 (June 2004), 249–257.
Donner, Fred. "The Sources of Islamic Conceptions of War," in *Just War and Jihad: Historical and Theoretical Perspectives on War and Peace in Western and Islamic Traditions*, ed. John Kelsay and James T. Johnson (New York: Greenwood, 1991), 31–69.
Euben, Roxanne. *Enemy in the Mirror: Islamic Fundamentalism and the Limits of Modern Rationalism* (Princeton, NJ: Princeton University Press, 1999).
European Council for *Fatwa* and Research. *Fatāwā al-majmūʿa al-ūla* (Cairo: Islamic Publishing, 1999).
———. "Elections in Non-Muslim Countries: Role of Muslims" (May 2004), at http://www.islamonline.net/fatwa/english/FatwaDisplay.asp?hFatwaID=78491.
Fadel, Mohammad. "The Social Logic of *Taqlīd* and the Rise of the *Mukhataṣar*," *Islamic Law and Society* 3:2 (1996), 193–233.
———. "The True, the Good and the Reasonable: The Theological and Ethical Roots of Public Reason in Islamic Law," *Canadian Journal of Law and Jurisprudence* 21:1 (2008), 5–69.
Faḍl Allāh, Muḥammad Ḥusayn. *Uslūb al-daʿwa fī'l-Qur'ān* (Beirut: Dār al-Zahrā', 1986).
———. *al-Hijra wa'l-ightirāb: ta'sīs fiqhī li-mushkilat al-lujū' wa'l-hijra* (Beirut: Mu'assasat al-ʿĀrif li'l-Maṭbūʿāt, 1999).
al-Fatāwā al-Hindiyya (Beirut: Dār Iḥyā' al-Turāth al-ʿArabī, n.d.).
al-Fawzān, Ṣāliḥ ibn Fawzān ibn ʿAbd Allāh. *Muḥāḍarāt fī'l-ʿaqīda wa al-daʿwa* (Riyadh: Dār al-ʿĀṣima, 1992).
Fish, Stanley. *There's No Such Thing as Free Speech (. . . and It's a Good Thing Too)* (New York: Oxford University Press, 1994).
Frank, Richard M. "Moral Obligation in Classical Muslim Theology," *Journal of Religious Ethics* 11:2 (Fall 1983), 204–223.
Friedmann, Yohanan. *Tolerance and Coercion in Islam: Interfaith Relations in the Muslim Tradition* (Cambridge: Cambridge University Press, 2003).
Galston, William. "Who's a Liberal?" *Public Interest* (Summer 2001), 100–108.
———. *Liberal Pluralism* (Cambridge: Cambridge University Press, 2002).

Garsten, Bryan. *Saving Persuasion: A Defense of Rhetoric and Judgment* (Cambridge, Mass.: Harvard University Press, 2006).
Gaus, Gerald F. "The Rational, the Reasonable and Justification," *Journal of Political Philosophy* 3:3 (1995), 234–258.
———. *Justificatory Liberalism: An Essay on Epistemology and Political Theory* (Oxford: Oxford University Press, 1996).
Geertz, Clifford. "Anti Anti-Relativism," *American Anthropologist* 86:2 (June 1984), 263–278.
al-Ghannūshī, Rāshid (Rachid Gannouchi). *Huqūq al-muwāṭana: Huqūq ghayr al-muslim fi'l-mujtama' al-Islāmī* (Herndon, VA: International Institute of Islamic Thought, 1993).
———. "Participation in Non-Islamic Government," in *Liberal Islam: A Sourcebook*, ed. Charles Kurzman (Oxford: Oxford University Press, 1998), 89–95.
———. "al-Islām fi'l-gharb wa 'alāqātuhu bi'l-anẓima al-gharbiyya," in *Risālat al-Muslimīn fī bilād al-gharb*, ed. Majdī 'Aqīl Abū Shamāla (Irbid, Jordan: Dār al-Amal, 1999).
al-Ghazzālī, Abū Ḥāmid. *On Enjoining Good and Forbidding Wrong*, trans. Muhammad Nur Abdus Salam (Chicago: Kazi, 2003).
Gray, John. *Post-Liberalism: Studies in Political Thought* (London: Routledge, 1993).
Guillaume, Alfred. *The Life of Muhammad: A Translation of Isḥāq's* Sīrat Rasūl Allāh (London: Oxford University Press, 1955).
Gutmann, Amy. "Civic Education and Social Diversity," *Ethics* 105 (April 1995), 557–579.
Habermas, Jürgen. "Struggles for Recognition in the Democratic Constitutional State," in *Multiculturalism: Examining the Politics of Recognition*, ed. Amy Gutmann (Princeton, NJ: Princeton University Press, 1994), 107–148.
———. *Moral Consciousness and Communicative Action* (Cambridge, MA: MIT Press, 2001).
al-Haddad, Sheikh Haytham bin Jawwad. "An Advice to British Muslims Regarding the Coming Elections," (n.d).at http://www.as-sahwah.com/viewarticle.php?articleID=1150&%C2%A0.
al-Hakim, Abdul Hadi. *A Code of Practice for Muslims in the West (In Accordance with the Edicts of His Eminence Grand Ayatullah As-Sayyid Ali al-Husaini as-Seestani*, trans. Sayyid Muhammad Rizvi (London: Imam Ali Foundation, 1999).
Hallaq, Wael. *A History of Islamic Legal Theories: An Introduction to Sunni* Uṣūl al-Fiqh (Cambridge: Cambridge University Press, 1997).
al-Hanooti, Muhammad. "Immigration to a Non-Muslim Country" (August 2002), at http://www.islam-online.net/fatwa/english/FatwaDisplay.asp?hFatwaID+77860.
———. "Voting in a Majority Non-Muslim Country" (August 2003), at http://www.islamonline.net/fatwa/english/FatwaDisplay.asp?hFatwaID=14795.
Hansen, Randall. "The Danish Cartoon Controversy: A Defence of Liberal Freedom," in "The Danish Cartoon Affair: Free Speech, Racism, Islamism, and Integration," *International Migration* 44:5 (2006), 7–16.
Hashmi, Sohail, ed. *The Islamic Ethics of War and Peace* (Ph. D. diss., Harvard University, 1996).
———. "Interpreting the Islamic Ethics of War and Peace," in *The Ethics of War and Peace*, ed. Terry Nardin (Princeton, NJ: Princeton University Press, 1996), 146–66.
———. *Islamic Political Ethics* (Princeton, NJ: Princeton University Press, 2002).
Hourani, George. "Ghāzalī on the Ethics of Action," *Journal of the American Oriental Society* 96:1 (January–March, 1976), 69–88.

———. *Reason and Tradition in Islamic Ethics* (Cambridge: Cambridge University Press, 1985).

Ibn ʿAbidīn, Muḥammad Amīn ibn ʿUmar (d. 1836). *Radd al-muḥtār alā'l-Durr al-mukhtār sharḥ Tanwīr al-abṣār* (Beirut: Dār al-Kutub al-ʿIlmiyya, 1994–1998).

Ibn Bayya, ʿAbd Allāh ibn al-Shaykh al-Maḥfūẓ. *Ṣināʿat al-fatwā wa-fiqh al-aqalliyāt* (Jedda/Beirut: Dār al-Minhāj, 2007).

Ibn Hajar al-Haythamī, Aḥmad ibn Muḥammad (d. 1566). *al-Fatāwā al-kubrā al-fiqhiyya* (Beirut: Dār al-Kutub al-ʿIlmiyya, 1997).

Ibn Ḥanbal, Aḥmad ibn Muḥammad (d. 855). *al-Musnad* (Cairo: Dār al-Maʿārif, 1950).

Ibn Hishām, ʿAbd al-Mālik (d. 834). *al-Sīra al-nabawiyya* (Cairo: Muṣṭafā al-Bābī al-Ḥalabī, 1936).

Ibn al-Humām, Muḥammad ibn ʿAbd al-Wāḥid al-Sīwāsī (d. 1460). *Sharḥ fatḥ al-qadīr* (Beirut: Dār al-Fikr, n.d.).

Ibn Kathīr, Ismāʿīl ibn ʿUmar (d. 1373). *Tafsīr al-Qur'ān al-ʿAẓīm* (Beirut: Dār al-Kutub al-ʿIlmiyya, 1998).

Ibn Nujaym, Zayn al-Dīn ibn Ibrāhīm ibn Muḥammad (d. 1563). *al-Baḥr al-rā'iq* (Beirut: Dār al-Maʿrifa, 1993).

Ibn Qudāma, Muwaffaq al-Dīn (d. 1223). *al-Mughnī* (Cairo: Hajar, 1990).

Ibn Rushd, Abū al-Walīd ibn Muḥammad ibn Aḥmad (Averroës, d. 1198). *Bidāyat al-mujtahid wa-nihāyat al-muqtaṣid* (Beirut, Dār al-kutub al-ʿilmiyya, 1996).

Ibn Rushd, Muḥammad ibn Aḥmad (d. 1122). *al-Muqaddimāt al-mumahhidāt*, ed. Saʿīd Aḥmad Aʿrāb (Beirut: Dār al-Gharb al-Islāmī, 1988).

Ibn al-Siddīq, Abd al-ʿAzīz ibn Muḥammad. *Ḥukm al-iqāma bi-bilād al-kuffār wa-bayān wujūbihā fī bʿaḍ al-aḥwāl* (Tangiers: Maṭābiʿ al-Būghāz, 1985).

Ibn Taymiyya, Aḥmad ibn ʿAbd al-Ḥalīm (d. 1283). *Majmūʿ fatāwā Sheikh al-Islām Aḥmad Ibn Taymiyya* (Rabat: Maktabat al-Maʿārif, 1980).

Jā'billāh, Aḥmad. "Qawāʿid al-taʿāmul bayn al-muslimīn wa-ghayrihim fi'l-mujtamaʿāt al-awrubiyya," in *Risālat al-Muslimīn fī bilād al-gharb*, ed. Majdī ʿAqīl Abū Shamāla (Irbid, Jordan: Dār al-Amal, 1999).

Jād al-Ḥaqq, ʿAlī Jād al-Ḥaqq. "Fatwā fī baʿḍ aḥkām tataʿallaq bi'l-aqalliyyāt al-muslima fī ghayr diyār al-muslimīn," *Majallat al-Azhar* 63:6 (1991).

Jackson, Sherman. "Jihad and the Modern World," *Journal of Islamic Law & Culture* 7:1 (Spring–Summer 2002), 2–26.

al-Jadīʿ, ʿAbdallāh. "Risālat al-Muslim fī bilād al-gharb" in *Risālat al-muslimīn fī bilād al-gharb*, ed. Majdī ʿAqīl Abū Shamāla (Irbid, Jordan: Dār al-Amal, 1999).

Jamal, Amaney. "The Political Participation and Engagement of Muslim Americans: Mosque Involvement and Group Consciousness," *American Politics Research* 33:4 (May 2005), 521–544.

al-Jarbūʿ, ʿAbd al-ʿAzīz ibn Ṣāliḥ al-Jarbūʿ. "al-Iʿlām bi-wujūb al-hijra min dār al-kufr ilā dār al-Islām." (July 15, 2001) On file with author.

———. "Al-ta'sīl li-mashrūʿiyyat ma ḥasala li-Amrīka min tadmīr." On file with author.

Johansen, Baber. *Contingency in a Sacred Law: Legal and Ethical Norms in the Muslim* Fiqh (Leiden: Brill, 1999).

Johnson, James Turner, and John Kelsay, eds. *Cross, Crescent and Sword: The Justification and Limitation of War in Western and Islamic Tradition* (London: Greenwood, 1990).

Jones, Peter. "Respecting Beliefs and Rebuking Rushdie," *British Journal of Political Science* 20:4 (October 1990), 415–437.

———. "Toleration, Recognition and Identity," *Journal of Political Philosophy* 14:2 (2006), 123–143.

Kahf, Monzer. "Refusing to Pay Taxes to the US due to Its Anti-Muslim Policy" (June 2002) at http://www.islamonline.net/fatwa/english/FatwaDisplay.asp?hFatwaID=70581.

Kamali, Mohammed Hashim. *The Dignity of Man: An Islamic Perspective* (Cambridge, UK: Islamic Texts Society, 1999).

———. *Freedom, Equality and Justice in Islam* (Leicester, UK: Islamic Texts Society, 1999).

al-Kāsānī, Abū Bakr ibn Mas'ūd (d. 1191). *Kitāb Badā'i' al-sanā'i' fī tartīb al-sharā'i'* (Beirut: Dār al-Kutub al-'Ilmiyya, 1986).

Kekes, John. *The Morality of Pluralism* (Princeton, NJ: Princeton University Press, 1993).

Kelsay, John, and James Turner Johnson, eds. *Just War and Jihad: Historical and Theoretical Reflections on War and Peace in Western and Islamic Traditions* (Westport, CT: Greenwood, 1991).

Khadduri, Majid. *War and Peace in the Law of Islam* (Baltimore: Johns Hopkins University Press, 1955).

———. *The Islamic Conception of Justice* (Baltimore: Johns Hopkins University Press, 1984).

Khalil, Mohamed. *Islam and Democracy: Religion, Politics, and Power in the Middle East* (Washington, DC: USIP, 1992).

al-Khamlīshī, 'Abd Allāh al-Ṭā'i'. *al-Janna wa-tarīquhā al-mustaqīm wa'l-nār wa-tarīquhā al-dhamīm* (Rotterdam: Masjid al-Naṣr, 1995).

Khan, Shaykh Aurangzeb. "Joining Political Parties in Non Muslim Countries: According to Islamic Shariah" (December 2004), at http://www.mpacuk.org/content/view/211/.

Klosko, George. "Political Constructivism in Rawls's Political Liberalism," *American Political Science Review* 91:3 (September 1997), 635–646.

Krasnoff, Larry. "Consensus, Stability, and Normativity in Rawls's Political Liberalism," *Journal of Philosophy*, vol. 95 (1998), 269–292.

Kukathas, Chandran. "Are There Any Cultural Rights?" *Political Theory* 20.1 (February 1992), 105–139.

Kutty, Sheikh Ahmad. "Is *Hijrah* (Emigration) Still Necessary?" (February 2005) at http://www.islamonline.net/fatwa/english/FatwaDisplay.asp?hFatwaID+99040.

Kymlicka, Will. *Multicultural Citizenship: A Liberal Theory of Minority Rights* (Oxford: Oxford University Press, 1996).

Lewis, Bernard. "Legal and Historical Reflections on the Position of Muslim Populations under Non-Muslim Rule," *Journal of the Institute of Muslim Minority Affairs* 13:1 (January 1992), 1–16.

Macedo, Stephen. "Liberal Civic Education and Religious Fundamentalism: The Case of God v. John Rawls?" *Ethics* 105 (April 1995), 468–496.

———. "Transformative Constitutionalism and the Case of Religion: Defending the Moderate Hegemony of Liberalism," *Political Theory* 26:1 (February 1998), 56–80.

Mahmood, Saba. "Questioning Liberalism, Too," *Boston Review: A Political and Literary Forum* (April/May 2003), 18–20.

Mahmoud, Mohamed. "Mahmud Muhammad Taha's Second Message of Islam," in *Islam and Modernity: Muslim Intellectuals Respond*, ed. John Cooper, Ronald L. Nettler, and Mohamed Mahmoud (London: I. B. Tauris, 1998).

al-Majlis al-Awrubbī l'il-Iftā' wa'l-Buḥūth. *Fatāwā al-majmū'a al-ūlā* (Cairo: Maktabat al-Īmān, 1999).

Manṣūr, 'Alī 'Alī. *al-Sharī'a al-Islāmiyya wa al-qānūn al-duwalī al-'ām* (Cairo: Lajnat al-Khubarā', 1971).

March, Andrew F. "Liberal Citizenship and the Search for Overlapping Consensus: The Case of Muslim Minorities," *Philosophy & Public Affairs* 34:4 (Fall 2006), 373–421.

———. "Islamic Foundations for a Social Contract in Non-Muslim Liberal Democracies," *American Political Science Review* 101:2 (May 2007), 235–252.

Masud, Muhammad Khalid. "Being a Muslim in a Non-Muslim Polity: Three Alternative Models," *Journal of the Institute of Muslim Minority Affairs* 10:1 (January 1989), 118–128.

———. *Shatibi's Philosophy of Islamic Law* (Islamabad: Islamic Research Institute, 1995).

al-Māwardī, Abū al-Ḥasan (d. 1058). *Tafsīr al-nukat wa al-'uyūn*, at http://www.altafsir.com.

Mawdūdī, Sayyid Abul 'Alā. *Towards Understanding the Qur'ān* (Leicester, UK: Islamic Foundation, 1990).

Mawlawī, Fayṣal. "al-Mafāhīm al-asāsiyya li al-da'wa al-islāmiyya fī bilād al-gharb," in *Risālat al-Muslimīn fī bilād al-gharb*, ed. Majdī 'Aqīl Abū Shamāla (Irbid, Jordan: Dār al-Amal, 1999).

———. "How Should Muslims in the West Deal with the Iraqi Crisis?" (March 2003), at http://www.islamonline.net/fatwa/english/FatwaDisplay.asp?hFatwaID=97351.

Mayer, Ann Elizabeth. "War and Peace in the Islamic Tradition and International Law" in *Just War and Jihad: Historical and Theoretical Reflections on War and Peace in Western and Islamic Traditions*, ed. John Kelsay and James Turner Johnson (Westport, CT.: Greenwood, 1991), 195–226.

Michot, Yahya. *Mardin: Hégire, fuite du péché et «demeure de l'Islam»* (Beirut/Paris: al-Bouraq, 2004).

Modirzadeh, Naz K. "Taking Islamic Law Seriously: INGOs and the Battle for Muslim Hearts and Minds," *Harvard Human Rights Journal* 19 (Spring 2006), 191–233.

Modood, Tariq. "The Liberal Dilemma: Integration or Vilification," in "The Danish Cartoon Affair: Free Speech, Racism, Islamism, and Integration," *International Migration* 44:5 (2006), 4–7.

Muḥammad, Jamāl al-Dīn 'Aṭiya. *Naḥwa fiqh jadīd li'l-aqalliyyāt* (Cairo: Dār al-Salām, 2003).

al-Munajjid, Muhammad Salih. "Living in a Non-Muslim Country Seeking a Better Life" (February 2004), at http://www.islamonline.net/fatwa/english/FatwaDisplay.asp?hFatwaID+110859.

Murad, Khurram. *Da'wah among Non-Muslims in the West* (Leicester: Islamic Foundation, 1986).

Muslim ibn Hajjāj al-Qushayrī, Abū al-Ḥusayn (d. 875). *Ṣaḥīḥ Muslim* (Beirut: Dār Iḥyā' al-Turāth al-'Arabī, n.d.).

Nadwi, Syed Abul Hasan Ali. *Muslims in the West: The Message and Mission* (Leicester, UK: Islamic Foundation, 1983).

Nagel, Thomas. "Moral Conflict and Political Legitimacy," *Philosophy and Public Affairs* 16: 3 (Summer 1987), 215–240.

an-Na'im, Abdullahi. "The Rights of Women and International Law in the Muslim Context," *Whittier Law Review* 9:3 (1987), 491–516.

———. *Towards an Islamic Reformation: Civil Liberties, Human Rights, and International Law* (Syracuse, NY: Syracuse University Press, 1990).

al-Nasā'ī, Aḥmad ibn Shu'ayb (d. 915). *al-Sunan al-Kubrā* (Beirut: Dār al-Kutub al-'Ilmiyya, 1991).

al-Nasafī, 'Abd Allāh ibn Aḥmad (d.1310). *Tafsīr al-Nasafī : Madārik al-tanzīl wa haqā'iq al-ta'wīl* (Beirut: Dār Ibn Kathīr, 1998).

al-Nawawī, Abū Zakariyyā' (d. 1277). *Sharḥ Ṣaḥīḥ Muslim* (Beirut: Dār al-Qalam, 1987).

———. *al-Majmūʿ sharḥ al-Muhadhdhab* (Beirut: Dār al-Fikr, 2000).
"Need It Be "Us and Them?" at http://www.islamonline.net/english/introducingislam/Tolerance/article02.shtml (December 2003).
Nielsen, Jørgen S. *Muslims in Western Europe* (Edinburgh: Edinburgh University Press, 1992).
———. *Towards a European Islam* (New York: St. Martin's, 1999).
———. *Muslim Networks and Transnational Communities in and across Europe*, ed. with Stefano Allievi (Leiden: Brill, 2003).
Nussbaum, Martha. *Frontiers of Justice: Disability, Nationality, Species Membership* (Cambridge, MA: Belknap, 2007).
Opwis, Felicitas. "*Maṣlaḥa*: An Intellectual History of a Core Concept in Islamic Legal Theory" (PhD diss., Yale University, 2001).
———. "*Maṣlaḥa* in Contemporary Islamic Legal Theory," *Islamic Law and Society* 12:2, 2005, 182–223.
Packer, George. "Fighting Faiths: Can Liberal Internationalism Be Saved?" *New Yorker*, July 10, 2006.
Parekh, Bhikhu. *Rethinking Multiculturalism: Cultural Diversity and Political Theory* (Cambridge: Harvard University Press, 2000).
———. "Barry and the Dangers of Liberalism," in *Multiculturalism Reconsidered:* Culture and Equality *and its Critics*, ed. Paul Kelly (Oxford: Polity, 2002).
Peters, Rudolph. *Jihad in Classical and Modern Islam* (Princeton, NJ: Markus Wiener, 1996).
Pew Research Center, *Muslim Americans: Middle Class and Mostly Mainstream*, http://pewresearch.org/assets/pdf/muslim-americans.pdf.
Powers, David S. "Fatwās as Sources for Legal and Social History," *al-Qanṭara* 11 (1990), 295–341.
al-Qara Dāghī,ʿAlī Muḥyī al-Dīn. "Tax Evasion in Non-Muslim Countries: Permissible?" (January 2004), at http://www.islamonline.net/fatwa/english/FatwaDisplay.asp?hFatwaID=35886.
al-Qaraḍāwī, Yūsuf. *al-Khaṣāʾis al-ʿāmma liʾl-Islām* (Cairo: Maktabat Wahba, 1991).
———. *Min fiqh al-dawla fīʾl-Islām* (Cairo: Dār al-Shurūq, 1997).
———. "al-Infitāḥ ʿalāʾl-gharb: muqtaḍayātuhu wa-shurūṭuhu," in Majdī ʿAqīl Abū Shamāla, ed., *Risālat al-Muslimīn fī bilād al-gharb* (Irbid, Jordan: Dār al-Amal, 1999).
———. *Priorities of the Islamic Movement in the Coming Phase* (Swansea, UK: Awakening, 2000).
———. *Fī fiqh al-aqalliyyāt al-muslima* (Cairo: Dār al-Shurūq, 2001).
———. "Ulama's Fatwas on American Muslim Participating in US Military Campaign" (October 2001), at http://www.islamonline.net/fatwa/english/FatwaDisplay.asp?hFatwaID=52014.
———. *Fatāwā muʿāṣira* (Beirut: al-Maktab al-Islāmī, 2003).
———. "American Muslim Soldiers Participating in US Attacks against Muslims" (October 2003), at http://www.islamonline.net/fatwa/english/FatwaDisplay.asp?hFatwaID=49987.
———. "Backing the Wronged Afghans" (October 2003), at http://www.islamonline.net/fatwa/english/FatwaDisplay.asp?hFatwaID=51564.
———. "Muslims' Participation in the US Political Life" (November 2003), at http://islamonline.net/fatwa/english/FatwaDisplay.asp?hFatwaID=4743.
———. "Cooperating with Non-Muslims in Fighting Evil" (February 2005), at http://www.islamonline.net/fatwa/english/FatwaDisplay.asp?hFatwaID=8514.

Quong, Jonathan. "The Rights of Unreasonable Citizens," *Journal of Political Philosophy* 12:3 (2004), 314–335.

al-Qurṭubī, Muḥammad ibn Aḥmad (d. 671/1273). *al-Jāmi' li-aḥkām al-Qur'ān* (Beirut: Dār al-Kutub al-'Ilmiyya, 1996).

Quṭb, Sayyid. *Fī ẓilāl al-Qur'ān* (Beirut: Dār al-Shurūq, 1979).

———. *In the Shade of the Qur'ān*, Adil Salahi and Ashur Shamis, trans. and eds. (Leicester: Islamic Foundation, 2001).

Rahman, Fazlur. *Islam and Modernity: The Transformation of an Intellectual Tradition* (Chicago: University of Chicago Press, 1982).

Ramadan, Tariq. *To Be a European Muslim* (Leicester, UK: Islamic Foundation, 1999).

al-Ramlī, Muḥammad ibn Aḥmad (d. 1595 or 1596). *Nihāyat al-muḥtāj ilā sharh al-Minhāj fī al-fiqh 'alā madhhab al-Imām al-Shāfi'ī* (Beirut: Dār al-Kutub al-'Ilmiyya, 1993).

Rawls, John. *A Theory of Justice* (Cambridge: Harvard University Press, 1971).

———. "Kantian Constructivism in Moral Theory," *Journal of Philosophy* 77 (1980), 515–572.

———. *Political Liberalism* (New York: Columbia University Press, 1993).

———. "The Idea of Public Reason Revisited," in *The Law of Peoples* (Cambridge: Harvard University Press, 1999).

Raz, Joseph. *The Morality of Freedom* (Oxford: Clarendon, 1986).

———. "Multiculturalism: A Liberal Perspective," in *Ethics in the Public Domain* (Oxford: Clarendon, 1994).

al-Rāzī, Fakhr al-Dīn (d. 1149). *Mafātīḥ al-ghayb* (Beirut: Dār al-Kutub al-'Ilmiyya, 1990).

Reinhart, A. Kevin. "Impurity/No Danger," *History of Religions* 30:1 (August 1990), 1–24.

———. "Islamic Law as Islamic Ethics," *Journal of Religious Ethics* 11:2 (1993), 186–203.

Riḍā, Muḥammad Rashīd (d. 1935). *Tafsīr al-Qur'ān al-ḥakīm al-shahīr bi-tafsīr al-manār* (Beirut: Dār al-Ma'rifa, 1973).

———. *Fatāwā al-Imām Muḥammad Rashīd Riḍā*, ed. Ṣalāḥ al-Dīn al-Munajjid and Yūsuf Q. Khūrī (Beirut: Dār al-Kitāb al-Jadīd, 1980).

Rorty, Richard. *Contingency, Irony, Solidarity* (Cambridge: Cambridge University Press, 1986).

Rousseau, Jean-Jacques. *The Social Contract*, in *The Basic Political Writings* (Indianapolis, IN: Hackett, 1988).

Sachedina, Abdulaziz. "The Development of *Jihad* in Islamic Revelation and History," in *Cross, Crescent and Sword: The Justification and Limitation of War in Western and Islamic Tradition*, ed. James Turner Johnson and John Kelsay (London: Greenwood, 1990), 35–50.

———. *The Islamic Roots of Democratic Pluralism* (Oxford: Oxford University Press, 2001).

Safi, Louay. *Peace and the Limits of War* (London: International Institute of Islamic Thought, 2003).

Saḥnūn, 'Abd al-Salām ibn Sa'īd (d. 854). *al-Mudawwana al-kubrā* (Cairo, Dār al-Fikr, n.d.).

Sajid, Abduljalil. "Joining Political Parties in Non Muslim Countries: According to Islamic Shariah," *Muslim Public Affairs Committee UK* (December 2004), at http://www.mpacuk.org/content/view/211/.

Sandel, Michael. "*Political Liberalism* (Review)," *Harvard Law Review* 107:7 (May 1994), 1765–1794.

al-Sarakhsī, Muḥammad Ibn Aḥmad (d. 1090). *Kitāb al-Mabsūṭ* (Beirut: Dār al-Kutub al-'Ilmiyya, 2001).

al-Ṣāwī, Aḥmad (d. 1825). *Bulghat al-sālik* (Cairo: Muṣṭafā al-Bābī al-Ḥalabī, 1952).

Scheffler, Samuel. "The Appeal of Political Liberalism," *Ethics* 105 (October 1994), 4–22.

Schlag, Pierre. "The Empty Circles of Liberal Justification," *Michigan Law Review* 96:1 (1997), 1–46.

Schwartzman, Micah. "Political Justification Beyond the Limits of Public Reason." Unpublished manuscript.

Shadīd, Muḥammad. *al-Jihād fī'l-Islām* (Cairo: Mu'assasat al-Maṭbū'āt al-Ḥadītha, n.d.).

Shadid, W. A. R., and P. S. van Koningsveld, eds. *Political Participation and Identities of Muslims in Non-Muslim States* (Kampen, Netherlands: Kok Phaos, 1996).

———. "Loyalty to a Non-Muslim Government: An Analysis of Islamic Normative Discussions and of the Views of Some Contemporary Islamicists," in *Political Participation and Identities of Muslims in Non-Muslim States,* ed. W. A. R. Shadid and P. S. van Koningsveld (Kampen, Netherlands: Kok Phaos, 1996).

———. *Muslims in the Margin: Political Responses to the Presence of Islam in Western Europe* (Kampen, Netherlands: Kok Pharos, 1996).

———. *Religious Freedom and the Neutrality of the State: The Position of Islam in the European Union* (Leuven; Sterling, VA: Peeters, 2002).

———. *Intercultural Relations and Religious Authorities: Muslims in the European Union* (Leuven: Peeters, 2002).

———. "Religious Authorities of Muslims in the West: Their Views on Political Participation," in *Intercultural Relations and Religious Authorities: Muslims in the European Union,* ed. W. A. R. Shadid and P. S. van Koningsveld (Leuven: Peeters, 2002).

al-Shāfi'ī, Muḥammad ibn Idrīs (d. 820). *Kitāb al-Umm fī furū' al-fiqh* (Beirut: Dār al-Ma'rifa, 1986).

Shaltūt, Maḥmūd. *al-Qur'ān wa'l-qitāl* (Beirut: Dār al-Fatḥ, 1983).

al-Shanqiti, Sheikh Muhammad al-Mukhtar. "Muslims' Participation in US Elections" (November 2003), at http://www.islam-online.net/fatwaapplication/english/display.asp?hFatwaID=106769.

al-Sharqāwī, 'Uthmān al-Sa'īd. *Sharī'at al-qitāl fī'l-Islām* (Cairo: al-Zahrā', 1972).

al-Shāṭibī, Abū Iṣḥāq (d. 1388). *al-Muwāfaqāt* (al-Khubar, Saudi Arabia: Dār Ibn 'Affān, 1997).

al-Shaybānī, Muḥammad in al-Ḥasan (d. 805). *The Islamic Law of Nations: Shaybānī's Siyar,* Majid Khadduri, trans. (Baltimore: Johns Hopkins University Press, 1966).

al-Shīrāzī, Abū Isḥāq (d. 1083). *al-Muhadhdhab fī fiqh al-Imām al-Shāfi'ī* (Beirut: Dār al-Fikr, n.d.).

al-Shirbīnī al-Khaṭīb, Muḥammad ibn Aḥmad (d. 1570). *al-Mughnī al-muḥtāj ilā ma'rifat ma'ānī alfāẓ al-Minhāj* (Beirut: Dār al-Kutub al-'Ilmiyya, 2000).

al-Shithrī, Ṣāliḥ ibn Muḥammad. *Ḥukm al-lujū' wa'l-iqāma fī bilād al-kuffār* (Riyad: Dār al-Ḥabīb, n.d.).

Siddiqi, Muzammil H. "Immigration to a Non-Muslim Country" (August 2002), at http://www.islamonline.net/fatwa/english/FatwaDisplay.asp?hFatwaID+77860.

———. "Muslims Participating in the US Local Councils" (October 2003), at http://www.islamonline.net/fatwa/english/FatwaDisplay.asp?hFatwaID=62236.

al-Sīstānī, 'Alī al-Ḥusaynī. *al-Fiqh li'l-mughtaribīn* (London: Mu'assasat al-Imām 'Alī, 2002).

Spinner-Halev, Jeff. *The Boundaries of Citizenship: Race, Ethnicity, and Nationality in the Liberal State* (Baltimore: Johns Hopkins University Press, 1994).

———. "Cultural Pluralism and Partial Citizenship," in *Multicultural Questions*, ed. Christian Joppke and Steve Lukes (Oxford: Oxford University Press, 1999), 65–87.

Spivak, Gayatri. "Can the Subaltern Speak? Speculations on Widow Sacrifice," *Wedge* 7–8 (Winter–Spring 1985), 120–130.

al-Suyūṭī, Jalāl al-Dīn 'Abd al-Raḥmān (d. 1505). *al-Durr al-manthūr fī tafsīr al-ma'thūr* (Beirut: Dār al-Kutub al-'Ilmiyya, 1990).

Swaine, Lucas. *The Liberal Conscience: Politics and Principle in a World of Religious Pluralism* (New York: Columbia University Press, 2006).

al-Ṭabarī, Abū Ja'far (d. 923). *Jāmi' al-bayān fī ta'wīl al-Qur'ān* (Beirut: Dār al-Kutub al-'Ilmiyya, 1999).

al-Ṭaḥḥān, Muṣṭafā. "al-Muslim al-dā'iya yaḥsun al-ta'āmul ma' al-muslim wa ghayr al-muslim," in *Risālat al-Muslimīn fī bilād al-gharb*, ed. Majdī 'Aqīl Abū Shamāla (Irbid, Jordan: Dār al-Amal, 1999).

Taseer, Aatish. "A British Jihadist," *Prospect* 113 (August 2005), 18–24.

Taylor, Charles. "The Politics of Recognition," in *Multiculturalism: Examining the Politics of Recognition*, ed. Amy Gutmann (Princeton, NJ: Princeton University Press, 1994), 25–73.

Tibi, Bassam. "War and Peace in Islam," in *Islamic Political Ethics*, ed. Sohail Hashmi (Princeton, NJ: Princeton University Press, 2002), 128–145.

al-Tirmidhī, Muḥammad ibn 'Isā (d. 892). *al-Jāmi' al-ṣaḥīḥ* (Beirut: Dār al-Kutub al-'Ilmiyya, n.d.).

de Tocqueville, Alexis. *Democracy in America* (New York, Penguin, 2003).

Tūbūlyāk, Sulaymān Muḥammad (transliteration from Bosnian of "Sulejman Topoljak"). *al-Aḥkām al-siyāsiyya li'l-aqalliyāt al-muslima fi'l-fiqh al-Islāmī* (Beirut: Dār al-Nafā'is, 1997).

'Ulaysh, Muḥammad ibn Aḥmad (d. 1882). *Fatḥ al-'alī al-mālik fi-al-fatwā 'alā madhhab al-Imām Mālik* (Cairo: Dār al-Fikr, 1937).

Walzer, Michael. *Obligations: Essays on Disobedience, War, and Citizenship* (Cambridge: Harvard University Press, 1970).

al-Wansharīsī, Aḥmad ibn Yahya (d. 1508). *al-Mi'yār al-mu'rib wa al jāmi' al-mughrib 'an fatāwā ahl Ifrīqiya wa'l-Andalus wa'l-Maghrib*, ed., Muḥammad Hajjī (Rabat: Ministry of Religious Endowments and Islamic Affairs, 1981).

Weiss, Bernard G. *The Search for God's Law: Islamic Jurisprudence in the Writings of Sayf Al-Din Al-Amidi* (Salt Lake City: University of Utah Press, 1992).

———. *The Spirit of Islamic Law* (Athens: University of Georgia Press, 1998).

Wenar, Leif. "*Political Liberalism*: An Internal Critique," *Ethics* 106 (October 1995), 32–63.

Young, Iris Marion. "Polity and Group Difference: A Critique of the Ideal of Universal Citizenship," *Ethics* 99 (January 1989), 250–274.

al-Zamakhsharī, Maḥmūd ibn 'Umar (d. 1144). *al-Kashshāf* (Beirut: Dār al-Kitāb al-'Arabī, n.d.).

al-Zuḥaylī, Wahba. *al-'Alāqāt al-duwaliyya fī al-Islām* (Beirut: Mu'assasat al-risāla, 1981).

———. *al-Tafsīr al-wasīṭ* (Damascus: Dār al-Fikr, 2001).

Zysow, Aron. "The Economy of Certainty: An Introduction to the Typology of Islamic Legal Theory" (PhD diss., Harvard University, 1984).

Index

'Abd al-Qādir, Khalid, 125, 126–27, 248, 253–54, 263, 265
on Muslim minorities, 233–35
on solidarity, 129
abode of Islam (*dār al-Islam*), 104, 109, 126, 127, 137, 177, 310n38
abode of unbelief (*dār al-kufr*), 104, 137, 307n49
abode of war (*dār al-ḥarb*), 126, 127, 173, 181, 219, 267, 295n15, 308n10
abode of witness (*dār al-shahada*), Tariq Ramadan's concept of, 265
Abou El Fadl, Khaled, 169, 264–65, 301n102
Abrahamic fraternity, 15, 158, 209–10
Abū Dāwūd, 166
Abyssinia, 190, 248
affection (*'āṭifa*), Fayṣāl Mawlawī's conception of, 223, 240
alienation (critique of conjecture), 57–59. *See also* conjecture
aliens. *See* resident aliens
alms tax (*zakāh*), 108, 238
amān (guarantee of security), *ḥadīth* reports on, 185
amān (contract of security), 118–19, 121, 183–89, 245, 261–62, 266, 267, 322n19
Apel, Karl-Otto, 35–36, 38, 44
apostasy, 18, 98, 101, 115–16
approach. *See* methodology
argumentation, 65–66, 81–82. *See also* conjecture; discourse; *da'wa, jadal*; justification; persuasion
jadal as, 221, 224–25
army, Muslims serving in non-Muslim, 113–16, 140, 147–48, 150–51, 190–96, 297n47
arranged marriage, 40, 41
association, right to, 138
Audi, Robert, 69
authenticity, 58–59, 72–73, 81
beliefs, 278n8
authoritarian traditions, 54, 269
authority
classical text, 80, 213
communal, 55
cultural, 92
legal, 128
autonomy
communal, 104, 107, 138, 169
of comprehensive doctrines within political liberalism, 78
culture and, 51
individual, 43, 50–52, 52, 88, 99
justice and, 247
axiomatic beliefs, 87

Baier, Kurt, 93
bearing witness (*shahāda*), Tariq Ramadan's concept of, 174–76
Benhabib, Seyla
and discourse ethics, 37–42
on equality/"other," 153–54
historicism of, 42–43
on importance of moral dialogue, 37–39
on universal respect, 38
Bilgrami, Akeel, 278n4, 281n7
Black Nationalists, 143
blasphemy, 18, 247, 267, 278n8, 279n14
Bosnia, 171
Brown, John, 144, 145–46
burdens of judgment, 26, 30–32, 94, 272, 273, 283n34
in Rawls, 26, 30–32
Islamic doctrine of citizenship and, 143
justificatory comparative political theory and, 55–56
methodology and, 89, 90, 94
moral conflict and, 158
moral pluralism and, 213, 215

Canada, 6
categorical imperative, Habermas's transformation of, 33–34
charity, 238–39, 240
Christian pacifists, 151
citizens
resident aliens versus, 136, 139, 151, 208, 227, 236
unreasonable, 302n7
Western, non-Western beliefs embraced by, 12
citizenship. *See also* Islamic affirmations, of liberal citizenship; Islamic doctrine of citizenship; liberal citizenship
charity and, 239
Islamic ethics and, 7–8
liberal conception of, 98–102, 135–136
loyalty and, 140–151
solidarity and, 157–160
versus justice, 135–36, 301n1
violence and, 145
voting and, 161–162
civil disobedience, 143–46, 187
civil rights. *See* rights
classical texts, Islamic, 184–85, 191, 263, 264. *See also specific issues; specific texts*
authority of, 80, 213
coercion, 98, 101, 125
non-, 221, 225–26
Cohen, Joshua, 32, 284n35
collective duties (*farḍ kifāya*), 117
communal authority, 55
communal autonomy, 104, 107, 138, 169
communities. *See also* Muslim communities; readership, overlapping consensus
belonging to several, 286n75
justice across, 216–21
Scripturary ("People of the Book"), 210, 301n103
comparative ethics, 13–14, 88. *See also* conjecture; justificatory comparative political theory
authenticity and, 58–59, 72–73, 81
consensus goal of, 4
ethics of, 14, 65–96
language of, 74–76
manipulation and, 69–70, 72, 79, 289n9
moral dialogue and, 70–73
objections to, 67–73
paradox of, 74, 88
persuasion and, 65–66
plausibility standard in, 68–69, 95
principles of conjecture/, 73–77
compatibility *See also* overlapping consensus
defense of non-Muslim state and, 123–24, 192
determining, 87–96
Islamic ethics/recognition, 218
liberal citizenship requirements and, 97–102
non-Muslim army service by Muslims, 190–96
comprehensive ethical doctrines, 12, 18
autonomy of, 78
emphasis on, 17
Islam as, 80–87
justice independent of, 29
justification based on, 24, 25, 90
societal stability/justice based on, 24, 25
conception of good, 255–56
Islamic, 131, 153
liberalism's, 97–98, 284n37
overlapping positions on, 161

participation and, 161
social cooperation and, 97–100, 140
conflict. *See* moral conflict
conjecture *See also* comparative ethics; objections to justificatory comparative political theory
critiques of, 19–22, 53–64 (*see also* alienation; cultural hegemony; liberal bias)
diagnostic stage of, 78, 95, 102
evaluation of reasons in, 79
operationalizing, 77–79
orthodoxy and, 73–76, 84–85
overlapping consensus search using, 17–22, 50, 60–63
persuasion versus, 42, 48, 50, 63, 65–66, 70, 270
polyvalent traditions and, 67, 68
principles of, 73–77, 290n14
Rawls' definition of, 13, 65, 291n40
religious integrity and, 67
synthetic stage of, 79
conscientious objection, 147
consensus. *See also* overlapping consensus
comparative ethics goal of, 4
dimensions of, Baier on, 93
among Islamic jurists, 169
consequentialist-utilitarian approach, to moral obligation, 220, 268–69
Constructivism, 220, 280n2
contract of loyalty, 183–89, 267. *See also* contract of security (*amān*)
contract of security (*amān*), 118–19, 121, 245, 261–62, 266, 267, 322n9
classical texts on, 184–85
moral recognition/Muslim-non-Muslim relations based on, 219–20
contractualist approach, to ethics, 220, 280n2
contribution, to non-Muslim welfare, 139–40, 237, 238–42
defense, 190
solidarity based on, 159–60
substantive, 151, 159–60
conversion, 139, 257, 261, 270. *See also* coercion
non-Muslims as prospects of, recognition based on, 138, 158
tactical acceptance of liberal citizenship and, 138
Cook, Michael, 318n25
cruelty, historicist/relativist critiques and, 45
cultural authority, 92
cultural hegemony (critique of conjecture), 57–62. *See also* conjecture
culture
autonomy and, 51
background versus public, 40
neutralization of illiberal, 56–57
research on, 60

Danish cartoon controversy, 5, 6, 37, 61, 278n9, 279n9, 288n105
dār al-ḥarb (abode of war), 126, 127, 173, 181, 219, 267, 295n15, 308n10
da'wa (proselytizing/calling to Islam), 15, 138, 172–78, 221–29, 262
al-maw'iẓa al-ḥasana (good-willed exhortation), 221–24
argumentation (*jadal*) in, 221, 224, 270
as basis of moral obligation, 269–70
charity and, 241
civic friendship and, 271
comparison with Habermas's discourse ethics, 227–229
jadal (argumentation) in, 221, 224–25
methodology for, 221–23, 224–25
noncoercion (*lā ikrāh*) in, 221, 225–26
recognition and, 202, 221–26
declaration, witnessing versus, in Rawls, 42
defense, non-Muslim state, 190–96
democracy
discourse ethics and, 33–42, 56
public moral dialogue in, 38
democracy, Islamic ethics/moral conflict and, 3–16
deontological approach, to moral obligation, 109, 220, 236, 266, 269
diagnosis
as stage of conjecture, 78, 95, 102
ideal discourse as, 34–35
discourse(s). *See also* moral dialogue
apologetic, 7, 13, 209–10
ideal, 34–35
moral obligation, three main, 220–21
Muslim minorities in West, 4, 277n1
normative force of, 34, 35, 275–76
pragmatics in, 35, 38, 48

discourse ethics
democracy in, 33–42, 56
Habermas's, 33–38, 56, 153, 227
doctrines. *See also* comprehensive ethical doctrines; pluralism; reasonable doctrines; revelation; *specific doctrines*
authenticity concerns and, 58–59
diversity within, 211
features of secular versus religious, 66–67
internal Islamic debate over, 9
justice relation to, political liberalism interest in, 33
justification based on single, 24, 25, 99
legitimizing secularism, 11
"pluralism as divine injunction," 215
of recognition, 152, 157–58, 208
reinterpretation of, 80
duties, civic. *See also specific duties*
collective, 117
exemption from, 54–55, 149–50
honoring of contracts, 187
individual, 116–17, 118
manifesting religion (*izhar al-dìn*), 166–72
toward non-Muslims, 110, 252
recognition, 155
sentimentality and, 139–40
spread of Islam, 172
Dworkin, Ronald, 45, 74

education, 23, 40, 100, 292n4, 292n42
religious, 180
egalitarian reciprocity, 38, 39–40
empirical overlapping consensus, 29–33, 273
enemies
friendship with, 216–21, 237
justice toward, 216–21, 313n21
England, 40, 117
epistemic abstinence, 235
equality
Benhabib on "other" and, 153–54
justice and, 216–21
recognition of, 152–54, 262, 311n52
equilibrium, for Islamic doctrine of citizenship, 135–51
ethics. *See also* comparative ethics; discourse ethics; Islamic ethics
of comparative ethics, 14, 65–96
contractualist/constructivist approaches to, 220, 280n2
Europe, 6, 9, 173–74
evaluation of reasons, conjecture through, 79
exemption, from duties, 54–55, 149–50
existentialists, 49–50

Fadel, Mohammad, 279n16
Faḍl Allāh, Muhammad Husayn, 217–18
farḍ 'ayn (individual duty), 116–17
farḍ kifāya (collective duty), 117
fasting, 108
fiqh al-aqalliyyāt (jurisprudence/ethics of Muslim minorities), 80, 263. *See also* Muslim minorities; 'Abd al-Qādir; Ibn Bayya; Mawawlī; al-Qaraḍāwī; Topoljak
Fish, Stanley, 44–46, 47, 48–49, 53
France, 6, 40, 117
freedom
of exit/association, 39–40
intrasocietal disagreement in conditions of, 24
liberal citizenship's protection of, 98–99
to manifest one's religion, 110, 166–72
to refuse arranged marriage, 41
seduction from religion, 167, 168, 171, 172, 203
free speech, 5, 18, 37, 278n8, 278n9, 279n9, 280n18
Fish on nonexistence of, 45
separation of church/state and, 10, 280n18
friendship, 216–21, 237
da'wa and, 271
with enemies, 237
with non-Muslims, 111–12, 127–33, 152, 229–36
fundamentalism, 31, 62, 277n2

Galston, William, 155
Gaus, Gerald F., 281n6
Geertz, Clifford, 47
al-Ghannūshī, Rāshid, 247, 251
God's law. *See* sharī'a
good, conception of, 255–56
Islamic, 131, 153
liberalism's, 97–98, 284n37

Muslim participation and, 161
social cooperation and, 97–100, 140
good-willed exhortation (*al-maw'iẓa al-ḥasana*), 221–24
group punishment, 119

Habermas, Jürgen, 44, 47–48
discourse ethics of, 33–38, 56, 153, 227
ideal discourse, 34, 35
impartiality and, 36
ḥadīth reports
amān in, 185
hijra in, 105, 166
Ḥanafī school, 106, 113, 122, 169, 186
Ḥanbalī jurists, 112
al-Hanooti, Muhammad, 169, 250
headscarf, 6, 40
Hegel, Wilhelm Friedrich, 34, 35
hegemony, ideological, 46. *See also* cultural hegemony
Heidegger, 49
hermeneutics, 19, 60, 72, 81
hijra (migration), 103–7, 110, 111, 171, 295n15
context of law on, 166–68
ḥadīth reports on, 105, 166
Ibn Taymiyya's conception of, 176–78
interpretation and, 168, 176–78
Islamic texts from pre-, 211–15
Meccan period and, 211–15, 305n12
Muhammad's, 190, 248, 304n5
obligation versus recommendation for, 166–67
oppression basis of, 166, 168
punishment as, 177
Qur'ānic verses on, 105, 106, 165, 309n22
ḥikma (wisdom), 221, 226
historicism, justification using, 42–53
historicization, of texts, 167
ḥudūd (punishments), 91–92

ibāḥiyya (permissiveness), 112–13
Ibn Bayya, 'Abd Allāh, 230–33, 244–45, 265
Ibn Kathīr, 130
Ibn Qudāma, Muwaffaq al-Dīn, 111, 188
Ibn Taymiyya, Aḥmad ibn, 111, 120–121, 171, 177–178, 217, 219, 234, 248, 253–254, 264, 268–269
ideal discourse (Habermas), 34–35
identities
beliefs versus, 9–10
derivation of, 8–9
ideological hegemony, 46
immigration, 63
impartiality, Kant versus Habermas on, 36
inauthenticity, religious doctrine and, 58–59
individuals
autonomy of, 43, 50–52, 88, 99
duty of (*farḍ `ayn*), 116–17, 118
obligations to political systems versus, 155
inequality, radical, 209
infinite regress, 44
injustice, two kinds of in Islam, 247
intrasocietal disagreement, freedom allowing for, 24
ironists, liberal, 45, 49
Islam
as comprehensive doctrine, 80–87
duty to spread. See *da'wa*
Islamic affirmations, of liberal citizenship, 15
challenges to, 103–133
da'wa and, 221–29
friendship/*muwālāh* for, 229–36
loyalty to non-Muslim state, 181–206
Meccan period texts as, 211–15
political participation, 242–58
recognition/moral pluralism, 207–36
religious disagreement and, 209–15
residence in non-Muslim state, 165–79, 260–61
self-restraint and, 248
Islamic arguments, against liberal citizenship, 9, 103–33
autonomy and, 52, 88
contributing to self-defense of non-Muslim state, 121–24
danger of strengthening non-Muslims, 110–11, 121–22
da'wa, 269–70
defined by what is not Western, 73
friendship with non-Muslims, 111–12
jihād against own non-Muslim state, *116–21*
living in sinful environments, 112–113
loyalty to non-Muslim state, 113–27, 181
Muslim service in non-Muslim army, 140, 147, 148, 150–51, 297n47

Islamic arguments (*continued*)
  non-Muslim permissiveness, 112–13
  non-Muslims' predominance over Muslims, 109–10
  participation in non-Islamic political system, 242–243
  promotion of virtue/morality, 113
  recognizing inviolability of non-Muslim state, 124–27
  residence in non-Muslim state in, 107, 112, 137, 141, 260–61
  six explanatory, for prohibiting residence, 165, 178–79
  solidarity with non-Muslims, 127–33
  subjection to non-Muslim laws, 107–9
Islamic doctrine of citizenship. *See also* doctrines; Islamic affirmations, of liberal citizenship; residence in non-Muslim states; loyalty to non-Muslim states; solidarity with non-Muslims; political participation
  burdens of judgment and, 143
  conclusions about, 205–6, 260
  crucial components of, 242
  equilibrium in, 135–51
  interest in, 41
  Muslim political participation and, 160–62, 242–58, 260
  need for, 23–24
  summary of, 260–263
Islamic ethics
  citizenship and, 7–8
  interpretation of, 12–13
  Islamic law as, 80–87
  moral conflict/democracy and, 3–16
  moral obligation discourses in, 220–21
  political liberalism recognition compatibility with, 218
Islamic good life, 131, 153
Islamic law. *See also* sharī'a; *fiqh al-aqalliyyāt*; *specific laws*
  definition of, 80
  friendship with non-Muslims in, 111–12, 127–33, 152
  as main source for inquiry, 80–87
  Muslim minorities in, 80
  Muslim service in non-Muslim army opposed by, 140, 147, 148, 150–51
Islamic texts, 13–14, 19, 80–87, 166, 280n23
  diversity/religious pluralism and, 211
  Meccan period, 211–15, 305n12
  selection of, 59, 80–87
Islamization, 138, 139, 162, 172, 174, 221, 244. *See also* conversion
IslamOnline, 241
Islamophobia, 96
Islam, political liberalism and. *See* overlapping consensus
Iẓhār al-dīn (manifesting religion), 110, 166–72

Jackson, Sherman, 62, 80, 199
jadal (argumentation), 221, 224–25
Japan, 192, 299n80
jihād, 261, 298n64, 311n50
  belief in, 9
  classical doctrine of, 125–127
  defensive interpretation of, 197, 203
  expansive, 201
  interpretations of, 125–26, 197, 203
  offensive, 198, 202
  Ottoman fatwa on, 117, 122
  against own non-Muslim state, 116–21
  reformulated doctrine of, 262
Jones, Peter, 64
Joseph, story of, 245, 246, 247–48, 249
jurists
  consensus among, 169
  Ḥanbalī, 112
  Malīkī, 107, 112, 137, 166, 169, 200, 231–32, 240, 295n15
  neoclassical, 263
justice, 19, 302n5, 313n21
  autonomy and, 247
  belief and, 246–47
  citizenship requirements versus requirements of, 135–36, 301n1
  across communities, 216–21, 313n21
  doctrine's relation to, political liberalism interest in, 33
  enemies/unbelievers and, 216–21, 313n21
  equality and, 216–21
  between equals, 216–21
  independent of comprehensive ethical doctrines, 29
  minimal standards of, 159
  political conception of, 21
  Rawlsian stability and, 27–28
  stability and, 24, 25, 26–33

transcending differing beliefs through, 208
witnessing versus declaration of, 42
justification. *See also* Islamic affirmations, of liberal citizenship; justificatory comparative political theory
comprehensive doctrine basis of, 24, 25, 90
empirical overlapping consensus and, 29–33, 282n17
participation, 242–58, 260
popular acceptance distinguished from, 25, 281n3
"pro tanto," 27–28
public, 28, 61, 282n16
purpose of, 14, 23–64
radical inequality, 209
war, 120, 124–27, 132, 173, 261, 293n2, 297n41, 297n44
justificatory comparative political theory, 17–22, 95
alienation charge against, 57–59
burdens of judgment and, 55–56
conjecture methodology in, 17–22, 50, 60–63
as cultural hegemony, 57–62
in defense of, 53–64
doctrinal authenticity concerns in, 58–59
hermeneutics versus, 19, 60
modus vivendi and, 94
need for, 19
purpose of, 23–64
relativist/historicist critiques of, 42–53
self-restraint and, 92
stigmatization/marginalization charge against, 62–64
traditional hermeneutics versus, 19
justificatory gap, 28, 85
just war doctrine, 142–46, 182, 191–96, 201–5, 297n40, 302n5

Kant, 33–34, 35, 36
Kutty, Shaykh Ahmad, 173, 191
Kymlicka, Will, 43, 98, 286n90

La ikrah (noncoercion), 221, 225–26
laws. *See also* Islamic law; sharīʿa
Muslim subjection, to non-Muslim, 107–9
legal authority, 128
legal texts, Islamic, 80–87
Letter Concerning Toleration (Locke), 56
leveraging by reasons, Audi's, 69
Lewis, Bernard, 306n28
liberal bias (critique of conjecture), 19–20, 57, 59–62. *See also* conjecture
liberal citizenship. *See also* Islamic affirmations, of liberal citizenship; Islamic arguments, against liberal citizenship; Islamic doctrine of citizenship
communal authority limits in, 55
conversion potential and, 138
defining feature of, 98–99
Islam and, 18, 97–102
Islamic affirmations of, 15
minorities in, first requirement of, 101
minority rights in, 18, 40–41, 98, 100, 101–2
moral conflict and, 3–16
passive acceptance of, 139
punishment and, 98
from within religion, 11, 13
requirements of, 97–102
six explanatory Islamic arguments against, 165, 178–79
tactical acceptance of, 138
liberal contract theorists, 262, 267
liberal democracies, social cooperation in, assumption of, 59, 63
liberalism
conception of good in, 97–98, 255–56, 284n37
neutrality and, 100, 130–31, 215, 284n37, 303n17
questioning, 288n102, 288n104
religion and, 98–102
Locke, John, *Letter Concerning Toleration*, 56
London, 2005 attacks in, 119
loyalty
absolute, impossibility of, 145
amān /civic, 183–89, 267
contract of, 183–89, 267
to non-Muslim state, 113–27, 140–51, 181–206, 262
wartime, 132, 187

Mālikī jurists, 107, 112, 137, 166, 169, 200, 231–32, 295n15
on charity, 240

manifesting religion (*iẓhar al-dīn*), 110, 166–72
manipulation, comparative ethics and, 69–70, 72, 79, 289n9
marginalization objection, 62–64
marriage, 40, 41, 98
Marx, Karl, 24
Maudoodi, Syed Abul 'Ala. *See* Mawdūdī, Sayyid Abul 'Ala
al-maw'iẓa al-hasana (good-willed exhortation), 221–24. See also *da'wa*
Mawdūdī, Sayyid Abul 'Ala, 118, 198
Mawlawī, Fayṣal, 222, 240, 241
Mecca, Muslims remaining in, 110
Meccan period, texts of, 211–15, 305n12
methodology, comparison, 273. *See also* conjecture; justification
  burdens of judgment in, 89, 90, 94
  conjecture, 17–22, 50, 60–63
  da'wa, 221–23, 224–25
  ethics of comparative ethics in, 14, 65–96
  Islamic ethical traditions and, 60–61
  liberal bias in, 19–20, 59–62
  objections to justificatory comparative political theory, 17–22, 53–64
Michot, Yahya, 171
migration. *See hijra*
Mill, John Stuart, 23
minorities
  liberal citizenship requirement for, 101
  mutual recognition from, 156
  political philosophy and, 17
  rights of, 18, 40–41, 98, 100, 101–2
minorities, Muslim
  Islamic law and, 80
  'Abd al-Qādir on, 233–35
  in West, 4, 277n1
modus vivendi, 27, 29, 78–79, 88, 89, 272
  justificatory comparative political theory and, 94
moral conflict, 3–10
  burdens of judgment and, 158
  context and, 5, 6
  democracy/Islamic ethics and, 3–16
  objections to inquiry into, 4–10, 279n16
moral dialogue
  Benhabib on importance of, 37–39
  comparative ethics and, 70–73
  open, 37–41
morality, promotion of virtue and, 113
moral obligation, to non-Muslims
  approaches to, 220, 266–70
  consequentialist-utilitarian approach to, 220, 268–69
  creativity/tradition in affirming, 259–76, 309n22
  da'wa basis of, 221–229, 269–70
moral pluralism, 70, 132, 207–36, 272
  burdens of judgment and, 213, 215
  reasonable, 18, 26, 32–33, 57, 143, 211, 273
  recognition and, 207–36
moral psychology, political theory addressing, 23
moral recognition. *See also* recognition
  contractual basis of, 219–20
  general, 267
Muḥammad (Prophet)
  cartoon controversy, 5, 6, 61, 278n9, 279n9
  migration (*hijra*) of, 190, 248, 304n5
  oppression of, 198
multiculturalism, liberal, 17–18, 43, 286n90, 293n9, 293n13
Münchhausen trilemma, 35, 44
Murad, Khurram, 317n16
Muslim Brotherhood, 83
Muslim communities, autonomy of, 104, 107, 138
Muslim minorities, Islamic law and, 80
Muslims, in West/non-Muslim societies, 18, 100, 101–2. *See also* Islamic arguments, against liberal citizenship; Islamic doctrine of citizenship; *specific topics*
  al Wansharīsī on, 109–10
  civil disobedience and, 143–46
  contribution concerns regarding, 139–40, 151, 159–60, 190
  Islamic affirmations of liberal citizenship and, 165–206
  non-Muslims predominance over, 109–10
  rights of, 18, 40–41, 98, 100, 101–2
mutual recognition, 156
muwālāh verses, 152, 229–36

Nadwi, Syed Abul Hasan Ali, 173–74
Nagel, Thomas, 280n2, 283n31

al-Nawawī, Abū Zakariyyā', 169–71, 187–88
neutrality, 215, 284n37, 303n17
  appeal of liberalism's, 100, 130–31
  Ibn Bayya endorsing secularism and, 232
  nonendorsement of, 131
neutralization, illiberal culture, 56–57
Nietzsche, 49, 50
noncoercion (*Lā ikrāh*), *da'wa* recognition theme, 221, 225–26
non-Muslims
  da'wa as basic principle for relations with, 221–22
  duties toward, 110, 252
  duty to criticize, 110
  friendship with, 111–12, 127–33, 152, 237
  Islamic arguments for liberalism by, 68–73
  loyalty to state of, 113–27
  moral obligation to, 259–76, 266–70
  nonrecognition of, 126
  permissiveness of, 112–13
  as potential converts, 138, 158
  predominance of, 109–10
  recognition of, 152–62
  serving in army of, 113–16
  solidarity with, 127–33, 152–62, 263, 313n21, 317n10
non-Muslim state. *See also* contribution, to non-Muslim welfare
  amān /contract of security with, 118–19, 121, 261–62, 266
  defense of, 190–96
  inviolability of, recognizing, 124–27
  Islamic arguments against residence in, 137
  jihād against one's own, 116–21
  loyalty to, 113–27, 140–51, 181–206, 262
  Muslims' military service to, 113–16, 147–48
  political participation in, 160–62, 242–58, 260, 316n86, 318n27, 321n73
  recognition of, permanent, 196–205
  residence in, 294n5
nonparticipation, 160–62
nonpublic justification, 28, 282n16
nonrecognition, 126, 219
norms/normative concerns
  Benhabib's three, 39–40
  discourse and, 34, 35, 275–76
  stability as, 29–30
  universal respect, 38–39
North American Fiqh Council, 169

objections, to inquiry into Islamic doctrine of citizenship, 4–10, 53–64, 279n16. *See also* Islamic arguments, against liberal citizenship
  authenticity, lack of, 58–59, 72–73, 81
  banality, 67–68
  liberal bias, 19–20, 59–62
  marginalization, 62–64
  polyvalent traditions, 67, 68
  religious integrity, 67
objections to justificatory comparative political theory, 17–22, 53–64, 67–73
  alienation charge, 57–59
  cultural hegemony, 57–64
  justificatory force absent, 53–57
obligation. *See also* moral obligation, to non-Muslims
  to individuals versus political systems, 155
  migration (*hijra*) as recommendation versus, 166–67
operationalizing, of conjecture, 77–79
oppression, 142
  migration duty based on, 166, 168
  of Muhammad, 198
orthodoxy, 242
  conjecture and, 73–76, 84–85
  identifying, 84–85
Ottoman, 1914 *jihād fatwa of, 117, 122*
overlapping consensus, 10–13, 87–96. See also compatibility; Islamic doctrine of citizenship
  apologetic discourse and, 7, 13, 209–10
  conjecture in search for, 17–22, 50, 60–63
  contesting, method of, 65
  definition of, 27
  detail/precision in, 94–95
  empirical, 29–33, 273
  endogenous nature of, 10
  evidence against, transparency principle for, 76
  expanding, 90–94
  generic nature of, 3, 10, 288n103
  goal of, 7–8, 28–29, 52

overlapping consensus (*continued*)
Islamic texts and, 13–14, 59, 60–61, 80–87, 280n23
main questions of, 11, 93–94
model case of, 89–90
objections to, 4–10, 279n16
orthodox texts and, 75
philosophy and, 93
political duty and, 124
Rawls's conception of, 10–13, 23–33
Scheffler on, 86–87
social cooperation assumption and, 59, 63
sociology and, 32, 273
stability and, Rawls's political liberalism on, 26–33, 282n11
sympathy and, 76–77
utilitarianism opposed to, 86–87

pacifists, 150, 151
Palestine, 186
paradox of comparative ethics, 74, 88
Parekh, Bhikhu, 21–22
participation, political. *See also* contribution, to non-Muslim welfare
contracts and, 186
conversion and, 257
non-, 160–62
in non-Muslim state, 160–62, 242–58, 260, 316n86, 318n27, 321n73
overlapping consensus and, 124
perfectionism, 43, 54
permissiveness (*ibāḥiyya*), 112–13
persuasion
comparative ethics and, 65–66
da'wa and, 221–229
Plato, 23
plausibility standard, for overlapping consensus, conjecture, 68–69, 95
pluralism
moral, 70, 132, 207–36, 272
Qur´ānic verses supporting religious, 210
reasonable moral, 18, 26, 32–33, 57, 143, 273
religious, 210–11
"pluralism as divine injunction" doctrine, 215
pluralistic consensus test, 31
policy, public profession versus, 264–65
political conception, justice, 21
political constructivism, 20, 267
political liberalism. *See also* justification; justificatory comparative political theory
autonomy of comprehensive doctrines in, 78
comprehensive doctrines viewed in, 78
education and, 292n4, 292n42
as freestanding, 28
friendship/*muwālāh* not required by, 235
Islam and, 272
main virtue of, Rawls on, 272
Meccan texts affirming, 213–15
participation concerns in, 160–62
political duty in, emotional attachment with, 124
self-restraint in, 28, 58
social unity problem in, 29
stability problem in, 24
supported by purely political values, 27–28
Political Liberalism (Rawls), 11–12, 259, 293n13
overlapping consensus/stability in, 26–33
political obligation, individual versus, 155
political participation. *See* participation, political
political theory. *See also* justificatory comparative political theory
comparative, 14
justice versus citizenship requirements in, 135–36, 301n1
moral psychology addressed by, 23
philosophy of contemporary, 17
political vision, Islam's claim to, 99–100
polyvalent traditions objection, 67, 68
popular acceptance, justification distinguished from, 25, 281n3
power
accommodation of, 19, 277n2
imbalances in, 5, 6
pragmatics, 35, 38, 48
Habermas/Apel on moral principles in, 38

prayer, Islamic law on, 108–9
predominance, non-Muslim, 109–10
presumption of consensus, 38–39
principles, of conjecture, 73–77
orthodoxy, 73–76
restraint, 77
sympathy, 76–77
transparency, 76
Prophet (Muhammad)
cartoon controversy, 5, 6, 61, 278n9, 279n9
migration (*hijra*) of, 190, 248, 304n5
oppression of, 198
proselytizing. *See da'wa*
"pro tanto justification," 27–28
public justification, 28, 61, 282n16
public profession, policy versus, 264–65
punishment
group, 119
hijra/migration as form of, 177
ḥudūd as, 91–92
liberal citizenship and, 98

al-Qaraḍāwī, Yūsuf, 116, 173–75, 190, 223, 269
Meccan Qur´ān viewed by, 213
on participation, 252
Quakers, 151
quietist approach, 187
Qur'ān, 113, 199
amān in, 184
charity addressed in, 238
da'wa in, 221, 225, 226
friendship with non-Muslims in, 111–12, 127–28, 130, 152, 229, 237
hijra (migration), 105, 106, 165, 309n22
humankind addressed in, 242, 317n17
killing between Muslims in, 114–16
loyalty to non-Muslim state prohibited by, 181, 262
non-Muslim predominance and, 110
participation and, 245
pre-*hijra*, 211–15
provisional/final rulings in, 126
reciprocity in war cited in, 120
recognition of non-Muslim state in, 196–98
religious pluralism in, 210
self-defense in, 202
Qur'anic interpretation, *hijra* (migration), 106, 171
Quraysh, 166
al-Qurṭubī, Muḥammad Ibn Aḥmad, 240, 319n36
Quṭb, Sayyid, 106, 111, 196–97, 198, 200–201, 202
provisional rulings of peace, 126
on solidarity with non-Muslims, 129–30, 313n21

Rahman, Fazlur, 72
Ramadan, Tariq, 9–10, 73, 92, 241, 249
abode of witness idea of, 265
on contracts of civic loyalty, 183–84
on *da'wa*, 174
Sarkozy and, 91
rationality, 44, 50
rationalization, secular, 69
Rawls, John, 17, 48, 68, 97, 98
burdens of judgment, 26, 31
conjecture defined by, 13, 65, 291n40
fact of reasonable pluralism of, 26, 211, 273
justice and, 27–28
later work of, 24, 42
overlapping consensus requirements of, 11, 88, 89–90
Political Liberalism, 11–12, 259, 293n13
political liberalism's main virtue viewed by, 272
reasonable citizen concept of, 55
reasonable comprehensive doctrine defined by, 30–31, 89
reciprocity viewed by, 159
on self-respect, 154
stability viewed by, 26–33, 282n11
A Theory of Justice, 26, 86, 293n13
Raz, Joseph, 43
readership, overlapping consensus, 68–69
reality, debate versus, 14
reason(s), 30
evaluation of, conjecture through, 79
historicism/relativism and, 45–47
leveraging by, 69
meta-, 45
reasonable citizen, 55, 89
reasonable doctrines, 55
Rawls's definition of, 30–31, 89

reasonable moral pluralism, 18, 26, 32–33, 57, 143
Rawls's "fact" of, 26, 211, 273
reciprocity
egalitarian, 38, 39–40
Rawls on, 159
violence and, 189
in war, 119–20
recognition
conversion potential basis of, 158
doctrine of, 152, 157–58, 208
of equality, 152–54, 262, 311n52
four *da'wa* values in support of, 221–26
general moral, 267
Islamic affirmations on, 207–36
moral pluralism and, 207–36
mutual, 156
permanent, 196–205
solidarity and, 152–62, 208–9, 227
recommendation, migration *(hijra)* as obligation versus, 166–67
reflective equilibrium, 43
reformulation, *jihād* doctrine, 262
relativism
fear of, 47
justification using, 42–53
justificatory comparative political theory and, 42–53, 59
religion. *See also* comprehensive ethical doctrines; doctrines; fundamentalism
apostasy and, 101, 115–16
denial of, 10
exaltation of, 151
liberal citizenship from within, 11, 13
liberalism and, 98–102
manifesting one's, 110, 166–72
seduction away from, 167, 168, 171, 172, 203
separation of church/state based on importance of, 51–52, 286n89
religious disagreement, human nature and, 208, 209–15
religious education, 180
religious integrity objection, 67
religious pluralism, 210–11
religious sensitivity, free speech and, 5, 279n8, 279n9
research
culture, 60
future, 272–76
residence, in non-Muslim states, 103–13, 136–40, 294n5
Islamic affirmations of liberal citizenship for, 165–79, 260–61
Islamic arguments against, 107, 112, 137, 141, 260–61
legitimating, 139–40
passivity and, 139
permission confusion/question of, 294n5, 294n10
predominance, non-Muslim in, 109–10
strengthening unbelievers and, 110–11, 121–22
subjection, to non-Muslim laws in, 107–9
al-Wansharīsī prohibition on, 107, 112
resident aliens, 136, 139, 151, 208, 227, 236
respect
self-, 154
universal, 38–39, 41
restraint, 88, 248, 260, 292n42
conjecture principle, 77
revelation, 80, 108–9, 128–31, 198–99, 209, 211–213, 215, 218, 229, 233, 262, 266–67, 300n99, 312n6, n10
context and, 129
final, texts as, 128
Riḍā, Muḥammad Rashīd, 115, 171–72, 192–94, 233
fatwa on hijra, 171–172
muwalah verses interpreted by, 229–36
rights
to association, 138
minority, 18, 40–41, 98, 100, 101–2
natural, 218–19, 220, 286n88
recognition and, 154
of unreasonable citizens, 302n7
Rorty, Richard, 44, 45–46, 48–49, 53, 281n7
Rousseau, Jean-Jacques, 24, 303n22
rulings
general/aḥkām 'āmma, 129
provisional versus final Quranic, 126
Rushdie, Salman, 37, 279n10
Russia, 117
Russo-Japanese War, 192, 299n80

Salafī groups, 274
al-Sarakhsī, Muḥammad Ibn Aḥmad, 117, 185
Sarkozy, Nicolas, 91
Saudi Standing Committee for Scientific Research and Religious Guidance, 110
Scheffler, Samuel, 86–87
Scripturary communities, 210, 301n103
secular doctrines, features of religious versus, 66–67
secularism/secularization, 48, 51–52, 142
  Ibn Bayya on values of, 231, 232
  religion validating, 11
secular rationalization, 69
security, contract of *(amān)*, 118–19, 121, 183–89, 261–62, 266, 267, 322n9
self-defense, 202
  Muslim fighting in, 122
  non-Muslim state, Muslims contributing to, 121–24
self-description, Muslims, 50
self-respect, Rawls on, 154
self-restraint, 236, 253, 260, 272. *See also* restraint
  Islamic affirmations of liberal citizenship and, 248
  justificatory comparative political theory and, 92
  political liberalism's, 28, 58
  solidarity and, 152–53
sensitivity
  to Islamic ethical traditions, 60–61
  religious, 5, 279n8, 279n9
sentimentality, 139
separation of church/state
  free speech and, 10, 280n18
  philosophy and, 10–13
  religion's importance making necessary, 51–52, 286n89
September 11 attacks, 119–20
shahāda (bearing witness), 174–76
al-Shanqiti, Sheikh Muhammad al-Mukhtar, 249
sharī'a (God's law), 81, 100, 251
  conclusions and, 264
  contracts and, 184
  interpretation and, 81, 169
  migration under, 103–7
al-Shātibī, Abu Ishāq, 253<?>
Siddiqi, Muzammil, 254
social cooperation
  assumption of, 59, 63
  "conception of the good" and, 97–100, 140
  worldly versus spiritual purpose of, 15–16
socialization, 24
social unity
  fragile, 28
  political liberalism problem of, 29
  Rawls on reasonable doctrines and, 30
sociology, overlapping consensus and, 32, 273
solidarity
  contribution basis of, 159–60
  excessive, 157
  human, 50, 99, 102
  with non-Muslims, 127–33, 152–62, 263, 313n21, 317n10
  recognition and, 152–62, 208–9, 227
  self-restraint and, 152–53
sources. *See* texts, Islamic
South Africa, 155–56
space of testimony (*dar al-shahada*), 175
speech. *See* free speech
spirituality
  migration (*hijra*) interpretation, 176–78
  social cooperation and, 15–16
stability
  justice and, 24, 25, 26–33
  as normative concern, 29–30
  Rawls on, 26–33, 282n11
statutory approach, 220
stereotypes, of Muslims, 4, 62, 68, 96, 155, 277n2
stigmatization objection, to justificatory comparative political theory, 62–64
subjection, to non-Muslim laws, 107–9
substantive contribution basis, 159–60
Sunni schools, 125, 185, 187, 267
sympathy, conjecture principle, 76–77
synthesis, conjecture with, 79

Tāhā, Maḥmūd Muḥammad, 213
tax, 238, 308n15
Taylor, Charles, 153

terrorism, justification of, 119–20
texts, Islamic, 13–14, 59, 129, 166, 280n23
  authenticity and, 81
  classical, 263, 264
  classical, authority of, 80, 213
  contextualization/historicization of, 167
  final revelations, 128
  legal, 80–87
  Meccan period, 211–15, 305n12
  orthodox, conjecture principle of, 73–76, 84–85
theories. *See also* conjecture; justificatory comparative political theory
  justice, 19
  liberal contract, 262, 267
  liberal political, 135
  political comparative, 14
A Theory of Justice (Rawls), 26, 86, 293n13
  revision of, 26
toleration, 56, 225
Topoljak, Sulejman, 121, 123–24, 194–195, 263, 265, 296n35, 298n53, 299n80, 309n29
tradition(s). *See also* comprehensive ethical doctrines
  authoritarian, 54, 269
  creativity and, 259–76, 309n22
  hermeneutic, 19, 60, 72, 81
  polyvalent, 67, 68
  residence viewed in most dominant Islamic tradition, 261
translation, 94
transparency, conjecture principle, 76, 290n14

unbelievers
  danger of strengthening, 110–11, 121–22
  justice toward, 216–21, 313n21
universalism, 35, 36, 40
  enlightened, 39
  "historically self-conscious," 42–43
  moral, 271
universal respect, 38–39, 41
utilitarianism, 86–87, 220, 268–69

violence
  citizenship and, 145
  justification of, 198
  reciprocity and, 189
  terrorism, 119–20
virtue, promotion of morality and, 113
voluntary self-ascription, 39–40
voting, 243, 318n27

al-wafā' bi'l-'aqd (duty to honor contracts), 187
Wahhabis, 266
Walzer, Michael, 136
al-Wansharīsī, 112–13
  on prayer in non-Muslim lands, 109
  residence prohibition of, 107, 112
  subjection to non-Muslim law viewed by, 108
war, 115, 181, 267
  abode of, 126, 127, 173, 181, 219, 267, 295n15, 308n10
  conscientious objection to, 147
  context and, 199–200
  doctrine of just, 142–46, 182, 191–96, 201–5, 297n40, 302n5
  justification for, 120, 124–27, 132, 173, 261, 293n2, 297n41, 297n44
  loyalty during, 132, 187
  between Muslims, 114–16
  in name of Islam, 114
  "reciprocity" in, 119–20
  Russo-Japanese, 192, 299n80
  unjust/aggression, 144
Warren, Earl, 243–44
wisdom (*ḥikma*), 221, 226
witnessing. *See also* abode of witness, Ramadan's conception of; bearing witness
  declaration of support versus, 42
World War I, 115

zakāh (alms-giving), 108
al-Zuḥaylī, Wahba, 312n11, 313n17

1721922R00192

Printed in Germany
by Amazon Distribution
GmbH, Leipzig